$\mathcal{A}$ LETTER OF INTRODUCTION:

The Life and Films of

JAMES
STEPHENSON

DAVID A. REDFERN

"A Letter of Introduction: The Life and Films of James Stephenson"
By David A. Redfern

Published in USA:
BearManor Media
P.O. Box 1129
Duncan, OK 73534-1129
www.BearManorMedia.com

ISBN—978-1-59393-754-6

Printed in the United States of America.
Book and cover design by Jacquelin Brough
Cover photo courtesy of Stephenson Archive

DEDICATION

To

DENNIS, DOUG, GEOFF & MAURICE
who unwittingly initiated the idea.

PETER
who graciously sanctioned its execution.

CLYM
may this piece of family history inspire his own future.

Above all to the
MEMORY OF LORNA
her love and devotion made it all possible.

FOREWORD

By CATHERINE WYLER

Casting was always a difficult process for my father; he hated making those decisions, because once accomplished, they limited his options. However, when he found someone who coincided with his vision, he would go to great lengths to secure them. That certainly was the case with Jimmy Stephenson and the role of Howard Joyce in *The Letter*, resulting in much drama between Willy and Warner Bros. before Jimmy eventually got the part.

Actors often found Willy intimidating at first. He was demanding, but he didn't tell them what to do. He pushed them to find the reality in their character without giving verbal instructions that might trigger false responses. In this case, as in so many others, Stephenson gave a marvellous performance which resulted in an Oscar nomination. (Unmatched by any other director, Willy's actors' performances received thirty-five Oscar nominations and fourteen statues.) As Charlton Heston once said: "Working for Willy is like getting the works in a Turkish bath: you think you're going to drown, but you end up smelling like a rose."

Given Willy's appreciation of Stephenson's talent and hard work, I'm sure they would have had many more successful collaborations had it not been for Jimmy's untimely death at such an early age. It is past time for a serious look at Jimmy Stephenson's life and work, and this book reinforced my awe and respect for the creative process in making movie magic.

ACKNOWLEDGMENTS

For their invaluable assistance and expertise in various guises: Peter Allen, Malcolm Arthur, Donovan Brandt, Pam Brooks, Philip Carli, Tony Davison, Graham Fisher, Tony Fletcher, the late Clive Garner, Agnése and Bob Geoghegan, the late David Gillespie, David Haley, the late Roger Hambleton, Gordon Hobbs, Dennis Howells, Tony Hutchinson, Jeremy Jago, Colin Jellicoe, Phil Johnson, Alun Lettsome Jones, Alan Kibble, Russell F. Knott, Phillipa Lewis, Lee Mannering, the late Neil Packard, Laurie Ringrow, Professor Frank Scheide, Astor Sklair, Dennis Sykes, Keith Teanby, Harriett Thistlethwaite, Tony Walker, Jim Wild, the late David R. Williams, Keith Withall, Elaine Mae Woo.

Special thanks to local Burnley historians: James Howell, Dennis Murtaugh's column in the *Burnley Express*, Jack Nadine and exceptionally Ken Spencer.

The following individuals and institutions have been generous with their time: Snowden Becker at Academy of Motion Picture Arts and Science Film Archive, Stacey Behmler and Barbara Hall at the Academy of Motion Picture Arts and Sciences Margaret Herrick Library Special Collections, for pulling out several pertinent items, Jeff Walden at BBC Written Archives Caversham Park, Birkenhead Archives, Blackburn and Bolton Local History Libraries, Bruce Boyer at the Fred Astaire Conference held at Oriel College, Oxford in 2008, John Oliver curator at the British Film Institute, Janice Healey formerly at the British Film Institute Library, The British Library, Reference Librarian Susan A. Halstead and staff at Burnley Local History Library, Richard Chatten for his assiduousness and eagle eye in uncovering relevant material, Colindale Newspaper Library, Coventry City Archives, Patrick Moules, editor of *Flickers*, Dennis Hagen wizard of the golden age of radio, Halifax and Heysham Libraries, John Rylands University Library, Lancashire Record Office, Karen Fishman at the Recorded Sound Division of the Library of Congress, Kay Parrot at Liverpool Record Office, David Taylor former librarian at the Local Studies Department Manchester Central Library, David Fallows Emeritus Professor of Music at Manchester University for deciphering the musical voice of James Stephenson, The Michael Redgrave Archives, Morecambe Library, The National Archives, Kew, London, Fiona Aitken secretary of Association of Old Brightonians, Major Farrington at The Queen's Lancashire Regiment Museum, Ronald Grant Archives, Julie Bott secretary of The Rugbeian Society, Selby, Southport and Todmorden Libraries, Mike Townend Keeper of History at Towneley Hall Burnley, Wallasey Central Library, Ned Comstock University of Southern California Archivist at The Doheney Library for his expertise and generosity in bringing several nuggets of vital information to my attention, Hayden Guest and Randi Hockett formerly at Warner Bros. Archive at the University of Southern California, for collating valuable source material often at short notice.

Peter von Bagh, Guy Borlée and Gian Luca Farrelli of *Il Cinema Ritrovato* and Livio Jacob and David Robinson of *Le Giornate del Cinema Muto* for their unrivalled abilities in programming rare and remarkable archive film festivals over several decades that continue to instruct and delight – *il miglior fabbro*.

Thanks also to: Maureen Alexander, Diana Serra Cary, Edith Corner, Anne Dickson, Betty Goodwin, Elizabeth Hardman, Julia Hatfield, Shirley Haworth, Muriel Jobling, Rosella Kronman, the late Moira Lister, the late Jack Lord, the late Lesley Spencer, the late David Stephenson, Richard Stuttard, Mence and Ruth Wilkinson for delving into their past and sharing their insights.

The late Dame Beryl Bainbridge, Sam Beazley, the late George Melly, Graham Stark and the late John Williams for reminiscences of Liverpool Playhouse.

John Rathbone and John Steane for their memories of Alan Stephenson, the late Vincent Sherman for his exceptional recall, George Suter for sharing memories of his mother Betty, Jane for her keen support under difficult circumstances, Leon in his capacity as chauffeur and courier, Helen and Jackie – their resolute patience an inspiration.

Students on the various film history courses I have taught during the last thirteen years.

Film historian Kevin Brownlow for reiterating the maxim of Hamlet's old friend Polonius: "I must be cruel to be kind."

Lastly, a warm thank you to Dorte-Lis and Peter for their unstinting hospitality, kindness and patience and not forgetting Scamp, the best mascot a project of such magnitude ever had.

PREFACE

Ask any film aficionado about screen actor James Stephenson and you are more than likely to receive a non-committal answer. Indeed, his name is often confused with Henry Stephenson, an elderly British character actor who also worked extensively in Hollywood during the 1930s and 1940s. [1] Consult various standard cinema reference books on any bookshelf and entries for this actor are either hard to come by or are, at best, rudimentary. In Ephraim Katz's *Encyclopaedia of Film*, for instance, Stephenson is conspicuous by his absence. Look in David Thomson's *The New Biographical Dictionary of Film* (5th ed.) and his name is to be found, albeit somewhat belatedly, inserted between composer Max Steiner and director George Stevens. Thomson welcomes him into the latest edition with much enthusiasm describing his performance in *The Letter* (Warner Bros., William Wyler, 1940) as being: ". . . one of the great performances in film history." [2] Unfortunately the accompanying biographical essay is sketchy and the filmography is incomplete. Another biographical entry in *The Encyclopaedia of British Film* asserts, incorrectly, that he had only one starring role among his eight English pictures. [3] In *Quinlan's Film Stars* the entry describes him in somewhat enigmatic terms as being: "One of the cinema's more extraordinary figures." [4] The annotation goes on to relate how this tall, distinguished-looking actor, having toiled away for several years playing run-of-the-mill parts in A pictures and suave villains in B pictures, was finally given the chance to show his acting mettle in the role of Howard Joyce in Wyler's film, only for his promise and talent to be curtailed by a premature death, aged just fifty-two.

All this indicates the name of James Stephenson stands fairly inconspicuous in contemporary media and yet, in the annals of Hollywood, he remains an intriguing personality. Given he entered the acting profession rather late in life, and had no formal acting training, save experience in amateur dramatics, he achieved a considerable amount in a career of less than ten years, including the remarkable distinction of being Oscar nominated just prior to his tragic death. His untimely demise leaves a whole set of unanswered questions. How, for example, does someone from a conventional and modest English background end up working at Burbank studios during the so-called "golden age" of Hollywood cinema? What did he do before entering the acting profession? How did his previous life experiences enhance his acting roles, and what other influences did he draw upon? How would his career have developed had he lived?

It is with the intention of setting the record straight in these and other matters and attempting to disentangle the reality from the myth Hollywood spins, however prosaic that reality maybe, that I have undertaken to chart his life with as much fidelity as the passing years permit. Having been granted access to the surviving family archives I have sought, wherever possible, to let the subject "speak" for himself by drawing upon archival letters, diaries, news cuttings, extant films, oral witnesses and other primary source materials. Where necessary, I have provided a historical background to help explain and understand his life in a wider context.

In drawing back the veil, as it were, and putting Stephenson into the public domain it is with the aim of assessing his film legacy and thereby stimulating the appreciation of historians and enjoyment of viewers of 1930s and 1940s British and Hollywood cinema. As such, I assume responsibility for any mistakes or omissions that may occur within these pages.

INTRODUCTION

That's all there is to life, just a little laugh, a little tear.
LON CHANEY - *THE UNHOLY THREE*
(METRO-GOLDWYN-MAYER, JACK CONWAY, 1930)

Monday July 28, 1941: the war in Europe, almost two years in duration, is entering a crucial phase. Adolf Hitler's greatest gamble, Operation Barbarossa, the invasion of Soviet Russia by Nazi Germany, gathers momentum since being unleashed the previous month on June 22, 1941. His frenzied attack on Russia was designed to secure yet another lightning victory and consolidate his already massive military successes. The offensive tactic of blitzkrieg, with its track record of breaking the fighting spirit of nation states and producing destruction on a brutal and devastating scale, seemed invincible. German troops began an offensive to encircle Soviet forces in the city of Smolensk. Despite stiff resistance and several counter-attacks the race to capture Leningrad and Moscow, and the rout of Soviet armies by German forces, within the year appeared within Hitler's grasp. Hitler's vision of conquest knew no bounds, as he confidently told his generals: ". . . a campaign against Russia would be like a child's game in a sandbox . . . ." [1]

In a bid to strike back at the Nazi aggressor, war-planes intended for the bombing of German cities in retaliation for Luftwaffe air-raids over English cities such as Bristol, Coventry, Liverpool, London and Manchester, were supplied to Britain from America under the US Lease-Lend Agreement. Elsewhere, the Empire of Japan had recently invaded French Indochina, territories formerly under the control of Vichy France. This successful incursion by the Japanese military would prompt future offensive action, notably the devastating attack on the United States Pacific Fleet at Pearl Harbor on December 7, 1941. Britain, alone, battered, but undaunted, stood firm under the shock of German bombing and the threatened invasion of her shores.

Some five thousand miles away on the United States West Coast in Hollywood such horror seemed far removed. Official US foreign policy was still staunchly isolationist, although President Franklin D. Roosevelt viewed American involvement in a European conflict as both inevitable and impending, given that the fighting had become, in all but name, a global war. At this time over eighty million Americans visited the cinema every week eager to escape the humdrum realities of daily urban living and rumours of entanglements in foreign wars. The Hollywood studios were producing escapist packages based on slick, no-nonsense entertainment interspersed with images of national revival and an unflinching optimism – now the worst of the United States deep economic depression appeared over. All across the country film fans queued outside their local theatres and waited in anticipation eager to see engaging stories inhabited by striking characters, acting out improbable scenarios – the best of which were brought to life with a dedication, skill, flair and panache rarely matched since. In return for what they paid at the box office the masses experienced a sense of shared identity and strong vicarious emotions. Such was the era that film historians today define as "Classical Hollywood Cinema."

The major Hollywood studios were turning out several films per week on an industrial assembly line basis. Walt Disney studios, despite being embroiled in a bitter labour dispute, had just released *The Reluctant Dragon* and were midway through producing *Dumbo*. Another of Hollywood's iconic creators, Charles Chaplin, had just released his own personal film project – a satirical warning of the dangers of modern totalitarianism – *The Great Dictator*. Appearing on screen in the double guise of a Jewish barber and Adenoid Hynkel, dictator of Tomania, Chaplin's lampoon of Germany's dictator provoked both controversy and praise in equal measure. By coincidence both Hitler and Chaplin were born in the same month and year – April 1889. Another who shared this date of birth was James Stephenson.

The final few hours of James Stephenson's life that July Monday were spent with his beloved family, his wife Lorna and their young son Peter, at the family home at 839 Toyopa Drive, Pacific Palisades, Los Angeles, California. During the following morning of Tuesday July 29 he suffered a massive and fatal heart attack.

Among his last acts were to write down his daily expenses in a small pocket cash-book diligently maintained out of necessity and habit. Money, always a concern amongst actors, weighed heavily on his mind. After dinner, served by Violet the housemaid, he had telephoned his secretary, Maud B. Bowman, who was temporarily laid up in hospital with a broken pelvic bone. He was pleased to hear she had received the basket of fruit he'd sent her, but dismayed to learn the cigarettes he'd specifically requested had been omitted. "I phoned the order and they sometimes forget these things," [2] Stephenson had said apologetically. Though he had been visiting her several times a week he was sorry, but at this moment he didn't feel quite fit. He'd come in a couple of days when he was better. As usual he tried to reassure those around him by declaring he'd be okay if he took things easy and rested a while. Innate courtesy and a concern for others were very much a part of his personality.

He had begun to see a decline in his health a month before on a week's vacation at Lake Arrowhead. [3] Whilst there he began to feel unwell and on his return went to see his doctor who didn't like the look of the situation and so sent him to a vascular specialist for tests.

In the meantime he had continued to maintain his daily work schedule, checking in as usual on the Warner Burbank sound stages for make-up and costume tests on the studio's forthcoming big budget melodrama *Kings Row* (Warner Bros., Sam Wood, 1941). [4] People on the set had noted the absence of his usual ready wit and smile. Instead, his face was drawn and displayed an anaemic look. In an effort to secure a financial future for his young family, he had visited his agents and tried haggling for a raise of salary. They were at a loss to explain his sudden acquisitive attitude, given the recent upturn in his career. Perhaps, they guessed, he needed to send a large share of his savings to his brother Alan, chief chorister and organist at Coventry Cathedral, in financial difficulties as a result of the bombings of the English city back in November 1940 and April 1941.

November 1940 was the month that saw the release of William Wyler's adaptation of W. Somerset Maugham's "The Letter," which had launched Stephenson on the path to stardom. He'd proved himself in two star vehicles and, now in demand by the studio, was looking forward to the challenge of more exacting and better roles. No one would have expected this sudden pressure to provide for the future for his wife and child.

The California weather on that July Monday was benevolent even by Hollywood standards. As usual the short-wave radio in the living room of the Stephenson home would have been tuned in to receive news broadcasts from London. Copies of the *Los Angeles Times* and a weekly US edition of *The Times* newspaper, providing news of the international situation, would also have been spread about the house. Reports on the precarious British wartime predicament (especially relevant for the community of ex-patriots in Hollywood's film colony) were a vital lifeline.

Suffering and privation back in Britain were extremely unsettling for the Stephensons. Private trepidation about their families over in England was compounded by murmurs from certain sections of the British media, who questioned the attitude of British personnel in Hollywood. In contrast to the unstinting duty and loyalty of countrymen back in Britain, who had answered the national call-to-arms and given heroic sacrifice in the name of King and Country, their allegiances, at least in some quarters, appeared suspect and unpatriotic. [5] For the British community in Hollywood, the geographic isolation of the United States West Coast made such criticism difficult to fend off. During this early period of the British war effort the British government was torn between tacit support of a visible and high profile British presence in American life (proven to act as a powerful beacon in the allied propaganda war against fascism) and inflaming American domestic feelings against the war raging in Europe. To bolster British interests and encourage American goodwill, Lord Halifax, British Ambassador in Washington, had recently paid a visit to California to inspect US armament plants as part of a nationwide charm offensive gauging diplomatic opinion of a vital, if still neutral, ally. [6]

During his last few days and hours Stephenson had struggled to keep up a daily routine. The heart specialist had phoned Stephenson's doctor to report his findings, which weren't too good. They had agreed to wait until the morning before telling Stephenson that his condition was serious, and he should take a complete rest for three months. Though unaware of the official result from his cardiac tests, his intuition, gained from experience on the Western Front during the First World War, would have told him time was fast running out. He had entered into an understanding with his wife that when either died, what remained to be done should be done as simply as possible. They didn't see why people should be burdened by the heaviness of funeral ceremonies. "I'd rather have them remember me," said Stephenson, "as they last saw me - as if I'd gone off on a trip." [7]

To the end he was paradoxically, for someone in a business that is renowned for egocentricity and vanity, a modest man possessed of a natural reserve and an undemonstrative temperament. His restrained conduct was properly inbred, part of his late Victorian and early Edwardian upbringing in Lancashire, England. He exemplified the values associated with his social background: courtesy, dependability, hard work and a belief in social responsibility, and loyalty to family and friends. For contemporary moviegoers these attributes, with help from the vast resources of the Hollywood studio system, appeared to represent the very essence of an English gentleman. Although he naturally acted the part, he cared little for overt demonstrations of social distinction, the demarcations of class and rank, or the formalities of social deference as expressed in the British class system. Though ambitious he did not, by instinct, take to the limelight, and he disliked "personal appearances" which, as a contract player of a major Hollywood studio, he was obliged to undertake. As an actor his best performances project a gravitas and they exert authority. His delivery was as intense as it was measured. Yet all this was achieved often under circumstances of extreme stress borne of the demanding rigours of tight budgetary shooting schedules. These challenging conditions called for a concentration of physical stamina and mental discipline in order to achieve a sense of credibility, seamlessness and spontaneity in the face of the arduous reality of the piecemeal and fragmented processes of mass studio film production.

Since his death Stephenson, the man, has all but been misplaced and assimilated within a manufactured screen persona perpetuated down the decades. It is with the intent of discovering the individual and exploring his life and times that this monograph is concerned. This is his story.

James Albert Stephenson aged one year and eight months.

1
EARLY LIFE
(1889-1932)

There is genius in persistence.
O.S. MARDEN
THE SECRET OF ACHIEVEMENT (1899)

James Albert Stephenson was born at 1 New Church Terrace, New Lane, in the English town of Selby in The West Riding of Yorkshire. [1] His mother, Emma Longbottom, born 1868, was the youngest daughter of Ann and James Longbottom, a local blacksmith in the Ousgate district of the Yorkshire town. His father, John Gathorne Stansfield [JGS] Stephenson, a trainee chemist born 1868, came from Todmorden in the county of Lancashire. The couple had married in Selby Abbey on October 6, 1888 [2] and James was born on April 14, 1889. [3]

Matrimonial convention demanded that Victorian notions of inheritance and legitimacy be observed and any moral, religious or social objections directed against a child born out of wedlock would be rectified by subsequent marriage. Nevertheless, there were those on the Stephenson side of the family who were of the opinion JGS had married beneath him, a suggestion proved groundless by a long and happy marriage. However, as a consequence of starting a young family, James's father, though he had attained a good standard of education, was forced to give up attending evening classes studying chemistry at Owen's College, a civic institution later to become the University of Manchester. He never qualified as a chemist, and was therefore obliged to employ suitably qualified staff to undertake dispensing of prescribed drugs.

JGS's birth in 1868 coincided with the appointment of Gathorne Hardy, 1st. Earl of Cranbrook, as Home Secretary in the Earl of Derby and Benjamin Disraeli governments. The presence of such a grand name as Gathorne in JGS's forenames was repeated in the name of Stansfield. Family history implied a connection with the wealthy land-owning Stansfields of Halifax in the county of Yorkshire. Whatever the validity of this genealogical claim it was taken in earnest, and to this day the name of Stansfield survives in the family.

During the first few years of his life James and his family moved around the counties of Yorkshire and Lancashire numerous times. In 1891 the family turned up (somewhat appropriately) in Stansfield, a district of Todmorden, at 20 White Platts, where a second son, Alan, was born on July 5. [4] The Stephenson family moved again to Hebden Bridge, Yorkshire where a third son, Norman Douglas, was born on July 9, 1894. [5] Ultimately *circa* 1895 the family of three children and three adults, (JGS's widowed mother Isabella - known affectionately as "Grannie" - also joined the extended family) settled in the town of Burnley in East Lancashire. Old Mr. Stephenson bought a chemist shop at 109 Parliament Street in the Burnley Wood district of the town. [6] The business prospered and by 1906 the family had vacated their accommodation above the shop and moved into a seven room house situated at 162 Todmorden Road, a short walk from the business premises. [7] Looking back James Stephenson stated he had a: ". . . very happy boyhood, roaming every summer in the surrounding countryside." [8] There is nothing surviving in the Stephenson family archive that appears to disprove this assertion.

The township of Burnley was part of the hub of the Lancashire cotton industry. From the mid nineteenth century cotton was king and Burnley's population had risen exponentially from a mere 3,305 in 1801 until by 1899 it was over 100,000. At the turn of the last century the social geography of Burnley was constituted in classic Victorian mode. There were two main arteries leading into the town. The premier route was Manchester Road, home of the professional middle-classes engaged in the mercantile service sector of accountancy, banking, insurance and legal services. Commensurate with its ambience of middle-class affluence a municipal park had been opened on August 8, 1895. Scott Park, situated on the southerly side of the town adjacent to the prosperous occupants of Manchester Road was a public space where the well-connected habitués engaged in social "promenading" among the eighteen acres of well-groomed grass verges, flower beds, memorial fountain, bowling green and band-stand, all maintained by a diligent park keeper and recreation ground staff.

By contrast, Todmorden Road, North-East of the town though respectable enough (Towneley Park, a former private estate with a hall and sixty-one acres had been purchased by the borough council in 1901 from Lady O'Hagan for the benefit of the local town population), can best be described as the tradesmen's entrance. It was here the lower middle-classes: craftsmen, artisans, small-business proprietors and their ilk were to be found. The Stephenson home on Todmorden Road was located on the side of a hill. At the top of the hill lived well-to-do mill owners living in grand detached houses with large grounds and domestic quarters for servants. Meanwhile, at the foot of the hill dwelt the town proletariat who subsisted in rows of cramped, grimy, terrace houses set among the belch of phosphorous smoke and gas that hung in the air from the "dark satanic mills," mines and factories. This display of urban, industrial sprawl, though demonstrably obnoxious, was tolerated by the self-made worthies in the town as incontrovertible manifestations of enterprise and productivity. Such utilitarian traits were viewed as bulwarks in preserving social stability and staving off the perils of revolution from below. The old saying: "idle hands are the Devil's plaything" underpinned the social order of the day.

Though neither James nor his siblings ever laboured at a textile loom, worked down a coal mine, or sweated in an engineering foundry, they would have been only too aware of what could befall them should circumstances take a turn for the worse, the family business experience an economic downturn, or family members suffer the misfortunes of long-term sickness or bereavement. The shadow of the workhouse (described euphemistically in the local Burnley directory as "commodious") and high child mortality were stark facts of life a century ago when welfare provision and a health and safety culture were rudimentary in comparison to contemporary standards. Life, at its worst, in Lancashire's cotton towns could be a "nasty, brutish and short" existence. [9]

This then was hardly the background for a cosseted upbringing providing an insouciant charm which would propel one forward effortlessly in life. James Stephenson's gentlemanliness was therefore derived not from birth nor inherited through great wealth, rather it was created through individual effort and moulding of character. By dint of personal endeavour and self-application it was possible to aspire to better things and get on in life. For the Stephenson brothers, a measure of social affluence and progression were available if they took heed and aimed outward and upward in life. Ambition was a social necessity, and not an optional life-style choice.

The first institution to make an indelible impression on James and his siblings was the local church of St. Catherine's. All three brothers became members of the choir and were thus acquainted with hymns "ancient and modern" and familiar with the scriptures proclaiming the apostolic creed of the Christian faith as professed in the sermons of the Reverend Alfred B. Eddleston (1858-1926), the first vicar of St. Catherine's. Both parents were affiliated to the local church, with Mrs. Stephenson serving on the parochial church council.

The second institution to leave a lasting imprint on their identity was the local borough grammar school. Burnley Grammar School advertised itself in the local press as providing: "Higher Scientific and Commercial Education, Preparation for the Universities and Professions." To be accepted into this august establishment meant a ticket to social mobility. Here the Stephenson brothers were schooled in the middle-class shibboleths of duty, service and self-abnegation. The covenant between school and pupil stressed the value of intellectual rigour, the virtues of sporting prowess, social obligation to kin, duty to King and Country and veneration of: "An empire upon which the sun never sets," or so the maxim ran. Such dedication to "gentlemanly" conduct would forge meritorious achievement, social prestige and personal honour.

In early 1900, as a pupil of Fulledge Wesleyan Day School, James sat and passed examinations for a Burnley Borough Corporation Grammar School Scholarship and the Howarth Prize of £5. He was among thirteen who gained entrance scholarships and exhibitions at the Burnley Grammar School during that annual intake of scholars. [10] He was lucky, for in 1900 there were only places for a hundred pupils. Between 1900 and 1901 the school was modernised and new classrooms were built with temporary provision for girls made available in an otherwise all-male institution. In 1901 the register rose to 150 scholars and in 1909 to 183. [11]

The family archive contains a book marking this rite of passage. It was presented to the young scholar by R. Simpson Esq., Treasurer of Fulledge School. *The Secret of Achievement* subtitled: *A Book Designed to Teach*, written by American author Orison Swett Marden (1850-1924), is a self-help book inspired by the self-improvement ideals of Samuel Smiles. The text sets about generating optimistic self-motivation dedicated to willpower and mind over matter derived from the work of French psychologist Émil Coué (1857-1926). It was Coué who coined the popular mantra: "*Tous les jours à tous points de vue je vais de mieux en mieux*" [Every day, in every way I'm getting better and better]. [12]

Although to modern taste Marden's book reads as pompous and politically incorrect, his archaic prose style seeks to combine a didactic exaltation of heroes with the exhortations and platitudes found in contemporary managerial training manuals. The book is filled from cover to cover with exemplars of, predominantly, great men of modern history compiled according to the tenets of nineteenth-century historian and sage Thomas Carlyle and his code of hero worship. Among the great and the good cited within the book's covers are: Prime Minister Gladstone; presidents Lincoln and Washington; soldier Grant; inventor Watt; historians William H. Prescott and, naturally, Thomas Carlyle; Emperor Napoleon; biographers and poets Holmes and Johnson; evangelist Dwight L. Moody. These notabilities are selected for their qualities of moral leadership, selfless courage, duty under adversity and all-round exemplification of superior talent and crusading excellence. Chapter headings in the book are written in quasi-religious fashion dispensing moral sentiment interspersed with cautionary warnings. Examples include:

"Moral Sunshine – We carry with us the beauty we visit, and the song which enchants us." [13]

"Blessed be Drudgery – Keep the watch wound, or the dark rust assaileth." [14]

"The Conquest of Obstacles – To know how to wring victory from defeat, and make stepping stones of our stumbling blocks, is the secret of success." [15]

"Self-Control – The perfect victory is to triumph over oneself." [16]

Warnings against the emergence of vanity also abound:

"Being and Seeming–"Let us abandon the miserable, false artificialism and take up again with the good wholesome sincerity that will stand by us in the time of need." [17]

"Decide – Success rides upon the hour of decision." [18]

"Making the Most of Life – Our to-days and yesterdays are the blocks with which we build." [19]

These moral homilies were designed to preach the gospel of hard work, energy and growth. "God (or Heaven) helps those who help themselves" was the axiom given to assist individuals, keep them on the straight and narrow and stop them falling into bad habits of lassitude, indecision and debilitation of mind and body.

At the annual grammar school prize day in December 1906, guest speaker Sir John O.S. Thursby set store on the qualities required for demonstrating the effortless push and self-assured ease necessary for attaining high-achievement. After referring to Pope's: "A little learning is a dangerous thing," and Tennyson's: "Self-reverence, self-knowledge, self-control, These three alone lead life to sovereign power," he spoke, at length, of the motto of Winchester School: "Manners makyth man. Culture gives good manners. Bad manners show lack of culture. It is not fine to be rude, to be courteous is not to be servile. One may show respect without loss of self-respect. To be a gentleman is to be gentle in thought, in word and act." [20]

School Headmaster, Mr. Henry Lincoln Joseland, BA (London) MA (Cambs.) (1866-1949), a Cambridge Wrangler, was not tolerant of academic failure or misconduct that would reflect badly on the high reputation of the school. In the paternalistic universe of "Joss," as Mr. Joseland was known to his pupils, a stern warning in his study assisted by the ministering of corporal punishment would suffice to bring boys whose "work left something to be desired" to their senses and persuade them to achieve the ideal scholastic standards.

All pupils were instilled with the need to be attentive and show a concerted effort to present themselves, and thereby the school, to good advantage. Self-restraint, correct speech, formal dress and the suppression of any base impulse of desire precluded any talk of feelings or emotions. Adherence to a rigid social order dictated social deference, compliance and obligation even in the face of rapid socio-economic change. Everything was ranked and stratified with one's role in society designated according to a prescriptive social hierarchy. "Know your station in life" was the watchword of English Edwardian culture.

Receiving a book prize written by an American author was indicative of economic and cultural relations between colonial Britain and the burgeoning colossus of the United States, already flexing its economic muscle in the international arena. British supremacy in world trade markets and as a military power a century ago was being challenged, and already in danger of eclipse.

In November 1900, American ambassador Joseph H. Choate visited Burnley. In an official speech at the town's Mechanics Institute he expressed his views on the benefits and desirability of education on international competitiveness and the opportunities for peace:

"Mr. Choate believes that the conflicts of the future between the great nations of Christendom will not be conflicts in arms. He declared amid approving cheers that any nation which spent too much of its time and substance and energy in the destructive luxury of war would fall sadly behind its rivals in the arts of peace. That is a lesson which the people of this country are only gradually learning to their great cost to-day [An allusion here to the Second Boer War (1899-1902) already a year old and in its third and final phase] Mr. Choate warned us that it will not do for Great Britain and America to look upon themselves as the sole competitors. Germany is in many respects a little ahead of us in its educational enterprise and all the other nations are alive to the importance of the subject. We have reached a period in our history now when the country will have to make up its mind to keep abreast with other countries in this important subject... And for seeing that our sons and daughters have at least an equal chance with our competitors in the race which is before them." [21]

A century later when major economies of the world have entered a third industrial age in their transformation into global, digital and knowledge-based entities, Choate's words have a striking resonance.

The era of so-called "splendid isolation" in which the bastions of empire and gunboat diplomacy ruled, was by now passé. An American presence had taken steady and irreversible root in the British economy. Henry Ford had established his first assembly plant at Trafford Park in Manchester in 1908. By the outbreak of the First World War in 1914 the United States had outstripped Britain as the world's largest manufacturing nation. There were those like journalist F. A. McKenzie who saw the American invasion of modern mass production as a threat to every aspect of British society. In a journalistic fantasy he wrote:

"The average citizen wakes in the morning at the sound of an American alarm clock; rises from his New England sheets and shaves with his New York soap and a Yankee safety razor. He pulls on a pair of Boston boots over his socks from West Carolina (sic) fastens his Connecticut braces, slips his Waterbury watch into his pocket and sits down to breakfast . . . Rising from his breakfast table the citizen rushes outs, catches an electric tram made in New York, to Shepherds Bush, where he gets into a Yankee elevator, which takes him on to the American-fitted railway to the city. At his office of course everything is American. He sits on a Nebraskan swivel chair, before a Michigan roll-top desk. Writes his letters on a Syracuse typewriter, signing them with a New York fountain pen, and drying them with a blotting sheet from New England. The letter copies are put away in files manufactured in Grand Rapids." [22]

James's younger siblings also completed their elementary education at Fulledge Wesleyan Day School, from where they too gained scholarships to the local grammar school. Alan Stephenson was awarded a William Milner Grant Scholarship in 1902 to enter the Burnley Grammar School and, whilst his health was not nearly as robust as his brothers, he excelled intellectually as a scholar in both mathematics and music. [23]

Alan Stephenson's musical aptitude was developed by several critical mentors in Burnley. Mr. A[lfred]. W[ilfred]. Hedges (1862-1934), organist at Fulledge Wesleyan Chapel, provided him with personal music instruction. Mr. W[illiam].A[lexander].C[ampbell]. Cruickshank (Mus. Bac. Oxon) (1854-1934), a Scottish born musician, also instructed him in private tuition on the theory and practice of ecclesiastical music. Cruickshank was organist and preceptor of St Peter's the local parish church for many years. He had himself been trained under both Sir George Martin and Sir Frederick Bridge. His compositions were sung at many national music festivals, in Westminster Abbey, St. Paul's, Winchester and many other cathedrals. As a result of such consummate teaching Alan Stephenson competed in many musical festivals, including a piano competition for under-sixteen year olds held in October 1904 at Blackpool. He achieved second place out of twenty-three candidates, playing Tchaikovsky's *Chant Sans Parole*. The adjudicator, Dr. McNaught, remarked: "Touch perfect, a splendid performance." [24] Such generous praise and diligent application won Alan Stephenson a music scholarship to Keble College Oxford, and he graduated with a Bachelor of Music on November 30, 1911, aged just twenty-one.

Norman Douglas Stephenson completed a trio of scholarship success and took his place on the grammar school register in 1906. He excelled at sports and achieved notable feats during the annual school sports day held on the cricket ground at Turf Moor. [25] Compared to his older brothers, Norman struggled academically. However, after successful matriculation he found suitable employment as a clerk with Proctor and Proctor, a local firm of chartered accountants. His sporting prowess would later be transferred from the playing field to the stoical resilience of the battlefield. Henry Newbolt's poem *Vitai Lampada* immortalised the spirit of Anglo Saxon hardiness in the famous refrain: "Play up! Play up! And play the game!"

The second phase of industrialisation began to hit Britain at the turn of the last century as new technological innovations threatened to usurp the older industries. The world of a century ago was one based on the science of invention, novelty and gadgetry. Electricity, chemistry, the internal combustion engine, aviation were all revealed as scientific wonders of the age. In 1896 the first motor vehicle made its debut in the town of Burnley. In the same year the cinematograph, the last invention of the Victorian age, was first introduced in the town at The Burnley Empire Theatre. The new medium captured for posterity, the highpoint (and end) of the era: the 1897 Diamond Jubilee of Queen Victoria. The first electric tramways began running in Burnley town centre in 1901. The Stephenson family shared in this growth of technical progress for c.1902 a telephone was installed in the chemist shop. [26]

After completing his education at the grammar school young master

James spent several years in search of a suitable occupation. A stint as a pupil teacher at the grammar school produced no particular yearning or burning ambition. Nor was the position of a trainee dentist any more satisfactory as he didn't find fillings enthralling. He finally settled for a position as a bank cashier at the local branch of The Manchester and County Bank Ltd.. Banking was then considered a safe, solid, and even "respectable" profession. Bank manager W. H. D. Flack Esq., a scion of high-minded rectitude, had risen steadily through the tiers of banking management until attaining the elevated position of senior manager in charge of a designated financial domain. "Mr. Flack is well-known and highly esteemed in the district," commented the local papers upon his appointment as successor to Mr. N.[athan] P.[arr] Gray as branch manager in 1909. [27] Indeed, for Mr. Flack a pillar of the Burnley Establishment exemplified perfectly the virtues of the nineteenth-century mindset with its emphasis on character, sympathy, self-interest compatible with moral sentiment, and social cohesion. [28] Victorian values based on thrift, sound money and a basic family decency, interspersed with socially progressive Christian good works, being the order of the day. Financial prudence wasn't just preached but practised, with stringency. Mr. Flack's position of authority and probity made him known to everybody in the town deemed worthy of doing honest business.

It is difficult to overestimate the importance music played in the lives of people in those days. Music was live and not supported by mechanical reproduction. In order to hear music you would attend a live performance. The early phonograph machines, first cylinders and later discs, with their horns were an expensive luxury restricted to the homes of the affluent. Promenading in the park on a Sunday afternoon after morning church service, and listening to local bandmaster Dan Duxbury conducting on the band stand in Towneley Park were social highlights of the week. Perhaps a smart restaurant or a café in one of the fashionable departmental stores might have a small live orchestra. Whit Walks and processional marching were other occasions when the presence of music was necessary and desirable. To appreciate music people were encouraged to study musical composition and play an instrument. Attendance at the Victoria Theatre or "The Vic" as it was known was also available for those able to afford the price of tickets for the latest operatic star celebrities. The non-conformist Methodist background in northern England emphasised choral singing over musical instruments. Hardly surprising then that James should reminisce: "I, myself, did quite a bit of singing in churches when I was a boy." [29]

Church music was something which occupied his leisure activities a great deal. Performance of Handel's oratorio *Messiah* was a venerable tradition stretching back many years. James also sang bass in amateur concerts and local music societies. He was a member of the Burnley Vocal Society and in its fifth season, during January 1913, the society gave a concert programme devoted to selections from the works of "Maestro Wagner." James appeared on stage at the Burnley Mechanics Institute in a fragment taken from Act III, Scene V of *Die Meistersinger* in the small part of Pogner. Of his singing, the local paper remarked:

> "Although Mr. Stephenson had little to do, he did his portion with great credit to himself." [30]

James was particularly enthralled by the music of Richard Wagner. Wagner's music was given particular approbation by the middle-classes of the day. His musical compositions were prodigious, being both exhausting and challenging in their length and performance. His works provided a cutting edge experience in terms of scale, and stylistic innovation.

Yet even as James participated in the respected traditions of choral singing and the classical music repertoire, he also experienced modernity in other activities. Professing to be of a mechanical bent, James followed the rise of motoring for the masses with interest, and in 1911 he acquired a new motorcycle. The records show a twin cylinder five horsepower Rex Cycle was registered in his name on April 24, 1911, the month of his twenty-second birthday. By the following year, James had sold the machine on to John Basil Fletcher, a tailor shop assistant of 18 Harriet Street, Burnley, who on May 17, 1912 added a detachable side car to the Rex cycle. [31] These were up-market machines manufactured in Coventry. Additional archives show James then progressed to a second-hand motor car. A 1904 Humberette, six horsepower, open two-seater, complete with klaxon, crank handle starter and a maximum speed of twenty-five mph, was registered in his name on March 27, 1912. [32]

In addition, reference to the polling register of 1912-13 reveals James was now eligible to vote by virtue of being classed as a lodger who paid his father a weekly rent of 16 shillings (c.£61.80 worth at today's retail prices) to contribute to the upkeep of the family property on Todmorden Road. Sharing in the financial management of the property entitled him to voting rights. [33] At this juncture in his early life James had already achieved a degree of mobility both social and geographical.

The Stephenon's next door neighbour, housed at 164 Todmorden Road, Lieutenant-Colonel Charles Henry Cowling was an old soldier of local distinction. His military rank and social standing provided an irresistible role-model particularly for Norman Stephenson. Following retirement from the army Lieutenant-Colonel Cowling had become an H.M. inspector of schools. The local press on the eve of his departure from Burnley in 1928 gave him a cordial and reverential valedictory in terms that would not have disgraced the venerable English actor C[harles]. Aubrey Smith, or cartoonist David Low's famous political caricature, Colonel Blimp.

> "Colonel Cowling is a fine mixture of the scholar, the soldier, and the saint. With his courtly manners, his high ideals, his love of King and Country and his old-fashioned Toryism, he might perhaps best be described as a typical English gentleman of the old school." [34]

If the merits of self-improvement brought success for a minority at home, at an international level self-aggrandisement was marching apace in the guise of imperialism, a web of international alliances, an Anglo-German naval arms race and the emergence of two armed camps on the European continent.

The British Empire had by the early years of the twentieth century reached a point where its geopolitical reach extended to a quarter of the earth's surface. The presumption of moral authority and racial supremacy lay at the heart of empire building with its proclaimed benefits of Christianity, commerce and governance to the civilisation of conquered populations. The British, with their vast empire in tow, adopted a supercilious didactic mindset. "Foreigners begin at Calais" remained a deep-rooted and pervasive idea. [35] The British saw themselves as the elect, pre-eminent above all other nations by virtue of their dependability, based on classical stoicism and keeping a proverbial stiff upper lip in circumstances of confrontation or trouble. Foreigners, in contrast, were viewed as suspect and unreliable. They should, like everyone else, know their station and if they became too irksome they should initially be ignored and if they still refused to know their station then they must be taught a harsh lesson by use of gunboat diplomacy.

Along with Britain, Europe in 1900 exercised direct rule over large parts of the globe. In Asia there was French Indo-China, the Dutch East Indies, German New Guinea and the great British Raj in India, Burma and Malaya. Africa too was almost entirely divided between several European nations. In cultural, economic and military affairs European domination was implicit, and was expressed through the medium of European languages operating right across the world. Europe's historic centre was Vienna, her religious centre Rome, her economic and military centre Berlin, her trade and financial centre London and Paris, her artistic centre.

Britain had led the way in the first industrial revolution during the nineteenth century, but now international rivalry threatened peaceful and prosperous co-existence. The European dynastic empires of Habsburg Austro-Hungary, Romanov Russia and Hohenzollern Germany, whose autocratic leaders decorated themselves in resplendent uniforms replete with ostrich plumes, regimental swords and militaristic helmets, such as the Pickelhaube, may have appeared remote figures of Ruritanian pantomime, but behind the strutting bombast and disproportionate ostentation lay power politics writ large. In a chilling prophecy, the philosopher Friedrich Nietzsche had written in 1886:

> "The time for petty politics is over: even by the next century, we will be battling for mastery over the earth – "forced" into politics on a grand scale." [36]

As international events began to unravel during the long hot summer of 1914 this impression of rising violence amongst nation states would become fully apparent. The established order began to dissolve into a frenzy of bellicose nationalism as the lure of a short decisive victory, as foretold in a previous conflict, the Franco-Prussian War of 1870-1871, caught the imagination of Europeans everywhere. In Britain domestic industrial strife (a general strike was scheduled to occur in September 1914), increased direct action by the militant arm of the women's suffrage movement, and threatened civil war in Ireland over the issue of Home

Grand old folk: James Stephenson's parents,
Emma and John Gathorne Stansfield Stephenson on the eve
of their retirement from Burnley, East Lancashire in 1936.
Photo courtesy of Stephenson Archive Photo

Rule were all overshadowed by an approaching European war. The local Burnley press declared:

> "The outlook is indeed serious. Trade is bad; the country is menaced by civil war and a war has broken out on the Continent the outcome of which it is impossible, at present, to foresee." [37]

From surviving archival material it is possible to ascertain that the status of the Stephenson family in the years leading up to the outbreak of war was relatively stable, reasonably content, moderately prosperous and fairly ambitious for the future. The family archive contains a dictionary belonging to old Mr. Stephenson who appreciated words and used them judiciously. On the eve of his retirement in 1936 he declared with some self-satisfaction: "I made three fortunes: one I lived on, one I used to educate my sons and the other I saved." [38]

There can be little doubt that the experience of war left an indelible mark on a generation of combatants. Unlike British film director James Whale, who took the opportunity to reinvent his identity during the war, James Stephenson's wartime experiences consolidated and refined his character. His sharp intellect, already demonstrated through the traditional channels of religious instruction and formal education, was now exposed to the rigours of leadership and the strains of military combat. The middle-class belief system of duty and service would now be tested to the very limit with self-sacrifice on a scale hitherto unimaginable. Both Church and State stood shoulder-to-shoulder fighting under the banner of Empire, King and Country.

The first in the family to enlist in the army was Norman who joined the 20th Royal Fusiliers some two months following the outbreak of war. Later he was sent to Sandhurst Royal Military College and received a commission serving in the 1st. Loyal North Lancashire Regiment. He arrived in France in January 1916 and after some seven months at the front he was involved in heavy fighting during the Somme offensive to take High Wood, a small forest near Bazentin Le Petit. This area saw intense fighting for two months from July 14 to September 15, 1916. Surviving war diaries of 1st Brigade, Loyal North Lancashire Regiment record the strength of the Battalion for Thursday August 17, 1916, as sixteen officers and 522 other ranks. The report for the following afternoon of Friday August 18, 1916 stated:

> "In conjunction with troops on our flanks, the Battalion attacked the German trenches just west of High Wood. Casualties: Captain M.A. Cross and Captain D.O.H. Tripp D.S.O. killed. Lieutenant Nichol, Second Lieutenants Ware, Stephenson, Harrison, Heaton and Bulling wounded. Other ranks: killed thirty; wounded 110; missing fifty." [39]

Norman sustained shrapnel in the shoulder, and had become yet another of the hideous casualty rates of officers and men who suffered great sacrifice on the Western Front. He was admitted to the Second Red Cross Hospital, Rouen, on August 21, 1916 and transported back to England to the Worsley Military Hospital near Manchester where the shrapnel was removed. On recovery, he returned to the front and was subsequently made a first lieutenant. For gallantry in the field Lieutenant Norman Douglas Stephenson was awarded the Military Cross in the King's Birthday Honours List in June 1918.

Meanwhile, James enlisted in the army in late December 1914 as a junior officer (second lieutenant direct commission) in the 2/5th East Lancashire Regiment. He spent the first year of his army service at University of London officer's training school where on July 25, 1915 he attained the rank of captain. He also undertook a staff college course at Camberley, Surrey in December 1915. In September 1916, he applied for transfer to the Army Service Corps in the motor transport division. His application papers, submitted with due deference, stated:

> "Sir,
>
> I have the honour to make application for transfer to the A.S.C. M[otor]T[ransport] Class B Road Officer. I have the honour to be, Sir,
>
> > Your obedient servant
> > James A. Stephenson
> > Capt.
> > 2/5th East Lancs. Regiment
> > Colchester
> > 4.9.16" [40]

This application proved successful due to his competence with mechanical vehicles both pre-war and during his army training. He signed an affidavit to the effect that he had maintained and ridden several makes of both two and four wheel vehicles:

> "I certify that I have driven various makes of motor cycles for the past six years – heavy issues and lightweights – and that I am able to carry out running repairs to the same.
>
> I also certify that, during the past two years and six months, I have driven three makes of cars – two and five seaters and am able to carry out road repairs to the same." [41]

This being the British Army, a testimonial substantiating the application was forthcoming from Captain H. Wallwork, 2/10 Battalion, Manchester Regiment. [42]

A surviving photograph featuring an assembly of army officers of

Officers of 2/5th East Lancashire Regiment at Colchester in March 1916. Captain James Stephenson, wearing a slight moustache, is seated extreme left on the front row. He emerged from the war unscathed, but others were not so fortunate. Of the thirty-one men in the photograph at least three were killed in action. Claude Oliver Boswell [Passchendaele 10/9/1917]; Thomas William Battock [3/21/1918]; Denham Walker [9/19/1916]

PHOTOGRAPH PUBLISHED BY ELLIOTT & FRY LTD, PHOTO COURTESY OF BURNLEY BOROUGH COUNCIL, TOWNELEY HALL ART GALLERY AND MUSEUMS

the 2/5th East Lancashire Regiment shows a rather raffish young man sporting a slight moustache. His appearance provides evidence of the military esprit de corps and his rite of passage into the military world. Having successfully transferred to the Army Service Corps he was posted to Grove Park and then Bulford Motor Transport Depot and finally joined the expeditionary force for France on March 29, 1917, his motor transport unit being attached to 285th Siege Battery Royal Garrison Artillery.

Compared with his brothers, Alan Stephenson had a relatively quiet

Captain James A. Stephenson attached to 12 Battalion Royal Garrison Artillery on motorcycle somewhere in France between March 1917 and November 1919
PHOTO COURTESY OF STEPHENSON ARCHIVE

war. He was the last to join up and become a private in 5th Battalion, The East Lancashire Regiment on December 11, 1915. Later in September 1916 he applied for a commission and became lst. Lieutenant in the 2/5th East Lancashire Regiment and was seconded for duty as an assistant bomb instructor in a Corps Bomb and Trench mortar school. He never saw active service in France, and on December 13, 1916 he married Ethel May Wileman (1895-1974), the daughter of a mechanical engineer's clerk in Gainsborough. [43] The wedding took place just before the death, a week later, of paternal grandmother Isabella Stephenson who died aged eighty-one on December 23, 1916. [44]

Surviving evidence in the form of a handful of photographs, taken after the November Armistice, and various military documents show James had a "good war" in the sense that he managed to come through it without any physical or mental impairment. His transfer into the Army Service Corps meant he was spared the danger of front line trench warfare on the Western Front.

In the Stephenson family archive two orders of the day, signed by Commander-in-Chief of British Armies in France, Field-Marshal Douglas Haig, are preserved. It includes Haig's famous stoical and uncompromising order of April 11, 1918.

"Many amongst us now are tired. To those I would say Victory will belong to the side which holds out the longest . . . There is no other course open to us but to fight it out. Every position must be held to the last man: there must be no retirement. With our backs to the wall and believing in the justice of our cause each one of us must fight on to the end." [45]

This document is a testament to a reversal of fortunes during the final year of the war. The year began with Allied demoralisation and defeat and yet, miraculously, ended with the complete collapse of the Central Powers of Germany, Austria-Hungary, Bulgaria and the Ottoman Empire. James appears to have shared Haig's resilience and belief that though the war had been bloody and horrific in its human cost, it was just and did produce, via conviction and resolve, an ultimate and necessary victory for the allied forces.

The evidence in the family archive is at variance with today's common image of Field Marshal Douglas Haig as an incompetent bungler reviled for his futile butchery of countless lives, which were lost in wave after wave of senseless slaughter. During his life he was respected and revered as a national hero. Such popular vilification began following his death in 1928, as the war memoirs of former premier Lloyd George records:

> "He was a painstaking professional soldier with a sound intelligence of secondary quality. He had the courage and stubbornness of his race . . . But he did not possess the necessary breadth of vision or imagination to plan a great campaign against some of the ablest Generals of the War. I never met a man in a high position who seemed to me so utterly devoid of imagination." [46]

By the late 1930s, with the approach of another European conflict, the great victory of 1918 and mantra of "the war to end all wars" seemed hollow and Haig's image, and that of fellow senior officers, began to be the subject of popular disparagement. As military historian Basil Liddell Hart suggested:

> "The figure of Haig has become enfolded in a dual legend – one might describe it as a 'Jekyll and Hyde' legend. On the one hand there has grown the conventional picture of a great commander – far-sighted, profound in reflection, quick of decision, unshakeable in resolution, moved solely by a sense of duty. On the other hand, there is the picture of a soldier moulded to a different yet not less popular pattern – short-sighted, dull, slow, obstinate and callous. This also follows a convention of popular caricature. It has left Haig a wooden effigy, at which the man in the streets shrugs his shoulders . . . Is there any way of reconciling such contrasting pictures, and of discovering the real form which lies hidden underneath them?" [47]

Since the 1960s Haig's image has been presented, overwhelmingly, in a negative light. This can be chiefly traced to historian Alan Clark's controversial book about the British high command, *The Donkeys* (1961) and the savage anti-war satire, *Oh What a Lovely War* (1963). By the time of the transmission of the BBC Television situation comedy *Blackadder Goes Forth* in 1989, the Haig myth was ripe for mocking satire.

The debate over Haig's reputation (was he a lion or a donkey?) rumbles on to this day. There is little doubt of the appalling conditions endured by troops on the Western Front; it was the antithesis of what the glory of warfare had hitherto envisaged. The mass mechanisation of warfare produced slaughter on a scale not previously conceived or imagined, even in the worst possible case scenario. It is estimated between 722,785 and 772,000 Britons died in military service during the First World War. It is these casualties and the myth of Haig's "indifference" and High Command "incompetence" that continue to cause controversy. At the time, Haig had led the British army to final victory and his hard work for ex-servicemen after the war counted for something with most people. This certainly appears to be the case with James Stephenson.

James remained stationed in France following the November armistice and continued in service for a further twelve months (aside from extended leave on "private matters") before being discharged on November 5, 1919. A war diary entry for August 8, 1919 states:

> "Capt. J.A. Stephenson RASC taken on strength from 25 vehicle repair park." [48]

His final unit of service was RASC Motor Transport 21st M[otor] A[mbulance] C[onvoy]. This indicates, following the armistice, his duties and responsibilities changed from command of artillery to ambulance convoys transporting patients to evacuation reliefs.

His surviving army discharge papers are heavily creased, suggesting he carried them around on his person either in his pocket or, more likely, in his wallet. They refer to:

> "A very good officer who has always carried out his duties in a very efficient manner. Did excellent service in the Kemmel Wyschaete fighting in April-May 1918 - inspires confidence in both his superior officers and those under his command. Has commanded RASC attached to 18 Bdt. Royal Garrison Artillery for four months during which heavy and arduous operations were in progress." [49]

The report goes on to ascertain his proficiency in other aspects of his war service:

> "Ability and professional knowledge – Very good
>
> Power to maintain discipline – Very good

Power of leadership – Very good

Knowledge, capacity and tact for training – Should consider exceptionally suitable

Suitability for staff employment – Very suitable and capable of demonstrating staff work

Any other special military qualification it may be necessary to mention – Good knowledge of military law and infantry training."

Although, unlike his younger brother, Norman, he was not awarded medals for gallantry, James's selfless attention to duty and his abilities in a tight spot is attested to by the remarkable survival of a small scrap of paper in the family archive containing the following inscription:

"Dear Eve

I very much regret

That your group are again leaving us as you lot have

Done magnificently and have been

The star performers all through

Stephenson has worked like a hero and

Is worthy of all praise

I would like to congratulate

All of your officers, NCOS, and men

For the splendid way in

Which they have stuck

It during the past few days

   Yrs. sincerely

   B.S.R. Cunningham." [50]

Counting the cost:
Scenes of devastation in the Ypres Salient
following the armistice of November 1918.
PHOTOS COURTESY OF STEPHENSON ARCHIVE

France, June 15, 1919. Captain James Stephenson, front row extreme left
with fellow officers and female civilian. The photograph is signed at the back:
"Smith gets a whizzbang in the eye, on the other films the smoke
from the burst screens Gale half the major and Mckie."
PHOTO COURTESY OF STEPHENSON ARCHIVE

The awful bloody war destroyed forever the illusion of stability in
Europe and produced repercussions in international affairs which still
affect us today. Commemoration, remembrance and memory of the
war became a cornerstone of British culture throughout the 1920s and
1930s. This collective sense of loss and scepticism would play a part in
undermining some of the received notions of British national identity
given carte blanche before the war. If churchgoing and formal schooling
were institutions of character building, then participation in the First
World War was an additional life changing event that would, forever,
mould the characters of the Stephenson siblings.

Hindsight and nostalgia tend to distort and obscure the steep
economic decline and deep social insecurities of Britain's former
Victorian eminence, exacerbated by the First World War. Upon James's
return to civilian life in Burnley, stark economic and social conditions
confronted him. In another surviving special order of the day, dated on
the fourth anniversary of the outbreak of war on August 4, 1918, Field-
Marshal Douglas Haig reported:

> "At the end of four years of war, the magnificent fighting qualities
> and spirit of our troops remain of the highest order. I thank them
> for their devoted delivery and unshaken resolution with which
> they responded to my appeal at the height of the struggle and I
> know they will show a like steadfastness of courage in whatever
> task they may yet be called upon to perform." [51]

These fine words during wartime were not matched by fine deeds in the years of peace which followed the final armistice of November 11, 1918. With the cessation of hostilities many northern English towns came to economic grief as unemployment began to rise precipitately. By January 1921 there were 43,000 unemployed in Burnley. The desperation of these hard times can be deduced from the prominent front-page headlines in the local press:

"There is Real Distress in Burnley

Hundreds of People are Short of Food

I do wish that all those who have dinners will try to support those who have none.

There is real need. At least £400 is required weekly

The present fund is exhausted

This is a testing time. I appeal to all out of goodness of heart to help the Relief Fund by giving all they can" [52]

This was a rare break with journalistic tradition during a time when use of the front page for banner headlines was still considered indecorous. This appeal for charitable aid signed by Burnley Lord Mayor, Edwin Whitehead, tells all one needs to know about the perilous state of the Lancashire economy at this time. There was no getting away from it; Northern England, East Lancashire and the town of Burnley were economically on the ropes.

As a former army officer James attended officer reunions (66th East Lancashire Division Dinner Club) held at Manchester's premier Midland Hotel. It was there that he made the acquaintance of Harold Collier (1891-c.1962). The name of Capt. Harold Collier 6th Manchesters is listed in an officer's dinner directory along with his parent's address, The Olives, Victoria Park, Rusholme, Manchester. [53] Collier, the second of four brothers, was son of Reverend Samuel Francis Collier (1855-1921), a famed Methodist preacher who worshipped in Manchester. Tragedy had struck the Collier family twice during the final year of the First World War. Captain Samuel Francis [Frank] Collier, the eldest son, died on the Western Front on March 22, 1918 leaving a young widow. His name appears on the Pozières Memorial. This tragedy was cruelly, and swiftly, followed by the death of Sidney Collier, the youngest son. Having fought in military campaigns on the Western Front and Gallipoli he had decided, in 1918, to transfer from the army to the Royal Flying Corps. This decision proved fatal; he was killed not in aerial combat, but in a flying accident while on training exercises on March 28, 1918. He was buried, just twenty-two years of age, at La Chaudière Military Cemetery, Vimy. [54]

Harold Collier, like James's brother Norman, had received a Military Cross for gallantry in the field. Like James he also arrived in France during March 1917, having already seen service in both Gallipoli and Egypt. He had recently married and lived in Prestbury, Cheshire.

Together Harold and James formed a cotton shipping business, Collier and Stephenson. A municipal rates book dated June 24, 1921 confirms Harold Collier and James Albert Stephenson as named occupiers of 29 Great Ancoats Street, Manchester. [55] These business premises were situated above a café and, significantly, a Methodist shelter. Harold Collier's family Methodist connections suggest it was he, rather than James, who was responsible for providing these premises. The names of Harold Collier and James Albert Stephenson also appear in a surviving Manchester business rates book for their new office premises on 30 Princess Street, Manchester. In a biography of Collier's father, Rev. Samuel Collier, there is a reference to Harold Collier who, ". . . eventually entered into business." [56] Like James Stephenson, Harold Collier was a product of middle-class schooling having been educated at Manchester Grammar School. Following the death of Collier's father in 1921, Collier, his wife and family, frequently stayed at a property owned by the late Rev. Collier in North Wales. The available evidence leads to the conclusion that a great deal of effort on James's part did not yield significant financial reward. There were several shifts in business addresses around the centre of the city of Manchester. [57]

International travel during the inter-war years involved long and arduous trips by boat-train. For example, on May 2, 1925, following a train journey from Manchester, James boarded the White Star Line, SS *Celtic*, at Liverpool and crossed the Atlantic bound for New York. From New York he sailed on the *President Monroe* down through the Panama Canal stopping over at Havana, Cuba and arriving at Los Angeles. There he sailed across the Pacific until finally docking at Shanghai, China. A Chinese passport dated March 25, 1926 shows he had official access to the province of Jiangsu. In China, James befriended Li Quong Hiu, a native servant who served him loyally and faithfully, which was as well for the climate in the province of Chapu was extreme with harsh freezing winters and stagnant tropical summers which made exploration of the countryside otherwise difficult. In business James was able to rely on his unfailing memory for currency quotations, production costs, exercise duties and shuffling exchange rates.

Whatever the challenges in James's business career it didn't dent his enthusiasm for his love of music. Live music was still the dominant form of musical education, enlightenment and entertainment. Following the

Crossing the equator during the 1920s. Cotton merchant James Stephenson
in shirt sleeves and arms folded with other passengers aboard ship.
PHOTO COURTESY OF STEPHENSON ARCHIVE

lead of other English northern towns, Burnley had decided in November
1919 to form an amateur music society known as the Clef Club. James,
intent on recapturing the musical taste and fraternity of the pre-war years,
signed up for membership. In October 1920 he performed in a concert
of famed Italian operatic pieces. There is a clue in the following critique
as to his transfer away from the provincial world of banking to that of
international cotton shipping in partnership with Harold Collier:

> "Mr. Stephenson sang "Garment Antique" with musical taste, but
> what impressed us most was the beautiful tone and rich colour
> of his glorious voice. Bass singers of Mr. Stephenson's class are
> so rare that we could not hope to keep him in this district had not
> business the first call on his services." [58]

And so, intermittently, as the cotton business permitted, he would
continue to support the Clef Club and its commitment to local singing
talent. In 1924 he appeared in Holst's opera *Savitri* as Death, and the
following year as Mr. Sharpless, the United States Consul, in *Madam
Butterfly*. Of the latter the local press reported:

> "Mr. James Stevenson (sic) has a fine bass voice which he
> effectively used in the dignified music allotted to "Sharpless."
> He looked the part of an august consul and a little stiffness

in movement did not detract from the impressiveness of his portrayal." [59]

In March 1927 he appeared in *A Persian Garden – A Fantasy* as an elderly Persian Prince. The *Burnley News* noted:

"Mr. James Stevenson (sic) is a singer whom we hear too little, for he has a magnificent bass voice and good style. His work here was impressive, for he made every phrase full of meaning, and every note a thing of beauty." [60]

Although to twenty-first century listeners the music of the inter-war years is renowned for its melodic tunes, at the time many people, including James, had little taste for the strident jazz chords being played at the local palais de dance and hitting the airwaves of wireless broadcasting. The "wah-wah-wah" of a jazz trumpet was to the late Victorian and Edwardian ear what the amplified cacophony of modern rock music is to contemporary middle-age sensibility.

It is likely that following the death of Harold Collier's mother, Henrietta, in early 1926 Collier had decided to leave the business to pursue other business interests at his parents' address in North Wales. In any case, by the end of 1926 Harold and James had agreed, by mutual consent, to dissolve the partnership with the business transferring with all debts due to and owing to James as sole partner who carried on the business in the same name and style from the same address. [61]

There is plenty of available evidence that trading conditions during the early and mid 1920s were not propitious. The name of Collier and Stephenson appears in a 1923 round robin letter published in the *Manchester Guardian* containing over four hundred firms of Manchester cotton merchants and suppliers protesting about the monopolistic practices of the Piece Dyers Association. [62] Two years later the partnership undertook legal proceedings to obtain payment in respect of outstanding debts owed to the business. At The King's Bench Division High Court the case of Collier and Stephenson of 5 Beaver Street Manchester versus John Robertson and Sons of 3 and 5 Booth Street Manchester was heard in Court No 3 on April 2, 1925 before Mr. Justice Roche. Beyond this bald statement contained in Legal Notices of several national newspapers, records of the court case do not survive, and this suggests that the case was not contested by the defendants, and did not alter any points of law. [63]

In the long term this incident was the least of Harold and James's worries, for in 1925 Chancellor of the Exchequer Winston Churchill, on the advice of the Governor of the Bank of England, Montagu Norman, returned Britain to the gold standard. The exchange rate for sterling was inaugurated at the pre-war parity of £1=$4.86c. The rate was set too high and proved disastrous for British industry, particularly for cotton export markets as this added an extra ten per cent cost to British goods. The old nineteenth-century stable industries such as cotton and coal suffered from foreign competition in international markets where demand had fallen off drastically. Not only on the economic front, but politically the Far East was subject to rising nationalism and the spread of dissident activity and political insurrection. In early 1927, five thousand British troops were dispatched to Shanghai. It was time for James to cut his losses, call it a day, and make a lateral career move.

James struck up an acquaintance with fellow businessman Ernest Bryce Clegg (1888-1962). Like James, Clegg had also set up a business partnership after the War. Being a keen cricketer he had set up, with John Hunt managing, a small sport's outfitters shop located on 48 Standish Street in Burnley. By October 27, 1923 J. Hunt & Co. had been dissolved by mutual consent. Clegg had then diversified, becoming a merchant (or sales representative as it would now be called) in the distribution of oil. *Spurrier Glazebrook & Co. Ltd.* was an oil refiner and manufacturer. 'Spur' Oil had several distribution outlets scattered around the northern region of England, including a branch based in Albert and Riverside Mills, Wyre Street in Padiham. [64] Together Clegg and Stephenson worked their respective geographic patches selling oil lubricants to those mills still managing to function in a depressed market.

In December 1927 James applied for a vehicle driving license and rented a garage at Towneley Villa, Todmorden Road near his home. The records reveal he had bought a brand new 11.9 horsepower Riley Lulworth Special Saloon from George W. Rushworth of Station Garage, Colne Road in Colne, East Lancashire. It cost approximately £350 (c. £16,300.00 worth at today's retail prices). A family saloon car, he often took his elderly parents to coastal seaside resorts and beauty spots in the Lake District. He later sold the vehicle on to a Mr. Abraham Pattison, 100 Highgate, Kendal. The transaction occurred at the Windermere Motor Boat Club on June 22, 1929. [65]

There is no surviving photograph of James in his motor car, but he would have cut a dashing figure dressed smartly in the new style of dress then popularised by such celebrities as His Royal Highness Edward, Prince of Wales and the new American popular elegance and grace of dancer Fred Astaire. Provision of personal comfort rather than demonstrating social authority was the concept behind the new clothing fashions between the wars. [66] When James wasn't out on business trips abroad he showed his mastiff dog, Bronx of Towneley, in local shows.

James Stephenson (right) wearing the smart casual dress of plus fours
with unidentified friends during the 1920s.
PHOTO COURTESY OF STEPHENSON ARCHIVE

To his delight, the dog won prizes consecutively at the Burnley local dog
show in November 1925 and the Royal Lancashire Show in July 1926. [67]

Meanwhile James's brother, Norman, had spent most of the 1920s
in the army as commissioner of police of the Upper Nile province in
the Sudan. It was during September 1927 that he met his future wife
Adela Riddlesdale Wilkinson (1898-1988). They met aboard the SS
Devanha embarking at Port Said where Norman was requested by the
captain to give up his cabin for a young female passenger. [68] Adela was
a determined young woman and by the end of the voyage they had come
to a romantic understanding and their engagement was soon announced.
Their wedding took place quietly amongst family and close friends
on November 17, 1928 at Leatherhead Parish Church followed by a
honeymoon at Cannes on the French Riviera. A discreet announcement
was published in *The Times* a few days later. [69]

Their marriage strengthened the Stephenson family connection to
colonialism, affiliations that are an integral part of Somerset Maugham's
short story, "The Letter," and James's most famous film role.

Born in Calcutta, India, a child of Empire, Adela was quite a few
notches above the social scale than Norman. [70] Her father, Mr. Mence
Wilkinson (1863-1939), was an East Indian merchant involved in a
diverse portfolio of colonial business interests. He became director
and chairman of the Scottish firm Whiteaway, Laidlaw and Company
following the death of Sir Robert Laidlaw in 1915. He was also a

Norman Douglas Stephenson, "Steve," and his wife Adela Riddlesdale
Wilkinson, "Toonie," on their wedding day: November 17, 1928.
Toonie was an elocutionist of local renown and a prolific diarist.
PHOTO COURTESY OF BLAIN ARCHIVE

director of a mining company, the Central Provinces Manganese Ore
Company, from 1915 and chairman in 1921. In this capacity he served
under Sir Reginald H[enry]. Craddock MP (1864-1937). Finally, he also
assisted in the management of The London Asiatic Rubber and Produce
Company Limited. As was the vogue among the upper middle-classes,
the Wilkinsons of Leatherhead, Surrey gave themselves private family
nicknames. So Adela was known as "Toonie" and her three siblings:
Mence (1894-1976), Amy Isabel (1897-1980) and Mabel Outram (1906-
1939) were known as "Menie," "Vanny," and "Bay." These names were
of a Kiplingesque *Jungle Book* derivation. Toonie took to calling her
husband by the affectionate nickname of "Steve" in preference to his
legitimate and more formal name of Norman.

Opera and singing were beginning to occupy a greater proportion of
James's time. The Burnley Operatic Society had been formed in 1928
and inaugural performances of three grand operas: *Cavalleria Rusticana*,

I Pagliacci and *Faust* took place week commencing December 3, 1928. During the week, three performances of each opera were given. Though unable to participate in these productions, due to winding up the cotton shipping business in Shanghai and attending his brother's wedding, James was drawn to the ideals of its foundation. The operatic society relied solely and heavily on local talent to function and, unsurprisingly, given his track record with the Clef Club, he was soon approached by members of the society with an invitation to join. James was persuaded, under some protest, by both John Grey and Clifford Parkinson to come on board. He had already taken part in a daytime BBC radio concert during February 1929 and delivered a performance as the commandant in a Clef Club production of *Don Giovanni* on the Burnley amateur stage in March 1929. This flurry of activity was capped by his appearance in The Burnley Operatic Society's second season. During November 1929 there were two productions: Bizet's *Carmen* followed by Mozart's *The Magic Flute*. In the latter, James played High Priest Sarastro. The *Northern Daily Telegraph* reported that he "used his pure bass voice with intensity particularly in 'Within these Hallowed Portals'." [71] The *Burnley News* went further opining that: "Mr. Jas. Stephenson impressed us with his Sarastro, which had dignity and power. His declamatory passages and stage deportment were even better than his singing." [72]

Such was the success of this production that James's good friend John Grey was emboldened to go and realise further ambitions. Picking up *The Times* newspaper he read an advertisement for the sale of scenery and the entire effects from a production of *Aida*. The old British National Operatic Company had gone into liquidation. He sent a telegram offering £20 and the answer came back: "Yours, collect." As he went on to explain:

> "There was seventeen tons of it. It had to be loaded at a store house at the back of Euston Station in special 40 ft. long trucks and it cost me £39 to bring it to Burnley where we stored it in a disused cotton mill. Perhaps the society's most outstanding production was that of *Aida* with a cast of ninety-six performers, a veritable Cecil B. De Mille epic!" [73]

Along with Verdi's *Aida* the Society also gave performances of Mozart's *The Marriage of Figaro*. John Grey's uncle, Councillor John Thornber, was president of the opera company and the ideal patron. He hosted champagne parties at his residence, Healey Hall, on the Friday and Saturday nights for the principals of each of the two operas given. Later there would be another party for over two hundred people connected with the shows at the Mechanics Institute.

There was a host of talent to call upon in the locality, and one of

The cast of the epic *Aida* produced by the Burnley Operatic Society
assembled on stage at the Palace Theatre in November 1930.
Lee Thistlethwaite, in business suit, is centre stage with James Stephenson
standing among the three male leads to his immediate left.
PHOTO COURTESY OF LANCASHIRE COUNTY LIBRARY AND
INFORMATION SERVICE: BURNLEY LIBRARY

the most versatile was Lee Thistlethwaite (1885-1973). He was a local
cotton manufacturer, but spent any spare time indulging his passion for
live music. A talented, semi-professional baritone singer and musician,
as an oboist he played with the Halle orchestra, he brought the best in
live music to Burnley, and was a prime organiser of musical recitals,
oratorio, ballads and opera. He was a founder member of the Burnley
Operatic Society and an early broadcaster on BBC radio. His son, Frank
Thistlethwaite (1915-2003), being intellectually astute and precocious,
won scholarships to Burnley Grammar School, Bootham School, York,
St. John's College, Cambridge, and later gained a Commonwealth Fund
Fellowship to the University of Minnesota. He became a distinguished
academic and historian of American history. The pinnacle of his career
was as one of the longest serving and founding vice-chancellors of the
University of East Anglia from 1961 to 1980. As a concert-class pianist he
found this accomplishment a useful antidote when managing the burden
of institutional bureaucracy, and dealing with student protests during the
late 1960s and early 1970s, something which he found perplexing and

disappointing. Inheriting his father's musical talent, Frank was pressed into playing the piano for rehearsals for the *Aida* ballet numbers during the school holidays of 1930. In old age he remembered:

> ". . . James Stevenson (sic) a true bass, tall with a strong stage presence, an impressive Ramphis in *Aida,* Sarastro in *The Magic flute* and Sparafucile in *Rigoletto,* he was already known in amateur dramatic circles. . . ." [74]

He also recalled the high demands made on his father in mounting the ambitious production of *Aida.* Not only was Lee Thistlethwaite in charge of all the music, but as theatre director he had responsibility for choreography of all principals, chorus, musicians and members of the ballet. When, during a dress rehearsal a climactic scene was bungled Lee, in emotional frustration, threw down his conducting baton, stopped the rehearsal, and let out such a stream of expletives that John Thornber himself was forced to intervene, and reprimand him in public on his abusive and threatening language.

In February 1932 the Operatic Society produced Verdi's *Rigoletto* and *Il Trovatore.* The role of Sparafucile in *Rigoletto* was the final operatic production in which James participated. The local press was ecstatic in its praise:

"Mr. James A. Stephenson was just right in the role of Sparafucile and gave the best histrionic performance of the evening." [75] "Mr. Stephenson made a fine Sparafucile, his commanding figure and weighty voice being particularly effective." [76]

Clifford Alwyn Parkinson, the doyen of amateur dramatic productions in Burnley, noting James could act as well as sing, asked him to play Sir Oliver Surface in *The School for Scandal* which Miss Shannon Leslie was producing at The Mechanics Institute. Despite having shared a concert platform with Clifford Parkinson at St. Catherine's Church back in November 1929, James appeared reluctant to appear in a non-singing part on the amateur stage. "I'm afraid I shall be no good," was James's reply "but I'll do what I can." [77] And so notably did he acquit himself that he was straightaway appropriated by The Burnley Players for their March 1930 production of *The Best People.* That performance established his reputation.

This period of two crowded years did not go unnoticed and attracted criticism as well as praise. In a letter to the local paper a theatre lover expressed a complaint about

> ". . . the glut of amateur theatrical productions with which Burnley is inflicted. I . . . see no justification for the public parade, within a few weeks, under different auspices, of the familiar faces

of our talented amateur actors and actresses. If they desire an amateur repertory company by all means have one, and proclaim it as such. As it is, it seems to be a competition they are taking part in." [78]

In the aftermath of the First World War farce enjoyed enormous popularity. *The Best People* staged at the Victoria Theatre was an American import which turned up as an early talkie re-titled *Fast and Loose* (Paramount, Fred Newmeyer, 1930). Similarly, another farce, *It Pays to Advertise*, by Walter Hackett and Roi Cooper Megrue, was put on by The Burnley Players in October 1930 and continued to enjoy local acclaim from patrons in the town.

Not every production James appeared in was an unqualified success. On February 7, 1931, five members of the Burnley Drama Guild, including James Stephenson, Clifford Parkinson, Shannon Leslie, Arthur Nightingale and Albert Smith, put themselves forward in a regional dramatic competition held at the Free Trade Hall Manchester against the Amateur Players Society, Manchester and the Bury Stage Society. Both these societies produced versions of the one act play *The Sister Who Walked in Silence* by Philip Johnstone. The adjudicator, Mr. L.A. Coles of Huddersfield, said of the Burnley Drama Guild's presentation of Shaw's one act play *Annajanska, The Bolshevik Empress*:

> "Of the Shaw play the adjudicator expressed surprise that it had been chosen, as it was not at all a good Shaw play. It should have been treated more as a burlesque than with the seriousness all save one of the players had shown. The part of the lieutenant [Clifford Parkinson] had however been very finely taken." [79]

Another gifted individual in the town was elocutionist Miss Shannon Leslie who arrived in Burnley, from London, in 1926 with her father-in-law, John Brown, a chemist. An idealistic woman, she worked tirelessly with local dramatic and musical organisations in the town. Her open air performances as Titania in scenes from Shakespeare's *A Midsummer Night's Dream*, in which she resembled the dancer Isadora Duncan, garnered local acclaim. This was given initially at an outdoor festival staged in the countryside of Reedley Hallows, a suburb of Burnley near Pendle Hill. On June 20, 1931 branches of the English Folk Dance Society in Blackburn, Burnley, Colne and Nelson in conjunction with the Drama Guild, Burnley, converged upon Four Oaks, Reedley, the home of Alderman Harry Aitken for traditional folk song and dance. Apart from Miss Shannon Leslie's Titania, John Grey was Quince and James played Bottom in an open air production of Shakespeare's play. So successful was this open air production of *A Midsummer Night's Dream*, that the performance was repeated some twelve months later on June 18, 1932 at Quernmore Park, Lancaster.

By early 1932, on the back of this intense amateur dramatic activity, James had decided to throw in his lot and become a professional actor. His reasons, as we shall see, were part emotional and part a belated chance to show his resolve in a field of his own choosing.

2
PROFESSIONAL STAGE ACTOR
(1932-1937)

England is the most class-ridden country under the sun.
It is a land of snobbery and privilege, ruled largely by the old and silly.
- GEORGE ORWELL.
THE LION AND THE UNICORN (1941)

Financial difficulties, dole queues, hunger marches, political agitation, a welter of foreign crises and social anxiety are proverbial characteristics embedded in the collective memory of the 1930s. Yet the Stephenson archive somewhat contradicts this common perception, for then, as now, the effects of the economic slump were uneven and disproportionate. Even within depressed districts of England like East Lancashire, where many mill towns such as Burnley bore the brunt of Britain's industrial decline, the middle-classes continued to enjoy relative prosperity. To ask what life was like in the town of Burnley in 1932 depended upon which side of the social fence you were from. For James Stephenson, his middle-class friends and acquaintances, life during the early thirties could be quite congenial. If you were fortunate enough to be in full-time employment there was comfort to be had. Falling food and material prices meant cheaper imports, rising living standards and the extended choice of new consumer goods (the motor car, the radio) and flourishing leisure facilities (the cinema palace, the dance hall).

On the surface there appeared a whole set of environmental proposals, social improvements, economic aspirations and civic goodwill to commend the town of Burnley. There was, for instance, much talk about adopting a clean air zone in the town but, as a political cartoon in the local press pointed out, there was a stark economic cost attached to attaining the goal of an atmosphere free from industrial pollution. [1] In the event, Burnley Council decided to fall back on a tried and tested social amenity by opening yet another public park, Thompson Park, in July 1930.

The town had embarked on major slum clearance and a new public library provided by the Carnegie Trust had been built. The opening ceremony on July 3, 1930, officiated by the Earl of Elgin and Kincardine, was broadcast on BBC radio. His speech was greeted with a chorus of loud applause.

> "Mr. Mayor, we are living in hard times . . . Over this town and neighbourhood there has been a particularly black cloud, but in the act we are accomplishing to-day, and in the interesting development of your art gallery and museum at Towneley, you are giving evidence of a policy of progress founded on wisdom and it is refreshing and invigorating to find that, in spite of these grave difficulties, you and your Council are facing the future with courage and hopefulness. In the honest belief that in these actions you are showing not a wild extravagance, but a sound investment, I have much pleasure in declaring this building open." [2]

This was indeed a fighting rebuff to those naysayers and doubters in the town, but despite such pockets of prosperity and bubbles of optimism there was no real solution available for staving off the ravages of a world economic slump. For the working masses the harsh realities of life seemed far removed from any signs of recovery or improvement. Labour unions were militant in their demands for retention of basic wages, and following an acrimonious cotton strike lasting nine weeks workers were forced to undergo a 12 ½ per cent reduction in wages. Mills, when they were employing people, worked short-time and unemployment was endemic in the town as indeed it was throughout the county of Lancashire. In August 1930 it was reported 42.1 per cent of 47,000 insured workers were unemployed. [3] In June 1931 local unemployment in Burnley stood at nearly 19,000. [4] Government assistance, in the form of an unemployment means-tested benefit, was severe and punitive and was responsible for several suicides in the town. There were also fears expressed about a breakdown of law and order with accusations of "mob law in Burnley" reported in the local press. [5]

In the family archive a copy of Lytton Strachey's satirical work *Eminent Victorians* (1918) survives. Strachey's scepticism regarding religion and debunking of notabilities of the Victorian era - once sacred cows – became a distinctive characteristic of the modern age. Reverence for Church and State, once received wisdom, was now subject to challenge and negotiation. In 1934 Reverend Harry Battye, the new vicar of St.

Catherine's Church from 1929, complained about dwindling parishioners in his pews and the onset of a phenomenon he described as "wireless religion." He declared:

> "The majority of Englishmen have an entirely wrong conception of the purpose of churchgoing. The Church of England has allowed people to think that they go to church to hear good music or 'good' sermons . . . Consequently the majority of English people nowadays stays at home and listens to 'wireless religion', for here they get good music and famous oratory. If Mr. and Mrs. John Bull do not happen to be in the mood for this kind of entertainment on any particular Sunday, they switch off the wireless or get the car out and "go for a run." The less wealthy members of the community are content to go cycling or hiking on Sundays." [6]

This sermon produced little effect, for four years later Rev. Battye again admonished the public on the decline of his flock. [7] Throughout the European continent the verities and assurances of organised religion were being eroded and appropriated by political ideologies. Marxist cultural critic Walter Benjamin in his 1936 essay *The Work of Art in the Age of Mechanical Reproduction* examined the cultural effect of mass reproduction on works of art, and in particular cited the consequent waning function of sacred ritual:

> "An analysis of art in the age of mechanical reproduction . . . leads us to an all important insight: for the first time in world history, mechanical reproduction emancipates the work of art from its parasitical dependence on ritual. To an ever greater degree the work of art reproduced becomes the work of art designed for reproducibility.
>
> From a photographic negative, for example, one can make any number of prints; to ask for the "authentic" print makes no sense. But the instant the criterion of authenticity ceases to be applicable to artistic production the total function of art is reversed. Instead of being based on ritual, it begins to be based on another practice – politics." [8]

Intellectual thought between the wars was permeated by a morbid anxiety concerning disease within races. From Oswald Spengler's pessimistic tome *The Decline of the West* (1918) to The Third International Eugenics Congress held in New York City in August 1932 it was widely held that civilisation was collapsing, lurching from crisis to crisis, and in terminal decline. Only radical politics, drastic social measures or a scientific cure appeared to offer renewal, revival or, at the very least, a reversal of fortunes.

During the early thirties the British Board of Film Censors banned outright the showing of *Island of Lost Souls* (Paramount, Erle C. Kenton, 1932). The film, based on the HG Wells story *The Island of Doctor Moreau*, depicted scenes of vivisection in a locked room, referred to as "the House of Pain." Its lurid storyline culminated in a chilling climax involving semi-human creatures devouring their mad creator, played by Charles Laughton complete with dapper moustache and trim beard, attired in white suit and whip in hand, was deemed inappropriate. Today, the film's scenario is just as unsettling, but for reasons of political correctness rather than its capacity to deprave, offend or corrupt against the then accepted canons of decency. The film's allusions to the breeding of the races and the science of eugenics were played for cheap horror, yet these were lively and popular issues of the day.

This sort of thing wasn't just the province of a few eccentrics and fanatics, but found favour with eminent scientists and intellectuals of the period. People such as playwright George Bernard Shaw, whose popularity at the time rivalled that of Shakespeare. In old age, Shaw's opinion on a wide range of topics was avidly sought and freely given. Several of his pronouncements, even allowing for his redoubtable contentiousness and mischievousness, appear wide of the mark. Disconcerting in both sentiment and hindsight was Shaw's call for the mass extermination of those in society deemed to be unfit - he was a supporter of the eugenics movement. In a 1934 BBC radio broadcast he declared:

> "If you are a humanitarian, like myself, appeal to the chemists to discover a humane gas that will kill instantly and painlessly; in short, a gentlemanly gas, deadly by all means, but humane not cruel." [9]

Such attitudes not, alas, unique were accorded wide media circulation. A correspondent writing in the letter's column of the *Burnley Express* advocated sterilisation for the unfit:

> "While I am not unmindful of the fact that a return to happier trade conditions would work untold wonders upon the health of our peoples, I also believe that, like all good buildings, a solid foundation is the main essential, and that we could, to our advantage, adopt the principle of sterilisation." [10]

Not only was Christianity in peril but so too was that other bedrock of Western civilisation, market capitalism. With failing market economies, many on the intellectual left saw salvation in the guise of a Marxist Socialist Utopia. In misguided naivety Shaw, and a party of other liberal-minded intellectual fellow-travellers, undertook a tour of Soviet Russia in 1933. On their return in a round-robin letter addressed to the letters page of the *Manchester Guardian* they declared with assured fervour:

"Particularly offensive and ridiculous is the revival of the old attempts to represent the condition of Russian workers as one of slavery and starvation, the Five Year Plan as a failure, the new enterprises as bankrupt and the Communist regime as tottering to its fall. Some of us travelled throughout the greater part of its civilized territory. We desire to record that we saw nowhere evidence of such economic slavery, privation, unemployment and cynical despair of betterment as are accepted as inevitable and ignored by the press as having "no news value" in our own countries. Everywhere we saw a hopeful and enthusiastic working class, self-respecting, free up to the limits imposed on them by nature and terrible inheritance from the tyranny and incompetence of their former rulers, developing public works, increasing health services, extending education, achieving the economic independence of a woman and the security of the child . . .

We would regard it as a calamity if the present lie campaign were to be allowed to make headway without contradiction and to damage the relationship between our country and the USSR. Accordingly we urge all men and women of good will to take every opportunity of informing themselves of the real facts of the situation and to support the movements which demand peace, trade and closer friendship with and understanding of the great Workers Republic of Russia." [11]

Soviet General Secretary Joseph Stalin had carefully constructed an itinerary emphasising what he wished his distinguished visitors to see and report on. The terrible truth of starvation and famine in the countryside, caused by the draconian policy of farm collectivisation, was proscribed. Stalin's crusade to bring modernity to the USSR, via industrial planning and scientific management, aimed at total and radical social transformation with brute speed at whatever the cost. His challenge to Russians was blunt and uncompromising:

"We are fifty or a hundred years behind the advanced countries. We must make good this distance in ten years. Either we do it, or we shall go under." [12]

While convulsive chaos around the world spawned several dictatorships, the British wrapped themselves in their imperial dignity. Following the Versailles Peace Settlement Britain's colonial territories had increased several-fold, and on paper the Empire gave Britain

One foot in the nineteenth century and one foot in the twentieth century. A group of James Stephenson's Lancashire business associates during the early 1930s.
PHOTO COURTESY OF STEPHENSON ARCHIVE

immense prestige on the world international stage. Yet behind this façade the political reality revealed Britain as overstretched, and struggling to maintain an effective global presence. There were loud calls for independence and secession from the mother country from many quarters of the empire. Britain retreated into a perturbing insularity both at home and abroad. A photograph from the Stephenson archive, showing a group of Freemasons/Rotarians standing outside a civic building, captures perfectly a demonstration of high complacency and obstinate resistance to modernisation in British business circles during the inter-war period. A mixture of lethargy and caution dominated. Britain desired to be left to its own devices and not be drawn into any further foreign entanglements. The political slogan "Safety First!" used by the Conservatives during the 1929 General Election campaign and the avuncular, emollient, pipe-smoking, figure of Prime Minister Stanley Baldwin, exemplified this state of inertia. As journalist William L. Shirer noted:

> "No one could accuse [Baldwin] of being sparkling or brilliant, though he was not unintelligent. He was as stolid as John Bull. The country seemed to like him for just muddling along – it was so rather British." [13]

Baldwin observed the phenomenon of continental fascism with

guarded disdain. At the end of 1936 he privately mused:

"With two lunatics like Mussolini and Hitler you can never be sure of anything. But I am determined to keep the country out of war." [14]

As dictators of various hues strutted on the world stage, a more benign form of "theatricality" was patronised by middle-class communities up and down Britain. The Burnley Players were an amateur dramatic group specialising in the staging of farces. In 1924 they put on their first production: *Wedding Bells*. The title is significant, for these amateur performances were, among other things, occasions for the middle-classes to socialise. Many were the relationships started and broken; some even developed into matrimony. Among the throng of amateur thespians was local businessman Alan Coppock (1898-1983) who proposed to Miss Eva Heap. Unfortunately, his prospective mother-in-law, Mrs. Heap, did not approve of their engagement and forbade the marriage. It appears that although Alan Coppock was a good all-round social animal: an excellent dancer, a fine amateur actor, and played a good round of golf, Mrs. Heap considered him unsuitable because he was a person of limited prospects who did not apply himself to the same degree in his business career.

In this intimate self-contained atmosphere friends relaxed and addressed each other on first name terms: thus James Stephenson was "Jim," John Grey "Jack," Clifford Parkinson "Cliff," Florence Moon "Flossie" and Dr. Hitchon Chadwick was nicknamed "Spike." In contrast, their daily work environment, white collar occupations, required full use of a formal style of address: Mr. Sir, or Miss, Mrs., Madam. However, even in this social circle, older members preferred social rank over individual informality. Producer Marjorie Croasdale, a former professional actress with Constance Bellamy's Company, insisted on remaining the Victorian *grande dame* and was addressed respectfully as Mrs. Croasdale rather than the familiar Marjorie. From this point in the chapter Stephenson's forename of James will be dispensed with and substituted by the informal Jim.

On Saturday June 20, 1932, following the close of the final performance of the Aldwych farce *Plunder* at the Victoria Theatre, Jim Stephenson was presented with an engraved cigarette case by Edward Harrison MacGregor "Jimmie" Landless (1900-1978) on behalf of the Burnley Players company. In reply Jim expressed his good fortune that he was able to "kick off" his professional career at the renowned Liverpool Repertory Company. He also recorded a debt of gratitude to Burnley born actor Herbert Lomas, who had expressed an interest in his desire to enter the acting profession by suggesting an introduction to William Armstrong of the Playhouse Liverpool. [15] This occasion prompted Jim's first published public speech:

"I shall leave Burnley with very many and very great regrets. I shall leave three artistic organisations which have helped in no small measure to make the past two years the happiest of my life – The Burnley Players, The Burnley Operatic Society and the Drama Guild. And I do appeal you, ladies and gentlemen, to support these organisations – to support all your amateur organisations in Burnley – the three I have just mentioned and the Garrick Club. They are worthy of your support. You have this company of players giving you farce with the lavishness of acting and dressing which you have seen to-night.

You have the Burnley Operatic Society giving you year by year grand opera on a scale which a town five times the size of Burnley might envy. You have the Drama Guild giving you fine plays, including the works of the greatest living dramatist of this or any other country, George Bernard Shaw. You have the Garrick Club giving you its own chosen type of play and giving it superlatively well. Surely four organisations of this kind are worthy of support of a town the size of Burnley. And this widespread amateur movement of to-day is the greatest asset the theatre has. Let us make no mistake about that – it is being realised to-day by professional managers, producers, and actors alike. In these days of canned music, of mutilated Americanised English and of screen plays, so many of which are entirely and utterly and absolutely debasing to the public taste, this movement which is fostering a love of all that is best in the drama and in music, fostering too, a love for, and appreciation of good acting, is invaluable.

Don't let the word 'amateur' keep you away from the theatre. It need not, for if you do not always get the same high standard of acting that you do from some professional touring companies, you do, very often, get a scale of production, of setting and of dressing, which the average touring company cannot afford. [A reference here to the recent epic production of *Aida* by the Burnley Operatic Society] And you get, too, very frequently, a sincerity from the players which is not always to be expected from professionals who are playing the same play week in week out for months on end. Support these amateur efforts. You know Burnley has a bad name. [16] One can think of so many artistic organisations which have come into being with a fanfare of trumpets, have flourished exceedingly for a year or two, or perhaps three, and then gone 'phut!' Don't let that happen to any of the organisations I have mentioned." [17]

Like Reverend Battye, Jim's plea to the Burnley public for patronage of these amateur societies fell on deaf ears. The march of modernity, in the form of popular consumerism, threatened the traditions of live entertainment. The talkies and wireless radio had already appropriated a significant share of the leisure market. Why then persist in the notion of putting on amateur productions during times of mass unemployment and social agitation? An answer may be found by reference to the ideas of the noted Victorian cultural commentator Matthew Arnold (1822-1888). Arnold spoke against the aristocratic barbarians and the middle-class philistines when he declared in the preface to his celebrated series of essays in *Cultural and Anarchy* in 1869:

> "Culture is a study of perfection. It seeks to do away with classes; to make the best that has been thought and known in the world current everywhere; to make all men live in an atmosphere of sweetness and light . . . to recommend culture as the great help out of our present difficulties; culture being a pursuit of our total perfection by means of getting to know, on all the matters which most concern us, the best which has been thought and said in the world, and, through this knowledge, turning a stream of fresh and free thought upon our stock notions and habits . . . ." [18]

Far from the Burnley middle-classes merely fiddling while the working-classes burned, these amateur productions were devised as acts of compassionate enlightenment dedicated to setting an example to those below whilst maintaining the paternalistic status quo. By doing their civic duty, the Burnley petty bourgeoisie were rising above local difficulties such as high unemployment, bad industrial relations and class antagonism. Jim, being gainfully self-employed was spared the first two but, as we shall see, he could not evade the class divide. Though the First World War had helped to expose and censure pre-war class divisions, social distinctions remained sharp and stubborn with socio-economic inequality still prevalent.

In subsequent press interviews, Jim gave several plausible reasons for deciding to enter the acting profession. For instance, he spoke of his affection for dramatist George Bernard Shaw:

> "Shaw has always been my idol, for which reason I've never ceased to marvel at my colossal cheek. I did the part [John Tanner in *Man and Superman*] quaking, but I did it. The thing caused a local furore, so from then on I did nothing but act in my spare time and began to filch time from my business to make it spare,

with the inevitable result that business felt the effects. Finally I said, 'The hell with it. I like this better than anything else. In fact, I love it. I'll try to get a job as a professional actor'." [19]

Reporting his role in Shaw's *The Devil's Disciple* the local press noted his high abilities as an amateur actor:

> "Mr. James A. Stephenson, as Richard Dudgeon, emerged with flying colours from a strenuous role. Mr. Stephenson is an excellent Shavian actor . . . His complete self-possession and mastery of the dialogue gave the part a genuine interest." [20]

In the *Beaux' Stratagem* playing Archer, a gentleman of fortune, his sense of dramatic technique was readily apparent:

> "Mr. James Stephenson was again outstanding. He has a wonderfully easy stage presence, knows the value of a gesture, and can speak his lines effectively, without appearing to exert himself. The part also gave him an opportunity to delight us with his singing, and in every respect he gave a most delightful performance." [21]

These comments by Jim and by reviewers go some way to suggest why he decided to become an actor. Beyond an obvious natural enjoyment of the stage, acting requires a lot of nerve. Jim's motives were rooted in strong inclination, a powerful agent of ambition.

On the face of it, giving up the security of a regular job during the very depths of the economic depression for a life on the professional stage appeared a touch foolhardy at the very least. As a fully paid-up member of Burnley's middle-classes Jim had the means to realise his career ambitions and effect a change of occupation. Two of his friends in the amateur dramatic fraternity also gave up traditional jobs for new careers. Clifford Parkinson had worked on the floor of Manchester's Corn Exchange, but decided the vocation of the church suited him better and was ordained as a member of the clergy in 1934. "Jimmie" Landless found working in the transport department of Bank Hall Colliery, managed by his father, Richard Landless JP Esq., similarly unfulfilling. Instead, he used his management skills to run the Tivoli Cinema on Colne Road, Burnley.

To attain his goal of becoming an actor Jim did some social networking in the town. During 1930 he was inducted into the Burnley Freemasons and also the Burnley Rotary Club. [22] Charitable fundraising dominated these organizations and with these activities came many useful contacts. Rotary lunches provided the opportunity to approach various speakers invited to talk on specific topics. All the amateur stage work was given free with no fees exacted. They relied solely on local patronage. Within a span of two years Jim was increasing his social standing by becoming

Members of the Burnley Rotary Club prepare for dinner at the Empress Hotel
in the town centre of Burnley c.1931. Rotarian James Stephenson is seen
standing at the back of the room, behind a pillar to the right of the picture.
PHOTO COURTESY OF STEPHENSON ARCHIVE

affiliated to various Burnley social circles. Jim's best friend during this
period of his life was John Grey (1904-1993). He was by all accounts
"a gifted amateur actor, a very good public speaker, a fine singer, and
accomplished painter." [23] Apart from these natural talents he was well-
connected being the son of Edwin Morley Grey, a local banker, and Annie
Thornber whose father was a former Lord Mayor of Burnley. His uncle,
John Thornber JP, a local councillor and benefactor, typified the non-
conformist middle-classes which still held sway over the life of the town.
Rather than follow his father into the banking profession he had qualified
as an insurance broker, the first to do so in the town in 1928. [24] Speaking
many decades later about Jim Stephenson he recalled:

> "He didn't begin on the stage until he was forty-three. If I can
> be immodest for a moment, I was instrumental in getting him to
> play a part in 1929 in the Burnley Operatic Society's *The Magic
> Flute*. He was a natural." [25]

Due to his insistence Jim became involved in the farce *The Best
People*, produced by the Burnley Players from March 31 to April
2, 1930. This also marked a turning point in his personal life. The
plotline of *The Best People* dealt with the matrimonial visions of a son

Amateur Burnley actor
John Grey as the Captain
in Strindberg's *The Father*
produced at the
Victoria Theatre,
Burnley, Lancashire
in February 1931.
PHOTO COURTESY OF
HAWORTH ARCHIVE

and daughter of an old established family - "the Lennoxes." The son had engaged himself to a chorus girl and the daughter to the family chauffeur, the son of a Canadian Rancher. The local press was most enthusiastic about Jim's efforts:

> "One would almost unhesitatingly give the palm to Mr. Stephenson for his masterly rendering of Masters the Chauffeur. The cool plain speaking, man-to-man candour of the fellow was embellished with the necessary accent, and what one would take to be the native gesture of the Canadian of the plains." [26]

This enthusiasm was shared by local audiences in the town and particularly by patrons of The Burnley Players. These included Mrs. Willie Stuttard and her daughter Dorothy, who would shortly enter Jim's life. Maud Martha Stuttard nèe Chadwick (1878-1953) was the daughter of a publican who had married Willie Stuttard, a cotton director in 1902. Willie Stuttard (1873-1955) was the third son of Richard Stuttard (1829-1895), a prominent Burnley cotton manufacturer who had founded the business during the 1860s. By 1904 the Stuttard Empire consisted of Byerden, Old Primrose and New Primrose Mills, employing approximately two thousand looms and all managed by the Stuttard dynasty of five sons. Dorothy Maude Stuttard (1905-1987) was their only daughter and her brother Harold Stuttard (1903-1947) was a good friend of Jack Grey. The

Dorothy Stuttard
aged twenty-one in 1926.
PHOTO COURTESY OF
HARDMAN ARCHIVE

Stuttards lived at "Grasmere" a semi-detached suburban house situated in Reedley a well-to-do suburb near the boundary of Burnley and Colne.

As befitted a member of the middle-classes, Dorothy's education consisted of early learning at the local primary school succeeded by several terms spent at a boarding school in Southport on the Lancashire sea coast. Her education was confined to that of a prospective wife and homemaker. An excellent cook, she adored children, was proficient in needlework and played the piano with competence. After completing full-time education she was able to draw upon a monthly allowance enabling her to purchase the latest dress and cosmetic fashions. She also learnt to drive at an early age, enjoyed hiking with like-minded friends, and was proficient in playing games of golf and tennis at local sporting clubs. When not otherwise occupied, she spent her time being chaperoned by her redoubtable mother, Mrs. Willie Stuttard, to various social soirees patronised by the elect of the district, with the ideal of finding a suitable marriage partner. It seemed this aim had been achieved when, around 1926, at the age of majority, it was announced she was engaged to [John] Gilbert Nelson (1904-1948), grandson of prominent cotton magnate Sir Amos Nelson (1860-1947). Sir Amos Nelson was the most significant and progressive employer in Lancashire during the inter-war years. He had invested in new technology and was particularly keen to bring an end to the many disputes plaguing the Lancashire cotton industry of the period. Nelson lived in palatial style at Gledstone Hall, Skipton in Yorkshire, designed by renowned architect Sir Edwin Lutyens. For the socially ambitious Mrs. Willie Stuttard it seemed the perfect match of

Jim Stephenson with female companion out in the Far East during the 1920s.
PHOTO COURTESY OF STEPHENSON ARCHIVE

mercantile with gentry. However, it was not to be. It seems Dorothy did not relish the prospect of becoming such a grand member of local society. The engagement was eventually called off and Gilbert Nelson went on to marry Margaret Mercia Heywood on April 16, 1930.

The precise circumstances of Jim's romantic past prior to meeting Dorothy are not known. However, as pictures in the family archive indicate, he wasn't averse to female company. Though not as wealthy as Gilbert Nelson he was older and worldly-wise, having fought as an officer on the Western Front for King and Country. A decade on since the armistice, the memory of the First World War was still very strong and instilled mixed emotions of respect and regret for the great sacrifice exacted. As an international businessman he had travelled extensively across several continents and had already broadcast on BBC radio. Though he suffered from bouts of lumbago and sciatica, Jim, in his early forties, was still strikingly handsome and possessed an engaging manner both on and off the amateur stage.

His two younger brothers had gone on to bigger and better things. In April 1933, Alan Stephenson had been elected an honorary member of the Royal College of Music for "valuable service" to music. He also attained a top position as organist and leading chorister at Coventry

Musician Alan Stephenson Bac.
Mus. (Oxon) Hon. R.C.M., F.R.C.O.,
F.R.S.A. Organist and Master of the
Choir Coventry Cathedral, BBC
Recitalist and Festival Adjudicator.
PHOTO COURTESY OF STEPHENSON ARCHIVE

Captain Norman Douglas
Stephenson MC
photographed c.1940.
PHOTO COURTESY OF
WILKINSON ARCHIVE

Cathedral, succeeding Dr. Harold Rhodes in June 1933. In this capacity,
he was heard on regular live concert broadcasts on BBC radio. He was
also a much sought-after adjudicator at musical festivals throughout
the country. [27] Norman Stephenson, as a Captain in the military police
undertook six months tours of duty at a British colonial outpost at Malakal
in the Upper Nile region of the Sudan. During his last two tours of duty,
in 1933 and 1934, Norman and his wife, Toonie, took advantage of the
technological breakthrough in aviation and booked a two hour flight on
an Imperial Airways Hercules passenger plane from Le Bourget Airport,
Paris across the English Channel to Croyden Aerodrome, London. Like
his elder brother, Norman had a penchant for motor cars and in April
1932 he acquired a second hand Wolseley Hornet for £165. In May 1934
he traded the Wolseley for a 1932 Humber saloon.

    Within a short period Dorothy and Jim were courting one another.
There is talk of Jim arranging to meet Dorothy at a local picture house

only to find she came accompanied by her mother. To avoid this Dorothy took to excusing herself on a pretext of seeing a show in the town, whereas she was in fact motoring to 212 Manchester Road, home of newly-weds Jack and Dorothy Grey, for an assignation with Jim in their front parlour. [28]

Jim thus had good reason to be bullish whilst on stage speaking his farewell to Burnley in preparation for starting his professional career on the Liverpool stage. Jim and Dorothy however would find the path of love to be anything but smooth for relationships are fragile and in breaking cause deep hurt and harm to all. In a lecture delivered to the Burnley Rotary Club on *The Play's of Bernard Shaw* Jim devoted a significant section to Shaw's John Tanner in *The Revolutionist Handbook* speaking of natural attraction rather than wealth or social class as being desirable in governing the selection of marriage partners. Jim and Dorothy's courtship certainly seemed based on personal attraction, not material motives. On December 23, 1932, after two years courtship their engagement announcement appeared in the local papers. [29] Eight months later during August 1933 Jim, having a few weeks off before resuming his second season with the Liverpool Playhouse, invited his brother Norman and wife Toonie to travel up from their Surrey home to Burnley to meet Dorothy and her family. Jim took Dorothy, his brother, and sister-in-law, to a celebratory dinner at The Moorcock Inn, an up-market country restaurant situated in a picturesque and prosperous area of Lancashire – Waddington in the Ribble Valley. A few days later Jim, Norman and Toonie were joined by Dorothy and her mother for morning coffee at the Savoy Café, a prestigious middle-class venue in the town. However, by the time Norman and Toonie had paid a return visit to Burnley during June 1934, the engagement had been called off on the orders of Mrs. Willie Stuttard. [30]

Unfortunately we are not privy to the precise details, but the nearest Jim comes to referring to the altercation is in one of several press interviews given when receiving the star build-up in Hollywood. Discussing the adjustment in culture between America and England he stated:

> "I detest class distinctions. We have them in England . . . our people have been divided into watertight compartments. I know that if I went back to England I'd hate to see again what I've seen there so often, emanating from that sub-conscious feeling of 'he is down there, I'm up here'." [31]

It is known that the family business, Richard Stuttard Ltd., was beleaguered by economic ills due to the decline in demand for British textiles after the First World War. On December 15, 1933 it was publicly announced that the business had sought recapitalisation. The capital of the business was reduced by half, its value falling from £150,000 to £75,000. This course of action had taken effect from November 28, 1933. [32] One can imagine the strain of anxiety and frustration this downturn in financial circumstances put the family, and particularly Mrs. Willie Stuttard under. Though this situation would have had a serious impact on Dorothy and Jim's intended matrimonial plans, it is by no means straightforward to suggest this was the only factor involved.

From the above it is easy to imagine Mrs. Willie Stuttard as a Lancashire matriarch who used her entitlement and obligation based on property status and social rank to make her daughter defer to familial duty and responsibility. However, Mrs. Stuttard had family relatives, "The Three Leslies," who worked in the entertainment business putting on live performances in seaside concert parties on the South Coast of England. Her nephew John [Hind] Stuttard (1908-1971) had been stage manager of the Burnley Players for many years. An avid reader, she is also said to have taken possession of a private and illicit copy of D.H. Lawrence's *cause célèbre Lady Chatterley's Lover*, but had to hand it back to the authorities before having the chance to read it. On this evidence she was anything but puritanical, but details remain too unclear to speculate further with confidence.

In private letters Jim writes of "adversity and disappointment." [33] A combination of catharsis in his public stage performances and inner private dignity kept him from falling into complete emotional turmoil following his separation with Dorothy Stuttard. Whatever the precise reason for the breaking of their engagement, this revelation at least acknowledges Dorothy Stuttard's crucial part in Jim Stephenson's decision to give up the day job and become a professional actor. Without her emotional support and the intervention of other close friends, such as Jack Grey, it remains doubtful whether he would have been capable of quelling his doubts, fulfilling his aspirations and realising his self-potential. One of the few survivors from this period, actor Sam Beazley, recalled Jim Stephenson to be serious-minded and keenly ambitious while acting alongside him at the Liverpool Repertory Company. [34] This would be in keeping with the sense of rejection, pride and anxiety arising from his altercation with his prospective mother-in-law.

Jim, with a combination of stoicism and diligence, saw the Stuttard episode through. Though torn emotionally, his burning ambition remained intact. His private disillusionment was finally resolved when, at New Brighton during the summer season of 1935, he was introduced to a young woman by the name of Lorna Dinn whom he would later marry.

William Armstrong (1882-1952) had been producer at the Liverpool

The Liverpool Playhouse en masse on the afternoon of Thursday July 30, 1936. Sir John Joseph Shute Playhouse chairman (left) escorts manager Maud Carpenter (middle) and director William Armstrong (right) to Thurstaston Church on the occasion of the marriage of James Albert Stephenson to Lorna Hewitt Kilby Dinn. Note the large crowds gathered on either side applauding politely.
PHOTO COURTESY OF STEPHENSON ARCHIVE

Playhouse since 1922 and would remain in post until 1940. During his long tenure he directed some 355 productions, many as double bills. A genial Scot, former actor and once factotum to the legendary Mrs. Patrick Campbell, he was canny in finding and nurturing acting talent. His "discoveries" were a roll-call of the English theatrical stage: Harry Andrews, Robert Donat, Robert Flemyng, Deryck Guyler, Rex Harrison, Elizabeth Inglis, Megs Jenkins, John Justin, Rachel Kempson, Cecil Parker, Michael Redgrave, Graham Stark, Alan Webb, Hugh Williams, Diana Wynyard, were all given their early apprenticeships courtesy of William Armstrong. Many of these would later grace the American film screen and came to be known affectionately as "The Hollywood crowd." The Playhouse opened in 1911 and its first director, Basil Dean, set the seal by offering adventurous, interesting and stimulating fare. Dean left in 1913 to join Birmingham Repertory, and later in 1928 entered the British film industry as a producer. Unfortunately at the time of his departure the budget was grossly overspent, and the theatre nearly closed. William Armstrong gave much needed stability by installing a permanent company which stabilised the situation. On the business side the remarkable Maud Carpenter (1895-1977) was licensee and administrator at the theatre from 1922 until 1962. [35] Completing the sense of continuity, Chairman of the Playhouse from 1913 until 1948 was Colonel Sir John Joseph Shute CMG, DSO, TD, JP, DL (1873-1948), a British army officer, businessman, philanthropist and Conservative Party politician.

At the time of Jim's arrival during the summer of 1932 there were six other newcomers to the playhouse. They included: Prudence Magor who had toured in Canada with Sir Barry Jackson's company, played at the Old Vic and Sadler's Wells. Ena Burrill had played leads at The Apollo, Amabel Gibson, who came from the Leeds repertory Theatre. Eric Noels had been performing in London and on tour. Robert Flemyng had toured with Violet Vanbrugh in *After All* and appeared in *Dangerous Corner* at the Lyric. Richard Carey had been with the Bristol Repertory company and also toured with *Bitter Sweet*. Jim, making his first professional appearance at the Playhouse, was described as having undertaken "a great deal of broadcasting work." [36]

In 1932 the British Broadcasting Corporation celebrated its first anniversary. From a mere 18 thousand license holders the number had quadrupled to over 5 million licenses. Audiences had risen from 12 million to 45 million. Director General John Reith wrote: "In the early days one of our earnest desires was to be taken seriously." [37] Reith wanted no part of the commercial model used in the United States where consumer choice was delivered through open competition. This, as far as he was concerned, was a recipe for unregulated chaos, and playing to the lowest common denominator would lead inexorably to low standards in broadcasting. Using "the brute force of monopoly" he set about devising a national and unified radio network that would give listeners access to "the best which has been thought and said in the world," to use the Arnoldian notion. Raising and maintaining high standards of broadcasting would be achieved through the promotion of education and enlightenment, with religious and cultural improvement and national unity taking precedence over public choice. As a consequence of Reith's idealistic and lofty stance, the staple diet of British wireless broadcasting in the early 1930s was decidedly prescriptive, high-minded, top-down and very bland. Controversy was to be avoided at all cost. Talks were scripted and submitted for official approval prior to broadcast, and any speaker who deviated or ad-libbed from their script risked the indignity of being faded out from the airwaves. Syncopated hot American jazz was frowned upon and instead British dance musicians served up sentimental fare. Henry Hall's BBC Radio Dance Orchestra was heard broadcasting daily at 5:15pm, beginning with the signature tune: "It's Just the Time for

Dancing" and signing off with the refrain "Here's to the next time." It was all disarming pap, but the public eagerly lapped it up. If something livelier was preferable, then Harry Roy's orchestra with its "hot-cha-ma-cha-cha" scat style of playing would fit the bill. His band was to be found broadcasting live late in the evening, initially from London's fashionable Café de Paris and then later at the Grosvenor Hotel.

In a special tenth anniversary edition of *Radio Times* the worthy ideals of the BBC wireless broadcasting service were in celebratory mode, and on full display for all to read. His Grace the Lord Archbishop of Canterbury, Cosmo Lang, spoke mindfully of the danger and blessing of broadcasting: "I am most thankful that here in England this wonderful influence has been controlled and guided by high ideals" he concluded somewhat warily. [38] The President of the National Free Church Council opined: "Britain has been fortunate in having men in control who are inspired by the highest ideals of public service, and who have vision and imagination linked to executive ability of a very high order." [39]

Jim's deep bass singing, though it possessed some sonority, appears to have been limited in its capacity to sustain major operatic roles, or provide full resonance on the concert platform. A press report of his performance at a Burnley municipal concert noted: "He has a pleasing, deep and resonant voice, though we doubt whether we heard it in its fullness. A little self-consciousness, coupled with nervousness, robbed it of its strength, but there was always richness and expression, if somewhat subdued." [40]

The family archive contains a recording of his vocal singing with no musical accompaniment. Recorded on an RCA Victrola machine and played back on early vinyl disc, at 78rpm the recording is a miscellany of opera and lieder.

The two pieces on the recording are taken, first, from the prologue of the overture to Ruggero Leoncavallo's 1892 opera *I Pagliacci*. Next is "Ludgate Hill" taken from *Bow Bells: Five London Silhouettes*, a piece of British lieder composed in 1900 by Charles Willeby (1865-1955). An examination of this recording by John Fallows, Emeritus Professor of Music at Manchester University, in September 2007 confirmed the voice lacks richness and tonality. This appears to be indicative of being recorded near the end of Jim's life.

His one and only performance as a bass vocalist in front of a radio microphone occurred in a live BBC concert broadcast in the early afternoon of February 25, 1929. His name appears in surviving broadcast logs at the BBC Written Archives at Caversham, but there appears to be no traceable review, either in the local Burnley papers or the regional

James Stephenson at his home using an RCA Victrola machine to record his voice.
PHOTO COURTESY OF STEPHENSON ARCHIVE

Manchester papers, of the broadcast, bar a photograph of his profile in the *Manchester Evening Chronicle*. [41] His subsequent decline to appear again on radio as a vocalist reinforces the notion that his vocal range was somewhat limited. In contrast, his speaking voice was distinctive and rich. He is on record confirming the importance he attached to the mellifluous quality of his voice. His clarity of enunciation was a calling card for entry into the acting profession and well-suited for sound reproduction on radio and later on film soundtracks.

British class distinctions of the day were dictated through standards of formal dress, codes of manners based on social class and gender, but the pre-eminent marker of class was the emphasis placed on speech. Jim would have been trilingual. Speaking his regional Lancashire dialect to his family and contemporaries in Burnley, Received Pronunciation, or the refined accent used by educated persons, for his work on stage, wireless radio and, finally, an American vernacular from idioms picked up from his business travels and the talkies exported from Hollywood. When interviewed in Hollywood he expressed, with some regret, the need to disregard his native accent:

"... most of my growing years were lived in Lancashire, England

and if ever a man had a broad accent, it's the Lancashire man . . . I've made a conscious effort to overcome the idiomatic in my speech, and in so doing, strained out some other things as well." [42]

His first dramatic speaking role on BBC radio occurred on July 5, 1932 in a half hour historical drama based on an Isle of Man legend relating the execution of William Christian. The radio play was entitled *The Spectral Dog*.

Of Jim's playing of Scriven, a seventeenth-century soldier in the Earl of Derby's force, the *Burnley News* declared: "Mr. Stephenson's voice proved to be admirably suited to the medium and it came through with wonderful clarity." [43]

Of the radio play itself, the *Manchester Guardian* with slight reservations, declared it a creditable broadcast:

"Occasionally the seventeenth-century soldiers garrisoned at Peel Castle, in the Isle of Man, where the scene was laid, reeled off speeches of great length and clarity in order, one felt, to inform the listener of certain happenings and circumstances and this awkwardness of structure tended to destroy realism. But otherwise both atmosphere and tension were well sustained. The play showed all the signs of being well rehearsed and the actors were happy in their parts." [44]

Such was the impact of being heard on the radio that when Jim spoke as a guest speaker at the Burnley Rotary Club on August 8, 1932 on the subject of "Art and the Box Office," the private meeting was full to capacity. As in his previous speech on the eve of his departure from the amateur stage back in June, he restated his magnanimous intentions regarding the integrity of true artistic endeavour, in contrast to the vulgar popularism of "the jazz merchants." [45] The bulk of his BBC broadcasting career consisted of four appearances on the *Children's Hour* programme, various historical and contemporary dramas either adapted from well-known plays and novels or original scripts commissioned for radio. These included an adaptation of Alexandre Dumas's *Twenty Years After*, a sequel to the saga of *The Three Musketeers*. Jim played Athos, and in the cast were two stalwarts of British radio drama Norman Shelley as Oliver Cromwell and Carleton Hobbs as Porthos. In a BBC celebration of Strauss's *The Blue Danube* broadcast the following month, Jim appeared opposite Charles Sanders, elder brother of George Sanders who from 1936 began a successful film career, usually playing cynical cads and urbane bounders, in Britain and Hollywood. When Charles followed his brother George to Hollywood in 1939, the brothers tossed a coin to decide which would change their name, their voices and appearances being almost identical. Charles lost, and took the name of Tom Conway. The Sanders brothers were a byword for suave sophistication, and they plied their polished charms over many decades on film, television and radio.

These broadcasts were transmitted from BBC North at the Piccadilly Studios, Manchester and later BBC National at Portland Place, London. All transmissions were live, and unlike commercial radio stations in the United States, British broadcasting was slow to introduce recording devices and use them. Thankfully, in Jim's case posterity was bestowed one broadcast recording of November 29, 1936. In a letter to Lorna Stephenson Jim wrote: "I wonder if you picked out my voice in the broadcast. First, tho,' I wonder if you remember to listen. Tho' I says it as shouldn't, I recorded far better than anyone else!!" [46]

Scotland Yard was an early actuality drama produced by the BBC in co-operation with the London Metropolitan Police. Scenes involving members of the police force were recorded on location and this material was later incorporated with scripted scenarios back in the broadcasting studio.

This ambitious broadcast was a timely exercise in shoring up public support for the police authorities, following severe criticism of their heavy-handed clashes with anti-fascists protesters, during Oswald Mosley's British Union of Fascist's march in London's East End on October 4, 1936. This incident became known as the Battle of Cable Street, and led to the passing of the Public Order Act 1936, designed to control extremist political movements by banning the wearing of political uniforms.

The broadcast consisted of ten parts dealing with organisational issues and the working environment of the Metropolitan Police Force. Jim appeared briefly in part seven, "Traffic Patrol," as continuity announcer reading a few lines of factual and statistical details relating to the policing of traffic, public highways, and motorists. The broadcast offers a consensual and deferential representation of a dedicated and professional organisation keen to show itself as being on the public's side and taking an even-handed lead in the fight against crime. Great care was taken by the BBC to exclude any suggestion of bias, and it strove hard to achieve impartiality in its editorial policy. Though by contemporary standards the presentational style and content of the programme appear innocuous, there is a distinctive impression that the authenticity of the broadcast expresses a masculine preserve of command and control. In this context the programme's commentator and compère, Thomas Woodrooffe an ex-naval officer, is characteristic.

The following year on May 20, 1937 Jim took part in a BBC variety programme, *Palace of Varieties*, in which he delivered a monologue, *A Stationmaster's Story*, with organ accompaniment. However, the programme was overshadowed by another broadcast on the same evening. Throughout the day, BBC radio had commentated live coverage of the prestigious annual Royal Naval Review at Spithead. Commentary duties were shared between ex-naval officers Lieutenant Commander G.V. Knight at the quayside, with Commander D.A. Stride and Lieutenant Commander Thomas Woodrooffe on board HMS *Nelson*. The outside broadcast culminated with a final observation and commentary from Woodrooffe during the late evening on the illumination of the fleet. Allocated fifteen minutes of broadcast time, Woodrooffe's commentary consisted of prolonged hesitation, deviation in the form of slurred words, incoherent sentences, and repetition of such phrases as: "the fleet's lit up," "fairy lamps" and "fairyland." He also let slip a mild profanity on air, whereupon the broadcast was faded out prematurely after some four minutes of live broadcasting. Record numbers of perplexed listeners rang the BBC to complain. In fact, Woodrooffe had over indulged himself in hospitality during the interval between his penultimate and final broadcast. He was ordered to take a short period of sick leave, and upon his return was allocated other duties rather than speaking at the microphone. Eventually, suitably chastened, he was allowed to resume broadcasting. Remarkably, a recording of this infamous episode in the early annals of BBC radio broadcasting survives.

Back at the Liverpool Playhouse, Jim, now installed in a flat at 24 Canning Street in North Liverpool City near the Anglican Cathedral, was creating something of a stir during his first season, 1932-1933. He had been taken on at a standard rate of £3 per week less deductions totalling £2.18s.5d. In his second play *Lean Harvest* he played Nigel Trent, a stockbroker who, in the thrall of ambition to money, loses his reason and his wife. In this modern variation of the Faust legend, Jim received unanimous good notices. "The production is noteworthy for the utterly unexpected brilliance of the acting of James Stephenson. He acted throughout with unfaltering confidence." [47] He also exhibited "skill in the progressive development of the character and so gets inside the part that the breakdown scene in its realist-romantic intensity acquires real dramatic power." [48] Among the twenty parts, four were of major importance. Three of them were played by newcomers to the Playhouse. Apart from Jim, Ena Burrill played his wife Celia, and Eric Noels was Nigel's feckless brother Steven. This three act play had fifteen scenes and experimented with quick curtains to offset the impact of rapid cutting in the cinema. The settings were deemed very accomplished. "The stage settings are among the best seen at the Playhouse – Nigel's study in his prosperous Park Street House being the essence of smart modernity. The dresses are also above the ordinary level." [49]

The Playhouse also premiered new plays such as J.B. Priestley's *The Roundabout* which made its debut on stage during Christmas 1932. Jim played Lord Kettlewell, a harassed father to his daughter Pamela played by Jane Vaughan, who brings home an objectionable Bolshie friend Comrade Staggles played by Geoffrey Edwards. A much worried lord listening to his daughter mouthing a lot of communist theories at one point exclaims: "Oh Bunk!" The theme of a clash between Russian communism and hard-boiled British convention tried to attain Shavian paradox. Yet, despite clever witticisms it only succeeded in achieving a trivial social comedy. Marjorie Fielding played a common sense aristocrat, with Wyndham Goldie as Churton Sanders a society idler and friend of Lord Kettlewell, and Lloyd Pearson as Parsons the butler. The stage setting was designed by Leon Berger and painted by Augustus Trout.

In those days there were essentially four different styles of theatrical acting: modern, Shavian, Restoration and Shakespearean. Though there was a certain amount of experimentation and innovation, the English repertory theatre was essentially conservative, being content in challenging the operation of the social system rather than the system itself. At this time it was still the drawing room that dominated the English theatre rather than the kitchen sink. The Liverpool Playhouse was renowned for the quality and range of its output, due in no small measure to lengthy three week rehearsals which were held almost daily from 10.30 in the morning until at least 3.30 in the afternoon, thus guaranteeing thorough preparation. Its nearest rival was the Birmingham Repertory Company under Barry Jackson. The atmosphere of the Playhouse Company was congenial, loyal and diligent and aimed to ensure high quality acting for a discerning public. Most of the company referred to each other by forename or else a genial nickname such as "Lindy" for Lindisfarne Hamilton and "Doylie" for Deidre Doyle. However, as in all organisations there were times of tension when members of the company took it upon themselves to be disobliging and egotistical.

In the summer of 1934 there came to the Playhouse a tall, young, talented and gifted actor by the name of Michael Redgrave. Fresh from university and a spell as a schoolmaster at Cranleigh School, an independent English boarding school, he not only took to acting with great self-possession but, in a streak of precociousness, wrote several plays whilst at the Playhouse, including a one act drama *The Seventh Man* and a

The Liverpool Playhouse Repertory Company assembled backstage during
December 1933. Jim Stephenson is seated extreme right. Next to him sits
Marjorie Fielding, Sir John Shute, Maud Carpenter, and Ena Burrill.
Standing extreme left is Lloyd Pearson, Jim's best man at his wedding.
Standing next to him is Anthony Hawtrey and his wife Marjory Clark,
and three unidentified actresses. Behind Jim stands Stephen Jack.
PHOTO COURTESY OF STEPHENSON ARCHIVE

Christmas family entertainment *Circus Boy*. In his memoirs, he referred
in passing to Jim Stephenson in somewhat dismissive terms as: "a dark
horse" and "an honest, earnest nonentity." [50] Redgrave belonged to a
generation schooled in the codes of reticence where questions of personal
identity and sexuality were concerned. He was doubtless aware that Jim,
like everyone, had something to conceal in their private lives, but was
disinclined to probe too deeply. Not only was Jim considerably older,
but this generation gap was marked in particular, as with other senior
members of the company such as Lloyd Pearson, by Jim's participation
in the First World War. Redgrave's sporadic diary entries for the period
1935-1936 make reference to Jim in just two instances. Once, when in
the company of Deidre Doyle, Rachel Kempson and Lloyd Pearson,
he noted with mild disdain: "J.S's perfectly frightful room" referring
to Jim's Liverpool flat at 14 Huskisson Street. [51] On another occasion

Redgrave and Jim were involved in an altercation. This began when Redgrave refused to appear in a production of the romantic drama *Death Takes a Holiday* scheduled for the end of January 1936. A member of the company, Charles Thomas, informed him of Jim's displeasure at hearing this news. When they eventually confronted each other over the matter Redgrave appeared to get the better of Jim:

> "So early to theatre and have it out with J.S. on subject. July leaving cast. He is mulish, but I score some time and retire." [52]

Redgrave's reference to Jim leaving the company in July referred to his recent announcement of his engagement to Lorna Dinn of West Kirby. They had met backstage at The Winter Gardens, New Brighton the previous year during the annual summer season, when the Liverpool Company put on a selection of their best received plays of the previous season. Lorna Hewitt Kilby Dinn (1908-1967) was the only daughter of Charles Kilby Dinn (1876-1949) a dentist, whose practice was based in Hoylake on Merseyside. Her mother Ethel Marion Hewitt Dinn (1876-1947) was the daughter of a Liverpool iron merchant. The couple had married on May 14, 1905. The Dinns, "Pop" and "Dinny" and their children Lorn' and Gil,' resided at Abbey Lodge, a semi-detached middle-class Edwardian house, in the affluent and prosperous coastal town of West Kirby on the Wirral Peninsula at the mouth of the River Dee. In its own grounds, half the house was once occupied by the famous English conductor Sir Adrian Boult (1889-1983). Situated on top of a hill the house overlooked the River Dee, and this magnificent view was accompanied by distant views of the North Welsh coast. The family enjoyed a secure middle-class lifestyle employing a maid and a gardener, and took annual holidays to the Welsh resort of Criccieth. "Pop" as Lorna affectionately christened her father, enjoyed playing the role of a country gentleman and was partial to hunting, shooting, fishing and a round of golf at the nearby Royal Birkdale Golf Club at Hoylake.

Although Lorna demonstrated intelligence beyond the education she received at Brighthelmston School in Southport, the family would not pay for her to attend either college or university. Despite the passing of the Representation of the People Act of 1928 granting women universal suffrage, discrimination and inequality in education, employment and legal services for women remained. The family set little ambition for their daughter beyond expecting her, in due course, to take on the traditional role of a "dutiful wife." A young, idealistic woman with a mischievous sense of humour, she was somewhat shy and self-conscious outside of her immediate social circle of family and friends. She appreciated the use of language and was an articulate and able writer. Her older brother, Gilbert

Hewitt Kilby Dinn (1906-1953), a commercial artist by profession, once requested her assistance in composing a letter for a job application. On the strength of her written testimony he secured an interview. However, it soon became apparent there was a discrepancy between the expressive letter of application and his performance at interview. At one point the interviewer observed: "You know, you're not like your letter!" Needless to say, on that occasion he wasn't successful in securing the job.

A monthly allowance allowed Lorna to drive and maintain a motor car and she enjoyed an active social life with interests in theatre and sport. An enthusiastic and exceptional player of tennis, Lorna belonged to the Hoylake Tennis Club. Within her circle of friends was Dr. William Dickson (1891-1979), a General Practioner whose quiet manner endeared him to his patients, and his vivacious wife Eleanor May Dickson (1901-1989), who organised amateur stage revues (the Hoylake Racketeers) at the tennis club. "Bill" and "Bobbie" Dickson and possibly Constance [Mary] Marwood (1884-1946), a neighbour of Jim's who lived at Cathedral Mansions on Huskisson Street, appear to have been among the party of people who accompanied Lorna backstage to meet Jim. The couple soon met again at Bill and Bobbie Dickson's home, Sea Bank, in West Kirby.

His courtship of Lorna was assiduous, intense and accomplished with boundless enthusiasm. "I fell. Then she fell." is how he later described it. [53] When their engagement was announced in the local Liverpool papers, on September 23, 1935, Jim even managed to obtain two news sheets displayed by street newspaper vendors announcing their engagement. [54] Yet this romantic mood was compromised by time constraints, for he would shortly be resuming his work schedule at the Liverpool Playhouse. He most likely realised this was a stroke of good fortune, and a chance to recover the emotional contentment and psychological well-being formerly denied him. He had to act swiftly though, if the opportunity was not to slip irretrievably through his grasp. As he went on to explain:

> "Well, it seems to me love at first sight is the best and truest kind of love. It's very instinctive, explosive, and spontaneous and sets in motion vibrations which a man does well not to ignore. I'm by no means a reckless, imprudent man, but a week after I met her I proposed to her. That was fast work. She took a bit longer to make up her mind. Yes, a week later I proposed. But it was six weeks before she came through."[55]

Given Jim's romantic past, Lorna seems to have reacted cautiously to his advances. Her instincts were to pause and consider her long-term future: Was he honest? Was he true? The answers to these questions were not long in coming. Quite early in their relationship Lorna was taken seriously ill. In those days, before widespread availability of antibiotics, organ transplants, scans, vaccinations etc., an accurate diagnosis was hard to come by and major operative surgery was an uncertain procedure with no guarantee of success or complete recovery. Medical care at this time was neither free at the point of use, nor comprehensive as a service and indeed promotion of public health issues by government was still evolving. Surviving letters show their anxiety at being apart for long periods of time and the uncertainties about Lorna's health.

To be granted access to the cache of private letters in the family archive is to be instantly transported back in time. Spanning the years 1935 until 1939 there are rather more letters written in England than from the United States simply because the international post, the bulk of which was still transported by ship rather than by plane, was slow and unreliable. Jim's letters are written in an off-the-cuff style suited to a jobbing actor. He is to be found snatching a few moments writing backstage at Liverpool Playhouse, or The Garrick Theatre, with a borrowed ink pen, or between takes at Warner Bros. Teddington British and Welwyn Film Studios, and later after a hard day's toil at the Warner Bros. Burbank Studios in Hollywood. His writing style, though sometimes lapsing into his native Lancashire dialect, is plain and direct, and exhibits genuine period touches such as apologising for writing in pencil, because he has no ink in his pen. When he takes the occasion to use intemperate language – an expletive, for example, is written with the first letter followed by a dash. However, this practice does not extend to racial remarks which from today's perspective of multiculturalism would invite the charge of racism. Such remarks are symptomatic of received opinions based on the dominant values of the day rooted in colonialism and monoculturalism. When he wishes to place emphasis on a phrase or word he will underline using either a single or double line. Similarly, he hyphenates such compound words as in "to-night." All in all, his style is that of "a gentleman of letters."

Though he performed with the Liverpool Company within the usual walls of the Playhouse or the Winter Gardens at New Brighton, Jim occasionally performed in other venues. Such was the case in February 1933 when the company, at the suggestion of Wyndham Goldie, gave a reading for the Overseas League Sunday Circle of the first part of Eugene O'Neill's *Mourning Becomes Electra*, *Homecoming*, in which Jim played the role of Captain Brant.

For his final appearance of the 1932-33 Playhouse Season Jim played Smith, a jewel thief, in the Frederick Lonsdale comedy *Never*

Come Back. His character was archetypical of the debonair nefarious gentleman thief he would later impersonate during his film career. The play had its concluding performance on June 2, 1933 and the play itself would be filmed that year as *Just Smith* (Gaumont-British, Tom Walls. 1933). As was noted at the time:

> "James Stephenson, as Smith the gentlemanly burglar shows how gentlemanly a burglar can be, even when beset by a none the less polite detective. He gives the part the necessary social distinction, which makes it fit in with the other characters, yet he let the audience know that the real brains of the party are possessed only by him . . . From Mr. James Stephenson comes an admirable sketch of the adventurer, Smith, who, like so many people of the really wicked people on this earth, is really a charming fellow." [56]

Twenty-three plays had been produced during the 1932-33 season, and Jim had appeared in seventeen productions. The *Stage* offered congratulations on his work so far in the profession: "Mr .James Stephenson ends a season's work that must have given him considerable satisfaction . . . ." [57]

The 1933-1934 Playhouse Season brought Jim in a succession of leading roles beginning with a strong performance in Ronald Jean's three-act comedy *Smoke Screen*. He played Dr. John Poynter, a Harley Street specialist psychologist. It was the first time the play was performed on any stage. A satire on Harley Street, the story revolves around a young country general practitioner, Dr. Hugh Gaitley [Geoffrey Edwards] who visits the consulting room of Dr. Poynter followed soon after by his wife, Valerie Gaitley [Ena Burrill] about their domestic troubles. The following weekend is spent at the Gaitley's home in which Poynter gives a diagnosis of their marital jealousy. As in his earlier role of stockbroker Nigel Trent in Jeans' *Lean Harvest*, Jim scored another hit in this play. The *Birkenhead News* averred: "The important role of Dr. John Poynter is allotted to James Stephenson who is completely master of the part from the rise of the curtain." [58] The Liverpool *Evening Express* noted: "Mr. Stephenson must add this to his list of Playhouse triumphs." [59] At one point during the play's run Ronald Jeans himself was persuaded to say a few words of appreciation to the audience.

Such was the play's success that a special matinee performance was given in aid of charity. Apart from the civil dignitaries of Liverpool attending, the occasion brought Dame Sybil Thorndike, (her son Christopher Casson had a small role in the play) and other members of the acting fraternity including: Mr. and Mrs. Owen Nares, Mr. and Mrs.

Sebastian Shaw and Dora Barton. In the interval several members of the theatre company sold confectionary and programmes to patrons. In all, the event raised £117 for charity. The play was selected for the 1934 summer season at New Brighton. During this period Jim's salary rose from £3 to £4 less deductions totaling £3.18s.5d.

There followed a three week production of *Gallows Glorious* by Ronald Gow. A lengthy play to stage, it involved a cast of twenty-three, four changes of scene and elaborate stage effects and costumes. Jim brought "gravity and simple grandeur" to the role of John Brown and was "the backbone of the play." [60] Another critic remarked: "Mr. Stephenson's John Brown dominated the evening; he held the stage, with gripping power, and deserved the series of curtains so enthusiastically accorded to him." [61] Another critic gave him a back-handed compliment on: ". . . a marvel of consistent character acting, but why he should have imagined that the Lancashire dialect had invaded America in 1860, left me guessing. He well earned his persistent curtain calls." [62] Such was the success of this production that members of the cast were invited to reprise their roles in a half hour BBC radio adaptation broadcast on October 13, 1935.

True to the spirit of a theatrical repertory company, *Gallows Glorious* was followed immediately by Shakespeare's tragedy *Macbeth*. Producer William Armstrong divided the play into three parts with the aim of speed and simplicity. The settings by Marjorie Brooks and William Holford of Liverpool were constructed to be unobtrusive in quality enabling them to be used as an effective background for interesting groupings of the players on stage. The tragedy was played using revolving curtains meaning no change of scenery required more than thirty seconds. The Holfords also designed the costumes using rubber, and gramophone music was used with effect to bridge, close and introduce successive scenes. Of thirty-two parts only two insignificant ones were doubled. Jim played a "rough-hewn" Macduff and was especially admirable in the scene with Malcolm in which he hears of his wife's death, rendered with a sincerity that was intensely human and poignant. Among the starry cast was a twelve-year old Graham Stark as Macduff's son making his stage debut. Stark later became a good friend of actor comedian Peter Sellers and was a regular performer in *The Pink Panther* films. The play was rehearsed in less than a fortnight with *Gallows Glorious* being played each evening and all the original costumes were designed and executed within three weeks.

It was during this time Jim moved from his flat in Canning Street to a more comfortable flat at 14 Huskisson Street, situated again near the vicinity of the Anglian cathedral, North Liverpool City. This move was prompted by a raise in salary to £8 with no theatrical deductions. Apart from Deidre Doyle in an adjoining flat, William Armstrong lived at 18 Huskisson Street and prior to her departure from the Playhouse in 1935, Ena Burrill lived at 50 Huskisson Street.

The 1934-35 season began with high expectations, as the Playhouse Theatre auditorium had undergone refurbishment. A new drop curtain of silver velvet with a pelmet of green and silver and curtains of similar shades of green and silver decorated the entrance to the foyer and the boxes inside the theatre. The decoration to the auditorium was carried out in cream and gold with tints. On the opening night a capacity audience applauded spontaneously at the entrance of each member of the company.

The part of lawyer George Simon in Elmer Rice's three-act play *Counsellor-at-Law* provided another fillip in Jim's burgeoning theatrical experience. Paul Muni had taken on the role in New York and Hugh Miller in London, while John Barrymore had taken on the part in the film version. "As a piece of high-speed American character-acting, Mr. Stephenson's study was, however, both rapid and consistent," noted the *Liverpool Post*. [63]

In November 1934 the Playhouse mounted a production of Somerset Maugham's play *Sheppey*. This is the story of "Sheppey" Miller, who works as an assistant at a Jermyn Street hairdressing salon. Upon learning he has won a considerable amount on a big sweep prize, he decides to the consternation of his family – wife and daughter – to proceed to give away his fortune to the undeserving poor. Maugham aimed the barbed shafts of his cynical wit at the Church, the Medical Profession and the Press. Jim played the sententious Dr. Jervis who is determined to certify Sheppey. The *Evening Express* thought it: ". . . the best production The Playhouse has so far given us this season." [64]

In March 1935 Jim went onto play another successful part in Edward Wooll's court-room drama *Libel* as Thomas Foxley K.C., counsel for the defendants opposing Sir Wilfred Kelling K.C. counsel for the defendant played by Lloyd Pearson. Playwright Edward Wooll (1878-1970), a barrister of the Inner Temple and Recorder of Carlisle, had written the play under the pen name of Ward Dorane. It was produced on the London stage at the Playhouse in April 1934 with Malcolm Keen as Sir Mark Loddon and Audrey Mather as the judge with Thomas Foxley K.C. played by Leon M. Lion, and making his first professional appearance on stage as a speechless junior counsel, Alec Guinness. An instant hit it also enjoyed considerable success on the European continent as well. Wooll himself, after viewing Jim's performance, sent him a congratulatory note backstage.

"Dear Mr. Stephenson, I did not have a proper opportunity on Wednesday night of thanking you for the brilliant manner in which you played the part of counsel for the defendants in my play. It has never previously been properly played in England, though you won't mind my saying your rendition was surprisingly reminiscent of the very talented actor who played the part in Paris – the first production of the play I really enjoyed. I am looking forward to having another opportunity of seeing you play this long and exhausting role. With best wishes, Yours sincerely Edward Wooll." [65]

When, during the 1935 season William Armstrong came to stage another Shakespearean tragedy, *Hamlet*, he again, as in *Macbeth*, made cuts in the text, often ruthlessly sacrificing famous lines in order to save time and advance dramatic interest. A fortnight was spent in devising the April stage production. Again, Marjorie Brooks and William Holford designed Elizabethan style costumes and, as in *Macbeth*, use was made of curved curtains to effect changes of scenery. Thirty-five players were cast and were led by Geoffrey Edwards who, at only twenty-three, gave a technically assured performance as the Prince of Denmark. Jim played the ghost of Hamlet's father and provided a fine piece of oratory that had a true Shakespearean ring. Actor Howard Marion Crawford was brought up from London not only to play the small part of Marcellus, but more importantly to arrange the fight in the final scene of the play.

For its twenty-fifth season, 1935-1936, William Armstrong secured a coup by persuading film star Jane Baxter to join the Playhouse Company. [66] She made her debut on the Liverpool stage in *Youth at the Helm,* a three act comedy by Hubert Griffith based on a German original by Paul Vulpius. A satire on big business and modern banking, Randolph Warrender [Michael Redgrave] an unemployed young man uses his considerable charm and the weakness of human nature to bluff his way into the world of banking. He invents a mythical transaction, and as he is the only one who knows anything about it he is put in charge of it. He deceives two senior bankers, Lloyd Pearson and Jim, playing the pair in a conspiracy they didn't understand, and members of the government. Despite many near scrapes, he manages to turn a commercial venture into profits for all. Jane Baxter appeared as the bank typist and was warmly received by audiences.

This comedy was followed by *Barnet's Folly* by Jan Stewer in which Jim played a character part, farmer Mark Lannacott. Herbert Lomas had taken the role in its West End debut at the Haymarket in February 1935. The plot concerns a West Country farmer who is inveigled into financing a farm produce marketing scheme, and brought to near ruin. Critics complained about the various individual interpretations of a Devonshire dialect given by members of the cast. Jim as the farmer brought to near ruin, was deemed to have given a finely chiselled and vigorous character study. For his part, Jim appears to have had difficulty with the role as in a letter he writes: ". . . after dinner I did my best to break the back of the first two acts of *Barnet's Folly!*" [67]

This was followed by J.B. Priestley's *Cornelius* in which Jim played the lead. Alfred Sangster was Biddle and the young and clear-headed typist, Judy Eivson, was played by Jane Baxter. The tale is of the history, the bankruptcy and dissolution of an old established city metal firm. The play had been produced in the West End in March 1935 at the Duchess Theatre by Basil Dean, and the lead role taken by Ralph Richardson. Critics in Liverpool complained the transition from comedy to drama was too abrupt, as much the fault of Priestley's material, "something of a potboiler," as the playing of the actors. Nevertheless, the critics asserted Jim's role gave him "a supreme opportunity which he seized." [68] Moreover, he acted with "a strength that is singularly compelling and his Merseyside admirers will feel that they have never seen him to more artistic advantage." [69] In a letter he writes of the audience's reaction during the play's first performance:

> "Last night something happened which has only happened once before at the Playhouse I am told. At the end of my "cup of bitterness" speech in the last act I got a round of applause! Which astonished me – nearly threw me off my balance – and pleased me no end!" [70]

In a later letter, he explains his thoughts about the serious intentions of the Priestley play:

> "*Cornelius* is a good show . . . But it's not going to be a popular success. I think it is because it goes down and down and the last act is unrelieved gloom, until the nit-wits laugh in the wrong places. Last night I felt like breaking off – looking out at them and saying "go to hell." They even giggle when the poor faded typist is saying her pathetic goodbye – [they] think, I suppose, that she is "vamping" me. Oh what a lot the films have to answer for! They want comedy all the time so that they can open their foolish mouths and laugh!" [71]

Despite Jim's serious attitude, he recounted a risible incident which occurred whilst performing the play, and this revived memories of his military service:

> "I wonder if you remember where Biddle is talking to me about figures and numbers just before the creditor's meeting? He says

- there is more in numbers - than meets the eye – then 'Take number nine' and then there is a knock at the door. Last night there was a continuous guffaw in the stalls and chuckling went on for a long time. I couldn't make it out – and then it struck me – 'number nine' in the army is the universal remedy – a purgative pill! And I saw the funny side of it and had all my work cut out to refrain from chuckling myself." [72]

Miss Linley of Bath by Dr. Mary Sheridan, marked another premiere of a brand new comedy play. Set in the eighteenth century, audiences found the play dealing with a trivial episode in the life of Richard Brinsley Sheridan amusing, but Giles Playfair writing for the *Evening Express* was far from pleased. He found the acting heavy where it should have been light and frothy. The dialogue and situation did not in general suggest

Jim Stephenson extreme right as the villainous circus master Gasper Boom in the children's play *Circus Boy*. It was written by Michael Redgrave and staged at the Liverpool Playhouse during the Christmas holidays of 1935. Next to Jim is Betty Fleetwood as Janet, Patricia Hayes as Ludo the circus boy, Brian Blades as the spoilt rich boy, and Louise Frodsham as Miss McTatty. On the recommendation of Rachel Kempson, Patricia Hayes was brought up to Liverpool from London. She was paid £3 and 5 shillings per week for her trouble!
Photo courtesy of Stephenson Archive

Jim Stephenson as Prince Sirki and Penelope Dudley Ward as Princess Grazia in
the Liverpool Playhouse production of *Death Takes a Holiday* in January 1936.
Photo courtesy of Stephenson Archive

the eighteenth century, tending to wander aimlessly up and down the
years, sometimes too modern and at other times laboriously Victorian. In
conclusion he felt "The grace, the elegance, the acid and polished wit of
the eighteenth century are lacking." [73] Jim played the role of Mr. Linley
with stiff dignity and pride.

The year 1935 rounded off with the traditional children's Christmas
holiday play. These were of an especially high standard, and Michael
Redgrave's play, *Circus Boy*, was a fast moving affair. Thirty-three parts
were cast with Redgrave playing the small role of a BBC official. On

Rachel Kempson's recommendation, Patricia Hayes was brought up, at some expense, from the Duchess Theatre in the West End to play the part of Ludo the gypsy boy. The story revolves around Ludo's attempt to reclaim ownership of a travelling circus, cruelly filched from him by the villainous Gasper Boom played in delightfully melodramatic fashion by Jim. The production had elaborate set designs including the circus scenes, the Sussex Downs and an Old Mill all by Charles Thomas. The gypsy caravan itself was artfully constructed by Norman Hawkins and the Playhouse property staff. *Circus Boy* was first staged on Christmas Eve 1935. Redgrave was congratulated by the critics on a very keen appreciation of the juvenile mind.

Jim's final season with the Liverpool Company brought a production of *Death Takes a Holiday* based on Alberto Casella's 1924 play *La Morte in Vacanza* which had been filmed in Hollywood as *Death Takes a Holiday* (Paramount, Mitchell Leisen, 1934) with Fredric March cast as Prince Sirki and Evelyn Venable as Grazia. Jim was cast as immortal Death and Penelope Dudley Ward as Grazia. There were marked differences of opinion about this production. Michael Redgrave, as we have already learned, was decidedly unimpressed by this production. David Webster, reviewing the play in the *Liverpolitan*, agreed with Redgrave's sentiments, declaring:

"On his first appearance, Mr. James Stephenson, instead of making the blood run down our spines, hinted only too clearly at a rather pompous aldermaniac type of creature, who later developed into a rather stagey strong man. Here was a Messenger from Mars rather than a blood-curdling coldness. Obviously Mr. Stephenson was mis-cast, a misfortune liable to befall any popular member of a resident company, but so far as a play is concerned, disastrous when it happens to its central character." [74]

Other critics though were more positive, describing Jim's performance as "A capable piece of acting. It had strength and dignity." [75] "James Stephenson in the title role gives a masterly and vivid performance. He registers no false note. His splendid voice and build have rarely been used to better advantage." [76] On the strength of this performance Jim was invited by the Reverend David Douglas of St. Andrew's Church Rodney Street, Liverpool to read the scripture lesson of a service at the church. [77]

Boyd's Shop, a St John Ervine play was premiered at the Playhouse. The story is set in a grocer's shop run by Andrew Boyd [Lloyd Pearson] who is up against John Haslett, an ambitious rival competitor, played by Jim, who in turn has also competition from the young ambitious Reverend

Dunwoody [Michael Redgrave] who also covets the position of an older curate, the Rev. Arthur Patterson played by Alfred Sangster. Both men have designs on Agnes, Boyd's daughter played by Rachel Kempson. This comic play, with its tale of modernity in the retail trade and the impetuousness of youth, captured life in an Ulster village. Jim conveyed just the right impression of clumsy sincerity. St John Ervine himself was on hand, and responding to enthusiastic calls, spoke to the audience and paid tribute to William Armstrong and his company's rendition of the play. He also remarked of the Playhouse with deliberate flattery: "If you live in London and wish to see a play nowadays, you have to make the journey to Liverpool." [78]

Jim was able to bring strength and sincerity to his many theatrical roles at Liverpool, and, overall, Jim's time at the Liverpool Playhouse had been invaluable training giving him an excellent grounding in memorisation of parts, timing, blocking, motivation, characterisation and the ability to perform a diversity of parts from classical Shakespeare, to

On the left, Jim Stephenson [5ft, 11"] as John Haslett, alongside Michael Redgrave [6ft, 3"] as the Rev. Eric Dunwoody and Rachel Kempson as Agnes Boyd in the 1936 Liverpool Playhouse production of *Boyd's Shop*.
PHOTO COURTESY OF STEPHENSON ARCHIVE

dramatic leads and supporting roles in new and traditional plays. He also demonstrated stamina, coping with the unexpected, and using, if required, improvisation, providing personal make-up and costume fittings. These all came with the job and were skills he honed to perfection. This was the secure foundation on which his subsequent film work would be based.

During his final season with the Company he was earning £10 per week with no deductions. One of the final productions before Jim's departure from the Liverpool Company was James Bridie's Anglo-Scottish comedy *Storm in a Teacup* taken from Bruno Frank's play *Sturm im Wasserglas* in which he took the role of the provost.

While all this was going on, Lorna and Jim were searching for suitable accommodation down in London and planning their wedding to take place just prior to the August bank holiday of 1936. The couple took a London flat, in Charlbert Court, near Regents Park where they employed a maid, Amy, to look after the domestic side of things.

The location of Lorna and Jim's wedding on Thursday July 30, 1936 was St Bartholomew's Parish Church in the picturesque village of Thurstaston on the Wirral Peninsula. In a mild transgression of sartorial convention of the day, Jim substituted the usual "tails" for a short black jacket, black and white checked trousers and grey cravat. Unsurprisingly, most of the wedding guests were family and friends of the bride. Apart from his immediate family, Alan Stephenson played the organ at the wedding service, invited guests of the bridegroom were drawn exclusively from the Liverpool Playhouse Theatre Company. Lloyd Pearson was best man, and other high profile figures included Playhouse Chairman of directors Colonel Sir John Shute MP, board director Professor Henry Cohen, artistic director William Armstrong and manageress Maud Carpenter. Indicative of the pre-television age there were throngs of people outside the church ready to spot their favourite Playhouse personalities, and there was much cheering and applauding. The wedding made noteworthy regional news, and was even accorded a prominent place in a local high-society periodical, the *Liverpolitan*, which stated: "No Wirral wedding this season has attracted greater interest than the marriage of Mr. James Stephenson . . . to Miss Lorna Hewitt Kilby Dinn . . . ." [79]

With Lorna's support, Jim decided to take his chances and go to London to see what work he could find on the West End Theatre, BBC radio and more especially in the lucrative, though precarious, film industry based in and around London and the South East of England. While in Devonshire, on honeymoon, his agent contacted him. He was offered the part of the provost in the West End hit *Storm in a Teacup* at the Garrick Theatre, where it had a long successful run of 450 performances.

Jim and Lorna Stephenson on their wedding day, July 30, 1936.
PHOTO COURTESY OF STEPHENSON ARCHIVE

The *Daily Telegraph* declared it: "The most amusing play of 1936," and in March 1937, following its West End run it transferred to the Streatham Hill Theatre and Golders Green Hippodrome. *Storm in a Teacup* was later filmed in 1937 by Alexander Korda, directed by Victor Saville, and starred Vivien Leigh and Rex Harrison. Jim made his London stage debut at the Garrick on August 17, 1936.

But despite all this run of luck Jim was perturbed about Lorna's health and this uncertainty cast a sense of self-doubt in his stage work, as this brief letter extract suggests:

> "Anmer Hall and Miss Schaife were at the show last night and I
> met them afterwards. And altho' I felt very Monday nightish
> they were very congratulatory . . . and Mason [stage director
> R. Halliday Mason] said I was in very good form too – so I'm
> no judge." [80]

A few days later he was hitting his stride and settling into the role:

> "Last night I gave what I thought was a dashing performance.
> Fay [Actor William George Fay (1872-1947)] told me Anmer
> Hall [pseudonym of impresario Alderson Burrell Horne (1863-
> 1952)] was mightily pleased with me on Monday." [81]

In his dressing room at The Garrick he wrote:

> "The matinee is going well – I've just come off from the first
> act. An understudy is playing for Lisbet – quite good but a deal
> slower than Ethel Glendenning. [Roger] Livesey and I seem to
> be getting quite matey!" [82]

Though he was grateful for the offer to appear in a familiar role he
decided to keep his options open, and not sign up for the run of the show.
As in any long running show audience reactions were varied, and a few
weeks later he wrote:

> "We had rows and rows of dead cod-fish at the theatre last night.
> Two of them laughed about twice. The rest were in a state of
> coma. Takings were £26 down last week – altho' last Saturday
> was the biggest house we've had £150." [83]

During October 1936 Jim went along to the St. Martin's Theatre for
preliminary discussions of a part in a new play, *Till the Cows Come Home*
by Geoffrey Kerr; in the event, Leslie Banks got the role. [84]

In the family archive there are surviving details of the readings
he selected for stage and radio auditions. These included two modern
pieces: speeches from *Gallows Glorious* and *Libel*; Act I Scene V from
Shakespeare's *Hamlet* "Thus was I, sleeping . . . ." and a piece of comic
Lancashire dialect. [85]

Jim, in keeping with many actors, was very sensitive about his
looks and overall health. At one point, in some dismay, he wrote:
"I combed out such a lot of hair this morning and I'm really getting
depressed about it." [86] Luckily he applied several hair tonics and this
appeared to rectify any encroaching baldness. His general health was also
causing him concern, as the onset of middle-age found him putting on
weight. Half-heartedly he took up physical exercise ". . . in my green and
white "creation" - having done my ups and downs and pedalling . . . ." [87]
Needless to say, despite his fitness regime, he was still smoking heavily.

During December 1936 the issue of Edward VIII and the constitutional crisis over his affair with American divorcee Wallis Simpson finally was revealed to the British public after a news media blackout on the subject. The issue divided the country with support for the King amongst the working and middle-classes, and opposition from the aristocracy and the political establishment. As an ex-serviceman Jim was fully supportive of the King, impressed with Mrs. Simpson, and critical of Prime Minister Stanley Baldwin's handling of the situation.

"The King? Well, I think I'm going to take the [*Daily*] *Mail* in future! I bought one when I was out and have just read the leading article which expresses exactly what I feel in the matter. One of the few times when the *Mail* does not exasperate me. I think it would be a <u>catastrophe</u> if the King were forced to abdicate. There is no one else with one tenth part of his qualification for the job, or his influence, or his popularity. I think Wedgewood is right and if it comes to the <u>people</u> choosing they will send Bishops <u>and</u> Politicians about their business and say 'Give us our king!' I think Mrs. Simpson looks a charming, intelligent woman – as she apparently is." [88]

Lorna, still seeking a diagnosis of her illness, took the opposite view; the King had shirked his duty. Jim ended the topic on a humorous note: "Well, well – I can see we'll have arguments about it. Come back quick and let's have them!" [89]

In fact Lorna's coolness towards the King and Mrs. Simpson was proved correct in the light of abdication documents released on January 1, 2003 at the National Archives in London. A special branch report, dated July 3, 1935, revealed that while Mrs. Simpson was openly seeing the Prince of Wales she was also seen both socially and secretly in the company of Guy Marcus Trundle (1899-1958). He was described as: "a very charming adventurer, very good looking, well bred and an excellent dancer." Trundle, a married man, was an engineer and car salesman and was said to be in the employ of the Ford Motor Company. [90]

By April 1937, in addition to having embarked upon a film contract at Warner Bros. First National Teddington Studios, Jim had secured a role in another West End play. *Post Road* was a successful comedy-thriller by Wilbur Daniel Steele and Norma Mitchell which ran on Broadway for over 200 performances between December 1934 and June 1935. Two members of the original cast, Percy Kilbride, making his debut on a British stage, and Edmon Ryan along with Sara Seeger joined British members of the cast. These included Louise Hampton, Mary Merrall and Jim. After a week's try out at Golders Green Hippodrome, the two act play opened at The Queens on April 20, 1937. It didn't stay there long because the

Emlyn Williams / John Gielgud production *He Was Born Gay: A Romance in Three Acts* was scheduled to play at the Queens during May. The plot of *Post Road* concerned Emily Madison's Connecticut home on the old post road between New York to Boston. Dr. Spender and Nurse Martin, in reality professional kidnappers, view her home as the perfect place to stage a kidnapping act. Reviews of the piece were mixed. Many critics judged the play as too much of a hybrid. The *Birmingham Post* argued that to gain true success, the cast needed to be drawn either from wholly English or American Companies and concluded: "The different styles of a mixed cast do not seem to blend satisfactorily." [91] The last surviving cast member of *Post Road*, the late Moira Lister (1923-2007) recalled:

> ". . . dear Percy Kilbride who was devastated when his sure-fire "laughs" did not materialise, and the ladies Mary Merrall and Louise Hampton who were both very kind and motherly towards me and I remember James Stephenson being Dr. Spender and playing a very impressive doctor! But to a star struck thirteen year old everyone seemed to have lights round their heads!" [92]

When his work permitted, Sundays, summer breaks and bank holidays, Jim visited his two younger brothers; Alan in Coventry:

> "Coventry . . . went down with Alan to the cathedral in the afternoon to practice for his recital in the evening. And after tea we all went in the organ loft for service and just had time to hear the first piece in the recital afterwards before I went off for my train at 8.30. Here at 11.15!" [93]

And Norman in Great Bookham, Surrey: "We [Norman, Toonie and Jim] went to "Thorncroft" for lunch and tea yesterday and in the evening just the three of us had dinner and a few drinks at "Riddlesdale." [94]

On his penultimate day before sailing across the Atlantic Jim went with Lorna, his brother Norman, and sister-in-law Toonie to the cinema in London to see *Victoria the Great* (Radio-Keith-Orpheum/Herbert Wilcox, 1937). As a matter of form, patrons were obliged to stand while the national anthem played prior to, and at the end of, the film programme. It was a final adieu to the stiff formality and conservative tradition dictated by British mores and customs before beginning a new life in the United States. He would never set foot in Britain again. [95]

A FIRST ENCOUNTER WITH THE MOVIES IN APRIL 1932.
Jim Stephenson, oil merchant (left) and Jack Grey, insurance broker (right)
have an impromptu acting test. They act out a scenario
from a Sherlock Holmes and Dr. Watson scenario.

Behind the camera George Dunkerley, shoe retailer, captures "shots" on his black and white, silent 16mm baby ciné camera in preparation for an a non-commercial film produced by The Burnley and District Amateur Ciné Society.

Jim did not appear in the final film, and given the expense of processing and developing a roll of 16mm film, 20 shillings, or £54.10p at today's retail prices, this is probably a staged photo opportunity.

PHOTO COURTESY OF THE BURNLEY EXPRESS

3
BRITISH AND HOLLYWOOD SCREEN ACTOR
(1937-1941)

I hope I don't trip on the road to stardom!
- JAMES STEPHENSON TO LORNA STEPHENSON
(AUGUST 17, 1937)

Amateur ciné was all the rage among the well-to-do middle-classes during the inter-war years. Jim Stephenson's sister-in-law Toonie, for instance, had purchased a 16mm home movie camera during the early 1930s. Images of her family, relations and friends back home in Surrey, England, dominate these domestic films. Amongst this footage, however, are shots of Norman Stephenson's final tour of duty as Captain of the Nile Military Police in April 1934 captured for posterity. Unsurprisingly, given this background, Jim's first recorded venture into film was that of amateur film-making. At the turn of the 1930s several Lancashire towns such as Blackburn had already produced short amateur films. Anxious not to be outdone, The Burnley Amateur Ciné Society had been formed in early 1932 by a group of the town's entrepreneurs. The society's first production, *The Second Stain*, was a two reel, black and white, silent adaptation of a Conan Doyle detective story produced by, and starring Burnley's professional middle-classes. It was a rather expensive affair shot not on amateur 9:5mm film, but on semi-professional 16mm gauge. In April 1932 the enterprise attracted several reports in the local press, including a couple of photographs showing Jim and his good friend Jack Grey at work behind, and in front of, the camera.[1] By the time of the film's premiere in December 1932 Jim was six months into his stage career at Liverpool Playhouse. Given the high cost of shooting and processing 16mm film, it is reasonable to conclude that these press reports were primarily intended as publicity for the ciné society and, perhaps, Jim's ambitions to enter the acting profession. It is clear from the outset of his professional acting career that Jim aimed for work in British films and, had the hand of fate dealt with him differently, it is conceivable he would have entered the film business at an earlier time. When in February 1932 he paid £1 18s 6d to be placed in *Spotlight*, the actor's directory, he was described as seeking stage, screen and radio work.

Relocating from a provincial northern English mill town to the exotic distance of Hollywood was, even back then, not wholly inconceivable. In 1929 a Burnley born girl, Mary James, who had emigrated to Detroit in the United States, had managed to become a stand-in for Dolores Costello in the part-talkie epic *Noah's Ark* (Warner, Michael Curtiz, 1929) using the screen name of Mary Lowes. [2]

During the early 1930s Hollywood came to the North of England in the guise of famous comic duo Stan Laurel and Oliver 'Babe' Hardy. Having arrived at Southampton on board RMS *Aquitania* on July 23, 1932, the pair toured the British Isles before their departure across the channel to Paris. On August 1, 1932 Laurel and Hardy appeared in the Lancashire seaside resort of Blackpool. The following day "the boys" arrived by train at Victoria Station, Manchester to be greeted by large enthusiastic crowds.

Only after meeting his fiancée Lorna Dinn during the summer of 1935 did Jim begin to think seriously of breaking into the film business. As one of his film co-stars, Lesley Brook, confirmed, film work may have lacked the kudos of the English theatrical stage: "I considered films to be 'selling your face.' It wasn't acting you know in those days." [3] However, it was not to be ignored for it not only provided regular work but, more importantly, the financial remuneration compared to that of the legitimate stage, was very lucrative and would provide sufficient investment for Jim's impending marriage. With this attitude in mind, and moderating his earlier protestations of "screenplays . . . debasing to the public taste," [4] Jim swallowed his pride and made several attempts to begin a film career.

He approached Crusade films, a small independent company which distributed their films through Paramount and New Realm Pictures. Over two days, from Wednesday August 7, 1935 to Thursday August 8, 1935, he made a series of tests for director Donovan Pedelty (1903-1989) on behalf of the Rowson brothers Simon (1877-1950) and Harry (1875-1951), producers of New Realm Pictures Company. A journalist by profession, Pedelty wrote film articles for various English papers including the *Manchester Evening News* and was later editor of

Picturegoer fan magazine. In 1933 he entered films as a scenarist, and in 1935 had directed his first film, *Flame in the Heather*, a historical romantic drama set in Scotland. Released in September 1935 it was critically panned. [5] At the time Jim made contact with Pedelty he was a talent scout for Paramount British.

While Jim waited anxiously for the outcome of his tests, word leaked out and a local reporter was soon backstage at the Liverpool Playhouse pressing him for comments on signing an impending film contract. It was reported: "he preferred not to discuss the matter at this juncture. No contract had been signed. He did not wish to say anything about it in fairness to all concerned." [6]

Unfortunately, the tests did not prove satisfactory for either party and the outcome was delayed due to Pedelty falling ill. After this abortive attempt, a year later Jim resumed efforts to break into films. Now performing in London's West End, and broadcasting on BBC radio he had instructed the theatrical agency O'Bryen, Linnit and Dunfee to begin searching for film work on his behalf. [7] At the beginning of September 1936 he was invited by his agent, Bill Linnit, to go along and see contacts about possible film work.

> "Linnit rang up for me yesterday and I went and saw him. Criterion Films (D.[ouglas] Fairbanks Jnr.) want someone for a Scottish part in a film and they (two of them) were to come to the theatre last night to see my performance. Linnit sent me out to the studio at Isleworth yesterday afternoon in his brand new Rolls, with chauffeur! and I saw the two blokes concerned. I am waiting to hear from Linnit what the result is. Even if it comes off I'm very exercised in my mind as to what I should do. It would mean coming out of the show." [8]

On the following day, after a matinee performance of *Storm in a Teacup* at the Garrick Theatre, he renewed his acquaintance with Burnley born actor Herbert Lomas in the Green Room Club at 46 Leicester Square to discuss acquiring film roles.

> "I had a meal with Herbert Lomas . . . to have a talk about things. At the club (The Green Room) I met a lot of well-known people, including Howard Rose of the BBC whom I am going to see at Broadcasting House on Friday. Herbert, after a good many fulminations against agents in general said he thought I had done the right thing in getting in with O'Bryen's and that they are certainly the best people in town. He's going to put in a word for me where he can with film people but he says introductions are really no good – they want to see your work, and from that point

of view it is an excellent thing that I am in this show. No word from Linnit yet about the Criterion people." [9]

Later in the afternoon of the same day, writing in his dressing room he referred again to his visit to Criterion Films: "No news from Linnit yet. I'm afraid it looks bad." [10]

The following month, October 1936, there was still nothing in the wind, but a chance meeting with an ex-colleague from Liverpool Playhouse, Robert Flemyng, galvanised him into lobbying contacts in the film industry again.

> "I looked out of the window and saw Bobby Fleming (sic) walking up the street so I called him in and we've been talking. He is going to ask Harold Huth the casting manager of GB [Gaumont-British Picture Corporation] to come and see me [at the Garrick]. Says he has heard from many people who have seen the show that I am splendid in the part" [Provost Thompson in *Storm in a Teacup*]. [11]

Later in November 1936 he wrote: "I went and saw Dunfee – told him to keep these film people warm." [12]

Jim's persistence finally paid off, for at the beginning of 1937 he was offered a contract making budget feature film programmers at Teddington Studios, the British arm of Warner Brothers' First National. Studio chief Irving Asher (1903-1985) had seen Jim on stage and had liked what he saw. A forgotten figure today, the fast-talking, sharp-dressed Asher knew all the film business angles and set store on bringing profit and prestige to the operations of the Warner British studios. In his memoirs, the celebrated British director Michael Powell recalled:

> "I liked Irving. What he knew, he knew, but he didn't know very much. On the other hand, he didn't pretend that he did. Our relations were always happy." [13]

Warner Bros. had acquired the Teddington Studios on lease in 1931, and for the first couple of years produced undemanding quota-quickies destined for the bottom half of double bill programmes. In 1934 they purchased the Teddington studios outright and, mindful of the bad press these low-budget second features were attracting, with accusations of American distributors bringing the industry into disrepute and ruining its prospects of future international expansion, began a process of modernisation. Bigger budgets were allocated and better technical facilities were installed resulting in fewer films being produced, but with longer running times and higher production values. There was also a step change in the calibre of directors hired. Ralph Ince, long in Hollywood as an actor and director, and Roy William Neill, who would later direct all but one of the Sherlock Holmes second features at Universal studios during the 1940s, were brought over from Hollywood to bring "pizzazz" to the product. Michael Powell also cut his directorial teeth by making five pictures at Warner Bros. Teddington Studios of which three are today considered "missing believed lost." [14]

Though made chiefly to comply with the 1927 Cinematograph Films Act stipulating a percentage of films shown had to be distributed and exhibited by British cinemas, Warner Bros. put a good deal of effort into these second features, and the handful that survive warrant re-evaluation for their craftsman-like appeal in bringing solid unpretentious genre pictures to the screen. They were an excellent training ground for native talent to learn the craft of film-making using American "factory" know-how. Michael Powell remembered these budget films, or "quota-quickies," as they were known at the Warner studio, as being journeyman assignments, but backed up with well-focused talent and resourceful studio facilities:

> "The quota-quickies that I made . . . at Warner Brothers' British Studios at Teddington were a damn sight more honest and more entertaining, because they were not trying to be anything but what they were." [15]

Asher had an instinct for finding suitable photogenic talent not only to serve the British market, but for export to the Burbank Studios over in Los Angeles, California. Occasionally there were blips in persuading talent to come over to his way of thinking. Robert Donat, for instance, was wary of Asher's confident chutzpah, and declined the assurances of a long-term Hollywood contract which Asher dangled in front of him. Donat's first film for Warners was to have been *Captain Blood*, but when he refused the script, citing charges of type-casting, Asher went one better and substituted, what would prove his biggest discovery, a young Tasmanian by the name of Errol Flynn. Flynn's athleticism, swagger and bravado fitted perfectly into the swashbuckling genre. During the late 1930s and early 1940s Flynn invested his own colourful personality in the legendary heroes he portrayed on screen with the result he dominated the genre completely for almost a decade. Other lesser Asher discoveries exported to Burbank included: Paul Graetz (1889-1937), Ian Hunter (1900-1975), child-star Sybil Jason (1927-2011), Warner's attempt to tap into the Shirley Temple phenomenon, and Patric Knowles (1911-1995). After many years at the helm of Warner Bros. Teddington, Asher quit his post as managing director in March 1938. In May 1938 he joined London Films Productions to become associate producer for Alexander Korda over at Denham Studios. During his time with Korda, Asher produced the highly regarded spy thriller *The Spy in Black* (London, Michael Powell, 1939). Asher was in the room when director Powell was introduced to Hungarian screenwriter Emeric Pressburger, brought in to rewrite the film scenario. Thus began a partnership that would produce some of the most original and innovative films of the 1940s, notably: *A Matter of Life and Death*, also known as *Stairway to Heaven* (General Film Distributors / The Archers, Michael Powell and Emeric Pressburger, 1946), *Black Narcissus* (General Film Distributors / The Archers, Powell and Pressburger, 1947) and *The Red Shoes* (General Film Distributors / The Archers, Powell and Pressburger, 1948).

Jim Stephenson made a total of eight British second features, seven at Warner Bros. First National-British, Teddington Studios, and one loan out to Rialto Productions based at Welwyn Studios. All were produced in nine months during 1937, and of these five films are considered missing believed lost, but three films are known to have survived. Looked at today, these films may appear feeble and naïve in their construction and attitude. Yet upon closer examination, it is clear their scripts were censored for any hint of salacious detail or topical reference that might, however inadvertently, offend the prevailing social and political consensus. Love was therefore portrayed as being in the head rather than the body and crime, however minor, was subject to swift retribution to counter any suggestion of a breach of the moral codes and social mores of the day. Because film scenarios were sanitised, this created a peculiar sense of emasculation as exhibited by often stilted dialogue spoken in cut-glass accents, pedestrian characterisation and indifferent plotting. British films of this period were further beleaguered by a lack of ambition and finance which thwarted the prospects of the film industry in general. As we will see, this strategy of censorial policing compromised the structure of at least two of the eight films in which Jim appeared. However, whatever their deficiencies as films, Jim's performances were no disgrace, and of sufficient merit to enable him to set off on the road to Hollywood.

Luckily, his debut film, *Perfect Crime* (Warner, Ralph Ince, 1937), has survived. A well-turned out crime melodrama, it owes a great deal of its appeal to sure-footed direction from industry veteran Ralph Ince. He not only directed the film, but also acted on screen, thus demonstrating two essential qualities for B picture production: economy and versatility. [16] Ince endorsed Asher's decision to hire Jim when, after only two days of filming, he gave an assessment of the studio's latest acquisition to the press:

"James Stephenson is one of the most important discoveries we

Jim Stephenson
as the villainous
Parker in his
1937 debut film
Perfect Crime.
PHOTO COURTESY
OF STEPHENSON
ARCHIVE

have yet made. He can act well, speak well, and wear his clothes
well. He has a fine camera face and as one of the villains of the
piece is plumb full of menace. In my view James Stephenson is
going to be a real big bet." [17]

The tale of *Perfect Crime* involves an inept, myopic clerk who
embezzles money from his employer, books two berths on a passenger
liner, sheds his former identity, assumes the guise of a debonair man-
of-the-world, falls in love and finally confesses his hidden past to the
authorities. At a melodrama level the scenario has an ingenuity and
novelty which is engaging and amusing. Romantic interludes between
Glen Alyn and Hugh Williams don't carry particular conviction, nor do
footling deck games on board ship or flirtatious frivolity from Iris Hoey
either, but these are all commendably brief and are no serious obstacle to
the progression and vigour of the narrative.

Jim plays the character of Walter Parker who spends the duration
of the film looking suave and being affable, whilst simultaneously
endeavouring to conceal his shady past from American detective Jim
Lanahan (Ralph Ince). Whilst on screen, Jim produces a cigarette case.

This was the parting gift given him by the amateur dramatic company [The Burnley Players] some five years previously and was a reminder of both good and bad luck he had sustained in the intervening years. Jim, like Ronald Colman, had the luck of being blessed with a pair of brown eyes capable of being very photogenic and expressive on black and white film. Unlike those who had pale blue eyes, they suffered less from the studio arc lights which were capable of burning the skin of the eyeballs. [18] Overall, discounting a slight tremulousness in his voice and a hint of rigidity in his blocking, he acquitted himself admirably in his first film appearance.

Jim's next film, *The Man Who Made Diamonds* (Warner, 1937), was also directed by Ralph Ince and is, unfortunately, a lost film. However, a detailed 149 page script survives at the University of Southern California Warner Bros. Archives and indicates it was a fast-paced thriller full of action and atmosphere with artless humour, supplied by Renee Gadd, and confected romance from Lesley Brook and George Galleon, added for mass appeal. [19] Jim played crook Ben Errol, described as "a well-dressed man of about thirty," who, along with Wilfred Lawson, was in cahoots with arch villain Noel Madison who had flooded the market with fake diamonds. Several atmospheric scenes were set in a laboratory where, using pseudo-scientific methods, diamonds were contrived using an electrical apparatus. These special effects, showcasing electricity, are a reminder of an age when the national grid, wireless and electrical appliances were modern marvels. Even electricians working in film studios were known as "sparks" with suggestions of cutting-edge virtuosity, excitement, mystery and something to be appreciated.

Unfortunately the release of the film was overshadowed by the tragic death of Ralph Ince which occurred just after the film was completed on Saturday April 10, 1937. In the early hours of Sunday April 11, 1937, Ince was killed outright in a motor-car accident in London. The two-seater car, driven by his wife Helen, came into collision with an obelisk in Kensington Road outside the Albert Hall as they were returning home from a bridge party. In a witness statement Helen Ince recalled: "We were driving along quite peacefully as I wanted to see the dawn, when suddenly this happened." [20] A statement by Mrs. Ince was read out at the coroner's inquiry which suggested that Mr. Ince might have been talking to his wife and might have distracted her attention.

Jim had been taken on by the studios at $75 (£15) per week for no more than fifty days per year so leaving plenty of time to supplement his salary from stage and radio work. It was intended that initially he would be called upon to perform as a character player. So it was that

Jim as Ben Errol with unidentified player in a scene taken from
The Man Who Made Diamonds 1937.
PHOTO COURTESY OF STEPHENSON ARCHIVE

Jim showed his versatility by appearing in minor character roles in two
Claude Hulbert comedies: *You Live and Learn* (Warner, Arthur Woods,
1938) and *It's in the Blood* (Warner, Gene Gerrard, 1938). Claude Hulbert
(1900-1964), whether pursuing a solo career on radio, London stage
revue, cabaret, pantomime or in partnership with his older brother, Jack
Hulbert (1892-1978), in British films was hugely popular.

In *You Live and Learn* Jim played farmer Sam Brooks and in *It's
in the Blood* he was cast, yet again, as a gangster who went by the
improbable name of "Milky Joe." Though neither of these films survives
for posterity, *You Live and Learn* had the curious distinction of pairing
the comic silly-ass Claude Hulbert with Glenda Farrell, brought across
from Hollywood with her trademark wise-cracking Brooklyn idiom.
Theirs was one of the more incongruous Anglo-American screen comedy
partnerships since the teaming of Will Hay (the master of the double take)

with Edgar Kennedy (the king of the slow burn) in *Hey! Hey! U.S.A!* (Gainsborough, Marcel Varnel, 1938). If contemporary reviews are to be believed, Claude Hulbert's and Glenda Farrell's comic thunder was stolen by character player Charlotte Leigh who delighted audiences with her rendition of the Cuckoo Song in the film. Leigh, a revue artist on the London stage, is also to be seen scene-stealing in the camp short *The Fairy of the Phone* (GPO, William Coldstream, 1936). She plays the government "Fairy of the Phone" who advises telephone subscribers on GPO protocol when dialling a call. In the film's musical finale she puts her back out by falling down stairs and is offered some wilted flowers!

A genuine legend of British comedy variety, "The Cheeky Chappie," Max Miller's saucy stage patter and inimitable way with innuendo gave him an unrivalled ability to work audiences. Inevitably the racy material used in his stage routines was bowdlerised for mass film consumption, and the absence of a live audience, the essence of his act, also restricted his success as a film star. Nevertheless, Max made a total of fourteen films between 1933 and 1941 of which eight star vehicles were produced at Warner Bros. Teddington Studios. Three of the eight survive but the other five are missing believed lost and include: *Transatlantic Trouble* also known as *Take It From Me* (Warner, William Beaudine, 1938). [21] This lost film was a seemingly harmless farce involving a smart-aleck boxing manager, Albert Hall [Max Miller], whose chief fighter (played by Buddy Baer the younger brother of former heavyweight boxing champion of the world Max Baer) is taken up by the wealthy lovelorn Lady Fairhaven [Zillah Bateman] on a voyage from New York. As in *Perfect Crime*, part of the story is set on board a passenger liner, and Parisian settings, used in *You Live and Learn* and *It's in the Blood*, were utilised again for the film's finale. Amidst all the gags and cross-talk Jim appeared in a supporting role as Fred Lewis, a rival English big-time prize-fight manager.

Despite the innocuousness of such anodyne screenplays and the best efforts of film companies, trade bodies and censors, films could, and often did, cause offence. Such was the case with *Transatlantic Trouble*. The film made banner headlines, for no sooner had the film been released at the Empire Theatre, Leicester Square on a double bill with *Madame X* (M-G-M, Sam Wood, 1937) than a libel suit was brought by Cara Leland, Baroness Fairhaven of Park Street, London. The scenario writer had intended to use a fictitious name, but due to an oversight had used instead the name of the plaintiff Lady Fairhaven. Warner Bros. issued a public apology, paid damages to charities nominated by the plaintiff and the film was hastily withdrawn. Actors were recalled for re-dubbing with the character name changed to Lady Foxham and the film was re-launched under the title of *Take It From Me*. [22]

Part of the interest in these Warner Bros. British productions is seeing anglicised versions of Hollywood scenarios reprised in a British setting. Based on the 1931 story *From this Dark Stairway* by the prolific thriller writer Mignon G. Eberhart, *The Dark Stairway* (Warner, Arthur Woods, 1938) was a remake of an earlier Hollywood B mystery film *The Murder of Dr. Harrigan* (Warner, Frank McDonald, 1936) starring Kay Linaker, Ricardo Cortez and Mary Astor. Although all prints of *The Dark Stairway* appear to have vanished, a final story script survives at the USC Warner Archive. The story, involving professional jealousy over the discovery of a formula for an anaesthetic leading to murder in a hospital, was rather convoluted, but brisk efficiency was brought to bear on the plot and good acting opportunities were taken up by a capable cast. Chili Bouchier (1909-1999), a minor leading lady in British films of the late silent era, had made her first appearance at the Warner Bros. Teddington studios in 1934. In the film she played the female lead, and prime suspect, Sister Betty Trimmer. Hugh Williams was again pressed into service playing the main protagonist, Dr. Thurlow, who was kept busy trying to deflect suspicion from Chili Bouchier's character. As the murder victim the prolific and reliable character player, Garry Marsh, was neatly cast. Marsh had appeared in Warner Bros. earliest Teddington studio feature release, *Stranglehold* (Warner, Henry Edwards, 1931). Reginald Purdell, not for the first or the last time, provided light comic relief as an inebriated patient. In the role of Scotland Yard's Detective Inspector Clarke, Jim brought the same authority and gravitas to bear as he had displayed in previous stage roles. For this particular characterisation his wartime experiences in the British army came in handy for issuing brusque directives to subordinates.

Picture Show magazine thought: "James Stephenson, as the Scotland Yard detective, makes his role worth watching by sheer personality." [23] Jim had also built up a good rapport with director Arthur Woods, who was assigned to his next picture *Mr. Satan* (Warner, 1938). It was around this time, that the studio began to see him as potential star material and started to promote him with well-organised publicity. He was described as "the British Walter Huston" with the rider of being "younger and better-looking." [24] This news coverage boded well for his career and offered the prospect of greater financial remuneration for the future. In a letter to his wife, Lorna, he remarked on the hyperbole of the press coverage:

"... when I have the money to keep pace with you!! And with the

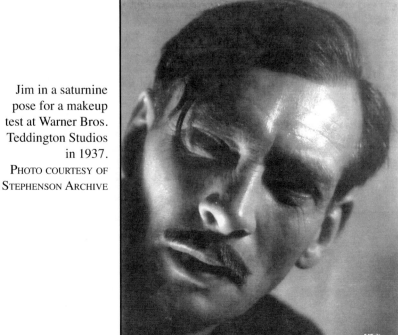

Jim in a saturnine pose for a makeup test at Warner Bros. Teddington Studios in 1937.
PHOTO COURTESY OF STEPHENSON ARCHIVE

publicity I'm getting that shouldn't be soon!! How do you like this *Evening News* dope?" [25]

In a 1937 interview Irving Asher discussed what was required of the studio's players:

"We believe in keeping a stock company of some thirteen or fourteen people under contract. Of these, perhaps three or four are rated as stars. These are our heavy artillery; each has his own line of attack; stories are fashioned to fit them.

That leaves us with our supporting players – our mobile troops, ready and able to take any part that may come their way. We encourage our people to play as many widely different roles as possible. We avoid 'typing' them as we would avoid the plague. We release them, if they wish, for seasons at neighbouring theatres. If they play gilded youth in one picture, we knock the gilt off them for the next. If they have to eat caviar for a scene this week, we try and fix them up with crusts and a coffee stall for the week after.

Only in that way do we consider a player can find his real metier. Then, and only then is he ready to be groomed for stardom." [26]

Due to Jim's favourable impression on the Warner high command and his compliance with the studio ethos of flexibility, the management took to addressing their latest protégé by the fraternal nick-name of "Jimmy." Thereafter, indicative of the "can-do" culture of American enterprise, Jim Stephenson, for the rest of his acting career, became known around the Warner Bros. Teddington British and Burbank Hollywood studios, as Jimmy Stephenson. Lorna Stephenson, who had a cheeky sense of humour, took to calling Jim by the private nick-name of "Jimmy James."

As foreign correspondent Tim Garnet, Jimmy was given the nominal lead in *Mr. Satan*. However, because he had yet to make a name for himself with the paying public his name does not appear above the title. He cuts a debonair, if mature, hero and was given lively support from American import Richard "Skeets" Gallagher and, hedging their bets, the studio included a dog [Bob the dog] as mascot for good measure. Chili Bouchier provided the main romantic interest which didn't quite

The English custom of a tea break is observed at the Warner Bros. Teddington Studios. Everything stops for tea on the set of *Mr. Satan*. From left to right: Skeets Gallagher, Jimmy Stephenson, Mary Cole and Chili Bouchier.
PHOTO COURTESY OF STEPHENSON ARCHIVE

come alive as it should. In a secondary role as a fiery Conchita was Betty Lynne. Having been educated in France she would have been a stronger candidate for the casting of the romantic lead. The villain of the piece, Franklyn Dyall, is suitably suave and malevolent as Zubova a devious armaments dealer.

As luck would have it, a print of this film survives, so a judgement can be made about Jimmy's suitability to carry a picture. He is certainly on the go with quick changes of costume and there is diversity of locales with scenes shot at Brookland's Aerodrome (the Brookland's Aero Clubhouse was adapted to appear as a Spanish style airport building) and on the banks of the River Thames. The Surrey countryside stood in for the rural pastures of an unspecified Mitteleuropa. [27] These elements, for the most part, are successfully integrated with artful studio model work, and well-constructed and lit studio sets. Particularly effective is Zubova's hideout den with its globe as a signifier of megalomania and, in a display of modernity, a tele-visual apparatus transmitting fiendish plans of sabotage and destruction to agents of subversion. However, these positive points aside, critical reservations were expressed concerning the film. *The Times* reported:

> "The methods of an unscrupulous manufacturer of armaments are exposed, but the necessary concession to romance robs the film of much of its force." [28]

In fact, constraints of political censorship combined with over-ambitious direction from Arthur Woods, produced a film which, though slick in production values, has a tendency to overstate the action, often at the expense of plot coherence and rounded characterisation. As a qualified pilot, Woods assisted in the staging of an air attack in the film by piloting a blue Stinson monoplane. In the end the story is just too tenuous and fails to carry conviction. Like the contentious *Blockade* (United Artists / Walter Wanger, William Dieterle, 1938), released in Hollywood in the same year, all direct references to the Spanish Civil War were omitted and this exclusion lessens the scenario's credibility. Though the story tends to move from situation to situation at a rapid pace, as in the style of a film serial, there are jumps in film continuity. Photographs in the family archive show several deleted scenes indicating that the film was originally considerably longer.

In this production, tucked away in a crowd scene, was a general purpose British actor by the name of Bruce Lister. Since 1936 Lister had been a minor contract player at Warner Bros. British Teddington Studios and would soon accompany Jimmy across the pond to Burbank Studios in Hollywood, California. [29]

As surviving letters reveal, Jimmy was filming *Mr. Satan* back-

A rare production shot of outdoor filming on Warner Bros. Teddington film *Mr. Satan* shot during August 1937. Here "the sparks" led by photographer Robert La Presle wait while the sound technicians arrange their equipment. In the car at the wheel sits a patient Chili Bouchier with Jimmy Stephenson alongside her in swim costume. The continuity girl sits directly behind director Arthur Woods.

PHOTO COURTESY OF STEPHENSON ARCHIVE

to-back with his next starring film *Dangerous Fingers* (Pathe, Rialto, Norman Lee, 1938), which was shot on loan out at Welwyn Studios only a half hour train journey from central London. Reciprocal arrangements involving film companies loaning stars to other studios and thereby reducing cost by processes of quick product turnaround, was the nature of second feature studio production. In high dudgeon Jimmy wrote about the gruelling pace of B picture film-making and his attempt to rearrange the shooting schedule to a more congenial work pattern:

"I got home [1, Charlbert Court, London, NW 8] at midnight last night. And those b—s at Welwyn actually wanted me to start at 9 this a.m. So I saw red, stuck both heels in the ground, told 'em I was a human being and not a horse and that I just could not do it. So they gave in and rearranged their schedule and I start at 9 a.m. tomorrow. Even that's too soon for I'm beginning to feel very tired and it's very hot and sultry and tiring weather." [30]

Chili Bouchier's death scene in *Mr. Satan* with Jimmy
was filmed on the evening of Monday September 6, 1937.
Photo courtesy of Stephenson Archive

Having aired his grievances, Jimmy then goes on to describe his
approval and relief at completing a key scene on *Mr. Satan*.

"We did Chili's death last night – the last scene – and everyone
thought it was grand. It felt good." [31]

The depiction of the criminal underworld which is the setting of
Dangerous Fingers is a derived caricature half-way between British
music hall, and an English schoolboy comic magazine. One of the
reasons for its coy depiction of criminal sub-culture was the imposition
of moral censorship laws drawn up in 1916 by President of the British
Board of Film Censors, T[homas].P[ower]. O'Connor. O'Connor listed
"forty-three grounds for deletion" and rule six forbade the depiction of
"the modus operandi of criminals." [32]

Though Jimmy is again cast as the lead, the film's structure and
design does little to enhance his star status. Indeed, the production seems
intent on placing a great number of obstacles in his path. Norman Lee's
direction is mechanical and uninspired; the script is obtuse providing
flat characterisations, schematic situations and its editing style is often

slapdash in delineating action and continuity. Yet, despite these hindrances there are compensations. The scenario, modelled on E.M. Hornung's gentleman crook Raffles, involves ex-convict Ronnie "Fingers" Elliott, amateur cracksman and talented musician, and his attempt to keep on the right side of the law when released from prison. Despite his protestations to the contrary, Jimmy's capacity to perform light comedy with understated delivery in several scenes are noteworthy. His scenes with "Kitty," his feline partner in crime, whom he carries secreted in a small case, and produces to walk on the keys of a piano giving the pretence of piano tuning whilst he is busy cracking open safes, are especially novel and engaging. This, in tandem with his love of music, is successful, and a minor delight.

Jimmy's musical competence was tested as he was seen playing Chopin "Polonaise for piano No. 6 in A Flat Major, L'Héroique," during an emotional scene where he finds his girlfriend murdered in her flat. This scene, where he swears vengeance by reverting to his former life of crime, contains a very intense close-up. Later he is seen performing Rachmaninov "Prelude No. 1 in C Sharp minor Op. 3 No. 2." Dressed immaculately, he is both raffish and urbane in evening dress. He also adopts the disguise of a bearded Scots reporter with slick competence. However effortless it all appeared on screen, in reality it was arduous work as Jimmy testified when writing in his dressing room off set:

> "I'm starting this but I may be called any moment. I've been working hard all day until just now. Everyone is very nice and I think I have this part in my pocket – so far at any rate. Most of

Jimmy in his convict uniform as he appears in the opening scenes of *Dangerous Fingers*.
PHOTO COURTESY OF STEPHENSON ARCHIVE

Jimmy as "Fingers" the urbane jewel thief in *Dangerous Fingers*.
PHOTO COURTESY OF STEPHENSON ARCHIVE

my shots have been "put in the can" with one take. The piano playing is a bit of a trial – I have a lot of difficult stuff to 'play' – I have a dummy piano and the sound will be put in afterwards but I have to look as if I were actually playing it. And often talking at the same time!

I think I've created an impression here by telling 'em I couldn't start yesterday. The floor staff etc. and the man I spoke to on the telephone, all seem kind of respectful!" [33]

As befitted its budgetary status, the movie is decidedly spare in its construction. John Reynerd's score played over the opening credits was recycled by the studio again as credit music in the Welwyn release, *Dead Men are Dangerous* (Pathe, Harold French, 1939), which also starred Betty Lynne. In line with the emphasis on cost consciousness, the camera is under-cranked during the climatic car chase to speed-up the action. Overall, despite the production's many deficiencies, Jimmy ably negotiated all the pitfalls. He emerged with flying colours, and he managed to turn base metal if not exactly into gold then material conducive to fair amusement. The process was made doubly difficult by the illness of his wife Lorna and his difficulty with recurring lumbago and sciatica:

> "I doubt if this will be more than the very scrappiest of notes darling – I've been in every shot so far and am now in my room to change suits and go down to start some more.
>
> I've played another love scene to-day. Not nearly so good as the one with Chili, but still it ought to be effective I think. With a girl I'm sure can't weigh more than six stone! I had to pick her up and carry her . . . I hope I don't have to carry Betty Lynne when the love stuff with her happens – because she's a big bouncing lass!" [34]

Unlike comparable scenes with Chili Bouchier in *Mr. Satan*, there is a better rapport between Betty Lynne and Jimmy in the romantic and dramatic situations in the film. [35] The picture was successful and given a release in the United States under the title of *Wanted by Scotland Yard*. [36]

All this sterling work came to the attention of movie mogul Jack L. Warner who had arrived in London from Hollywood on October 1, 1937. As Jimmy recalled:

> "Around this time Mr. Jack Warner arrived in London. I'll never

Jimmy and D.A. Clarke-Smith in *Dangerous Fingers*. The cigarette case in the photograph was given to him by the amateur dramatic company The Burnley Players as a farewell present in June 1932.
PHOTO COURTESY OF STEPHENSON ARCHIVE

Jimmy and Betty Lynne in *Dangerous Fingers,*
his second leading role in British films.
PHOTO COURTESY OF STEPHENSON ARCHIVE

forget my first conversation with him. He's easy to talk with you know, and he just asked me to tell him about myself." [37]

Warner was in fact a lively, cocky, belligerent, egocentric despot. A former song plugger in his youth, he was ridiculed by his competitors as a purveyor of corny jokes, but respected and feared by his employees for his shrewd instinct and tough-minded bargaining. Jack, as vice-president in charge of production, was the person who had responsibility for managing expenditure at the Burbank Studios in Hollywood and was renowned for keeping tight-fisted control of production costs, and demanding lean efficiency and high productivity. Behind this resilient front, however Warner was hyper-sensitive and vulnerable. He had come to check out the studio operations in Britain in response to the Moyne Report, commissioned in May 1936 and presented to Parliament on November 23, 1936, to consider changes to the original Quota Act of 1927. The second Cinematograph Films Act of 1938 linked the quota to a quality threshold. Part of the press coverage presaging Warner's visit talked of extending and renovating the existing three stages at the Teddington studios.

Warner offered Jimmy and two other Teddington contract players, Chili Bouchier and Bruce Lister, the chance of going out to Hollywood to shoot tests and, subject to a satisfactory outcome, the prospect of long-term Hollywood film contracts. They would also be travelling to the United States in the company of Irving Asher, his wife, the actress Laura La Plante, and their baby daughter, Jill. Jimmy took the precaution of signing a further contract with O'Bryen, Linnit and Dunfee, to run for five years from November 16, 1937, to act as his representatives in dealing with Warner Bros. in Hollywood. [38]

Unlike today's mass budget jet flight schedules across the Atlantic, with cordons of airport security making for a frustrating and routine travel experience, back then a voyage on a passenger liner such as the SS *Normandie* was a luxurious, exclusive and opulent (with a capital "O") affair. The lavish interior of such a ship was the envy of even the most flamboyant and profligate Hollywood art director. [39] Though Jimmy had travelled first-class back in his cotton shipping days, sailing on the *Normandie* in de luxe class was an experience all of its own.

The *Normandie* entered service in 1935 and was the longest ship at 1,028 feet and the largest afloat at a tonnage of 79,280. The luxurious interiors were marvels of Art Deco and the Streamline Moderne style. The roster of Art Deco masters who worked on the ship's furnishings included: René Lalique, Jean Dupas, Jean Patou, and Emile-Jacques Ruhlmann. Jean de Brunhoff, creator of Babar the Elephant, decorated the children's dining room. The most dazzling of all was the first-class dining room. Three hundred and five feet long, forty-six feet wide and twenty-eight feet high, this was by far the largest room afloat. It could seat seven hundred diners at a time with 150 tables, serving them with some of the best meals in the world. This ship was a floating promotion of the most sophisticated French cuisine of the period. However, due to the design of the ship, no natural lighting could get in. The designers illuminated the room with a combination of twelve tall pillars of Lalique glass and along the walls stood thirty-eight columns equally bright. In addition, two chandeliers hung at each end of the room. From this gorgeous display of lights came the nickname "Ship of Light." There were also twenty foot tall entrance doors adorned with bronze medallions by artist Raymond Subes.

The long voyage sailing from Le Havre, France, across to New York City via Southampton, England involved catching a boat-train from London to Southampton, then embarking on a tender to board the *Normandie*, some way out in the English Channel. Then, after crossing the Atlantic and docking at New York, there were a few days recuperation.

The journey recommenced by rail on board the 20th Century Limited, the latest in express trains, to Chicago, and then another express train connection out West to Los Angeles. The journey for Jimmy (aged forty-eight) began on Wednesday November 17, 1937 and finished on Sunday November 28, 1937. In a despondent tone, he described the beginning of the journey with travel companions Bruce Lister (aged twenty-five) and Chili Bouchier (aged twenty-eight) as they left behind the familiar landmarks to sail into the unknown:

> "The train journey and the tender were a pretty ghastly business and nobody was in any mood to talk or "be company." Chili had left her "boy friend" and Bruce his mother. We had a meal – and got on board about midnight.

The "*Normandie*" looked beautiful as we approached it in the tender. All lights on, and the three funnels floodlit so that they looked as if they were red hot. And such a huge bulk of a ship. When we got alongside and looked up, it was like looking up the side of a skyscraper. And so on board and to my stateroom which is about the size of our lounge-dining room and has a beautiful bathroom off it. And, after unpacking some of my things, to bed." [40]

Despite his sense of apprehension he was given a good send off by various members of the family, friends and business associates all wishing him "bon voyage."

"I had telegrams from Norman and Toonie, Constance Marwood, Jack and Dorothy Grey, Arthur Woods, and John Ware in addition to yours. So I have all of them to write to. I've cleared off all my arrears of letters – thirteen of them." [41]

Jimmy went on to describe the sumptuous interior of the ship and the opulence on board:

> "The ship is magnificent – a floating palace in truth. The most palatial hotel I've ever seen is nothing to it. And it seems incredible that it should be floating in mid-Atlantic – or rather forging through it at nearly thirty knots. I haven't seen nearly all of it yet. But where I am writing this is on the promenade deck just between the cinema and the huge lounge. Between me and the cinema, where a show is now going on, is a great square with four huge lifts cased in gilt and wrought-iron. And looking to the right the lounge, and the stewards walking about at the other end of it look like pygmies, they are so far away. The restaurant is bigger than any hotel restaurant I've ever seen – a colossal place all decorated in gold and Lalique glass. And the doors and the ceiling are gold and the walls are completely covered in Lalique

with huge pillars of Lalique and gold for lighting. The service and the food are wonderful." [42]

On the coat-tails of Irving Asher and his wife, Laura, Jimmy and his companions were introduced to several personalities:

"To-day has been rather rough and I have been on deck all day until now – 7.15. Last night Irving gave a cocktail party in his suite. He has either three or four bedrooms, each with a bathroom, a dining room, a lounge and a serving pantry. So that will have cost him a bit!

The three of us were there and Harry Richman, the cabaret singer cum Atlantic flier! And Greer Garson and her mother and some assorted men. Dietrich should have come but did not. Greer Garson gave me a pain in the neck – in fact she produces that effect on all of us including Irving and Laura. Putting on the "dog" you know!" [43]

Jimmy went on to describe his impressions of the legendary Marlene Dietrich:

"I've just remembered I've only casually mentioned Dietrich. She's here and, to me, is a great disappointment to look at. She has pretty legs and feet and a certain "air" but she's not by any stretch of imagination pretty. A couple of Frenchmen seem to keep her pretty "warm!" We sat behind her at the cinema the other evening. There are various other celebrities, of all nationalities, on board."[44]

Even mixing with such exorbitant affluence and rubbing shoulders with flamboyant company didn't turn Jimmy's head. As ever, he was preoccupied with more mundane, but essential matters such as accommodation issues:

"I was talking to Irving to-day about where to live in Hollywood and he says I ought to go to the Roosevelt but only until I can get an apartment somewhere. He says we'll make enquiries at the studio and that an apartment is cheaper and much more comfortable than the hotel." [45]

As the time approached to disembark at New York the schedule for completing the journey West to Hollywood became clearer and more pressing:

"We are to arrive tomorrow at a very awkward time, 8 in the morning. Passport examination at 7 o'clock, heavy baggage to be packed by 2. I shall cable you as soon as I get to the hotel: The Ambassador's, I think, is the one we're going to." [46]

Later installed at the Ambassador's Hotel New York City, he writes:

"We are still here, where we finally came to rest about midnight on Monday. I sent you the cable at the end of the gangplank just as we disembarked. Before we left the *Normandie* there was an orgy of photographing and press interviews, in Irving's suite, where we had all assembled before being invaded. Then we went into the Winter Garden where Dietrich was engaging the attention of about twenty newspaper cameramen, and had some more photographs taken. Then disembarkation and waiting on the quay under, for me, a large 'S' until all my baggage reached there and could be examined. The actual examination was very short and cursory and I soon got clear once I had got all my baggage together – but that took a long time. This is a beautiful hotel and I have a very nice big room on the seventh floor with bath. We leave here on Thursday about five and get to Los Angeles on Sunday about midday. And I think for the time being we shall be at the Roosevelt." [47]

A sense of trepidation begins to set in and he confessed: ". . . [I think] I'm not good enough for what I shall have to face in a few days – I hope I shall be." [48]

This feeling soon passed, however, as Irving Asher took his three protégés on a whirlwind tour of New York City:

"Yesterday Irving took us out and we had a very full day. We went to the 21 Club for drinks before lunch and then to Jack Dempsey's Café from whence I sent you the menu. After lunch we went to the top of the highest building in the world – The Empire State Building and had the most wonderful view of New York. 104 floors up and the lifts just shoot to the top. It was a clear sunny day and the view of all the other skyscrapers, the river (with The *Normandie*, *Berengaria* and other ships), Central Park etc. was marvellous. Four big navy air ships were flying down river and we were well above them. Then we took a taxi and drove to Wall St., and then along the docks and thro' Central Park – which to my mind does not compare with the London Parks – and so to Warner's office where we met Sam Morris The Vice President of the company and other big noises in Warners – all very "matey" blokes – as all Americans are – even taxi drivers, hotel and café porters, cloakroom attendants, barbers and all the rest. I like them this time more than I have ever done before – and the whole atmosphere. And Irving is grand. And Laura. Well we came back and changed and went to the 21 Club for a very nice dinner and then on to the 'Cort' Theatre for *Room Service*. [49] The show was rotten we all agreed – tho' it is one of the big successes of New York – and having met Roland Young in the foyer during the first interval, we left at the end of the second act and went along to his "apartment" – a lovely and palatial flat – and had a drink and stayed about an hour and then drove to "Radio City," which is a bunch of huge skyscrapers, where we went to "The Rainbow Room" – right at the top of one of the buildings, which is a café and cabaret. [50] There we looked out over New York by night – a beautiful sight – saw the cabaret, and left about 2 to go to "The Cotton Club," another night resort where the band is of niggers with one "Cab Calloway" "conducting" – and all the waiters etc. are niggers. [51] It was however, very slow and we did not stay long but moved on to "Reubens" where we had real American sandwiches - "four deckers" with turkey, tomato, cheese, bacon – enough in one sandwich for a meal for anyone. And so at about 3.30, back here. I got up at 9 but I think all the others are still abed. I feel a bit tired but otherwise O.K. – no head!

To-day Irving has to spend [time] at Warners and I don't suppose we shall do anything much until to-night when we go to a show "*The Women*," and, I hope earlier to bed. I shall cable you to-day as soon as I'm sure about the Hollywood address. [52]

And now I think I'll see if anyone else has come to life. This will get the *Berengaria* sailing tomorrow. And I will write to you on the train – tho' you probably won't be able to read it." [53]

Before leaving New York and beginning the second stage of the long journey to Hollywood Jimmy had a welcome interruption:

"On the morning before we left New York I had a telephone call from Ed Ryan – of "*Post Road.*" And Lister and I went to The Little Theatre, where he was rehearsing, to see him also Dick Mervyn who stage managed "*Post Road.*" [54]

Jimmy's journey across country turned out to be something of a pleasant surprise, due, in large part, to the comfort and amenities on board the express train:

"We left at 5.30 and had a most comfortable journey, and one that I hope you will love when you do it. The cars are splendid – you have your own little compartment with <u>everything</u> in it. In the daytime it is a comfortable little room where you can be very quiet – and the trains are quiet – and at night the seats fold down and into the most comfortable bed I've ever slept in in a train – far better than the Wagons-Lits Cars on the continent. Irving has a "drawing room" where we had most of our meals, but the dining cars are splendid – the food delightful and the service (all black) beyond reproach. All the "porters" (what we should call car stewards perhaps) are so obliging, and the same applies to the waiters. There is a "club car" and an observation car and all together you can't imagine a long rail journey like that being so comfortable." [55]

Upon arrival in Chicago there was much frantic activity with press junkets. Irving Asher in an expansive mood encouraged his protégés to raise their game and be uninhibited when talking to the press, but natural British reserve and uncertainty dictated otherwise:

"We arrived in Chicago at 9:00 a.m. on Friday and were at once whisked off by a Warner's publicity man to a hotel for interviews with journalists and photographers. It seems Jack Warner on his return talked quite freely about our being definitely fixed up, so Irving said "you can let yourselves go as much as you like." Not that we did, any of us, but I suppose the Chicago papers will make a story out of it. Chicago is a fine city with long wide boulevards and skyscrapers – though not as colossal as the latter, as New York. We drove to the hotel along the shore of Lake Michigan and rejoined the train at noon." [56]

After this interlude the long trek recommenced:

"From then on we have passed through all types of country. The towns with the exception of Kansas City are small and sprawling and as the poorer districts are always by the railroad track you see a queer assortment of shacks and mud huts. A great deal of the country, in Colorado, and especially Arizona, is desert with no vegetation except "sage brush" and no rivers. You climb the Rockies – though they don't seem very high or impressive to me – and it takes three huge engines to do the job. Then later on, and nearer the coast, come the Sierra Nevada and presently the vegetation gets more plentiful – cactus and pepper trees and olives and then vineyards and olive groves." [57]

When he finally arrived in Los Angeles he was underwhelmed by the topography of the city, compared to previous sights encountered. The fatigue from the long trip also began to affect him.

"And then into Los Angeles – the ugliest of cities, apparently surrounded by tin cans! From Los Angeles to Hollywood is about half-an-hour – all distances here are by car.

We got into Los Angeles at 12:45 and drove along here in a studio car, and the three of us have just had lunch together and are now in our rooms alongside each other. I have a small, but quite nice room with bath,

An aerial shot of the Warner Burbank Studios taken in 1937.
PHOTO COURTESY OF STEPHENSON ARCHIVE

and the bed – I have at length discovered – is behind two glass doors in the wall, and swings round and pulls down somewhat à la Canning Street. My trunks have not yet arrived. When they do, and when I have finished this letter, I shall steep myself in the first bath for three days and change my clothes. It is quite as hot here as a late June day at home! Home!

We go to the studio tomorrow and perhaps in a day or two I may know how things stand." [58]

Despondency returned, as he tried to adjust to the new and rather alien environment:

"I'm feeling dreadfully lonely in this crazy place. I have a touch of my back problem to-day and don't feel very well altogether.

I've just had lunch with Chili down below – a glass of orange juice and a fruit salad – and I'm waiting for a call to go and see O'B[rien]L[innit and] D[unfee]'s representatives here.

I don't feel like doing a thing. We were warned yesterday that it takes some people a while to get acclimatised and I think I'm one of them." [59]

Jimmy and his colleagues were finally taken by Irving Asher to the 135 acre lot of Warner Bros. First National, Burbank Studios. Compared to the minor studio facilities back in England, the scale and magnitude of American industrial film enterprise were striking:

> "Irving picked us up at the hotel yesterday at 11 and took us along to the studio and showed us around. It is a colossal place – there are twenty sound stages and the place is like a town. We wandered around the offices seeing people – all of them very nice and none of them, I am convinced, meaning anything they said. We spent quite a long time in the casting office and the arrangement is that we are left alone until about Thursday to get use to the place a bit, and then we go along and have photographs and makeup tests, and early next week we make real tests which will decide our fate. When we left the casting office Irving stayed inside for about a quarter of an hour to talk about us and I haven't had a chance since to try and find out something of what was said." [60]

The interval from his arrival in Hollywood on Sunday November 28, 1937 until beginning work at the Burbank studios on Saturday January 8, 1938 was a fallow period in Jimmy's life. He was marooned in Hollywood waiting, with increasing anticipation and apprehension, to start his screen tests, and then kept in the dark until the results finally came through. Then, further delays while he was assigned work. Hollywood in its productive prime was akin to a ride on a boisterous fairground carousel revolving at speed, and not predisposed to slowing down. This meant an actor had to pick his or her moment to clamber on board, and stay on board, lest they be thrown off and come to grief. Jimmy was given a foretaste of the systemic processes and procedures involved in the promotion of star personality, and the studio's abilities to determine and redesign the personal identity of their contract artists:

> " . . . we went to the publicity department and had to fill in long questionnaires asking the most varied and, to me, absurd questions, for "domestic" and "foreign" publicity. What is your favourite dish? (Give the recipe if you can). Your favourite colour, flower? What are you able to do in Hollywood which you could not do in England? What characteristic or atmosphere would you like to see transplanted from England to Hollywood and vice versa? What foreign countries have you visited and what impressed you most about them? And so on and on." [61]

Jimmy then relates encounters with star personalities, his continuing difficulties with finding suitable accommodation, and the blasé attitude of Bruce Lister:

> "We met Errol Flynn and Patric Knowles and with the latter,

all went off to lunch at the "Vendome" where all the stars congregate when not working. [62] There did not seem to be many there though. Loretta Young, and Basil Rathbone are the only two I can remember.

Then we went back to the studio and Patric Knowles took us to his house for tea. A very pretty house in, well I suppose, a sort of Spanish style – only about two minutes from the studio. He says he goes to the studio in pyjamas when he has a 9 o'clock call. [63] He's very nice and says he will help me find a house whenever we are ready – he's moved about a good deal and knows all the agents. Apparently a furnished house about our size would be £20 to £30 a month. But an apartment is the first thing I must have and Laura is collecting a list of addresses for Chili and I to go around and look at. I say Chili and I because Bruce – who annoys us both terribly – has already taken the first apartment he's looked at, bought a radio, and is talking about a car. I want to know a bit more before I do any of these things. Anyhow I'm staying here for a week or ten days at least.

Bruce went off with Patric Knowles on a bit of a "jag" last night and Chili and I had supper here and I was in bed by 9:30." [64]

Trepidation, concerning the ordeal of his impending screen tests, began to get the better of him:

> "Talking to Bruce and Pat Knowles yesterday, Bruce said that he had always said that of all the people under contract at Teddington I was the only one who would do anything. And Pat Knowles said he would change places with me. But I'm less sure of myself than I have ever been in my life. And I have a feeling that Chili and Bruce will "click" and I shall not. For the money, I hope I'm wrong, but for everything else I would willingly take the next train. I shall try and find out just as soon as I can, so that if I am to stay I can cable you . . . It is a beautiful place and a lovely climate. But just at present – oh dear." [65]

Jimmy later acquired further details about his impending screen tests:

> "We've been to the studio Friday and Saturday and have settled the bits we are to do for tests. I'm doing a scene from *Counsellor-at-Law*, in a dinner jacket, a comedy scene from a film script, in a lounge suit, and a scene from *Journey's End* in uniforms. We are not to work together – which I'm sorry about. Some strange woman will be thrown at me. And we are to rehearse on Tuesday and make tests on Wednesday. Unless they change their mind!" [66]

In the interim Jimmy and his two companions were taken on more cultural sight-seeing by the ever affable and obliging Irving Asher:

"We were taken to a football game Saturday at the Los Angeles Coliseum (where the Olympic Games have been held). It was an amazing business the press of cars was unbelievable. 78,000 people there. Two college teams playing, and portions of the amphitheatre reserved for what are called "routing sections" – students in college colours, who cheer their sides under leaders or conductors. Each routing section has a band and the bands march on to the arena during the interval and play. The crowd went mad on occasions. And although at first I found it a dull game I found myself getting really excited later. We had dinner at the "Cock n' Bull," a so called English restaurant, and later Irving and Robert Young picked us up and took us to the latter's house in Beverly Hills. Young is a <u>very</u> nice chap but none of us liked his wife. [67]

To-day all I have to do is learn my lines. It's a beautiful day and we <u>ought</u> to be out somewhere. But without a car it's quite impossible. And I must make up my mind about moving. The only reason I hesitate at all is because of Chili. She is as lonely for her Teddy Joyce as I am for you . . . And we have been a certain amount of "company" for each other. Having most of our meals together, whilst Bruce has been out on the jag on many occasions." [68]

The night before the tests, along with Chili and Bruce, he attended a studio radio broadcast:

"Last night there was a big broadcast from the studio, sponsored by "Lucky Strike" Cigarettes. And we were invited, and on to the Trocadero afterwards as Jack Warner's guests. The Trocadero is <u>the</u> swell restaurant here and they charge the earth for a meal. We only stayed until 10 p.m. – because of our work to-day. The broadcast was very good – Dick Powell was the compére – a big orchestra – a choir of sorts – Gary Cooper did a sort of monologue (not very well) and Bette Davies (sic) Basil Rathbone, Olivia de Havilland and Pat Knowles did a scene from a film." [69]

Finally the day of the dreaded screen tests, Thursday December 9, 1937, arrived:

"Well the tests. Bruce and I got up at 7 and were at the studio at 8:45 where we got into officer's uniforms and at 10:10 started to work on the *Journey's End* scene together. I think it went very well – I did not feel nervous and really felt I had a grip on the thing. I think the director was very pleased with it – he let me do it exactly in my own way – did not alter an inflection. He had a bit of trouble getting Bruce to put what he wanted into it.

So after that I felt quite pleased. I had to go and change, and be made-up. (We played *Journey's End* without make-up – except for a little glycerine and water for sweat!) They did Bruce's two tests with girls next, which I didn't see. After lunch came the one I was afraid of – the little comedy scene. I rehearsed it once with the girl and the director said "That's fine!" But when we came to shoot it I was like a jellyfish with nerves and for the first time in my life felt camera shy. I fluffed a couple of times and then we got it. But it did not feel good to me. The *Counsellor-at-Law* bit I did with Betty Compson – she didn't know the lines, and stumbled and dried up all over the place. So that wasn't a help. I think I was "pretty good" only – I didn't feel there was the ease and freedom in it that I usually get (or think I do). However, I maybe quite wrong – and I do hope I am. For though I so often feel I must get out of here or bust I would hate to get out because I have failed. We finished at about 3.30 and at that time Chili had still to begin her tests. So I suspect she will still be at it. I don't know how soon they will be ready – tomorrow possibly. Anyway within the next few days I imagine I shall know my fate." [70]

Finally Jimmy was able to view his screen tests and was also given feedback on Bruce and Chili's tests.

"I saw my tests this afternoon. The *Journey's End* scene was grand. The other two good, but not so good. Lister was not too good – Irving told me he has only scraped through, but that everyone is delighted with me. And Arnow introduced me to someone to-day as "A very fine actor!" Chili has yet no definite answer. Apparently Jack Warner did not really want her and would only consent to her being sent over on an expenses allowance. No salary. They are still testing her for make-up and hairdressing." [71]

In fact Chili Bouchier hated Hollywood, finding the atmosphere alien and the people unappealing. Her sense of discomfort and loneliness was certainly not helped by this incident recounted by Jimmy.

"In the evening I went to the pictures with Chili and had a shemozzle with the car. I put it on a parking lot and locked the doors. When we came out I could not unlock them – nearly midnight. So Chili had to go home in a taxi and I struggled for some time with the doors, then rang up the Buick people – only a janitor there – then called up a locksmith and got a sleepy refusal to turn out. So I had to leave it – the park attendant ran me home in an 1897 Chevrolet." [72]

She later ran away, sailing back to England where, naively, she resumed her work at Teddington studios, but when her six month option came up the studio did not renew her contract. Not only that, but she was unable to find any further work in British films and resumed her career working in the theatre. Only many years later did she find out she had been blacklisted by Jack Warner from working in any other film studio. The axiom was clear; Warner Bros. could walk all over their artists, but nobody walked out on a Warner Brother.

Meanwhile, Bruce Lister seemed unconcerned by the slow progress in the beginning of his career but, as Jimmy makes clear, in the meantime he was having a splendid time slacking and otherwise enjoying himself:

> "Young B. Lister has transferred himself to a more sumptuous apartment – in this building at $120 a month, plays golf every morning and goes out to the Santa Anita racetrack each afternoon, and has an accommodating sweetie on the spot for his evenings! I very occasionally see him and have been up and had drinks with him on two occasions. He has no sign of work yet – but does not seem to worry." [73]

On August 20, 1938 Lister returned to England at the company's expense, for six months travelling on the Pacific Grove and returned to the United States on February 21, 1939 sailing on the SS *Ile de France* at his own expense.

Jimmy had a long wait for news regarding his wife's impending passage to the United States.

> "No news yet as to whether Warners will pay your passage. I do hope they will, but I'm realising all the time how tight-fisted they are.
>
> Anyway after next week I shall really be able to put money away, so that when you arrive they'll be a nice little nest egg. The thing I'm hoping for is to be really well cast in my first picture and make a success of it and then we can go to work on them about salary when the first notices come along.
>
> They say I shall not be confined to English parts because my accent is not obtrusively British!! Which is a very good thing. They little know that I was trying my damndest to be American! It is a mistake to be too English here. And certainly unless you are playing a purely English part, at which people are meant to laff, you must say can't and afternoon and past with short 'A's." [74]

Jimmy's fondness for dogs continued unabated, and in the same letter he recommended Lorna should catch the film, *The Awful Truth* (Columbia, Leo McCarey, 1937). This film featured Skippy, a wire-haired terrier, whose prowess on screen as "Mr Smith" was shown to great advantage

Jimmy and Lorna Stephenson outside their first Hollywood home,
4429 Clybourne Avenue, Los Angeles in 1938.
PHOTO COURTESY OF STEPHENSON ARCHIVE

during a legal custody dispute between characters played by Irene Dunne and Cary Grant. Among Skippy's finest performances were as "Asta" in the detective comedy *The Thin Man* (M-G-M, W.S. Van Dyke, 1934) and its sequel *After the Thin Man* (M-G-M, W.S. Van Dyke, 1936).

> "If you get a chance to see a picture called *The Awful Truth* with Cary Grant and Irene Dunne, do see it. It is the funniest thing ever, and has sent Cary Grant rocketing right to the top." [75]

It was the prerogative of the studio contract system to alter a person's personal identity often quite radically. In Jimmy's case his name remained intact on theatre marquees, but for publicity purposes the studio was "generous" regarding his date of birth, often giving out he was born in 1899. Two personal items appear regularly on the screen. A signet ring, dating around 1928, is worn on his small left finger and also on his left wrist is a watch, given by his wife Lorna as a wedding present. From time to time, as in the pictures at Warner Bros. Teddington, he also produces on screen the cigarette case given to him as a farewell present by the Burnley Players amateur dramatic group back in 1932.

Lorna finally arrived in New York on February 7, 1938 sailing across the pond on the RMS *Queen Mary*. The Stephenson's first home was a rented apartment on 4429 Clybourne Avenue, Los Angeles, North

California. By September the following year they had relocated to what was to be their final address, 839 Toyopa Drive, Pacific Palisades, Los Angeles, California. Some twenty miles or so from the studio, it was not the most convenient location, but the Stephensons liked the house and the sea nearby.

The Stephensons didn't play the social scene, preferring to spend time at their home, or at the homes of friends such as: Eileen and Roy Forkum; animators who had worked as background artists on Disney's *Fantasia* (1940); journalists Albert and Betty Blair Treynor (1888-1967); Albert M. Treynor (1884-1948), a screen playwright who spent fifteen years in Hollywood, had provided the story for *Dancing Co-Ed* (M-G-M, S. Sylvan Simon, 1939), a so-so romantic comedy starring band leader Artie Shaw and the pulchritudinous Lana Turner at the beginning of her career. His wife, Betty, wrote several crime novels and her first, *She Ate Her Cake*, was published in 1946 and survives in the Stephenson archive. Busy British character actor Melville Cooper (1896-1973) and his second wife Rita Page (1905-1954) were also good friends. However, their closest friends were Enid and Pat Knowles.

The dashing and urbane Reginald Lawrence Knowles had a long

From left to right: Eileen Forkum, Jimmy, Melville Cooper, Roy Forkum and Lorna at Laguna Beach, California during the summer of 1939.
PHOTO COURTESY OF STEPHENSON ARCHIVE

From left to right: Enid Knowles, Jimmy and Lorna Stephenson and Pat
Knowles in a small corner at Pete and Billy Synder's Band Box Café
on 135 Fairfax Avenue, Hollywood.
PHOTO COURTESY OF STEPHENSON ARCHIVE

career in films, from an unbilled appearance in the missing believed lost
British feature, *Men of Tomorrow* (London Film, Zolta Korda, Leontine
Sagan, 1932) until small roles in two exploitation horror films shot back-
to-back: *Arnold* (George Fenady, 1973) and *Terror in the Wax Museum*
(George Fenady, 1973). His long list of some 124 films, TV and radio
work contains an A to Z of major and minor Hollywood celebrities. He
played foil to Abbott and Costello in *Who Done It?* (Universal, Erle C.
Kenton, 1942) and *Hit the Ice* (Universal, Charles Lamont, 1943) and was
billed below Efrem Zimbalist Jnr. in *Band of Angels* (Warner, Raoul Walsh,
1957). After appearing in some fourteen films in Britain he and his wife,
Enid Percival, went out to Hollywood in 1936. Whilst working at Warner
Bros. British Teddington studios, Patric met and befriended Errol Flynn.
He later played opposite Flynn in four Hollywood pictures: *The Charge
of the Light Brigade*, (Warner, Michael Curtiz, 1936); *The Adventures of
Robin Hood* (Warner, Michael Curtiz, William Keighley, 1938); *The Sisters*
(Warner, Anatole Litvak, 1938) and *Four's a Crowd* (Warner, Michael
Curtiz, 1938). Always in the shadow of Flynn, he spent much of his film
career typecast as an amiable second lead. After signing initially with
Warner Bros. he later freelanced, and during the 1940s had small roles in

such revered pictures as *How Green Was My Valley* (Twentieth Century-Fox, John Ford, 1941). At Universal he was involved in the final gasp of the studio's horror genre: *The Wolf Man* (Universal, George Waggner, 1941) and *Frankenstein Meets the Wolf Man* (Universal, Roy William Neill, 1943). He took the leads in two mystery B horrors: *The Mystery of Marie Roget* (Universal, Phil Rosen, 1942) and *The Strange Case of Dr. Rx* (Universal, William Nigh, 1942). He also excelled in costume dramas such as: *Kitty* (Paramount, Mitchell Leisen, 1945), *Monsieur Beaucaire* (Paramount, George Marshall, 1946), *Ivy* (United Artists, Sam Wood, 1947) and a whole plethora of colonial dramas such as *Heart of the North* (Warner, Lewis Seiler, 1938), *Storm over Bengal* (Republic, Sidney Salkow, 1939) and *Kyber Patrol* (Edward Small, Seymour Friedman, 1954). He ended the 1940s as a villain playing opposite Robert Mitchum in *The Big Steal* (RKO, Don Siegel, 1949). During the early 1950s he saw the potential of the up and coming television medium, embraced it with enthusiasm and consequently his film appearances were fewer. Later in retirement, he was fiercely loyal and protective of the former industry he had worked in so prodigiously.

There was another practical reason why Jimmy and Lorna were reluctant to socialise at prominent night spots, as Jimmy explained:

> "Binnie Barnes has just rung me up and asked me to get Bruce and go along to her place at twelve tomorrow to play tennis. I hope Bruce can't go! Because she's an awful woman – not to say a common b —. And I can't cope with her and don't want to get involved, so that I shall have to ask her back, and so spend money!!" [76]

He later enlarges:

> "I have not seen or heard anything of Binnie or Jean since last weekend and I don't particularly want to. I would rather let the acquaintance die down a bit. I've come to the conclusion that you run into expense out here chiefly if you start going out." [77]

The Stephensons' were thus not part of the famed British colony of actors, but they did attend war benefit charity events such as those held at the home of titular head of the Hollywood colony of British film actors, C. Aubrey Smith.

As an actor, Jimmy was a shrewd observer of character and this is evident when he visited the family of his friend, Belfast born Dr. Bill Dickson of West Kirby back in England.

> "I don't think I told you that I went out to the Dicksons the other night for the first time did I? They live out in the direction of the studio in quite a nice house (I don't know if you would think houses nice here – they're very different from ours and the furniture would be called "old-fashioned"

at home). They are very nice folk, but oh so boring and Presbyterian! The old man talked me stiff all night and he hums and haws and can't get his words out. And the sons are very stodgy. What Bill might have been I imagine, if he had not married Bobbie! I was asked for 7 o'clock so imagined it was for dinner. I was mistaken! We talked – then we played snooker, and at about 9.30 Mrs. D. (who has no regular maid) produced tea and cakes, and I went off about 10.00. Not a drink in the place. They asked me to spend Christmas with them, but I really felt I could not, so next day called up and said I had a previous engagement – of which I had warned them of the possibility. They really are nice folk according to their likes – but, oh! Not for me." [78]

Writing to his wife during Christmas 1937 Jimmy had written of impending film work finally assigned to him in the New Year after his successful test:

"I'm to play in what they say (although you can never believe 'em) is quite a nice part in an A picture with Dick Powell and Pat O'Brien starting about the middle of January. I'm told the director is very good to work with – which is a blessing. So I'm impatient to start – not only to fill my days a bit until you come but to get a chance of showing whether I'm any good or not." [79]

The studio released fifty-one feature films during 1938 and of these Jimmy appeared in six releases: three A films and three B films. The scepticism expressed in his letter concerning his film debut at the Warner factory was justified. His role in *Cowboy from Brooklyn* also known as *Romance and Rhythm* (Warner, Lloyd Bacon, 1938) playing magician/hypnotist and pseudo psychologist Professor Landis, was an inauspicious beginning. Conceived of as a spoof on the glut of singing cowboys heard on radio (Tex Ritter), and seen on film (Gene Autry), *Cowboy from Brooklyn* manages to pack in six pleasant, if unremarkable, Johnny Mercer songs for its principal singing star Dick Powell. Unfortunately the story of Brooklynite Powell, who becomes an overnight singing cowboy sensation in spite of himself, lacks a firm satirical edge and the screenplay spends too much time offering familiar slapstick and contrived farcical situations for the film to be wholly convincing or outstanding in its appeal. Pat O'Brien is often reduced to comic "mugging" ad infinitum and, unlike Dick Foran who excelled in musical westerns, Dick Powell's performance, though amiable enough, doesn't quite surmount the undistinguished script in this studio attempt to broaden his appeal. For all these reasons, the film must be adjudged disappointing, routine fare.

Appearing in just two scenes, Jimmy's role in the picture is hardly memorable and could easily have been a major embarrassment. Disaster is

A photographer snaps Jimmy Stephenson (left) in early 1938
on the set of his first Hollywood film, *Cowboy from Brooklyn*, with director
Lloyd Bacon (middle) and associate producer Louis Edelman (right).
PHOTO COURTESY OF STEPHENSON ARCHIVE

averted because his role is marginal and peripheral to the plotline. Dressed initially in an incongruous dude cowboy outfit, he sits around an ersatz camp fire surrounded by cowpokes on a studio soundstage masquerading as a western set. Before being called upon to produce a white dove from a Stetson, he can be seen briefly rubbing his hands, indicative not so much of anticipation, but more of nervous tension. In a later scene, dressed in conventional business suit, he leans over a desk with a look of sheer bewilderment as the plot demands he hypnotise Dick Powell, while all around him is pure pandemonium, with characters darting across the screen etc., trying to stop Powell's character from making a fool of himself. The desk would become a familiar prop in Jimmy's Hollywood films and a metaphor for his authoritative performances of middle-class professionals, depicted as either legitimate/straight or illegitimate/crooked roles.

Produced in association with Cosmopolitan Films, set up by media mogul William Randolph Hearst, the film is an A picture even though its running time is just seventy-seven minutes. Some of the characters on screen such as musicians "Spec," Candy Candido, and "Louie," Harry Barris, who have prominent roles in the early part of the film, disappear suddenly as the story progresses. This appears indicative of an earlier, longer studio cut before the final theatrical release print. For his efforts, Jimmy appears tenth billed, out of twenty-two cast names, on the end credits.

In addition to the film roles offered him, the studio sought to fill his time with the allocation of stand-in and general factotum work for the shooting of studio screen tests. In the following letter he provides an example of this type of work:

> "I have got myself the script for the picture but have not looked at it yet, and I have to learn some lines for a test for Barbara O'Neill (sic) on Friday – I am to play a definite part in a picture. Here they are always testing people in this way – quite different from England." [80]

> "I have just got back from the studio – 3.30 – having worked from 10.00 a.m. on the test with Barbara O'Neill (sic). The picture is called *White Banners* I think, and Claude Rains is actually to play the part I was playing. Edmund Goulding is directing – <u>very</u> nice and a splendid director – <u>what</u> a difference from Arthur Woods for example. We did just two little scenes and when we had finished he asked me if they had fixed me up in anything yet. I told him about the little part in *The Dude Rancher* and he said "They ought to give you *Clitterhouse*. – why don't you make a test for it – you'd be <u>grand</u> for the part." I said I'd love to and he said he would speak to the director at once. It is the lead of course – and a grand part – Ralph Richardson plays it in the play. [81] Of course it may come to nothing – but it's nice to have attracted the attention of one of the best directors in Hollywood and may do me good in other directions and at some other time even if I don't get this. If only I <u>could</u> get it!! <u>Then</u> we could stand up to Mr. J[ack].W[arner]. and <u>make</u> him alter the contract! Mustn't go counting chickens.

> But apart from everything else – oh how <u>grand</u> it has felt to be <u>working</u>. I was in a dressing gown and pyjamas with my hair all guffie-ish – a feckless inventor 'guy'." [82]

Compared to the business-like Arthur Woods, Goulding was not only genial, but went out of his way to make actors comfortable by often acting out scenes himself on the set for their benefit. Along with "Willy" Wyler, "Eddie" Goulding was a key personality in the development of Jimmy Stephenson's Hollywood career.

The presence of Edmund Goulding on the studio roster was indicative of a structural shift in the diversity of subject matter the Warners Studio was seeking to promote. Renowned for its spate of gangster pictures and hard-hitting social exposé films during the early 1930s, it had from the mid 1930s striven to broaden its product beyond the action and adventure-oriented films it was renowned for. To this end, in 1935 the studio took a gamble and produced *A Midsummer Night's Dream* (Warner, William Dieterle, 1935) and the following year produced the biographical picture *The Story of Louis Pasteur* (Warner, William Dieterle, 1936). The positive box office success and the critical kudos of reviewers for these super productions persuaded the studio to invest in further prestigious quality dramas and "women's" pictures. When in 1937 Edmund Goulding became available, having departed in problematic circumstances from M-G-M, Warner Bros. had added him to their register of directors. Though outwardly affable, amusing and multi-talented, the personality of British born Goulding was anything but straightforward. His private life was beset with numerous traumas, doubts and demons. In certain Hollywood circles he was known for his bisexual affairs, wild parties, bouts of alcoholism and drug addiction. Whatever proclivities and orientations he may have nurtured privately, his films are, with the notable exception of *Nightmare Alley* (Twentieth Century-Fox, 1947) a roll-call of decorum and discretion, offering the splendour of tender human emotion with a dramatic quality that stands the test of time. [83] It is worth seeing such films as: *Love* (M-G-M, 1927), *Grand Hotel* (M-G-M, 1932), *Dark Victory* (Warner, 1939) and *The Razor's Edge* (Twentieth Century-Fox, 1946) as reminders of what poignant, expressive accomplishments Hollywood was once capable of, but can no longer manage with ease. Despite his personal problems and volatility, Goulding was professionally astute, and did his best to assist Jimmy's career at Warners by offering him suitable roles whenever they became available. Goulding had suggested Jimmy for the role of Major Brand in the remake of *The Dawn Patrol* (Warner, Edmund Goulding, 1938). Though he had tested successfully and even had uniforms fitted, the front office decided to proceed with caution and the day before shooting was due to commence Jimmy was informed a "name" had been given the role; Basil Rathbone was to play opposite Errol Flynn instead. Writing to his wife, Lorna, Jimmy found Goulding's interest a welcome contrast to the "double-dealing" of studio bosses Irving Asher and Jack Warner:

> "I went to the studio this morning to have some portraits done and afterwards was sitting in the casting office when Edmund Goulding called there and asked if I would go up and see him. So up I went. Well it appears that the test I did for him with Barbara O'Neill (sic) has already produced results and may produce more. Goulding was so pleased with it that he talked to the producer of *Clitterhouse*, to [Maxwell] Arnow, (head of the casting

department) to [Hal] Wallis, J. Warner's second man, and finally
to Jack Warner himself. Then <u>all</u> went and had another look at <u>all</u>
my tests and, in Goulding's words, the whole thing is "steaming
up." The immediate result is that a very good part in Goulding's
picture which goes into production soon, another A picture *White
Banners* (for which the test with Barbara O'Neill (sic) was done)
– a part for which they were considering Ian Hunter (quite a big
noise out here), is <u>mine!</u> And on Tuesday I make a test with a
girl – I think Helen Twelvetrees, – with me playing Clitterhouse.
The test is officially for her – but unofficially for me as well.
Goulding is <u>very</u> keen on it and says if I get it I am a star at once.
And he wants the credit of being my "discoverer." He says he has
something of a reputation for being able to "smell" talent a mile
off and <u>knows</u> it is my part. Which it <u>is</u>. – I could <u>play</u> it. Anyhow
there seems to be a lot of "movement" behind the scenes and if
only the gods are good to me on Tuesday I may get my chance
much earlier than in our wildest dreams we have ever hoped . . .
One thing is certain. Goulding is very keen on me and even if <u>this</u>
does not happen he'll certainly get me anything that he possibly
can in my "line"!! And I'm so lucky to be in <u>two</u> A pictures so
soon. Some people hang about for six months or more and don't
do a thing. Bruce Lister has no sign of anything yet – has not even
been called upon for tests." [84]

In the event, Jimmy's role in *White Banners* (Warner, Edmund
Goulding, 1938) was small, but pivotal. The story was written by Lloyd C.
Douglas whose first best-selling novel, *Magnificent Obsession* published
in 1929, had been a prestigious hit for Universal studios back in the mid
1930s. *Magnificent Obsession*, (Universal, John Stahl, 1935) co-starred
Irene Dunne and a young Robert Taylor. Warner Bros. went on to purchase
the Douglas novel *Green Light* which became a vehicle for Errol Flynn
in *Green Light* (Warner, Frank Borzage, 1937). Other films adapted from
Douglas's works included: *Disputed Passage* (Paramount, Frank Borzage,
1939); *The Robe* (Twentieth Century-Fox, Henry Koster, 1953); a remake
of *Magnificent Obsession* (Universal-International, Douglas Sirk, 1954)
and *The Big Fisherman* (Centurion Films, Frank Borzage, 1959).

Today *White Banners*, a domestic drama of small town values with
religious overtones, is overlooked even amongst film historians. Set in
1919, the story involves a failed middle-aged inventor Paul Ward, Claude
Rains, who is cheated out of a patent for a refrigerated ice-box he has
devised. Undaunted, he goes on to create an even better, more sophisticated
gas ice-box. A mysterious housekeeper Hannah Parmalee, Fay Bainter,

Jimmy as Thomas Bradford (left), with Fay Bainter as
Hannah Parmalee (middle) and Claude Rains as Paul Ward (right)
in Edmund Goulding's 1938 production of *White Banners*.
PHOTO COURTESY OF STEPHENSON ARCHIVE

arrives at the family home and engenders compassion, trust and courage
in those around her. In response to her sagacious advice and cheerful
homilies, every adversity and crisis encountered by the Ward family in
their small Indiana town is approached with positive affirmation and all
domestic tragedy is averted. The studio brought in three screen writers to
adapt the Lloyd C. Douglas *Cosmopolitan Magazine* story. Playing safe,
the familiar disclaimer: "The story, all names, characters, incidents and
institutions, portrayed in this production are fictitious. No identification
with actual persons, living or dead is intended or should be inferred,"
was tacked onto the credits. The film's simple, uncomplicated moral of
"turn the other cheek" was shaped into something commendable by a
sterling cast lead by Rains and Bainter. Both were fresh from appearing
in substantive roles in landmark Warner productions of 1938, the former
as Prince John in *The Adventures of Robin Hood* and the latter as Aunt
Belle in *Jezebel* (Warner, William Wyler, 1938). Edmund Goulding's

expert direction accentuated tasteful decorum over vapid religiosity, and Max Steiner's score supplied the customary overlay of musical cues to invigorate the dramatic impact of the story. The film's inspirational, albeit improbable story would have struck a chord with audiences struggling to emerge from the ravages of a deep economic depression.

Jimmy played Thomas Bradford, a wealthy businessman from Chicago, who turns out to be the long-lost father of Peter Trimble, an adopted child played by Jackie Cooper. Neither Peter nor anyone else, except Ward and Bradford, is aware that his real mother is the mysterious Hannah. Warner executive Hal B. Wallis expressed concern to associate producer Henry Blanke about treatment of the incredulity of Bradford and Hannah's first meeting when they are alone in a sensitive way. Jimmy plays his scenes with tact and discretion, showing Bradford change from a detached, shrewd businessman, to a concerned and repentant partner and father, struggling to fully comprehend the dilemma of his past actions and deciding on a correct course of action to safeguard the future for all concerned. This early role is a key performance and one that, given correct casting, demonstrates his consummate ability in putting over a complex character. Although his time on screen is short, a little over seven and a half minutes, and the story has progressed some seventy-five minutes before he appears, Jimmy makes the most of his part and turns in a credible and noteworthy performance. Wallis duly noted Jimmy's handling of the part and, while mindful of his reliability and usefulness as a stock player for the Warner Company, he couldn't, as yet, foresee anything further on the horizon other than his continuing to be cast in smallish roles in suitable character parts.

Jimmy's performance in this film caught the eye of English film critic C.A Lejeune. Compiling an end of year report for the cinema of 1938 in her weekly column in the Sunday *Observer*, she requested: "Father Christmas" to "Give better parts to James Stephenson." [85]

Unfortunately, at this early stage in his Hollywood career no such luck was forthcoming. The seemingly positive step forward in his career prospects, prompted by his appearance in *White Banners*, proved a false dawn. The studio continued to cast him in roles well beneath his potential. Surviving letters show his frustration at the lack of good roles and being denied the chance to show his true capabilities. The unfairness of the standard "option contract" used by all the Hollywood studios at this time was something which preoccupied him to the exclusion of much else in these surviving letters.

It was part of the Hollywood studio business model; once an aspiring actor sought employment at a studio he or she was confronted with a contract of employment that progressed in steps over a seven year term. Every six months the studio reviewed the actor's progress or otherwise and decided whether or not to renew the option. If the studio dropped the option, the actor was unemployed; if the studio renewed the option the actor continued on the pay roll for a further six months and received a fixed raise in salary. It was the studio and not the actor that had the right to drop or pick up the option. The contract did not stipulate any reciprocal rights, meaning that a player had no right to quit and join another studio, could not stop work and could not renegotiate a higher salary. In essence, the contract to all intents and purposes compelled a performer to remain at a studio for seven years. As far as the studios were concerned, the option contract was necessary because developing talent was costly and precarious. If a new artist proved successful then the studio was justified in cashing in on its investment. If new players did not show potential then it made no sense keeping them on for a full seven years. Even when players were signed up they had little control over what roles were assigned or the quality of scripts. This situation was a proverbial grievance shared by all stars and particularly those higher in the studio firmament such as Cagney, Davis, Flynn and later Bogart. A name which occurs on most surviving Warner memoranda files is Roy [John] Obringer (1897-1967). A senior official in the company, he was the leading attorney and comptroller at Warner Bros. and responsible for drawing up and negotiating the contracts for all talent at the studio. [86]

Jimmy signed a customary stock player contract guaranteeing him twenty-six weeks of work within which to prove himself at a salary of $250 per week and $75 expenses. While waiting to sign the contract before his screen tests he writes apprehensively of the frugal expense allowance allocated by the studio:

> "Our living allowances have been fixed at $75 (£15 per week) which is a bit of a shock: although I imagine I can save £5 out of that I hoped we should get at least a $100. The agent talked glibly of $125. A way the agents have over here as well as at home apparently." [87]

In one of his letters Jimmy talks of possibly standing up to Jack Warner and making him "alter the contract!"

> "I have, innumerable times, been on the point of cabling you not to come, throwing the whole thing up, and coming back. I saw my agents this a.m and they agree that it is all vastly unfair but that unless I am prepared to risk the collapse of everything I had better sign the contract (after the expenses clause has been

added) and hope to get my own back later. They say that if you are important – a star or thereabouts – they'll tear up the contract and give you the earth, but that as things are now Warner's know they have me in a fix and are trading on that. One thing I've learnt – never to take any verbal promise ever again in this business, but to have it down on paper. Bill Linnit ought to have had it in the contract about any return passage. Thank heaven there's nothing in the writing about the wardrobe. And Vincent says "say nothing about it until we get the contract signed and then we can talk." [88]

In common with other stars signed up by the studio, Jimmy was beginning to learn how "tight-fisted" the studio was in respect of salary and expenses. When he made the trip out to Burbank an outstanding bill of $743.19, money advanced in respect of wardrobe purchased during his time at the Teddington studio, followed him. It seemed that back in England, at Irving Asher's suggestion, Jimmy purchased a wardrobe commensurate with his status as a rising star in films. Asher took Jimmy to his own personal tailors, Kilgour and French, for suits at sixteen guineas a time, to McAfee for shoes at five guineas and Fortnum and Mason for an overcoat. When challenged about the expense of acquiring such a wardrobe, Asher suggested the studio would pay for these items and then recoup it back later when he was earning a great deal more than his then current modest salary. To his chagrin now in Hollywood, it transpired the amount was to be repaid to the studio with immediate effect at $50 per week deductable from his salary. [89]

This incident aroused his indignation and in the heat of the moment he wrote a condemnatory letter to casting director, Bill Drury, back at the Warner First National Teddington Studios:

"I wrote a long letter to Bill Drury the other day telling him just what I thought of Warners and of Irving and all his work. "And slept on it" and tore it up. Now I've written another which is just as intemperate in language and I can't make up my mind whether to send it or not. Maybe I'll keep it till you come and maybe I'll get a sudden fit of rage and post it. I do feel I want to get it off my chest to someone at Teddington. You bet I will kick like hell if and when I get on. I'll fight for myself and no sentiment about it." [90]

Later in the same letter, in a more reflective frame of mind he concludes that discretion is the better part of valour:

". . . I've decided to try and put all grievances at the back of my mind for reproduction at the right time – and be as nice as I possibly can to everybody. I've also decided not to post

> my very heated letter to Bill Drury, but to keep it safely for
> production later." [91]

The issue of the contract was still uppermost in his mind when
he later confronted John Sloan of Teddington Studios who was in
Hollywood on vacation.

> "I went to tea at Pat Knowles, having met him at the studio.
> John Sloan, Teddington production manager, is staying with Pat
> on holiday for a few weeks. I had been talking to Pat about my
> contract and the treatment I have had etc. when John came. Pat
> advised me to tell him about it. So I did – and missed out nothing.
> He would not of course commit himself, but was very sympathetic
> and advanced no arguments whatsoever against me. And fully
> admitted what a "cinch" for the firm our Teddington contract was.
> He advised me to have a talk in private with Irving before he goes
> – but chiefly, now that the contract is signed, to forget it all and
> show 'em what I can do. – He said – "I <u>know</u> you're going to do
> well here Jimmy and when you do you can talk to them." [92]

Despite all these misgivings when he was finally given the opportunity
to begin work he became more focused, and more optimistic about his
chances for the future.

> "I saw my test with Barbara O'Neill (sic) to-day and liked it. And
> they have given me "*Clitterhouse*" to read and [Steve] Trilling in
> the casting office says he wants to arrange for me to do a test as
> Clitterhouse, with Helen Twelvetrees. He says Robert Lord, the
> producer, saw my first tests and thinks I'm a damned good actor,
> and that although a star is really required for Clitterhouse you never
> know! <u>Oh Gosh</u> I wish I could get it. And <u>then</u> for Irving Asher." [93]

His sense of anxiety and loneliness led him to search for something
recognisably nostalgic and mythical. As he explained: "I'm going out to
get a good but cheap dinner and then to a 25 cent cinema to see *Prisoner of
Zenda*" [United Artists / Selznick International Pictures, John Cromwell,
1937]. [94] What could be a better antidote than viewing a quintessentially
English film with its chivalric code and esprit de corps? Indeed, a perfect
companion to his final film watched in a London cinema - *Victoria the
Great*. Still pining for English tradition and convention he later wrote:

> "I had lunch at the [Athletic] club and then saw *Goodbye Mr.
> Chips* by James Hilton, which I had got at the library on the
> way to the club (it only takes about an hour to read and is very
> beautiful, though a bit sad) . . . ." [95]

Being part of the Warner Studio stock company, the bulk of Jimmy's
work was devoted to B films. Since 1936 the studio B unit had been

headed by producer Bryan Foy. As "the Keeper of the Bs," his remit was to produce around twenty-five films per annum using a budget of $5 million. His pragmatic response was to ensure cheap and cheerful films were churned out to order, on time and within, or preferably under, budget. This quick turnaround meant that scenarios were devised on the spot by studio scriptwriters such as the prolific Raymond Schrock, rigid shooting schedules of between fifteen to twenty-five days were adhered to, and casting for these films drew upon new studio contract players, the services of reliable outside talent, or former stars whose popularity at the box office had plunged. Referring to this "pile 'em high, sell 'em cheap" mentality, studio co-star Ronald Reagan recalled: "They were movies the studio didn't want good, they wanted 'em Thursday." [96]

Despite the impression of standard uniformity, the B films produced by Warner Bros., like those of the other Hollywood studios, were on closer inspection, protean and came in all shapes and sizes. Though convention dictated many B films were shot on the back lot at Burbank Studios, outdoor locations were sought and used, and even on occasion the expense of Technicolor was permitted. Jimmy appeared in half a dozen B picture series including: *Nancy Drew, Detective*; *Torchy Blane in Chinatown*; *The Adventures of Jane Arden*; *Calling Philo Vance*; *Secret Service of the Air*; *Murder in the Air,* as well as a string of other programmers. In doing so he honed his screen craft, working alongside emerging talent such as Janet Chapman, Nanette Fabray, Priscilla Lane, William Lundigan, Ronald Reagan, Rosella Towne, Maris Wrixon as well as seasoned professionals: Glenda Farrell, Kay Francis, Boris Karloff, Henry O'Neill, Robert Warwick, Pierre Watkin and Anna May Wong. Behind the camera were veteran directors: William McGann, William Clemens, Lewis Seiler and Noel Smith. Proficient technicians: photographer Ted McCord, scenarist, and later director, Vincent Sherman, also brought their craft to bear. As the 1930s wore on fewer B films were produced at Warner studios and once the United States entered the Second World War the major studios cut back on their supply of B films drastically. Jack Warner's emphasis on keeping costs low, whilst maintaining solid craftsmanship was the secret of business success. On a broader economic level, these films served to fuel the smooth running of the studio, whereby all three functions of film-making; production, distribution and exhibition, were fully utilised to deliver sustained employability for studio personnel, a steady stream of new material to sell to movie exhibitors and their patrons and thereby maximise profitability. As anthropologist Hortense Powdermaker noted in her study of the Hollywood studios, the studios tended to place great reliance on tried and tested formulas. "The old hokus pokus," as Jack Warner like to call these conventions, were held to deliver "sure-fire" successes in mainstream films.

More outlandish and prestigious, but unpredictable and therefore expensive projects were saved for their super productions. [97]

To inspect surviving primary source material detailing production, distribution and exhibition records contained in the USC Warner Bros. Archive in Los Angeles, is to recapture the highs and the lows of the classical film making process; the sense of energy, frustration and triumph of the Hollywood studios at their peak of popularity and creative output. Memos, production schedules and other studio records were written and circulated daily from department to department. These fascinating records clearly demonstrate there just weren't enough hours in the day to supply the insatiable demand of the movie-going public. For the movie experience was run on industrial systemic processes and procedures, based on immutable business principles: cost, efficiency and productivity.

When Were You Born (Warner, William McGann, 1938) was an astrological thriller starring Anna May Wong, based on a story by author and mystic Manley Hall, who also appeared on screen introducing this contrived tale of horoscope and murder, which lacks both mystery and excitement. Principal shooting began on February 23, 1938. There was dismay at the studio when Anna May Wong was taken ill with a cold at the beginning of the production. Bad weather also meant the film slipped behind schedule despite having initially shot six and a half pages of script. In her absence, scenes were shot around her character until her recovery and return to the set. The script gave little acting opportunities for its star beyond feigning subdued suspicion. Nevertheless, the film wrapped up on schedule on March 15, 1938. Jimmy's performance as murder victim Phil Corey is all on one note. He often delivers his lines speaking from the side of his mouth in a *faux* gangster drawl. With the exception of some banter between Shields, his manservant played by British character actor Eric Stanley, there is little rapport between Jimmy's character and the main protagonists. Jimmy received $1,667 salary as against $10,290 salary paid to Margaret Lindsay and $5,250 drawn by Anna May Wong. This, his first B film, was the first of his thirty-one Hollywood films to be released.

Heart of the North (Warner, Lewis Seiler, 1938), a tale of the Royal Canadian Northwest Mounted Police, represented a distinct change of pace for a film programmer. The film was made as Warner's part riposte to the recent success of *Renfrew of the Royal Mounted* (Grand National Pictures, Albert Herman, 1937) starring radio vocalist James Newell as Sergeant Renfrew, a "Singing Mountie" who burst into song when he wasn't apprehending fugitives from justice. The new three-strip Technicolor process, though it had enhanced Warner's prestigious

Portrait of Bruce Carruthers, technical adviser on the 1938 Mountie film *Heart of the North*. It is inscribed: "To James Stephenson, a truly realistic RCM Police Inspector. May you portray one again, Jim!"
PHOTO COURTESY OF STEPHENSON ARCHIVE

The Adventures of Robin Hood, was an expensive gamble. By itself Technicolor couldn't lift a routine western such as *Gold is Where You Find It* (Warner, Michael Curtiz, 1938) from the response of public apathy. Despite this, the studio was loath to waste the opportunities colour photography promised, so factoring in the bright red uniforms of the Canadian Mounties and the splendour of outdoor location scenery, Mountie "Westerns" appeared a ready-made opportunity. It marked Jimmy's first appearance in Technicolor. As Inspector Stephen Gore he looks suitably well turned-out in uniform and he exudes a natural air of authority, even if in one scene he is seen fidgeting with his signet ring while he sat at his desk. A minor transgression perhaps, but retakes were anathema to the tight schedule exacted by B films, and the high cost of shooting in Technicolor only served to reinforce this rule. So Jimmy's few seconds of apparent nerves remain in the final release print. In order to keep down costs, location shooting took place at Big Bear in California, while B. Reeves Eason took a second unit crew to the Mammoth Lakes to shoot the action scenes. At one point, the set in the lake had to be shot and cleared urgently as another production shot back-to-back, *Torchy Blane in Chinatown*, required a submarine in the lake as well! In comparison to other expensive epics, the gamble paid off as the film received praise from film exhibitors and did good business. Jimmy's impersonation of a Royal Canadian Mountie Officer did not go unnoticed. The family archive has a signed photograph from Bruce Carruthers, a former Royal Canadian Mountie Police corporal based in Hollywood, who acted as a freelance technical consultant on Mountie films. In this capacity Carruthers corrected details of dress, behaviour and other concerns on the film. His approval provides credibility to the authenticity and stature of Jimmy's performance. Warner Bros. were determined to ensure the success of the film could be further exploited in other scenarios. Using this criterion the opening scene of *Heart of the North* with its Mountie Song on the soundtrack was reused in a two reel Technicolor short *Romance Road* (Warner, Bobby Connolly, 1938). This musical adventure short was devoted to the exploits of the Royal Canadian Northwest Mounted Police, and the studio secured the services of operatic baritone Walter Cassel (1910-2000). Once again, Bruce Carruthers was brought in as a consultant to provide technical assistance in the staging of the film scenario.

James Cagney was not only one of Warner Bros. biggest stars, but also one of the most truculent. Cagney had tried lobbying for a greater salary, and the right to select the roles offered to him without automatically being suspended if he chose to reject parts assigned to him. Determined to prove his point, he struck out on his own by producing and starring in *Great Guy* also known as *Pluck of the Irish* (Grand National, John G. Blystone, 1936) and *Something to Sing About* (Grand National, Victor Schertzinger, 1937). Lacking the budgetary resources or distribution network of a major Hollywood studio, these independent ventures were not commercially successful, and poor box office receipts left both Grand National and Cagney in financial straits. He eventually returned to Burbank on improved terms and conditions and the first production waiting for him was *Boy Meets Girl* (Warner, Lloyd Bacon, 1938). Based on Bella and Sam Spewack's Broadway play, it ran from 1935 until 1937 at the Cort Theatre and was produced by George Abbott. Some of Cagney's frustrated energy was channelled into a hyper-active performance as a Hollywood screenwriter opposite Pat O'Brien. Set in a movie studio, there is the fascination of seeing the Warner Burbank Studio standing in for the fictitious Monumental Pictures. Bruce Lister, now renamed by the studio Bruce Lester, was given seventh billing and played the romantic lead, Rodney Bevan, son of an English lord, opposite Susie a waitress in the studio commissary, played by Marie Wilson. In contrast to Lester, Jimmy is on screen under a minute and a half and is

Led by Bonita Granville, the cast and crew of *Nancy Drew, Detective*
give a surprise birthday party to director William Clemens while on
location. The gifts were dime store toys which were bought by Bonita with
dimes collected from each member of the company. Jimmy Stephenson is
extreme left next to Frankie Thomas who is wearing a nurse's uniform as
part of a disguise he wears in the film. Next to Frankie is Bonita Granville,
and behind her in white hat is cameraman Lu O'Connell. Dick Purcell is
holding a glass while director William Clemens is extreme right.
PHOTO COURTESY OF STEPHENSON ARCHIVE

given fourteenth billing at the bottom of the cast list.

His part was a walk-on cameo as Major Thompson, "Hollywood
representative for Teddington British." This caricature is modelled on the
monocle-wearing English upper-class "silly ass" created to perfection by
Aldwych farceur Ralph Lynn. Jimmy speaks in the appropriate vernacular
of to the manor born. His character is there to bring about the plot resolution
of the film. Jimmy's function being to recognise Lester as the son of an
English lord, thereby freeing Marie Wilson to marry, and the elaborate
deception concocted by scenarists Cagney and O'Brien is thus revealed
to studio boss Ralph Bellamy. Having achieved this plot device Jimmy's
character promptly disappears. Inconsequential in itself, this piece of comic

playing is rooted in his amateur dramatic experiences with the Burnley Players, and their interpretations of the Aldwych farces back in England. Despite Jimmy's protestations in an interview: "Someone in the publicity department wrote that I was dying to do a comedy. Hell, no – I'm no comedian," this short scene is suggestive of how he might have looked and sounded on the Burnley amateur dramatic stage during the early 1930s. [98]

This brief scene was shot at lot nineteen at the Burbank studios on Saturday March 19, 1938 from 9:00 to 16:55. Amidst all the screen mayhem, former radio sports reporter Ronald Reagan appeared appropriately as a radio announcer at a film premiere.

Nancy Drew, Detective (Warner, William Clemens, 1938) was the first in a series of four films based on the fictional character of Nancy Drew, who appeared in many mystery fiction series. Bonita Granville played the amateur sleuth, assisted by her boyfriend, Ted Nickerson, played by Frankie Thomas. Like the books in which she appeared, the Nancy Drew films were conceived of as a positive role model for juveniles. The screenplay appears uncertain as to how to represent and treat her childish escapades in an adult world. At various times during the course of the narrative she wavers between active and passive, fearless and fearful. Dialogue between Nancy and Ted indicates that he is older than her. Yet her competence and initiative easily match, and often outstrip, his. There is a tendency in the film to undercut her inquisitive feminine ingenuity, independence and self-sufficiency (she drives a car) by reverting to comic by-play. Monkey wrenches, instead of being weapons of violent assault, are neutralised into comic props and, as such, are dropped several times on Ted's feet. There is also the use of comic masquerade with Ted taking on the guise of a nurse in a bogus sanatorium. Jimmy is third billed, as criminal boss Challon. He sits behind his perennial desk, from which he issues orders to henchman Dick Purcell. When a member of his criminal gang [Charles Trowbridge] threatens desertion Challon orders him killed before he can leave the room. Allocated an eighteen day shoot, the production began on August 29, 1938 and was completed on September 24, 1938, five days behind schedule. Exteriors were shot at the Camarillo Ranch.

Torchy Blane in Chinatown (Warner, William Beaudine, 1939) was also part of another profitable second-feature series produced by the Warner Studio, in which smart-talking, resilient news reporter Torchy Blane [Glenda Farrell] pursues headline scoops come what may. Lieutenant Steve McBride, a loud mouth police detective, played by the ever reliable Barton MacLane was the object of her affections. Usually cast as the villain or heavy, MacLane in the *Torchy Blane* series plays the boyfriend hero in a similar manner except he doesn't shout as loud when spitting out his dialogue.

Amid the mayhem of industrial film production at the Warner Bros. Burbank
Studios, Jimmy and Patric Knowles have an impromptu tea break
on the set of *Torchy Blane in Chinatown*. Marie Wilson joins them
from another sound stage. Given she is wearing a riding costume,
Sweepstake Winner seems the likely parallel film in production.
Note the busy studio technicians (grips) in the background. Time is money!
PHOTO COURTESY OF STEPHENSON ARCHIVE

Throughout the series McBride's assistant, Police Sergeant Gahagan, was
played by Tom Kennedy as a dumb incompetent who offers little help, save
for reciting pieces of doggerel verse to camera. The seventh in a series of
nine second feature films, *Torchy Blane in Chinatown* was bankable box
office, aimed specifically for mass popular consumption. Produced in an
unpretentious and slick manner it was a B movie to its core. Standing sets,
stock footage and a well-oiled script were all utilised to advantage. These
modestly conceived film series ensured regular contract players were kept
active, and new talent, such as Jimmy, was trained up. Unsurprisingly, the
script was derivative, being a remake of two previous mystery films: *The
Purple Cipher* (Vitagraph, Chester Bennett, 1920) and *Murder Will Out*
(Warner, Clarence G. Badger, 1930). Stalwart director William Beaudine
was a seasoned practitioner at shooting exactly what was required in just
one take. Allocated twenty-one days, principal shooting began on August 8,
1938 and was finished five days ahead of schedule on September 1, 1938.

Signed portrait of Kay Francis to Jimmy on the occasion of their work together on *King of the Underworld* in 1939: "To "Bill" - from "Doc Nelson" – really my best to Jim - Kay." PHOTO COURTESY OF STEPHENSON ARCHIVE

By lunchtime on the first day of shooting Beaudine had already shot some four and a half pages of script. During filming, however, two problems emerged. Noise from overhead aircraft meant the production had to undergo some rescheduling. More cause for concern was Beaudine's request that a four o'clock tea break, with the dialogue director and whole cast, be charged to the company. This was a precedent the studio would not concede. Such a concession would mean giving every company throughout the studio the same privilege. Jimmy received the same level of salary as Tom Kennedy, $1,500, whereas star Glenda Farrell received $7,500, Barton MacLane $5,000 and Pat Knowles $4,500. In the opening scene where Jimmy and his three associates sit in the interview room of a precinct police station, he leans back in his chair, which lifts momentarily from the ground, a sign of boredom perhaps? The scenario involves an "oriental gang" of jade thieves, and their attempt to extort ransom money by committing homicide. The plotline doesn't bear too much analysis, but the production's snappy delivery and a willing cast compensate for any implausibility. In a sad ironic twist Jimmy's character, Mansfield, "dies" through smoking a poisoned cigarette.

As has already been noted, Hollywood and major US tobacco companies liaised with one another in terms of publicity and sponsorship. Lucky Strike Cigarettes, for example, were sponsors of the radio series *Your Hollywood Parade* which Warner Bros. used to promote their new studio players. The studio went on to produce one film, *Bright Leaf* (Warner, Michael Curtiz, 1950), in tribute to tobacco.[99]

King of the Underworld (Warner, Lewis Seiler, 1939) was started on May 24, 1938 and finished on June 17, 1938, with additional scenes being completed in September. The studio was playing politics, by casting star Kay Francis in a lurid gangster melodrama in the belief she would refuse the role, and by doing so the studio would then be able to claw back her $200,000 annual salary. Her previous position as the prime female box office star at Warner Bros. had by the late 1930s been usurped by Bette Davis. Whatever the politics of the situation Francis, ever the professional, declined to be goaded by the studio's behaviour and accepted the role without rancour or complaint. The film was in fact a disguised remake of an earlier Paul Muni vehicle, *Dr. Socrates* (Warner,

Humphrey Bogart as Joe Gurney with Jimmy as Bill Stevens and Joe Devlin as a henchman lurking in the background in a scene from *King of the Underworld*.
PHOTO COURTESY OF STEPHENSON ARCHIVE

Jimmy as Colonel Armand Lucien with Nedda Harrigan as Madam Lucien
and unidentified actor in the much delayed *Devil's Island* shot in 1938,
but held back for two years due to censorship problems.
PHOTO COURTESY OF STEPHENSON ARCHIVE

William Dieterle, 1935), with Francis recast in the Paul Muni role and
Jimmy in a role previously occupied by Ann Dvorak. As a signed portrait
in the Stephenson archive indicates Francis appreciated Jimmy's mutual
professionalism on the film. Jimmy's first appearance as Bill Stevens, a
travelling hobo seen at the side of a freeway following the breakdown
of mobster Humphrey Bogart's car, bears a resemblance to the character
of British intellectual writer turned alcoholic drifter, Alan Squier, played
by Leslie Howard in *The Petrified Forest* (Warner, Archie Mayo, 1936).
Bogart gives a competent, if unremarkable performance as gangster Joe
Gurney, who has a Napoleon complex – a vague reference to the growing
menace of European dictatorships.

Even in the best of circumstances film productions go awry, in this
case several scenes were found to have been photographed out of focus.
This was due to a camera defect, and not picked up until the dailies,
or rushes were shown. In this instance the studio made light of such a
production error, and even used the mishap in pre-publicity promotion of

the film. Bogart, not Kay Francis, was billed above the title and Jimmy was given third billing in the film.

Devil's Island (Warner, William Clemens, 1940) began production on June 22, 1938 and shooting finished on July 22, 1938. Jimmy was paid $2,000 as against $10,000 paid to Boris Karloff. The film is significant in terms of Jimmy's evolving movie persona. This was the first occasion in which his characterisation called for the wearing of a moustache. The moustache would reappear in many of his future film appearances. However, audiences were denied immediate opportunity to view this melodrama as it didn't receive a general release until almost a year after production was completed. Given a limited release in January 1939 the film was withdrawn due to numerous objections from the French government about the depiction of the notorious French penal colony and the dispensing of French justice. Only with the outbreak of war in the autumn of 1939 followed by the occupation of France was the film finally released in domestic and foreign markets. [100]

The film itself delivers durable if uninspired entertainment. Though it is hinted at throughout the film, the expected showdown between

Jimmy and Lorna Stephenson adopt a pose on the set of *Calling Philo Vance*, his first star vehicle at Warner Bros. produced during the summer of 1939.
PHOTO COURTESY OF STEPHENSON ARCHIVE

Jimmy as Philo Vance disguised as Fritz Snaubel, with Henry Blair
and Marion Lessing as his assumed son and wife at the dockside
while Hans Schumm as a state officer looks on.
PHOTO COURTESY OF STEPHENSON ARCHIVE

the two central protagonists, sadistic Col. Lucien and the wrongly
convicted brain specialist Dr. Charles Gaudet [Boris Karloff], never
really materialises. During their scenes of confrontation in the film,
Jimmy brings a concentrated integrity to his role that matches the quiet
authority Karloff always brought to his playing of misunderstood victims.
Jimmy's character is first seen cutting a cigar via a model guillotine, and
although on the plump side, he cuts a distinguished figure of authority
sitting behind his official desk in colonial costume. Perhaps the weakest
character in the film is Madame Lucien [Nedda Harrigan]. She begins the
film as a devoted wife to her husband, and appears unconcerned about
the brutality and inhumane treatment he metes out to the convicts in the
penal colony. Following Gaudet's life-saving operation on their daughter,
she becomes all too willing to report her husband to the authorities, and
thus ruin his career. Her change of motivation appears vague, and her
behaviour is lacking in realism.

A prologue tacked on at the beginning is a clear indicator of the many
unexpected changes inflicted on the film by complicated and lengthy

Jimmy as sleuth Philo Vance and Terry,
as Vance's faithful dog McTavish, make a winning duo.
PHOTO COURTESY OF STEPHENSON ARCHIVE

censorship issues. These problems account for the often elliptical nature of the final film scenario. The soundtrack relies too often on overused stock music (the tune of "La Marseillaise" is never far away) and this tends to labour rather than enhance the visuals on the screen. Nevertheless, the professionalism of cast and technicians is apparent, and even various re-editings by the studio, prompted by censorial intervention, cannot deny a level of pace and vigour still evident in the film when examined today.

As a minor reward for his accommodating attitude in taking on the work the studio assigned him, Jimmy was given the nominal lead in *Calling Philo Vance* (Warner, William Clemens, 1940). Though cast in the eponymous role, as a regular contract player in a second feature his name does not appear above the title. This remake of *The Kennel Murder Mystery* (Warner, Michael Curtiz, 1933) starring William Powell, commenced shooting on July 27, 1939 and concluded August 16, 1939. Like *Nancy Drew, Detective* the direction was assigned to the reliable William Clemens; Jimmy turns in a thoroughly decent star performance. Running just over an hour, the film moves at a brisk tempo

"Bob the Wonder Dog who has spent his life acting for British films,
is such a conscientious artist that he does not allow play to interfere
with work, although Skeets Gallagher and James Stephenson who
played important roles in the same film *Mr. Satan* tried their hardest."
PHOTO COURTESY OF STEPHENSON ARCHIVE

and the content is among the most varied and active of all the B films
he appeared in during his Hollywood career. Jimmy has at least half a
dozen changes of costume, along with a great deal of blocking involving
the handling of props, model planes, murder weapons, etc. The Vance
character, in order to make good his escape after having stolen secret
plans, uses disguise as a subterfuge. His alias, Fritz Snaubel a Viennese

peasant, is played initially straight and dramatic, but later ends on a wry and comic note. Although William Powell had played sleuth Philo Vance on four successive occasions, the role was thereafter given to various actors and as a result the series of films suffered in comparison to other film detectives. Jimmy's portrayal was the twelfth occasion of the Vance character appearing on film. The supporting cast includes solid, comic support from Edward Brophy as Ryan and Jimmy once more played opposite Henry O'Neill as J.P. Markham. Chief among his co-stars was canine Terry, a Cairn terrier who "plays" McTavish with a knowing assurance. Unlike her British canine counterpart, Bob the Dog (a collie) in *Mr. Satan*, who is on the margins of the narrative and is by comparison rather pedestrian, Terry is never dull. She is centre stage throughout the action, an integral part of the plotline and not above scene-stealing. But, then Terry was fresh from her most famous part of Toto in *The Wizard of Oz* (M-G-M, Victor Fleming, 1939). There is nothing in *Calling Philo Vance* to suggest any anxiety on the part of Jimmy as he takes on his first chance to impress as the lead in a Hollywood B picture programmer. However, in the theatrical trailer during a scene where he is interrogating a witness Jimmy is seen, as in *Heart of the North*, fidgeting with the ring on his finger. In the final theatrical release print an alternate take is used and consequently the unintentional behaviour with the ring is eliminated. Despite the density of clues and red herrings in the plot, making the detection difficult to follow, critical approval of Jimmy's portrayal was generally positive: "James Stephenson is a worthy successor to the other interpreters of the Vance role – including William Powell. He has a Ronald Colman touch about him, and acts with easy assurance." [101]

In *Secret Service of the Air* (Warner, Noel Smith, 1939) Jimmy appeared on screen, fourth billed, as the villainous Jim Cameron. As already noted, although he had already appeared on screen with a moustache in *Devil's Island,* censorship issues meant the film was not released until 1940. Therefore, this was the first occasion when audiences had the opportunity of seeing him on screen with a moustache. This was the second of four secret service B movies featuring secret agent Lieutenant "Brass" Bancroft performed by the young Ronald Reagan. Raymond Schrock's story involves people trafficking from Mexico across the United States border. The film is an opportunity to put together a series of industrial conventions involving lots of action: fist-fighting in bars, prison breaks, car chases, flying escapades - all edited together with stock footage, and copious instances of sequences shot utilising visual montage and back projection. Jimmy ensured Cameron's dialogue is delivered in an appropriate curt and snarling manner. There is a suspenseful fight

Ronald Reagan (left) as government agent Brass Bancroft, Ila Rhodes
(middle) as Pamela Schulyer and Jimmy (right) as Jim Cameron -
a despicable, but accomplished villain in *Secret Service of the Air* 1939.
Photo courtesy of Stephenson Archive

between hero Brass Bancroft and Jim Cameron, in which Cameron
comes off worse and is handed in to be dealt with by the appropriate law
enforcement agency. Location shooting was at Van Neuys Airport, Los
Angeles. Allocated an eighteen day production schedule, filming began
on September 26, 1938 and concluded on October 20, 1938.

Murder in the Air (Warner, Lewis Seiler, 1940) was the fourth and final
entry in the Ronald Reagan "Brass" Bancroft series of heroic espionage
thrillers devoted to rooting out Un-American subversives. Eddie Foy Jr.
was again Lieutenant Brass Bancroft's comic sidekick Gabby Watters,
and John Litel was Chief Saxby. Allocated twelve days, filming began
on September 10, 1939 and finished on September 18, 1939 - on
schedule. Jimmy was fourth billed playing villain Joe Garvey, an alien
reincarnation of Jim Cameron in *Secret Service of the Air*, except now
the subversive activity was taking place within the United States rather
than on its borders. Garvey, "a citizen of foreign birth," is of unspecified
extraction and Jimmy speaks in a suspect accent appropriate to received
notions of an undesirable alien engaged in un-American activities. In this
populist vein the story is replete with instances of skulduggery including:

initiation tattoos, secret writing and use of aliases and codes. For a third time, Jimmy is seen fidgeting with his signet ring on his left hand. Like Jim Cameron, Joe Garvey has a moustache but unlike Cameron he carries a cane, wears a homburg hat and conducts himself with suave malevolence. The film is fascinated and alarmed by the promise and threat of air technology. A piece of technological kit known as the Inertia Projector is able to harness powerful beams to disengage and destroy aircraft in mid-air. This was a direct reference to the development and use of radar, something which would be of vital significance in the Royal Air Force's winning of The Battle of Britain during the summer of 1940. During his Presidency the idea of a missile defence system, the Strategic Defence Initiative informally known as "Star Wars," would quite likely have reminded Reagan of this early phase of his film career. Unlike Jim Cameron, who is apprehended by the "fair play" of fisticuffs and placed into FBI custody, Joe Garvey puts up fierce resistance using underhanded tactics whilst absconding in the air. He is paid back in kind, however, and is fatally shot down using the Inertia Projector. The enthusiasm for national defence was never so palpable. The Bryan Foy B unit was beginning to wind down and so for this final entry in the Brass Bancroft series the cast list was reprised at the film's closure.

The scenarios of these B pictures may have been fictious and rooted in popular culture, but they were underpinned by notions of personal and national identity. For Jimmy and Lorna Stephenson this was all very resonant, given they had paid a brief trip to Ensenada, Mexico in late November 1938, and then walked back across the US border and requested permanent residence, declaring their intentions of becoming naturalised United States citizens.

By the time Jimmy came to appear in *The Adventures of Jane Arden* (Warner, Terry Morse, 1939) he was well settled into the role of playing suave gentlemen of dubious means. Among his gallery of villains, Dr. George Vanders ranks as the apogee of urbane nastiness. From the beginning of this tale of jewel thieves and smuggling Vanders displays a deadly charm shooting, without compunction, debutante "Martha Blanton" [Maris Wrixon] in the back. Vanders is more agile than Challon in *Nancy Drew, Detective*, more ruthless than Joe Garvey in *Murder in the Air* and even more manipulative than Jim Cameron in *Secret Service of the Air*. At a short running time of under an hour, the film forgoes any pretence of presenting any rounded characters. Everything revolves around the action of the melodramatic plot, and consequently there is never any doubt about the direction of travel of this schematic piece of comic strip caper. Nevertheless, there are some interesting diversions along the way before its inevitable conclusion.

From the beginning heroine Jane Arden [Rosella Towne] operates in a blatant masculine environment of wheeling and dealing. In an attempt to confiscate a set of dice from a group of news delivery employees, she ends up joining them in their game instead. The theme of ruse and fabrication is carried on throughout the film. After apparently being fired by her city editor boss, "Ed Towers" [William Gargan] Jane Arden is assured this is just a ploy to put her on a special assignment. She is sent as an undercover reporter on the tracks of European jewel thieves. She is accompanied on her travels by a female side-kick "Teenie Moore," played in the manner of a lower-berth Gracie Allen by Dennie Moore. This character supplies more than ample comic shtick as does her boyfriend "Marvin Piermont" [Benny Rubin] and also Vander's henchmen played by Joe Devlin and a youthful Raymond Bailey. During the 1960s Raymond Bailey would be in high demand for TV work, and is best remembered today for his playing of banker Milburn Drysdale in the TV situation comedy series *The Beverly Hillbillies* (CBS, 1962-1971).

Former editor Terry Morse, making his directorial debut, lends a dynamic that brings momentum to the film, and brushes aside all the improbabilities of the script. Based on comic strip characters, the situations are serial-like in their fluency. To disarm any criticism from the jewellery trade, the front office inserted the usual cautionary all persons fictitious disclaimer to the credits.

In contrast to everything else in the film which, by melodramatic convention, is overstated, Jimmy plays Vanders with understated poise. In the office of jeweller Albert Thayer [Pierre Watkin] Vanders beats his hand against the chair indicative of impatience, but this is tempered by his relaxed posture as he leans back in his chair. The action filled climax is set in Bermuda and involves an equestrian chase, shot, as in *Heart of the North,* by the renowned master of second unit action sequences "Breezy" Reeves Eason. While not remotely on the scale of his famous second unit work on *Charge of the Light Brigade* or *Gone with the Wind* (M-G-M / Selznick International Pictures, Victor Fleming, 1939), the sequence still possesses all the excitement the occasion demanded and it successfully integrates studio back projection with carefully crafted location footage. However, there is a violation of continuity editing when Vanders is thrown from his speeding open carriage. In one shot he is seen without his hat, in the next shot it reappears only to disappear again in the following shot. Retribution is soon displayed, for when Vanders is about to board a waiting getaway plane he is shot dead in the back. With proper justice having been exacted, there only remains the obligatory

Jimmy as Dr. George Vanders, suave, but deadly (left) with Rosella Towne
as Jane Arden (middle) and Peggy Shannon as Lola Martin (right)
in *The Adventures of Jane Arden* 1939.
PHOTO COURTESY OF STEPHENSON ARCHIVE

kiss between Rosella Towne and William Gargan before a fade to the final
credits. Despite his moral turpitude and the inevitability of his demise,
Vanders is a striking villain and lingers in the memory. Jimmy was given
third billing. Rosella Towne, who bears a passing resemblance to Loretta
Young, is self-assured and level-headed in the lead role. Working with
Jimmy during this period of her career, Rosella recalled:

> "I was nineteen when I knew James, and he became something
> of a father figure for me. He was a kind man, although I do
> remember once when he reprimanded me in a most fatherly
> style. I used a word that is not considered 'bad' in America, but
> it is in England. He looked quite stern and said, 'Rosella, I never
> want to hear you use that word again!' I never used it again. The
> word was 'bloody.' " [102]

Although *The Adventures of Jane Arden* had all the hallmarks of
initiating a film series the market was already crowded with installments
of the *Torchy Blane* films, and, in any case, Rosella left the studio in early
1940 and so a series never materialised. Rosella married radio writer

Harry Kronman in January 1942, and gave up her film career soon after to raise a family.

On Trial (Warner, Terry Morse, 1939) is a moderate programmer with Jimmy as murder victim, financier Gerald Trask. Receiving fifth billing, he is reunited on screen with John Litel, as Robert Strickland, the accused on trial for murder, Margaret Lindsay as Stickland's wife, Nedda Harrigan as his own wife, Joan Trask, and Janet Chapman as Strickland's young daughter. Based on Elmer Rice's 1914 play, the plot structure of this murder mystery relies on extensive use of flashback. This was the third film adaptation of Rice's play. A previous version, produced by Warner Bros. in 1928 and, apart from the theatrical trailer, is now missing believed lost. It starred Pauline Frederick and Holmes Herbert had played Gerald Trask. As in Rice's *Counsellor-at-Law* there is much preoccupation with legal court procedure. As the revelation of court testimony unravels Trask is found to have been a womanizer, a blackmailer and a thoroughly loathsome individual. For his playing of a suave bounder, Jimmy was paid $763. Running just over an hour, the narrative is vigorous in execution, but is otherwise an undistinguished piece of film-making with most of the action confined to the courtroom and other studio interiors in the flashback scenes. To keep costs to a minimum just a few location shots, an airport terminal and a train station, appear in the film. Jimmy wears a wardrobe similar to other films he had previously appeared in.

The Old Maid (Warner, Edmund Goulding, 1939) came with impeccable credentials, indicative of a star production for Bette Davis at the peak of her popularity. It had a Civil War setting; was based on an Edith Wharton novella, and had been brought to the Broadway stage by Zoë Akins' Pulitzer Prize play. It was one of the highest grossing films produced by Warner Bros. at that time. Yet, at the time of its production, the film was fraught with difficulties and it took much of Edmund Goulding's creative energy, and considerable resource on the part of the Warner studio machine before this troubled production was turned around. At the outset both Bette Davis and Miriam Hopkins displayed antipathy towards each other and battled incessantly, each one trying to upstage the other and this, combined with bouts of sickness, real or imagined, suffered by both stars put the film behind schedule. Casting difficulties were also encountered over the male lead, Clem Spender. Several suggestions including Alan Marshal, David Niven and George Sanders, were passed over in favour of Humphrey Bogart who had been cast opposite Bette Davis in *Dark Victory*. It soon became apparent he was miscast. The bland, but capable George Brent, who like Ralph Bellamy alternated with ease between A and B pictures, stepped into the role of Clem. Goulding tested Jimmy with Ila Rhodes on February 15, 1939 and Jimmy secured the small role of Jim Ralston billed seventh. In the film's scenario representations of masculinity are depicted either as deficient or absent. Jimmy's character is seen hovering in the background; has two scenes speaking a few inconsequential lines, and then promptly dies. Despite the tumult suffered by all during the making of the film, its treatment of Charlotte Lovell's development from indiscreet youth to embittered old age remains of interest to contemporary audiences. Script writer Casey Robinson dealt again with issues of personal and social identity in the iconic Davis vehicle *Now Voyager* (Warner, Irving Rapper, 1942) in which another Charlotte is transformed. On this occasion the process was reversed beginning from a repressed, guilt-ridden old maid and then through psycho-analysis emerging as a self-confident articulate, liberated young woman.

As with *White Banners*, the film is preoccupied with circumstances surrounding the antecedents of a child and how this is to be reconciled with future destinies. The opportunity to view Bette Davis age over many years is irresistible, and there is dramatic poignancy in her soliloquies to her unacknowledged child Tina, played by Jane Bryan, that remain especially moving and memorable. Goulding's camera is forever gliding through open doorways as if eavesdropping on a bygone world.

Because of moral censorship issues arising from the subject of an unmarried mother giving up her illegitimate child to her cousin, and production problems already mentioned, the progression of the narrative is somewhat elliptical and terse, but it always remains captivating in its emotional range.

During September 1939 Warners sent some of its young featured players, including Gloria Dickson, on a junket up and down the United States West Coast. This culminated with the stars at Oakland's Esquire Theatre, home of the Warner Theatre under recent agreement with the Laws-Blumenfeld exhibition chain, in order to celebrate the premiere of *The Old Maid*. Included on the studio junket were: Lya Lys, Ronald Reagan, John Payne, Lucille Fairbanks, Jane Gilbert, James Stephenson, William Lundigan, Rosella Towne, Barbara Pepper, Claire Windsor, and Jean Parker. They arrived in Oakland and were met at the train station with pomp and circumstance. They were given an official welcome at City Hall, taken on a motor tour of the city, and attended a luncheon at Hotel Lake Merritt. At 2:00 p.m., the stars made the first of two personal appearances at the theatre, returning to their rooms at the Hotel Leamington for tea and then a subsequent appearance at the theatre. Afternoon and evening entertainment consisted of a visit in secret to the

During September 1939 James Stephenson and other members of the Bryan
Foy Warner B picture unit toured the United States West Coast by road and rail
making personal appearances. Here standing alongside the Lake Merritt Monu-
ment at Oakland, California (inscribed: "Lake Merritt was secured for Oakland in 1891 through the personal efforts of Melvin C. Chapman Mayor") are
extreme left: Lya Lys, James Stephenson, Ronald Reagan, Rosella Towne and
Maris Wrixon. William Lundigan can also be clearly seen next to an unidentified road manager. At the front seated on the ground are from left:
Lucille Fairbanks, Barbara Pepper and unidentified male personality.
PHOTO COURTESY OF STEPHENSON ARCHIVE

practice of the Bears Football Team at Edwards Field in Berkeley and a
dinner at the Claremont Hotel. They departed the next day from the 16th
Street station at 8:00 a.m. for Hollywood. Writing about the experience
Jimmy found it all a lot of tiring nonsense:

"We arrive in Portland in about an hour – 2:30 – darling. So, tho'
it's a long time and a long way back, we're on our <u>way</u> back at any rate.

We left Seattle yesterday after lunch by cars, for Olympia, the State
capital of Washington; on arrival there we went to the State capital
building to meet the governor. Then back to the hotel to change for a
cocktail party at 6, attended by all the "notables" of Olympia, and given
by the owner of the theatre.

At 6:30 dinner, with about 150 invited guests and from which the speeches were broadcast. Then in cars to the theatre, preceded by the local band in resplendent uniform. A mob of people outside the theatre, and the 500 seat house packed to suffocation. After the show by cars to Tacoma where our railway car was waiting! And, for me, straight to bed.

The car remained in the station all night so I had a good night's sleep until the jolting of coupling up awoke me about nine.

When we arrive at Portland we go to meet the mayor and make two appearances to-night leaving tomorrow for Eugene Oregon. Each time I go on a stage and say the old blare over again it becomes more irksome, and the whole business is very tiring.

Unless something happens to alter things we leave Oakland Salem a.m. Saturday and arrive at Glendale at about 7:30 p.m. so I'm counting the days." [103]

"I'm getting more and more, weary of the whole thing and longing to be back – on Saturday. We made our appearance at Portland at 11 p.m. last night, then had a snack and got back to our car, which again was parked in a siding. By the time I had, in the confined space of a compartment, undressed, packed up everything for this morning, it was 2 a.m.

The train pulled out at 8:00 a.m. and to-day we have all left everything in the car and we make appearances here and at Eugene without putting on Tuxedos etc.

Last night was again a very successful appearance – but each time now I feel – "oh hell I can't go on and repeat the same old "guff." I don't make a speech – it's just a little "interview" with Ronnie – He makes the introduction and then asks me a few questions to which I reply, and say goodnight to the folks." [104]

Warner Bros. gave Jimmy his first loan out to Paramount for a prestigious remake of P.C. Wren's tale of high adventure in the French Foreign Legion *Beau Geste* (William A. Wellman, 1939) in which he appears as Major Henri de Beaujolais. The script was based on the 1924 novel by Percival Christopher Wren and had been produced as a silent under the same title by Paramount in 1926 directed by Herbert Brenon and starring Ronald Colman. In the original version Major de Beaujolais was played by Norman Trevor. With the tremendous critical kudos and box office success of the 1926 silent version still relatively fresh, the sound remake drew heavy comparisons from critics and public alike.

"Keep it up, you scum! Keep shooting! You'll get a chance yet to die with your boots on!" These machismo orders bawled out by Brian Donlevy's sadistic Sergeant Markoff might easily have applied to the film's director, William A[ugustus] Wellman. A former First World War pilot and a specialist of action movies, including the very first Oscar winning film *Wings* (Paramount, 1927), he was often referred to as "Wild Bill" Wellman for his impatience with actors, fast shooting and a boisterous, reckless, aggressive approach to life.

The film contains the memorable foreword: "The love of a man for a woman waxes and wanes like the moon, but the love of brother for brother is steadfast as the stars and endures like the word of the prophet." A paean to all-male camaraderie, loyalty and breeding, *Beau Geste's* code of honour dictates that acts of bravery are to be made light of, if indeed they are to be discussed at all. This attitude had personal resonance for Jimmy given, as we have seen, the near fatal sacrifice of his younger brother, Norman, on a battlefield in France back in 1916. [105]

Originally, the famous opening of the deserted fort manned by dead legionnaire soldiers was to have been preceded by a brief scene in which Major de Beaujolais is awoken in his desert tent, as a report by a dying scout from Fort Zinderneuf comes through. Wisely, this was dropped as it only served to hinder rather than improve the suspenseful opening of the narrative. The staging of the ensuing Arab attack is superbly

Unsung stuntman Joe Rogers standing in for Jimmy as
Major Henri de Beaujolais climbing the wall of Fort Zinderneuf
in William Wellman's rousing *Beau Geste* 1939.
PHOTO COURTESY OF STEPHENSON ARCHIVE

choreographed, and the dramatic hold of the story is helped immeasurably by Alfred Newman's splendid score. Under Wellman's gripping direction this was no slavish copying of the original silent version.

Unlike many films of the era, extensive location shooting took place on the production of *Beau Geste*. Scenes of Brandon Abbey were shot at Busch Gardens in Pasadena, California, a location much used in films of the 1930s such as *Dr. Jekyll and Mr. Hyde* (Paramount, Rouben Mamoulian, 1931) and *Gone with the Wind*. The setting for Fort Zinderneuf was shot in the Yuma Desert, Arizona. Although location shooting provided a marker of authenticity it came at a cost. Overcast light and desert sandstorms combined to complicate and delay the filming process. At the beginning of the picture Major de Beaujolais is seen scaling the wall of the deserted fort. Stuntman Joe Rogers, who appears in long shot, substituted for Jimmy which, given his recurring lumbago and sciatica, must have been of some relief.

As storm clouds began to gather on the diplomatic stage with the international crisis over Czechoslovakia in September 1938, the Warner Brothers gave their own urgent response to the threat of Hitler's Germany. Many were taken in by Hitler's cunning skills of dissembling and his regime's spell-binding use of propaganda, but there were others such as Harry Warner, the elder of the four Brothers, consistently hostile to Hitler's Germany. The studio had first-hand knowledge of the regime's brutality when their Berlin representative, Joe Kaufman, was murdered by Nazi thugs. From 1936 the Warner studios produced a series of Technicolor historical shorts such as: *Sons of Liberty* (Warner, Michael Curtiz, 1939) and *The Monroe Doctrine* (Warner, Crane Wilbur, 1939) to warn of the dangers of European totalitarianism and anti-Semitism. These historical allegories appealed to American solidarity and vigilance and offer fascinating cultural insights into the construction and maintenance of nationhood and national identity.

Sons of Liberty traces the story of Hyam Saloman, American patriot and financier of the American Revolution. Forced to leave his native Poland due to religious persecution, he fled to New York then under control of the British. There he was active in a secret group known as The Sons of Liberty which had been established to oppose British rule. Handsomely produced, this short film benefited from the excellent cinematography of Ray Rennahan fresh from his triumphant work as principal cinematographer on *Gone with the Wind*. *Sons of Liberty* won the 1940 Oscar for best short subject. *The Monroe Doctrine* refers to President James Monroe's foreign policy statement proclaimed on December 2, 1823, warning that the United States would not permit any European intervention in the newly independent states of Latin America. The film traces this doctrine and its application across decades of national crisis, culminating with the rumbustious figure of Theodore Roosevelt. His "speak softly and carry a big stick" speech spelled out the clear message of the United States as a sleeping industrial, political and military giant capable of being roused and willing to defend its independence and integrity against any European sabre rattling.

Although the studio was giving him exposure in varying roles, Jimmy's participation in these short films was hardly an optimum use of his acting talents. In the former, *sans* moustache he is billed sixth playing Colonel Tillman, fighting with Washington in the American Revolutionary War. It is 1781 and Tillman is sent on horseback to bring an urgent dispatch from General Washington to Hyam Saloman. He is found in a Philadelphia synagogue in the middle of sacred worship. Tillman apologises, but insists on presenting the urgent message of appeal for monies of $400,000 to pay Washington's disintegrating army militia, without which the ability to carry on the struggle for independence would be in jeopardy.

In the latter he received second billing in his playing of Signor de La Torre, a deposed governor of a South American province. Wearing a Van Dyke beard and equally artificial moustache and monocle he is paterfamilias to Nanette Fabares, who is in love with John Sturgis [George Reeves] secretary to Henry Clay, Democratic-Republican Speaker of the House of Representatives. Although he cannot conceive of Sturgis as a son-in-law, he encourages affection between the two as Sturgis is a useful source of "insider information" for his political scheming involving European powers in South America. However, much to his chagrin his daughter and Sturgis decide to marry. Behind all these scenarios, lay the notion of war contingencies in the event of an attack on the United States. These shorts were historical representations of contemporary threats posed by spies and saboteurs.

The spy thriller, *Confessions of a Nazi Spy* (Warner, Anatole Litvak, 1939) was based on factual events of a series of spy trials held throughout 1938. Though rightly cited as a landmark film in bringing Nazism to book, it can also be seen more widely as the culmination of a cycle of films produced by the Warner studio that campaigned implicitly against Nazism prior to the United States entering the Second World War in December 1941. Other titles in this series of pictures include: *Black Legion* (Archie Mayo, 1937), *They Won't Forget* (Mervyn LeRoy, 1937), *Juarez* (Anatole Litvak, 1939), and *Sergeant York* (Howard Hawks, 1941). Indeed, the concept of such a film can be traced back even further to *My Four Years in Germany* (William Nigh, 1918), Warner

Bros. first important syndicated feature released shortly after the studio's foundation in 1917. The story recounted the experiences of the American ambassador, James Gerard, in Germany during the period 1913-1917 and was taken from his best-selling book of the same title. Like *My Four Years in Germany*, *Confessions of a Nazi Spy* adopts the format of reconstructed scenes shot in a studio incorporating contemporary newsreel footage. G-man Leon G. Turrou was assigned to the film as a special adviser. Its exposé format is apparent from the beginning. The usual convention of opening credits is suspended and replaced with just a bald title card. A stentorian commentator and newsreel footage are used throughout the film to further underline the urgency of its message. The film's closure is deliberately low-key when, in a diner over coffee, the conversation of two FBI agents about the smashing of a Nazi spy ring is interrupted by strident but commonsensical remarks of a couple of "ordinary" diners in the restaurant. It is the common people in an everyday situation who are deliberately given a presence and a prominent voice in this carefully crafted final scene. The delayed credits finally unfurl to the martial strains of "America the Beautiful." Despite the sterling efforts of all those involved, the film on its original release was not an outstanding box office success in the United States. Isolationism was a prevalent force in the United States at this time and the America First Committee, a pressure group set up in 1940 against American entry into the Second World War, had a high profile membership which included such celebrities as aviator Charles Lindbergh and actress Lillian Gish. Only through subsequent reissues did the film's earnest message translate into box office receipts.

Jimmy appears in two short sequences playing a British military intelligence officer apprehending spies in a Scottish village, or rather a mid-European looking standing set borrowed to suit the particular circumstances of the script. Following the arrest of an unsuspecting villager, he is next seen and heard speaking on the transatlantic telephone reading a captured coded letter to FBI operatives in Washington. He speaks in an English accent, enunciating his vowels in the refined style of John Reith's BBC radio news readers. Hung on the wall directly behind him is a portrait painting of the British sovereign King George, not George VI however, but his father George V. This dates the dramatic action to May 1936 when a Dundee hairdresser, Mrs. Jessie Jordan, was discovered to be relaying messages from German Intelligence to an address in New York City. Convicted of breaching the official secrets act she was gaoled for four years. Jimmy was in fact portraying Guy Liddell, the military intelligence officer involved in the real spy tip-off.

Espionage Agent (Warner, Lloyd Bacon, 1939) was a lower berth variant of *Confessions of a Nazi Spy*. The film began production on May 17, 1939 and finished considerably behind schedule on September 11, 1939. International events in Europe were jumping ahead of the script which was being rewritten day-by-day. Billed sixth on the cast list Jimmy plays Dr. Rader, the leader of a pack of nefarious spies, all wearing conspicuous dark suits with handkerchiefs protruding from their top pockets. Jimmy's make-up provided by Perc Westmore is particularly prominent in emphasising his villainy. He is given a streaked blond hairpiece, an equally false moustache, and, for good measure, his deviancy is made explicit by providing his left facial profile with lacerations. He sneers his way through cliché dialogue on the level of: "We have ways of making people like you talk." He marches into a spy's hideout holding a cane, totes a gun and carries himself with distinction and, in line with cinematic convention of the day, is always tastefully attired and scrupulous in his menace. At the film's climax he suffers a knock-out blow to the head by hero Joel McCrea in a trans-European rail compartment, but he soon regains consciousness and is quickly on the telephone attempting to stop McCrea from escaping the country. Needless to say, his attempts prove futile. There is copious stock footage of the bombing of factories lifted from the original version of *The Dawn Patrol* (Warner, Howard Hawks, 1930), which had already been recycled in the recent 1938 remake of *The Dawn Patrol*.

We Are Not Alone (Warner, Edmund Goulding, 1939) was a prestigious production based on the 1937 novel by famed writer James Hilton, then very much in vogue with his two bestsellers *Lost Horizon* and *Goodbye Mr. Chips*. He also adapted his novel for the screen with screenwriter Milton Krims, and Hilton's profile occupies a prominent position in the film's theatrical trailer. Edmund Goulding was again at the directing helm and Paul Muni starred as an English country doctor, Dr. David Newcombe. Muni's star popularity at Warners, like Al Jolson before him, had begun to slip, and though the studio still continued to support him the film did little to prop up his flagging box office reputation. Though a very worthy effort, it unfortunately happened to be produced and released at the wrong time, and as such it does disappoint. Like *White Banners* it has a pacifist message, with its Austrian heroine, ex-dancer and housekeeper Leni, [Jane Bryan] who becomes embroiled in ugly scenes of vengeance following the announcement of the outbreak of war in 1914. Such depictions of violence were a more noteworthy departure from the usual sentimental fare served up by James Hilton. In fact, incidents of public disorder in English towns during the outbreak of war were widespread, although under-reported at the time. It is known several premises with German names were damaged in the town of Burnley during the early months of the First World War. Whether intentional or not, there are no surviving photographs or little else relating to this film in the Stephenson family archive. The main protagonists, Newcome and Leni, are both condemned to death and such a sombre downbeat ending had repercussions and inevitably the film did not fare well at the box office. Jack Warner referred to the project as unnecessary, both in its downbeat attitude and its huge cost. The film was budgeted at $710,000 and Jimmy received his standard $1,600 salary whilst Paul Muni received a stratospheric $112,500.

Jimmy is eighth billed and appears in three brief scenes as a titled general, Sir William Clintock, in the governor's office playing opposite Montague Love slumped in a wing-backed chair in heavy make-up. He is later on his feet moving room to room smoking a cigar. At an early stage of pre-production he was scheduled for the role of Archdeacon played in the film by British newcomer Alan Napier.

In *Wolf of New York* (Republic, William McGann, 1940) Jimmy is third billed as Hiriam Rogers, a crooked investment broker who poses ostensibly as an upright pillar of society. This, his second loan out, was to Republic Studios. Unlike the veneer of continental sophistication offered by Paramount studios, Republic was renowned for specialising in low budget genre films predominantly B westerns; the studio became identified with screen cowboys Gene Autry and Roy Rogers, and film serials with their cliché cliff-hanger endings. In the film, Jimmy takes on another sedentary role, exchanging his desk on Warner Bros. sets for another studio desk, and goes through the motions of shuffling paper and issuing deviant orders with specious calm. He is the very acumen of suave self-assurance, and the plot is built around the 'Wolf' in sheep's clothing and his denouement as the brains behind a crooked bond-selling ring. Titular star Edmund Lowe as cynical lawyer Christopher Faulkner, succeeds in routing out Rogers's criminal racketeering. There are standard car chases and gun shoot-ups, but even with a fairly competent cast (Rose Hobart, Jerome Cowan, reteamed with Jimmy again after their previous encounter on *The Old Maid*, William Demarest, Charles D. Brown, Edward Gargan, Andrew Tombes and Ben Welden) this is routine fare. In England, this film was shown on a double bill with the comedy *My Little Chickadee* at the Odeon Leicester Square, London during May 1940. [106]

The Private Lives of Elizabeth and Essex (Warner, Michael Curtiz, 1939) was a prestigious exercise designed to showcase two major Warner studio stars, Errol Flynn and Bette Davis, and to tap into the success of *The Adventures of Robin Hood*. Flynn and Davis had already been teamed in *The Sisters*, an attempt to cash in on the success of *San Francisco* (M-G-M, W.S. Van Dyke, 1936) starring Clark Gable and Jeanette McDonald. The film was based on a Maxwell Anderson play, *Elizabeth the Queen*, with Lynn Fontanne and Alfred Lunt which had played on Broadway for 146 performances during the early 1930s. Yet despite Sol Polito's pleasing Technicolor photography, Erich Wolfgang Korngold's stirring score and all round effort from a sterling cast, the film lacks pace, is often pedestrian and refuses to respond to any cinematic finesse with the result its theatrical origins are apparent throughout. Too much time is spent on court intrigue, and too little devoted to outdoor action sequences. The scenes of battle set in Ireland are disappointingly stage-bound.

Davis made it known she wanted Laurence Olivier for the role of Essex and did not conceal her disappointment when Flynn was cast instead. As a consequence, Flynn and Davis seem ill at ease in their dramatic and romantic scenes together, and display little spontaneity.

In the minor role of Sir Thomas Egerton, Jimmy appears several times on screen, usually in an ensemble of courtiers paying homage to Queen Elizabeth, but often without uttering a single line of dialogue. At one stage the studio had considered him for the key role of Francis Bacon. Unfortunately, he was yet again passed over and the part was played, with unintentional pun, by Donald Crisp. In the middle of production, Errol Flynn was reported as turning up at the studio some thirty-five minutes late. In the context of a big budget Technicolor film this type of behaviour was costing the studio dearly, and for Flynn's fellow actors, stood around waiting on set in full costume with no air conditioning, under the harsh glare and humidity of strong studio lighting demanded by the processes of early Technicolor, such misconduct was considered bad form and very unprofessional. Davis in particular, a stickler for thorough preparation and a consummate professional, took a decidedly dim view of this sort of misbehaviour. Though the film was a top grosser of its day the two stars, save for incidental star cameos in separate musical numbers in the wartime musical *Thank Your Lucky Stars* (Warner, David Butler, 1943), were never reunited on screen again.

Warner Bros. mounted a prestigious, rousing and highly entertaining piece of cinematic swashbuckling in *The Sea Hawk* (Warner, Michael Curtiz, 1940). On prominent display in the film was the studio's newly acquired studio tank, installed as part of capital investment on the back of the studio's success of *The Adventures of Robin Hood*. Errol Flynn stepped into the lead playing Captain Geoffrey Thorpe in Howard Koch's adaptation of a former studio success. Rafael Sabatini's *The Sea Hawk* had been first filmed in 1924 by the studio and starred Milton Sills and was directed by Frank Lloyd. There is a shift in emphasis in the telling of this tale of piratical adventures on the high seas. With war clouds ranging over Europe, Howard Koch's screenplay is a thinly disguised attempt to draw parallels with the contemporary situation of a Europe under German domination with sixteenth century Spain standing in the place of Germany. Indeed, the stirring final speech delivered by Elizabeth I [Flora Robson] at Tilbury Docks bears comparison to the drum-rolling oratory of Winston Churchill's wartime speeches. As Jimmy stood in the background with other anglophiles in the cast listening to this speech it is not inconceivable that subconsciously his thoughts might have turned to his family and friends back in Britain undergoing privation and adversity during those testing times as the country sought to rebuff the Nazi aggressor.

Surviving studio memos again complain of Flynn's lateness and not knowing his lines. Unlike his chilly relationship with Bette Davis, Flynn's relationship with co-star Flora Robson was based on mutual respect. Because Robson was committed to appear in a Broadway production of *Ladies in Retirement* her scenes were shot immediately. When Flynn kept fluffing his lines she explained this would delay her trip out to New York. From that moment he ensured he was word perfect, and she was able to fulfil her commitment on time. Although Jimmy was eighth billed in the small role of Abbott, he had been considered for the substantial role of Lord Wolfingham, but lost out to the more established actor, Henry Daniell. [107]

One of the film's many highlights is the climatic sword duel that deploys panache of action along with brilliant costumes and stylised sets lit with chiaroscuro lighting, all peerlessly photographed by Sol Polito. In taking on the role, Daniell was certainly the epitome of a sneering villain and delivered his lines in a sardonic manner befitting the role. However, there was one major drawback. He could hardly hold a sword, much less adequately feign prowess as a sword-fencer. It is a tribute to the skill of editing in the capable hands of George Amy and dexterity of master swordsman Fred Cavens (who choreographed the whole sequence) that the lengthy duel comes off with such aplomb. The long shots (using stand-in doubles Don Turner for Flynn and a combination of Ned Davenport and Ralph Faulkner for Daniell) are deftly integrated into close-up shots of the principal actors. On seeing the final cut, and being aware of the problems confronting the production team, one cannot but be full of admiration and wonder at the expertise and dedication that went into such a scene. If there is a need to point out the abilities of the old Hollywood studio system to pull incredible rabbits from implausible hats, then this surely is a case in point. It certainly wins the day, whereas contemporary Hollywood prefers the bankable option of computer generated imagery to parade its special effects. However, used too often digital manipulation is at best uninspired, and at worse it demeans the imagination and curiosity of the audience.

When Paul Muni decided not to renew his contract and left the Warner studio, Edward G. Robinson stepped forward to carry on the studio's tradition of historical biographical pictures. *A Dispatch from Reuter's* also known as *The Man from Reuter* (Warner, William Dieterle, 1940) tells the story of nineteenth-century entrepreneur Paul Julius Reuter who, with perseverance and determination, managed to build an international news agency renowned for speed and accuracy. Jimmy's character, Carew special courier of the London Times, is a distinguished gent who appears in a few brief scenes at the start of the film. Jimmy is accoutred in suitable Regency dress purloined from the wardrobe of a concurrent Bette Davis vehicle *All This and Heaven Too* (Warner, Anatole Litvak, 1940) which was set in 1840s France. Studio make-up artist, Perc Westmore provided him with false sideburns to emulate the look of a dashing dandy. In the film he is without moustache and his facial makeup is rudimentary, a natural mole on the side of his left temple is visible on screen. The first scene where Carew arrives by coach was shot on a standing set used in *Tovarich* (Warner, Anatole Litvak, 1937). It is all done with the expedient efficiency that came with the resources of the studio system operating at full capacity.

South of Suez (Warner, Lewis Seiler, 1940) is a preposterous, albeit watchable, pot-boiler with shifting melodramatic affiliations. It utilises standing sets, including those used in *The Letter* and even a refugee from *The Sea Hawk*, in the form of Errol Flynn's pet monkey, turns up in comic support. Among the British contingent of the cast, Jimmy is given the subsidiary role of Inspector Thornton of Scotland Yard and was fourth billed. Yet again, he sat at a desk in an office during three cursory scenes shot on October 3, 1940. The film gives far more opportunities for character players such as George Tobias and Lee Patrick than the nominal leads George Brent and Brenda Marshall who are somewhat plain and unappealing. Brent's part had originally been offered to George Raft, who rejected the story and turned down the role. This meant the script had to be considerably altered. The story begins in the African Colony of Tanganyika, with unexpected pre-credits action as a native from a diamond mine attempts to escape, but is gunned down. The credits then unfurl to the accompaniment of native choral chants composed by Frederick Hollander and orchestrated by Leo Forbstein. George Tobias plays villainous mine owner Eli Snedeker, who bears a passing resemblance to Albert Dekker's Dr. Alexander Thorkel in *Dr. Cyclops* (Paramount, Ernest B. Schoedsack, 1940). Snedeker is resentful of ex-foreman John Gamble [George Brent], for not only did he stop him from taking over the mine from its kindly but drunken owner Roger Smythe, but his wife [Lee Patrick] harbours affections for Gamble as well. When Smythe is killed by Snedeker the crime is blamed on Gamble. Fleeing Africa to England, Gamble adopts a new identity and begins a fresh start. Meanwhile, he meets and falls in love with Smythe's daughter Katherine who harbours hatred for John Gamble, the man she believed killed her father. At the film's climax, there takes place a trial where the truth is revealed and justice of a contrived kind is meted out.

River's End (Warner, Ray Enright, 1940) was a remake of an earlier 1930 version directed by Michael Curtiz and starred Charles Bickford and Evelyn Knapp. Dennis Morgan and Elizabeth Earl were cast as the main leads in the remake, and Jimmy took over the role of Inspector McDowell previously taken by David Torrence. Billed fifth on the cast list, he is yet again a figure of authority sitting in an office behind a desk. This time without moustache, he is later seen enjoying himself dancing at a square dance. As in *Heart of the North* his final act before the closure of the narrative is to present a citation that acknowledges injustice. Photographed in black and white, this "Mountie Western" proved a sturdy if predictable crowd-pleaser. Singer Dennis Morgan played both the fugitive from justice and the Mountie in pursuit who takes his place when he dies. Though in a straight dramatic role, he manages to sing a few melodic bars. Impressive second unit exteriors shot at Huntington Lake, Fresno County, California are used to good effect, particularly during the obligatory climatic chase. In medium close-up with studio back projection Dennis Morgan grapples with the arch villain, the prolific and dependable Victor Jory, while stunt doubles are visible in long shot location exteriors. Film montages are used extensively to facilitate changes of locale, indicate the travel of distance taken by the pursued and pursuer, and provide segue into studio interiors. Amongst the cast was Stuart Robertson, older brother of British actress Anna Neagle, who as a baritone singer had appeared on the concert platform in Jimmy's home town of Burnley back in 1928. Elizabeth Earl had come to Hollywood from England, where during the late 1930s she had appeared for a few seasons on stage at Jimmy's old alma mater The Liverpool Playhouse. The shooting schedule, like the film proceeded at a rapid pace. Jimmy in particular had a great deal on his mind, and was anxious to complete the job on time as Lorna was heavily pregnant. On May 16, 1940 Lorna gave birth to a son, Peter Stansfield Stephenson, at the Good Samaritan Hospital, 1225 Wiltshire Boulevard, Los Angeles. The proud parents with their new baby were caught on camera by a studio photographer at the hospital maternity ward. In tandem with this

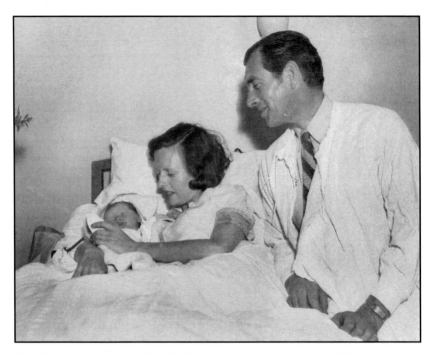

Proud parents Lorna and Jim Stephenson celebrate the arrival of their new baby.
PHOTO COURTESY OF STEPHENSON ARCHIVE

momentous event, Jimmy was also busy preparing for what would prove to be the performance of his acting career.

The Letter, in its various incarnations, has a long and interesting history. William Somerset Maugham's "The Letter" first appeared in magazine form in *Hearst's International* in April 1924. The story was later published in *The Casuarina Tree*, an anthology of seven short tales, in 1926. In these stories, Maugham probed the identity of the English colonial expatriate in remote Malay outposts of empire caught in circumstances of adultery, class division, racial difference and social hypocrisy. At the core of these stories lies the tension between overt calm composure and emotional control and inner concealed torrid desire and passionate sensuality.

"The Letter" was inspired by a real life *cause célèbre*. During the early 1920s, on his travels in the Malay States, Maugham was given an account of an earlier incident in Kuala Lumpur while staying with Mr. and Mrs. Courtney Dickinson. Dickinson was a well-known Singapore attorney and his wife a prominent society hostess. The story involved the shooting of Mr. William Crozier Steward, a manager of the Salak South tin mines, by Mrs. Ethel Mabel Proudlock, wife of Mr. William Proudlock acting headmaster of the Victoria Institution, Kuala Lumpur, on April 28, 1911.

In her subsequent trial beginning on June 7, 1911, and presided over by Mr. Justice Sercombe Smith, Mrs. Proudlock said she acted in self-defence and, to resist outrage, shot Steward with a Webley revolver six times on the veranda of her home. Contemporary news reports of the trial demonstrate that all the elements necessary for Maugham's tale were ready to hand:

"After dinner, [Mrs. Proudlock] was finishing a letter about nine o'clock, when she saw Steward getting out of a rickshaw. He enquired for Mr. Proudlock, and she told him her husband was dining out. Steward then told his rikisha to wait some distance off and she asked Steward to allow the coolie to wait there because of the rain. Steward said it was not nice to hear the coolie spitting, so he sent the man away. Steward came on to the veranda. During the conversation Mrs. Proudlock rose to get a book. Steward also got up and put his arm around her and told her he loved her, and said "let me have you." Steward turned out the light and put his hand up Mrs. Proudlock's clothes. Mrs. Proudlock struggled and reached towards the switch. Steward seized her hand which came in contact with the revolver and she seized it. Steward tried to put her down. She was frightened and feeling sick she fired once, but remembered two reports. She remembered stumbling and nothing more, till she came to herself again on the veranda. Then she went out to call the boy, and then saw the revolver in her hand and threw it down." [108]

"In cross examination defending counsel, Mr. Pooley, called upon Dr. Cooper to explain why he based his opinion on the assumption the assailant was in front of the woman. The range would have been one to twelve inches. He repeated his opinion that the wounds upon the deceased could not have been caused by a person struggling their hardest to resist an attempt at rape. The rickshaw coolie spoke of taking a man to the Proudlocks' house on the night of April 23. The tuan entered the veranda and the witness went off thirty or forty paces and sat with his back to the house. Ten minutes afterwards, he heard "pop-pop-pop" and looking round he saw that the veranda was dark. The tuan came out running towards the rickshaw, accused running behind. When witness first saw the accused, she was running down the step. The tuan was halfway to the rickshaw. The tuan fell near the rickshaw, accused being two or three paces from him. She walked up and stood by tuan, witness being still there." [109]

Mr. A.E. Mace, miner of Kuala Lumpor, said he was an intimate friend of Steward. They lived together at Salak South for eighteen months.

Cross-examined, Mr. Mace stated Steward drank very moderately and had never seen him under the influence of drink. He had kept a Chinese woman about three months before he died. Witness stressed Steward was a temperate man and had generally accepted standards of morals.

The counsel asked the Court to find that the accused, as a consequence of shock, lost all power, not only of self control, but of knowledge of what she was doing. On that point there would be medical evidence showing that the accused was an emotional hysterical woman and that the effect of shock might result in the loss of knowledge; loss of consciousness was not absolutely the same thing as absolute fainting.

On June 15, 1911 the jury returned a verdict of guilty. Though she was sentenced to death, the jury gave a recommendation for mercy. Mrs. Proudlock wrote a letter petitioning the Sultan of Selangor in which she protested her innocence and her inability to bear the horror and suspense of her situation and the prospects of yet another trial. This direct appeal, accompanied by separate overlapping petitions for a pardon including one signed by "220 Europeans," rescuing their own, and another signed by "over 500 Asiatics" was followed by a cable signed by "the women of Kuala Lumpur requesting Queen Mary to pardon Mrs. Proudlock in view of the Coronation." [110] Leading firms in the district also placed petitions on display for signatures. All this activity was successful in her being granted a free pardon on July 10, 1911.

The twists and turns of the documented crime and subsequent trial fascinated Maugham and he constructed a short story making cursory changes: using fictitious names, placing the action in a modern setting and changing the location of both crime and trial.

Set in the Malay Archipelago Maugham's story begins in the office of lawyer Mr. Joyce (his appellation in the story remains formal throughout). Though the writing style of the story is crisp and suspenseful the shooting is only reported and therefore the plot lacks the melodramatic opening and the equally famous confessional finale for which the stage and film versions would gain their lasting fame. The attitudes and views expressed on race are faithful to the era in which the story is set, but the language and opinions, in the context of twenty-first century post-colonial and multicultural sensibilities, are untenable and deeply suspect.

In 1927 "The Letter" was successfully adapted as a play by Maugham for the London stage. Directed by Gerald du Maurier, *The Letter* made its West End debut on February 24, 1927. The production ran for 338 performances at the London Playhouse Theatre, plus another 150 on the post London tour. Gladys Cooper appeared as Leslie Crosbie,

Nigel Bruce as Robert Crosbie, S[tanley]. J. Warmington as Geoffrey Hammond, James Raglan as John Withers and Leslie Faber played Howard Joyce. [111] During its tour of the provinces the play came to Burnley during February 1929. [112]

Gladys Cooper (1888-1971), an actress whose radiant beauty as a Gaiety Girl had made her a pin-up during the First World War, was among the first performers to go over to France to entertain the British troops. She also accepted a lucrative offer to lend her name to endorsements of beauty products. So successful were these creams, shampoos and rouges that they were stocked at many chemists throughout England. Unlike her contemporaries Sybil Thorndike and Edith Evans, Gladys (or G. as she preferred to be called) had carved out a stage career in the inter-war years, not by giving interpretations of the classical theatrical repertoire, but by starring in a stream of commercial theatrical successes in tandem with spells as a theatrical producer. She had been managing the Playhouse following the illness and death of theatre manager Frank Curzon. This provided a unique opportunity for her to exploit commercially attractive plays with popular appeal. No playwright of the era was more commercial than Maugham who supplied her with several adapted stage versions of his stories beginning with *Home and Beauty* in 1919. Over the next ten years Gladys appeared in three other Maugham plays (including *The Letter*, *The Sacred Flame* and *The Painted Veil*) and came to represent the perfect composed Maugham leading lady.

A Broadway production of *The Letter* was produced by Messmore Kendall at the Morosco Theatre with Katherine Cornell and J.W. Austin playing the leads. Allan Jeayes played Howard Joyce. The play ran 104 performances from September to December 1927.

As several of Maugham's stories had already been successfully adapted for the screen and proven to be popular box office, it was predictable that Hollywood would buy the story. Paramount studios purchased the rights to the story and play on February 28, 1928 and *The Letter* was shot at their small Astoria studio in Queens, New York during November and December 1928. It was, in fact, the first all-talking feature to be made in New York. In the lead role starred Jeanne Eagels who had already played another Maugham heroine, Sadie Thompson, in an acclaimed Broadway production of *Rain* running during 1922, and revived again in 1924-26. Reginald Owen played her husband, the role of the lover was taken by Herbert Marshall in his first American film, and Australian actor, Oliver Peters Heggie, played the part of Joyce, the lawyer. [113] French director Jean de Limur, with the un-credited assistance of supervising producer Monta Bell, created a moody oriental atmosphere. The camera is surprisingly mobile, at a time when the stasis of early sound technology dictated a glut of photographed plays, whose substance was restricted to insipid dialogue and stilted acting. [114] Not only was the film above the usual technical benchmark of the time, but its content proved controversial in the light of the later reinforced 1934 Hollywood production code. The lover, Geoffrey Hammond, unlike the stage adaptation or the later Wyler film version, is on screen for a considerable period of time and Hammond's Chinese mistress Li-Ti appears alongside him in the film.

In contrast to the Wyler version, there is an explicit scene where Leslie Crosbie, alone, visits Hammond's mistress, a madam at a local brothel. Her precarious descent down a flight of dark labyrinthine stairs has the feeling of a Gustave Doré engraving of Dante's Vision of Hell. Once inside, she witnesses a brutal Darwinian fight between two animals: a snake and a mongoose, in which the snake triumphs. When she delivers the ten thousand dollars to her former lover's mistress in exchange for the incriminating letter, she is degraded by being forced to retrieve the letter from the floor at the feet of a native Chinese woman. Her humiliation is complete when a group of prostitutes look on, laughing in derision at the spectacle of a colonial European reduced to such abject ignominy. This is a riposte to an earlier racially insensitive remark uttered by her lawyer, Mr. Joyce. Actor O.P. Heggie provides the character of Joyce with plenty of professional gravitas, but there is a conspicuous absence of any sense of inner turmoil that Jimmy Stephenson would later bring to the role.

Apart from *The Letter* there are curious parallels in the professional acting careers of Jeanne Eagels and Bette Davis. After her appearance in *The Letter,* Eagels was reunited with director Jean de Limur in her next, and what turned out to be her final film, she died of a drug overdose, *Jealousy* (Paramount, 1929). Based on a Broadway property, the story was later picked up by Warner Bros. and resurfaced under the title of *Deception* (Warner, Irving Rapper, 1946) as a vehicle for Davis. Further back in Davis's career *The Girl from 10ᵗʰ Avenue* (Warner, Alfred E. Green, 1935) was a remake of the *The World and the Woman* (Pathe, Frank Lloyd, 1916) in which Eagels took the lead. Davis's second Oscar winning role as a broken down actress, Joyce Heath, in *Dangerous* (Warner, Alfred E. Green, 1935) is said to be taken from Eagels own tragic life. Eagels, like Davis was given her career break by George Arliss, who requested her to appear opposite him in three Broadway revivals. *The Professor's Love Story*; *Disraeli;* and *Hamilton* were all performed consecutively during 1917 at the Knickerbocker Theatre. Doubtless Arliss saw similar potential in both young actresses. On the strength of this evidence it appears whether by accident or intent Davis went on to use Eagels as a touchstone throughout her subsequent career. In *The Letter* Jeanne Eagels enunciates her lines in a clipped mid-Atlantic accent reminiscent of that famous exponent of the American stage of the 1920s, Tallulah Bankhead.

Some ten years later Warner Bros. were searching for suitable film properties which would celebrate and exploit their latest top female star. Director Edmund Goulding thought Maugham's story ideal material for Bette Davis. The studio set about purchasing the rights of *The Letter* from Paramount for a negotiated $25,000. Others who expressed interest in acquiring this property included David Selznick and Samuel Goldwyn. The executive handling the purchase of the story warned all interested parties that censorship issues arising from the material would be a major obstacle. In a memo dated 1938 chief censor, Joseph L. Breen cautioned the studio on negative reactions from the British Board of Film Censors in Britain. There were three main objections. Firstly, the story revolved around adultery and lacked a suitable morally retributive punishment. Secondly, not only is a murder committed and goes unpunished, but it brings about a perversion of justice. Finally, as Leslie's lover keeps a Chinese mistress there were questions of miscegenation. Selznick International Pictures sent the British Board of Film Censors a scenario for *The Letter* in June 1939 and the reaction was, as predicted, doubtful in the extreme. [115]

Despite these obstacles, on May 23, 1938 Merle Oberon, Walter Huston, Ralph Forbes and Eric Snowden took part in a radio broadcast of *The Letter* on the popular long-running *Lux Radio Theatre,* a classic radio anthology series. The favourable reaction to this adaptation was proof the story was fundamentally sound, and would deliver a commercial success for the Warner studio if handled appropriately.

Bette Davis had begun her film career rather unpromisingly as an ingénue at Universal studios in the early 1930s. She was not considered anything special and after six pictures her contract was not renewed. As already indicated, the celebrated English actor George Arliss personally requested Davis should appear in his forthcoming picture *The Man Who Played God* also known as *The Silent Voice* (Warner, John G. Adolfi, 1932). He had met her previously as a guest lecturer at a drama school in New York. On the strength of her performance opposite Arliss, Warner Brothers signed her for a five year contract. After scores of routine and undistinguished films she gained her first big success in a loan out to RKO studios for the Somerset Maugham story *Of Human Bondage* (John Cromwell, 1934) in which she excelled as the shrewish slatternly Mildred Rogers. This was followed by her first best actress academy award performance playing in *Dangerous*. Still dissatisfied with the quality of the material she was being assigned by the studio, Davis baulked and travelled to England to try to have her contract with the studio annulled in the English courts. Despite losing her case she returned to the studio and was given better scripts. Davis made it known she wanted the coveted role of Scarlet O'Hara in *Gone with the Wind*. Though considered unsuitable by producer David Selznick, Warner Bros. by way of compensation produced *Jezebel*. The story of a head-strong southern belle, Julia Marsden, who shocks convention by appearing at the Olympus Ball in a brazen red dress marked Davis's first appearance under the direction of William Wyler on loan from Samuel Goldwyn. Although Davis and Wyler had both worked at Universal Studios earlier in their careers their paths had crossed only briefly. The Davis Wyler collaboration would yield a total of three unforgettable films: *Jezebel, The Letter* and *The Little Foxes* (Samuel Goldwyn, 1941).

The production of *Jezebel* was fraught with tension and significant delay. Although studio publicity sought to represent Warner Brothers as socially progressive and responsible in its corporate governance, ("Good films mean good citizenship" was prominently displayed on a bill board near the studio gates), within the walls of the studio the credo of "Time is money" was deemed infallible and applied rigorously in the pursuit of profit. Wyler's perfectionism and extreme care to make a story "play" was often at odds with the Warner orthodoxy of speed, recycling and penny-pinching. Despite the undoubted skill and polish Wyler put into his film-making, Warner Bros. were most concerned about his tendency to go over the agreed budget and production schedule. His meticulous execution began to slow down the rate of progress on the production of *Jezebel*, and in the film business this represented unproductive cost. When the filming finally finished on January 17, 1938 it was twenty-eight days over the agreed forty-two days shooting schedule, and the budget had inflated from $783,000 to $1,073,000. Nevertheless, *Jezebel* was a big box office success and accrued critical kudos, winning three academy awards including providing Davis with her second Oscar. Wyler and Davis collaborated closely in their work on screen, and this also extended to a tempestuous off screen relationship.

Director William Wyler was born in 1902 in Mulhouse, originally a French speaking region of Alsace-Lorraine; then, following the Franco-Prussian War, was under the control of the German Empire. Wyler's German mother was a cousin of movie mogul Carl Laemmle of Universal Studios in California. She had written to her uncle in desperation as young Willy, as he was known, had developed into something of a youthful tear-away. Wyler was offered passage to America with Paul Kohner in 1920 where he obtained a job at Universal's New York offices as a messenger boy. He then moved to the west coast and began his career at Universal Studios as a film cutter. He then started at the bottom of the directorial ladder cranking out two reel silent westerns. Combative and ambitious he then progressed to full dramatic features. One of Wyler's earliest surviving silent dramas *The Shakedown* (Universal, 1929) has all the hallmarks of his later prestigious film's; great dramatic detail, riveting camerawork, superb editing, a capable cast and a sense of empathy and uplift. It bears similarities in plotline to *The Champ* (M-G-M, King Vidor, 1931) and *The Kid* (First National, Charles Chaplin, 1921) in its story of an itinerant boxer [James Murray] on the make, who is redeemed by a small-town girl [Barbara Kent] and spunky urchin [Jack Hanlon]. Wyler even appears on screen, à la Hitchcock, in a brief cameo as a boxing referee. [116] Wyler's breakthrough came with his direction of *Counsellor at Law* in 1933. The Elmer Rice play was graced by fabled star John Barrymore who was beginning his decline into alcoholism. This caused the director, cast and crew innumerable problems and led to the production slowing down and overrunning its shooting schedule and budget.

This then is the background prior to what would become the definitive filming of the Maugham story. Originally Edmund Goulding had been considered for direction of *The Letter* which, given his previous assistance in Jimmy Stephenson's Hollywood career, was no bad thing. However, producer Robert Lord found Goulding's thoughts on the Maugham play too "radical." In any case, Goulding became ill with pneumonia and was taken off the project.

William Wyler, having refused the offer of directing Ginger Rogers in *Kitty Foyle* over at RKO, was able to negotiate a loan out to Warner Bros. from Sam Goldwyn when he learned that Davis was to be cast in the Maugham story. At the Goldwyn Studios, Wyler had produced several prestige films dealing with, for their time controversial social themes. These included: *These Three* (1936) (a love triangle); *Dodsworth* (1936) (adultery); and *Dead End* (1937) (delinquency). It was an ideal track record to approach Maugham's torrid tale and he did so with relish.

By the time *The Letter* was offered to him Wyler's relationship with Davis was over. However, there remained mutual respect between the two, although with such high-powered personalities, both arguably at the peak of their careers, there were bound to be occasions when sparks flew. During filming there were arguments between director and star over artistic differences and approaches to creative interpretation. At one point Davis called in sick for a few days. [117]

Wyler came to the project with his formidable reputation for meticulous detail and perfection unsullied. He would again, as in *Jezebel*, attempt to push to the very edge all the technical capabilities of studio film-making to make the story play, but in a tempo and manner all his own using long tracking shots, deep focus, low key expressionistic set-ups which were all expensive and difficult to justify to the cost conscious studio. Wyler was also unafraid of taking risks in shooting set-ups where the lead players are often positioned with their backs to the camera at crucial moments in the film.

Like Hitchcock, he was insistent on long script conferences and with the various writers assigned to a particular film he functioned as script doctor. In this instance, the highly capable Howard Koch managed to incorporate the visual suggestions offered by Wyler into the script, and also convey Maugham's original conception of the material in an exceptionally intelligent and suspenseful screenplay. [118] Koch provided numerous changes to several of the characters. The middle-age matron in the visitor's room at the jail is changed from Mrs. Parker to Mrs. Cooper. Together with producer Robert Lord, Koch also placated the censor's objections by changing Geoff Hammond's Chinese mistress to an Eurasian wife. At the film's end Hammond's widow would kill her husband's murderess, but censorship also demanded that this homicide should be punished too. This involved the incongruous appearance of a police official who, torchlight in hand, apprehends both Mrs. Hammond and her accomplice just around the corner from the murder scene. Looking suitably chastened, the transgressors are led away by the long arm of the law.

Wyler also preferred meticulous rehearsals, and he was able to extract a concession of two days rehearsals. Jimmy with other cast members gave over twelve hours of arduous blocking and line readings during May 24 and 25 before shooting began on May 27, 1940. Wyler was allowed to bring along his script girl, Freda Rosenblatt, but on the understanding that her high salary (by Warner's standards) would be paid only if Wyler made up the difference from his own pocket; the studio being unwilling to make good the difference.

Wyler's request to use top cameraman Gregg Toland was refused. Instead, studio cinematographer Tony Gaudio was pressed into service to deliver the exceptional chiaroscuro lighting and expressionistic shadows Wyler demanded. Gaudio's superior photography is the overlay for a simulated Singapore rubber plantation, colonial bungalow, English club and courtroom etc. All these settings were quickly constructed either on bare studio sound stages or improvised from existing sets on the Burbank back-lot. The impeccable art

In this scene from *The Letter* Leslie Crosbie (Bette Davis),
her lawyer (James Stephenson) with guide Ong Chi Seng (Sen Yung)
travel to Chinatown to retrieve the incriminating letter in the possession
of the widow of the deceased. There they encounter
a local resident (Willie Fung) casually inhaling an illegal substance.
PHOTO COURTESY OF STEPHENSON ARCHIVE

direction was supervised by resourceful veteran Carl Jules Weyl.

Weyl conjured up a stereotypical Chinatown underworld complete with illicit opium den for a highly charged scene where Leslie Crosbie and her lawyer go to Chinatown to exchange the $10,000 for the incriminating letter supplied through Hammond's Eurasian wife. In phlegmatic style the lawyer ignores a native smoking opium, and remarks instead on the fetid atmosphere, requesting the opening of a window to let air circulate in the room. This sets the scene for the second dramatic appearance of Mrs. Hammond from behind bamboo streamers, silent and statuesque with a piercing stare from "eyes like a cobra's," preceded by the tinkling sound of wind chimes on the soundtrack. This memorable sequence is something of a throwback to the high stylisation of late silent cinema, in the mould of the renowned partnership of director Josef von Sternberg and cinematographer Lee Garmes. It is the equal of *The Shanghai Gesture* (United Artists, 1941), von Sternberg's eccentric revisiting of outlandish exotic melodrama.

The use of cinematic framing in the film is outstanding. Characters are displayed on camera in a style that emphasises not only their height and physique relative to one another as unequal, but also displays the disparity of their social status and power based on tenets of class, gender and race.

The shifting concept of social authority in the film with its dominant and subordinate characteristics is shown in the character of Mrs. Hammond. The casting of a European rather than an Asian actress, such as the Chinese-American Anna May Wong, in the role of Hammond's wife would have given a different interpretation to the character from the standard depiction of a creature seen as evil and threatening, the stereotypical "Dragon Lady," to one of a noble and dignified woman mired in circumstances not of her making. The role was played by Danish-American actress Gale Sondergaard, the first actress to win an Oscar for best supporting actress in *Anthony Adverse* (Warner, Mervyn LeRoy, 1936). Sondergaard recalled collaborating with Wyler to offer a different interpretation of the character from that envisaged in the original script. She considered the character's original wardrobe demeaning. Instead, with Wyler's agreement, she was able to change the costumes to bring some semblance of dignity and honour to the character: "We began to design some gorgeous fashions, gave her dignity – which made the picture so much more interesting." [119] Despite this attempt to break away from stereotypical connotations of sly deceitfulness, there is a tendency to undercut Sondergaard's playing of the character by the overuse of dramatic staged entrances and exits in the film. Such devices convey exotic otherness and denial, suggestive of misogyny and miscegenation.

The film has early noir credentials due in part to its stylised approach to lighting, décor and framing. Symbols of Leslie Crosbie's guilt are everywhere in the film's *mise-en-scène* blinds in the bungalow, bars in the prison, and stripes on chair covers and emblazoned on dress patterns. This was a deliberate attempt to emulate effects such as Nathaniel Hawthorne's use of the symbolic letter A in the novel *The Scarlet Letter*. Leslie Crosbie possesses all the hallmarks of the later femme fatale: a strong female protagonist who brings destruction on the dominant patriarchal order and pays the ultimate price (a violent death) for her transgression. Her final doom-laden walk in the garden as she walks inexorably towards her death is indicative of her predestined fate.

Critic Philip Jenkinson cited *The Letter* as: "a fine example of Warner Bros. know-how at its peak." [120] Whilst the film has the look and feel of a typical Warner production of the studio era, on closer examination the description fails to account for the hybrid nature of its execution and style.

The film owes its suspense to the economy driven pace of the Warner house-style just as much as to Wyler's characteristically taut control and understanding in adapting a literary property. There is less material to go awry in translating a short story to the screen than is the case in realising a lengthy novel. Though the dialogue is often solemn and risible, such as when Leslie Crosbie's killing is compared with the shooting of "a mad dog," it is made to appear earnest and credible through the interpretation of skilled actors, and a director sensitively attuned to the material in Maugham's short story.

From the outset Wyler stamps his authority on the film by devising a scintillating opening that interrelated mood and character instantaneously in purely cinematic terms. Behind the opening credits tropical trees point diagonally upwards and cast their shadows over a moon-lit sky. As the credits progress, a colonial bungalow and garden are glimpsed in the background, locations where key moments of drama will unfold. There follows an optical camera wipe to signage declaring: "L. Rubber Co. Singapore Plantation No. 1." Another optical wipe and the camera pans, ever so furtively, at ground level to soak in the sight and sound of latex tapped from a rubber tree. Nearby, in segregated quarters, native workers rest, many suspended in their hammocks asleep, while a few indigenous musicians play an incantatory dirge. Wyler here primes the audience responses by presenting information in one shot that leads and ties into the next shot. This introductory scene setting reveals a world where everything has been assigned a particular place in the social order. This social arrangement is about to be shattered forever by the sound of shots - six bullets are fired into Leslie Crosbie's lover. To shoot a man once may be considered as a mistake, to shoot him twice may be considered carelessness, but six shots is pure homicide.

The deployment of thirty-five extras and five dogs woken from sleep plus a cockatoo flying off in fright adds to the dramatic impact of the suspense. Unsurprisingly, given the complex set-up, it took fourteen takes before Wyler gave the okay. Shot in a studio-controlled environment the audience is immediately plunged into an exotic Far Eastern locale deliberately stylised to emphasise melodramatic situations, in preference to plain realism. It is one of the defining moments of classical Hollywood cinema by virtue of its cinematic élan, its meticulous planning and fluidity of execution. It sets the tone for the ensuing drama, for Wyler manages to imbue a stage play with many scenes devoid of dialogue using instead the pure essence of cinema; light, shadow and movement to convey character and atmosphere.

The studio was well versed in staging similar foreign backdrops.

One Way Passage (Warner, Tay Garnett, 1932), for instance, begins in a studio recreation of a Hong Kong saloon bar, and in its own brief manner succeeds in generating just as much atmosphere as the opening of Wyler's *The Letter*. However, unlike the Wyler film the dramatic action is presented using the preferred studio convention of unifying, connective editing, ensuring each scene segued swiftly and securely together to maximise dramatic impact and narrative progression. Producer Hal B. Wallis understood Wyler's aim of transforming a stage property into something unmistakably cinematic, but he was still critical of the picture's tempo and chided Wyler on being too slow and laboured. [121]

Trying to sustain this level of technical proficiency was always going to be difficult. Just how difficult became apparent during the filming of the interrogation scenes when the lawyer presents the compromising letter to his client in jail. Wyler tried using long continuous takes when shooting these lengthy dialogue scenes, but found pivotal moments in the unfolding of the drama required the insertion of reaction shots of the two principals. These were edited into the final cut, and though Davis and Jimmy had the technical expertise to hold a shot with poise, their static poses are noticeable transgressions of continuity studio editing, but do not interfere with the dramatic suspense of the scene. [122]

In the scenes of cross-examination the lawyer is always calm, firm and inquisitional in the probing of Leslie Crosbie's motives, even as he and the audience come to recognise that he is irresistibly being drawn into the web of lies, conspiracies and complicities. Nobly suffering and silent, the lawyer comes to realise there is no way out as bit by bit his professional integrity is compromised. At some point he will have to "pay the piper" for the expediency of his actions. Jimmy underplays these scenes with consummate skill.

Wyler used parallelism to structure the film. In the lengthy interrogation scene when the lawyer confronts Leslie Crosbie with a copy of the letter the proceedings are interrupted by her faint. The resumption in another area of the prison uses the same cinematic framing as in the previous scene. The lawyer and his client occupy the left portion of the screen and the emphasis on deviance is reinforced by the presence of dark shadows, refraction from the serrated blinds. This deliberate structure of one scene being dovetailed into another is part of a wider visual pattern established to create mood and motivate characterisation. Thus, characters are framed with their backs to the camera indicative of concealment, dishonesty and hypocrisy. The reoccurrence of moonlight at crucial moments in the film serves to remind Leslie Crosbie and the audience of the enormity of her transgression and guilt. During the film's

Client Leslie Crosbie (Bette Davis) a cold-hearted predator
is taken on by lawyer Howard Joyce (James Stephenson) whose
sense of loyalty and duty to his profession is tested to the limits.
PHOTO COURTESY OF STEPHENSON ARCHIVE

closure moonlight appears from behind a night cloud and reveals the
corpse of Leslie Crosbie on the ground. The moving camera follows the
sound of dance music in full swing coming from the house-party. In the
distance are glimpsed the colonial elite, oblivious as one of their own lies
dead nearby. Inside the deceased's bedroom, strewn over a chair, is a lace
veil bathed in moonlight. Momentarily a slight breeze stirs the delicate
material wistfully. Then, a final shot of the moonlit tropical skyline and
fade to the end credits. Notwithstanding the short sequence attributable
to ludicrous moral censorship which damages an otherwise imaginative
and skilful conclusion, this is a piece of captivating high drama delivered
in consummate cinematic style.

It is arguably among Davis's finest screen presentations. Her
performance as Leslie Crosbie is diva-like oscillating, as it does, from cool
calculating stratagems to frenzied appeals for clemency. The role allows her
to blow hot and cold on screen, as and when the machinations of the plot
demand, but with less of the usual indulgence and overkill of gestures and
mannerisms prominent in other earlier films. Wyler brought a redefining to

her handling of the melodramatic form. Not only does she rein back on the usual stridency associated with her star personality, but she also manages to circumvent the usual demands of melodrama, by calibrating the pace of her performance and simmering her emotional delivery. Indeed, it can be argued it is the camera itself rather than the star that needs reining in, indulging, as it does, in much stalking and prowling around. Unlike contemporary lightweight photographic equipment, cameras during the studio era were restricted by bulk and weight. To bring extensive camera movement to scenes was a conscious and expensive decision requiring a dolly shot, which meant laying the camera on tracks and also the labour of several technicians, or grips, to move the camera around.

Her characterisation successfully captures the personal vanity and hypocrisy of Leslie Crosbie and her attempts to use and abuse her social privileges in order not to lose face and compromise her social standing among the elite in colonial society. Davis plays the character as a congenital liar who maintains her cool steady disposition whilst performing delicate embroidery, weaving and spinning out her version of the truth to serve her own deviant ends. Her demeanour of quiet confidence, self-control and controlled motivation is a cause for concern rather than congratulation. Davis's saucer eyes, considered a liability by the studio, are put to prominent use by Wyler in the course of the drama. At several crucial junctures in the film narrative Davis's character rears her head and faces the camera full on. Following the shooting of Hammond, the sky darkens as moonlight retreats behind the clouds. As the moonlight reappears, showing Hammond's body, Leslie Crosbie, her back to the camera, swivels around violently with her eyes pointed towards the sky. Her defiant look straight to camera is again paralleled when she delivers the celebrated finale line to her husband.

Davis's sang-froid playing of Leslie Crosbie is a direct, cold and distant interpretation, one of the least outrageous performances the actress gave. In the *Lux Radio Theatre* broadcast of *The Letter* Jimmy's character speaks of Leslie Crosbie as "an erupting volcano" in his response to her exclamation of being an evil woman. This strong emotion is something Olivia de Havilland talked about during a BBC television interview about Davis. [123] The film was presold as a vehicle for its star and in contrast to Jeanne Eagels interpretation, her performance is restrained. Whereas Eagels positively spits and hisses the infamous last line, not once but twice, gloating in defiance as she does so, mocking in her triumphalism of having the last words before the film concludes. Davis, by comparison, is fatalistic, resigned to her final walk of death before she takes leave of the world. She does so in complete silence.

Orry-Kelly's gowns worn by Davis in the film are classic and sleek in their design and significantly shoulder pads are seen protruding through the fabric suggestive of the steely predator lurking beneath a façade of middle-class hauteur and respectability. She is sphinx-like and statuesque following the murder with her dress blowing from an unseen tropical fan as she stands icily calm. Davis as Leslie Crosbie was never more selfish and cruel and yet beautiful and self-possessed.

In keeping with British colonial mores which forbad women smoking, lest it demean their social standing, Davis was deprived of the cigarette, her stock-in-trade screen prop. In contrast, Jimmy's character is seen with several cigarettes during the course of the film. Compared to those two iconic star smokers of 1940s Hollywood cinema Bogart, in *Casablanca*, and Davis, in *Now Voyager*, the presence of cigarettes in the film appears not too prodigious. In the original short story the lawyer smoked a pipe only.

The cigarette was a prop of preference for screen actors of the era. It gave them a veneer of glamour and made them appear self-assured, sophisticated and, more importantly, their star status was used to endorse and promote the purchase and consumption of cigarette brands to mass audiences. Smoking also added mystery and rakishness when creating the code of the cad or villain. Smoking was depicted as soothing and calming and, even without the assistance of mass advertising it cut across class and gender boundaries. The effects of smoking on health were not yet established, although scientists in Germany during the 1930s were carrying out research that suggested a causal link between smoking and addiction. [124]

Given their previous experiences with Wyler, there was from the beginning of the film project nervousness on the part of Jack Warner and Hal Wallis. Wallis stressed adamantly that the picture should be shot in a maximum of seven not eight weeks. Looking at the dailies, Warner took exception to line readings spoken by the British male acting contingent. Dialogue between Bruce Lester, Herbert Marshall and Jimmy was not being picked up adequately by the studio microphones; on the soundtrack it apparently registered as no more than garbled mumbling. [125]

Continual problems regarding the recording of lines demanded retakes of the scene at the English club with Herbert Marshall and Jimmy sitting at the table. During this tense scene, the lawyer informs his client of the existence of a piece of incriminating evidence and the need for its purchase. Jimmy traces his index finger back and forth along the edge of the table, suggestive of anxiety. Though the film script is comprehensive and detailed, this piece of business does not

A tense moment in *The Letter* as lawyer Howard Joyce
(James Stephenson, left) breaks the news of an incriminating letter
to his client Robert Crosbie (Herbert Marshall, right).
<small>PHOTO COURTESY OF STEPHENSON ARCHIVE</small>

appear in the final script. A slight touch, but the kind of nuance Wyler
was willing for his actors to come up with.

Despite the work of research assistant, Herman Lissauer, the film
contains the odd continuity hiccup. During the scene in the jail sick
room an unscheduled dark shadow from the camera apparatus is seen
briefly. The cars are left hand drives rather than right hand and similarly
are driven on the left side of the roads rather than the right, as was the
custom in British colonial territories. In the final scene Bette Davis is
shown locking the door of her bedroom and placing the key in a drawer.
Moments later, Herbert Marshall opens the door and walks into the room
with no apparent difficulty.

As already indicated the studios regarded Wyler as someone
who brought delay and tardiness to the filming process. This was in
fact an undeserved reputation, for although there were indeed delays
on *The Letter* they were unintended. The chief causes of delays were
reshooting of the inspection of Geoffrey Hammond's body in a rubber

shed outside the plantation bungalow because it was felt the rubber looked unconvincing, as was Gale Sondergaard's make-up, at one stage insufficient to cover her hairline over her wig.

Wyler's direction of *The Letter* is exemplary on both technical and aesthetic levels. Even when there are inconsistencies and compromises in the narrative due to studio policies and moral censorship this does not diminish his achievement in bringing out the hypocrisy and anxiety of the characters. An early scene where Leslie Crosbie retraces her actions leading to the killing of her lover Geoffrey Hammond has her pointing to show where in the room the scene had taken place. The camera becomes mobile, animated even, as it adopts the first person point of view while accompanying Leslie Crosbie's recollections on the soundtrack. Such a touch is compelling and transcends the theatrical boundaries of the original drama.

Jimmy was reunited, on screen, with Bruce Lester for the third time in what was, for Lester, a fairly substantial role. His playing of Assistant District Attorney, Mr. Withers, is fittingly all on one note. Accompanying the husband and the lawyer as they investigate the shooting, Lester

Jimmy as Howard Joyce with Bruce Lester as John Withers in *The Letter*.
PHOTO COURTESY OF STEPHENSON ARCHIVE

presents the audience with a young, supercilious, eager-to-please, colonial chap. He offers polite encouragement to Leslie Crosbie as the "civilized" white middle-class administrators and planters all begin closing ranks, certain in the knowledge of her innocence. Withers for all his polite airs, remains an impressionable, callow and sycophantic lightweight. In the post trial party scene, his vapid chitchat as he dances and socializes is just as annoying as the slightly askew dress-tie he wears. [126]

Other minor characters in the film, particularly the two female supporting players Elizabeth Earl and Frieda Inescort, are mere ciphers for Davis's main protagonist. Both Wyler and screen writer Howard Koch were concerned that the gravity of her crime of murder would render the character too unsympathetic for a mainstream audience. They were persuaded to soften the impact of her crime by introducing the superfluous character of Adele Ainsworth, played by Elizabeth Earl, over from England who does little else aside from trilling and fluttering moth-like around the aura of Leslie Crosbie. Mrs. Dorothy Joyce, as played by Frieda Inescort, is potentially interesting, but there isn't much available by way of character development for the actress to work with. Both characters are brought into the plot to lend credence to the view expressed in Maugham's original story of Leslie Crosbie as someone beyond reproach, who: ". . . wouldn't hurt a fly." [127]

At least these two characters made it to the release print, but another minor character, Prescott played by Cecil Kellaway, had all his dialogue scenes cut. Careful viewing does reveal the appearance of Kellaway in brief shots during the trial, and again tendering congratulations at the house-party. Contractual reasons obliged the studio to retain his name on the film credits. Small-part actress Doris Lloyd played Mrs. Cooper and, in the true "waste not, want not" style of the Warner treadmill, small part actor David Newell, who played murder-victim Geoffrey Hammond, reappeared as a courtroom extra in the trial.

Herbert Marshall was excellent as the cuckolded husband Robert Crosbie. Marshall's forte was a hard to beat expression of both tenderness and silent suffering when playing a love scene. This capacity is fully in evidence in the famous last scene of denunciation. [128] The scene begins with the two protagonists resigned to mutual indifference and a broken relationship. There follows an all too brief attempt at reconciliation, in which the pair confront each other as though about to perform an aria in a grand opera, and then they give a final embrace. (The surge of Max Steiner's musical *leitmotif* in designating emotive feeling, as this action takes place on screen is peerless). This is a crucial scene for Leslie Crosbie, who must finally confront her own actions and their consequences for others around her. It is well publicised that Davis and Wyler had an altercation over this vital scene. The actress wanted the line delivered with her face averted from the camera, whereas Wyler's insistence she deliver the line in full view of the camera is consistent with the revelatory nature of the scene, and the final confession of her crime of passion.

Some critics have complained about Max Steiner's musical score claiming it "demeans" the film. [129] Steiner's score is an amalgam of styles that serves to compliment Wyler's taut direction. On the one hand there are Wagnerian crescendos which are fully applied and, fresh from his recent triumph in *Gone with the Wind*, Steiner cannot resist recycling some of the motifs that appear in that epic film. Though florid, the music does provide verve and passion in profusion on the soundtrack. It propels the action forward even if, at times, it is overbearing. There are also several key passages where, in the absence of dialogue, the dramatic progression is accompanied and supported by the sonority of Steiner's music.

Wyler's carefully staged and edited exercises in adapting literary properties for cinematic finesse drew great admiration and praise during his lifetime. French critic Andre Bazin argued Wyler's lack of discernible style in his films created its own pure cinema. [130] Rather than spend time infusing his own directorial style on the films he directed, Wyler objectively concentrated on the script's sources; novel, play, short story etc. for inspiration and created an aesthetic and tone most suited to enhancing a film's source material. This approach is at odds with the later Auteur theory, which lauded the personal creative vision of a director throughout a distinct body of work consistent to film per se. Today Wyler has become underrated and unfashionable. The skill of Wyler's direction in translating a literary story incisively and vividly to the cinematic medium is deserving of more than Andrew Sarris's backhanded compliment of: "meticulous craftsmanship." [131]

The Letter would prove to be Jimmy's finest cinematic hour and he was justly proud of his performance, but the assignment of the role had been anything but straight forward. As he recalled:

> "I had been thoroughly fed up. I, too, knew they were looking for someone to play the role of Howard Joyce, the lawyer. I couldn't see the sense of hiring an outside player for the part when they had me under contract. And what was even more – I wanted to do that role very badly. If you know how we Englishmen feel about Somerset Maugham and his works, you can understand my anxiety." [132]

Jimmy had been considering leaving the security of the Warner

Studio to try free-lancing, like his good friend Pat Knowles had done, for better parts when his option came up for renewal. Both his wife and agent had argued against this. To acquire the coveted role his agent, Charles E. Trezona (1905-1958) of 400 North Camden Drive Beverly Hills, lobbied the studio hard on Jimmy's behalf. Jimmy had issued him with an ultimatum: either he be given better roles or he would change his agent. Trezona proved himself doggedly loyal to his clients, and in gratitude Jimmy referred to him thereafter as being "straight as a die." Through his intervention Jack Warner was convinced that the role of lawyer Howard Joyce would play to his client's strengths. [133] Warner was initially happy to recommend Jimmy to Wyler. The studio suggested Wyler look at Jimmy's work in *White Banners* as well as shoot a test for the role of Howard Joyce. Wyler liked what he saw and immediately contacted Warner saying he was impressed and would like to use Jimmy in the film. [134] Warner then began to raise all sorts of objections and suggested several other well-established names to play the part. Wyler would not be dissuaded and held his ground arguing for Jimmy to be used in the film. Eventually, with some reluctance, Warner agreed. Had he bothered to read the script he would readily have understood that though Leslie Crosbie has the first and last acts all to herself, the lawyer takes centre stage in the rest of the film.

On May 7, 1940 *The Letter* was assigned production #315 and a budget totaling $696,000. On May 8, 1940 actor Laird Cregar tested for the role of lawyer Howard Joyce [135] and contract player George Brent was pencilled in for the role of Robert Crosbie. In the event Cregar, a Twentieth Century-Fox contract player, was dropped and Sen Yung, also from Twentieth Century-Fox studios, was loaned instead to Warners to play the role of wily clerk Ong Chi Seng.

Co-star Frieda Inescort recalled times during filming on set when "tensions could be very strong," not unusual in the playing of an emotional melodrama and especially one where expectations were high, and of a top director whose reputation preceded him. Though Wyler could be disarming company away from the studio, when on the studio floor he was unyielding, often brusque, and, as often as not, just plain difficult. When asked by Jimmy: "How did I do?" his bruising reply was: "Jimmy, I could understand it if you did too much. But you don't do anything!" [136] In point of fact, Jimmy's ability to underplay his role is a central strength of the film's success and marks his performance as exceptional. This is further commendable because he is hardly ever off screen. As usual he was able to bring ineffable, calm and authority to his role in any scene that warranted it.

A rare example of light relief on the set of *The Letter* Jimmy (left) watches
Elizabeth Earl and dog being fed cake by director William Wyler,
while cinematographer Tony Gaudio offers ice cream.
PHOTO COURTESY OF STEPHENSON ARCHIVE

Not only was there a prodigious amount of dialogue to remember
and deliver word perfect, but technical difficulties had also to be
overcome. For instance, putting the camera on tracks in several key
scenes to permit movement in and around the actors threw up all sorts
of logistical problems such as timing the action to ensure the camera
recorded the relevant details, whilst still realising spontaneity in pace
and performance.

When first confronted, for instance, with the existence of the
incriminating letter by chief clerk Ong Chi Seng (superbly played by Sen
Yung), Jimmy's considered response of unperturbed calm and feigned
unconcern is a perfect example of understated acting. The subtext of
the scene, the relationship between master and servant, is later explored
very effectively when the arrangement for retrieving the letter is set up
in the shady milieu of a parking lot. [137] At the very end of their long
conversation when it is known that the incriminating letter held by the
dead man's widow need not go to the public prosecutor, it can be obtained
for $2,000 cash, there follows a final vigorous verbal exchange between

Jimmy as lawyer Howard Joyce strides with indignation as he enters the car parking lot followed by Sen Yung as confidential clerk Ong Chi Seng.
PHOTO COURTESY OF STEPHENSON ARCHIVE

the lawyer and his clerk. The lawyer's reaction (etched on his face) is a combination of offhand resentment at the clerk's impertinence and disgust at the sordidness of discussing such matters in a grubby car-park. The lawyer's car situated in prominent view drives off at some speed. In contrast the car driven by the wily clerk is hidden from view by other parked vehicles and is heard starting with a comic putt-putt before appearing on screen as a small diminutive model of car. The car-park scene is an intricate vignette; it is satiric in its quality and delineates, with precise aim, the legal, moral and political power relationships within the drama. The natives appear to be challenging the social and economic order of things, but it is a cat and mouse game, in which those who rule and those who serve are each depicted as fully understanding the complicity at the heart of the story.

Rather remarkably the character of the lawyer, having compromised his professional status, is allowed to walk away, albeit marginalised, without any retribution. At the end of the film he suddenly disappears only to be heard once more as he bids Leslie Crosbie, off camera, a final goodnight. [138]

It took all of Jimmy's English reserve and self discipline not to rise to Wyler's seemingly implacable manner. Davis later recalled Jimmy had difficulty with Wyler, losing his temper and walking off the set more than once. [139] Jimmy found, as did others, that Wyler had a penchant for wearing people down. For Jimmy it was all disconcerting and difficult to fathom. As he later confessed:

> "By the end of the first week, I'd been convinced that I was the worst damn actor in the world. I dreaded leaving home for the studio in the morning. I envied every man I met on the road who didn't have Willie (sic) Wyler to face that day." [140]

If Wyler was pulling out all the stops technically then he expected his actors to do likewise. On a Wyler picture it was simply not good enough to just turn up, know your lines, and hit the chalk marks. Wyler's legendary perfectionism insisted you had to give your all and not merely reproduce a surface effect. He was always looking to his actors to deliver something special in a given scene. Being part-intuitive in his approach meant he was often reluctant to offer any practical assistance when encountering difficulty with a scene. Conversely, a successful outcome didn't warrant any praise from him either. Actor David Niven, when speaking of directors and "their little idiosyncrasies," recalled that Wyler would think nothing

An autographed photograph to Jimmy from Herbert Marshall, co-star in *The Letter* 1940 using his nickname: "To Jimmy with much liking. Bart."
PHOTO COURTESY OF STEPHENSON ARCHIVE

of making up to forty takes and then print the first. [141] Hyper-critical and demanding he thrived on delivering a quality product and would brook no obstacles. Both Bette Davis and Herbert Marshall, veterans of Wyler pictures, coached and supported Jimmy through the demands of a far from easy and often difficult shoot. Not until all three principals were summoned to the projection room to see the finished picture did Wyler finally give his verdict. As the lights were switched on, he turned to them: "You three have done first-class jobs" and with a bashful grin added, "I feel mine wasn't a bad one either." [142]

Looking back on the whole experience Jimmy was philosophical about the uncomfortable mauling meted out to him: "What if he did give me a hell of a time? With it he gave me a new lease of life, for which I shall be everlastingly grateful." [143] He had taken up the gauntlet of Wyler's stiff challenge to "be better" and won his acting spurs.[144] In later years, when Wyler reminisced about the film he spoke warmly of Jimmy's performance and abilities. [145] *The Letter* stands head and shoulders above any other piece of work Jimmy delivered in his short time in Hollywood. His performance has the power to enthral which was noted at the time of the film's reception and remains undiminished with the passing of time.

"James Stephenson almost runs off with the honours in a fine performance as her legal adviser," [146] was typical of the press reaction.

> "James Stephenson is superb as the honest lawyer who jeopardizes his reputation to save a friend – a shrewd, dignified reflective citizen who assumes a sordid business with distaste. He is the strongest character in the film, the one person who really matters . . . ." [147] wrote Bosley Crowther, in the *New York Times*.

In similar vein the London *Times* wrote:

> "Mr. James Stephenson, the counsel who risks his career for a beautiful woman or for a friend's wife (the point is not clear), puts up such an impressive show of silent torture that we are rather more interested in his problem than in his client's." [148]

Among the many critical plaudits that came his way, Jimmy was particularly proud of comments by renowned writer Damon Runyon:

> "In *The Letter* [Bette Davis] has a fellow working with her who is no sucker in the acting racket and who makes her hustle to keep up with him. His name is James Stephenson and he reads line for line and plays scene for scene with Miss Davis. Only she could escape larceny of the picture at his hands. He is one of those sophisticated looking gees with a suave manner, a marvellous

speaking voice and a little mustachio. He does a bit of struggling with his conscience that is as nice a spot of acting as you have ever seen. He is a superb performer." [149]

Perhaps the critique most apposite came from English critic James Agate who in June 1941 wrote:

> "The writing is taut and spare throughout, never a word too much or too little. The unravelling of Maugham's story is masterly, and the presentation by William Wyler is visual and cinematic. The film runs an hour and a half and the audience at the trade show – and it is a fairly hard-boiled audience – did not move a finger. . . I liked very much James Stephenson's lawyer; this is an actor of whom we should see more." [150]

The success of the Wyler film prompted a second radio transcription on the radio series *Lux Radio Theatre* on April 21, 1941 with Bette Davis, Herbert Marshall and Jimmy reprising their roles along with radio stalwart Eric Snowden. [151] In between the obligatory commercial breaks for sponsor Lux Soap Flakes (". . . so kind to your hands!") there is extensive use of interior monologue as Leslie Crosbie's inner anxiety and frustration is played out on the airwaves. Though these broadcasts were heavily scripted there is a brief indication of the simulated relaxed atmosphere of Jimmy's burgeoning stardom. Before the final curtain call at the end of the broadcast Bette Davis addresses him fraternally as "Jimmy." On March 6, 1944 Bette Davis and Herbert Marshall teamed up again in a fourth and final version of *The Letter* on *Lux Radio Theatre* with Vincent Price in the role of the lawyer.

This was the second occasion Jimmy had appeared on American radio. His previous broadcast on March 23, 1938 consisted of a half-hour condensed version of an earlier Warner Bros. film hit *I Found Stella Parish* (Mervyn LeRoy, 1935). Gale Page played the part of the eponymous actress, [played in the original film by Kay Francis] and Jimmy took the male lead played by Ian Hunter in the film. When the drama had concluded, there were interviews from studio guest stars including newcomer Marie Wilson and B picture producer Bryan Foy. This was an episode in a short-lived radio series of thirteen programmes known as the *Warner Brothers Academy Theatre Programme*. The format was a dramatic anthology showcasing only Warner Bros. productions and promising studio players each week. The series was sponsored by Gruen Watches, ("A Gruen watch is more than ever a thing of rare beauty and a pleasure to wear, a joy to behold!") but the series didn't last beyond the summer of 1938. This suggests the listening ratings did not make the grade, or that the supply of young

Jimmy, flanked to his right by guest star Marie Wilson and to his left by
Gale Page, at the microphone with script in hand during a *Warner Brothers
Academy Theatre* Broadcast of *I Found Stella Parish* on March 23, 1938.
PHOTO COURTESY OF STEPHENSON ARCHIVE

studio talent was beginning to diminish.

Though these broadcasts were transmitted live, it was customary
for the networks to record their broadcasts on disc to allow for the time
difference between the United States east and west coast and to restore
the loss of revenue this would otherwise mean. Unfortunately a transcript
of this particular programme appears missing, awaiting rediscovery.

In succeeding years, Warner's couldn't resist the temptation to recycle
the story of *The Letter* yet again, in another scenario manufactured by
noir writers David Goodis and James Gunn. *The Unfaithful* (Warner,
Vincent Sherman, 1947) found Ann Sheridan as the woman on trial for
the murder of a man in self-defence, with Zachary Scott substituting in
the Herbert Marshall role. Lew Ayres took the part of the lawyer. The
property proved too popular to pass up and so in 1950 it made the jump
to the small screen. A half hour version appeared on American television
as part of the first season of *Robert Montgomery Presents*. Madeleine
Carroll portrayed Leslie, Howard Wierum, Robert, Theodore Newton,
Joyce and William Post Jr. played Geoffrey Hammond. In 1952 there
was a Broadway Television Theatre presentation starring Sylvia Sidney

as Leslie Crosbie and Gene Raymond as Robert Crosbie. In 1982 there was a forgettable TV movie with Lee Remick as Leslie Crosbie, Jack Thompson as Robert Crosbie and Ronald Pickup as Howard Joyce.

In subsequent years the play has been often revived on the English theatrical stage. Most recently, in a 2007 production, the director Alan Strachan goes beyond the surface themes of racism and the colonial mentality and brings out a homoerotic subtext by supplying an answer to the question, why does Howard Joyce defend a woman he so blatantly detests? The answer being that he loves the husband. Maugham's story also turned up as a "noir opera" performed by the Santa Fe Opera during the summer of 2009. As a singer himself Jimmy would have been intrigued and pleased to learn that Maugham's stories are still capable of finding a variety of modern audiences. [152]

Despite all the critical acclaim the role in *The Letter* brought him there was a dark shadow cast over Jimmy's screen triumph. Over the radio flashed the first terrible news of the bombing of the city of Coventry back in England. Heavy bombing in November 1940 had turned Coventry Cathedral to ruins and with it went the career of Jimmy's younger brother, Alan Stephenson, chief chorister and organist at the city cathedral. Jimmy was frantic for news to confirm if his brother and family were safe. He didn't dare cable his elderly parents knowing the adverse effect such a cable would have on his mother. Instead he cabled a friend of his brothers in Coventry. As luck would have it, Alan was with this friend when the message arrived and he sent back word that he and his wife, May, were both safe. In an interview Jimmy mused on the devastation of Coventry Cathedral: "I used to spend hours there listening to the choral and organ music. It seems impossible that anything could have touched the lovely old place." [153] Alan's home, though habitable, suffered significant damage and he was, of course, unable to continue with his occupation. As a result Jimmy sent a considerable amount of money back home to England to ensure Alan was able to seek another position and find alternate accommodation. Alan and his wife May took a flat in Heysham situated at the back of the retirement home of old Mr. and Mrs. Stephenson. He was also able to secure a temporary position as organist at Lancaster Priory. Through all of this the strain on his health was immense and later on he had to give up a teaching position at Lancaster Grammar School due to a decline in his health.

While this trauma was being gone through back in England, in Hollywood Jimmy was being groomed for stardom. His slight pencil-thin moustache which had first appeared on screen in *Devil's Island* was now a permanent feature. Though unorthodox, he was a useful "type," but the

Jimmy receives the highly stylised star treatment of classical Hollywood.
The portrait exudes notions of gentlemanly charm
with a dash of masculine sophistication.
PHOTO COURTESY OF STEPHENSON ARCHIVE

studio appeared at a loss as to how to market him with distinction. He was promoted as being in the mould of the suave, reserved and conservative Englishman, such as Ronald Colman, Laurence Olivier, David Niven among many others. He was also seen as having a passing resemblance to the up-and-coming stars James Craig and John Carroll.

In February 1941 the Academy of Motion Pictures Arts and Sciences held their annual academy award banquet at the Biltmore Hotel. Because of the deteriorating situation of hostilities in Europe and the Far East the ceremony was comparatively low profile. Even so, various innovations were made that year. For the first time the announcements were made via use of sealed envelopes, and the assembled throng of some 1,500 guests heard President Roosevelt deliver a live radio broadcast in which he praised the United States film industry for its indelible contribution to national life. Jimmy and Lorna took their places at the tables and a studio photographer was on hand to capture their presence for posterity. Notice how Jimmy appears to change appearance from one shot to another. Jimmy along with Jack Oakie for his performance as Napoloni in *The Great Dictator* was tipped to win the Oscar for best supporting actor. To the consternation of everyone present, and to his own embarrassment, Walter Brennan won a third time for Judge Roy Bean in *The Westerner* directed by William Wyler – a heavy irony.

Flight from Destiny (Warner, Vincent Sherman, 1941) provided an early directorial assignment for studio writer Vincent Sherman, who had worked in this capacity on *Heart of the North*, *King of the Underworld* and *The Adventures of Jane Arden*. Jimmy was given fourth billing in the supporting role of physician Lawrence Stevens, who explains to the elderly Professor Todhunter [Thomas Mitchell] he is terminally ill and has only six months to live. Discussing his situation with friends, Todhunter decides to conduct a "social murder," killing someone who society would be better off without. He decides to reunite two young people, a struggling young artist, [Jeffrey Lynn] and his girlfriend [Geraldine Fitzgerald] who are being blackmailed by a conniving seductress, Ketti Moret, [Mona Maris]. Jimmy reappears towards the end of the story where incarcerated in jail on a charge of murder, Todhunter pleads with his doctor to give testimony at the ensuing trial. Following the trial Jimmy goes to see Todhunter a final time. He reads out Todhunter's last statement about crime in a letter written while waiting to be taken to the electric chair. This was among the more unusual dramas to emerge from Warner Bros. at this time, the film marks a distinct shift in the morality of the era; to discuss the possibility of social murder was quite an innovation and doubtless was brought about by the spread of another world conflict; though not a complete success as the objections from the Hays Office were not overcome, it is a worthy effort deserving of some reappraisal. Though Jimmy gives a fine performance, he is given all too little to do. With hindsight, it is deeply ironic he was cast as a medical doctor, given the film scenario deals with issues of mortality. Jimmy's sincerity shines throughout, and this was recalled over sixty years later by director Vincent Sherman:

> ". . . he was an actor I admired. His quiet intensity and interior emotion always carried him thru in his performances and he was a pleasure to work with, a gentleman and an artist in all respects. I am happy to be asked something about him." [154]

Though Jimmy had failed to win the Oscar for best supporting actor, the studio finally gave him the chance of a "big meaty part" and cast him as a star lead in *Shining Victory* (Warner, Irving Rapper, 1941). It was based on the play *Jupiter Laughs* by Scottish physician and writer

A tense moment for James and Lorna Stephenson seated among more than 1,500 guests on the evening of Thursday February 27, 1941 at the Biltmore Bowl of the Biltmore Hotel in Los Angeles. The 13 Academy Awards annual dinner banquet given by the Academy of Motion Picture Arts and Sciences is hosted by producer Walter Wanger. Though Oscar nominated best supporting actor for his role of Howard Joyce in *The Letter* James lost to Walter Brennan who played Judge Roy Bean in *The Westerner*. Note his passing resemblance to Clark Gable.
PHOTO COURTESY OF STEPHENSON ARCHIVE

Dr. Archibald Joseph Cronin (1896-1981), whose popular novels and stories were adapted to film from the 1930s onwards with success both in Britain and Hollywood. *The Citadel* (M-G-M, King Vidor, 1938); *The Stars Look Down* (Grafton Films, Carol Reed, 1939); *Vigil in the Night* (RKO, George Stevens, 1940) and *Hatter's Castle* (Paramount British, Lance Comfort, 1941) were just a few among many others. His 1935 novella *Country Doctor* formed the basis for the popular BBC TV and radio series *Dr. Finlay's Casebook* (1962-1971). *Jupiter Laughs* had been first performed on stage in Glasgow in March 1940 with James Mason playing the male lead. It also ran on Broadway during September 1940 with Alexander Knox and Jessica Tandy in the leads at the Biltmore Theatre. *Shining Victory* is a splendid example of astute playing over average and conventional material. Even with Howard Koch working on the scenario, its substance is somewhat conventional; meretricious rather than meritorious. Jimmy's earnest playing of Dr. Paul Venner only

Seconds later with Lorna Stephenson still clutching matches, James has morphed into a passing likeness to Tom Conway.
PHOTO COURTESY OF STEPHENSON ARCHIVE

Jimmy as Dr. Paul Venner and Geraldine Fitzgerald as Dr. Mary Murray
in a romantic love scene from *Shining Victory* 1941.
PHOTO COURTESY OF STEPHENSON ARCHIVE

accomplishes so much in overcoming the age disparity between himself, Geraldine Fitzgerald, (young enough to be his daughter rather than his sweetheart) and Donald Crisp (old enough to be a contemporary rather than a father-figure) in the story. The film may be described as a nervous A picture in the sense that Warners were playing safe and not taking chances in heavy promotion of their new stars – Geraldine Fitzgerald and Jimmy. Making his directing debut was Irving Rapper whose directorial mentor at the studio was the remarkably efficient and versatile, Michael Curtiz. Needless to say, there is spontaneity and bounce in the pace and delivery style of the narrative which is supported by a rousing score from Max Steiner. As with *The Letter* Hal Wallis and Robert Lord were producers, and Carl Weyl again was art director, which achieved assured competence rather than inspirational heights.

As in many of A.J. Cronin's stories, the film centres on an idealistic individual, Dr. Paul Venner, an English medical student played by Jimmy, who succeeds despite numerous setbacks in doggedly pursuing a just cause for the greater good. There is thus a sense of predictability about the scenario from the beginning with Barbara O'Neil playing an ersatz Mrs. Danvers housekeeper (Miss Leeming) in an old grim Scottish castle called Hopewell Towers, converted into an unimportant sanatorium. The building is populated by recognisable English types: Donald Crisp as Dr. Drewett, a loyal old friend of Venner's, George P. Huntley Jr. as the music loving and garrulous Dr. Thornton, and Billy Bevan as a chirpy cockney entrepreneur Chivers. Also appearing in the background, is Bruce Lester as Dr. Bentley. His dialogue appears to have ended up on the cutting room floor. When asked by Dr. Drewett where Dr. Venner is, he merely motions a reply with his head. When Venner requests a research assistant he is initially chagrined to be assigned the young and charming Dr. Mary Murray [Geraldine Fitzgerald]. Her hard working and painstaking efficiency soon makes him realise that he loves her and cannot let her leave to become a medical missionary in China. She consents to stay for she loves him, too. They celebrate their engagement by going on a picnic. They both work on a hasty post-mortem for establishing evidence for Venner's new method of brain treatment. Though the post-mortem proves his theories, it violates the coroner's laws of Scotland. Miss Leeming, who has slowly developed a strange mixture of love and hatred for Dr. Venner, confronts him saying he must renounce Dr. Murray. Venner reacts by telling her she needs treatment for mental disorder. Later when Venner leaves his laboratory, Miss Leeming starts a fire. Dr. Mary Murray is consumed by the fire as she successfully rescues case-papers proving Venner's innocence. Dr. Venner decides to go to China to combat an outbreak of cerebro-spinal meningitis, thus undertaking the task which Dr. Murray had originally assigned to herself. Just before his final exit from Hopewell Towers to begin an exiled life in China, Venner turns a sad farewell glance at the rooms where Mary and he had shared happy times. At this point on screen, Jimmy momentarily has the look of Warner Baxter playing the haggard producer, Julian Marsh, at the end of the backstage depression musical *42nd Street* (Warner, Lloyd Bacon, 1933). In this instance Jimmy's expression was not altogether acting, for his heart condition was already beginning to be apparent.

The final scene in which Venner returns to the beauty spot where Mary and he had spent private moments together during their picnic draws on symbolic imagery. In pouring rain, branches of a willow tree brush against his face, suggesting feminine sensibility and the power of dreaming and enchantment. The willow puts him in touch with personal feelings and deep emotions and assists him by allowing him to feel sadness and pain. Jimmy's pained expression to camera and the upsurge of Max Steiner's flamboyant score combine to transcend the studio-bound artifice in which this closing scene takes place.

Director Irving Rapper recalled, he preferred to pre-plan each

On the set of *Shining Victory* in 1941. From left director Irving Rapper,
actress Ida Lupino visiting the set, Jimmy with newspaper in hand,
his signet ring and wrist watch clearly visible and Geraldine Fitzgerald.
Photo courtesy of Stephenson Archive

scene and follow the script to the letter, but was open to a good deal of
improvisation. Jimmy was loath to hold up proceedings, even though
suffering some discomfort. Called upon in the film to wear a high collared
surgical dress, the collar stud dug into his neck, but he did not reveal this
until confronted by director Rapper.

Jimmy was paid $6,000 as opposed to $10,000 paid to Barbara
O'Neil, and Donald Crisp $10,833. O'Neil was taken ill with swelling
of the lips due to a cold, and this delayed the film with the studio chiefs
sending a doctor to check when she might recover. A minor defect of the
film was the tendency of the actors to mispronounce medical terms in the
script which, given Irving Rapper's previous experience as a dialogue
director, must have been a personal disappointment. [155] As this was
both Irving Rapper's directorial debut and Jimmy's first starring film of
real substance, Bette Davis contrived to appear in the film in a cameo
appearance dressed as a nurse. There are surviving stills of her on the film
set, but it cannot be ascertained with absolute certainty if she appears in
the final release print. During the opening scene, in the outer office of a

Budapest hospital there is a shot of a figure, back to the camera, dressed in nurse's uniform carrying medical notes walking towards the door, but the shot is so transitory as to rule out firm identification.

Jimmy was by inclination a serious actor rather than a star personality, and the sudden transformation in his career fortunes brought with it some surprise, and also alarm.

> "Never did I dream of the results it would bring . . . All this is very surprising . . . How quickly things change. A few weeks ago, I could go anywhere without getting a second glance from people. But now, if I want to go shopping I have to go on days when the stores are crowded so that people will overlook me in the throngs. And even if they do recognize me, they insist on calling me "the man from *The Letter*." [156]

After all the stiff and starched clothing he had been required to wear in his previous occupations (during his time as a bank cashier or in the military for instance) the chance to dress down and put on the casual clothes of Southern California when in private, and off duty was something he genuinely welcomed. His predisposition was to wear shades of brown or tan in his sports jackets and slacks, and he disowned collars and ties, and wore the short sox which did not require garters. He spent some of his hard-earned income on building a library of books. English literature prose, poetry and plays – See bibliography – and also collecting classical records. When not otherwise occupied, he spent time at home "mucking about" with the car which, with its automatic transmission and car radio, offered refined ease, comfort, and novelty for him. Occasionally the Stephensons would take in a classical concert at the renowned amphitheatre, the Hollywood Bowl.

One day Lorna Stephenson with her infant son, Peter, motored to the Warner lot. While waiting for Jimmy to clock off, Marlene Dietrich, then working on the set of *Manpower* (Warner, Raoul Walsh, 1941), came along and was so charmed by the Stephenson's baby, she placed him on her knee and gave him some affectionate attention.

Jimmy's screen career ended prematurely with a tribute to Royal Air Force wartime pilots in *International Squadron* (Warner, Lothar Mendes / Lewis Seiler, 1941). The theatrical trailer for this film had the main participants, including Jimmy, address the camera directly appealing for war bonds. Sadly, at the time of writing it has not been possible to locate a copy of this trailer with which to gain a rare glimpse of the man unimpeded by the requirement to act in character. [157]

The film began shooting at the beginning of April 1941 and was completed, albeit fourteen days behind schedule, on May 6, 1941. The studio's original directorial choice, Lothar Mendes, was considered too pedantic and slow, and was taken off the picture and the reliable Lewis Seiler was brought in to shape-up a beleaguered production.

The final film is well enough made, but suffers in comparison to another celluloid tribute to the RAF made at the behest of Darryl Zanuck. *A Yank in the RAF* (Twentieth Century-Fox, Henry King, 1941) offered audiences the irresistible allure of two top flight stars; Tyrone Power and Betty Grable both in fine form.

Jimmy dressing down in casual outfit typical of Southern California.
PHOTO COURTESY OF STEPHENSON ARCHIVE

Jimmy, Ronald Reagan and William Lundigan exemplify esprit de corps in a
production still from his final film *International Squadron* 1941.
PHOTO COURTESY OF STEPHENSON ARCHIVE

In *International Squadron* the unassuming poise and fortitude of his
screen character, Squadron Leader Charles Wyatt, is played with heightened
empathy by Jimmy. The *New York Times* reported: "James Stephenson has
added another clipped performance as the squadron leader." [158] Throughout
the film, he appears somewhat gaunt and bears a pallid expression indicative
of his final illness. The closing scene in the officer's mess was, appropriately,
a melancholy one. Wyatt [Jimmy] walking up to the mess bar takes the
empty glass offered and places the glass upturned behind the bar – an
honourable tribute to flier Jimmy Grant [Ronald Reagan] just shot down by
enemy action - followed by a symbolic toast to the memory of Grant from
his old squadron. It is a scene which honours quiet dignity, conscientious
duty, selfless service and sacrifice. These same qualities were exemplified
by Jimmy Stephenson the actor and the man and as such the scene, with
hindsight, offers a suitable valediction.

Lorna and Jim Stephenson photographed together on their final vacation at Lake Arrowhead in June 1941. Note Lorna shows solidarity for the British war effort by wearing the fashionable turban style of head dress worn by women in wartime munition factories.

PHOTO COURTESY OF STEPHENSON ARCHIVE

4
ENVOI

To live is to be lonely
TAKI NO SHIRAITO / THE WATER MAGICIAN
(IRIE, KENJI MIZOGUCHI, 1933)

In the early hours of Tuesday July 29, 1941 James awoke, asphyxiated, gasping for breath. A doctor was called who immediately ordered an oxygen tent, but by the time of its arrival it could no longer serve any useful purpose. James Stephenson's demise, aged fifty-two, was reported at 5:30 a.m. and the cause of death given as "shock due to coronary occlusion." [1]

Good friends Enid and Pat Knowles immediately rallied round and took charge in organising the funeral arrangements. The simple ceremony attended by his widow, young son and a few close friends took place at 11:30 a.m. on Thursday July 31 at the Wee Kirk of the Heather in Forest Lawn Memorial Park. Rev. Wesley Havermale, of the Westwood Episcopal Church, officiated at the service. James's final departure, though tragic and premature was, in keeping with his disposition and wishes, private and unobtrusive.

Back in England at his old church, St Catherine's in Burnley, the Rev. Harry Battye gave this moving tribute:

> "The news of the death of James Stephenson came as a terrible shock to all of us here. Only recently, we had rejoiced to hear that he was nearing the top rung of the ladder as a Hollywood film star. We have admired his acting on the films, and with great pride said: "He is an old St. Catherine's choir boy." It appears to be so tragic that a man who had such great gifts should so suddenly, be called away. His fine acting has given such pleasure to so many." [2]

Lorna Stephenson showed great empathy and presence of mind in the breaking of the tragic news to Jim's mother and father, now in their seventies and living in quiet retirement in the English seaside resort, Heysham. She ensured her cable notifying the family of Jim's death was sent to Norman's wife, Toonie, who drove immediately from her home in Surrey to Lancashire where, surrounded by other members of the extended family, she broke the terrible news to Mr. and Mrs. Stephenson. [3] In a tragic coincidence when news of Jim's death arrived by cable from Hollywood, The Empire Theatre in nearby Morecambe was showing *The Letter* while *Calling Philo Vance* was being screened over at The Plaza, Morecambe. His father went to see *The Letter* at The Empire, his mother being too overcome with grief to go. It is probable his father was the only one among the Morecambe audiences who saw the film who knew that James Stephenson was dead. The death came as a terrible blow to the family because there had been no suspicion that Jim had suffered from heart trouble.

Meanwhile in Hollywood, Jimmy Stephenson's loyalty to the Warner Company and his compliance with its dictates were acknowledged in the annual compilation of blooper reels edited for Jack Warner's Christmas Parties. In *Breakdowns of 1941* he is seen rehearsing on the set of *Shining Victory*. Delivering his lines, back to camera, co-star Barbara O'Neil fails to respond with her lines and he simultaneously turns to the camera and breaks into spontaneous laughter. These few seconds are a rare glimpse of the private man rather than the representation manufactured by Hollywood's dream machine.

In homage to his memory the studio, through his recently installed fan club, compiled a series of valedictories written by various Warner associates, co-workers and ordinary fans. A brief selection serves to illustrate the high-regard in which Jimmy Stephenson was held around the Burbank lot and indeed the picture business in general.

The first tribute, written by an aspiring actor on the brink of stardom after years playing the studio's number one heavy dying a myriad of melodramatic deaths, speaks succinctly of Jimmy's loyalty to the profession and his qualities as an actor:

> "*To the members of the James Stephenson Fan Club*
> Dear Club Members,
>
> I wish to express my very deepest sympathy to the family of James Stephenson and to join with all of you, who were his friends, in a tribute of appreciation to his memory.
>
> It had been my good fortune to work with Mr. Stephenson and I found him a very fine actor and one of great ability and

sincerity. His loss will be felt very keenly in the industry.

        Very truly yours

        Humphrey Bogart" [4]

Another tribute from a colleague who appeared in *The Letter* reiterates the sense of shock, felt by many, at the suddenness of his passing:

    "Dear Ellen:

        You asked me for a few words about Jim Stephenson and frankly I find them hard to write. When he and his charming wife, Lorna first came over from England we met casually at the home of mutual friends and prior to playing with him in *"THE LETTER"* I don't suppose we had seen each other more than a half a dozen times. I had enjoyed [his] excellent expert performances of various small roles and liked his quiet unactory manner socially. He never was one to enjoy large so-called Hollywood gatherings and neither am I. During our three weeks together at Warner Bros. last summer I came to know him better and admire him more. At times on any set tension can become very strong and particularly is that true in the direction of an emotional drama. But although he felt deeply Jim never once let it disturb his conception of the job to be done and the resulting three-dimensional characterisation is proof how right he was. He was unostentatiously generous with both his money and his time and never a flag waving Britisher, he responded to War Relief appeals which I made in behalf of the unit for which I work. I think he planned eventually to become an American citizen because I remember a long talk we had on that subject which my views as a naturalized voter seemed to interest him keenly.

        His sudden completely unexpected death was a great loss to his friends and family and I know that all his fellow workers will miss him keenly as an actor but above all as a man.

        Sincerely,

        Frieda Inescort" [5]

However, among the many tributes there is one that strikes a note of *faux* sentiment:

    "Dear Jim:-

        Since we made our test a few days ago, I see you have changed studios. The production manager where you are now is infinitely better than any for whom you have worked before. I know you must have talked to HIM many times because it seems that all great artists, (and I include you among them), when in doubt, asked HIS advice. I wish to compliment you on having taken it so often. HE certainly is a GREAT PRODUCER, isn't HE? It is wonderful to work for a GUY who can figure out how to give every one top billing; I envy you a great deal your new contract.

Sam Wood, Ann Sheridan and the entire company send their love and are sorry you had to leave just before *"KINGS ROW."* Claude Rains just the other day was telling me how much he admired you and said he felt honoured to be able to play DOCTOR TOWER since you are on your way to the top. Say Hello to your new studio manager for us. We shall be plugging for you.

> See you at the final World's Premier.
> Your Friend,
> Bob Cummings" [6]

Rather than writing a simple, straightforward condolence to the family of a colleague, Cummings becomes preoccupied with the great hereafter and his hyperbole descends into mawkishness. During the Second World War the same florid style resurfaced in Hollywood scenarios that concocted celestial fantasy as a compromise in dealing with the stark reality of high wartime military and civilian casualties. Similar divine interventions are apparent in such celluloid apparitions as: *Here Comes Mr. Jordan* (Columbia, Alexander Hall, 1941), *A Guy Named Joe* (M-G-M, Sam Wood, 1943); not to mention the heavenly prologue and epilogue from *The Ziegfeld Follies* (M-G-M, Vincente Minnelli, 1944 / released 1946).

Despite its demerits, the tribute's mention of a final role that never was brings into focus the question of what path Stephenson's career would have taken had he, for instance, lived on for another decade? It is, of course, impossible to say with any assurance just how his professional life would have developed. However, a series of educated guesses does provide some fascinating scenarios. In the fullness of time it may be assumed he would, later rather than sooner, have forsaken romantic leads for character roles. [7] If today the role of Dr. Tower in *Kings Row* is seen as a highpoint in the screen career of Claude Rains then his playing of Dr. Jacqueth in *Now Voyager* (Warner, Irving Rapper, 1942) remains archetypal. Yet, given Stephenson's penchant for playing authoritative figures in an understated manner and his previous rapport with both Bette Davis on *The Letter* and Irving Rapper in *Shining Victory*, it is not inconceivable he would have been a strong contender for the Jacqueth role. The character's mixture of professional integrity and sincerity, aligned with avuncular charm, were certainly qualities well within

Stephenson's capabilities as an actor.

Post Pearl Harbor the personal appearances he so disclaimed as pointless took on new and urgent meanings. Eager to prove itself in the national call-to-arms the movie colony, in a fit of moral righteousness and civic responsibility, sponsored coast-to-coast war bond drives designed to rally national solidarity and bolster wartime consensus.

Given this background Stephenson might have been persuaded to sing at a troop concert, or for a benefit on radio. Another possibility would have been a cameo appearance in a dramatic sketch or musical number in those all-star studio flag-wavers specifically envisaged for this time of national emergency. Studio stars were usually only too willing to descend from their pedestals and become plain Jo/sephines for the duration in order to do their bit during a nation's hour of need. Wartime camaraderie was a powerful inducement for stars to "step out of character" and guy their screen image. [8]

Looking further ahead, there would have been a place for Stephenson in early American television especially in the genre of crime detection in a series such as: *The Adventures of Ellery Queen* (1950-1952). By then in his sixties it may be assumed he would have played the father figure Detective Inspector Queen rather than the male lead. [9]

It is reasonable to suggest that, all conditions being equal, Jimmy might well have found himself working again for both Edmund Goulding and William Wyler. Though illness curtailed Goulding's output during the 1940s, Jimmy could have been put to good use as a member of the supporting cast in *The Constant Nymph* (Warner, 1943). The quiet stoicism displayed in *The Letter* would not have been out of place as the stiff upper-lip spouse of *Mrs. Miniver* (M-G-M, William Wyler, 1942). Though the previous success of *Blossoms in the Dust* (M-G-M, Mervyn LeRoy, 1941), the first film to pair Walter Pidgeon alongside the redoubtable Greer Garson, would have probably prohibited Jimmy from attaining the role. [10]

In any case, Wyler again directed *The Letter* for television in an episode in the prestigious TV series *Producer's Showcase* broadcast on November 15, 1956. This, his television debut, featured Siobhan McKenna as Leslie and John Mills as Robert Crosbie, Cathleen Cordell as Mrs. Joyce and a particularly acclaimed performance from Anna May Wong as the Chinese woman.

The casting of English actor Michael Rennie in the part of attorney Howard Joyce (there is a noticeable passing resemblance in looks between both stars) suggests Wyler felt vindicated in using Jimmy in the original film. He certainly never forgot Jimmy's "first-rate" contribution.

Assuming Jimmy had lived to return to England, Alexander Korda might have used him as the stern cuckold, Alexei Karenin, in his 1948 version of Tolstoy's *Anna Karenina*, a part taken in the film by Ralph Richardson.

Though necessarily speculative and intriguing, all these hypotheses argue his talent and capacity as an actor would have coped with the challenges experienced by the American motion picture industry during the decade following his demise. It was a time of radical change in which the re-conversion of wartime to peacetime film production was accompanied by a precipitous decline in theatrical movie attendance, as the domestic mass-market was eaten away by the rise of television. There can be little doubt his early death robbed him of the opportunity to develop his screen career, and denied audiences the chance to enjoy further intriguing performances.

Back in Burnley, his old friends had ample opportunity to see him again on the silver screen and pay their respects. Just a week after his passing a local cinema was showing a double bill: John Garfield in *Flowing Gold* (Warner, Alfred E. Green, 1940) paired with *The Man Who Made Diamonds*. In the next few years a succession of his pictures played around cinemas in the town, including the Tivoli Cinema managed by "Jimmie" Landless – presenter of the silver cigarette case from the Burnley Players almost a decade before. The anniversary of his death was marked in memoriam, in the local Burnley Press, by his grief-stricken parents.

Meanwhile the world moved on. As the economic fortunes of Burnley declined and social circumstances changed so one-by-one his middle-class friends moved out of the town. The idealism of elocutionist Shannon Leslie fell into a benign eccentricity and following retirement in 1971 she moved to Warrington to live with her sister, a retired headmistress, where she died in 1979. Alan Coppock remained single and unmarried and died in an East Lancashire retirement home in 1983. Former friends Jack and Dorothy Grey retired to The Isle of Man in 1972, where, still hankering after the amateur stage, Jack Grey continued his theatrical interests almost up to the time of his death. Among his appearances on the Manx amateur stage was a 1986 production of Joao Bethencourt's farce: *The Day They Kidnapped the Pope* playing the part of the pope. His death on March 4, 1993 followed by his wife Dorothy on November 28, 1993 brought down the final curtain on those who had intimate knowledge of Jim Stephenson's years spent as an amateur actor in Burnley.

Ernest Bryce Clegg, Jim's former business partner relocated to The

Craggs Hotel in Morecambe, and later ran for public office becoming a conservative councillor in 1946. He ended up as Lord Mayor of Morecambe from 1954-55 and in his official capacity met HRH Queen Elizabeth on a Royal Tour of Lancashire in April 1955.

Saddest of all, Jim's former fiancée, Dorothy Stuttard, died in a Lancashire nursing home on July 31, 1987 aged eighty-two. Despite a succession of suitors and a short-lived marriage she revered Jim to the last. After his death she continued to maintain contact with the Stephenson family and was given a cigarette lighter belonging to Jim as a keepsake. During the 1960s and 1970s she would avidly watch sporadic showings of his films as, and when, they were revived on television.

Unfortunately for his surviving family the future proved hard and unkind. In the cruellest of ironies the day of his passing, instead of mourning and sadness, should have been spent in celebration and joy. Jim's death occurred less than twenty-four hours before what would have been the couple's fifth wedding anniversary on July 30. Counselling or therapy then being none-existent, his widow diverted her grief and sense of injustice into a tireless stoical pride and an unwavering fidelity to his memory.

Jimmy left a modest estate of $11,271.00. This financial reality meant fundamental adjustments had to be made for life to carry on. The sense of physical and emotional upset, caused by Lorna's departure from Toyopa Drive, is suggested by architectural blueprints in the family archive showing structural alterations to the small house; Thus there had been plans for the future comfort of family life so tragically curtailed.

Lorna Stephenson began the difficult readjustment to her new life as a single parent. An intelligent young woman, she studied Gregg shorthand and stenography and began full-time work as a secretary at KMPC, a local Los Angeles radio station. Lorna and her infant son Peter moved into a small apartment: 1528 South Bentley Avenue, Westwood, Los Angeles. There, Mrs. Florence Kaylin and her family took Lorna and Peter under their wing.

It was Jim's dying wish that the family back in England would be looked after, but a return voyage across the Atlantic during wartime hostilities was out of the question. Nevertheless, Lorna's family immediately begged her to return home: - "Come back, come back home Lorn'" the letters implored. Following the cessation of the war in Europe she immediately pulled some strings with the authorities. The result was that Peter and she crossed the Atlantic on the SS *Franconia* docking at Liverpool on June 8, 1945 where they returned to her parents at Abbey Lodge in West Kirby, England. Unfortunately what should have been a happy family reunion proved otherwise. In stark contrast to America's wartime economic boom and victorious prosperity, Britain was near bankrupt, exhausted and diminished by the hard slog of five years fighting. Confronting Lorna's homecoming was bleak economic austerity, depleted infrastructure, and severe rationing. Even the British weather turned hostile, with 1947 set to become one of the coldest winters on record.

Of more immediate concern was the decline of both the Dinn and Stephenson families. Soon after her return Lorna's mother, who had never fully recovered from a serious operation, died in 1947. Lorna, her brother now married and living in Scotland, was left to administer the estate and relocate her father to nearby Hoylake on Merseyside where he died, shortly after, in 1949. In 1953 her brother Gilbert also died.

On the Stephenson side things were just as sad. Emma Stephenson had died after an illness lasting seven weeks on October 26, 1944 aged seventy-eight at the Queen Victoria Hospital, Morecambe. [11] Norman, Jim's younger brother, suffered an early death aged only fifty-five on July 30, 1949. [12] Alan Stephenson never completely recovered from the loss of his prestigious position at Coventry Cathedral. During the late 1940s his physical health began to deteriorate and, like his elder brother, he too died of a fatal heart attack on May 2, 1950 at his flat in Heysham aged fifty-eight. [13] Finally, his family having predeceased him, John Gathorne Stansfield Stephenson died alone aged eighty-two on October 22, 1950. [14]

By the early 1950s Lorna and Peter had relocated to Georgina Cottage in the village of Hemingford Abbots, Huntingdonshire. Though a genteel sounding place it was in fact a rudimentary one-up and one-down dwelling and lacked all the amenities and ambience of the former Dinn middle-class residence, Abbey Lodge. Although life during this period was spartan and difficult a few choice reminders of happier times presented themselves. There were occasional visits to the Patric Knowles's when they came over from the States to stay with relatives in England. Lorna and Peter also met Lloyd Nolan backstage in London during a theatrical run of Herman Wouk's *The Caine Mutiny* in 1955 and reminisced about the days with Jimmy at Warners. [15]

Lorna still kept up her interest in writing and often submitted short articles for broadcast on the BBC Radio programme *Womans' Hour*. A surviving manuscript on the subject of beginning a career in the city of London resonates with the memory of Jimmy. The title, *Something in the City*, recalls one of his plays at Liverpool Playhouse. There is also reference to "such mighty sums have "stand-ins," as the films call it." [16]

The sense of profound loss would remain to the very end of her life, cut short tragically by cancer.

Opportunities to catch any of Jimmy's old films were few and far between but, fortunately, during the mid-1950s a reissue of *Calling Philo Vance* came to a local cinema. Lorna took Peter along to view his late father whose portrait, along with the Oscar nomination citation, hung proudly on the parlour wall in Hemingford Abbots. Unfortunately, youthful inattention meant Peter missed the beginning of the picture at the precise moment when Jimmy's face appeared underneath his character name during the credits. A golden chance to see his "legendary" father, appearing out of character as it were, was missed. As the years went by opportunities to learn more about the man seemed to slip away and his memory lapsed into pomp without any circumstance.

In 1965 Peter Stephenson re-crossed the pond to become a student and instructor of the University of California, Davis. Upon graduation in 1967 he declined to attend the graduation ceremony presided over by the Governor of California. Back in 1941 the holder of this state office had put pen to paper and given Peter's father a final valediction. It read:

"Dear Friend:

> This letter you have asked me to write is very difficult. Not because I'm at a loss for things to say about Jim but because I'm at loss to express what is in my heart.

> We made several pictures together, more perhaps than either of us made with any other actor so I can tell you Jim was honored and happy when you formed this club and felt deeply grateful to all of you.

> And I can assure you, he was completely worthy of your decision to organise a club in his behalf. Worthy as to talent and ability in his profession and worthy as to character and high standards as a man.

> As a friend may I thank you for the honor you did him.

> Sincerely,

> Ronald Reagan" [17]

Needless to say, the turns of history give this particular eulogy an added significance.

The party may be over and the parade may have long gone by but, on celluloid at least, the scenarios of the past are preserved ready to be seen again and re-interpreted by future generations. As Shakespeare reminds us the path to immortality is achieved either through bequeathing heirs or producing a body of work. Jimmy Stephenson accomplished both.

Having sifted through the surviving evidence and presented all the relevant facts how stand the final conclusions on James Albert Stephenson?

Compared to many other stars, he did not exhibit manifestations of petulance or egocentricity, traits common among the acting fraternity. Instead his overriding characteristic was an old-fashioned reticence. Understatement and discretion were his watchwords. This is in stark contrast to contemporary twenty-four/seven media culture based on celebrity saturation and hyper surveillance where confession and immodesty are the order of the day. The myth of the English gentleman, though still palpable, has, of late, become the object of some derision and parody. However, back then in this vanished culture self-deprecation, discipline, good manners, civility and a certain obligation to others were all admirable and saleable qualities much in demand by cinema audiences of the day. Representations of such English gentility were many and various. In the premier league stood Ronald Colman (upright and decent), Leslie Howard (dreamy and intellectual), Herbert Marshall (dogged and faithful) and Basil Rathbone (formidable and incisive). Among a plethora of second lead gentleman players were: Ian Hunter, Patric Knowles, John Loder and Reginald Denny – all solid, dependable English types and cache at the box office.

In succeeding years since his death the glamorous star imagery of James Stephenson, matinee idol, manufactured by the Hollywood studio system has been displayed, duplicated and revived in perpetuity through television and contemporary digital media. An English television broadcast of *The Letter* in January 1968 prompted a series of articles about amateur dramatics in the Burnley local press. John Grey was invited to talk briefly about his old friend: "It was quite eerie to see someone whom one [had] known so well coming back after all those years," he recalled. [18]

In contrast, for his surviving family there is the unresolved limbo of seeing their next of kin revived on screen but without any tangible memories. Trying to discover some personal private reality that cuts through the fictional make-believe presents difficulties. Despite all these deficiencies his family has sponsored a dedication plaque, secured surreptitiously to the back of a seat, in a local cinema arts venue in England. It reads simply: "Remembering James Stephenson, Oscar Nominated, *The Letter* (1940)."

The journey from 162 Todmorden Road, Burnley Wood, Burnley, Lancashire to 839 Toyopa Drive, Pacific Palisades, Hollywood, California, via war service on the Western Front, cotton shipping in Shanghai, amateur dramatics in Burnley and professional acting on the English theatrical stage in Liverpool and London, had been a long and circuitous one. His time at the top of his chosen profession had been

Jimmy captured whistling on the Warner Burbank lot.
PHOTO COURTESY OF STEPHENSON ARCHIVE

barely six months. During this brief spell his capabilities had been widely recognised among his peers and within the industry he had finally won the hard sought after kudos and esteem that had, for so long, eluded him. His cultivated, well-bred and distinguished presence brought a solid sensibility to the screen, someone for audiences to identify with and admire during those turbulent times of global instability.

This narrative has striven to provide a picture of the man and his era. In casting light on this "dark horse of Hollywood" it is conceded there are still areas of his life that remain shrouded in mystery. If, through the lapse of time, the reticence of the man has not been penetrated sufficiently then so it must, with regret and reluctance, remain. There are, I believe, no complicating motives in regard to his decision to become an actor. Through a combination of determination, sheer hard work, perseverance and a couple of lucky breaks he did manage to reach near to the top rung of the ladder of stardom, only to miss his footing suddenly and tragically be taken away.

All things being equal, many decades after his passing, he deserves to be acknowledged and remembered. "A grand bloke," as the English say, or to use the American equivalent, "A swell guy."

Jimmy and Lorna Stephenson at the dining room table of their home
839 Toyopa Drive, Pacific Palisades.
Note Jimmy's passing resemblance to actor Warner Baxter.
Photo courtesy of Stephenson Archive

Jimmy and Lorna with their son, Peter, at home on the lawn.
Photo courtesy of Stephenson Archive

Jimmy at home reading his film script. The shot may be posed,
but his preparation for a film part was always diligent and thorough.
PHOTO COURTESY OF STEPHENSON ARCHIVE

Jimmy stood outside his home.
PHOTO COURTESY OF STEPHENSON ARCHIVE

NOTES AND REFERENCES

PREFACE

[1] Harry Stephenson Garraway (1871-1956) took his middle forename and adopted it as his stage name. Born in Grenada, British West Indies, he spent his education at Rugby School followed by a period in the British army before making his Broadway stage debut in 1901 in *Messenger from Mars*. He entered films in 1917, but found his metier in Hollywood from 1932 onwards. Unusually he was cast as a murderer in *Guilty as Hell* (Paramount, Erle C. Kenton, 1932), but reverted to type by repeating his Broadway stage role as an English aristocrat in *Cynara* (Goldwyn, King Vidor, 1932). By this time in his sixties, he tended to play either crusty but benevolent patriarchs such as Emperor Franz Josef in *Spring Parade* (Universal, Henry Koster, 1940) or venerable avuncular gentlemen of which, among his final films, Mr. Brownlow in *Oliver Twist* (Cineguild, David Lean, 1948) was typical. Although unrelated, both Henry and James appeared on screen together in *The Private Lives of Elizabeth and Essex* (Warner, Michael Curtiz, 1939)

[2] Thomson, p.926

[3] McFarlane, p.637

[4] Quinlan, pp.486-87

INTRODUCTION

[1] Speer, p.250

[2] Undated manuscript written by Ida Zeitlin and published in abridged form in *Photoplay* October 1941

[3] Lake Arrowhead is situated on the San Bernardino Valley ninety-five miles north of Los Angeles. Its picturesque scenery has been used to effect in many Hollywood films. Noteworthy examples include: *Flesh and the Devil* (M-G-M, Clarence Brown, 1926); *Sunrise: A Song of Two Humans* (Fox, F[rederick] W[ilhelm] Murnau, 1927) and *Magnificent Obsession* (Universal-International, Douglas Sirk, 1954).

[4] As a rule ofa thumb, during the 30s and 40s a film was considered a major "A" or super production if costs approached or exceeded $1,000,000. In the case of Kings Row the production exceeded its initial budget of $850,000.

[5] In a caustic fulmination, verging on the libellous, Michael Balcon, British producer of A[ssociated]T[alking]P[ictures] Studios, Ealing, accusingly stated:
"I am surprised and disgusted by the attitude of the British people at present in Hollywood. . .These people have in the past enjoyed the advantages and the profits of working in Britain. When things become tough here, they immediately desert the country and the British film industry, and take cover in Hollywood. With them go an assortment of Central Europeans who have been given refuge in this country, who have in many cases gained the benefits of British naturalization, but who have no intention of repaying Britain in return."
[Here Balcon may have had in mind the recent relocation to Hollywood of the entire cast and crew of the lavish spectacular fantasy *The Thief of Bagdad* (London Films, Alexander Korda, et al, 1940). Stars Sabu, Conrad Veidt and June Duprez, stayed on in Hollywood as did composer Miklos Rozsa and producer Alexander Korda. During his stay in Hollywood Korda would produce *That Hamilton Woman* also known as *Lady Hamilton* (London Films, Alexander Korda, 1941), allegedly Winston Churchill's favourite film, and *Jungle Book* (London Films, Zoltan Korda, 1942)]
" I am not a recruiting sergeant . . . But I do maintain that they should return to this country and help with the war effort, instead of cavorting about in Hollywood, evading all indirect taxation and - if they were clever enough to get to Hollywood more than twelve months ago – evading even direct income tax as well. They do not work for their country; they do not even contribute their share of the expense of

defending it. . . There have been many excuses put forward on behalf of the Britains who have run to find a safe and luxurious haven in California. One of the most fantastic is that they have been advised by our ambassadors and consuls in America that their services are not required in this country." [Balcon, p.11]

It should be noted that as Balcon vented his spleen, the military and political fortunes of the British war effort were at their lowest ebb, having just suffered the humiliating debacle of the Norway expedition, and the resignation of Prime Minister Neville Chamberlain. On taking over wartime leadership Winston Churchill told the country, in his maiden speech on May 13, 1940, he had nothing to offer but: "blood, sweat and tears". Eric L. Wigham in an article, "Britain Needs Her Fine Film Team Here," [Manchester Evening News, May 8, 1940 p.4], blamed the British Government for its lack of vision in supporting the film industry since the war began. Another notable j'accuse article, written in June 1940 in the *Sunday Pictorial*, was provocatively titled "Gone with the Wind Up," and penned by venerable English actor Sir Seymour Hicks.

[6] Though given the plain name of Edward [Frederick Lindley] Wood (1881-1959) Halifax was, as son of Charles the Viscount Halifax, born into the English aristocracy. He overcame disability, he was born without a left-hand and also spoke with a slight lisp, and went on to forge a career as a Tory grandee, and achieve the glittering prizes of high political office. His impressive CV included: The Viceroyalty of India; President of the Board of Education; Secretary of State for War; Lord Privy Seal and Leader of the House of Lords; Lord President of the Council; Foreign Secretary and Ambassador to Washington. Viewed by his critics as patrician, pious, aloof and snobbish the tall, lugubrious Halifax was certainly prone to social gaffes, such as mistaking the diminutive Hitler for a footman when greeting him at the Berghof, the Fuhrer's Alpine retreat at Berchtesgaden, on November 19, 1937. Halifax found Hitler to be: "a very nasty little man, but inspired". [Roberts, p.48] Hitler, in return, referred to England's ambassador contemptuously as: "diesen englischen 'Pfarrer' / the English parson." [Schmidt, p.76] Hitler, however, was delighted to inform Halifax that his favourite film, *Lives of a Bengal Lancer* (Paramount, Henry Hathaway, 1935), was compulsory viewing for the SS as "that was how a superior race must behave" [Kirkpatrick, p.97].

[7] Zeitlin, p.109

CHAPTER ONE

[1] Although the property in Selby survives both the exterior and interior of the building have undergone extensive structural alteration and today would be unrecognisable to former occupants.

[2] General Register Office Register of Marriages: October-December 1888, Selby, 9c, 1205

[3] GRO Register of Births: April-June 1889, Selby, 9c, 810.
As already noted Stephenson's birthday coincided with that of two historical figures. Hitler was born on April 20, 1889. In his autobiography Chaplin claimed to have been born on April 16, 1889. However, his parents being travelling stage performers neglected to register his birth and, therefore, there is no official record of his birth. [Robinson, p.10] It has been suggested Chaplin's birth date is taken from his mother's father, Charles Frederick Hill, born on April 16, 1839. On February 17, 2012 newly declassified records released by the National Archives, in London, revealed the British Security Service, MI5, mounted an investigation into the mysterious circumstances of Chaplin's birth. File KV 2/3700 shows, despite extensive searches by MI5, at the request of the US authorities; British intelligence could find no birth certificate.

[4] GRO Register of Births: July-September 1891, Todmorden, 9a, 236
Stephenson's forename is recorded as "Allan" (sic)

[5] GRO Register of Births: July-September 1894, Todmorden, 9a, 221

[6] The former chemist shop on Parliament Street still stands today. Though somewhat dilapidated, the property is conspicuous from adjacent terraces by virtue of being built two storeys high rather than the conventional one storey.

[7] During the 1960s the local council changed the building numbers on Todmorden Road and today 162 is now 172.

[8] Surmelian, p.96

[9] For a visual representation of northern England in the Edwardian era see the films of Sagar Mitchell and James Kenyon who roamed the British Isles filming the everyday lives of ordinary people at work and play.

Presented as "Local Films for Local People" and "We take them and make them" Mitchell and Kenyon's films capture the traditions of a bygone era in huge quantity and with pristine clarity. These early films were all but forgotten when they eventually turned up, all 826 nitrate rolls, stored in seventeen sealed barrels in the cellar of a Blackburn shop nearly a century later. Taken from the original camera negatives these films are, in terms of quality and scope, an unparalleled window on a lost world. See *The Lost World of Mitchell and Kenyon: Edwardian Britain on Film*, (eds.) Vanessa Toulmin, Patrick Russell and Simon Popple, London, British Film Institute, 2004

[10] *Burnley Express*, July 11, 1900, p.4

[11] Bennett, p.47

[12] Coué, p.18

[13] Marden, p. v

[14] Marden, p. v

[15] Marden, p. v

[16] Marden, p. vi

[17] Marden, p. vi

[18] Marden, p. vi

[19] Marden, p. vi

[20] *Burnley Express*, December 22, 1906, p.16

[21] *Burnley Gazette*, November 17, 1900, p.4

[22] Dimbleby and Reynolds, pp.142-43

[23] WO 374 / 65170, National Archives
According to Alan Stephenson's army service records he was, at 5ft 7¼, the smaller in height of his siblings. He was also short-sighted and had been ill with appendicitis.

[24] *Burnley Express*, October 16, 1904, p.5

[25] *Burnley Express*, June 30, 1906, p.5
In 100 yards (under fourteen) Norman Stephenson came first place and in the half-mile bicycle handicap he took third place

[26] Barrett (8th Ed.), p.212

[27] *Burnley Express*, September 18, 1909, p.4

[28] A grand old man of Burnley William Henry Douglas Flack (1858-1936), eldest son of Captain Flack of Burnley, was head boy of Burnley Grammar School. He began his tenure in banking aged eighteen in 1870 and at the time of his retirement in 1922 had clocked up fifty-two years in the profession. From 1905 he served as a local borough magistrate and was affiliated to various charitable committees and cultural societies in the town including honourable treasurer to The Burnley Victoria Hospital Fund, the Burnley Chamber of Commerce, the Police Court Mission and The Burnley Clef Club. His esteemed position of local magistrate in the community entitled him to provide the necessary character references for James Stephenson's application as a British Army Officer in 1914 by certifying his good moral character during his eight year record of employment at the bank. [See War Records: WO329-65205, National Archives]

[29] Surmelian, p.96

[30] *Burnley Express*, January 18, 1913, p.7

[31] VLBU 2/6 P.12, Lancashire Record Office

[32] VLBU 2/3, Lancashire Record Office. A model of Humberette has the distinction of being the main attraction in one of the earliest film's featuring a motor car. The British silent short trick film *The ? Motorist* (Robert W. Paul, Walter Robert Booth, 1906)

[33] ERB 20 / R.P.E. 11 p.85; ERB 22 / K1757 p.65, Burnley Local History Library

[34] *Burnley News*, July 21, 1928, p.9

[35] For a contemporary rendering of this colloquial expression see Richards, 1973, p.187

[36] Nietzsche, Section 6, Aphorism 208, p.101

[37] *Burnley Express*, August 1, 1914, p.9

[38] *Burnley Express*, February 22, 1985, p.18

[39] WO 95 / 1270, National Archives

[40] WO 374 / 65205, National Archives

[41] WO 374 / 65205, National Archives

[42] WO 374 / 65205, National Archives

[43] GRO Register of Marriages: October – December 1916, Gainsborough, 7a 1526

[44] GRO Register of Deaths: October - December 1916, Burnley, 8c, 302

[45] Order of the Day, April 11, 1918, Stephenson Archive

[46] Lloyd George, *War Memoirs*, Vol. IV, pp.2266-2267

[47] Hart, pp.40-41

[48] WO 95 / 411, National Archives

[49] Discharge Form A.F. W.3723, Stephenson Archive

[50] Stephenson Archive

[51] Order of the Day, August 4, 1918, Stephenson Archive

[52] *Burnley Express*, January 29, 1921, p.1

[53] Beaumont, p.29

[54] See Commonwealth War Graves Commission Website

[55] M9/40/2/10563, Manchester Central Reference Library Archives

[56] Jackson, p.158

[57] Slaters, p.770

[58] *Burnley News*, October 16, 1920, p.13

[59] *Burnley News*, March 28, 1925, p.15

[60] *Burnley News*, March 23, 1927, p.6

[61] *London Gazette*, January 4, 1927, *The Times*, January 5, 1927, p.19; *Manchester Guardian*, January 1, 1927, p.4

[62] *Manchester Guardian*, October 19, 1923, p.12

[63] *The Times*, Law Notices, April 2, 1925, p.5

[64] UDPA 32/3; UDPA 32/4; UDPA 32/5, Lancashire Record Office

[65] VLBU 2/12; VLBU/4/1: CW7918, Lancashire Record Office

[66] For details in changing male fashion styles see G. Bruce Boyer, Elegance: *A Guide to Quality in Menswear*, New York, Norton, 1986. As a bank cashier in the early years of the twentieth century James Stephenson would have been obliged to adhere to a strict occupational dress code. Any deviation, such as the removal of a jacket without prior permission of his superiors, would have resulted in instant dismissal. The received notion of sartorial formality would have consisted of a starched collar and tie, a three piece suit, with watch and chain. The latter survives in the family archive.

[67] *Burnley News*, December 2, 1925, p.3; Burnley News, August 4, 1926, p.7

[68] BT26 / 849/79, National Archives

[69] *The Times*, November 20, 1928, p.1

[70] The 1911 Census (RG14PN2992 RG78PN104 RD32 SD1 ED11 SN316)

reveals a small army of servants were employed to run the Wilkinson household at the fourteen room Outram House, St George's Avenue, Weybridge, Surrey. To facilitate their comfortable Edwardian lifestyle the Wilkinson family had call upon a cook and three domestic servants. There was also a governess for Adela and her younger sister Mabel Outram Wilkinson.

[71] *Northern Daily Telegraph*, November 20, 1929, p.4

[72] *Burnley News*, November 23, 1929, p.15

[73] *Burnley Express*, February 27, 1968, p.9

[74] Thistlethwaite, p.265

[75] *Burnley Express*, February 10, 1932, p.5

[76] *Burnley News*, February 10, 1932, p.4

[77] *Liverpool Echo*, June 1, 1936, p.10

[78] *Burnley Express*, June 3, 1931, p.6

[79] *Bury Times*, February 11, 1931, p.2

CHAPTER TWO

[1] *Burnley News*, August 17, 1929, p.5
A political sketch headed *Cost of a Clear Atmosphere*, depicts smoking chimneys obscuring the skyline of the town. A caption reads: "We often have a lot to say about Burnley's smoky chimneys," underneath another sketch of smokeless chimneys the caption continues: "But when they do cease to smoke, as at the present time, we read an unwelcome message in the clearer atmosphere" In the drawing the words: "LOST TRADE" are spelt out in the form of chimney stacks.

[2] *Burnley News*, July 5, 1930, p.12

[3] *The Times*, August 23, 1930, p.10

[4] *Burnley Express*, June 3, 1931, p.6

[5] *Burnley News*, July 30, 1932, p.9

[6] *Burnley Express*, June 2, 1934, p.3

[7] *Burnley Express*, August 27, 1938, p.3
Reverend Battye proclaimed seven reasons for Sunday worship: "Worship of God; To obey the Lord; To attend as a family through worship; To witness our faith; To receive help and inspiration; To learn about our faith; To progress after the example of the Lord."

[8] Benjamin, pp.11-12

[9] *The Listener*, February 7, 1934, p.216

[10] *Burnley Express*, December 2, 1933, p.15

[11] *Manchester Guardian*, March 2, 1933, p.18.
Among the twenty-one signatories were architect Clough William-Ellis (1883-1978) and his wife Amabel William-Ellis (1894-1984); creators of the Italianate village of Portmeirion in North Wales setting for the cult British TV series *The Prisoner* (ITC, Patrick McGoohan *et al*, 1967-68)

[12] Stalin, p.530.
"The Tasks of Economic Executives" Speech delivered at the first All-Union conference of Leading Personnel of Socialist Industry on February 4, 1931

[13] Shirer, p.77

[14] Jones, p.191

[15] Thomas Herbert Lomas was born on January 17, 1887 [GRO Register of Births: January- March 1887, vol. 8a, p.217, Burnley] at 10 Hargreaves Street, Burnley. Lomas was the third son of Thomas Henry Lomas (1851-1910) master confectioner and Phoebe Lomas née Smith. He attended Bellingham's School in Colne Road and Red Lion Street Higher Grade School in Burnley. After completing his formal education he worked for Joseph Henry Howarth, an auctioneer on Manchester Road. Lomas, unlike Jim Stephenson, had caught the acting bug early and was determined to enter the profession. Showing no aptitude for the auctioneering trade he enrolled at The Royal Academy of Dramatic Art, and began his

professional acting career aged nineteen in 1906. He was for many years a member of Miss Annie Horniman's Company. Lomas at 6ft 1½" tall was gaunt and lugubrious with a hollow voice, and though only two years older than Stephenson, he excelled in character parts. Early success on the stage included John Rutherford in *Rutherford and Son* and Nat Jeffcote in *Hindle Wakes*. Lomas married Clarissa Nancy Nutter (1882-1977) a music teacher on July 11, 1911 at Padiham Unitarian Church [GRO Register of Marriages: July-September 1911; vol. 8e, p.644, Burnley.] A daughter, Nancy, was born in 1912. During the First World War Lomas served for two years as a gunner in the Royal Garrison Artillery. From 1922 to 1927 he was an outstanding member of the Liverpool Repertory Theatre. He was particularly effective in Lancashire pieces by Stanley Houghton, *Hindle Wakes*, and Harold Brighouse, *Hobson's Choice*. Though he never made the trip out to Hollywood he played the Broadway Stage in four productions. These included a short run at Maxine Elliot's Theatre in *Hindle Wakes* (1912-13) accompanied by Roland Young also making his Broadway debut. *The Skin Game* (1920-21) directed by Basil Dean at the Bijou Theatre; *Fanny Hawthorn* 1922 at the Vanderbilt and the successful comedy, *Bird in the Hand*, at the Booth (1929-30) playing Thomas Greenleaf, with Ivor Barnard and Roddy Hughes. As a character player he was active in films from 1931 until the mid-1950s. Among his more memorable film appearances were two Arthur Wontner Sherlock Holmes vehicles: *The Missing Rembrandt* (Twickenham, Leslie Hiscott, 1932) and *The Sign of Four* (Associated Talking Pictures, Graham Cutts, 1932); Sir Ensor Doone in *Lorna Doone* (ATP, Basil Dean, 1934); Vladinoff in the underrated Alexander Korda production *Knight Without Armor* (London Film, Jacques Feyder, 1937), coroner Thomas Knight in *Inquest* (Charter, Roy Boulting, 1939), a bogus coastguard in *Ask a Policeman* (Gainsborough, Marcel Varnel, 1939) and the stationmaster in *The Ghost Train* (Gainsborough, Marcel Varnel, 1941). He also appeared in small roles in other Alexander Korda productions: *The Ghost Goes West*, (London Film, René Clair, 1935) *Rembrandt* (London Film, Alexander Korda, 1936) and *South Riding* (London Film, Victor Saville, 1938). There were also minor film roles for such major directors as: Hitchcock in *Jamaica Inn* (Mayflower, 1939), Michael Powell in *The Phantom Light* (Gainsborough, 1935), Powell and Pressburger's *I Know Where I'm Going!* (The Archers, 1945) and the Boulting Brothers all-star *The Magic Box* (British Lion, 1951). Tom Herbert Lomas of 3 Brookfield Close, Golvers Hill Road, Kingsteignton, Devon. Died April 11, 1961 at Hawkmoor Chest Hospital, Bovey Tracey, Devon. Effects of £12268 2s were bequeathed to his daughter Nancy Lomas, spinster. [GRO Register of Deaths: April-June 1961 07a 539 Newton Abbot]

[16] It was during a BBC radio broadcast of December 10, 1930 that contentious opinions about the town were expressed in a discussion programme in which Mr. L. Du Garde Peach contended: "I like the Northern Country" whilst Mr. E.M. Lustgarten., opined, "I prefer the Northern Town". According to Peach, Burnley was "a blot on the landscape" and "some of the dregs of humanity lived in it." His aspersions culminated: "It is a town to be avoided, its inhabitants being on the whole of a low moral and intellectual standard, lacking in the milk of human kindness." This outburst was met with a mixture of indifference (prominent townsmen such as the mayor and the Bishop of Burnley refused to comment) others brushed it aside as a cheap comic remark: "He is talking daft" noted Mr. W.M. Whitehead A.R.C.A. Principal of the Burnley Municipal School of Art. While Dr. Howarth M.A. Director of Education explained away Peach's onslaught: "He has said Burnley is a blot on the landscape before. He is a comedian, or, at least, he tries to be!" L[awrence] Du Garde Peach (1890-1974) was a prolific writer of history with his finger on the pulse for popularising historical subjects primarily on radio. He had started his working life as a school teacher, and had taught English for a time at the Burnley Grammar School, but had detested the job and had left the teaching profession as soon as he was able to support himself as a writer. Later, from 1933 until 1943, he wrote screenplays for many British films including: *Red Ensign* (Gaumont-British, Michael Powell, 1934); the Anglo-American *The Tunnel* (Gaumont-British, Maurice Elvey, 1935); *Turn of the Tide* (British National, Norman Walker, 1935) - flour magnate and would-be movie mogul J. Arthur Rank's initial foray into feature film production; *His Lordship* (Gaumont-British, Herbert Mason, 1936) in which George Arliss played a dual role; the delightful comedy-thriller *Seven Sinners* (Gaumont-British, Albert de Courville, 1936) with Edmund Lowe and Constance Cummings playing light comedy in the mould of *The Thin Man* series. The worthy, but dull, *The Great Mr. Handel* (GHW, Norman Walker, 1942) and the George Formby comedy *Get Cracking* (Columbia British, Marcel Varnel, 1943). Its home guard setting provided the archetype for the later successful British television situation comedy series *Dad's Amy* (1968-1977) produced by the BBC. Edgar Marcus Lustgarten (1907-1978) was a Manchester barrister turned crime writer, best remembered for hosting two crime film series: *Scotland Yard* (1953-1961) thirty-nine episodes and *Scales of Justice* (1962-1967) thirteen episodes all produced at Merton Park Studios.

[17] *Burnley News*, July 2, 1932, p.13
The Burnley Players and the Drama Guild disbanded in the mid 1930s.
The Burnley Operatic Society also ceased in 1937

[18] Arnold, pp. 45, 70, 6

[19] Karr, p.74

[20] *Todmorden Advertiser*, February 26, 1932, p.3
A surviving letter dated December 13, 1930 from Fred Smith of 48 Plumbe
Street, Burnley offered congratulations: ". . . upon your splendid portrayal
of Jack Tanner in "*Man and Superman*" I may say that an Esme Percy or
a George S. Wray could not have handled the part more efficiently. The
whole company deserve unstinted praise for the masterly way in which
they tackled an undoubtedly difficult play in such an efficient manner." -
Stephenson Archive
Esme Percy (1887-1957) was a celebrated British stage actor much
associated with the plays of Bernard Shaw. He appeared in British films
from 1930 until the late 1940s and also appeared in early BBC television
plays. He is chiefly remembered for two roles: as the murderer, Handel
Fane, in Hitchcock's *Murder!* (British-International-Pictures, 1930) and
Professor Higgins suspicious pupil, Karpathy, in Anthony Asquith's
Pygmalion (Gabriel Pascal, 1938). George S. Wray (1889-1950) was
another British stage actor who specialised in performing Shavian Plays.
He came to Burnley in March 1923 in a touring production of *Pygmalion*
with the Macdona Players and returned again in March 1930. On March 3,
1930 Wray along with popular Scottish music hall entertainer Will Fyffe,
were guests of the Burnley Rotary Club. Wray addressed the Burnley
Rotarians on: "A Few Remarks on Shaw." He was active in the British
theatre c.1918 until c.late1940s.

[21] *Burnley Express*, December 13, 1930, p.4

[22] Ashlar Lodge Papers No 4858, Stephenson Archive
At a regular lodge meeting on October 1, 1930 members were asked to
ballot the following candidate for initiation: James Albert Stephenson 162
Todmorden Road, Burnley oil merchant, aged 41 years. Proposers were
Brother Ernest Bryce Clegg and seconded by Brother Arthur S. Leedam.
At an Emergency lodge on October 22, 1930 he was duly initiated having
been previously elected by members. He joined the Burnley Rotary club
in early 1930 and resigned, after taking to the stage, in late 1932. He was

especially in demand as a singer assisting John Pickles and Laurie Lord in "Songs of the Old World" at the rotary Christmas concert, December 22, 1930. [Cunliffe, p.259] On June 29, 1931 he led in song following Rotarian President Job Hartley's Valedictory Address. [Cunliffe, p.260] He also gave two talks at the Burnley Rotary Club on the subjects of: "The Plays of George Bernard Shaw" on November 30, 1931 followed by "Art and the Box Office" on August 8, 1932. Other speakers invited to address rotary dinners included Miss Shannon Leslie speaking on "The Drama and Its Relation to the Community" [Cunliffe, p.257] and Mr. H.J. Dunkerley on the topic of "BBC Programmes and Group Listening" [Cunliffe, p.261]

[23] Conversation with John "Jack" Lord (1912-2010) to the author on October 17, 2009

[24] *Burnley News*, July 20, 1929, p.9.
A party from Burnley including Jack Grey, Alan Coppock and Alan Shaw had sailed across to the French port of Boulogne. On this crossing the group met two young women from Gillingham, Kent. Dorothy Eleanor Eade, a pianist by profession, and her sister. Upon reaching Boulogne they took the opportunity to view a Casino to "satisfy a legitimate curiosity." On their way out they were approached by an English speaker who recommended a nearby restaurant. Though the three course meal was satisfactory, when the bill was presented to the party it proved an expensive mistake. Jack Grey married Dorothy Eade on July 12, 1931.

[25] *Burnley Express*, March 12, 1968, p.9
Grey was a veritable one-man band of cultural pursuits in Burnley. A founder member of the Burnley Operatic Society in 1928, he was also stage manager and secretary. With Jim he was a founder member of the Burnley Drama Guild in the early 1930s. He helped form Burnley Artist's Society (1949-1951) with painter Noel Harry Lever ARCA (1889-1951). He instantly spotted and assisted Jim's acting talent. A letter dated February 23, 1931, written from his business address, 1A Yorke St. Burnley, praises Jim's invaluable contribution in staging Strindberg's *The Father*. "With many thanks for all your help in putting over, what I feel sure, was an excellent show and one which at any rate as far as I am concerned, gave a great deal of pleasure in a good thing well done" [Stephenson Archive]. Jack, like Jim, was an active Rotarian in the town and assisted him during his talk on "The Plays of Bernard Shaw" at a Rotary Lunch on November 30, 1931. Jack Grey was the conduit that ensured copy appeared in the

local press c.1924-1940 regarding the activities of amateur dramatics and musical opera in the town. His cordial relations with the press, especially with *Burnley News* editor Arthur Rought-Brooks (1880-1947), proved decisive in providing Jim Stephenson with contacts and opportunities. Rought-Brooks had interviewed actor Herbert Lomas back stage in 1919 [*Burnley News*, December 17, 1919, p.5]. A decade later, following the success of John Drinkwater's long running comedy *Bird in the Hand* on the Broadway stage, Lomas and his family sailed back to England on the SS *Samaria*, docking at Liverpool on June 23, 1930 [BT26/925/13, National Archives]. It was later reported in the local press "Bert" Lomas had returned to his Burnley home at 365 Clone Street. [*Burnley News*, July 5, 1930, p.9]

[26] *Burnley News*, April 2, 1930, p.4

[27] "Alan Stephenson was probably the strongest formative influence in my youth. He was a man who set standards. He was always 'Mr Stephenson' or sometimes 'Steve' or possibly 'Stevo' in choirboy-talk; never, as he might be today 'Alan'. When I came, many years later, to meet his widow, we talked quite freely about him, but always it was of a man whose high standards and strong character put him at a remove; and I personally was still under [his] spell. Everybody sang their best at his practices and there was no messing-about. Sometimes it seemed we could never satisfy him. Occasionally he would go so far as to remark that something, the introit perhaps, in the previous Sunday's services had been "Quite Lovely". That was the furtherest it ever went: "Quite Lovely". Usually there were grumbles and sometimes rages. Yet it could also happen that when we thought the thunderbolt must fall, we were somehow spared. One morning a treble lead was unaccountably missed in the *Te Deum*. I daresay we all knew when we should have sung; we just never came in. Retribution seemed inevitable and nobody was surprised when we were summoned to be in our places after service. But Steve simply ordered a run-through; this time all went well, and having been told not to do it again we were sent home to our Sunday dinners. No doubt he had one waiting as well.

He was sharp-eyed (beneath thick authoritarian spectacles), rather aquiline of nose, dangerously red of cheek, not a hair out of place, he wore a black cassock with a stern black belt. He mouthed our vowels and clipped our consonants as he conducted the introit in the side-chapel, after which we watched as his black heels disappeared up the steps to the organ. He was square-shouldered and physically rather formidable though of no more than average height. Nobody ever thought of him as small, and, in the eyes of at least one small choirboy, he was immense." Letter from John Steane to the author dated June 25, 2007 and conversation with John Rathbone to the author at Coventry Cathedral July 4, 2007

[28] A letter dated November 19, 1931 written by Walter G. Boys contains thirty-three signatures of members of the Burnley Drama Guild. It was written on the occasion of Jim's indisposition, (performing the role of Malvolio at the central library for the Drama Guild), due to illness. Next to John Grey's signature are the esoteric words "with kisses." Against Dorothy Grey's signature the word "ditto??" appears. This is indicative of the blossoming romance between Jim and Dorothy Stuttard. Stephenson Archive

[29] *Burnley Express*, December 24, 1932 p.9; *Burnley News*, December 24, 1932 p.16.
An editorial leader in the *Burnley News*, "Congratulations, Jim!" tendered hearty felicitations: "My readers will join me in congratulations to Mr. James A. Stephenson, first on his engagement to Miss Dorothy Stuttard (daughter of Mr. and Mrs. Willie Stuttard), and secondly, on his latest success in his chosen profession." [*Burnley News*, December 24, 1932 p.9.]

[30] Wednesday August 9, 1933: Dinner at the Moorcock Inn; Friday August 11, 1933: Meeting of Dorothy and Mrs. Stuttard at the Café Royal; Friday June 29, 1934: "Mrs. S[tephenson]. and I met Dorothy Stuttard by appointment at Towneley Gate at 4pm – But her mother came too! The meeting was a waste of time." - Diaries of Adela R. Stephenson: 1933-1937, Blain Archive.
When in October 1939 Norman Stephenson rejoined the army, following the outbreak of the Second World War, he was billeted at Fulwood Barracks, Longridge, Preston, Lancashire. Consequently, there are numerous subsequent meetings between "Toonie" Stephenson and Dorothy Stuttard noted in the diaries during the period 1940-41.

[31] Surmelian, pp. 33, 91
A scrapbook in the family archive contains only one page of this interview. It ends with an abrupt notation written by Jim in ink: "and so on!" Though referred to implicitly, the subject of their former relationship clearly remained raw and still rankled with him.

[32] *London Gazette*, December 15, 1933, p.8151

[33] Letter to Lorna Stephenson, March 10, 1936, Stephenson Archive

[34] Conversation with the author backstage at National Theatre, South Bank, London August 4, 2005. "I never got to know James Stephenson well. He was more serious and withdrawn than most members of the company, and therefore, to a young actor rather forbidding and serious, but always courteous and friendly, and always quiet and, I would say, very ambitious."

[35] When interviewed, Sam Beazley had no specific recollection of the legendary Maud Carpenter: "I never had much direct contact with her, but I was very much aware she was there." Conversation with the author backstage at National Theatre, South Bank, London August 4, 2005. As a sixteen-year-old actress at the Playhouse in 1949, writer Beryl Bainbridge, did have vivid memories of her. "Tall, bulky, always well dressed grey hair set in waves and curls as was the fashion. She always wore high heels and her walk was somewhat clumsy on account of them. She had a sort of Lancashire accent, not Liverpudlian . . . Husband David [Farrington] was very handsome, and charming. To me they were somewhat ill-matched. I believe she started out when very young in the bar of a Liverpool variety theatre, long since pulled down. Then she went to the box office of the Playhouse and upwards. I can see Maud now on the first night of the new season wearing her long black frock, and the way she strode up the corridor from her office." Letter to the author, August 6, 2005. Bainbridge's experiences at the Playhouse were the basis of her book *An Awfully Big Adventure* which was later filmed under the same title in 1995 and directed by Mike Newell. The character of Rose was based on the formidable Maud who ruled the Playhouse with a firm hand.

[36] *Liverpool Echo*, August 30, 1932, p.5

[37] *Radio Times*, November 11, 1932, p.413

[38] *Radio Times*, November 11, 1932, p.409

[39] *Radio Times*, November 11, 1932, p.409

[40] *Burnley News*, October 11, 1930, p.15

[41] *Manchester Evening Chronicle*, February 23, 1929, p.3

[42] Proctor, *Screen Life*, March 1941

[43] *Burnley News*, July 9, 1932, p.9

[44] *Manchester Guardian*, July 6, 1932, p.10

[45] *Burnley News*, August 10, 1932, p.5; *Burnley Express*, August 13, 1932, p.4

[46] Letter to Lorna Stephenson, November 30, 1936, Stephenson Archive

[47] *Liverpool Express*, October 12, 1932, p.6

[48] *Southport Guardian*, October 12, 1932, p.4

[49] *Southport Guardian*, October 12, 1932, p.4

[50] Redgrave, p.85

[51] Friday November 29, 1935, THM/31/4/1/3 – 1935, Redgrave Archive

[52] Thursday January 23, 1936, THM/31/4/1/4 – 1936, Redgrave Archive
Jim and Redgrave obviously overcame their disagreement, for a book of Redgrave's play *The Seventh Man* survives in the family archive. It is autographed: "Jim with best wishes Michael Redgrave 9.5.36."

[53] Karr, p.74

[54] These identical news quad sheets are taken from the *Liverpool Echo*. They are inscribed; "Another Playhouse Actor's Romance – Pictures."

[55] Surmelian, p.92

[56] *Southport Guardian*, June 7, 1933, p.3; *Birkenhead News*, June 7, 1933, Stephenson Archive

[57] *Stage*, June 8, 1933, Stephenson Archive

[58] *Birkenhead News*, March 3, 1934, Stephenson Archive

[59] *Liverpool Evening Express*, March 1, 1934, p.6

[60] *Liverpool Post*, April 12, 1934, p.5

[61] *Southport Guardian*, April 14, 1934, p.9

[62] *Liverpool Evening Express*, April 12, 1934, p.8

[63] *Liverpool Post*, August 31, 1934, p.5

[64] *Evening Express*, November 22, 1934, p.5

[65] The Playhouse Scrapbook Vol. III, August 1934 to June 1935, Stephenson Archive

[66] Jane Baxter had first appeared in the quota quickie *Bed and Breakfast* (Gaumont-British, Walter Forde, 1930). Having recently completed her only Hollywood feature *We Live Again* (Goldwyn, Rouben Mamoulian, 1934) she went on to appear opposite Richard Tauber in *Blossom Time* (British-International-Pictures, Paul L. Stein, 1934)

[67] Letter to Lorna Dinn, September 9, 1935, Stephenson Archive

[68] *Daily Dispatch*, October 10, 1935, Stephenson Archive

[69] *Liverpool Evening Express*, October 10, 1935, p.5

[70] Letter to Lorna Dinn, October 9, 1935, Stephenson Archive

[71] Letter to Lorna Dinn, October 11, 1935, Stephenson Archive

[72] Letter to Lorna Dinn, October 26, 1935, Stephenson Archive

[73] *Evening Express*, October 31, 1935, p.8

[74] *Liverpolitan*, February 1936, p.23

[75] *Evening Express*, January 30, 1936, p.10

[76] *Liverpool Echo*, February 4, 1936, p.11

[77] *Liverpool Post*, February 17, 1936, p.4

[78] *Liverpool Post*, February 20, 1936, p.5

[79] *Liverpolitan*, August 1936, p.21

[80] Letter to Lorna Stephenson, August 31, 1936, Stephenson Archive

[81] Letter to Lorna Stephenson, September 3, 1936, Stephenson Archive

[82] Letter to Lorna Stephenson, September 3, 1936, Stephenson Archive

[83] Letter to Lorna Stephenson September 29, 1936, Stephenson Archive

[84] Letter to Lorna Stephenson, October 18, 1936, Stephenson Archive

[85] These details are written on Letterhead paper with the address of the Stephenson's London flat: 1, Charlbert Court, Regents Park, N.W. 8. Stephenson Archive

[86] Letter to Lorna Stephenson, August 31, 1936, Stephenson Archive

[87] Letter to Lorna Stephenson, August 31, 1936, Stephenson Archive

[88] Letter to Lorna Stephenson, December 4, 1936, Stephenson Archive

[89] Letter to Lorna Stephenson, December 4, 1936, Stephenson Archive

[90] MEPO 10/35 Report by Special Branch, July 3, 1935, National Archives

[91] *Birmingham Post*, April 22, 1937, Stephenson Archive

[92] Postcard to author in 2003

[93] Letter to Lorna Stephenson, October 5, 1936, Stephenson Archive

[94] Letter to Lorna Stephenson, November 30, 1936, Stephenson Archive. Thorncroft Manor, south of Leatherhead, Surrey is an eighteenth century manor house situated in twenty-three acres of grounds with extensive frontages to the River Mole. Once described as "a country estate in miniature," the Wilkinson family during their tenure of the premises (c.1916-1938) had access to fifteen bedrooms, an impressive entrance hall leading to five reception rooms, including library, smoking and billiards rooms, a main dining room with a table seating sixteen people, and three bathrooms. In its grounds

were perfectly maintained rose and walled kitchen gardens, Paddocks and grazing land, an Entrance Lodge, Two Cottages and an extensive range of outbuildings. From the house, it was forty-five minutes by road to the town centre of Leatherhead, and a thirty minute rail journey to Waterloo Station, Central London. [*The Times*, May 26, 1938, p.31] Norman and Toonie and their three children lived at a smaller residence, "Riddlesdale" situated in Great Bookham, Surrey.

[95] Thursday November 16, 1937: "Very foggy. Drove to Liverpool Station. Parked the car. Train then to London. Fog soon cleared. Steve and I picked up Lorna and Jim at the club then went after to *Victoria the Great* – good film. Anna Neagle & Anton Walbrook." Diaries of Adela R. Stephenson: 1933-1937, Blain Archive.

The film was viewed at Leicester Square Theatre and the supporting programme included the latest Disney animated short, *The Old Mill* (Walt Disney, Wilfred Jackson, 1937). It won an Academy Award Winner for Best Short Subjects: Cartoons, in the Silly Symphony series.

CHAPTER THREE

[1] *Burnley Express*, April 16, 1932, p.8

[2] *Burnley News*, October 5, 1929, p.9

[3] Conversation with the author at Odiham, Hampshire, February 22, 2003

[4] *Burnley News*, July 2, 1932, p.13

[5] Other undistinguished second features scripted and directed by Donovan Pedelty include: *The Luck of the Irish* Sports drama released December 1935; *The Early Bird* Comedy released August 1936; *Irish and Proud of It* Irish comedy released November 1936; *Landslide* Crime drama released January 1937; and *Murder Tomorrow* crime drama released February 1938. Pedelty also provided the script for *Radio Pirates* also known as *Big Ben Calling* (Sound City, Ivar Campbell, 1935). Its storyline, involving a group of people who set up a pirate radio station, was a slim excuse for putting together a motley collection of wireless radio stars on screen. Apart from xylophonist Teddy Brown and Roy Fox and his band, the film contains the immodest, and unappealing sight of wireless juvenile Hughie Green (1920-1997) performing a *faux* impersonation of Maurice Chevalier. His caricature was achieved wearing a straw boater

perched at an angle on his head, pursing his lip whilst dressed in short trousers, and all accomplished with little shame or humility. The same brash, go-getting attitude would serve Green well throughout his career as host of radio and TV quiz game shows on British television from the 1950s to the 1970s.

[6] *Liverpool Evening Express*, October 10, 1935, p.1

[7] Theatrical agents Messrs. O'Bryen, Linnit and Dunfee had offices at 28 Brook Street, London W1. W J O'Bryen (1898-1977) married actress Elizabeth Allan in 1932. Known as Bill O'Bryen his full name was James Wheeler O'Bryen; Sydney Edmonds Linnit (1898-1956) or Bill Linnit, as he was known, once managed the writer Edgar Wallace; Jack Dunfee (1901-1975) was a former racing driver whose elder brother Clive, also a racing driver, was fatally injured at Brooklands racing track in 1932. At the time of his tragic death he was married to actress Jane Baxter.

[8] Letter to Lorna Stephenson, September 2, 1936, Stephenson Archive.
The Anglophile Douglas Fairbanks Jnr. (1909-2000) was not only an accomplished actor who managed to step out from his legendary father's shadow, but he also involved himself in the business side of the film industry. Criterion Films was the first of six companies created by Fairbanks. Four films were produced under the Criterion banner: *The Amateur Gentleman* (Thornton Freeland) a regency adventure released January 1936; *Accused* (Thornton Freeland) a crime drama released July 1936; *Crime over London* (Alfred Zeisler) a crime drama released October 1936; *Jump for Glory* also known as *When Thief Meets Thief* (Raoul Walsh) crime drama released March 1937. By coincidence, the offices of Criterion Film Productions Ltd were based at 28 Brook Street, London, W.1 the same building shared by agents O'Bryen, Linnit and Dunfee

[9] Letter to Lorna Stephenson, September 3, 1936, Stephenson Archive.
At the time of their meeting Herbert Lomas was appearing in a West End production of Ian Hay's *The Frog* based on the novel by Edgar Wallace, at the Princes Theatre. Gordon Harker, Jack Hawkins, Christine Barry, Percy Parsons and Cyril Smith also appeared in the cast. [Matthew] Howard Rose OBE, MC (1882-1978) had been appointed drama producer for the BBC station 2LO at Savoy Hill in 1925. He remained with the BBC for twenty-four years producing radio plays of every type. Among actors, Howard Rose was something of a legend in his own day. He knew the exact effect he wanted from every line of a play and was single-minded

in his determination to get it. Tall and distinguished, always well-dressed with a rose in his button-hole, he could be an awe-inspiring figure when the dramatic temperature in the studio began to rise. To some he remained a martinet; but to others he was an inspiration. He can be glimpsed directing a radio production of *Macbeth* in the documentary film *BBC – The Voice of Britain* (G-P-O, Stuart Legg, 1935)

[10] Letter to Lorna Stephenson, September 3, 1936, Stephenson Archive.

[11] Letter to Lorna Stephenson, October 6, 1936, Stephenson Archive. Harold Huth (1892-1967) had been a prolific stage and screen actor, but had retired from acting to become a casting director at Gaumont-British and later for M-G-M-British.

[12] Letter to Lorna Stephenson, November 16, 1936, Stephenson Archive.

[13] Powell, p.239

[14] The whole library of over 140 Warner Bros. British shorts and features produced at their Teddington Studios from 1931-1944 was once offered to the British Film Institute. These titles, predominately comedies and thrillers, were considered to possess little artistic merit or historical significance, and consequently it was decided to retain only a few films as a gesture to posterity. Ironically, in 1992 the British Film Institute launched a campaign called "Missing Believed Lost: A search for one hundred lost British feature films." A book with the same title listing all the sought-after films was published, and of these fifty-seven were the same Warner British films rejected as irrelevant several decades before. Among the surviving thirty plus titles that have surfaced in recent years are: *They Drive by Night* (Warner, Arthur Woods, 1938) a "noirish" thriller, *Man of the Moment* (Warner, Monty Banks, 1935), a screwball romantic comedy starring Douglas Fairbanks Jnr. and, much to his chagrin, several of Michael Powell's early films including: *Something Always Happens* (Warner, 1934) and *Crown v. Stevens* (Warner, 1936). *The Church Mouse* (Warner, Monty Banks, 1934), based on a Hungarian play by Ladislas Fedor, was filmed previously in Hollywood as *Beauty and the Boss* (Warner, Roy Del Ruth, 1932). It starred former silent actress Laura La Plante, who would later marry studio boss, Irving Asher, in 1936, and boasts the distinction of being given a general release in the United States, though this was an unusual exception.

[15] Powell, p.238 The quota quickie stigma is apparent in one of the earliest surviving quota films from the Teddington studios. *Illegal* (Warner, William McGann, 1932) lists actor D.A. Clarke-Smith erroneously on the main credits as D.E. Clarke-Smith!

[16] Co-star Lesley Spencer née Brook in conversation with the author February 22, 2003: "I think, to be quite honest, one didn't have nearly enough really good direction in those days. I mean to say, Ralph Ince was a good director because he was much more competent than Reggie Purdell was, but one really didn't get much direction." Jim Stephenson paid tribute to the expertise and help he received from Ince noting: "I was very lucky in having a good director in my first film. He helped me tremendously when I wasn't feeling very sure of myself in films" [*Manchester Evening News*, August 20, 1937, p.7].

[17] *Burnley Express*, February 10, 1937, p.5

[18] Niven (1975), p.175

[19] Box 2078, USC Warner Bros. Archive

[20] *The Times*, April 17, 1937, p.16

[21] An incomplete sixty-three page shooting script detailing seventy-nine scenes survives in the British Film Institute Special Collections [SCR-1800 / S286]. The script shows the original name of the libellous character had been changed from Lady Sappington Smythe to Lady Fairhaven. This would prove a costly mistake, and all the more ironic given there are numerous instances in the scenario where alternate takes are suggested for use by directors in case of "censor trouble."

[22] "A Film Withdrawn," *The Times*, October 28, 1937, p.14; *The Times*, November 25, 1937, p.4

[23] *Picture Show*, July 16, 1936, p.26

[24] *World Film News*, October 1937, p.32; *Manchester Evening News*, August 20, 1937, p.7 Born in 1883, Walter Huston had recently appeared in two British films: *The Tunnel* (Gaumont-British, Maurice Elvey, 1935) a science-fiction drama in which he played the American president, and *Rhodes of Africa* (Gaumont-British, Berthold Viertel, 1936) in which he played the lead role.

[25] Letter to Lorna Stephenson, August 17, 1937, Stephenson Archive

[26] *World Film News*, October 1937, p32

[27] *Flight*, September 23, 1937, p.316

[28] *The Times*, August 22, 1938, p.8

[29] Rowland Bruce Somerset Lister was born in Johannesburg South Africa on June 6, 1912. He was the son of Arthur Lindsay Lister a British mining engineer born in India. Following education at a minor English public school, Brighton College, he undertook a grand tour of Europe. As a proficient player of golf and tennis he toyed with the idea of becoming a professional sportsman, but instead decided to enrol at the Academy of Dramatic Arts in London. Lister's theatrical agent was former actor John Gliddon who operated from 106 Regent Street, London, WC1. He made his debut on the London stage in 1931. His stage work included Franz in *Mrs. Fischer's War* at the Ambassador's Theatre (1931); Ed Rimplegar in *Three Cornered Moon* (1934) at Westminister Theatre. He was given a screen test by actor/director Miles Mander (1888-1946) and made his debut in British features in a small un-credited role in *The Girl in the Flat* (Paramount-British, Redd Davis, 1934). He co-starred opposite Valerie Hobson in the now missing, believed lost British quota quickie *Badger's Green* (Paramount-British, Adrian Brunel, 1934). In all, he appeared in just over twenty feature films in pre-war Britain. Lister's sporting prowess won him the Oscar Asche Challenge Cup and Prize at the autumn meeting of the Stage Golfing Club Society in October 1937 shortly before his voyage across to the United States.

[30] Letter to Lorna Stephenson, September 7, 1937, Stephenson Archive. During this period of his life, Lorna Stephenson was undergoing difficult and painful post-operative convalescence.

[31] Letter to Lorna Stephenson, September 7, 1937, Stephenson Archive

[32] Hunnings, p.408.

[33] Letter to Lorna Stephenson, September 8, 1937, Stephenson Archive. The letter was written following a reassuring phone conversation with his wife Lorna during her convalescence.

[34] Letter to Lorna Stephenson, September 9, 1937, Stephenson Archive

[35] Born Margaret Helen Betty Karklinnis in Berlin on May 16, 1911 she was the fourth daughter of August Wilhelm Paul and Alice Karklinnis of Hendon, London. 5ft 6" in height, she spoke fluent French and German. She studied at the Royal Academy of Dramatic Art where she won the Bancroft medal and took the stage name of Betty Lynne. She appeared twice on the New York stage. Firstly, in *The Animal Kingdom* at the Broadhurst Theatre in 1932 produced by, and starring Leslie Howard. Then in 1935, she was an understudy for Elizabeth Bergener in *Escape Me Never* in both London and at the Shubert Theatre on Broadway. She also appeared in a production of *Will You Love Me Always?* with Yvonne Arnaud playing the lead at the Globe in London, and was a member of the new Bournemouth Repertory company for one season. Between 1934 and 1949 she appeared in sixteen films, and retired from acting shortly after marrying businessman Basil George Suter (1912-1997) in 1946. During her later years she suffered from macular degeneration. She died peacefully in her sleep at a retirement home in France on March 2, 2011, just a few months before what would have been her hundredth birthday.

[36] When *Dangerous Fingers* was distributed by Monogram in the United States in 1939 under the title *Wanted by Scotland Yard*, the states of Kansas, Ohio, Massachusetts and Pennsylvania demanded the elimination of the word "hell" spoken in three instances during the course of the film. New York was more liberal, as the film was released there without any deletions.

[37] Wallace, March 30, 1941, Stephenson Archive

[38] On the contract alongside Jimmy's signature appears the signature of agent Sydney "Bill" Linnit. For their services Messrs. O'Bryen, Linnit and Dunfee exacted a commission of ten per cent on all artists' earnings. Stephenson Archive

[39] The *Normandie* appears briefly on screen in gaudy Technicolor grandeur in *Vogues of 1938* (United Artists / Walter Wanger, Irving Cummings, 1937). Newsreel footage of the ship's sad demise in February 1942, after having caught fire and capsizing on its side at its pier in New York, appears momentarily in the spy thriller *Saboteur* (Universal, Alfred Hitchcock, 1942)

[40] Letter to Lorna Stephenson, November 20, 1937, Stephenson Archive

[41] Letter to Lorna Stephenson, November 20, 1937, Stephenson Archive
Born in 1904 at Liverpool, director Arthur Woods, a fully qualified pilot,
had joined the Royal Air Force Volunteer Reserve as a navigator on the
outbreak of war in 1939. Flight Lieutenant Arthur Bickerstaff Woods
A.F.C. of the Old Mill House, Byfleet, Surrey, died February 8, 1944 on
war service. His effects of £14938 10s 6d were bequeathed to Clifford
Lely Mollison Captain H.M. army and his wife Muriel Agnes Mollison
on September 13, 1944.
    John Ware was born c.1904 in Bradford, Yorkshire. After working
as a reporter and assistant editor in Fleet Street, he entered the British
film industry in 1936 and was put in charge of the press copy room at
Gaumont-British studios. In May 1937 he was appointed studio publicity
manager at the Warner First National Teddington studios. He later worked
as publicist for Alexander Korda and Twentieth Century-Fox. During the
Second World War he was publicity relations officer for fighter command
in the RAF and un-credited, supplied the story for the propaganda war
film *The Lion Has Wings* (London Films, Adrian Brunel, Brian Desmond
Hurst, Michael Powell, 1939). He died in 1969.

[42] Letter to Lorna Stephenson, November 20, 1937, Stephenson Archive.

[43] Harry Richman (1895-1972) was an American entertainer and night-club
owner who, as an accomplished aviator, flew across the Atlantic with
co-pilot Dick Merrall in 1936. The flight from New York to Wales was
completed in eighteen hours, thirty-nine minutes.
    BT27/1489: Passenger List November 17, 1937 gives the name of
"Greer Snelson (Garson) aged twenty-nine." Eileen Evelyn Greer Garson,
born in Essex, was, in fact, thirty-three years old [GRO Register of Births,
Oct-Dec 1904, West Ham, Essex, 4A p.250] and had married senior civil
servant Edward Alec Abbott Snelson in 1933. Her tendency to adopt
the hauteur of aristocratic sensibility, and cultivate airs and graces was
borne of an attempt to cover up her massive insecurity and inexperience.
Later in her career this *faux* regal demeanour was transformed into
Churchillian invincibility in her iconic playing of an extra/ordinary
middle-class British housewife, Kay Miniver, in *Mrs. Miniver* (1942).
This, her best remembered role, resembles the persona of the implacable
British Prime Minister Margaret Thatcher. Like Thatcher, Garson invited
strong responses. Critic Sherdian Morley, assessing her career, thought:
". . . that she wasn't really an actress at all; she was a sort of unofficial

ambassadress reminding Americans why they had fought their War of Independence and sold more war bonds than other stars of the 1940s." Morley went on to declare: "I defy anyone watching her . . . now to do anything more than wonder how she managed to fool so many million people for so many years." And he concluded she was: ". . . a bizarre accident of war." *The Sunday Times: Books*, December 13, 1998, p.5. However, she did have her ardent defenders. Michael J. Wild pointed out that in the film *When Ladies Meet* (M-G-M, Robert Z. Leonard, 1941) in a scene between Joan Crawford and Garson: "Crawford turns herself inside out, rolling her eyes and emoting full blast, while Garson, doing 100 per cent less achieves 100 per cent more, and completely takes the scene from her." *The Sunday Times: Books*, January 3, 1999, p.2. Actor Hubert Gregg, who had incidentally worked with Jimmy Stephenson on BBC radio in 1937, agreed with Morley's scathing assessment. He recalled Garson, early in her career, appearing in Shakespeare's *The Tempest* at the Open Air Theatre in Regent's Park in June 1934: "As soon as Miss Garson opened her mouth at the first rehearsal, Robert Atkins, the director, muttered an obscenity about her plummy voice and stormed around the theatre enlarging upon his remark. If it hadn't been for the producer he would have sacked her on the spot." *The Sunday Times: Books*, March 7, 1999, p.2

[44] Surviving passenger lists show Dietrich listed as Marlene Sieber-Dietrich [New York Passenger Lists, *Normandie*, 1937 T715-6080 1/2] Dietrich and her husband, Rudolf Sieber (1897-1976), had an open marriage which by the ultramodern standards of the German Weimar Republic was not unusual. However, Dietrich was remarkable in being her own woman. Using masquerade, she delighted in transgressing and flaunting her own brand of exoticism and eroticism to the disbelief of a morally hidebound era. Like her constantly changing wardrobe, her personality alternated seamlessly between chanteuse, hausfrau and divine love goddess. Among the other celebrities onboard: James A. Fitzpatrick, producer of travelogue documentaries; Carl Dixon, Secretary Treasurer of Paramount, Rouben Mamoulian, renowned and innovative film and theatre director; Louis de Rochemont, foreign editor of *March of Time*; Albert Pinkovitch, French movie producer of such classic films as *Jenny* (Les Réalisations d'Art Cinématographique, Marcel Carné, 1936) and *La Grande Illusion* (Cinédis, Jean Renoir, 1937), Constantin "Tino" Rossi, French tenor singer of cabaret and radio, French writer Jean Prevost, Michel de Brunhoff editor–in–chief of *Vogue Paris* magazine and Andre de la Varre, film artist who worked for Burton Holmes the

father of Travelogue. There was also a whole assembly of international diplomats and businessmen on board.

[45] Letter to Lorna Stephenson, November 20, 1937, Stephenson Archive

[46] Letter to Lorna Stephenson, November 21, 1937, Stephenson Archive

[47] Letter to Lorna Stephenson, November 24, 1937, Stephenson Archive. The letter is written on letterhead paper from the Ambassador Hotel 51-52nd Street, Park Avenue, New York.

[48] Letter to Lorna Stephenson, November 24, 1937, Stephenson Archive

[49] Letter to Lorna Stephenson, November 24, 1937, Stephenson Archive. On May 19, 1937, producer George Abbott ushered in his production of a raucous farce, *Room Service,* by John P. Murray and Allen Boretz at the Cort Theatre. With such expert farceurs as Sam Levene, Teddy Hart, Philip Loeb, Eddie Albert, Donald McBride and Betty Field, the comedy chronicled the plight of a group of hungry actors, and some shoestring producers living in a seedy hotel while trying to get backing for the play they wish to put on. It was a Cort favourite, and ran for 500 performances before closing on July 16, 1938. It was later made into a film, *Room Service* (RKO, William A. Seiter, 1938), with the three Marx Brothers supported by Lucille Ball and Ann Miller. From the original Broadway cast Alexander Asro, Philip Loeb, Philip Wood, Clifford Dunstan, and Donald McBride, were retained in the film.

[50] Roland [Keith] Young (1887-1953) had an apartment at 322, East 57th Street, New York City near the River.

[51] Disappointingly, the party did not stay to sample the tap, ballet, acrobatic, dance routines *par excellence* of the Nicholas Brothers, Fayard and Harold, who were among the premier African American artists billed to appear at the Cotton Club at this time. They had recently returned from Britain, where they appeared in the musical film revue *Calling All Stars* (British Lion, Herbert Smith, 1937). Their tap routines, with mid air splits and backward somersaults, not only defied the laws of gravity, but were executed, seemingly, with effortless grace. Their dance choreography, principally at the Twentieth Century-Fox studios, remains a master class of peerless technique and continues to astound and enthral succeeding generations of dance students and aficionados.

[52] *The Women* opened at the Ethel Barrymore Theatre in September 1936 and ran for 666 performances until July 1938. Phyllis Povah, Marjorie Main, Mary Cecil and Marjorie Wood repeated their Broadway roles in the lavish star laden Hollywood film *The Women* (M-G-M, George Cukor, 1939)

[53] Letter to Lorna Stephenson, November 28, 1937, Stephenson Archive. Posted at 10 a.m. and collected at 3 p.m. written c/o Roosevelt Hotel, Hollywood, California.

[54] Letter to Lorna Stephenson, November 28, 1937, Stephenson Archive.

[55] Letter to Lorna Stephenson, November 28, 1937, Stephenson Archive.

[56] Letter to Lorna Stephenson, November 28, 1937, Stephenson Archive.

[57] Letter to Lorna Stephenson, November 28, 1937, Stephenson Archive.

[58] Letter to Lorna Stephenson, November 28, 1937, Stephenson Archive.

[59] Letter to Lorna Stephenson, November 30, 1937, Stephenson Archive. Written on Hollywood Roosevelt Hotel letterhead paper and posted on December 1, 1937 at 1:30 p.m.

[60] Letter to Lorna Stephenson, November 30, 1937, Stephenson Archive.

[61] Letter to Lorna Stephenson, December 1, 1937, Stephenson Archive

[62] The Vendome Café was situated at 6666 Sunset Boulevard, and was opened in May 1933 by Hollywood Reporter's Billy Wilkerson. Originally planned as a gourmet paradise and speciality store, but soon after the opening Wilkerson made it a luncheon place and it soon became the most important place to lunch in town.

[63] Patric Knowles and his wife, Enid Percival, lived at 3286 Blair Drive, North Hollywood, California. The casual remark concerning Patric turning up at the studio in pyjamas aligns with the plotline of a B film he was starring in at this time. *The Patient in Room 18* (Warner, Bobby Connolly, Crane Wilbur, 1938) was a tall tale of Lance O'Leary (Patric Knowles) who is hospitalised for a nervous breakdown. During the course of the story he is seen sleepwalking in his pyjamas.

[64] Letter to Lorna Stephenson, December 1, 1937, Stephenson Archive

[65] Letter to Lorna Stephenson, December 1, 1937, Stephenson Archive

[66] Letter to Lorna Stephenson, December 5, 1937, Stephenson Archive.
Written at the Roosevelt Hotel, Hollywood

[67] Letter to Lorna Stephenson, December 5, 1937, Stephenson Archive.
The Cock n' Bull was a mock British tavern located on 9170 Sunset
Boulevard, Hollywood. It had a bar and dart board in the manner of the
tavern inhabited by Claude Rains at the opening of *The Invisible Man*
(Universal, James Whale, 1933). Opened in 1937 by brothers John and
Percy Morgan it ceased trading in 1987. The building is now used as an
automobile dealership. Robert Young (1907-1998) was married to Betty
Henderson from 1933 until her death in 1994.

[68] Letter to Lorna Stephenson, December 5, 1937, Stephenson Archive.
Nearly sixty years after this letter was written Chili Bouchier, interviewed
on BBC radio's *Desert Island Discs* January 21, 1996, professed her
undying love for the Canadian dance bandleader Teddy Joyce (Edmund
John Cuthbertson 1904-1941) and was moved to tears by his memory.
In February 1941, Joyce had just opened a season with his band at the
Playhouse Ballroom, Glasgow when he was taken ill with cerebro spinal
fever and died in a Glasgow hospital within a few days.

[69] Letter to Lorna Stephenson, December 9, 1937, Stephenson Archive. The
letter is written on The Hollywood Athletic Club notepaper.
On Wednesday December 8, 1937 Jimmy Stephenson, Chili Bouchier
and Bruce Lister were taken to sound stage nine at the Warner Burbank
Studios for an hour radio broadcast. *Your Hollywood Parade* was
sponsored by Lucky Strike Cigarettes. Dick Powell was master of
ceremonies, Leo Forbstein conducted The Lucky Strike Orchestra
and vocal arranger Dudley Chambers led the Lucky Strike Singers
known as The Lucky Seven. Powell began the show by introducing
casting director Mrs. Bernice Saunders affiliated to the Central Casting
Corporation responsible for the hiring of movie extras. Central Casting
had over twelve thousand registered extras on its books, but only a mere
five hundred obtained any work on a daily basis. The organisation was
celebrating its twelfth anniversary. Powell then promoted his latest film
Varsity Show (Warner, William Keighley, 1937) by introducing Leo
Forbstein conducting the Lucky Strike Orchestra accompanied by "vocal

swingsters" the Lucky Seven (a close harmony group identified by Jimmy as "a choir of sorts") singing "Have You Got Any Castles, Baby?" a hit song from the film. After the first commercial break the next item on the programme was resident comedian Rufe Davis, whose speciality act was making imitation sound effects using his voice. Next on the programme came the Gary Cooper sketch, followed by conversional banter between Powell and Cooper in which the radio audience were reminded of Cooper's coming picture release *Bluebeard's Eighth Wife* (Paramount, Ernst Lubitsch, 1938). There was also the obligatory endorsement of Lucky Strike Cigarettes. Powell then sang "Once in a While" a popular tune in the United States hit parade for Tommy Dorsey and his orchestra at this time. After a commercial break, Rosemary Lane sang "Roses in December." Following another commercial break, Powell, along with the Lucky Seven, sang "Vieni Vieni." Finally, to conclude the broadcast, a dramatic spot in the programme, a radio adaption of a current film release; *It's Love I'm After* (Warner, Archie Mayo, 1937) with Bette Davis and Patric Knowles reprising their film roles as Joyce Arden and Henry Grant. Basil Rathbone as Basil Underwood and Eric Stanley as Underwood's valet Digges substituted for Leslie Howard and Eric Blore in the original film. This show attracted audiences of over fifteen million listeners.

[70] Letter to Lorna Stephenson, December 9, 1937, Stephenson Archive written on Hollywood Athletic Club notepaper.
Betty Compson (1897-1974) was a former silent actress who began her career in 1915 and appeared in many major productions throughout the 1920s. Her career reached its apogee during the late 1920s, appearing opposite George Bancroft in *Docks of New York* (Paramount, Josef von Sternberg, 1928); *The Barker* (First National, George Fitzmaurice, 1928) for which she was Oscar nominated. She survived the sound period and went on to appear in *The Great Gabbo* (Sono Art-World Wide, James Cruze, 1929). As the remarks in the letter indicate by the mid 1930s her career had begun to plumet, due to financial mismanagement resulting from her first marriage to director James Cruze. Many of her silent films are missing believed lost, but three reels of *The White Shadow* (Gainsborough, Graham Cutts, 1924) were recovered in the New Zealand film archive in 2011. A young Alfred Hitchcock worked on this film as script writer, art director and assistant director.

[71] Letter to Lorna Stephenson, December 15, 1937, Stephenson Archive

[72] Letter to Lorna Stephenson, December 30, 1937, Stephenson Archive

[73] Letter to Lorna Stephenson, January 9, 1938, Stephenson Archive.
Jimmy's allusion to "Young B. Lister's" blasé attitude is confirmed by his
subsequent film career in Hollywood. Beginning in 1938 with a minor
role in *Boy Meets Girl* his CV was a litany of small supporting parts.
Lister had by now been renamed Lester (perhaps after the fashion of
A Star is Born) by the Warner Studio. He appeared in some nineteen
films prior to his screen career being interrupted by war service in the
American army. Among the plethora of secondary roles two parts stand
out: John Withers in Wyler's *The Letter* and Mr. Bingley in *Pride and
Prejudice* (M-G-M, Robert Z. Leonard, 1940). He also had a fairly
substantive role in a forgotten B picture *Shadows on the Stairs* (Warner,
D. Ross Lederman, 1941)

[74] Letter to Lorna Stephenson, December 9, 1937, Stephenson Archive.

[75] Letter to Lorna Stephenson, December 9, 1937, Stephenson Archive

[76] Letter to Lorna Stephenson, December 9, 1938, Stephenson Archive.
At this time Binnie Barnes (1903-1998) was romantically involved
with writer Jean Negulesco (1900-1993) who went on to direct shorts
for Warner Bros. before making his feature debut at the studio in 1941.
He was nominated for an Academy Award for Best Director for *Johnny
Belinda* (Warner, 1948). From 1953 he directed many early CinemaScope
films such as: *How to Marry a Millionaire* (Twentieth Century-Fox,
1953); *Three Coins in the Fountain* (Twentieth Century-Fox, 1954) and
Woman's World (Twentieth Century-Fox, 1954)

[77] Letter to Lorna Stephenson, January 9, 1938, Stephenson Archive

[78] Letter to Lorna Stephenson, December 21, 1937, Stephenson Archive.
Samuel and Elizabeth Dickson of Belfast, Northern Ireland had
immigrated to the United States during the early 1920s and were followed
by their two sons. According to the 1940 United States California
Federal census [60-1317/160/61A/12/T627-377] the Dicksons, listed
on the census form as Dickinson (sic), Samuel and Elizabeth and their
sons Samuel and Harold lived at 4010 Fairway Avenue, Los Angeles.
Nearby at 4058 Fairway Avenue, Los Angeles, lived actor Charles
Middleton aged 60 and his wife Leora. Born in Kentucky, Middleton is
remembered as a specialist in portraying villainous screen heavies, and

is remembered as a foil for Laurel and Hardy. His Emperor Ming the Merciless in the Universal serial *Flash Gordon* remains iconic. He also appeared as Abraham Lincoln in several films. In 1940 he appeared in a total of thirteen features and one short. This busy schedule meant he was probably unavailable when the census enumerator visited his home.

Dr William Dickson and his wife Eleanor May Dickson had four children. Their youngest daughter, Fiona, became a dancer and married musican, and entertainer Roy Castle (1932-1994) in 1963. Fiona and Roy were introduced to each other by comic Eric Morecambe [See Castle, pp113-115]. At the time of Jimmy Stephenson's death, young comedian John Eric Bartholomew (1926-1984) had just decided to turn professional, and announced he would be known professionally as Eric Morecambe. [*Morecambe and Heysham Visitor and Lancaster Advertiser*, June 30, 1941, p.6.] In 1941 Eric also began his professional comic double act with Ernie Wise (Ernest Wiseman 1925-1999). The duo's BBC television comedy shows during the 1970s, and especially their annual Christmas show, became a benchmark of classic British television comedy entertainment.

[79] Letter to Lorna Stephenson, December 30, 1937, Stephenson Archive

[80] Letter to Lorna Stephenson, January 6, 1938, Stephenson Archive

[81] Ralph Richardson appeared in the title role of *The Amazing Dr. Clitterhouse* at the Haymarket Theatre in August 1936. Other members of the cast included: Joan Marion, Eric Stanley, Charles Mortimer, Charles Farrell (1900-1988) [not to be confused with the Hollywood star Charles Farrell], Meriel Forbes, Vincent Holman, Ralph Michael, S. Victor Stanley, Norman Pierce, Hugh E. Wright and Frederic Worlock. A successful production it ran for 491 performances and later transferred to the Savoy Theatre. It played on Broadway for eighty performances, March to May 1937, at the Hudson Theatre. Cedric Hardwicke took the lead and Frederic Worlock repeated his London stage role of Sir William Grant KC.

[82] Letter to Lorna Stephenson, January 8, 1938, Stephenson Archive

[83] Goulding's *Nightmare Alley* (Twentieth Century-Fox, 1947) remains a dark, dubious curiosity dealing with religious charlatanism, human degradation and the tawdry world of the circus carnival. For an assessment of Goulding's fascinating, if neglected career see Matthew

Kennedy's biography.

[84] Letter to Lorna Stephenson, January 16, 1938, Stephenson Archive

[85] *Observer*, December 18, 1938, p.10

[86] For a rare photograph of Obringer See Behlmer (1987) photo no 16 following p.238

[87] Letter to Lorna Stephenson, December 9, 1937, Stephenson Archive

[88] Letter to Lorna Stephenson, December 27, 1937, Stephenson Archive. Written at Montecito Apartments, Franklin Avenue, Hollywood

[89] Box 2746B, USC Warner Bros. Archive, Letter to Stuart Stewart of H.E. Edington – F.W. Vincent Inc., January 24, 1939

[90] Letter to Lorna Stephenson, December 14, 1937, Stephenson Archive

[91] Letter to Lorna Stephenson, December 14, 1937, Stephenson Archive

[92] Letter to Lorna Stephenson, December 30, 1937, Stephenson Archive. John Robert Sloan (1912-2001) had signed with Warner Bros Teddington studios as studio manager in June 1936

[93] Letter to Lorna Stephenson, January 14, 1939, Stephenson Archive

[94] Letter to Lorna Stephenson, December 14, 1937, Stephenson Archive

[95] Letter to Lorna Stephenson, December 27, 1937, Stephenson Archive

[96] Reagan, p.89

[97] For a descriptive analysis of the anthropological aspect to genre film-making see Powdermaker, pp. 40-41

[98] McFee, p.37

[99] At this time smoking was all-pervasive. In Britain eighty per cent of men and forty-one per cent of women smoked. The smoking habit crossed boundaries of social class, age and gender. Apart from Jimmy, his father and

younger brother, Norman, all smoked. For reference purposes an inventory of Jimmy's smoking consumption on film is included in appendix four

[100] For a detailed analysis and commentary of the censorship issues of *Devil's Island* see Vasey, pp.179-187

[101] *Kine Weekly*, March 7, 1940, Stephenson Archive

[102] Letter to the author, October 2012, from Rosella Kronman née Towne

[103] Letter to Lorna Stephenson September 13, 1939, Stephenson Archive

[104] Letter to Lorna Stephenson, September 14, 1939, Stephenson Archive. Written from the Hotel Marion, Salew, Oregon

[105] In the local press during the First World War it was reported in addition to a slight gunshot wound in the shoulder Norman Stephenson had also been: ". . . slightly gassed." [*Burnley Express*, August 26, 1916, p.4]

[106] *Manchester Guardian*, May 26, 1940, p.12

[107] Many decades later Peter Stephenson was invited to the Tarzana home of Patric and Enid Knowles for Christmas. In casual conversation Peter let slip he had attained a level of proficiency in fencing championships at his alma mater Lancing College back in England. At Patric's insistence the foils were brought out. In time-honoured fashion cries of *en garde* ensued and battle duly commenced. Peter administered the *coup de grâce* fairly swiftly whereupon Patric duly conceded defeat with good humour.

[108] *Singapore Free Press and Mercantile Advertiser*, June 8, 1911, p.7

[109] *The Singapore Free Press and Mercantile Advertiser*, June 13, 1911, p.10 Tuan is used in Malaysia as a form of respectful address for a gentleman the equivalent to sir or mister.

[110] *Singapore Free Press and Mercantile Advertiser*, June 20, 1911, p.4

[111] Like Jimmy Stephenson Leslie Faber died young aged only forty-nine on August 5, 1929 of pneumonia and pleurisy following an operation for an abscess on the lung. He too appeared posthumously on screen in the film *White Cargo* (British International Pictures,

J[ames].B[ailiff].Williams, 1929).

[112] Leslie Crosbie was played by Hilda Esty-Marsh, Howard Joyce by Gerald Fitzgerald, Robert Crosbie was played by A.F. Johnson, and Leslie Dwyer played Ong Sing Ching. Other parts were taken by Marie Makins, Dorothy Garth, Arthur Melville and Neil Waring. Among the cast there were also a couple of Chinese boys and Malay servants. The production was directed by Barry O'Brien. Only Leslie Dwyer (1906-1986) achieved national fame. Born in Catford London, Dwyer was a performer from the age of ten making his film debut in *The Fifth Form of St Dominic's* (I.B. Davidson/Granger, A.E. Coleby, 1921). During the 1940s he appeared in a steady stream of British films (often appearing uncredited) as a cheery cockney (typical is the role of able seaman Parkinson in *In Which We Serve* (Two Cities, David Lean, Noel Coward, 1942) and from the early 1950s he worked extensively in television. It was at the end of a long career that he achieved lasting fame in thirty-six episodes of the British situation comedy *Hi-de-Hi!* (1980-1984) produced by the BBC. His role of Mr. Partridge the Punch and Judy man who hated children was a memorable swansong for the veteran actor.

[113] Reginald Owen was also appearing on the Broadway stage as Cardinal Richelieu in a Florenz Ziegfeld musical, *The Three Musketeers*, which ran at the Lyric Theatre from March 15 to December 15, 1928. Dennis King played D'Artagnan and Douglas Dumbrille, Athos.

[114] Paramount produced several multi-lingual versions to cater for the international market including the French *La Lettre* (Louis Mercanton, 1930); German *Weib im Dschungel* (Dimitri Buchowetzki, 1931); Spanish *La Carta* (Adelqui Migliar, 1931) and Italian *La Donna Bianca* (Jack Salvatori 1931).

[115] Robertson, p. 79

[116] This exceptionally rare early film was discovered by private collector Jerry Haber and shown to acclaim at the Syracuse Cinefest in March 1998 and the Pordenone silent film festival on October 13, 1998. Originally shot as a part-talkie the surviving silent print was blown up from 16mm to 35mm.

[117] *Variety*, June 7, 1940 records Davis returned to the film set after ailing with laryngitis. However, it is suggested, but unconfirmed she may have

had an abortion during this time. See Herman, p.213. It is also alleged Bruce Lester had a romantic flirtation with Davis. They were, apparently, seen around the studio together. See Quirk, p.219

[118] Koch had come to Hollywood via American radio and was responsible for, among other things, the infamous 1938 Halloween radio broadcast of *War of the Worlds* which had panicked America into thinking the Martian Invasion was for real. Previous to his work on *The Letter* he had been working on *Virginia City* (Warner, Michael Curtiz, 1940) a Western featuring Errol Flynn, Miriam Hopkins and Randolph Scott in the leads. The theatrical trailer assured audiences: "Crowded with glorious moments you will remember for years!" However, the sight of Humphrey Bogart improbably miscast as a mustachioed Mexican bandit, complete with phony accent and leer, would hardly qualify as a "glorious moment" though it is remembered, by some aficionados, as a piece of high kitsch!

[119] McClelland, p.354

[120] Jenkinson, p.15

[121] *The Letter*, Production File, Margaret Herrick Library

[122] Some discarded shots from these scenes appear in the theatrical trailer of *The Letter*.

[123] BBC Arena: *Bette Davis: - The Benevolent Volcano*, A seventy-fifth birthday profile of the Hollywood actress first broadcast on November 2, 1983

[124] See Robert N. Proctor, *The Nazi War on Cancer*, New Jersey, Princeton University Press, 1999

[125] Box 2042, USC Warner Archive, Memo June 8, 1940 from Jack Warner to Hal Wallis

[126] Upon return from army service Lester had one credited role of interest as a British spy in the successful, if highly improbable, melodrama *Golden Earrings* (Paramount, Mitchell Leisen, 1947) He then returned to Britain and made three films of which *The Fool and the Princess* (Merton Park, William C. Hammond, 1949) is a curious lower berth revamp of *Brief Encounter* (Cineguild, David Lean, 1945), co-starring Lesley Brook who

he had last appeared with at Warner Bros. Teddington studios in *Quiet Please* (Warner, Roy William Neill, 1938). His remaining work in such series pictures as the Tarzan franchise and TV work in the 1950s remained undistinguished and, though he later took up screen writing, his career faded into obscurity. He and his wife Jane maintained properties in Palm Springs and Los Angeles. Despite numerous written requests and a visit to his Los Angeles home in 2006 by the author he steadfastly maintained a wall of silence. He died on June 13, 2008 aged ninety-six and was the last surviving cast member of *The Letter*.

Lester's polished dapper patrician English gentleman was complimented by another Anglo-Saxon upper-class type, that of the cruel cad personified by minor British actor Morton Lowry (1914-1987). Following his screen debut in *The Dawn Patrol* (1938) Lowry gained screen immortality for his villainous John Stapleton in *The Hound of the Baskervilles* (Twentieth Century-Fox, Sidney Lanfield, 1939) and as the cruel schoolmaster, Mr. Jonas, in *How Green Was My Valley* (Twentieth Century-Fox, John Ford, 1941). In fact the name Morton Lowry was a stage name, as he was born Edward Morton Lowater on February 13, 1914 in the district of Barton upon Irwell in the county of Lancashire, England. [GRO Jan-Mar 1914, V.8, p.1257] His parents, Edward Morton Lowater, Sr. (1884-1956) an engineer and Bertha née Holmes (1884-1968) were married April-June 1910 in Barton upon Irwell. Rakishly handsome Lowater began a career on stage as a chorus boy. Aged twenty-one "Morty" as he was known married Diana Whalley (1912-1990) at St Pancras Middlesex in 1934. "Dido" as she was known came from a wealthy Cheshire family. The marriage was short-lived and on July 12, 1937 divorce proceedings were instituted against him in the High Court [J77/3627/2411, National Archives, London] and a *decree nisi* granted to his ex-wife on January 25, 1938. Prior to going to Hollywood he was in a London stage revue *Hide and Seek* which opened at the London Hippodrome on October 14, 1937. Billed as Morton Lowater, the show starred Bobby Howes, Cicely Courtneidge, Patricia Burke, Guy Spaull and David Burns. In December 1937 he sailed to the United States on the SS *Berengaria* from Southampton to New York. [Microfilm: T715-6093, New York Passenger Lists] The passenger list describes him as 5ft 10" in height, fair complexion, blond hair, blue eyes and no marks of identification. He lived with his mother at 182 Brompton Road, London. Lowater had become friendly with socialite Virginia Barnato (1916-1980) the daughter of Woolf Barnato (1895-1948) a racing driver, one of the so-called Bentley Boys. She had preceded him to the United States on the RMS *Queen Mary*. Morton Lowater married Virginia Barnato on

February 14, 1938 in San Francisco. Between 1938 and 1947 he appeared in approximately twenty-nine Hollywood features, many without credit. He appeared in screen tests with Jimmy on March 20, 1939 for *The Knight and the Lady* later known as *The Private Lives of Elizabeth and Essex*. He was also recommended as a possible candidate for a small supporting role in *The Old Maid* however, this suggestion was never taken up. After returning to England in 1946 he divorced Barnato and married again in 1956. Moving back to America during the early 1960s he died in San Francisco from a heart attack on November 26, 1987. He died in poverty and his unclaimed remains were eventually buried at Pleasant Hills Cemetery, Sebastopol, California. He fathered two children, a son born in 1939 and a daughter born in 1958. Though the film careers of Lister/Lester and Lowater/Lowry are confined to the footnotes of film history, coincidentally both actors are cast in the same two films: *British Intelligence* (Warner, Terry O. Morse, 1940) and *A Yank in the RAF* (Twentieth Century-Fox, Henry King, 1941). In the former, Lester receives third billing and Lowry receives no credit. In the latter, Lowry receives sixth billing and Lester receives no credit. In neither film do they appear together in any scene.

[127]   Maugham, p.252

[128]   Though Marshall lost his right leg during the First World War the use of a prosthetic leg meant his disability, apart from a slight limp, went unnoticed by audiences. However, though he was quite capable of walking a few steps thereafter he developed a noticeable rolling gait. It was therefore necessary to devise imaginative and innovative ways of making reasonable adjustment to disguise Marshall's disability. A particular noteworthy example occurs during the brief exit scene following Leslie Crosbie's successful acquittal at the trial. As the Crosbies leave the courtroom arm-in-arm, the camera takes great care to choreograph the action to avoid direct continuous viewing of their exit. Instead the couple are shown stopping and posing for waiting photographers and well-wishers offering congratulations. Finally, as the couple brush past the camera out of frame there is a shot of Geoff Hammond's widow positioned in the corner of the courtroom stood silently in exotic malevolence. Such is the speed and economy of these actions, caught on camera in a matter of a few seconds, the viewer is liable to overlook the complexity and dexterity on a first viewing, and not realise the camera is shooting around Marshall.

[129]   Kael, p.324

[130] Bazin, pp.1-22

[131] Sarris, p.168

[132] Schrott, p.96

[133] Trezona was loyal to his many clients including the volatile actor Robert Walker (1918-1951). Apart from Walker's parents, Trezona and his wife were among the few people to attend the disregarded actor's funeral.

[134] Jimmy had appeared in Maugham's play *Sheppey* at the Liverpool Playhouse back in 1934, and had repeated the role of Dr. Jervis at the Winter Gardens, New Brighton in 1935. His other big success on the Liverpool stage as lawyer George Simon in *Counsellor-at-Law* in 1934 and again at the Winter Gardens, New Brighton in 1935 would not have gone unnoticed either in deciding his suitability for the role in *The Letter*.

[135] Box 1485, USC Warner Bros. Archive

[136] Schrott, p.96

[137] Shot on Dijon Street set on the studio backlot.

[138] A wild track of Jimmy's voice was recorded in October 1940. In the alternate end version of the film (available as an extra on the Warner DVD release) the lawyer is seen on an open terrace gazing pensively into the distance.

[139] Stine, p.117; Quirk, p.218

[140] Schrott, p.96

[141] Niven, (1994) p.318
       The lengths Wyler was prepared to go to extract the required effort and effect of *misé-en-scene* from his crew and cast were legion. In *Mrs. Miniver*, for instance, a short scene of the Miniver family leaving church involved a lengthy shoot. Only much later did the cast and crew discover that during an earlier rehearsal the child actor playing young Toby Miniver (Christopher Severn) had impudently placed his hand on the brass fixture of the church-door and Wyler, rather than explain he wanted this action repeating, preferred to keep shooting until the young boy of his own

accord repeated the action. Striving for such spontaneity and effect though technically commendable and laudable was, for the studio moguls, too time-consuming and, in their eyes, did not warrant the hideous expense.

[142] Karr, p.74

[143] Karr, p.73

[144] Niven (1994), p.197
David Niven recalled that on the set of *Wuthering Heights* (Goldwyn, 1939) Wyler instructed Laurence Olivier to play a scene again and again without any indication as to what changes he required. When, in some desperation Olivier requested how he should play the scene the reply, after a long pause was: "Just . . . just be better."

[145] Higham oral interview with Wyler in 1973

[146] *The Argus*, Melbourne Victoria, April 7, 1941, Stephenson Archive

[147] *New York Times*, November 23, 1940, p.12

[148] *The Times*, June 2, 1941, p.8

[149] *Los Angeles Examiner*, May 1941, Stephenson Archive

[150] Agate, pp221-222

[151] Box 2746B, USC Warner Bros. Archive, Memo April 11, 1941 Obringer to Warner. Jimmy's agent Charles Trezona requested his client appear on a Lux Radio broadcast of *The Letter*. A cable dated April 12, 1941 to Obringer from Bette Davis also requested Jimmy's appearance on the programme.

[152] The National Film Preservation Foundation was founded by the Library of Congress in 1988. This charitable foundation has a film registry for preservation in the Library of Congress. Since 1989 the national film registry recommends twenty-five films each year for inclusion on the registry. William Wyler's *Jezebel* was selected in 2009. It would be apposite for *The Letter* to be selected at some point, and ensure its preservation for posterity. A full restoration of the surviving 35mm elements would certainly bring out the full

lustre of its luminescent photography.

[153] Smith, p.70

[154] Letter to the author, April 30, 2003

[155] *Monthly Film Bulletin*, Vol. 9, No5 97/108, 1942, p.6

[156] Schrott, p.96

[157] *Kine Weekly*, July 3, 1941, p.6

[158] *New York Times*, November 14, 1941, Stephenson Archive

CHAPTER FOUR

[1] State of California Death Certificate Registration No: 10480, Stephenson Archive

[2] *Papers of Rev. Harry Battye*, DDX 2523/6, Lancashire Record Office

[3] In her diary entry for Wednesday July 30, 1941 Adela Stephenson records: "Had a cable from Lorna saying that Jim died yesterday. Left at once for Morecambe where I broke the news to Mr. and Mrs. S[tephenson]. Met Jessie Longbottom, [Mrs. Stephenson's niece] Alan and May [Stephenson]. With Mrs. Wildman [May Stephenson's mother] as guide went to the post office and sent cable to Lorna. Back to the flat & had lunch at Alan and Mays. I left at 2:25pm. Drove there through Trough of Bowland to Lancaster." – Diaries of Adela R. Stephenson: 1938-1942, Blain Archive

[4] *In Memoriam*, August 21, 1941, Stephenson Archive.
Humphrey Bogart had finished principal shooting (July 18, 1941) on *The Maltese Falcon* (Warner, John Huston, 1941) playing private detective Sam Spade, a role that would catapult him into a front-rank star at Warners following the film's premiere in October 1941. At the time of writing his dedication Bogart was working on *All Through the Night* (Warner, Vincent Sherman, 1941)

[5] *In Memoriam*, August 22, 1941, Stephenson Archive

[6] *In Memoriam*, August 27, 1941, Stephenson Archive

[7] In *Shining Victory* there is a twenty-four year age difference between Stephenson and Geraldine Fitzgerald. Leading Hollywood actors from the pre-war era continued to star opposite actresses half their ages during the closing decade of Hollywood's classical era with an impunity that smacks of a double standard in which masculinity is equated with the authenticity of narrative action while femininity is subordinate to the illusion of display and spectacle. [Mulvey, p.117] The ageist phenomenon is blatant in the following screen partnerships: Gary Cooper and Grace Kelly (twenty-eight years difference) *High Noon* (United Artists, Fred Zinnemann, 1952); Charles Chaplin and Claire Bloom (forty-one years) *Limelight* (United Artists, Charles Chaplin, 1952); Humphrey Bogart and Audrey Hepburn (thirty years) *Sabrina* also known as *Sabrina Fair* (Paramount, Billy Wilder, 1954); Fred Astaire and Audrey Hepburn (thirty-three years) *Funny Face* (Paramount, Stanley Donen, 1957); Gary Cooper and Audrey Hepburn (twenty-eight years) *Love in the Afternoon* (United Artists, Billy Wilder, 1957); Clark Gable and Sophia Loren (thirty-three years) *It Started in Naples* (United Artists, Melville Shavelson, 1960); Clark Gable, again, and Marilyn Monroe (twenty-five years) *The Misfits* (United Artists, John Huston, 1961)

[8] The fascinating spectacle of entertainers on the march can be viewed in: *Star Spangled Rhythm* (Paramount, George Marshall, 1942); *Thank Your Lucky Stars* (Warner, David Butler, 1943); *This is the Army* (Warner, Michael Curtiz, 1943); *Thousands Cheer* (M-G-M, George Sidney, 1943); *Stage Door Canteen* (United Artists, Frank Borzage, 1943); *Follow the Boys* (Universal, A. Edward Sutherland, 1944); *Hollywood Canteen* (Warner, Delmer Daves, 1944); and *All Star Musical Revue* (Warner, Jack Scholl, 1945). In the cause of democracy and freedom all these films banished partisanship and substituted images of national unity. There was also a wartime production given over specifically to the British contingent in Hollywood. The episodic historical drama *Forever and a Day* (United Artists, Rene Clair *et al*, 1943) featured a star-studded cast including over forty-five name players with over twenty-one writers and some seven accredited directors, including Edmund Goulding, who also contributed their services for the war effort. All profits went to the aid of the British Red Cross. Jimmy would almost certainly have been recruited to appear in this project.

[9] See Aaker, 2006 for a comprehensive survey of this detective television series

[10] In point of fact, paperwork deposited at the USC Warner archive suggests Jimmy would have been inundated with offers of work. [James Stephenson Legal File Box No 27463] At the time of his death the studio had negotiating a loan out to Sol Lesser's Independent company, Principal Artists Productions, in the role of Michael in a film to be called *Strange Victory*. In return, Warners were loaned Martha Scott for their forthcoming production *One Foot in Heaven* (Warner, Irving Rapper, 1941). *Strange Victory*, based on the book published by Rose Franken in 1939, was due to begin shooting mid August, but in the event of Jimmy's death the project was shelved indefinitely. Other loan out offers considered included Alexander Korda's production of *Lydia* (United Artists, Julian Duvivier, 1941) starring Merle Oberon. M-G-M were interested in casting him the role taken by Arthur Shields in the Judy Garland musical *Little Nellie Kelly* (M-G-M, Norman Taurog, 1940), in the remake of *Smilin' Through* (M-G-M, Frank Borzage, 1941) and also in the role of Dr. John Lanyon in the lavish remake of *Dr. Jekyll and Mr. Hyde* (M-G-M, Victor Fleming, 1941) - the role was given to Ian Hunter. Lux Radio also wished to use him in a radio broadcast of *Cyrano de Bergerac* alongside Geraldine Fitzgerald and Laurence Olivier. Perhaps the most tantalizing opportunity was an approach by Samuel Goldwyn for casting of the husband Horace Giddens in *The Little Foxes* (William Wyler, 1941) playing opposite Bette Davis. Had he been given the okay to play the role of the invalid husband (ailing with a heart condition) the sense of irony, especially during the chilling climax when the stricken man staggers upstairs for his medicine, would have been particularly affecting. These clues of how his career might have developed demonstrate beyond doubt Jimmy had more talented performances to give.

[11] GRO Register of Deaths: October-December 1944, Lancaster, 8e, 879

[12] GRO Register of Deaths: July-September 1949, Uckfield, 5h, 365

[13] GRO Register of Deaths: April-June 1950, Lancaster, 10c, 589

[14] GRO Register of Deaths: October-December 1950, Lancaster, 10c, 637

[15] Lloyd Nolan generously autographed a copy of *The Caine Mutiny* for Peter Stephenson. His dedication dated December 28, 1955 reminded Peter he had taken his mother and him on a tour of New York including a visit to The Empire State Building during their brief stay before departing for England on the SS *Franconia* in June 1945. It is probable Nolan was

in New York for the shooting of Louis De Rochemont's spy thriller *The House on 92nd Street* (Twentieth Century-Fox, Henry Hathaway, 1945). Of his father, Nolan in his dedication wrote: "I had such admiration for him – he was a great actor and a wonderful man". Stephenson Archive

[16] Three page typed manuscript dated November 22, 1958, Stephenson Archive

[17] *In Memoriam*, August 26, 1941, Stephenson Archive. Reagan was 33rd Governor of California from 1967 to 1975.

[18] *Burnley Express*, March 12, 1968, p.9

APPENDIX 1

AMATEUR PERFORMANCES
(1901-1932)

*The following consists of musical and dramatic
performances on the amateur stage, along with other
public appearances, given by James Stephenson*

1. *May Show* held in Burnley, East Lancashire, England. Following a pageant procession through the town of Burnley, watched by four thousand people, there were prize givings and other events held at the Burnley Athletic Grounds on the afternoon of May 4, 1901. This included plaiting of the May pole by a number of girls and boys organised by Mr. James M. Cunningham.

   Principals: Those taking part included: Misses: Florrie Keighley; Ethel Keighley; Pollie Cooke; Amy Cooke; Lizzie Holt; Nellie Holt; Florry Duerden and Polly Steele. Masters: Willie Dixon; B. Fletcher; G. Duckworth; V. Kenshaw; Chas. Clegg; **Jas. Stephenson**; Atkinson and B. Cooper

2. **Selections from Handel's Oratorio *Messiah***; St. Peter's Parish Church, Burnley, East Lancashire, England; December 22, 1907

   Principals: Miss Lord (*Soprano*); Fred Watson (*Tenor*); Mr. A. Newall (*Bass*); Mr. W[illiam].A[lexander].C[ampbell].Cruickshank (*Conductor*); Mr. Alan Stephenson (*Organist*) **James Stephenson (?)**
   [Although his name is not given this entry stands four-square for his

many un-recorded appearances as a choir boy in churches across East Lancashire]

3. **A Grand Conversazione and Concert**; Bethesda Church, Burnley; November 27, 1909

   Principals: Pearl Mystr (*renowned master of legerdemain or sleight-of-hand, paper manipulator and illusionist*) followed by: Miss Lily M. Tubb (*Contralto*); Mr. Alan Stephenson (*Solo Pianoforte*); **Mr. James Stephenson (*Bass*)** sang *"The Lute Player"* and *"Mountain Lovers"* by Fred[erick] Edward Weatherly and W[illiam] H[enry]. Squire, 1908; Mr. E.T. Astin (*Tenor*); Mr. Lambert (*Accompanist*)

4. **Selections from Handel's Oratorio *Messiah***; Burnley Parish Church; December 26, 1909

   Principals: Alan Stephenson (*Organist*); **James Stephenson (*Bass*)**; Fred Watson (*Tenor*); James Holt (*Bass*) and Master Shoesmith (*Soprano*); Mr. W[illiam].A[lexander].C[ampbell]. Cruickshank (*Conductor*)

5. **Concert & Dramatic Performance**; St. Peter's Girls School, Burnley; January 10, 1911

   Play: *The Crystal Gazer*

   Principals: Mrs. J.H. Watson and Miss E[velyn]. Pullon

   Tableaux

   Principals: Mrs. J.N. Grimshaw; Mrs. J.H. Watson; Miss M. Edmondson; Miss Grimshaw; Miss E[velyn]. Pullon; Master B. Lund; Mr. Geoffrey H. Sutcliffe; Dr. Wood; Dr. Taylor; Captain Riley; Mr. Philip Pullon; Mr. Ray; Mr. R.G. Ross; Mr. J. Stamp

   Concert

   Principals: Mr. Alan Stephenson (*Pianoforte solo*); Miss G. Proctor (*Violin Solo*); Miss E[velyn]. Pullon; **Mr. J. Stephenson (*Bass*)** and Mr. Fred Watson (*Tenor*) performed several songs.

6. **Organ Recital** by Alan Stephenson Mus. Bac. (Oxon), Miss C.B. Halstead, A.R.C.O.and Mr. A[lfred].R[eevers]. Nutter followed by **selections from Handel's Oratorio *Messiah***; Burnley Parish Church; December 31, 1911

   Principals: Madame Jessie Lord (*Soprano*); Fred Watson (*Tenor*); John Clegg (*Tenor*); **Mr. James Stephenson (*Bass*)**; An augmented Choir and Orchestra; Mr. W[illiam].A[lexander].C[ampbell]. Cruickshank Mus.

Bac., Oxon. (*Conductor*).

7. Selections from Handel's Oratorio ***Messiah*** at Burnley Parish Church; Augmented choir of 70 voices with orchestra; December 29, 1912

Principals: Madame Jessie Lord (*Soprano*); Fred Watson (*Tenor*); John Clegg (*Tenor*); **James   Stephenson** (***Bass***): James Holt (*Bass*); Organists: Miss C.B. Halstead A.R.C.O. and Mr. A[lfred].R[eevers]. Nutter; Conductor: Mr. W[illiam].A[lexander].C[ampbell]. Cruickshank Mus. Bac., Oxon.

8. ***Wagner Concert***; The Manchester Orchestra Conducted by Dr. T.G. Crump; Burnley Vocal Society, Mechanics Institute, Burnley; January 14, 1913

Part I

Overture: *Tannhauser*; March and Chorus (*Hail Bright Abode*): *Tannhauser*; Act III: *Tannhauser*

Principals: Miss Carrie Tubb (*Elizabeth / Venus*); Mr. Frank Mullings (*Tannhauer*); Mr. Herbert Brown (*Wolfram*)

Part II

Trauermarsch: *Gotterdammerung*; *Wotan's Abschied und Feurzauber: Die Walkure*; Overture: *Die Meistersinger*; Prelude Act III: *Die Meistersinger*; Fragment from Act II, Scene V: *Die Meistersinger*

Principals: Miss Carrie Tubb (*Eva*); Mr. Frank Mullings (*Walther*); Mr. Herbert Brown (*Hans Sachs*); **Mr. J.A. Stephenson** (***Pogner***); Chorus of 120 Voices

9. Manchester Diocesan Church Music Society, Burnley Branch, **Annual Musical Festival**; Burnley Parish Church; November 20, 1913

Synopsis: Choir of 250 voices drawn from the following church districts: Burnley's: St. Peters, St. Pauls, St. James, Holy Trinity, St. Matthews, St. Stephens; Brierfield's: St Lukes; Colne's: St. Bartholomews, St George's, St James. Among the hymns sung: Wesley's "*Ascribe Unto the Lord*" and Brahm's "*How Lovely Are Thy Dwelling Fair.*"

Principals: Solos sung by masters A. Hoyle and F. Shoesmith and Messrs: Coates, Shaw, [John] Clegg, [Fred] Watson and [**James**] **Stephenson**. Organists: Mr. J.E. Gaul, Mr. James Armistead Mus. Bac. Oxon. F.R.C.O. (*Conductor*) Mr. W.[illiam]A.[lexander]C.[ampbell] Mus. Bac. Oxon.

10. **Selections from Handel's Oratorio** *Messiah*; St. Peter's Church Burnley; Orchestra leader: Mr. Albert Pollard with Mr. A[lfred].R[eevers]. Nutter presiding at the organ. Mr. W[illiam].A[lexander].C[ampbell]. Cruickshank (*Conductor*); December 28, 1913

    Principals: Mrs. Dobbing (*Soprano*); John Clegg (*Tenor*); Fred Watson (*Tenor*) James Holt (*Bass*); **James Stephenson (***Bass***)**

11. **Selections from Handel's Oratorio** *Messiah*; Burnley Parish Church; Orchestra Leader: Mr. Albert Pollard; December 27, 1914

    Principals: Miss Pollard; John Clegg (*Tenor*); Fred Watson (*Tenor*); **Jas. Stephenson**(*Bass*);Masters:ShoesmithandHoyle.Mr.A[lfred].R[eevers]. Nutter presided at the organ; Mr. W[illiam].A[lexander].C[ampbell]. Cruickshank, Mus. Bac. (Oxon.) (*Conductor*)

12. **Operatic Evening**; Burnley Clef Club, Mechanics Institute, Burnley; Musical Director: Mr. Tom Robinson; Piano Accompaniment: Mr. Arthur Baldwin; October 8, 1920

    Synopsis: An evening devoted to the evolution of the Italian school of opera.

    Part I - New Style: *1ˢᵗ Act from La Boheme* (Puccini) – Mr. Maurice Walton (*Marcel*); Mr. Scarboro Wilkinson (*Rudolph*); **Mr. James Stephenson (***Colline, a Philosopher***)**; Mr. Lee Thistlethwaite (*Schaunard*); Mr. Ernest Pollard (*Benoit*); Miss Lily Allen (*Mimi*); Act 4 of the same, duet *Ah Mimi Noble-hearted* – Mr. Fred Thistlethwaite and Mr. Rennie Nutter; **Song** *Garment Antique* (Puccini) **– Mr. James Stephenson;** Aria and duet from *Aida* (Verdi) – Miss Carrie Nutter Smith and Miss Evelyn Nicholson; *Prologue Pagliacci* (Leoncavallo) – Mr. Rennie Nutter; Song *Flantussa Romance, Cavalleria Rusticana* (Mascagni) – Miss Evelyn Nicholson

    Part II – Old Style: Selections from *The Barber of Seville* (Rossini) *The Barber's Song* and *Una Voce Poco Fa Romanza* – Mr. Lee Thistlethwaite and Miss Lily Allen; *Spirito Gentil La Favourita* (Donizetti) – Mr. Fred Thistlethwaite; Verdi Selection (early) *Ah Fore's Lui La Traviata* and *Fierce Now the Flames Il Travatore* - Miss Carrie Nutter Smith and Miss Evelyn Nicholson

13. **Operatic Evening** arranged by Mr. Tom Robinson; Burnley Clef Club, Mechanics Institute; February 22, 1924

    Synopsis: Concert featuring the opera *Savitri* by Gustav Holst and selections from Mozart's *The Magic Flute*

Part I: *Savitri*

Principals: Miss Lily Allen (*Savitri*); Mr. Wilfred Lord (*Satyanan Husband of Savitri*); **Mr. James A. Stephenson (*Death*)**; Ladies Choir: Mr. George Alston: *Piano*; Mr. Arthur Baldwin: *Organ*

Part II: *The Magic Flute - Act 2*

Principals: Miss Lily Allen (*Queen of the Night*); Miss Carrie Nutter Smith (*Pamina*); Frank Kippax (*Prince Tamino*); Arthur Tuck (*Papagano*); Dorothy Atkinson (*Papagena*); Annie Lord, Edith Rowbottom; Ada Morley; (*The Good Fairies*); Walter Haythornthwaite (*Sarastro, High Priest*); Walter Tout (*Monostatos*); Alan Wilmore, George Roylance and William Taylor (*Chief Priests of the Temple*); Edward Whittaker and Charles Preston (*Priests on Guard*); The Brierfield Male Voice Choir (*Chorus of Priests*); Conducted by A. Kippax; Mr. Baldwin: *Piano*; Mr. Altham: *Organ*

14. **Operatic Evening** arranged by Mr. Tom Robinson; Burnley Clef Club, Mechanics Institute; Accompanists: Pianoforte: Mr. Arthur Baldwin A.R.C.O.; Miss Mary Iveson; Miss Winifred Woods; Harp: Miss Winifred Woods; Stage Manager: Mr. Sydney Campion [Stage Manager of Palace Theatre]; Floral Decorations: Mr. W. Palmer; Curios and Idol Lent by Mr. L. Fairey [Art Dealer, Yorkshire Street]; Screen loaned by Mrs. Holden [Milliner, The Centre]; Makeup: Mr. Maddicks; Electric Effects: Thornton's [Bridge Street]; Costumes: Burkinshaws [Liverpool]; March 20, 1925

Synopsis: Concert featuring selections from two Puccini operas: *Tosca* and *Madam Butterfly*

Tosca

Principals: Miss Carrie Nutter Smith (*Floria Tosca*); Mr. F[rank]. Kippax (*Mario Cavaradossi*); Mr. A[lan]. Wilmore (*Baron Scarpia*); Mr. A[lfred]. Heap (*Spolleta*); Mr. W[illiam]. Taylor (*Sciarenne*); Mr. C[harles]. Preston (*Judge of the High Court*); Mr. W[alter]. Tout (*Roberti*); Miss Annie Aitken; Miss Gladys Sutcliffe; Miss Edith Rowbotham; Miss Annie Taylor; Miss Mary Rowbotham; Miss Florence Crossley; Mr. W.H. Miller; Mr. Thomas Hartley; Mr. Walter Trout; Mr. C[harles]. Preston (*Singers in the Queen's Palace*)

Madam Butterfly

Principals: Miss Lily Allen (*Madam Butterfly*); Miss Evelyn Nicholson

(*Suzuki*); Mr Frank Kippax (*Lieutenant Pinkerton*); **Mr. J.A. Stephenson** (*Mr Sharpless*); Mr C[harles]. Preston (*Prince Yamadorf*); Mr A[lfred]. Heap and Mr W[illiam]. Taylor (*His Two Attendants*); Mr W[alter]. Tout (*Goro, a Marriage Broker*); Nora Fielding (*Little Trouble, Butterfly's Child*)

15. *Song Recital*: Tudor Galleries, Sir Herbert Marshall & Sons Ltd., 69 and 71 Deansgate, Manchester; September 17, 1926

    1:15pm lunch time recital featuring Lily Allen and **James A. Stephenson**. Lily Allen gave a recital of songs by Mozart, Brahms and Wolf. George Altham, organist of St. Catherine's Church, was accompanist. A relaxed throat prevented James Stephenson from appearing.

16. **Operatic Evening**: Burnley Clef Club, Mechanics Institute, Burnley; Accompanists: Miss Mary Iveson A.R.C.M.; Mr Arthur Baldwin A.R.C.O; Stage Manager: Mr Sydney Campion; Director: Mr Tom Robinson; March 18, 1927

    Synopsis: Selections taken from *Othello* and *Aida* by Verdi and *A Persian Garden* by Liza Lehmann;

    Aida **Act II Scene I**

    Principals: Miss Gladys Hesketh (*Aida*); Miss Evelyn Howarth (*Amneris*); Miss Eva Halliwell; Miss Elsie Kirk; Miss Esther Knowles; Miss Teresa Russell; Miss Mary Rowbotham; Miss Gladys Sutcliffe; Miss Alice Spencer (*Chorus of Slaves*); Miss Ethel Wood (*Dancer*)

    Othello **Act IV**

    Principals: Irvine Howarth (*Othello*); Miss Carrie Nutter Smith (*Desdemona*); Miss Nora Rust (*Emila*); Mr Walter Tout (*Iago*); Mr Tom Hartley (*Cassio*); Mr William Taylor (*Ludovica*); Mr Alfred Head (*Montana*)

    A Persian Garden – A Fantasy

    Principals: **Mr James A. Stephenson** (*An Elderly Persian Prince*); Miss Evelyn Nicholson and Miss Lily Allen (*The Prince's Two Daughters*); Mr Wilfred Hindle (*Young Persian Nobleman*); Miss Ethel Wood (*Dancer*) [By arrangement with Miss Lofts]

17. **Grand Opera Night** arranged by Mr Tom Robinson; *Don Giovanni* by Wolfgang Amadeus Mozart; Burnley Clef Club, Mechanics Institute, Burnley; Accompanist: Mary Iveson L.R.A.M; Stage Director: Sidney Campion; March 16, 1928

Synopsis: Statue of a murdered man accepts an insolent invitation to banquet with his murderer appears at the feast and drags him down to hell.

Principals: Alan Wilmore (*Don Giovanni*); Douglas Kirk (*Laporello, Don Giovanni's Servant*); Wilfred Hindle (*Don Octavio, a Nobleman*); Gladys Hesketh (*Donna Anna, Betrothed to Don Octavio*); **James A. Stephenson (*The Commandant, Donna Anna's Father*)**; Miss Carrie Nutter Smith (*Donna Elvira*); William Taylor (*Masetto, a Stupid Peasant*); Miss Lily Allen (*Zertina, betrothed to Masetto*); Miss Teresa Russell, Mary Starkie, Nellie Dent, Esther Knowles, Arthur Hargreaves, Thomas Hartley, Laurence Lord, Thomas Duxbury (*Peasants*); Thomas Burrows, Leonard Green (*Footmen*)

18. **Operatic Evening**: Scenes from *Don Giovanni* by Wolfgang Amadeus Mozart; Burnley Clef Club, Mechanics Institute, Burnley; Director: Mr. Thomas Robinson; Piano: Miss Mary Iveson; March 1, 1929
    Synopsis: Don Giovanni, a young nobleman, after a life of amorous conquests meets defeat in his three encounters with Donna Elvira, Donna Anna and Zerlina.

    Principals: Mr. Douglas Kirk (*Leporello, Don Giovanni's Servant*); Miss Carrie Nutter Smith (*Donna Elvira*); Mr. Alan Wilmore (*Don Giovanni*); Mr. Irvine Haworth (*Don Octavio*); Miss Gladys Hesketh (*Donna Anna*); Miss Lily Allen (*Zerlina, a Peasant Girl*); **Mr. Jas. A. Stephenson (*The Commandant*)**; Mr. William A. Taylor (*Masetto*)

19. ***The Magic Flute*** by Wolfgang Amadeus Mozart; The Burnley Operatic Society; Victoria Theatre, Burnley; Conductor: Cecil H. Bateson; Stage Manager: John Grey; November 19, 21-22, 1929

    Synopsis: A prince and his companion battle evil forces to rescue a princess.

    Principals: Miss Carrie Nutter Smith (*Queen of the Night*); Miss Teresa Russell (*Pamina*); Florence Whitaker, Elsie Bond, Dorothy Todd (*Ladies of the Queen*); Frank Kippax (*Tamino*); Lee Thistlethwaite (*Papageno*); Eveline Nicholson, Elsie Kirk, Nellie Bradbury (*Genii of the Temple*); Sally Taylor (*Papagena*); James R[obert] Allison (*Speaker of the Temple*); **James Stephenson (*Sarastro*)**; Frank Kippax (*Tamino, Young Prince*); Arthur Nightingale (*Monostatos*); Alan Hoyle (*First Priest*); Arthur S. Baldwin (*Second Priest*)

    Chorus: Miss Clara Alfrey; Miss Jenny Allen; Mrs. Maria Allison; Mr. Louis Bannister; Mr. H. Barker; Mrs. Barker; Miss Madge Brown; Mrs.

C. Brown; Mr. Arthur Brett; Mr. F. Buckley; Miss M. Corbett; Miss Edna Duxbury; Mr. C. Frankland; Mr. H. Gale; Miss Maud E. Halstead; Miss F. Hartley; Mrs. N. Hindle; Mr. N.L. Holden; Mrs. D. Howarth; Miss E. Howarth; Miss M. James; Miss Amy Kellett; Mrs. Lathom; Mr. H. Layfield; Mr. Frank L. Lee; Mr. S. Lord; Mrs. Mercer; Miss Stella Moon; Mrs. Nicholas; Miss Florence Nightingale; Mr. R. Nutter; Miss Laura Parker; Miss D. Pate; Mr. A. Pilkington; Miss Dorothy Redding; Mrs. M. Robinson; Mrs. Elsie Ross; Miss Stott; Miss E. Shipley; Mr. T. Skipper; Mr. J. Thistlethwaite; Mr. W. Thornber; Miss E. Waterson; Miss V. Weston; Mr. A.H. Wheeler; Miss E. Whitehead; Miss Edith Whitaker

20. ***St. Catherine's Grand Concert*** arranged by Miss [Elizabeth] Woodhead L.R.A.M A.R.C.O (*Accompanist*); at the Schoolroom St Catherine's Church, Burnley; November 28, 1929

Principals: Miss Lily Allen (*Soprano*); Miss Eva Halliwell (*Contralto*); **Mr. J. Stephenson** (*Bass*); Miss M. Lambert (*Cello*); Mr. A. Baines (*Violin*); Mr. C[lifford]. Parkinson (*Humorist*); Master Ronald Welch and Miss Woodhead (*Piano Duets*)

Programme – Part I

1. Duet – *Danse Russe* – Tchaikovsky and *5th Ballet Music* from *Faust* [Miss Woodhead L.R.A.M. A.R.C.O. and Master R. Welch]
2. Song – *Waltz Song* from *Tom Jones* – E.German [Miss L. Allen]
3. Violin Solo – *Allegro Brilliant* – W. Ten Have [Mr A. Baines]
4. Song – *O Love from Thy Power* – Saint Saens from *Samson et Dalila* – [Miss E. Halliwell]
5. Cello Solo – *Dance Rustique* – W.H. Squire [Miss M. Lambert]
6. Selected Item – [Mr C. Parkinson]
7. **Song – *Invictus* – Bruno Huhn [Mr J. Stephenson]**
8. Trio – *In E. Minor Op. 159, No 2* – C. Reinecke [Misses Lambert and Woodhead and Mr. Baines]

Programme - Part II

1. Duet – *2nd Movement, 2nd Symphony* – Beethoven [Miss Woodhead L.R.A.M. A.R.C.O. and Master R. Welch]
2. Songs – a) *An Eriskay Love Lilt* – M.K. Fraser b) *Life and Death* – Coleridge Taylor [Miss E. Halliwell]
3. Cello Solo – *Romance* – A. Fischer [Miss M. Lambert]
4. **Duet – *The Voyages* – W. Sanderson [Miss L. Allen and Mr. J. Stephenson]**
5. Selected Item – [Mr C. Parkinson]

6. Songs – (a) *The Wren* – Liza Lehmann (b) *Down in the Forest* – Landon Ronald [Miss L. Allen]

7. Violin Solo – *Il Trovatore* – Verdi [Mr Baines]

8. Songs – (a) **Captain Stratton's Fancy** – Peter Warlock; (b) **The Sergeant's Song** (1803) – Gustav Holst [**Mr J. Stephenson**]

9. Duet – *Passing By* – H. Purcell [Misses Allen and Halliwell]

21. **The School for Scandal** by Richard Brinsley Sheridan; Burnley Clef Club, Mechanics Institute, Burnley; Piano: Wilfrid Lord; February 7, 1930

    Synopsis: Two brothers compete for the affections of a beautiful woman who happens to be their rich uncle's much younger wife.

    Cast: Greenwood (*Sir Peter Teazle*); **James Stephenson (*Sir Oliver Surface*)**; Clifford Parkinson (*Charles Surface*); Frank Lofthouse (*Joseph Surface*); George Alston (*Careless*); James Collinge (*Sir Harry Bumper*); Harry Thompson (*Sir Benjamin Backbite*); Arthur Nightingale (*Crabtree*); Donald Taylor (*Snake*); Alfred Maddicks (*Rowley*); Herbert Gregson (*Moses*); John Birley (*Trip, Charles' Servant*); Ernest Whittaker (*William, Joseph's Servant*); Shannon Leslie (*Lady Teazle*); Florence Broughton (*Lady Sneerwell*); Marion Atkinson (*Mrs. Candour*); Phyllis Sutcliffe (*Maria, Sir Peter's Ward*); Jennie Forsythe (*Maid to Lady Teazle*); Edith Broughton (*Maid to Lady Sneerwell*)

22. **The Best People** by David Gray and Avery Hopwood; The Burnley Players; Victoria Theatre, Burnley; Acting Stage Manager: John Stuttard; Stage Manager: Tom Pate;   Producer: Mrs. M.[arjorie] Croasdale; March 31, April 1-2, 1930

    Synopsis: The children of a wealthy family decide to marry beneath their class. Bertie falls in love with a chorus girl and Marion drops her rich suitors for her mother's chauffeur, much to their high-class family's disapproval.

    Cast: Nellie Down (*Mrs. Lennox*); Alan Shaw (*Edward Lennox*); Florence Moon (*Marion Lennox*); Stanley Haworth (*Bullock*); Hitchon Chadwick (*Lord Rockmere*); **James Stephenson (*Henry Masters*)**; Dorothy Whitaker (*Miss Tate*); James Pick (*George Grafton*); Edward Landless (*Bertie Lennox*); Albert Yates (*A Waiter*); Dorothy Kellett (*Millie Montgomery*); Muriel Eadie (*Alice O'Neill*); George Alston (*A Waiter*)

23. **Municipal Concert** Palace Theatre, Burnley; October 5, 1930

    Principals: The Municipal Symphony Orchestra Conductor: Archie Camden Miss Raya Garbousova (*Cellist*) Accompanied by Miss Lydia

Garbousova (*Piano*); **Mr. James A. Stephenson (*Bass*)** Accompanied by William A. Pollard (*Piano*) sang ***Through Faithless men*** from ***The Jewess*** (Jacques Fromental Halévy), followed by ***The Sergeant's Song*** (Gustav Holst) then two songs ***Four by the Clock*** and ***We Sway Along*** (Albert Mallison). Finally ***Captain Stratton's Fancy*** (Peter Warlock).

24. ***It Pays to Advertise*** a farce by Walter Hackett and Roi Cooper Megrue; The Burnley Players; Victoria Theatre, Burnley; October 13-18, 1930

Synopsis: Sir Henry Martin, a wealthy soap king, realising the fortune he has spent on his son's college education encourages his brash and callow son Ellery to go to work. Encouraged by the love of a girl and helped by press agent Ambrose Peale he eventually makes good.

Cast: Miss Florence Moon (*Mary Grayson*); Stanley Haworth (*Johnson, Butler of the Martins*); Mrs. Hilda Green (*Countesse de Beaurien*); Edward Landless (*Rodney Martin*); James Pick (*Ambrose Peale*); Miss Dorothy Kellett (*Marie, Maid at the Martins*); Alan Shaw (*William Smith*); Miss Alice Kay (*Miss Burke*); Clifford Parkinson; (*George McChesney*); Dr. Hitchon Chadwick (*Ellery Clark*); Eric Nayler (*George Bronson*); **James Stephenson (*Sir George Martin*)**

25. ***Aida*** by Giuseppe Verdi; The Burnley Operatic Society; Palace Theatre, Burnley; Conductor: Lee Thistlethwaite; Stage Manager: John Grey; Property Master: J.T. Pollard; Accompanist: Arthur Baldwin ARCO; November 17, 19, 22, 1930

Synopsis: An Ethiopian Princess is forced into slavery when captured by the Egyptians.

Principals: Miss Carrie Nutter Smith (*Aida*); Evelyn Haworth (*Amneris*); Reginald Trippier (*Radames*); **James Stephenson (*Ramphis*)**; Miss Laura Parker (*Chief Priestess*); Alan Wilmore (*The King*); William Smith (*Amonasro*); Tom Armer (*Messenger*)

Ladies and Gentlemen of the Chorus: Mrs. Allison; Miss Clara Alfrey; Miss Jenny Allen; Miss Madge Brown; Mrs. Barker; Mrs. Brown; Mrs. Nellie Bradbury; Miss Doris Brecknell; Mrs. Collinge; Miss Edna Duxbury; Miss M. Gutteridge; Mrs. Hindle; Miss Halstead; Mrs. Haworth; Mrs. Holden; Miss Rhona Howker; Miss Hartley; Miss Heap; Miss J. Horner; Miss Elsie Kirk; Miss Amy Kellett; Miss Dorothy Kellett; Mrs. Latham; Mrs. Mercer; Miss Stella Moon; Miss Florence Moon; Miss D. Pate; Miss Laura Parker; Miss Dorothy Redding; Mrs. Robinson; Mrs. Elsie Ross; Miss R. Stott; Miss Starkie; Miss Dorothy Todd; Mrs.

Thompson; Miss E[dith].J. Whitaker; Miss E. Whitehead; Tom Armer; Arthur Brett; Louis Bannister; Arthur S. Baldwin; H. Gutteridge; R. Gutteridge; Alan Hoyle; H.C. Holden; H. Layfield; Frank L. Lee; C. Mason; R[ennie]. Nutter; Arthur Nightingale; A. Proctor; H.S. Proctor; R. Mc. I. Ross; T. Skipper; W.E. Singleton;. F. Silcock; W. Thornber; J. Thistlethwaite; E.J. Taylor; J.L. Thompson; A.H. Wheeler

26. *Man and Superman* by George Bernard Shaw; The Burnley Drama Guild; Victoria Theatre, Burnley; Producer: Shannon Leslie; December 8-9, 13, 1930

    Synopsis: John Tanner, an earnest young revolutionary, flees to the Sierra Nevada when he discovers that his beautiful ward, Annie Whitefield, has plans to marry him.

    Cast: Paul Greenwood (*Roebuck Ramsden*); Florence Copeland (*Maid*); Harold Pollard (*Octavius Robinson*); **James Stephenson (*John Tanner*)**; Nellie Down (*Mrs. Whitefield*); Flossie Moon (*Annie Whitefield*); Dorothy Kellett (*Miss Ramsden*); Shannon Leslie (*Violet Robinson*); John Grey (*Henry Straker*); Clifford Parkinson (*Hector Malone Jnr.*); Alan Shaw (*Hector Malone Snr.*)

27. *The Beaux' Stratagem* by George Farquhar; The Drama Guild; Victoria Theatre, Burnley; Producer: Shannon Leslie; December 10-12, 1930

    Synopsis: After squandering their fortunes on drink and gambling, Tom Aimwell and Jack Archer seek refuge in the countryside. They hope to seduce two ladies of status and fortune, but true love and a band of thieves soon complicate their scheming.

    Cast: Alan Shaw (*Boniface, an Innkeeper*); Doris Foulds (*Cherry, his Daughter*); Clifford Parkinson (*Aimwell, a Gentleman of Broken Fortune*); **James Stephenson (*Archer, a Gentleman of Broken Fortune*)**; Albert Smith (*A Tapster*); Shannon Leslie (*Mrs. Sullen, Daughter-in-law to Lady Bountiful*); Florence Broughton (*Dorinda, Lady Bountiful's Daughter*); John Grey (*Squire Sullen, Lady Bountiful's Son*); Paul Greenwood (*Scrub, Sullen's Servant*); Donald Taylor (*Gibbet, a Highwayman*); Florence Copeland (*Gypsy, Lady Bountiful's Maid*); Grace Elford (*A Country Woman*); Dorothy Holgate (*Lady Bountiful, a Gentlewoman who Cures All her Neighbours of their Distempers*); Albert Smith (*Hounslow, Highwayman, Follower of Gibbet*); Arthur Nightingale (*Bagshot, Highwayman, Follower of Gibbet*); Harold Pollard (*Sir Charles Freeman, Mrs. Sullen's Brother*)

28. ***Selections from Handel's Oratorio Messiah***; St. Stephen's Church, Burnley; December 14, 1930

   Principals: Master G. Pickup (*Soprano*); Mr. T[om].L. Varley (*Alto*); Mr. J[ack]. Gomersall (*Tenor*); **Mr. Jas. Stephenson (*Bass*)**; Mr. J[ames]. Armistead Mus Bac FRCO FRMCM (*Organist*); Mr. F[rank]. Knight LCV (*Leader of String Orchestra*); Miss E[lizabeth]. Woodhead A.R.C.O. L.R.A.M. (*Conductor*)

29. ***Christmas Concert***; Burnley Rotary Club; Café Royal, Burnley; December 22, 1930 "*Music of the Old World*" sung by Mr. John Pickles; Mr. Laurie Lord and **Rotarian J. Stephenson**;

30. ***Man and Superman*** The Burnley Co-operative Players; Co-operative Hall, Todmorden, East Lancashire; January 17, 1931

   Cast: Paul Greenwood (*Roebuck Ramsden*); Doris Foulds (*Maid*); Harold Pollard (*Octavius Robinson*); **James Stephenson (*John Tanner*)**; Mrs. Nellie Down (*Mrs Whitefield*); "Flossie" Moon (*Anne Whitefield*); Dorothy Kellett (*Miss Ramsden*); Shannon Leslie (*Violet Robinson*); John Grey (*Henry Straker*); Clifford Parkinson (*Hector Malone Jnr.*); Alan Shaw (*Hector Malone Snr.*)

31. Readings of ***Merchant of Venice*** by Shakespeare at Burnley Central Library; January 21, 1931

   Cast: John Grey (*Antonio*); Florence Broughton (*Salarino*); Arthur Nightingale (*Salanio*); Clifford Parkinson (*Bassanio*); **James A. Stephenson (*Shylock*)**; Albert Smith (*Old Gobbo*); Doris Foulds (*Jessica*); Alan Shaw (*Gratiano*); Harold Pollard (*Lorenzo*); Shannon Leslie (*Portia*); Florence Moon (*Nerissa*); Grace Elford (*Servant to Portia*); Walter G. Boys (*Prince of Morocco*); Paul Greenwood (*Prince of Aragon*); Dorothy Holgate (*Tubal / Duke of Venice*); Norah Turley (*Salerio*)

32. Readings of ***Merchant of Venice*** by Shakespeare at Burnley Central Library; January 28, 1931

   Cast: John Grey (*Antonio*); Florence Broughton (*Salarino*); Arthur Nightingale (*Salanio*); Walter G. Boys (*Bassanio*); Harold Pollard (*Lorenzo*); Alan Shaw (*Gratiano*); Shannon Leslie (*Portia*); Florence Moon (*Nerissa*); Grace Elford (*Servant to Portia*); **James A. Stephenson (*Shylock*)**; A[rthur]. Rought Brooks (*Prince of Morocco*); Donald Taylor (*Launcelot Gobbo*); Albert Smith (*Old Gobbo*); Doris Foulds (*Jessica*);

Paul Greenwood (*Prince of Aragon*); Dorothy Holgate (*Tubal / Duke of Venice*); Norah Turley (*Salerio*)

33. ***Annajanska, The Bolshevik Empress*** a one-act play by George Bernard Shaw; Free Trade Hall, Manchester [National Festival of Community Drama]; Producer: Walter G. Boys; February 7, 1931

    Synopsis: A Shavian satire on the Russian revolution.

    Cast: Shannon Leslie (*Grand Duchess Annajanska, Bolshevik Empress*); **James A. Stephenson (*General Strammfest*)**; Clifford Parkinson (*Lieutenant Schneiderkind*); Arthur Nightingale (*Soldier*); Albert Smith (*Soldier*)

34. ***The Father*** by August Strindberg; The Opera Players' Dramatic Society, Victoria Theatre, Burnley; Producer: John Grey; Stage Manager: Mrs. L. Thistlethwaite; February 9, 1931

    Synopsis: The tragedy of a man and a woman struggling for the possession of their child.

    Cast: Eric Nayler (*Pastor*); John Grey (*Captain*); Alan Shaw (*Nojd*); Dorothy Kellett (*Laura*); **James Stephenson (*Dr Ostermark*)**; Shannon Leslie (*Nurse*); Flossie Moon (*Bertha*)

35. ***Oedipus, the King*** by Sophocles (in translation); Burnley Drama Guild; Burnley Central Library; February 18, 1931

    Cast: James A. Stephenson (*Oedipus*); Shannon Leslie (*Jocasta*); Clifford Parkinson (*Creon*); Paul Greenwood (*Tiresias*); Harold Pollard (*Priest of Zeus*); John Grey (*A Stranger*) [in disposed]; Albert Smith (*A Shepherd*); Alan Shaw (*A Messenger*); Walter G. Boys (*Chorus of Thebar Elders*); Betty W. Ashworth (*Leader*); (*Other Minor Roles Played by*): Florence Broughton; Florence Copeland; Hilda Davies; Grace Ilford; Mrs. [Marion] Foster; Doris Foulds; Jane Freeman-Smith; Dorothy Holgate; Dorothy Kellett; Florence Moon; Arthur Nightingale; Donald Taylor; Norah Turley

36. ***Plunder*** a farce by Ben Travers; The Burnley Players; Victoria Theatre, Burnley; Producer: Mrs. M[arjorie]. Croasdale; Stage Director: Dr. Sykes; Acting Manger: John Stuttard; March 9-14, 1931

    Synopsis: Mrs. Hewlett, a wealthy if unpopular woman, meets suave jewel thief Freddie Malone who is naturally keen to relieve the lady of her jewellery. An old school friend D'Arcy Tuck also wants to purloin Mrs. Hewlett's wealth. This compels Freddie to enlist his assistance as accomplice in the jewel theft.

Cast: Eric Nayler (*Oswald Veal*); Hilda Green (*Prudence Malone*); Mrs. Nellie Down (*Mrs. Hewlett*); James Pick (*Simon Veal, Mrs. Hewlett's brother-in-law*); **James A. Stephenson (*Freddie Malone*)**; Miss Gladys Naylor (*Mabel, the Maid*); Miss Florence Moon (*Joan Hewlett*); Edward Landless (*D'Arcy Tuck*); Hitchon Chadwick (*Sir George Chudleigh*); Mrs. Winifred Watson (*Lady Chudleigh*); Wilfred Newton (*Harry Kenward*); Tom Pate (*Buckley, the Butler*); Miss Dorothy Kellett (*Mrs. Orlock*); Alan Shaw (*Chief Constable Grierson*); Alan Coppock (*Chief Detective Inspector Sibley*); Walter Currie (*Police Constable Davies*); George Alston (*Detective-Sergeant Marchant / Oswald Hewlett*); Kenneth Vere (*Detective-Sergeant Bryant*)

37. ***Pompey the Great*** by John Masefield; Burnley Drama Guild; Burnley Central Library; March 18, 1931

Cast: Doris Foulds (*Antistis*); Arthur Nightingale (*Philip*); Shannon Leslie (*Cornelia, Wife of Pompey*); Florence Broughton (*Julia*); John Grey (*Metellius*); **James A. Stephenson (*Pompey*)**; Clifford Parkinson (*Theophanes*); Paul Greenwood (*Cato*); Alan Shaw (*A Horseman*); Albert Smith (*Domitius*); Donald Taylor (*Lentulus*); Alan Coppock (*Cotta*); Alan Shaw (*Aelius*); Walter G. Boys (*Captain*); Norah Turley (*The Boy*); Bannister Walton (*Third Hand*)

38. ***Scenes from A Midsummer Night's Dream*** by Shakespeare; Burnley Drama Guild; English Folk Dance Society; "Four Oaks," Reedley Road, Higher Reedley; Orchestra Leader: John Greenwood; June 20, 1931

Synopsis: An afternoon and early evening spent with members of English Folk Dance Society taking part in traditional country dancing, with a dramatized interlude based on the Cecil Sharp interpretation of Shakespeare's *A Midsummer Night's Dream* and played by members of The Drama Guild Burnley.

Cast: John Grey (*Quince, a Carpenter*); **James A. Stephenson (*Bottom, a Weaver*)**; Paul Greenwood (*Flute, a Bellows Mender*); Harold Pollard (*Starveling, a Tailor*); J.E. Deady (*Snout, a Tinker*); Albert Smith (*Snug, a Joiner*); Norah Turley (*Puck, or Robin Goodfellow*); Arthur Nightingale (*First Fairy*); J. Leslie Thompson (*Oberon, King of the Fairies*); Shannon Leslie (*Titania, Queen of the Fairies*); Doris Foulds (*Pease Blossom*); Florence Broughton

(*Cobweb*); Florence Copeland (*Moth*); Dorothy Holgate (*Mustard Seed*); Edith Whitaker (*Second Fairy*)

39. **Valedictory Address** from Job W. Hartley President of Burnley Rotary Club **J. Stephenson** led in several songs; Café Royal, Burnley; June 29, 1931

40. *Electra* by Euripedes; Burnley Drama Guild; Burnley Central Library; October 14, 1931

    Cast: Paul Greenwood (*Peasant*); Shannon Leslie (*Electra*); **James A. Stephenson** (*Orestes*); Arthur Nightingale (*Pylades*); Elsie Bird (*Clytemnestra*); John Grey (*Old Man*); Alan Shaw (*Messenger*); Alan Coppock (*Castor*); Dorothy Holgate (*Chorus Leader*); Jane Freeman-Smith; Grace Elford; Helen Fielden; Margaret Marshall; Doris Foulds; Florence Copeland; Elsie Hoyle; Edith Whitaker; Albert Smith and H. Starkie (*Chorus and Minor Parts*)

41. *The Plays of George Bernard Shaw* Burnley Rotary Club; Café Royal, Burnley; November 30, 1931

    Synopsis: 40-minute address to Burnley Rotary club by **Rotarian James Stephenson** with several dramatic illustrations assisted by John Grey; Rotarian Walter Boys in the chair.

42. *The Devil's Disciple* by George Bernard Shaw; Burnley Drama Guild; Victoria Theatre, Burnley; December 17-19, 1931

    Synopsis: In 1777, a colonial new town sits complacent and ignorant of its own danger under British rule as rebellion swirls around it. Only Richard Dudgeon, hard-living prodigal son of a leading family, sees the threat to those on the sidelines of war, but who will heed the warning of the Devil's Disciple?

    Cast: Jane Freeman Smith (*Mrs. Dudgeon*); Doris Foulds (*Essie*); Arthur Nightingale (*Christy Dudgeon*); John Grey (*Anthony Anderson*); Dorothy Kellett (*Judith Anderson*); Paul Greenwood (*Lawyer Hawkins*); Donald Taylor (*Uncle William*); Grace Elford (*Mrs. William*); Alan Shaw (*Uncle Titus*); Margaret Marshall (*Mrs. Titus*); **James A. Stephenson** (*Richard Dudgeon*); Alan Coppock (*The Sergeant*); Alan Shaw (*Mayor Swindon*); Paul Greenwood (*General Burgoyne*); Frank Lofthouse (*Chaplain Brudenell*)

43. ***Man and Superman*** by George Bernard Shaw; Burnley Drama Guild; Victoria Theatre, Burnley; Producer: Walter G. Boys; December 14-16, 1931

    Cast: Paul Greenwood (*Roebuck Ramsden*); Florence Copeland (*Maid*); Frank Lofthouse (*Octavius Robinson*); **James Stephenson (*John Tanner*)**; Elsie Bird (*Mrs. Whitefield*); Miss Flossie Moon (*Anne Whitefield*); Miss Marion Foster (*Miss Ramsden*); Miss Shannon Leslie (*Violet Robinson*); John Grey (*Henry Straker*); Eric Nayler (*Hector Malone Jnr.*); Alan Shaw (*Hector Malone Snr.*)

44. ***Act I of Man and Superman*** by George Bernard Shaw; Burnley Drama Guild; Burnley Central Library; Preceded by short Spanish play Sierta's *The Lover*; January 13, 1932

    Cast: Mr. Paul Greenwood (*Roebuck Ramsden*); Miss Flossie Moon (*Ann Whitefield*); **Mr. James A. Stephenson (*John Tanner*)**

45. ***Rigoletto*** by Giuseppe Verdi; The Burnley Operatic Society; Victoria Theatre, Burnley; Music Director: Cecil H. Bateson; Stage Manager: John Grey; Property Master: John Thornber Jr; February 8, 10, 13, 1932

    Synopsis: Seduction, betrayal, curses and vendettas end in the tragic death of Rigoletto's innocent daughter Gilda.

    Principals: Lee Thistlethwaite (*Rigoletto*); Miss Hilda Mitchell (*Gilda*); Reginald Trippier (*The Duke*); Miss Edna Duxbury (*Giovanna*); Miss Margaret Barker (*Maddelena*); Miss Dorothy Todd (*Countess of Ceprano*); James R[obert] Allison (*Count Monterone*); **James A. Stephenson (*Sparafucile*)**; Tom Armer (*Borsa*); Mr. H.E. Holden (*Count of Ceprano*);

    Ladies and Gentlemen of the Chorus: Mrs. Allison; Mrs. C. Alfrey; Miss Jenny Allen; Arthur S. Baldwin; Miss Nellie Bradbury; Mrs. Brown; Miss D. Brecknell; Miss M. Brown; R. Caldwell; M. Caldwell: Louis Bannister: Miss M. Gutteridge; Mrs. Dorothy Grey; C. Greenhalgh; J.R. Gutteridge; Mrs. K. Holden; Miss Rhona Howker; Miss A. Hartley; Mrs. N. Hindle; Miss M. Halstead; F. Haythornthwaite; Miss Amy Kellett; Miss Dorothy Kellett; Miss Elsie Kirk; Mrs. D. Latham; H. Layfield; F.L. Lee; Mrs. Mercer; Miss Florence Moon; Miss Stella Moon; A[rthur]. Nightingale; R[ennie]. Nutter; Miss Laura Parker; A. Pilkington; F. Pickles; Miss Dorothy Redding; Mrs. Elsie Ross; Mr. Ross; W. Singleton; J. Thistlethwaite; W. Thornber; J. Taylor; Miss E. Whitehead; Miss Edith J. Whitaker; A.H. Wheeler

46. *The Devil's Disciple* by George Bernard Shaw; Co-operative Hall, Todmorden, East Lancashire; February 20, 1932

Cast: Jane Freeman Smith (*Mrs Dudgeon*); Doris Foulds (*Essie*); Arthur Nightingale (*Christy Dudgeon*); John Grey (*Anthony Anderson*); Paul Greenwood (*Lawyer Hawkins*); Donald Taylor (*Uncle William*); Grace Elford (*Mrs William*); Alan Shaw (*Uncle Titus*); Margaret Marshall (*Mrs Titus*); **James A. Stephenson** (***Richard Dudgeon***); Donald Taylor (*The Sergeant*); Alan Shaw (*Major Swinden*); Paul Greenwood (*General Burgoyne*); Frank Lofthouse (*Chaplain Brudenell*)

47. *A Cup of Kindness* by Ben Travers; The Burnley Players; Victoria Theatre Burnley; Producer: Mrs. Marjorie Croasdale; March 14-15, 17, 1932

Synopsis: A long-standing feud between two families appears over when Charles Tutt marries Betty Ramsbotham. However the couple comes under suspicion of fraud and chaos ensues.

Cast: Alan Coppock (*Jim Finch*); Phyllis Dyson (*Kate*); Eric Nayler (*Ernest Ramsbotham*); Edward Landless (*Charles Tutt*); Hilda Green (*Mabel Ramsbotham*); James Pick (*Nicholas Ramsbotham*); Florence Moon (*Betty Ramsbotham*); **James Stephenson** (***Fred Tutt***); Marjory (*Phyllis Tutt*); Gladys Nayler (*Tillie Winn*); Hitchon Chadwick (*Stanley Tutt*); Walter Currie (*Mr Niblett*); Alan Shaw (*Mr Chivers*)

48. *Thark* by Ben Travers; The Burnley Players; Victoria Theatre, Burnley; March 18-19, 1932

Synopsis: Sir Hector Benbow sells the mysterious Thark Manor to Mrs. Frush who believes the place is haunted. To prove her wrong Benbow agrees to spend the night in the property.

Cast: Eric Nayler (*Hook*); Gladys Naylor (*Warner*); Dorothy Kellett (*Cherry Buck*); Hitchon Chadwick (*Lionel Frush*); Marjorie Croasdale (*Mrs. Frush*); **James A. Stephenson** (***Sir Hector Benbow Bart M.F.H.***); Edward Landless (*Ronald Gamble*); Winifred Watson (*Lady Benbow*); Florence Moon (*Kitty Stratton*); Stanley Haworth (*Jones*); Tom Pate (*Whittle*)

49. *Municipal Concert* Palace Theatre, Burnley; March 20, 1932

Principals: Miss Carrie Nutter Smith (*Soprano*); Miss Margaret Balfour (*Contralto*); Mr. Francis Russell [substituted [William] Heddle Nash indisposed] **Mr. James A. Stephenson** (*Bass*) *singing Dvorak's At the Foot of the Cross (Stabat Mater). Also sang The Wanderer and Ole Man River.*

50. *Scenes from A Midsummer Night's Dream* by Shakespeare; Quernmore Park, Lancaster Producer: Walter G. Boys; Stage Manager: Arthur Nightingale; June 18, 1932

    Synopsis: An interlude in the Lancashire Folk Festival of The English Folk Dance and Song Society

    Cast: John Grey (*Quince, a Carpenter*); **James A. Stephenson (*Bottom, a Weaver*)**; Paul Greenwood (*Flute, a Bellows Mender*); Leslie B. Chapman (*Starveling, a* Tailor); James E. Deady (*Snout, a Tinker*); Albert Smith (*Snug, a Joiner*); Elsie Chapman (*Puck, a Robin Goodfellow*); Edith Whitaker (*First Fairy*); Frank Lofthouse (*Oberon, King of the Fairies*); Shannon Leslie (*Titania, Queen of the Fairies*); Doris Foulds (*Peaseblossom*); Helen Fielden (*Cobweb*); Florence Copeland (*Moth*); Dorothy Holgate (*Mustardseed*) [*Fairies Attending on Titania*]; Mary Dyson (*Second Fairy*); Members of the English Folk Song and Dance Society

51. *Plunder* by Ben Travers; The Burnley Players; Victoria Theatre, Burnley; Producers: Mrs. Marjorie Croasdale and John Grey; June 20-22, 1932

    Cast: **James A. Stephenson (*Freddie Malone*)**; Edward Landless (*D'Arcy Tuck*); Mrs. Nellie Down (*Mrs. Hewlett*); Eric Nayler (*Oswald Hewlett / Chief Constable Grierson*); Stanley Haworth (*Simon Veal, Mrs. Hewlett's brother-in-law*); Miss Dorothy Kellett (*Prudence Malone*); Miss Florence Moon (*Joan Hewlett*); Alan Coppock (*Chief Detective Inspector Sibley*); Miss Phyllis Dyson (*Mrs. Orlock*); Mrs. Watson (*Lady Chudleigh*); Miss Gladys Nayler (*Mabel, the Maid*); Thomas Porter (*Sir George Chudleigh / Detective-Sergeant Marchant*); Tom Pate (*Buckley, the Butler / Detective-Sergeant Bryant*); Wilfred Newton (*Harry Kenward*); Walter Currie (*Police Constable Davies*)

52. *Art and the Box Office* **Rotarian Mr. James Stephenson** addresses the Burnley Rotary Club on the subject of *Art and the Box Office* at The Café Royal, Burnley; August 8, 1932

53. *The Second Stain* by Sir Arthur Conan Doyle; Burnley and District Amateur Cine Society; Non commercial film, 16mm, b/w, silent; *Producer*: Oliver Moffatt; *Cameraman*: G[eorge]. Dunkerley; *Electrician*: W.H. Harris; *Editors*: F.G. Shoesmith and G[eorge]. Dunkerley; *Direction*: W.A. Duckworth; Produced 1932 and exhibited at Phoenix Theatre, Burnley on December 2, 1932

    Synopsis: A Conan Doyle mystery story

Cast: Oliver R[obert]. Moffatt (*Sherlock Holmes*); H. Pilkington (*Rt. Hon. Trelawny Hope*); W.P. Brotherton J.P. (*Lord Bellinger*); E.W. Williams (*Doctor Watson*); Miss Betty W. Ashworth (*Lady Hope*); John B. Elce (*Detective-Inspector Lestrade*); G[eorge]. Dunkerley (*First Policeman*); J.H. Brotherton (*Second Policeman*); Jane Freeman-Smith (*Mrs Hudson*); Lucy Wright (*First Maid*); Stella Moon (*Second Maid*); Wynne Rowland (*Madame Fournaye*)

[Though James Stephenson is reported in the local press (April 1932) as appearing in this film in the lead role of Sherlock Holmes by the time of its completion in December 1932 he had left Burnley and his name does not appear among the named cast.]

APPENDIX II

RADIO BROADCASTING
BRITISH BROADCASTS
(1929-1937)

1. ***Musical Concert*** BBC Manchester 2ZY, Piccadilly Studios, Manchester; Northern Wireless Orchestra; Conductor: Mr. T.H. Morrison; Broadcast February 25, 1929

   Principals: **J.A. Stephenson** (***Bass-Baritone***); Gwen Rodgers (*Soprano*)

   Programme: A fifty minute afternoon concert in which he sang six songs: The Northern Wireless Orchestra: *Coriolanus Overture* by Beethoven; Selection from *Hansel and Gretel* by Humperdinck; **J.A. Stephenson**: ***Vulcan's Song*** from *Philemon et Baucis* by Charles Gounod; ***Morning Hymn*** by Sir George Henschel; ***Within These Sacred Bowers*** by Mozart; The Northern Wireless Orchestra: *The Emperor Waltz* by Johann Strauss; *La Czarine* [Mazurka] by Louis Ganne; Gwen Rodgers: *I Wonder if Love is a Dream* by Forster; *Be Still, Blackbird* by Wilfred Sanderson; *Down in the Forest* by Landon Ronald; The Northern Wireless Orchestra: *Le Roi s'amuse Suite* by Delibes; **J.A. Stephenson**: ***Old Barty*** by Douglas Grant; ***A Banjo Song*** by Sidney Homer; ***The Ringers*** by Hermann Lohr; The Northern Wireless Orchestra: *Three Dale Dances* by Wood; Gwen Rodgers: *A Brown bird Singing* by Haydn Wood; *One Morning Very Early* by Wilfred Sanderson; *The Kerry Dance* by J.L. Molloy; *I Know a Lovely Garden* by D'Hardelot; The Northern Wireless Orchestra: *March Medley* arranged by Winter

2. *"The Spectral Dog" – A Story of the Isle of Man* by Leslie W[illiam].A[lfred]. Baily; BBC North Region; Piccadilly Studios, Manchester; Producer: D[avid].E. Ormerod; Effects: A.G. Mitcheson; Broadcast July 5, 1932.

Synopsis: A half-hour radio historical drama adapted from Manx legend. The appearance of The Spectral Dog of Peel Castle heralds death or disaster in this depiction of the execution of William Christian. The scene is the guard-room of Peel Castle, Isle of Man, stronghold of the Derby family, in 1662. The characters are all soldiers, mostly in the Earl of Derby's force.

Cast: Ernest Retlaw (*Morkill*); G[eorge].B[ernard]. Smith (*Gilbert*); **James Stephenson** (*Scriven*); H.R. Williams (*Grant*); F[rank].A. Nichols (*Quayle*); J. Edward Roberts (*A Sergeant*)

3. *Boss* by Philip Wade; BBC North; Producer: D[avid].E. Ormerod; Broadcast August 3, 1932

Synopsis: A domestic-industrial drama set in the north of England and covering the years 1914-1929. The play opens in the office of a Lancashire machine works in August 1914. Boss Craddock, a Lancashire engineer, makes a big fortune during the war and thinks he can boss his family at home in the same autocratic way in which he bosses his workman at the factory. One of the early scenes takes place on the Fair Ground at Blackpool.

Cast: F[rank].A. Nichols (*John Craddock*); Lucia Rogers (*Mrs. Craddock*); Edith Toms (*Kathleen*); Harold Champion (*Harold*); Mary Brash (*Nancy Simpson*); J. Edward Roberts (*Ben Wilder*); **James Stephenson** (*Adams*); Michael Voisey (*Ronnie*); H.R. Williams (*Soldier*); Sheila Pallister (*Nellie*); D.W. King (*Sergeant*); Emily O'Brien (*Typist*); J. Crouch;

4. *The Children's Hour:* **play** *"The Shield of Malchus," The Magician* by Franklyn Kelsey; BBC North; Producer D[avid].E. Ormerod; Broadcast August 6, 1932

Synopsis: A tale of ancient Roman history.

Cast: **James Stephenson** (*Malchus*); F[rank] A. Nichols (*Nero*); D.W. King (*Marcus*); Ernest Retlaw (*Petronius*); Harold Champion (*Calpurnius*); Mary Eastwood (*Wise Woman*); Mary Brash (*A Woman*); A.G. Mitcheson

5. *The Children's Hour*: play *Tales of the Tower of London: "The Theft of the Crown Jewels"* by L[awrence]. Du Garde Peach; BBC North; Producer: D[avid]. E. Ormerod; Broadcast August 27, 1932

   Synopsis: In 1671 Colonel Thomas Blood attempts to steal the Crown Jewels from the Tower of London.

   Cast: F[rank].A. Nichols (*Narrator & Merton*); D.W. King (*King Charles*); **James Stephenson (*Colonel Blood*)**; Ernest Retlaw (*Sir Gilbert*); Helen Dixon (*Mistress Edwards*); G.H. Edwards (*Master Edwards*); Mary Brash (*Elizabeth Edwards*); H.R. Williams (*Master Gilbey*); J. E[dward]. Roberts (*Lieutenant Edwards*)

6. *His Magnum Opus* based on the story, '*Life*,' from the '*London Magazine*' A domestic play in one act by J. Logan-Darra; BBC North; Producer: D[avid].E. Ormerod; Broadcast August 27, 1932

   Synopsis: A writer, in love with his work, causes trouble through searching for "copy" among unsuspecting people. The scene is a living-room, poorly furnished, but clean and tidy, in a two-roomed hovel in the East-end of London. Liz is busy cutting bread and butter, while her father sits by the fire reading his newspaper.

   Cast: **James Stephenson (*Bill*)**; Emily O'Brien (*Liz*); F[rank].A. Nichols (*Dad*)

   [Previous BBC production broadcast August 29, 1927]

7. *Hunt the Tiger* by Henry A[ugustus]. Hering BBC North; Producer Victor Smythe; Broadcast September 24, 1932

   Synopsis: An inventor devises a game in which would-be suicides play dangerously until one of them is killed. The scene is a well-appointed salon in Paris, December, 1781.

   Cast: Helena Alexander (*Mademoiselle de Vincennes, a Lady of the Court*); Ernest Retlaw (*Monsieur Jules, an Inventor*); **James Stephenson (*Edmund Savine, a Poet*)**

   [This story was made into a short film in 1929]

8. *Robinson Crusoe - His Life and Adventures Reviewed in Eight Scenes* by Wyndham Goodden after the story by Daniel Defoe; BBC North; Producers: D[avid].E. Ormerod and T.A. Bowen; Incidental Music: BBC Studio Orchestra; Broadcast September 30, 1932

   Synopsis: Robinson Crusoe's life and curious adventures revised in eight scenes on the tercentenary of his birth September 30, 1632. Scene I – A gale at sea off Yarmouth; Scene II – Crusoe's home in York; Scene III – The Riverside London; Scene IV – Crusoe's coffee plantation in Brazil; Scene V – The Storm; Scene VI – On the island – the winds converse; Scene VII – The same; Scene VIII - London

Cast: J. Edward Roberts (*A Sailor and Cat*); A.G. Mitcheson (*Parrot and Effects*); Mary Eastwood (*Crusoe's Mother*); G.H. Dayne (*Crusoe's Father; Mate; Guitar Solo*); F[rank] A. Nichols (*Captain of Mutiny Ship; A Sailor*); Ernest Retlaw (*Captain; Partner*); Harold Champion (*Captain*); R.A. Morton-Martin (*Narrator*); K. Aston Murray (*North Wind*); G.[eorge] B.[ernard] Smith (*South Wind*); Emily O'Brien (*East Wind*); Muriel Roscoe (*West Wind*); D.W. King (*Friday*); James Stephenson (**Robinson Crusoe**)

9. ***The Pigeon*** A Play in Two Episodes by Ian Priestley-Mitchell; BBC North; Producer: D[avid].E. Ormerod; Broadcast October 8, 1932

Synopsis: A Lancashire man becomes ensnared by crooks in London, but proves to be less stupid than they think. The play opens in a busy lounge of the Popular Hotel and moves to Room 291 in the same hotel. It is shortly before midnight.

Cast: J. Hollinshead (*A Page*); F[rank]. A. Nichols (*John Bracewell*); Gladys Wilkes (*Hannah*); Ernest Retlaw (*A Stranger*); **James Stephenson** (***2nd Stranger***); G[eorge].B[ernard]. Smith (*A Man*)

10. ***The Children's Hour:*** **play *"Timkins Minor and the Vikings"*** by George D. Woodman; BBC North; Producer: D[avid].E. Ormerod; Broadcast November 12, 1932

Synopsis: A fantasy involving a young schoolboy and ancient Vikings.

Cast: F[rank].A. Nichols (*Headmaster & Cardoc*); G[eorge].B[ernard]. Smith (*Teasdale*); Ivor Heslop (*Timkins*); Harold Jagger (*Puggles*); Felix Milns (*Trevor*); D.W. King (*Thangbrand*); **James Stephenson (*Golthar*)**

11. ***The Ship***: A Play in Three Acts by St, John Ervine; BBC North; Producer: D[avid].E. Ormerod; Broadcast November 14, 1932

Synopsis: A stark Northern drama dealing with industry and family life.

Act I – A room in John Thurlow's country house, near the shipbuilding town of Biggport;

Act II- The living-room of Jack Thurlow's farm; Act III Scene I – The same as Act I; Scene II – A corner of the garden of John Thurlow's Country house; Scene III – The same as Scene I

Cast: Mary Eastwood (*Old Mrs. Thurlow*); Ernest Retlaw (*John Thurlow, her son*); Helen Gerrard (*Janet, his wife*); Ivor Heslop (*Jack, his son*); Edith Toms (*Hester, his daughter*); Wilmot Paul (*Captain Cornelius*); **James Stephenson (*George Norwood*) [*by arrangement with the Liverpool Playhouse*]**

12. ***Round the Northern Repertories 1 – The Playhouse Liverpool*** BBC North; Broadcast October 13, 1935

Synopsis: Half-hour adaptation of the last act of Ronald Gow's *Gallows Glorious* performed by the Liverpool Playhouse repertory company.

Cast: **James Stephenson (*John Brown*)**; Deidre Doyle (*Mrs. John Brown*); Michael Redgrave (*Owen Brown*); Denis Webb (*Watson Brown*); Jane Baxter (*Annie Brown*); Stephen Jack (*Mr Higginson*); John Kidd (*Colonel Lewis Washington*); William Armstrong (*Colonel Robert E. Lee*) and Derek Elphinstone; Cyril Lister; Larry Silverstone (*Minor Characters*)

13. ***Scotland Yard: Life in the Metropolitan Police*** BBC National; Devised and produced by Laurence Gilliam; Narrator: Thomas Woodrooffe; Broadcast November 29, 1936.

Synopsis: Early docu-drama depicting the work of the London Metropolitan Police, with descriptions by policemen and illustrations of police activities recorded on the spot. The following sequences were included: Joining the Force; Training at Peel House; The Policeman's Lot; On the Beat; Mounted Police; River Police; Traffic Patrol; C.I.D.; Information Room; Flying Squad

Cast: Those taking part include the following professional actors: **James Stephenson**; Wallace Evenett; Philip Wade; Mary Wakefield; Robert Holland; Vivienne Chatterton; Norman Shelley; Carleton Hobbs; Members of the public and personnel of the Metropolitan Police who took part were not identified.

[A recording of this broadcast survives in the BBC Sound Archives]

14. ***The Children's Hour*: play *Jack and the Beanstalk*** by Pat Hull; BBC London Region; Broadcast January 12, 1937.

Synopsis: A programme by young artists: *The Emerald Stone* a story by Elizabeth Smith Wright followed by *Jack and the Beanstalk* a play by Pat

Hull (aged 15) winner of a recent play writing competition.

Cast: Patricia Hayes; Ewart Scott; Cyril Nash; Mary O'Farrell; Dora Barton; John Ruddock; **James Stephenson**; Derek Smith (*Violin*); June Hitchcock (*Pianoforte*); Gillian Worsley (*Songs at the Piano*); William Crouch (*Mandolin*)

15. *Twenty Years After* Hour play adapted by Patrick Riddell from the novel by Alexandre Dumas; BBC National; Producer: Peter Cresswell; Orchestra conducted by Leslie Woodgate; Music by Victor Hely-Hutchinson; Broadcast January 25, 1937

Synopsis: A further adventure in Alexandre Dumas History of the Three Musketeers.

Cast: Barbara Palmer (*Anne, Queen of France*); Carleton Hobbs (*Oliver Cromwell*); Sebastian Shaw (*D'Artagnan*); **James Stephenson** (*Athos*); Norman Shelley (*Porthos*); Terence de Marney (*Aramis*); Wilfred Fletcher (*Louis XIII*); Robert Brooks-Turner (*Planchet, Lackey*); Cyril Nash (*Parry, Servant to King Charles*); Walter Fitzgerald (*Mardaunt, Cromwell's Secretary*); Robert Farquharson (*Cardinal Mazarin*); Jillian Sandlands (*Henrietta, Queen of England*); Ewart Scott (*Charles I of Scotland*); William Trent (*Bishop Juxon*); Cecil Calvert (*Groslow*); Theodore Mead (*Grimaud, Lackey*); A.B. Imeson (*Mousqueton, Lackey*); Michel Bazalgette (*Bernouin*)

16. *The Blue Danube* BBC London Region; Producer: Felix Felton; Broadcast February 19, 1937

Synopsis: A radio programme commemorating the 70th anniversary of the Johann Strauss waltz, and explaining why *The Blue Danube* was written.

Cast: *Speakers*: Neal Arden; Henry Hallett; **James Stephenson**; J.B. Rowe; Hubert Gregg; Robert Rendel; Charles Sanders; Eileen Tomlinson; Ronald Simpson; Fraulein Grossbard and Mr. Moray MacLaren

17. *Money With Menaces* A new radio play by Patrick Hamilton; BBC National; Producer: Lance Sieveking; Broadcast March 4, 1937

Synopsis: On a hot summer's day Andrew Carruthers, newspaper proprietor, is rung up at his office by a man whom he has never heard of in his life.

Cast: D.A. Clarke-Smith (*Andrew Carruthers*); Ernest Thesiger ("*Mr Poland*"); **James Stephenson** (*Macpherson*); Gabrielle Casartelli (*Miss Rough, The Girl at the Darts Stall, A Maid*); Nathalie Moya (*Miss Moyna*

Carruthers, Mrs. Sanderson); Carleton Hobbs (*The Commissionaire, The Bank Clerk, The Boy, The Tout*); Philip Wade (*The Shopkeeper, The Porter at the Club*); Spencer Trevor (*Hilliard*); Beatrice Gilbert (*Woman Phone Operator, Mrs. Carruthers, Woman on the Telephone*)

18. *News: The History of the Fourth Estate* by Kenneth Adam; BBC London; Producer: Laurence Gilliam; Broadcast March 8, 1937.

   Synopsis: The history of British news journalism.

   Cast: Norman Shelley; Carleton Hobbs; Leslie Perrins; Deering Wells; V.C. Clinton Baddeley; Eugene Leahy; Graveley Edwards; Patric Curwen; **James Stephenson**; G.F. Campbell Browne; Vivienne Chatterton; Robert Holland

19. *For the Children: The King's Chair* written by Lawrence Tanner; BBC London; Producer: Geoffrey Dearmer; Broadcast May 9, 1937

   Synopsis: A history, true in substance and in fact, of the coronation chair, from the day when it was installed in the abbey, by Edward I, to the coronation of King George VI. The voices of the boy king Richard II, King George III, Queen Victoria, bystanders at various coronations and Mr. Pepys will be heard.

   Cast: Hugh Dempster (*The Young Monk, The Bishop of Bath*); Ian Dawson (*Bishop of Durham, Will Hewer, Lord Melbourne*); Robert Holland (*Richard II*); Cyril Campion (*Reader*); Norman Shelley (*Master Walter, Lord Effingham*); Mary O'Farrell (*Widow Pipe*); **James Stephenson (*Edward I, Bishop of Durham, William Man*) [By Permission of Warner Bros. First National Pictures Ltd.]**; Beryl Laverick (*Queen Victoria*); Marcus Baron (*The Abbot, The Archbishop of Canterbury*) [By permission of Sydney Carroll]; Berkeley Mason (*Organist*)

20. *Palace of Varieties* BBC National; Devised Bryan Michie; Producer: Ernest Longstaffe; BBC Variety Orchestra; Conductor: Ernest Longstaffe; Broadcast May 20, 1937

   Synopsis: An old-time, music-hall variety programme featuring a host of popular entertainers.

   Cast: John Rorke (*Songs*); Warden and West (*Entertainers*); J. Rossi (*Accordian*); Mabel Constanduros (*Entertainer*); George Jackley (*Comedian*); **James Stephenson (*Monologue: A Stationmaster's Story by George R. Sims accompanied by Reginald Foort at the BBC Theatre Organ*)**; The Radio Ramblers [George Fairweather, Arthur Loader and

Phil Lester] (*Impressions*); Joe Young and Co. Sketch "Buying a Theatre" (Young); Marjorie Kirby and Ralph Truman (*Comperes*)

21. ***Death of a First Mate*** based on a novel by Charles Barry adapted by Jack Inglis; BBC London; Producer: Peter Cresswell; Broadcast November 13, 1937.

Synopsis: A drama of officers and crew aboard the SS Baynes, a small coasting steamer.

Cast: James Stephenson (*Captain Holloway, the Master*) [By Permission of Warner Bros. First National Pictures Ltd.]; Archibald McLean (*Hamish Fraser, Chief Engineer*); Charles Owens (*Tim Organ, Wireless Operator*); Clifford Bean (*Harden, First Mate*); Malcolm Graeme (*Raske, Second Mate*); Philip Wade (*Ling, A Chinese Waiter*); Carleton Hobbs (*Gunderton, Relief Mate*); Jack Allen (*Partridge, A Sailor*); Philip Wade (*Daniel Barton, Sailor*); Dudley Jones (*Perry, Relief Wireless Officer*); Beatrice Varley (*Mrs Harlen*); Howard Marion Crawford (*Detective Inspector Clancy*); Michael Cole (*Sergeant Casey, Irish Free State Police*); Christopher Steele (*Denis Brophy, A Publican*); Eugene Leahy (*O'Hara, The Coroner*); J. Adrian Byrne (*Michael Blake, A Stevedore*); Charles Maunsell (*Doctor Muloney, Police Medical Officer in Cork*); Doreen Heath (*Barmaid*); Nancy Rea and Ethel Lodge (*Crowd Work*)

AMERICAN BROADCASTS
(1938-1941)

1. *I Found Stella Parish* by John Monk Saunders; Encore Theatre; KFWB; Broadcast March 23, 1938 and later repeated on wax disc in various key cities of the United States.

Synopsis: An actress finds her lurid past catches up with her in this half hour adaptation of a successful Kay Francis film vehicle.

The Warner Brothers Academy Theatre was a short-lived programme running over the summer of 1938 and consisted of thirteen programmes. Nine programmes survive, but four, including this broadcast with Stephenson, remain missing. The programmes were sponsored by the Gruen Watch Company.

Cast: Gale Page (*Stella Parish*); **James Stephenson (*Keith Lockridge*).** Guests: Marie Wilson and Bryan Foy

2. ***The Letter*** by Somerset Maugham; Lux Radio Theatre; Columbia
   Broadcasting System; Director: Sanford Barnett; Adaptation: George
   Wells; Music: Louis Silvers; Sound Effects: Charlie Forsyth; Announcer:
   Melville Ruick; Host: Cecil B. De Mille; Broadcast April 21, 1941

   Synopsis: A Lux Soap sponsored radio adaptation of the Somerset
   Maugham story. The main film actors all reprised their roles.

   Cast: Bette Davis (*Lesley Crosbie*); Herbert Marshall (*Robert Crosbie*);
   James Stephenson (***Howard Joyce***); Sen Yung (*Ong Chi Seng, Lawyer's
   Assistant*); Richard Davis (*Withers*); Charlie Lung (*Head Boy*); Gloria
   Holden (*Mrs Hammond*) and Suzanne Kaaren; Wally Maher; Eleanor
   Stewart; Eric Snowden; Leila Hyams McIntyre

APPENDIX III

PROFESSIONAL STAGE
LIVERPOOL PLAYHOUSE
(1932-1936)

Unless otherwise indicated these are three-act plays produced by William Armstrong
Stage managers: Harry Bristow and Arthur Lawrence
Scenery painted by Augustus Trout.
Premiere date for each production is provided.
Cast lists are given in order of appearance

1. ***Hollywood Holiday*** A comedy by Benn W. Levy and John Van Druten; September 1, 1932

   Synopsis: Miss Pinnet, a governess who boards at a Bloomsbury boarding house, is bewildered to find herself in the febrile atmosphere of Hollywood.

   Cast: Amabel Gibson (*Mrs Bournemouth, Proprietress of 17 Aberfield Terrace*); Eric Noels (*Mr Lintish, a Bachelor*); Prudence Magor (*Gladys Petch, a Flapper*); John Kidd (*Mr Petch, a Widower*); Marjorie Fielding (*Miss Pinnet, a Governess*); Carmen Sugars (*Irene, a Maid*); Jack Allen (*Sam Bird, a Theatrical Agent*); Richard Carey (*King Pinto, Head of the Scenario Department at Phenomenal Pictures Inc.*); Geoffrey Edwards (*Eddie Blue, a Writer*); Julian Clay (*Jake Shoeman, Another Writer*); Eileen Oldham (*Mae Z. Pardee (Le Mosenthal's Secretary*); Stephen Jack (*Al Bantor, a Director*); Lloyd Pearson (*Mike Le Mosenthal, Head of Phenomenal Pictures, Inc.*); Neil Tuson (*Lou Katz, a Supervisor*); Ena Burrill (*Hedda Maelstrom, a Star*); Wyndham Goldie (*Earl Easter, Her*

Husband, a Song Writer); Jane Vaughan (*Jacqueline Kisse, an Extra Girl*); Harry Bristow (*King Eric of Bolania, an ex-King*); Robert Flemyng (*King Joseph of Ganaesgro, Another ex-King*); Louise Frodsham (*A Lady who Dances*); Alan Johnson (*A Gentleman who Swims*); Betty Langley (*A Drunk Lady*); Ted Dudgeon (*A Sleepy Gentleman*); Audrey Pimblett and Joan Lawson (*Two Guests*); Joy Erskine Young (*Eddie's Girl*); **James Stephenson (*Wal Sanscrit, Head of Phantastic Pictures Inc*.)**

2. ***Lean Harvest*** by Ronald Jeans in four acts consisting of thirteen scenes; October 11, 1932

   Synopsis: Stockbroker Nigel Trent makes a fortune but loses his wife to another man.

   Cast: Amabel Gibson (*Mrs Trent*); Eric Noels (*Steven Trent*); Jane Vaughan (*Anne Dornay*); Audrey Pimblett (*Gladys*); **James Stephenson (*Nigel Trent*)**; Ena Burrill (*Celia Hardman*); Jack Allen (*Alfred Tellworthy*); Eileen Oldham (*Mildred Tellworthy*); Wyndham Goldie (*Philip Downes*); Joy Erskine Young (*Miss Moggs*); Stephen Jack (*Duckit*); Brian Blades (*Richard*); Peggy Sparshott-Smith (*Anne*); Norman Waller (*Tommy*); Robert Flemyng (*Dr. Plumtree*); Betty Langley (*Leila Perritt*); Julian Clay (*Jack Crabb*); Prudence Magor (*Carmen Bracegirdle*); Lloyd Pearson (*Sir Morton Fisher*); Neil Tuson (*Mr. Featherstone*); Richard Carey (*Mr. McGowan*); Ted Dudgeon (*Mr. Porteous*)

3. **A Scene from Shakespeare's *Twelfth Night*** (Act II, Scene III); November 14, 1932

   Synopsis: The scene is the kitchen in the house of the Lady Olivia and Sir Toby Belch, her uncle, makes merry with his friend Sir Andrew Aguecheek, who is a suitor for the Lady Olivia's hand. They are joined by Feste, the clown and Maria, Olivia's maid. Their mirth is interrupted by the entrance of Malvolio, steward to Olivia.

   Cast: Lloyd Pearson (*Sir Toby Belch*); Geoffrey Edwards (*Sir Andrew Aguecheek*); Stephen Jack (*Feste*); Marjorie Fielding (*Maria*); **James Stephenson (*Malvolio*)**

4. ***The Long Christmas Dinner*** a one act play by Thornton Wilder; November 23, 1932

   Synopsis: Christmas dinners of a family over a period of ninety years enacted as a continuous event.

   Cast: Ena Burrill (*Lucia*); **James Stephenson (*Roderick*)**; Amabel

Gibson (*Mother Bayard*); Lloyd Pearson (*Cousin Brandon*); Joy Erskine Young (*The Nurse*); Stephen Jack (*Charles*); Eileen Oldham (*Genevieve*); Carmen Sugars (*Leonora*); Marjorie Fielding (*Cousin Ermengarde*); Harry Andrews (*Roderick, The Second*); Richard Carey (*Sam*); Joan Lawson (*Lucia, The Second*)

5. ***Lady in Waiting*** a comedy by Harry Graham; November 10, 1932

Synopsis: A Ruritania romance in which the typist daughter of a "working" family, on the strength of being given a ride in King Yovan's new car by a journalist friend, is instantly taken by the town's people as the King's mistress.

Cast: Amabel Gibson (*Julia Dengler*); Julian Clay (*Karel*); Jane Vaughan (*Lili*); Lloyd Pearson (*Ernest Dengler*); Stephen Jack (*Rosen*); Geoffrey Edwards (*Conrad Kanitz*); Louise Frodsham (*Sophia Metzel*); Betty Langley (*Madalina Gonda*); Edward Dudgeon (*Mirko*); Richard Carey (*A Photographer*); Harry Andrews (*Leiba*); Eric Noels (*Zimmerman*); **James Stephenson (*Blaskovics*)**; Jack Allen (*Count Cozonac*); Carmen Sugars (*Baroness Katchanski*); Eileen Oldham (*Madame Danitchich*); Neil Tuson (*A Reporter / A Footman*); Robert Flemyng (*King Yovan*)

6. ***The Roundabout*** a comedy by J.B. Priestley; December 14, 1932

Synopsis: Into the country house of Lord Kettlewell, who is on the verge of ruin owing to the world financial crisis, stalk two young communists fresh and enthusiastic from a visit to Russia. One is his daughter, whom he has not seen since she was a child, as he is separated from his wife, the other is an unpleasant young man, unshaven, rude and lecherous.

Cast: **James Stephenson (*Lord Kettlewell*)**; Wyndham Goldie (*Churton Saunders*); Lloyd Pearson (*Parsons*); Robert Flemyng (*Alec Grenside*); Jane Vaughan (*Pamela Kettlewell*); Geoffrey Edwards (*Comrade Staggles*); Jack Allen (*Farrington Gurney*); Marjorie Fielding (*Lady Knightsbridge*); Ena Burrill (*Hilda Lancicourt*); Amabel Gibson (*Lady Kettlewell*); Betty Langley (*Alice*)

7. ***What Happened to George***, a one act play for children by Vera Beringer; Matinee performance; December 26, 1932

Synopsis: Schoolboy George Maitland is suddenly summoned to meet his father, a colonel from India who he has not seen since babyhood. During the train journey to the country after the meeting it appears that his father is in the possession of a priceless ruby, which he is to restore to an Indian potentate. Despite the vigilance of the father and son and the father's Indian servant, the jewel is stolen by the butler and housekeeper at the country home the colonel has taken and young George is imprisoned in the cellars of the old house.

Cast: John Cranfield (*Robert Carnduff*); Geoffrey Laurence (*George Maitland*); Audrey Pimblett (*Annabel Prance*); Jack Allen (*Mr Prance*); Eve Mortimer (*The Maid*); Eric Noels (*Ticket Collector*); Joan Lawson (*An Excitable Lady*); Nancy Nuttall; (*Her Best Friend*); Carmen Sugars (*Hiking Hortense*); Joy Erskine Young (*An Exquisite Female*); Neil Tuson (*A Man With a Thirst for Knowledge*); Harry Andrews (*A Real Gentleman*); Julian Clay (*The Cheerful Porter*); Louise Frodsham (*A Muddle-Headed Lady*); Eileen Oldham (*A Mother from Poplar*); Edward Dudgeon (*A Worried Uncle*); **James Stephenson** (***Mahmoud***); Donald Pitman (*Georgie Bairstow*); Wyndham Goldie (*Colonel Maitland*); Robert Flemyng (*A Cross Old Gentleman*); Victor Dewhurst (*The Paper Boy*); Audrey Pimblett (*A Boy Who Sells Things*); Geoffrey Edwards (*Martin Eversleigh*); Stephen Jack (*Albert Pennyquick*); Marjorie Fielding (*Emmeline Pennyquick*); Betty Langley (*Annie*); Lloyd Pearson (*"Fatty Bill"*); Katrina Kaufmann (*Zara*); Robert Flemyng ("Mr. *Smith*); Julian Clay (*"Mrs. Smith*); Neil Tuson (*Doctor Dosewell*); Harry Andrews (*Inspector Katchem*); Eric Noels (*The Keeper of a Private Zoo*)

8. *Inquest* by Michael Barringer; January 19, 1933

Synopsis: Months after the death of her husband, a widow is suspected of his murder when a revolver and tins of weed-killer are discovered in her house. The local coroner is convinced she is guilty. Her future is bleak until her case is taken up by distinguished K.C. Norman O'Neale, who by clever deduction exposes the unexpected truth.

Cast: Louise Frodsham (*The Maid*); Geoffrey Edwards (*Richard Hannington*); Marjorie Fielding (*Mrs. Wyatt*); Ena Burrill (*Margaret Hamilton*); Wyndham Goldie (*Norman O'Neale, K.C.*); Lloyd Pearson (*The Coroner*); Harry Andrews (*Coroner's Officer*); Robert Flemyng (*The Constable*); Jack Allen (*Detective Inspector Mullin*); Eric Noels (*Sir Denton Hulme*); Stephen Jack (*Dr. Macfarlane*); Edward Dudgeon (*Foreman Juror*); Neil Tuson (*A Juryman*); **James Stephenson** (***William Trelease***); Arthur Lawrence (*Isaac Owen*)

9. *Don't Tell England* by Neil Grant; February 2, 1933

Synopsis: Young Dick Fayre, lively younger brother of the Earl of Duncaster, Secretary of State for the Middle-East, arrives at the minister's

London house about the same time that three sheiks descend on London. There are murmurs of a great war with the desert tribes.

Dick, as it happens, has been living among the Arabs and going about among them just as 'Lawerence of Arabia' is said to have done, so he takes a hand, entirely unauthorised in the game of diplomacy and the sheik returns home with the war clouds dissolved.

Cast: Eric Noels (*Philpotts*); Wyndham Goldie (*Richard Fayre*); Lloyd Pearson (*The Earl of Duncaster*); Marjorie Fielding (*The Countess of Duncaster*); Jane Vaughan (*Janetta Norton*); **James Stephenson (*Charles Stevenson*)**; Stephen Jack (*Lord Granton*); Geoffrey Edwards (*Abdullah Ibn Rashid*); Julian Clay (*Ibn Nahal*); Jack Allen (*Imbarak*)

10. ***A Bite of the Apple***, a comedy in one act by Vernon Sylvaine; February 11, 1933

    Synopsis: An erring husband tries to prevent his wife from carrying out a threat of divorce by getting a friend to "innocently compromise her."

    Cast: Carmen Sugars (*Anna*); Lloyd Pearson (*Charles Strephon*); Marjorie Fielding (*Jane Strephon*); **James Stephenson (*George Hope*)**

11. ***Mourning Becomes Electra*** by Eugene O'Neill; February 20, 1933 Playhouse company visit Overseas League performed at The Overseas Sunday Circle, Basnett Street, Liverpool

    Synopsis: General Mannon loses the love of his wife. She transfers her affections to his enemy, Captain Brant, and is discovered to have done so by their daughter Lavinia Mannon. Mannon returns from war suffering from heart trouble. Taking advantage of this circumstance, his wife poisons him in their bedroom during the early morning; but after his death she faints and her daughter discovers the bottle in her hand.

    Cast: Lloyd Pearson (*General Mannon*); Marjorie Fielding (*Mrs Mannon*); Ena Burrill (*Lavinia Mannon*); **James Stephenson (*Captain Brant*)**: Geoffrey Edwards (*Captain Peter Niles*); Carmen Sugars (*Hazel Niles*); Jack Allen (*Seth Beckwith*); Robert Flemyng (*Amos Ames*); Chloe Gibson (*Louisa*); Eileen Oldham (*Minnie*)

12. ***The Crime at Blossoms*** by Mordaunt Shairp; February 22, 1933
    Synopsis: Owners of an old-world cottage return from holiday to find the married couple they have let the cottage to are now dead murdered in the living room of the Blossoms cottage.

    Cast: Marjorie Fielding (*Mrs. Woodman*); Jane Vaughan (*A Laundry*

Girl); Ena Burrill (*Valerie Merryman*); Wyndham Goldie (*Christopher Merryman*); **James Stephenson** (*Mr. Palmer*); Neil Tuson (*Mr. Plummer*); Amabel Gibson (*Mrs. Carrington*); Edward Dudgeon (*Mr. Carrington*); Stephen Jack (*The Rev. Charles Stern*); Jack Allen (*A Charabanc Driver*); Eileen Oldham (*A Fat Lady*); Joan Lawson (*Her Daughter*); Audrey Pimblett (*A Child*); Eric Noels (*A Superior Husband*); Joy Erskine Young (*A Superior Wife*); Julian Clay (*A Boy with a Concertina*); Geoffrey Edwards (*An Artist*); Carmen Sugars (*His Friend*); Louise Frodsham (*A Dear Old Lady*); Robert Flemyng (*Her Son*); Betty Langley (*An Hysterical Lady*); Eve Mortimer (*A Nervous Girl*); Constance Jack (*A Keen Tripper*); Phyllis Garge (*Her Friend*); Harry Andrews (*A Disappointed Gentleman*); Lloyd Pearson (*A Very Late Visitor*)

13. ***Another Language*** by Rose Franken; March 14, 1933

Synopsis: The weekly Sunday foregathering of the Hallam Clan at Mrs. Hallam's home in a London suburb is a solemn and unbreakable tradition.

Cast: Amabel Gibson (*Mrs. Hallam*); Eric Noels (*Mr. Hallam*); Harry Andrews (*Henry Hallam*); Marjorie Fielding (*Helen Hallam*); Stephen Jack (*Walter Hallam*); Ena Burrill (*Grace Hallam*); **James Stephenson** (***Paul Hallam***); Carmen Sugars (*Etta Hallam*); Wyndham Goldie (*Victor Hallam*); Lucille Lisle (*Stella Hallam*); Geoffrey Edwards (*Peter Hallam*)

14. ***The Kingdom of God*** by G. Martinez Sierra; March 30, 1933

Synopsis: Sister Gracia's life is devoted to the service of humanities outcasts.

Cast - Act One: Arthur Lawrence (*A Pensioner*); Neil Tuson (*Another Pensioner*); Lloyd Pearson (*Trajano, a Pensioner*); **James Stephenson** (***Gabriel, Another Pensioner***); Marjorie Fielding (*Sister Gracia*); Betty Langley (*Sister Juliana*); Eileen Oldham (*The Mother Superior / Cecilia*); Eric Noels (*Don Lorenzo, Sister Gracia's Father*); Amabel Gibson (*Maria Isabel, Her Mother*); Jane Vaughan (*Lulu, Her Sister / The Dumb Girl*); Geoffrey Edwards (*Liborio, A Cuban Pensioner*); Jack Allen (*A Pensioner*);

Cast - Act Two: Carmen Sugars (*Candelas*); Eileen Oldham (*Cecilia*); Jane Vaughan (*The Dumb Girl*); Joy Erskine Young (*Sister Cristina*); Constance Jack (*Sister Feliciana*); Louise Frodsham (*Quica*); Marjorie Fielding (*Sister Gracia*); Joan Lawson and Phyllis Garge (*Two Laundry Girls*); Ena Burrill (*Margarita*); Stephen Jack (*Enrique, The Doctor*)

Cast - Act Three: Annabel Gibson (*Sister Dionina*); Audrey Pimblett (*Engracia*); Joan Lawson (*Lorenza*); Louise Frodsham (*The Innocent*);

Brian Blades (*Morenito*); Harry Andrews (*Policarpo, A Hunchback Tailor*); Geoffrey Edwards (*Vicente*); Marjorie Fielding (*Sister Gracia*); Eve Mortimer (*Paquita*); Robert Flemyng (*Juan de Dios, a Bull Fighter*); Julian Clay (*Felipe*); Jack Allen (*First Boy*); Norman Hawkins (*Second Boy*); Neil Tuson (*Third Boy*); Norman Waller (*Fourth Boy*); Joy Erskine Young; Betty Langley; Phyllis Garge; (*The Other Girls*); Kathleen Boutcher; Eunice Ferguson; Adela Ferguson; Doris Forrest; Margaret Hitchins; Olive Reid (*The Younger Girls*); William Cowley; Norman Fairburn; Ernest Faulkner; Ivor Rowlands; James Trayler; Ronald Woodrofe (*The Younger Boys*)

15. *Laying the Devil* by John Drinkwater; May 2, 1933

Synopsis: An honest, but limited husband forbids his wife to go to tea with a certain exotic foreigner.

Cast: Edward Dudgeon (*Benson's Manservant*); **James Stephenson** (***Roland Benson***); Lloyd Pearson (*George Fleming*); Wyndham Goldie (*Louis Constantine*); Lindisfarne Hamilton (*Betty Lingard*); Marjorie Fielding (*Hilda Benson*); Ena Burrill (*Louise Fleming*); Julian Clay (*Constantine's Servant*); Jack Allen (*Dr. Gosforth*); Stephen Jack (*Mr Spiller*)

16. *The Queen's Husband* by Robert E. Sherwood; May 17, 1933

Synopsis: A monarch of an imaginary kingdom is in fact a figurehead. Real rule and control is exercised by the queen along with the Prime Minister. During her majesty's absence however, the military statesman's bullying instincts carry him too far and the people revolt. Here is the king's chance for he not only makes peace, but he brings about the downfall of the premier and daringly frustrates the Queen's matrimonial scheme for the princess.

Cast: Robert Flemyng (*Frederick Granton*); Stephen Jack (*Phipps*); **James Stephenson** (***Lord Birten***); Edward Dudgeon (*Petley*); Lindisfarne Hamilton (*The Princess Anne*); Marjorie Fielding (*Queen Martha*); Eileen Oldham (*First Lady-in-Waiting*); Joy Erskine Young (*Second Lady-in-Waiting*); Lloyd Pearson (*General Northrup*); Wyndham Goldie (*King Eric VIII*); Harry Andrews (*Major Blent*); Julian Clay (*First Soldier*); Neil Tuson (*Second Soldier*); Eric Noels (*Doctor Fellman*); Jack Allen (*Prince William of Greck*); Geoffrey Edwards (*Laker*)

17. *Never Come Back* a comedy by Frederick Lonsdale; June 2, 1933

Synopsis: At a villa in Cannes a house party gathers and complications and misunderstandings ensue.

Cast: Julian Clay (*George*); Harry Andrews (*Morton*); Stephen Jack (*John Mortimer*); **James Stephenson (*Smith*)**; Amabel Gibson (*Mrs. Linkley*); Jane Vaughan (*Mary Linkley*); Wyndham Goldie (*Lord Trench*); Ena Burrill (*Susan*); Robert Flemyng (*Lord Redwood*); Lloyd Pearson (*Sir John Moynton*); Geoffrey Edwards (*Duke of Bristol*); Marjorie Fielding (*Lady Trench*); Lindisfarne Hamilton (*Lady Moynton*); Edward Dudgeon (*William*); Jack Allen (*Rolls*)

18. ***Winsome Winnie***, a romantic drama by V.C. Clinton Baddeley adapted from the story by Stephen Leacock; August 31, 1933

   Synopsis: Winnie, an orphan ward, is thrown upon the wicked world by Bonehead solicitor-guardian who loses all her fortune. She is rescued from abduction by a dissolute nobleman and a dissipated peer, by an unknown gentleman, captures the romantic interest of a diplomat and finally is restored to family and fortune and lover by the Marchioness Muddlenut.

   Cast: Stephens Jack (*Mr. Bonehead, an Aged Attorney*); Margaret Radcliffe (*Winifred Clair, a Beautiful Orphan*); **James Stephenson (*Lord Wynchgate, a Dissolute Nobleman*)**; Anthony Hawtrey (*An Unknown Gentleman*); Louise Frodsham (*Mrs Budge, a Landlady*); Harry Andrews (*Lord Dogwood, a Dissipated Peer*); Christopher Casson (*The Marquis of Frogwater, a Diplomat*); Joy Erskine Young (*Adelaide, Marchioness Muddlenut*);

19. ***The Road to Rome*** by Robert E. Sherwood; August 31, 1933

   Synopsis: Rome in 216 B.C. Amytis prevents Hannibal from fructifying his nearly complete conquest of Rome.

   Cast: Mardale Owen (*Varius*); Valerie Tudor (*Meta*); Marjorie Fielding (*Fabia*); Lloyd Pearson (*Fabius Maximus*); Ena Burrill (*Amytis*); Betty Langley (*Tanus*); Robert Dorning (*Cato*); Geoffrey Edwards (*Scipio*); Arthur Hutchinson (*Sertorius*); John Kidd (*Drusus*); Larry Silverstone (*Tibullus*); Harry Bristow (*The Sergeant*); Anthony Hawtrey (*First Guardsman*); Harry Andrews (*Second Guardsman*); Norman Threlfell (*Third Guardsman*); Arthur Lawrence (*Fourth Guardsman*); Harry Hughes (*The Corporal*); Neil Tuson (*Thotmes*); **James Stephenson (*Hasdrubal*)**; Stephen Jack (*Carthalo*); Christopher Casson (*Maharbal*); Robert Flemyng (*Mago*); Wyndham Goldie (*Hannibal*); Clifford Jones (*Bala*);

20. ***Britannia of Billingsgate***, a comedy in four acts by Christine Jope-Slade and Sewell Stokes; September 21, 1933

Synopsis: A humble cockney woman is chosen for a star part in a film.

Cast: Marjorie Fielding (*Mrs. Bolton*); Louise Frodsham (*Mrs Wigglesworth*); Stephen Jack (*Mr Britz*); Anthony Hawtrey (*Mr Jones*); Valerie Tudor (*Pansy Bolton*); Lloyd Pearson (*Mr Bolton*); Robert Flemyng (*Fred Bolton*); Ena Burrill (*Elf Russell*); Geoffrey Edwards (*A Journalist*); **James Stephenson (*Mr Elder*)**; Margaret Radcliffe (*Gladys*)

21. ***The Lake*** by Dorothy Massingham and Murray MacDonald; October 11, 1933

Synopsis: Mildred Surrege has reduced her husband to subservience, but her vaguely discontented daughter Stella conducts a liaison with Cecil Hessey, a married man as a gesture of revolt. Stella enters on a marriage of convenience with John Clayne, but discovers that she loves him. Her brief happiness dissolves in tragedy.

Cast: Margaret Halstan (*Mildred Surrege*); Harry Bristow (*Williams*); Marjorie Fielding (*Lena Surrege*); **James Stephenson (*Henry Surrege*)**; Valerie Tudor (*Marjorie Hervey*); Ena Burrill (*Stella Surrege*); Wyndham Goldie (*Cecil Hervey*); Anthony Hawtrey (*John Clayne*); Megs Jenkins (*Ethel*); Eve Mortimer (*Maud*); Betty Langley (*Dolly Braite*); Mardale Owen (*Stephen Braite*); Margaret Radcliffe (*Jean Templeton*); Joan Lawson (*Mrs. George*); Miss George (*Audrey Pimblett*); Joan Cooke (*Gwen Kurn*); Peggy Corkish (*Betty Marle*); Harry Andrews (*Dennis Gourlay*); Edgar Criddle (*Herbert Hemingway*); Constance Jack (*Pamela Hemingway*); Christopher Casson (*Sir Philip Stanway*); Joy Erskine Young (*Lady Stanway*); Nancy Nuttall (*Esther White*); Louise Frodsham (*Lady Kerton*); Larry Silverstone (*Arthur Carrington*); Neil Tuson (*Clarence Pybus*)

22. ***After the Event*** one act play by Hugh Boss; November 1, 1933

Synopsis: An essay in communism.

Cast: **James Stephenson (*William Preston, David's Father*)**; Christopher Casson (*Henry Knighton, David's leader*); Mardale Owen (*Richard Hapschott, David's Friend*); Megs Jenkins (*Margaret Calvert, David's Girl*); Louise Frodsham (*Miss Dorkington*); Valerie Tudor (*Frau Linz*)

23. ***The Cathedral*** by Hugh Walpole; November 21, 1933

Synopsis: Archbishop Brandon, a man obsessed by his ecclesiastical power, realises the ascension of a rival in the Cathedral Chapter and under the pathetic delusion that every man's hand is against him falls from grace.

Cast: Betty Langley (*Agnes*); Margaret Radcliffe (*Miss Milton*); Wyndham Goldie (*Adam Brandon*); Valerie Tudor (*Joan Brandon*); Marjory Clark (*Amy Brandon*); Anthony Hawtrey (*Frank Lockwood*); Marjorie Fielding (*Ellen Stiles*); Christopher Casson (*The Dean of Polchester*); Stephen Jack (*Canon Bentinck Major*); **James Stephenson** (***Canon Foster***); Robert Flemyng (*Lord St. Leath*); Lloyd Pearson (*Canon Ronder*); Geoffrey Edwards (*Falk Brandon*); Harry Andrews (*The Rev. Mr. Ryle*)

24. ***Shall We Join the Ladies?*** An uncomfortable play in one act by J.M. Barrie; December 12, 1933

    Synopsis: Sam Smith composes a house party of the possible murderers of his brother.

    Cast: Lloyd Pearson (*Sam Smith*); Valerie Tudor (*Lady Jane Raye*); Wyndham Goldie (*Sir Joseph Wrathie*); Marjorie Fielding (*Mrs. Preen*); Geoffrey Edwards (*Mr. Vaile*); **James Stephenson** (***Mr. Gourlay***); Margaret Radcliffe (*Mrs. Castro*); Ena Burrill (*Miss Isit*); Robert Flemyng (*Captain Jennings*); Joy Erskine Young (*Mrs. Bland*); Betty Langley (*Miss Vaile*); Anthony Hawtrey (*Mr. Preen*); Louise Frodsham (*Lady Wrathie*); Eve Mortimer (*Lucy*); Harry Andrews (*Dolphin*)

25. ***Is Life Worth Living?*** An exaggeration in three acts by Lennox Robinson; December 11, 1933

    Synopsis: The hotel in the sleepy village of Inish in the space of three weeks is revolutionised following the engagement of a gloomy repertory company at the local pavilion. There is a sudden outbreak of attempted suicides, thefts, and suspicion of crime all round, until the company is sent packing and peace returns to the town.

    Cast: Marjorie Fielding (*Lizzie Twohig*); Eve Mortimer (*Helena*); Valerie Tudor (*Christine Lambert*); Robert Flemyng (*Eddie Twohig*); Stephen Jack (*John Twohig*); Lloyd Pearson (*Hector de La Mare*); Ena Burrill (*Constance Constantia*); Louise Frodsham (*Annie Twohig*); Christopher Casson (*Peter Hurley, T.D.*); Geoffrey Edwards (*Michael*); **James Stephenson** (***John Hegarty***); Anthony Hawtrey (*William Slattery*); Harry Andrews (*Tom Mooney*)

26. ***Fun While It Lasts,*** a matinee adventure in two acts by Philip Johnson and Howard Agg; December 23, 1933

    Synopsis: Rex and Peter Malcolm, who with Mrs. Cuttle their house-keeper, are kidnapped and held to ransom by bandits.

Cast: Geoffrey Lawrence (*Rex Malcolm*); Miles Byrne (*Peter Malcolm*); Muriel Aked (*Mrs. Cuttle*); Betty Langley (*Ellen*); Larry Silverstone (*The Taxi-Driver*); Stephen Jack (*Mr. Jones*); Lloyd Pearson (*Number Thirteen*); Mardale Owen (*Number Fifteen*); Harry Andrews (*Number Sixteen*); Edgar Criddle (*Number Seventeen*); Neil Tuson (*Number Fourteen*); Christopher Casson (*Number Eighteen*); Peter Claughton (*Number Twelve*); Wyndham Goldie (Pongo); **James Stephenson** (*John Trueman*); Louise Frodsham (*Martha Trueman*); Geoffrey Edwards (*Jake*); Robert Flemyng (*Bill Andover*); Ena Burrill (*Mrs. Malcolm*); Anthony Hawtrey (*Mr. Malcolm*); Margaret Radcliffe; Megs Jenkins; Audrey Pimblett; Peggy Corkish (*The Little Chimpanzees*)

27. ***Dangerous Corner*** by J.B. Priestley; January 17, 1934

    Synopsis: In conversation the past of a dead man is recounted.

    Cast: Ena Burrill (*Freda Caplan*); Valerie Tudor (*Miss Mockridge*); Lindisfarne Hamilton (*Betty Whitehouse*); Marjory Clark (*Olwen Peel*); **James Stephenson** (*Charles Stanton*); Geoffrey Edwards (*Gordon Whitehouse*); Wyndham Goldie (*Robert Caplan*)

28. ***The Rose Without a Thorn*** by Clifford Bax; February 7, 1934

    Synopsis: A historical play based on Henry VIII's matrimonial ventures.

    Cast: Ena Burrill (*Katheryn Howard*); Valerie Tudor (*Katherine Tilney*); Robert Flemyng (*Francis Derham*); Lindisfarne Hamilton (*Margery Morton*); Margaret Radcliffe (*Anne of Cleves*); Anthony Hawtrey (*Thomas Culpepper*); Eve Mortimer (*Mary Lassells*); Wyndham Goldie (*Henry the Eighth*); **James Stephenson** (*Thomas Cranmer*); Lloyd Pearson (*John Lassells*); Stephen Jack (*Sir Thomas Audley*); Geoffrey Edwards (*The Earl of Hertford*); Christopher Casson (*Paris, Player in a Masque / Tom Tiler, Player in an Interlude*); Mary Daniel (*Juno, Player in a Masque*); Joy Erskine Young (*Minerva, Player in a Masque*); Betty Langley (*Venus, Player in a Masque*); Edgar Criddle (*Tom Taylor, Player in an Interlude*); Peter Claughton (*Strife, Player in an Interlude*); Harry Andrews; Neil Tuson; Peter Claughton, Audrey Pimblett; Nancy Nuttall, Guilda Strock, Peggy Corkish, Joan Cooke, Megs Jenkins and Judith Turner (*Soldiers, Servants, Warders, Ladies and Gentleman of the Court*)

29. ***Smoke Screen*** a comedy by Ronald Jeans; February 28, 1934

    Synopsis: A young, married couple invite a Harley Street psychologist to stay with them and he tries to sort out their tangled lives.

Cast: **James Stephenson** (*Dr. John Poynter*); Neil Tuson (*Mr. Grattle*); Mary Daniel (*Miss Harrison*); Geoffrey Edwards (*Dr. Hugh Gaitley*); Margaret Radcliffe (*Mrs. Arclifte*); Ena Burrill (*Valerie Gaitley*); Judith Turner (*Effie*); Louise Frodsham (*Mrs. Moot*); Joy Erskine Young (*Miss Hipkin*); Robert Flemyng (*Dennis Marle*); Lindisfarne Hamilton (*Vickie Fellowes*); Harry Andrews (*Mr. Crawford*); Joan Lawson (*Mrs. Crawford*); Betty Langley (*Pamela Crawford*); Christopher Casson (*Mr Staple*)

30. ***Cabbages and Kings***, a comedy by Giovacchino Forzano adapted by Emile Littler; March 21, 1934

    Synopsis: Don Geronimo is a priest in a hill village near Siena, at the time when Napoleon is at the peak of his power. Don Geronimo is informed that he is actually the uncle of the emperor, who desires him to go to Paris and become a cardinal.

    Cast: Marie Ault (*Agnese*); Anthony Hawtrey (*Maso*); Louise Frodsham (*Maria*); Stephen Jack (*The Doctor*); Valerie Tudor (*Mattea*); Lloyd Pearson (*Don Geronimo*); Edgar Criddle (*Spinoso*); Neil Tuson (*Cecco*); Mardale Owen (*Lorenzo*); Robert Flemyng (*Corporal Martiez*); Harry Andrews (*Captain Oddoredi*); **James Stephenson** (***General Miollis***); Wyndham Goldie (*Father Silverstro*); Christopher Casson (*A Lawyer*); Geoffrey Edwards (*Count Rosse*); Peter Claughton, Larry Silverstone, Arthur Lawrence, John Justin, J.G. Henderson, Betty Langley, Joan Lawson, Audrey Pimblett, Joy Erskine Young, Eve Mortimer, Guilda Strock, Megs Jenkins, Nancy Nuttall, Mary Daniel, Judith Turner, Peggy Corkish and Joan Cooke (*Soldiers, Peasant Men and Women*)

31. ***Gallows Glorious*** by Ronald Gow; April 11, 1934

    Synopsis: The last days of slave abolitionist John Brown.

    Cast: Ena Burrill (*Annie Brown*); Marie Ault (*Mrs. John Brown*); Audrey Pimblett (*Ellen Brown*); Robert Flemyng (*Owen Brown*); Stephen Jack (*Uncle Jeremiah*); Christopher Casson (*Salmon Brown*); John Justin (*Watson Brown*); Joan Lawson (*Bell, His Wife*); Anthony Hawtrey (*Oliver Brown*); Judith Turner (*Martha, His Wife*); **James Stephenson** (***John Brown***); Edgar Criddle (*Shields Green, a Negro*); Harry Bristow (*A Slave Owner*); Geoffrey Edwards (*John Kagi, Brown's Secretary*); Mardale Owen (*Stevens*); John Cresswell (*A Sentry*); Harry Andrews (*T.W. Higginson*); Lloyd Pearson (*Frederick Douglass, Negro Preacher*); Peter Claughton (*A Telegraph Operator*); Arthur Lawrence (*A Virginian Militiaman*); Larry Silverstone (*J.P. Gallagher, of the "New York Herald"*); Wyndham Goldie (*Colonel Robert E. Lee*); Sam Beazley (*Colonel Lewis Washington*)

32. *Macbeth* tragedy by William Shakespeare; May 2, 1934

Synopsis: A Scottish soldier attains power but kills most brutally to do so.

Cast: Valerie Tudor (*The First Witch*); Louise Frodsham (*The Second Witch*); Eve Mortimer (*The Third Witch*); Christopher Casson (*Duncan, King of Scotland*); Geoffrey Edwards (*Malcolm*); John Justin (*Donaldblain*); Harry Andrews (*A Sergeant*); Robert Flemyng (*Lennox*); Stephen Jack (*Ross*); Wyndham Goldie (*Macbeth*); Anthony Hawtrey (*Banquo*); Cyril Lister (*Angus*); Ena Burrill (*Lady Macbeth*); Sam Beazley (*Seyton*); Lloyd Pearson (*The Porter*); Peter Claughton (*Fleance*); **James Stephenson (*Macduff*)**; Edgar Criddle (*An Old Man*); Larry Silverstone (*First Murderer*); Mardale Owen (*Second Murderer*); Harry Bristow (*Third Murderer*); Lindisfarne Hamilton (*Lady Macduff*); Graham Stark (*Son to Macduff*); Derek Elphinstone (*Messenger*); Neil Tuson (*A Doctor*); Mary Daniel (*A Waiting-Gentlewoman*); Harry Andrews (*Menteith*); Dennis Rowland (*Caithness*); John Cresswell (*A Servant*); Leonard Clarke (*Siward*); Edgar Criddle (*A Messenger*); Mardale Owen (*Young Siward*); Derek Elphinstone; Leonard Clarke; Arthur Lawrence; Beranrd Robinson; John Cresswell; Dennis Rowland and Neil Tuson (*Lords, Soldiers*); Mardale Owen; Eve Mortimer; Audrey Pimblett (*Apparitions*); Joan Lawson; Betty Langley; Joy Erskine Young; Judith Turner (*Waiting-Women*)

33. *Lover's Leap*, a comedy by Philip Johnson; June 1, 1934

Synopsis: Two couples separate and then are reunited in surroundings of refined and sybaritic luxury.

Cast: Ena Burrill (*Helen Storer*); Harry Andrews (*Poynter*); Lindisfarne Hamilton (*Sarah Traille*); **James Stephenson (*Cedric Norreys*)**; Wyndham Goldie (*Roger Storer*)

34. *Counsellor at Law* by Elmer Rice; August 30, 1934

Synopsis: Professional and personal problems confront a successful New York lawyer.

Cast: Valerie Tudor (*Bessie Green*); Peter Claughton (*Henry Susskind*); Deidre Doyle (*Sarah Becker*); Cyril Lister (*Lunedi*); Bernard Robinson (*A Stout Man*); Edgar Criddle (*A Postman*); Carole Bradshaw (*Zedorah Chapman*); Elizabeth McCann (*Goldie Rindskopf*); Robert Flemyng (*Charles McFadden*); John Kidd (*John P. Tedesco*); Neil Tuson (*A Bootblack*); Lindisfarne Hamilton (*Regina Gordon*); Christopher Hippsley (*Herbert Weinberg*); John Justin (*Arthur Sandler*); Louise Frodsham

(*Lillian Larue*); Eve Mortimer (*An Errand Girl*); John Cresswell (A Messenger); Michael Redgrave (*Roy Darwin*); **James Stephenson** (*George Simon*); Netta Westcott (*Cora Westcott*); Joy Erskine Young (*Mrs. Gardi*); Edie Martin (*Lena Simon*); Lloyd Pearson (*Peter J. Malone*); Charles Thomas (*Johann Breitstein*); Larry Silverstone (*David Simon*); Geoffrey Edwards (*Harry Becker*); Harry Bristow (*Francis Clark Baird*)

35. *The Distaff Side* by John Van Druten; September 19, 1934

Synopsis: Mrs. Venables celebrates her 75th birthday with her family.

Cast: Lindisfarne Hamilton (*Mrs Venables*); Deidre Doyle (*Mrs Millward*); Ena Burrill (*Mrs Frobisher*); Louise Frodsham (*Mrs Fletcher*); Robert Flemyng (*Roland*); Valerie Tudor (*Alex*); Stephen Jack (*Christopher Venables*); Eileen Douglas (*Theresa Venables*); Joy Erskine Young (*Miss Spicer*); Judith Turner (*Rose*); Geoffrey Edwards (*Toby Chegwidden*); Michael Redgrave (*Charles Hubbard*); **James Stephenson (Gilbert Blaize)**

36. *A Sleeping Clergyman* by James Bridie; October 10, 1934

Synopsis: A study of heredity and breeding in the lives of three generations from the years 1867 to 1936.

Cast - Members of the Chorus: Stewart Baxter (*A Sleeping Clergyman*); Cyril Lister (*Dr. Cooper*); **James Stephenson (Dr. Coutts)**; Neil Tuson (*Wilkinson*)

Cast - People in the Play: Geoffrey Edwards (*Charles Cameron the First*); Deidre Doyle (*Mrs. Hannah*); Lloyd Pearson (*Dr. Marshall*); Ena Burrill (*Harriet Marshall / Wilhelmina Cameron*); Valerie Tudor (*Cousin Minnie*); Joy Erskine Young (*Aunt Walker*); Robert Flemyng (*John Hannah*); Edgar Criddle (*A Sergeant*); Bernard Robinson (*A Constable*); Geoffrey Edwards (*Charles Cameron the Second*); Larry Silverstone (*Donovan*); Mary Daniel (*Lady Todd Walker*); Stephen Jack (*Sir Douglas Todd Walker*); Ena Burrill (*Hope Cameron*); Louise Frodsham (*Little Thing*); Michael Redgrave (*Dr Purley*); Lindisfarne Hamilton (*Lady Katherine Helliwell*); **James Stephenson (Dr. Coutts)**; Christopher Hippisley (*A Medical Student*)

37. *Something in the City* a comedy by Neil Grant; October 31, 1934

Synopsis: A study of the lengths in a pretty and clever woman may go to get the price of some new hats.

Cast: Carole Bradshaw (*Ledgers*); Lindisfarne Hamilton (*Sheila Maynard*); Ena Burrill (*Cora Stratton*); Geoffrey Edwards (*Sidney Stratton*); Robert Flemyng (*Harry Maynard*); **James Stephenson** (**Harold Ayrton**); Lloyd Pearson (*James Garden*); Stephen Jack (*Sir Andrew Veitch*); Cyril Lister (*Macrae*)

38. *Sheppey* by W. Somerset Maugham; November 21, 1934

Synopsis: Sheppey Miller, an assistant in a Jermyn Street hairdressing saloon, wins £8,500 in an Irish Hospitals Sweepstake.

Cast: Eve Mortimer (*Miss James*); Peter Claughton (*Victor*); Derek Elphinstone (*First Customer*); Cyril Lister (*Albert*); Joan Lawson (*Miss Grange*); Neil Tuson (*Second Customer*); Lloyd Pearson (*Sheppey*); Stephen Jack (*Bradley*); Michael Redgrave (*Mr Bolton*); Charles Thomas (*A Reporter*); Stewart Baxter (*A Photographer*); Ena Burrill (*Bessie Legros*); Deidre Doyle (*Mrs Miller*); Valerie Tudor (*Florrie*); Geoffrey Edwards (*Ernest Turner*); **James Stephenson** (**Dr Jervis**); Robert Flemyng (*Cooper*)

39. *Laburnum Grove* by J.B. Priestley; December 12, 1934

Synopsis: A respectable man from the suburbs is revealed to be a forger.

Cast: Valerie Tudor (*Elsie Radfern*); Louise Frodsham (*Mrs. Baxley*); Stephen Jack (*Bernard Baxley*); Lloyd Pearson (*George Radfern*); Robert Flemyng (*Harold Russ*); Edgar Criddle (*Joe Fletten*); Deidre Doyle (*Mrs Radfern*); **James Stephenson** (**Inspector Stack**); Cyril Lister (*Sergeant Morris*)

40. *Ferry Inn* an Adventure by Alec Atkinson; December 22, 1934

Synopsis: The adventures of a couple of children who whilst staying in the Derbyshire hills fall in with Old Sam (who turns out to be a super detective in the disguise of a tramp) Ferdinand Gamble an arch-crook; Inspector Bellowes a pompous Scotland Yard man and Constable Rust a comic policeman.

Cast: **James Stephenson** (**Ferdinand Gamble**); Robert Flemyng (*Police Constable Rust*); Louise Frodsham (*The Nurse*); Stephen Jack (*Detective Inspector Bellowes*); Brian Blades (*Brian*); Betty Fleetwood (*Pat*); Peter Claughton (*A Boy*); Deidre Doyle (*Mrs Glenn*); Lloyd Pearson (*Old Sam*)

41. *Biography* a comedy by S.N. Behrman; January 23, 1935

Synopsis: A Bohemian young woman paints portraits of celebrities between her amorous indiscretions. Then she is induced to write the story of her life and loves for a cheapjack magazine and all is well until one of her earlier lovers, now aspiring to be a Senator, realises that if she mentions their particular affair the puritans in Tennessee would probably vote for someone else.

Cast: **James Stephenson** (*Leander Nolan*); Michael Redgrave (*Melchior Feydak*); Geoffrey Edwards (*Richard D. Kurt*); Louise Frodsham (*Minnie*); Ena Burrill (*Marion Froude*); Robert Flemyng (*Warwick Wilson*); Stephen Jack (*Orrin Kinnicott*); Lindisfarne Hamilton (*Slade Kinnicott*)

42. *Libel* by Edward Wooll; March 6, 1935

Synopsis: A libel action is taken against a newspaper by a Norfolk baronet, it being suggested that Sir Mark Loddon MP is a Canadian army imposter who has assumed a murdered man's identity.

Cast: Michael Redgrave (*Sir Mark Loddon Bart, MP, the Plaintiff*); Lindisfarne Hamilton (*Lady Loddon, his Wife*); Alfred Sangster (*The Hon. Sir Arthur Tuttington, A Judge of the King's Bench Division*); Lloyd Pearson (*Sir Wilfred Kelling, Counsel for the Plaintiff*); Neil Tuson (*William Bale, Counsel for the Plaintiff*); **James Stephenson** (*Thomas Foxley, K.C. Counsel for the Defendants*); Geoffrey Edwards (*George Hemsby, Counsel for the Defendants*); Cyril Lister (*Major Brampton*); Louise Frodsham (*Sarah Carleton*); Stephen Jack (*Patrick Buckenham*); Larry Silverstone (*Emile Flordon*); John Justin (*"Numero Quinze"*); Derek Elphinstone (*Gerald Loddon*); Walter Hawker (*Admiral Fairfax Loddon*); Bernard Robinson (*The Associate*); Stewart Baxter (*The Usher*); Harry Hughes (*General Winterton, C.B.*); Joy Erskine Young (*Millicent Winterton*)

43. *Flowers of the Forest* by John Van Druten; March 27, 1935

Synopsis: A modern pacifist is condemned to death from tuberculosis.

Cast: **James Stephenson** (*Lewis Jacklin*); Valerie Tudor (*Beryl Hodgson*); Louise Frodsham (*Mercia Huntbach*); Cyril Lister (*Matteson*); Alfred Sangster (*Rev. Percy Huntbach*); Deidre Doyle (*Mrs Huntbach*); Michael Redgrave (*Richard Newton-Clare*); Charles Thomas (*Thomas Lindsay*); Pauline Lacey (*Mrs Ettles*)

44. **Hamlet** tragedy by William Shakespeare; April 17, 1935

Synopsis: Intrigue and tragedy take a hand in the court of Denmark.

Cast: Simon Bach (*Francisco, a Soldier*); John Justin (*Bernardo, an Officer*); Howard Marion Crawford (*Marcellus, Another Officer*); Michael Redgrave (*Horatio, Friend to Hamlet*); **James Stephenson** (***Ghost of Hamlet's Father***); Stephen Jack (*Claudius, King of Denmark*); Denis Webb (*Laertes, Son of Polonius*); Alfred Sangster (*Polonius, Lord Chamberlain*); Geoffrey Edwards (*Hamlet, Prince of Denmark*); Oriel Ross (*Gertrude, Queen of Denmark and Mother to Hamlet*); Valerie Tudor (*Orphelia, Daughter to Polonius*); Stewart Baxter (*Reynaldo, Servant to Polonius*); Charles Thomas (*Rosencrantz*); Derek Elphinstone (*Guildenstern*); Larry Silverstone (*First Player*); Brian Blades (*Second Player*); Neil Tuson (*Third Player*); Edgar Criddle (*Fourth Player*); Cyril Lister (*Gentleman*); Andrew Cowan (*A Messenger*); Lloyd Pearson (*The First Gravedigger*); Peter Claughton (*The Second Gravedigger*) Neil Tuson (*A Priest*); Simon Bach (*Osric*); Mary Daniel, Eileen Douglas, Megs Jenkins, Betty Langley, Elizabeth McCann, Eve Mortimer, Joy Erskine Young (*Court Ladies*); John Cresswell, Arthur Hutchinson, Arthur Lawrence, Bernard Robinson; (*Courtiers, Soldiers*)

45. *The Seventh Man* by Michael Redgrave; May 8, 1935

Synopsis: Six sailors, one dying, are stranded in a hut built out of their ship wrecked by pack ice. Exhausted tensions steadily mount until they are aware of a "seventh man."

Cast: **James Stephenson** (*Snipe*); Alfred Sangster (*Ede*); Denis Webb (*Daniel Cooney*); Cyril Lister (*Tom*); Larry Silverstone (*George Lashman*); Stephen Jack (*Alexander Wilson*)

46. *Too Young to Marry* by Martin Flavin; May 8, 1935

Synopsis: Elaine Bishop's fiancée has neither present nor future prospects commensurate with her mother's idea.

Cast: Deidre Doyle (*Bessie Bishop*); **James Stephenson** (*A Stranger*); Joy Erskine Young (*Maggie Bishop*); Louise Frodsham (*Jane Bishop*); Cyril Lister (*Mr King*); Alfred Sangster (*The Rev. Dr. Greig*); Stephen Jack (*Sam Green*); Lloyd Pearson (*Sandy Bishop*); Michael Redgrave (*Bill Clarke*); Valerie Tudor (*Elaine Bishop*)

47. *The Matriarch* by G.B. Stern; May 29, 1935

Synopsis: The Jewish life and family tradition as viewed through the eyes of a matriarch between 1921 and 1935.

Cast: Eve Mortimer (*Sophie Maitland*); Pauline Lacey (*Mrs. Mitchell*);

Michael Redgrave (*Oliver Maitland*); Deidre Doyle (*Anatasia Rakonitz*); Louise Frodsham (*Wanda Rakonitz*); Valerie Tudor (*Toni Rakonitz*); Cyril Lister (*Simson*); Eileen Douglas (*Susan Rakonitz*); Denis Webb (*Danny Maitland*); Mary Daniel (*Val Power*); **James Stephenson (*Maximilian Rakonitz*)**; Lloyd Pearson (*Isaac Cohen*); Megs Jenkins (*Elsa Rakonitz*); Charles Thomas (*Felix Rakonitz*); Stephen Jack (*Louis Rakonitz*); Larry Silverstone (*Otto Solomonson*); Peter Claughton (*Gerald Rakonitz*)

48. ***Youth at the Helm***, a comedy by Hubert Griffith adapted from the German of Paul Vulpius; August 29, 1935

    Synopsis: A satire on modern banking.

    Cast: Denis Webb (*Fitch*); John Kidd (*William, a commissionaire*); Jane Baxter (*Dorothy Wilson*); Donald Mills (*The Office Boy*); Michael Redgrave (*Randolph Warrender*); Charles Thomas (*An Old Gentleman*); Lloyd Pearson (*Chairman of the London and Metropolitan Bank*); Stephen Jack (*Ponsonby, its Managing Director*); Rachel Kempson (*Yvonne, the Chairman's Daughter*); Peter Trent (*Nicholson, Joint Manager and Member of the Board*); Cyril Lister (*Hollman, Joint Manager and Member of the Board*); **James Stephenson (*Lord Farley, Chairman of the City Industrial Bank*)**; Derek Elphinstone (*Roberts, of the Board of Trade*)

49. *Barnet's Folly*, a comedy by Jan Stewer; September 18, 1935

    Synopsis: A comedy of West Country life set in a Devonshire farm.

    Cast: Louise Frodsham (*Hannah Mudge*); Lloyd Pearson (*George Growsell*); **James Stephenson (*Mark Lannacott*)**; Deidre Doyle (*Elizabeth Burridge*); Stephen Jack (*William Burridge*); Denis Webb (*Sam Burridge*); Rachel Kempson (*Hettie Burridge*); Michael Redgrave (*Richard Barnet*); Joy Erskine Young (*Lucy Lannacott*); Jane Baxter (*Nellie Lannacott*); Eve Mortimer (*The Young Girl*); Peter Trent (*The Young Man*); Cyril Lister (*The Father*); Megs Jenkins (*The Mother*); Eileen Douglas (*Mrs. Hammerton*); Sonia Garmian (*Mrs. Webber*); John Kidd (*The Single Man*)

50. ***Cornelius: A Business Affair in Three Transactions*** by J.B. Priestley; October 8, 1935

    Synopsis: The head of a business, despite the energy and integrity of the principal and the affectionate loyalty of the staff, goes smash.

    Cast: Louise Frodsham (*Mrs Roberts*); Donald Mills (*Lawrence*); Eve Mortimer (*Miss Porrin*); Alfred Sangster (*Biddle*); **James Stephenson**

(*Cornelius*); Victor Ledder (*Rug Man*); Denis Webb (*Eric Shefford*); Bernard Robinson (*Paper Towelman*); Derek Elphinstone (*Coleman*); Mary Daniel (*A Young Woman*); Peter Trent (*An Ex-Officer*); Jane Baxter (*Judy Evison*); Larry Silverstone (*Dr. Schweig*); Cyril Lister (*Fletcher*); Stewart Baxter (*An Elderly Man*); Eileen Douglas (*Mrs Reade*); Stephen Jack (*Pritchet*); John Kidd (*Mortimer*); Michael Redgrave (*Robert Murrison*)

51. *Miss Linley of Bath* by Mary D. Sheridan; October 30, 1935

Synopsis: The love story of Richard Brinsley Sheridan who elopes with Elizabeth, daughter of Thomas Linley, and a chaperone until the nuptial knot is tied.

Cast: **James Stephenson** (*Thomas Linley*); Pauline Lacey (*Mary Linley*); Denis Webb (*Charles Francis Sheridan*); John Kidd (*Captain Edward Knight*); Eileen Douglas (*Mere Marie Joseph*); Alfred Sangster (*Lecure*); Mary Daniel (*A Novice*); Cyril Lister (*The Landlord*); Louise Frodsham (*Alicia Sheridan*); Betty Fleetwood (*Polly Linley*); Rachel Kempson (*Elizabeth Linley*); Stephen Jack (*Captain Thomas Matthews*); Deidre Doyle (*Shelah O'Grady*); Lloyd Pearson (*Thomas Sheridan*); Michael Redgrave (*Richard Brinsley Sheridan*)

52. *Compromise,* a comedy in one act by Ronald Gow; December 11, 1935

Synopsis: Amusement is at hand when choosing the colour of paint in a new house.

Cast: Lloyd Pearson (*Wilf, a Painter*); Alfred Sangster (*Mr. Simmonds, a Joiner*); **James Stephenson** (*John, a Doctor*); Louise Frodsham (*Mary, his Fiancée*); Stephen Jack (*Gerald, an Architect*)

53. *Circus Boy* by Michael Redgrave; December 24, 1935

Synopsis: Ludo, a gypsy boy, fights to recapture ownership of a circus, which has been snatched from him by the villainous Gasper Boom.

Cast: **James Stephenson** (*Gaspar Boom*); Michael Redgrave (*A BBC Official*); Lloyd Pearson (*Bobo, a Clown*); Joy Erskine Young (*An Old Lady*); Mary Daniel (*The Lady in the Blue Hat*); Eileen Douglas (*The Lady in the Mackintosh*); Denis Webb (*Scoutmaster Smiley*); Donald Mills (*Watkins*); Stewart Baxter (*Biddle*); Doreen Deker (*The Bearded Lady*); Elwyn Lloyd-Jones (*Her Son*); Louise Frodsham (*Miss McTatty*); Brian Blades (*The Hon. Jeremy Poddington, Spoilt Rich Boy*); Victor Ledder (*The Policeman*); Letty Coupe (*Little Gladys*); Georgina Brent (*Her Mother*); John Kidd (*Hercules McTavish, Strong Man*); Patricia

Hayes (*Ludo*); Betty Fleetwood (*Janet*); Bernard Robinson (*Sophie, Chimp*); Rachel Kempson (*Columbine*); Deidre Doyle (*Tina, Fortune Teller*); Stephen Jack (*P.C. Appleby*); Cyril Lister (*Ricky Pollard*); Megs Jenkins (*Mrs. Gubridge*); Larry Silverstone (*Timber*); Sonia Garmian (*Gresla*); Eve Mortimer (*Wanda*); Rosalind Moore (*Greta*); Peter Trent (*Heinrich*); Derek Elphinstone (*Stepan*); Arthur Lawrence (*Bruiser*); Alfred Sangster (*Pan Tademus*)

54. ***Death Takes a Holiday*** by Alberto Casella, rewritten for English stage by Walter Ferris; January 29, 1936

    Synopsis: Death plays a jest with his own existence by taking a three days' holiday in mortal guise at the Duke of Lambert's Italian castle.

    Cast: Eve Mortimer (*Cora*); Larry Silverstone (*Fedele*); Stephen Jack (*Lambert, Duke of Catolica*); Sonia Garmian (*Alda Cesarea*); Mary Daniel (*Stephanie, Duchess of Catolica*); Deidre Doyle (*Princess of San Luca*); Lloyd Pearson (*Baron Cesarea*); Rachel Kempson (*Rhoda Fenton*); Peter Trent (*Eric Fenton*); Denis Webb (*Corrado*); Penelope Dudley Ward (*Grazia*); **James Stephenson (*The Prince Sirki*)**; Alfred Sangster (*Major Whitred*)

55. ***Boyd's Shop*** by St. John Ervine; February 19, 1936

    Synopsis: Andrew Boyd, a traditional small grocer in an Ulster village finds his way of life challenged by the arrival of John Haslett who opens a scientifically managed modern store in opposition.

    Cast: John Cresswell (*Andy Haveron*); Pauline Lacey (*Mrs McBrantney*); Eileen Douglas (*Mrs Clotworthy*); Lloyd Pearson (*Andrew Boyd*); Rachel Kempson (*Agnes Boyd*); Deidre Doyle (*Miss McClure*); **James Stephenson (*John Haslett*)**; Joy Erskine Young (*Miss Logan*); Michael Redgrave (*Rev. Ernest Dunwoody MA*); Stephen Jack (*William Henry Doak*); Louise Frodsham (*Carrie*); Alfred Sangster (*Rev. Arthur Patterson*)

56. ***And So To War***, satirical comedy in one act by Joe Corrie; March 11, 1936

    Synopsis: A satire on politics and dictators set in a broadcasting studio.

    Cast: Michael Redgrave (*A Radio Announcer*); Stanley Williams (*A Page Boy*); Stephen Jack (*The Archbishop of Bray*); **James Stephenson (*Lord Otterburn, National Newspaper Syndicate*)**; Lloyd Pearson (*The Right Hon. Benjamin Bolt, Leader of the Trade Unions*); Louise Frodsham (*Grace Manful, The Women's League of Justice Etc.*); Alfred Sangster (*Sir Percival Holdall, Amalgamated Banks*); Larry Silverstone (*Fanacci*);

Cyril Lister (*Viscount Hammersmith, Amalgamated Industries*); Donald Mills and Victor Ledder (*The Two Soldiers*)

57. ***Richard of Bordeaux*** by Gordon Daviot in twelve scenes; April 1, 1936

Synopsis: Richard II tries to persuade his minister's and his people that peace with France is preferable to war.

Cast: Peter Trent (*The Fair Page, Maudelyn*); Geoffrey Lumsden (*The Dark Page*); Michael Redgrave (*Richard II*); Rachel Kempson (*Anne Bohemia, His Queen*); **James Stephenson (*Thomas of Woodstock, Duke of Gloucester*)**; Alfred Sangster (*John of Gaunt, Duke of Lancaster*); Charles Thomas (*Sir Simon Burley, The King's Tutor*); Larry Silverstone (*Edmund of Langley, Duke of York*); John Kidd (*Michael De La Pole, The Chancellor*); Stephen Jack (*Richard, Earl of Arundel*); Lloyd Pearson (*Thomas Arundel, Archbishop of Canterbury*); Denis Webb (*Robert DeVere, Earl of Oxford*); Louise Frodsham (*Mary, Countess of Derby*); Mary Daniel (*Agnes Launcekron*); Edward Wheatleigh (*Henry, Earl of Derby, Son of Lancaster*); Thomas Reynor (*Thomas Mowbray, Earl of Nottingham*); Alan Judd (*Sir John Montague*); Donald Mills (*Edward, Earl of Rutland, Son of York*); Sonia Garmian (*A Waiting-Woman*); Deryck Guyler (*A Doctor*); Cyril Lister (*A Man in the Street*); Stewart Baxter (*A Second Man*); Bernard Robinson (*A Third Man*); Megs Jenkins (*Woman with Loaves*); Eileen Douglas (*Woman with Vegetables*); Eve Mortimer (*First Page*); Eileen Erskine (*Second Page*); Stanley Williams (*Lord Derby's Page*); Victor Ledder (*A Guard*)

58. ***Storm in a Teacup*** by James Bridie, based on *Sturm im Wasserglas* by Bruno Frank; April 29, 1936

Synopsis: The legal, political and matrimonial complications, which result from the failure of Honoria Flanagan, an Irishwoman, to pay the license for her little dog.

Cast: Rachel Kempson (*Victoria Thomson*); Joy Erskine Young (*Maggie*); Michael Redgrave (*Frank Burdon*); Deidre Doyle (*Honoria Flanagan*); Emma Trechman (*Lisbet Skirving*); **James Stephenson (*William Thomson*)**; Lloyd Pearson (*Mr. McKellar*); John Kidd (*Horace Skirving*); Bernard Robinson (*Court Officer*); Larry Silverstone (*Clerk of the Court*); Alfred Sangster (*Sheriff Murgatroyd*); Stephen Jack (*The Procurator Fiscal*); Alan Judd (*Mr. Menzes*); Stewart Baxter (*Solicitor*); Cyril Lister (*Policeman*); John Cresswell (*Mr Cassidy*)

59. *Twelfth Night or What You Will* by William Shakespeare; June 5, 1936

Synopsis: When two siblings are shipwrecked in a foreign country their identities and those around them becomes suspect.

Cast: **James Stephenson** (*Orsino, Duke of Ilyria*); Peter Trent (*Sebastian, brother to Viola*); Stephen Jack (*Antonia, a Sea Captain*); Alan Judd (*Valentine, a Gentleman attending on the Duke*); Donald Mills (*Curio, a Gentleman Attending on the Duke*); Lloyd Pearson (*Toby Belch, Uncle to Olivia*); Denis Webb (*Sir Andrew Aguecheek*); Michael Redgrave (*Malvolio, Steward to Olivia*); John Kidd (*Fabian, Servant to Olivia*); Harold Scott (*Feste, a Clown, Servant to Olivia*); Larry Silverstone (*A Priest*); Mary Daniel (*Olivia*); Rachel Kempson (*Viola*); Louise Frodsham (*Maria, Olivia's Woman*); Cyril Lister (*A Sea Captain*); Stewart Baxter, Bernard Robinson, Victor Ledder, Arthur Lawrence, Deryck Guyler, Geoffrey Lumsden, Joy Erskine-Young, Sonia Garmian, Eve Mortimer and Eileen Erskine (*Lords, Sailors, Officers, Musician and Attendants*)

SUMMER STAGE PRODUCTIONS
(1933-1935)
WINTER GARDENS, NEW BRIGHTON

1. *Inquest* by Michael Barringer; June 19, 1933

Synopsis: A coroner's inquiry is launched into the death of a man after he has been twelve month's dead. After an exhumation it is discovered that instead of heart failure Thomas Hamilton had died as the result of a shot from a revolver. His wife, Margaret, declares on oath that she was alone in the house at the time and that she did not hear the fatal shot fired. But when pressed in expert fashion by the K.C. who appears on her behalf she falters and the inquiry takes an entirely new turn.

Cast: Lloyd Pearson (*The Coroner*); Stephen Jack (*Dr. Macfarlane*); Harry Andrews (*Coroner's Officer*); **James Stephenson** (*William Trelease, Hostile Witness*); Ena Burrill (*Margaret Hamilton, Widow under Suspicion*); Marjorie Fielding (*Mrs. Wyatt*); Wyndham Goldie (*Norman O'Neale, K.C.*) Geoffrey Edwards (*Richard Hannington, Widow's Lover*); Neil Tuson (*Rigid Scientific Witness*)

2. *The Queen's Husband* by Robert E. Sherwood; June 26, 1933

Synopsis: A king of an imaginary kingdom is belittled by his queen and statesman.

Cast: Wyndham Goldie (*King Eric III*); Marjorie Fielding (*Queen Martha*); Lloyd Pearson (*General Northrup*); Ena Burrill (*Princess*); Robert Flemyng (*Royal Secretary*); Harry Andrews (*Prince William*); **James Stephenson (*Foreign Secretary*)**; Stephen Jack (*Footman*); Neil Tuson (*Revolutionary Leader*); Geoffrey Edwards (*Passionate Anarchist*)

3. ***Art and Mrs. Bottle*** or ***The Return of the Puritan*** by Benn W. Levy; July 3, 1933

Synopsis: An unmoral lady and her philandering artistic lover who deserts the wife he had filched from her husband and then twenty years later enjoys the thrill of the chase after his former mistresses young daughter.

Cast: Marjorie Fielding (*Celia Bottle*); Lloyd Pearson (*George Bottle, a Sanitary Engineer*); Jane Vaughan (*Sonia Tippet, Cockney Artist's Model*); Ena Burrill (*Judy Bottle*); Geoffrey Edwards (*Michael Bottle*); **James Stephenson (*Max Lightly, Ruthless Philanderer*)**; Robert Flemyng (*Charlie Dawes, Shy Young Lover*)

4. ***Anthony and Anna*** a comedy by St. John Ervine; July 10, 1933

Synopsis: Anthony makes love to the fair Anna who, for very sufficient reasons, scornfully rejects him.

Cast: James Harcourt (*George, Headwaiter at the Inn of St Peter's Finger*); **James Stephenson (*Jacob Penn, an American Millionaire*)**; Ena Burrill (*Anna Penn, His Daughter*); Geoffrey Edwards (*Anthony*); Lloyd Pearson (*English Businessman*); Robert Flemyng (*Mr Dunwoody, a Novelist*); Neil Tuson (*Waiter*); Mamia Hunt (*Earl's Daughter*)

5. ***The Cathedral*** by Hugh Walpole; June 18, 1934

Synopsis: An obstinate cleric looks upon Polchester Cathedral as his own and to have his way in everything. He regards as his enemy the recently appointed Canon Ronder, accuses him of personal antagonism, of undermining him, even in his household, calls him a liar and hypocrite and eventually collapses and dies after an ineffectual protest against the preferment of a modernist priest.

Cast: Lloyd Pearson (*Canon Ronder*); Ena Burrill (*Amy Brandon*); Valerie Tudor (*Joan Brandon*); Geoffrey Edwards (*Falk Brandon*); Robert Flemyng (*Lord St. Leath*); Louise Frodsham (*Ellen Stiles*); Joy Erskine Young (*Miss Milton*); Harry Andrews; **James Stephenson (*Archdeacon Adam Brandon*)**; Sam Beazley (*Mrs Brandon's Lover*); Geoffrey Bragg; Edgar Criddle; Frank Lockwood (*Minor Characters*)

6. *The Lake* by Dorothy Massingham and Murray MacDonald; June 25, 1934

Synopsis: Mildred Surrege, a domineering woman, who by her soulless managing of everything and everybody makes life a purgatory for her whole household. Her headstrong craze for "improvements," leads her to destroy a beautiful copse and replace it with the fateful lake, which makes a widow of her daughter on her wedding day.

Cast: Margaret Halstan (*Mildred Surrege*); Ena Burrill (*Stella Surrege*); Alisa Graham (*Lena Surrege*); Lloyd Pearson (*Henry Surrege*); **James Stephenson** (***Cecil Hervey, Country "Sportsman"***); Robert Flemyng (*John Clayne*); Geoffrey Edwards (*Williams*); Sam Beazley (*Minor Character*)

7. *Smoke Screen* a comedy by Ronald Jeans; July 2, 1934

Synopsis: A doctor dissolves the smoke screen, which has come between his friends whose matrimonial relations are badly strained by the nursing of grievances real or imagined.

Cast: Geoffrey Edwards (*Dr. Hugh Gaitley*); Ena Burrill (*Valerie Gaitley*); **James Stephenson** (***Dr. John Poynter***); Louise Frodsham (*Mrs. Moot*); Joy Erskine Young (*Miss Hipkin*); Valerie Tudor (*Vicki*); Megs Jenkins; Eve Mortimer; Betty Langley; Robert Flemyng; Geoffrey Bragg; Neil Tuson (*Minor Roles*)

8. *Britannia of Billingsgate* a comedy in four acts by Christine Jope-Slade and Sewell Stokes; July 9, 1934

Synopsis: A fishmonger's wife is "discovered" by a film studio.

Cast: Marjorie Fielding (*Mrs Bolton*); Lloyd Pearson (*Mr Bolton, a Fish Porter*); Ena Burrill (*Elf Russell, an Actresss*); Valerie Tudor (*Pansy Bolton*); Louise Frodsham (*Mrs. Widdlesworth*); Geoffrey Bragg (*Mr Jones*); Geoffrey Edwards (*A Journalist*); Robert Flemyng (*Fred Bolton*); **James Stephenson** (***Mr Elder, Transatlantic Film Magnate***); Megs Jenkins; Neil Tuson (*Minor Roles*)

9. *Libel* by Edward Wooll; June17, 1935

Synopsis: A libel action is taken against a newspaper by a Norfolk baronet, it being suggested that Sir Mark Loddon MP is a Canadian army imposter who has assumed a murdered man's identity.

Cast: Michael Redgrave (*Sir Mark Loddon, Bart, M.P., the Plaintiff*); Valerie Tudor (*Lady Loddon, his Wife*); Alfred Sangster (*The Hon. Arthur Tuttington, A Judge of the King's Bench Division*); Lloyd Pearson (*Sir

Wilfred Kelling, K.C.. M.P. Counsel for the Plaintiff); Neil Tuson (*William Bale, Counsel for the Plaintiff*); **James Stephenson (*Thomas Foxley, K.C, Council for the Defendants*)**; Denis Webb (*George Hemsby, Council for the Defendants*); Louise Frodsham (*Sarah Carleton*); Cyril Lister (*Patrick Buckingham*); Larry Silverstone (*Emile Flordon*); John Justin (*"Numero Quinze"*); Donal Rockmills (*Gerald Loddon*); Ronald M. Meldrum (*Admiral Fairfax Loddon*); Bernard Robinson (*The Associate*); Stewart Baxter (*The Usher*); Harry Hughes (*Gerald Winterton, C.B.*); Joy Erskine Young (*Millicent Winterton*)

10. ***Counsellor-at-Law*** by Elmer Rice; June 24, 1935

    Synopsis: Drama in the life of a successful New York Jewish lawyer.

    Cast: Lloyd Pearson (*Peter J. Malone, Political Boss*); Mary Daniel (*Cora Simon*); **James Stephenson (*George Simon*)**; Joy Erskine Young (*Mrs Lena Simon*); Michael Redgrave (*Roy Darwin*); Alfred Sangster (*John P. Tedesco*); Neil Tuson (*A Bootblack*); Denis Webb (*Harry Becker*); Deidre Doyle (*Sarah Becker*); Larry Silverstone (*David Simon*); Judith Turner (*Goldie Rindskopf*); Eve Mortimer (*Regina Gordon, Simon's Secretary*); Valerie Tudor (*Bessie Green, a Telephonist*); Louise Frodsham (*Mrs Zadorah Chapman*); Eileen Douglas (*Lillian La Rue*)

11. ***Too Young to Marry*** a domestic comedy by Martin Flavin; July 1, 1935

    Synopsis: A henpecked Scot lives under the dark shadow of a mysterious "might have been" of his wife's creation.

    Cast: Lloyd Pearson (*Sandy Bishop*); Deidre Doyle (*Bessie Bishop*); Valerie Tudor (*Miss Elaine Bishop*); Joy Erskine Young (*Miss Maggie Bishop*); Louise Frodsham (*Miss Jane Bishop*); Michael Redgrave (*Bill Clarke*); **James Stephenson (*The Suave Stranger*)**; Alexander Gauge (*Old Graveyard Worker*); Alfred Sangster (*The Rev. Dr. Greig*); Larry Silverstone (*Minor Role*)

12. ***The Distaff Side*** by John Van Druten; July 8, 1935

    Synopsis: A family saga presided by a mother on her 75th birthday.

    Cast: Deidre Doyle (*Mrs. Millward*); Valerie Tudor (*Alex, her Daughter*); Lorraine Cromarty (*Mrs. Venables*); Denis Webb (*Toby Chegwidden*); Mary Daniel (*Mrs. Frobisher*); Lloyd Pearson (*Christopher Venables*); **James Stephenson (*Gilbert Baize*)**; Louise Frodsham (*Mrs. Fletcher*); Judith Turner (*Rose*); Joy Erskine Young (*Miss Spicer*); Neil Tuson; Cyril Lister (*Minor Roles*)

13. *Sheppey* by W. Somerset Maugham; July 15, 1935

Synopsis: A barber's assistant wins £8,000 in a sweepstake and he determines to devote the money to helping the poor, despite the wrath of his family who seek to have him certified insane.

Cast: Lloyd Pearson (*"Sheppey" Miller, a Barber*); Deidre Doyle (*Mrs. Miller*); Louise Frodsham (*Bessie Legros*); Valerie Tudor (*Miss Miller*); Denis Webb (*Priggish Lover*); **James Stephenson (*Dr. Jervis*)**; Larry Silverstone (*Impertinent Sneak Thief*)

WEST END PLAYS
(1936-1937)

1. *Storm in a Teacup* a comedy by James Bridie (Adapted from Bruno Frank's *Sturm Im Wasserglass*); Producer W.G. Fay; The Garrick; August 16, 1936

Synopsis: When a young woman neglects to buy a license for her dog all manner of legal, financial, complications are meted out.

Cast: Ivy Des Voeux (*Victoria Thomson*); Anne Wilson (*Maggie*); Roger Livesey (*Frank Burdon*); Maire O'Neill (*Honoria Flanagan*); Ethel Glendinning (*Lisbet Skirving*); **James Stephenson (*Provost William Thomson*)**; Edgar K. Bruce (*Mr McKellar*); Norman Macowan (*Horace Skirving*); Craighall Sherry (*Court Officer*); Robert Drysdale (*Clerk of the Court*); C.M. Hallard (*Sheriff Murgatroyd*); R. Halliday Mason (*The Procurator Fiscal*); Rupert Siddons (*Mr Menzies, K.C.*); W.A. MacKersey (*Solicitor*); Alastair MacIntyre (*Policeman*); W.G. Fay (*Mr Cassidy*)

2. *Post Road* a comedy-thriller in two acts by Wilbur Daniel Steele and Norma Mitchell; Directed by Edmon Ryan; The Queens; April 14, 1937

Synopsis: Emily Madison has a house on the Old Post Road between New York and Boston. One night chance brings a gang of kidnappers, who pose as doctor, nurse, chauffeur and unmarried mother.

Cast: Percy Kilbride (*George Preble*); Edgar Driver (*Wesley Cartwright*); Louise Hampton (*Emily Madison*); **James Stephenson (*Dr. Spender*)**; Mary Merrall (*May Madison Preble*); Kenneth Duncan (*Matt*); Sara Seegar (*The Girl*); Leslie Bradley (*Bill*); Billie Dakin (*Celia*); Moira Lister (*Jeeby Cashler*); Pamela Henry-May (*Nurse Martin*); Edmon Ryan (*Virgil Bemis*); Marcus Merwin (*Jay*); Norma Winslow (*Mrs. Canby*); Dora Barton (*Mrs Cashler*)

APPENDIX IV

BRITISH AND HOLLYWOOD FILMOGRAPHY
BRITISH FILMS
(1937)

Films are placed in order of general release. Where possible all production credits and cast lists are taken from surviving film prints. Where available, publicity taglines used to promote a film have been appended.

"The strongest drama Teddington Studios ever made"
1. *Perfect Crime*
(Warner Bros., First National, Teddington Studios)

Credits: Director: Ralph Ince; Producer: Irving Asher; Screen Play and Dialogue: Basil Dillon; Editor: Leslie A. Norman; Photography: Basil Emmott; Art Director: Peter Proud; Sound: W.S. Nunn; Trade Show: April 28, 1937; Released November 1, 1937; Crime; 6,217ft; 69m; b/w

Synopsis: Tired of life as a bank clerk, Charles robs the bank and flees by ship, planning to leave behind a suicide note and some money and change his identity. A steward destroys the note, steals the money and is murdered for it. Charles confesses all to a girl he has met, and helps a detective corner the killer. Charles returns to face the music, but with the hope of a light sentence.

Cast: Hugh Williams (*Charles Brown*); Glen Alyn (*Fay Burton*); Ralph Ince (*Jim Lanahan*); Iris Hoey (*Mrs Pennypacker*); Philip Ray (*Newbold*); **James Stephenson** [***Walter***] (***Parker***); Wilfrid Caithness (*Rawhouse*); John Carol (*Snodgrass*); Reginald Purdell (*The Drunk*); [*Uncredited Cast*] Kate Cutler, Sam Springson, George Hughes, Ralph

Roberts, Madge White

Working title: *Copper Proof*

[Smoking inventory = eight cigarettes]

[35mm print held by the British Film Institute, National Film and Television Archive]

> "Teddington's twenty thousand volt thriller
> – the most amazing story ever told!"

2. *The Man Who Made Diamonds*
(Warner Bros., First National, Teddington Studios)

Credits: Director: Ralph Ince; Producer: Irving Asher; Script: Michael Barringer, Anthony Hankey based on a story by Frank A. Richardson; Photography: Basil Emmott; Trade Show: June 3, 1937; Released: December 6, 1937; Crime; 6,609ft; 73m; b/w

Synopsis: In a triumph of science, Professor Calthrop discovers the secret of manufacturing diamonds. However, his assistant Joseph harbours criminal intentions. In order to obtain the enormous quantity of electricty essential for the purpose Joseph has hit upon the plan of robbing the Electricity Company of power to supplement that generated in the Professor's own laboratories. Though the professor, a professional of unblemished character, is perturbed by this, his principles are sustained by the thought that in the near future he will have appeased and compensated such deranged notions. That night his years of labour and research merit their reward. The secret of the discovery is known only to the Professor and Joseph. Before day dawns it is known to Joseph alone.

Tompkins, the Professor's only servant, discovers Joseph's crime, but as he himself has a criminal record, Joseph succeeds in subduing him to his will. Tompkins proves useful to Joseph, as he has friends in the underworld who are receivers of stolen diamonds.

The following day the Professor's daughter, Helen and her friend Marianne, arrive at the house to spend their holidays and they are amazed to learn that the Professor has suddenly gone away on a journey, leaving no particulars of his movements. Becoming suspicious of Joseph, Helen telephones Mr. Warren, the family solicitor and friend, who is unable to visit her, but sends Tony a young man attached to Scotland Yard to see her. A few days later the diamond market is disturbed by a sudden influx of diamonds, the source of which is traced to a notorious gang who have long been under police surveillance. Tony is assigned a minor part in the investigation of their activities.

Diamond dealers become frantic and seek the aid of the police, but the authorities have no proof that the diamonds, which are flooding the market, have been obtained by illegal means.

Scotland Yard is also approached by the Electric Supply Company who complains that their supply is being tapped in a mysterious manner.

Worried by her father's mysterious disappearance, Helen is not slow to perceive that Joseph is not at all that he seems. Pursuing investigations on her own, she tracks him down to the secret laboratory and watches him make diamonds. He discovers her and determines that she too shall follow her father. He plans to electrocute her and to do so it is necessary for him to leave her while he goes to tap the electricity supply. Tompkins, now in his power, is called upon to assist him, but instead of obeying Joseph's orders he rushes from the house and meeting Tony implores him to save Helen, a task which the young man loses no time in embarking upon.

Then follows a dramatic and sensational struggle in which Joseph becomes yet another addition to the roll of victims that the invention of diamonds has claimed.

With him perishes the secret leaving the world richer by its ignorance of a process which it would seem that nature herself alone can accomplish.

Cast: Noel Madison (*Joseph*); Lesley Brook (*Helen Calthrop*); **James Stephenson** (*Ben Erroll*); George Galleon (*Tony*); Renee Gadd (*Marianne*); Wilfrid Lawson (*Gallanie*); Philip Ray (*Tompkins*); J. Fisher White (*Professor Calthrop*); Hector Abbas (*Nichols*); Jim Regan (*Wilson*); Dino Galvani (*Isotti*)

[Film is missing believed lost]

"He Trains "White Hopes" to Know the Ropes"

3. *Take It From Me* also known as *Transatlantic Trouble*
(Warner Bros., First National, Teddington Studios)

Credits: Director: William Beaudine; Producer: Irving Asher; Script: John Meehan Jr, J.O.C. Orton; Photography: Basil Emmott; Trade Show: September 16, 1937; Released: February 28, 1938; Comedy; 7,005ft; 78m; b/w

Synopsis: From Australia to New York, Albert Hall has managed Timber Wood, but boxing fights are not easy to arrange in New York, and Bert and Timber are on the rocks.

Bert's genius for bluffing fails to get him into contact with promoters. So he gives up the idea of an interview and resorts to claiming acknowledgment for Timber's boxing genius by staging a quarrel over a lady, with Kid Brody, the champion, after a big fight. The lady is unaware of any cause for a quarrel. She is Lady Foxham, a wealthy woman of society who has adopted the champion as her 'protégé'.

Immensely pleased with Timber's skill in knocking out Brody, she transfers her attentions to him. And she and Timber embark for Europe, intending to leave Albert in New York.

Albert follows them on board and the boat sails with the three of them arguing in the state room.

Bert, who cannot find accommodation on board, is rescued by Lilli, who offers him an adjoining stateroom booked for her fiancé who jilted her. They become friends, each thinking the other is wealthy. Lilli becomes violent when she discovers that Bert is penniless, but they agree to help each other to win a sweepstake on the time the ship passes Bishop's Light. As the ship nears the light it is far ahead of the time Lilli has drawn, so they hit on the brilliant idea of raising a "man overboard" alarm to delay its progress.

Their ruse works and Lilli wins the sweep, but she also wins Timsey from Lady Foxham. They pay Bert's bills and quietly slip off the boat before Bert recovers from his ducking.

Lady Foxham and Bert are joined by Kid Brody in trying to find Timber. When they succeed in tracing him Brody knocks Timber out and the picture fades out with Bert telephoning a boxing promoter in New York to arrange a contest for Kid Brody, whom he is now managing.

Cast: Max Miller (*Albert Hall*); Betty Lynne (*Lilli Maquet*); Buddy Baer (*Kid Brody*); Clem Lawrence (*Timber Wood*); Zillah Bateman (*Lady Foxham*); **James Stephenson *[Fred]* (*Lewis*) (*an English Fight Manager*)**; Charlotte Parry (*Mrs. Murphy*); Joan Miller (*Secretary*)

[Film is missing believed lost]

"High-spots of humour and heart-interest too"

4. *You Live and Learn*

(Warner Bros., First National, Teddington Studios)

Credits: Director: Arthur Woods; Producer: Irving Asher; Script: Brock Williams, Tom Phipps from a novel "Have You Come for Me?" by Norma Patterson; Photography: Basil Emmott; Trade Show: August 23, 1937; Released: March 21, 1938; Comedy; 7,230ft; 80m; b/w

Synopsis: Peter goes to Paris to collect a legacy left by his wealthy uncle, only to find that it takes the form of a smoking cap. To overcome his disappointment he makes a tour of the night-clubs. At one he meets Mamie, an American showgirl, who finds the show she is in is being closed and she will be left stranded in Paris. Mamie thinks he is a rich landowner. After a swift wooing and wedding they return to England. At Peter's tumbledown farm, Mamie finds he is a widower with three children. When she recovers from the shock she settles down but her appearance makes her a number of enemies. The straight-laced schoolma'am, Miss Tanner, hates Mamie. One day, Mamie's old theatrical friends call on her and indulge in mild revelry. Miss Tanner tries to turn her reunion with showbiz friends into an orgy through gossip, but Peter helps put her to flight and a new life for all at the farm begins.

Cast: Claude Hulbert (*Peter Millett*); Glenda Farrell (*Mamie Wallis*); Glen Alyn (*Dot Harris*); John Carol (*George*); **James Stephenson (*Sam Brooks*)**; George Galleon (*Lord Haverstock*); Arthur Finn (*Joseph P. Munro*); Margaret Yarde (*Mrs Biddle*); Gibb McLaughlin (*Monsieur Duval*); Pat Fitzpatrick (*Jimmy Millett*); Anna Murrell (*Anne Millet*); Wallace Evenett (*Amos Biddle*); Charlotte Leigh (*Miss Tanner*); Muriel Blatcher (*Peg Millett*)

Working title: *Have You Come For Me?*

[Film is missing believed lost]

"Burnley's Own Screen Star – In His Best Film to Date"
5. *Dangerous Fingers* also known as *Wanted By Scotland Yard*
(Pathe Pictures / Rialto)

Credits: Director: Norman Lee; Producer: John Argyle; Scenario: Vernon J. Clancey from the play by Ralph Stock, Percy Robinson, Terence De Marney; Photography: Bryan Langley; Art Direction: Duncan Sutherland; Sound Recordist: Frank Midgley; Film Editor: E. Richards; Assistant Directors: George Collins, Jack Martin, Peter Collin; Camera: Ronald Anscombe Anthony Scott; Dresses by Film Fashions Ltd; Additional Music: John Reynders; Trade Show: December 15, 1937; Released: June 27, 1938; Crime; 7,100ft; 79m; b/w

Synopsis: On his release from prison Ronnie Elliott or "Fingers," an accomplished cracksman, and a brilliant musican, intends to "go straight". He goes to the 13 Steps Club and discovers that his girl has fallen for someone else and she, realising her mistake and unable to face Fingers, commits suicide.

His dreams of settling down to a happy state of married bliss and honest toil are now shattered, and Fingers resorts once again to a life of crime. He poses as a piano tuner and with the aid of a kitten manages to gain entry into several houses on the pretence of coming to tune the piano. His latest efforts prove successful.

One day he manages to enter the house of wealthy Victor Standish, a man of influence in the music world. There he meets Standish's secretary Helen who falls in love with him. Standish arranges to hold a piano recital in Finger's favour thinking that Fingers really wants a chance to prove his mastery of the keyboard, when actually Fingers wants to explore the depths of the Standish safe which contains a valuable collection of rubies.

At the 13 Steps Club, Williams a detective from the Yard learns of the recital and goes to the Standish home to put them wise. Ben, Fingers' pal also goes to the house to warn his friend. Meanwhile during the interval Fingers makes toward the safe in the library and is intercepted by Standish. During their conversation Fingers discovers that it was Standish who carried on with his girl. A fight ensues and Ben from the confines of the French window, fearing for Fingers safety, seeing that Standish is brandishing a revolver, shoots Standish and inflicts a wound which proves to be fatal.

The pair make off across the roof tops as the police enter the house and escape into the country surrounding London. Days later Fingers leaves Ben in a disused cottage, and, disguised as a farm hand, comes back to London to seek out Helen and enlist her aid.

During his absence, Ben in self-defence shoots a gamekeeper and eventually manages to get back to the 13 Steps Club. The dragnet is drawing closer and closer and Williams with a posse of Scotland Yard men surround the Club. Fingers, leaving Helen, goes to the Club; while he is playing a melody on the piano Williams enters. Ben seeing this from the top of the stairs, switches off the lights and both of them escape. They get back to Standish's house and Helen takes them to the garage where a car is in readiness. Fingers hears Williams and his men enter the house realises it is too late, but Ben, now completely a nervous wreck, speeds away with the police in hot pursuit. His car turns somersault and bursts into flames. It is apparent the end is not far off for Ben, who confesses to the police and makes the way clear for Fingers to leave for South America with Helen, where he intends to do some real honest work, marry Helen and settle down.

Cast: James Stephenson (*Ronnie "Fingers" Elliott*) [**By Arrangement with Warner Bros. First National**]; Betty Lynne (*Helen*); Leslie Perrins (*Victor Standish*); D.A. Clarke-Smith (*Inspector Williams*); Phil Ray (*Ben*); George Merritt (*Charlie*); Nadine March (*Mabel*); Sally Stuart (*Molly*); Bryan Herbert (*Sherlock*); Florence Groves (*Maud*); Alfredo Campoli and his Orchestra; Eric Pavitt (*Boy*)

[Smoking inventory = six cigarettes and one pipe]

[35mm print held by the British Film Institute, National Film and Television Archive]

"Boasts One of the Strongest Casts
Ever to Grace a Teddington Production"

6. *The Dark Stairway*

(Warner Bros., First National, Teddington Studios)

Credits: Director: Arthur Woods; Producer Irving Asher; Script: Brock Williams; Basil Dillon from a novel *From What Dark Stairway* by Mignon G. Eberhart; Photography: Robert La Presle; Trade Show: January 9, 1938; Released: July 18, 1938; Crime; 6,588ft; 72m; b/w

Synopsis: Dr. Cresswell considers a new anaesthetic formula discovered at the Cresswell Institute to be his – but so do others. When Mortimer, a brilliant but unscrupulous surgeon, is found murdered in a lift, Scotland Yard's Inspector Clarke is called in and sorts out the killer from a tangle of suspects.

Cast: Hugh Williams (*Dr Thurlow*); Chili Bouchier (*Sister Betty Trimmer*); Garry Marsh (*Dr Mortimer*); Reginald Purdell (*Askew*); **James Stephenson (*Inspector Clarke*)**; Glen Alyn (*Isabel Simmonds*); John Carol (*Merridew*); Lesley Brook (*Mary Cresswell*); Robert Rendel (*Dr Fletcher*); Audrey Pollock (*Dr James B. Cresswell*); Ross Landon (*Frank*); Ivy Tresmand (*Mrs. Mortimer*); Elsa Buchanan (*Winifred*); Muriel Pope (*Desk Nurse*); Katie Johnson (*Old Lady Patient*)
Working Title: *From this Dark Stairway*

[Film is missing believed lost]

"There is Fast Action and Chucklesome Comedy"

7. *It's in the Blood*

(Warner Bros., First National, Teddington Studios)

Credits: Director: Gene Gerrard; Producer: Irving Asher; Script: Reginald Purdell, John Dighton, J.O.C. Orton, Brock Williams, Basil Dillon from a novel *"The Big Picture"* by David Whitelaw; Photography: Basil Emmott; Trade Show: March 8, 1938; Released: August 15, 1938; Comedy; 5,046ft; 56m; b/w

Synopsis: Mild Edwin Povey is plunged into adventures galore on a day trip to Boulogne. Robbed by English thieves, Edwin gets back home on an onion boat and tries to find the gang. He and his girl are trapped in a house where the crooks keep stolen valuables. But the police arrive, round up the criminals, and rescue Edwin.

Cast: Claude Hulbert (*Edwin Povey*); Lesley Brook (*Jill Borden*); **James Stephenson (*Milky Joe*)**; Max Leeds (*James Renton*); Clem Lawrence (*Dave Grimmett*); Glen Alyn (*Celestine*); Percy Walsh (*Jules Barres*);

George Galleon (*Young Gendarme*); Reginald Purdell

[Film is missing believed lost]

"It's Sensational! It's Thrilling! It's News!"

8. *Mr. Satan*

(Warner Bros., First National, Teddington Studios)

Credits: Director: Arthur Woods; Assistant Director: Peter Bolton [uncredited]; Producer: William Collier; Screen Play and Dialogue: J.O.C. Orton and John Meehan Jr; Editor: Terence Fisher; Photography: Robert La Presle; Art Direction: Peter Proud and Michael Relph; Sound: W.S. Nunn; Trade Show: January 26, 1938; Released: August 22, 1938 Crime; 7,192ft; 79m; b/w

Synopsis: Tim Garnet, a war correspondent and his photographer "One-More" Connelly, expose Zubova a big business magnate as the sinister figure behind several wars and revolutions and Zubova stages a suicide to escape the consequence.

A year later "One-More," who can't resist beautiful girls takes a photograph of Jacqueline at an airport; he boasts of his collection of beauties to Tim, who recognises in the background of Jacqueline's picture a face in the plane that he swears is Zubova. Zubova, who had kept his fake death a secret, realises the danger of his photograph in Tim's hands and sends gunmen after the passenger plane in which Tim and "one-More" are flying. The plane is shot down and Tim, "One-More" and their dog are injured in the crash. They are held under doctor's orders in a convent, where Tim's excitement at having discovered Zubova alive is taken for the ravings of a man mentally deranged by the crash. Ultimately he persuades the head of his newspaper to let him find Zubova in a given time and he and "One-More" set off on the trail.

He meets Jacqueline and suspects that she may be an agent of Zubova's and takes a room in the same hotel. He fixes a dictograph behind a picture in her room, but hears nothing.

Gradually during his investigations he and Jacqueline fall in love and she plans to leave Zubova's service. Before she can do so, Zubova finds out that she is in love with Tim and recalls her. Afraid that Tim's life is endangered Jacqueline makes him believe that she was only playing a part. Meanwhile, leaving "One-More" to spy in the hotel, Tim stores away in Zubova's airplane. He is discovered and taken to Zubova's house in the mountains. In a tense scene Tim is forced to watch Zubova planning the destruction of an ocean liner. He risks his life trying to overpower Zubova, and countermand the orders and as Zubova's revolver is levelled

Jacqueline enters behind him, and diverts his aim. Zubova spins round and both he and Jaqueline fire together. Tim does not wait to see what happens, but jumps to the wireless control to save the liner. He cannot make it work. Jacqueline, who understands it, sends his message and slumps forward across the controls. He lifts her up and finds that Zubova's bullet had not missed its mark. Jacqueline dies in Tim's arms.

Cast: **James Stephenson** (*Tim Garnet*); Chili Bouchier (*Jacqueline Manet*); Skeets Gallagher (*Connelly*); Franklin Dyall (*Emil Zubova*); Betty Lynne (*Conchita*); Mary Cole (*Billy*); Robert Rendel (*Seymour*); Eric Clavering (*Wilson*); Dino Galvani (*Scipio*); Cot d'Ordan (*Georges*); Brian Powley (*General Laska*); Victor Fairley (*Von Krako*); Bruce Lister (*Reporter*) [uncredited]; Bob the Wonder Dog (*Elizabeth*) [uncredited]; Patricia Medina (*Girl in Field*) [uncredited]

Working title: *Dr. Satan*

[Smoking inventory = five cigarettes]

[35mm print held by the British Film Institute, National Film and Television Archive]

HOLLYWOOD FILMS
(1938-1941)

"12 Suspects! One's Horoscope was a <u>Horror</u> Scope"

1. ***When Were You Born***
(Warner Bros., First National)

Credits: Director: William McGann; Producer: Bryan Foy; Screen Play: Anthony Coldewey; Original Story by Manley Hall; Dialogue Director: John Langan; Photography: L. William O'Connell A.S.C.; Film Editor: Doug Gould; Art Director: Hugh Reticker; Gowns by Howard Shoup; Sound by Stanley Jones; Music: Bernhard Kaun; Released June 18, 1938; Mystery; 65m; b/w; Production #208

Synopsis: As a notable expert of astrology Mary Lee Ling is convinced astrological science is able to solve crimes and provide accurate predictions of the future. During a voyage to San Francisco she predicts that passenger Philip Corey has less than forty-eight hours to live before he will die. The following day he is discovered dead in his apartment. The police authorities suspect murder and interview Mary Lee. To place herself above suspicion she volunteers to use her expertise in astrology to catch Corey's murderer. Though the police are initially dubious, she is able to satisfactorily present specific facts about the case deduced from astrological readings. The local police chief decides to give her a chance, and grants her authorisation to interrogate all the suspects on the Corey case. There are five main suspects: Corey's girlfriend Doris Kane, and an acquaintance of Mary Lee's; Corey's valet, Shields; Corey's business associate, Fred Gow; Corey's attorney, Peter Finlay and the man Doris loves, Lawrence Camp. Using astrological charts and dates of birth from each suspect Mary Lee is able to unravel the mystery of Philip Corey's death and identify his murderer.

Cast: Margaret Lindsay (*Doris Kane*) [*Leo*]; Anna May Wong (*Mary Lee Ling*) [*Aquarius*]; Lola Lane (*Nita Kenton*) [*Cancer*]; Anthony Averill (*Larry Camp*) [*Aries*]; Charles Wilson (*Inspector Gregg*) [*Tauris*]; Jeffrey Lynn (*Davis*) [*Gemini*]; Eric Stanley (*Shields*) [*Virgo*]; **James Stephenson (*Philip Corey*)** [***Libra***]; Leonard Mudie (*Fred Gow*) [*Scorpio*]; Olin Howland (*Peter Finlay*) [*Sagittarius*]; Maurice Cass (*Dr Merton*) [*Capricorn*]; Frank Jaquet (*Sergeant Kelly*) [*Pisces*]; Manley P[almer]. Hall (*Opening Narrator*); [*Uncredited Cast List*] Jack [Clayton] Moore (*Assistant District Attorney*); Sidney Bracey (*Juggler Barrows*); Sol Gorss (*Ship Passenger*); Carole Landis (*Passenger*); John Ridgely (*Crenshaw, Policeman*); Jack Mower (*Desk Sergeant*); Beal Wong (*Ship Waiter*); Cliff Saum (*Policeman*); Lottie Williams (*Passenger*); Paul Panzer (*Policeman*); James Nolan (*Ship Passenger*)

Film began production February 23, 1938 and finished March 15, 1938

[Smoking inventory = one cigarette]

[Original theatrical trailer available to download from Turner Classic Movies]

"A Thundering Symphony of Human Emotions
Tuned to the Brave Beat of a Woman's Love-scarred Heart"

2. *White Banners*
(Warner Bros., Cosmopolitan)

Credits: Director: Edmund Goulding; Screen Play: Lenore Coffee, Cameron Rogers, Abem Finkel; Story: Lloyd C. Douglas; Music: Max Steiner; Photography: Charles Rosher; Art director: John Hughes; Film Editor: Thomas Richards; Wardrobe: Milo Anderson; Sound: Oliver S. Garretson: Musical Director: Leo F. Forbstein; Producer: Hal B. Wallis [uncredited]; Associate Producer: Henry Blanke [uncredited] Released June 25, 1938; Drama; 88m; b/w; Production #199

Synopsis: In 1919 a science master teaching in a small town, Paul Ward, is a keen amateur inventor trying to discover an invention that will provide a secure financial future for his wife and family. Into the Ward house comes the mysterious Hannah Parmalee who offers her services to the family. As well as taking care of the domestic chores, she also inspires those around her with her practical wisdom. Hannah takes an interest in Peter Trimble a pupil at Paul's school. She suggests Paul should take Peter on as his assistant in his quest to develop an icebox that does not deep freeze. They develop a prototype model, but the details are given away unwittingly by Peter to competitors who steal the idea and take out a commercial patent. Though Paul becomes depressed and despondent Hannah advises him to turn the other cheek, and with Peter they go on to develop another superior version of the icebox. Fate intervenes in Hannah's own life when a figure from her own past turns up at the Ward home. Thomas Bradford, a wealthy businessman from Chicago, comes to inspect the new invention with a view to its investment potential. Hannah reveals to Paul that Peter is her son and Bradford the father. She was forced to give him up for adoption, and although Bradford now wishes to lay legal claim to Peter, Hannah manages to persuade Bradford that it is better for everyone that he should be left in his present circumstances. Assured that Peter is in a secure home environment, her work is done, and she leaves the Ward home in the firm knowledge that Peter and his adoptive family have a bright future ahead of them.

Cast: Claude Rains (*Paul Ward*); Fay Bainter (*Hannah*); Jackie Cooper (*Peter Trimble*); Bonita Granville (*Sally Ward*); Henry O'Neill (*Sam Trimble*); Kay Johnson (*Martina Ward*); **James Stephenson (*Thomas Bradford*)**; J. Farrell MacDonald (*Dr. Thompson*); William Pawley (*Joe Ellis*); John Ridgely (*Bill Ellis*); Mary Field (*Hester*); Edward McWade (*Sloan*); [Uncredited Cast List] John Harron (The Milkman); Cliff Saum (Mover); Frank Sully (Butcher's Delivery Man); Douglas Wood (The Dean)

Film began production mid January 1938 and finished mid March 1938

[Original theatrical trailer available to download from Turner Classic Movies]

"It's a Rootin' Tootin' Singin' Shootin' Laugh Rodeo!"
3. *Cowboy from Brooklyn* also known as *Romance and Rhythm* (Warner Bros., Cosmopolitan)

Credits: Director: Lloyd Bacon; Producer: Hal B. Wallis; Screen Play: Earl Baldwin From the Play "Howdy Stranger" by Robert Sloane and Louis Pelletier Jr.; Music and Lyrics: Richard Whiting and Johnny

Mercer; Song: "Cowboy from Brooklyn" Harry Warren and Johnny Mercer; Orchestral Arrangements: Adolph Deutsch; Musical Director: Leo F. Forbstein; Photography: Arthur Edeson; Art Director: Esdras Hartley; Film Editor: James Gibbons; Sound: Dolph Thomas and David Forrest; Gowns: Milo Anderson; Released July 9, 1938; Musical comedy; 77m; b/w; Production #198

Synopsis: Though he is afraid of animals Elly Jordan, a Brooklyn singer and his two musical partners find work at a Wyoming Dude Ranch run by the Hardy family. Such is Elly's success as a cowboy singer that he is immediately signed up by show business agent Ray Chadwick, who is down on The Hardys ranch for a vacation. Though Elly acts and talks like a real cowboy, Chadwick learns of his deception and fears the truth will jeopardise his chances of promoting Elly in Hollywood under the alias of Wyoming Steve Gibson. While at the dude ranch Jane Hardy develops a liking for Elly, much to the chagrin of Sam Thorne her steady boyfriend. Sam, in addition to being a cowboy at the ranch, is also an amateur singer. He auditions on a national radio talent show in New York, but before he goes on the airways Jane informs him she is truly in love with Elly. This news naturally upsets Sam's performance on the radio, and in anger he reveals Elly's true circumstances to Chadwick and his assistant. To dispel this revelation Chadwick suggests Elly enter a rodeo competition to prove he is a real cowboy. To make sure Elly can go through with this ordeal they drag him along to Professor Landis who is able to hypnotise Elly successfully. With new found confidence Elly is able to participate in the rodeo as though he were a natural cowboy. Only when he sneezes does the hypnosis disappear, and he realises he has spent time among animals. By then the crowd are enthralled by his rodeo skills and the movie people, also convinced by the adoration of the public, sign him to a picture contract. In celebration of their good fortune Elly and Jane embrace and kiss.

Cast: Dick Powell (*Elly Jordan / Wyoming Steve Gibson*); Pat O'Brien (*Ray Chadwick*); Priscilla Lane (*Jane Hardy*); Dick Foran (*Sam Thorne*); Ann Sheridan (*Maxine Chadwick*); Johnnie Davis (*Jeff Hardy*); Ronald Reagan (*Pat Dunn*); Emma Dunn (*Ma Hardy*); Granville Bates (*Pop Hardy*); **James Stephenson (*Professor Landis*)**; Hobart Cavanaugh (*Mr. Jordan*); Elisabeth Risdon (*Mrs. Jordan*); Dennie Moore (*Abby Pitts*); Rosella Towne (*Panthea*); May Boley (*Mrs. Krinkenheim*); Harry Barris (*Louie*); Candy Candido (*Spec*); Donald Briggs (*Star Reporter*); Jeffrey Lynn (*Chronicle Reporter*); John Ridgely (*Beacon Reporter*); William Davidson (*Mr. Alvey*); Mary Field (*Myle Sempie*); [*Uncredited Cast List*] Monte Vandegrift (*Brakeman*); Eddy Chandler (*Brakeman*); Cliff Saum (*Chief Brakeman*); Jack Wise (*Reporter*); Eddie Graham (*Reporter*); Don

Marion (*Bellboy*); Jack Mower (*Radio Station Manager*); John Harron (*Technician*); Wendell Niles (*Radio Announcer*); John T. Murray (*Col. Rose*); George Hickman (*Newsboy*); Jimmy Fox (*Photographer*); Stuart Holmes (*Doorman*); Emmett Vogan (*Loudspeaker Announcer at Radio*)
Working titles: *Dude Ranch*; *Dude Rancher*; *Howdy Stranger*; *The Brooklyn Cowboy*

Remade as Two Guys from Texas (Warner Bros, David Butler, 1948)

Film began production January 12, 1938

[Original theatrical trailer available to download from Turner Classic Movies and the feature film is available on DVD from the Warner Archive Collection]

> "Be There when Canada's Finest Swing into Action with all
> their Traditional Valor . . . In all their Imperishable Greatness!"

4. *Heart of the North*
(Warner Bros., First National)

Credits: Director: Lewis Seiler; Producer: Bryan Foy, Screenplay: Lee Katz and Vincent Sherman, based on a novel by William Byron Mowery; Dialogue Director: Frank Beckwith; Photography: L[ou] W[illiam] O'Connell; Technicolor Photography: Wilfrid M. Cline; Music: Adolph Deutsch; Musical director: Leo F. Forbstein; Art Director: Ted Smith; Film Editor: Louis Hesse; Sound: Stanley Jones; Gowns: Milo Anderson; Technical Adviser: Bruce Carruthers; Released August 12, 1938; Adventure; 74m; Production #226

Synopsis: Jim Montgomery, a Mountie in the North West Canadian Police Force, is gunned down brutally while on board a vessel shipping valuable cargo to Edmonton, the province of Alberta. Judy Montgomery, his young daughter is also abducted by the criminals and abandoned along the river. She is rescued by Sergeant Alan Baker and Corporal Bill Hardsack, who together promise to track down the perpertrators of their colleague's killing and bring them to justice. Their plans to seek out justice are frustrated by their superior, Inspector Stephen Gore, who possesses little knowledge of the local terrain, and Mac Drummond, owner of a local trading post and leader of the gang of thieves responsible for the murder. To throw the Mountie's off their trail the gang plant stolen furs in Dave MacMillan's cabin and he is arrested on suspicion of being an accomplice of the gang. Elizabeth Spaulding Alan's fiancée wrongly and maliciously identifies MacMillan as a member of the gang, hoping Alan will be dismissed from the Mountie force and return to the city. Believing MacMillan is guilty of the murder men at the trading post congregate and demand that he be turned over to mob justice. Despite attempts to stop them storming the jail Inspector Gore is knocked unconscious and tied up. Meanwhile, eager to pursue the thieves Mounties Baker and Hardsack seize a plane and abscond. After a ferocious battle with the gang they are rescued by a pursuing plane, and arrive back in time to intervene in MacMillan's public hanging. When Drummond is named as the ringleader responsible for Jim Montgomery's death he tries to escape, but is shot by a psychologically disturbed Mountie. Alan's ex-fiancée leaves and Alan is free to begin a new romance with Joyce, Dave MacMillan's daughter.

Cast: Dick Foran (*Sgt. Alan Baker*); Gloria Dickson (*Joyce MacMillan*); Gale Page (*Elizabeth Spaulding*); Allen Jenkins (*Corpl. Bill Hardsock*); Patric Knowles (*Corpl. Jim Montgomery*); Janet Chapman (*Judy Montgomery*); **James Stephenson (*Inspector Stephen Gore*)**; Anthony Averill (*Whipple*); Joe Sawyer (*Red Crocker*); Joseph King (*Mac Drummond*); Russell Simpson (*Dave MacMillan*); Arthur Gardner (*Larry Young*); Garry Owen (*Tom Ryan*); Pedro de Cordoba (*Father Claverly*); Alec Harford (*Lunnon Dick*); Robert Homans (*Captain Ashmum*); Anderson Lawler (*Burgoon*); Bruce Carruthers (*Pedeault*); [*Uncredited Cast List*] John Harron (*First Mate*); Harry Cording (*Miner*); Tom Wilson (*Miner*); Buster Wiles(*Johnny*); Nat Carr (*Clerk*); David Newall (*Pilot*); Lane Chandler (*Pilot*); Emmett Vogan (*Radio Operator*); Don Turner (*Trapper*); Paul Panzer (*Trapper*)

Locations used in the film Big Bear Lake California

Production began July 12, 1938

[Original theatrical trailer available to download from Turner Classic Movies]

"Funnier Than You Can Possibly Imagine!"
5. *Boy Meets Girl*
(Warner Bros., First National)

Credits: Director: Lloyd Bacon; Executive Producer: Hal B. Wallis; Associate Producer: Sam Bischoff; Screen Play: Bella and Samuel Spewack based on their 1935 Broadway play; Photography: Sol Polito; Art director: Esdras Hartley; Film Editor: William Holmes; Gowns: Milo Anderson; Music and Lyrics: M.K. Jerome and Jack Scholl; Sound: Dolph Thomas; Musical Director: Leo F. Forbstein; Released August 27, 1938; Satire; 86m; b/w; Production #207

Synopsis: Hollywood screenwriters, Robert Law and J. C. Benson, write scenarios at Monumental Pictures for conceited cowboy star, Larry

Toms, but their efforts please neither star nor producer C. Elliott Friday. One day, while arguing over lunch the writers learn their serving waitress is a divorcee called Susie, and she is expecting a baby. Her pregnancy inspires the pair to indulge in the tried and tested Hollywood scenario of: "Boy Meets Girl, Boy Loses Girl, Boy Gets Girl". They set about selling their idea to studio executives who take up the idea enthusiatically. Law and Benson decide Susie's baby should be placed under studio contract with the pair acting as godfathers / managers to the unborn child who has already been christened Happy. The new born infant becomes an immediate sensation in the picture business. Susie has flirted with a small part English actor, Rodney Bevin, who is trying to make it in Hollywood, but agents of screen cowboy star Toms aware of Happy's cache at the box office persuade Toms to consider his career and marry Susie. When Law hears of their engagement he coaxes Bevin into claiming he is the father of Happy. Unfortunately Happy catches measles, and also passes the disease on to Toms. In exasperation, the studio fires Happy, Benson and Law. Undaunted, Benson and Law use all their daffy chutzpah to reinstate Happy at the studio. Just as they achieve their goal Rodney Bevin appears and asks Susie to marry him. She initially refuses, but when Major Thompson, an old acquaintance from England, appears on the scene and confirms Bevin is in fact an English lord, she changes her mind. The couple decide they are to retire to England taking Happy with them. Following this unfortunate news, studio boss Friday receives news his wife is pregnant. A stand-in for Happy is in the pipeline.

Cast: James Cagney (*Robert Law*); Pat O'Brien (*J.C. Benson*); Marie Wilson (*Susie*); Ralph Bellamy (*C. Elliott Friday*); Frank McHugh (*Rossetti*); Dick Foran (*Larry Toms*); Bruce Lester (*Rodney Bevan*); Ronald Reagan (*Announcer*); Paul Clark (*Happy*); Penny Singleton (*Peggy*); Dennie Moore (*Miss Crews*); Harry Seymour (*Song Writer*); Bert Hanlon (*Song Writer*); **James Stephenson (*Major Thompson*)**; [*Uncredited Cast List*] George Hickman (*Office Boy*); Cliff Saum (*Smitty, Studio Policeman*); Carole Landis (*Commissary Cashier*); Curt Bois (*Dance Director*); Otto Fries (*Olaf, Masseur*); John Harron (*Extra Talking to Rodney*); Hal K. Dawson (*Wardrobe Attendant*); James Nolan (*Young Man Brought in for Susie*); Jan Holm (*Hospital Nurse with Letter*); Vera Lewis (*Studio Cleaning Woman*); Rosella Towne (*Hospital Nurse Wheeling Larry*); Paul Clark (*Happy Seabrook, the Baby*); Eddy Conrad (*Jascha Alexander*); Peggy Moran (*New York Operator*); Nannette Lafayette (*Paris Operator*); Bert Howard (*Director*); Bill Telaak (*Bruiser*); Dorothy Vaughan (*Happy's Nurse*); Pierre Watkin (*B.K. Whitacre*)

Film began production March 4, 1938
[Original theatrical trailer and film clips are available to download from Turner Classic Movies]

"You'll Hold On to Your Seats and Hang on to Your Hearts
When This Tiny Terror Goes Looking for Excitement"

6. *Nancy Drew, Detective*
(Warner Bros., First National)

Credits: Director: William Clemens; Producer: Bryan Foy; Original Screen Play: Kenneth Gamet based on the story "The Password to Larkspur Lane" by Carolyn Keene; Dialogue Director: John Langan; Photography: L[ou]. W[illiam] O'Connell; Music: Heinz Roemheld; Art director: Stanley Fleischer; Film Editor: Frank Magee; Gowns: Milo Anderson; Sound: Stanley Jones; Released November 19, 1938; Mystery/comedy; 60m; b/w; Production #235

Synopsis: A wealthy benefactor, Mary Eldredge, who is due to bestow a large donation to her former alma mater, the Brinwood School for Girls, goes missing. Nancy Drew who is a student at the school decides to investigate her disappearance. While driving home Nancy comes across a local physician, Dr. Spires, being kidnapped. Later during the evening Nancy's father Carson Drew receives a phone call from the doctor confirming he had been kidnapped and taken to treat an old woman who had been injured. The doctor remembered the kidnappers used the password "bluebells." Now convinced beyond doubt that Miss Eldredge is being held hostage, Nancy and her friend Ted Nickerson come upon a racing pigeon that carries a message containing the word "bluebells". The pigeon is released and it leads the pair to a country house where they find not Miss Eldredge, but her secretary Hollister. Still unconvinced Nancy and Ted hire an aeroplane to scout for the house described by Dr. Spires. They retrace the possible area on the ground, and drive to Larkspur Lane. Nancy wisely observes Larkspur is a synonym for bluebells. Later Nancy and Ted return incognito and gain access to the house in the grounds of Larkspur Lane. Inside the house they find Miss Eldredge who explains she is being driven insane in order Hollister and his associates can gain access to her wealth. Nancy and Ted are discovered and imprisoned in a cellar, but Ted is able to fix up a shortwave receiver to send a message for assistance. Before the gang can make good their escape Carson Drew arrives with the police and the gang are soon apprehended. Nancy and Ted receive the lion's share of the credit for bringing the gang to justice.

Cast: Bonita Granville (*Nancy Drew*); John Litel (*Carson Drew*);

James Stephenson (*Challon*); Frankie Thomas (*Ted Dickerson*); Frank Orth (*Captain Tweedy*); Helena Phillips Evans (*Mary Eldridge*); [*Uncredited Cast List*] Renie Riano (*Effie Schneider, Drew's Maid*); Charles Trowbridge (*Hollister*); Dick Purcell (*Keiffer*); Ed Keane (*Adam Thorne*); Brandon Tynan (*Dr. Raymond "Ray" Spires*); Vera Lewis (*Miss Van Deering*); Mae Busch (*Miss Tyson, the Nurse*); Tommy Bupp (*Spud Murphy*); Lottie Williams (*Mrs Ray Spires*); Tom Wilson (*Brennan the Gate Guard*); Joanne Tree (*Brinwood Student with Black Hat*); Cliff Saum (*Farmer*); John Ridgely (*Radio Station Technician*); Jack Mower (*Radio Station Technician*); Betty Jane Graham (*Brinwood Student*); Stuart Holmes (*Telegrapher*)

Production began August 29, 1938

[Smoking inventory = one cigarette]

[Original theatrical trailer available to download from Turner Classic Movies and the feature film is available in *the Original Nancy Drew Movie Mystery Collection* Box Set released on Warner DVD]

"Ruthless Killer vs. Lady Doctor! It's red-blooded action all the way!"
7. *King of the Underworld*
(Warner Bros., First National)

Credits: Director: Lewis Seiler; Producer: Bryan Foy; Screen Play: George Bricker and Vincent Sherman, adapted from the story "Dr Socrates" by W.R. Burnett; Dialogue Director: Vincent Sherman; Photography: Sid Hickox; Film Editor: Frank Dewar; Art Director: Charles Novi; Sound: E.A. Brown; Gowns: Orry-Kelly; Technical Adviser: Dr. Leo Shulman; Musical Director: Leo F. Forbstein; Music: Heinz Roemheld; Released January 14, 1939; Crime; 67m; b/w; Production #220

Synopsis: Dr. Niles Nelson and his wife, Dr. Carol Nelson, save the life of a wounded member of a criminal gang headed by big shot Joe Gurney. Due to his gambling debts Niles is forced to treat another member of the Gurney gang. When the police raid the gang's hideout Gurney kills Niles, because he suspects he may become an informant to the authorities. Carol comes under suspicion for being the gang's accomplice. While awaiting trial she sets up a medical practice in a small town in which two of Gurney's gangsters have been imprisoned. Gurney picks up a hitchhiker by the name of Bill Stevens who is a writer down on his luck. Gurney who likens his atavistic gangster tactics to the leadership skills of Napoleon Bonaparte orders Bill to write his grandiose biography. Carol and Bill soon become friends. When Gurney begins to complain his eyes are causing him concern, Carol contrives a plan to disarm Gurney and his gang by temporarily blinding them, giving them an eye solution which will reverse imminent blindness. Though Gurney is blind he tries to kill Carol and Bill, but the police arrive in time to kill him and rescue the couple. Carol and Bill are then free to begin a new life together.

Cast: Humphrey Bogart (*Joe Gurney*); Kay Francis (*Carol Nelson*); **James Stephenson (*Bill Stevens*)**; John Eldredge (*Niles Nelson*); Jessie Busley (*Aunt Josephine*); Arthur Aylesworth (*Dr. Sanders*); Raymond Brown (*Sheriff*); Harland Tucker (*Harland Tucker*); Ralph Remley (*Mr. Robert*); Charley Foy (*Slick*); Murray Alper (*Eddie*); Joe Devlin (*Porky*); Elliott Sullivan (*Mugsy*); Alan Davis (*Pete*); John Harmon (*Slats*); John Ridgely (*Jerry*); Richard Bond (*Interne*); Pierre Watkin (*District Attorney*); Charles Trowbridge (*Dr. Ryan*); Ed Stanley (*Dr. Jacobs*); [*Uncredited Cast List*] Sherwood Bailey (*Boy*); Clem Bevans (*Third Villager*); Sidney Bracey (*Bert, the Farmer*); Frank Bruno (*Gangster*); Nat Carr (*Second Villager*); Glen Cavender (*Deputy Shooting Bill*); Edgar Deering (*Police Detective*); Ralph Dunn (*First Policeman*); William Gould, (*Chief of Police*); John Harron (*G-Man*); Lew Harvey (*Chic, a Gangster*); Herbert Heywood (*Clem*); Max Hoffman Jr (*Second Policeman*); Stuart Holmes (*Doorman*); Al Lloyd (*Drug Store Clerk*); Paul M. MacWilliams (*Anaesthetist*); Jack Mower (*G-Man*); Jimmy O'Gatty (*Gangster*); Paul Panzer (*Gangster*); Richard Quine (*Medical Student*); Jack Richardson, Ann Robinson (*Second Nurse*); Cliff Saum (*Gangster*); Janet Shaw (*Blonde Nurse*); Carl Stockdale (*First Villager*); Doc Stone (*Gangster*); Charles Sullivan (*Gangster*); Lottie Williams (*Farmer's Wife*); Tom Wilson (*Deputy*)

Remake of *Dr. Socrates* (Warner Bros., William Dieterle, 1935)

Working title: *Unlawful*

Production began May 24, 1938

[Smoking inventory = two cigarettes]

[Re-issue theatrical trailer available to download from Turner Classic Movies and the feature film is available on DVD from the Warner Archive Collection]

"P.S. We Thinkee You Likee This Velly Much!"

8. *Torchy Blane in Chinatown*
(Warner Bros., First National)

Credits: Director: William Beaudine; Producer: Bryan Foy; Screen Play: George Bricker; Based on characters created by Frederick Nebel;

Original Story based on "*The Purple Hieroglyph*" by Murray Leinster, Will F. Jenkins; Dialogue Director: Harry Seymour; Photography: Warren Lynch A.S.C.; Film Editor: Frederick Richards; Sound: Lincoln Lyons; Art Director: Charles Novi; Gowns: Howard Shoup; Released February 4, 1939; Crime; 59m; b/w; Production #232

Synopsis: A series of death threats relating to missing precious jade tablets brought into the United States on behalf of a wealthy collector by three jade dealers, bring friends and rivals, newspaper reporter Torchy Blane and police lieutenant Steve McBride, with his slow-witted assistant Gahagan, together to investigate. On three occasions notes written in Chinese riddles are found demanding a paid ransom for each stolen tablet. Failure to comply with the extortionate payments will result in the deaths of each of jade dealers. The first representative, Fitzhugh, is machine-gunned in his car. The next, Mansfield, dies after smoking a poisoned cigarette, and then his body disappears mysteriously. The fiancé of the jade collector's daughter is then ordered to take a cash ransom to the edge of New York Harbor. Before the ransom can be taken by three masked villains, they are all apprehended by Torchy and Steve. When unmasked they turn out to be the same jade dealers who had feigned their own deaths in a scam to extort money from the wealthy New York jade collector.

Cast: Glenda Farrell (*Torchy Blane*); Barton MacLane (*Steve McBride*); Tom Kennedy (*Gahagan*); Henry O'Neill (*Baldwin*); Patric Knowles (*Condon*); **James Stephenson (*Mansfield*)**; Janet Shaw (*Janet*); Frank Shannon (*McTavish*); George Guhl (*Desk Sergeant Graves*); Anderson Lawlor (*Fitzhugh*); Richard Bond (*Staunton*); Eddy Chandler (*Captain McDonald*); [*Uncredited Cast List*] Alice Connors (*Hilda, Baldwin's Maid*); Joe Cunningham (*Maxie, City Editor*); Bud Geary (*Trooper*); Sol Gorss (*Taxi Driver*); Roger Gray (*Policeman at Cemetary Entrance*); John Harron (*Condon's Chauffeur*); Gordon Hart (*Minister at Funeral*); Charles Hickman (*Mike, a Policeman*); Stuart Holmes (*Club Member with Cigar/Party Guest*); Tetsu Komai (*Mayor Lem Kee*); Eddie Lee (*Chinese Adventurers Club Waiter*); Vera Lewis (*Dowager Attending Engagement Party*); Frank Mayo (*Submarine Captain*); Bruce Mitchell (*Tim, Policeman*); Edmund Mortimer (*Dowager's Party Escort*); Jack Mower (*Bill, Detective*); Paul Panzer (*Store Clerk*); Jack Richardson (*Party Guest*); John Ridgely (*Submarine Officer*); Cliff Saum (*Larry, Detective*); Leo White (*Party Waiter*); Eric Wilton (*Belden, Mansfield's Butler*); Jack Wise (*Party Guest*); Beal Wong (*Chinese Entertainer*); Victor Sen Yung (*Chinese Entertainer with Sword*)

Production began August 15, 1938

[Smoking inventory = two cigarettes & onscreen appearance of cigarette case]

[Original theatrical trailer available to download from Turner Classic Movies and the feature film is available on DVD in *Torchy Blane Collection* from the Warner Archive Collection]

"For the First Time the Authentic Adventures
of Uncle Sam's Ace Man-Hunters"

9. *Secret Service of the Air*
(Warner Bros., First National)

Credits: Director: Noel Smith; Producer: Bryan Foy, Original Screen Play: Raymond Schrock; Based on "Murder Plane" and the Files of ex-chief of the Secret Service William H. Moran; Dialogue Director: Frank Beckwith; Photography: Ted McCord; Film Editor: Doug Gould; Art director: Ted Smith; Gowns: Howard Shoup: Sound: Dolph Thomas; Music: Bernhard Kaun; [*uncredited*] Musical Director: Leo F. Forbstein; [uncredited] Released March 4, 1939; Crime; 61m; b/w; Production #238

Synopsis: Following the murder of a U.S. Secret Service agent, Service chief Tom Saxby recruits Lieutenant Brass Bancroft, a transport pilot, to infiltrate an organisation involved in human trafficking across the border of Mexico. To ensure his credentials with the criminal underworld are believed, Brass is deliberately arrested for counterfeiting and placed in a penitentiary with a member of the smuggling gang. Together they carry out an unsuccessful prison breakout and while the gang member is returned to jail, Brass is released to make contact with the smuggling ring. From information gleaned inside prison Brass secures a job at the Los Angeles Air Taxi company and is introduced to the boss of the smuggling racket, Jim Cameron. Matters become complicated when Brass's friend Gabby Watters appears at a fight in a Mexican bar. Later Brass's fellow prison inmate, having escaped from jail confronts Brass, but he manages to convince the gang and its leader Cameron that he is not a government agent. Lured by the pretext of obtaining valuable counterfeiting plates Cameron accompanied by a party of smuggled aliens takes a flight to Los Angeles. Before the plane reaches its destination there is a vicious fight between Cameron and Brass when the former discovers the true identity of the latter. Eventually Brass gains the upper hand and the plane lands safely at Los Angeles Aiport. Cameron is arrested by the border police and Brass is left in the arms of girlfriend Pamela Schuyler.

Cast: Ronald Reagan (*Lt. Brass Bancroft*); John Litel (*Saxby*); Ila Rhodes (*Pamela Schuyler*); **James Stephenson (*Jim Cameron*)**; Eddie Foy Jr (*Gaby Watters*); Rosella Towne (*Zelma Warren*); Larry Williams

(*Dick Wayne*); John Ridgely (*Joe LeRoy*); Anthony Averill (*Hafer*); Bernard Nedell (*Earl "Ace" Hemrick*); Frank M. Thomas (*Doc*); Joe Cunningham (*Agent Dawson*); Morgan Conway (*Edward V. Powell*); John Harron (*Agent Cliff Durell*); Herbert Rawlinson (*Admiral A.C. Schuyler*); *Uncredited Cast List*: Raymond Bailey (*Klune, Henchman Starting Fight*); Sidney Bracey (*John 'Joe'Vicary*); Pierre Watkin (*Chief Morrow*); John Hamilton (*Warden Jackson*); Davison Clark (*Deputy Warden*); George Sorel (*Captain Cortez, Mexican Police*); Alberto Morin (*Pedro, Mexican Bartender*); Richard Bond (*Buzzy, San Francisco Radio Operator*); Jack Mower (*Treasury Agent Aldrich*); Frank Mayo (*Treasury Agent Manning*); Henry Hollingsworth (*Guard*); Albert Lloyd (*Convict Bartell*); Edgar Edwards (*Convict Crowley*); Cliff Saum (*Alien, First Flight*); Duke Green (*Second Tough in Fight*); John Sinclair (*First Tough in Fight*); Jack Wise (*Ivan's Alien Pal*); Sol Gorse (*Patrol Pilot*); Paul Panzer (*Ivan, an Alien*); Don Turner (*Agent Harper*); Carlyle Moore Jr (*Glendale Radio Operator*); Eddy Chandler (*Captain King, Highway Patrol*); Emilio Blanco (*Mexican*); Lane Chandler (*US Border Patrol*)

Production began September 26, 193

[Smoking inventory = five cigarettes]

[Original theatrical trailer available to download from Turner Classic Movies and the feature film is available on DVD in *Brass Bancroft of the Secret Service Mysteries Collection* from the Warner Archive Collection]

"It's Really a Thriller-Diller
with Loads of Action Plenty of Romance and Comedy"

10. *The Adventures of Jane Arden*

(Warner Bros., First National)

Credits: Director: Terry Morse; Producer: Mark Hellinger; Screen Play: Vincent Sherman; Lawrence Kimble; Charles Curran; Based on Comic Strip characters Created by Monte Barrett and Russell E. Ross; Dialogue Director: Ted Thomas; Photography. L. William O'Connell; Film Editor: Harold McLernon; Art Director: Max Parker; Sound: Charles Lang; Gowns: Milo Anderson; Comedy Construction: Lex Neal Music: Howard Jackson [*uncredited*]; Released March 18, 1939; Crime; 53m; b/w; Production #224

Synopsis: Beautiful debutante Martha Blanton is brutally shot in the back before she can disclose her shady past. Reporter Jane Arden argues with her news boss Ed Towers about the Blanton news story only to find she is fired for alleged incompetence. It later transpires this was a deliberate ploy to ensure she can take on an undercover assignment relating to the

Blanton murder. It is suspected Martha Blanton was mixed up in the smuggling of valuable jewels and was killed when she tried to escape the smuggling ring. Suspicion centres on the respectable jewellery business of Thayer and Co. Jane incognito, trys to break into the gang by offering stolen goods to the Thayer Company. Criminal organiser Dr. George Vanders takes a liking to Jane, but Albert Thayer remains doubtful of her motives. Nevertheless, she is offered a job on board ship smuggling jewels from Bermuda. Before she sails Ed is seen visiting her cabin. Thayer shadows him and finds out he works for the newspaper media. On board ship Jane meets George Vanders and a female accomplice not realising they are involved in the smuggling ring. Vanders flirts with Jane and when he receives a cablegram from Thayer informing him of Jane's true identity he decides to go ahead with his nefarious plans and dispose of Jane when the jewels are safely brought back to the United States. Thayer decides to kidnap Ed to make sure Jane doesn't step out of line when assisting in the jewel robbery. However, Ed manages to escape and tricks Thayer into confessing about the planed robbery. Ed flys immediately to Bermuda where he catches up with Vanders who tries to make a getaway by speeding carriage to a waiting plane. Just as he is about to board the plane Ed shoots him dead in the back. On their return voyage home Ed reveals his love for Jane and the couple kiss.

Cast: Rosella Towne (*Jane Arden*); William Gargan (*Ed Towers*); **James Stephenson (*Dr. George Vanders*)**; Benny Rubin (*Marvin Piermont*); Dennie Moore (*Teenie Moore*); Peggy Shannon (*Lola Martin*); Edgar Edwards (*William 'Bill' Clifton*); Hobart Cavanaugh (*Suspect Killer*); Pierre Watkin (*Albert Thayer*); Maris Wrixon (*Martha Blanton*); John Ridgely (*Reporter*); [*Uncredited Cast List*] Raymond Bailey (*Vander's Henchman Driving Car*); Wade Boteler (*Police Sergeant O'Shaughnessy*); Ed Brian (*Newboy*); Nat Carr (*Mr Watson*); Davison Clark (*Police Sergeant Dan*); Hal Craig (*Policeman Arresting Thayer*); Laurence Criner (*Vander's Driver*); Joe Devlin (*Vander's Henchman*); Eddie Dew (*Wireless Operator*); Dudley Dickerson (*Elmer 'Sam' Jones, Elevator Operator*); Jack Gardner (*Crapshooter*); William Gillespie (*Driver*); Donald Goff (*Newsboy*); Jack A. Goodrich (*Bill, Billy*); William Gould (*Detective Looking for Pearls*); John Harron (*Airplane Pilot*); Albert Herman (*Taxi Driver*); Jose Mojica, Marins (*Cabin Boy*); Jack Mower (*City Editor*); Anthony Nace (*Thayer Jewelry Salesman*); George O'Hanlon (*Crapshooter*); Jack Richardson (*Steward with Radiogram*); Jack Santoro (*Reporter*); Cliff Saum (*Bartender at 612 River Street*); Earl Smith (*Driver*); Don Turner (*Crapshooter*); Claude Wisberg (*Bellboy*); Jack Wise (*Bill, Cigar-Counter Clerk*)

Production began October 20, 1938 [Smoking inventory = four cigarettes]

[Original theatrical trailer available to download from Turner Classic Movies]

"The Secret Story Behind the Murder of Gerald Trask
Revealed in all its Startling Details"

11. *On Trial*

(Warner Bros., First National)

Credits: Director: Terry Morse; Producer: Bryan Foy; Screen Play: Don Ryan based on the play by Elmer Rice; Dialogue Director: Ted Thomas; Photography: L[ou]. W[illiam] M. O'Connell; Music: Bernhard Kaun, Film Editor: James Gibbon; Sound: E.A. Brown; Art Director: Esdras Hartley; Gowns: Howard Shoup; Technical Adviser: Cecil Luskin; Released April 1, 1939; Drama; 60m; b/w; Production #252

Synopsis: At the murder trial of Gerald Trask the accused, Robert Strickland, appears resigned to his fate offering no attempt at self-defence or offering support for his attorney. He also shows little sign of anxiety or emotion when the prosecution proceeds to demonstrate how he murdered the wealthy Trask who, it is alleged, caught Strickland, an illegal intruder, in his home. As various witnesses take the stand, and are cross examined their testimony is conveyed through extensive flashbacks. The testimony of Stickland's daughter brings Strickland and crucial evidence to light and Strickland is eventually acquitted and his family is reunited in harmony again.

Cast: John Litel (*Robert Stickland*); Margaret Lindsay (*Mae Strickland*); Edward Norris (*Arbuckle*); Janet Chapman (*Doris Strickland*); **James Stephenson (*Gerald Trask*)**; Nedda Harrigan (*Joan Trask*); [*Uncredited Cast List*] Larry Williams (*Glover*); William B. Davidson (*Gray*); Earl Dwire (*Judge*); Gordon Hart (*Dr. Morgan*); Charles Trowbridge (*Henry Dean*); Sidney Bracey (*Joe Burke*); Kenneth Harlan (*Mr Trumbell*); Vera Lewis (*Mrs Leeds*); Nat Carr (*Clerk*); Stuart Holmes (*Mr Summers*); Cliff Saum (*Bailiff*); Jack Mower (*Court Stenographer*); John Dilson (*Jury Foreman*); Lola Cheaney (*Mrs Rosenblatt*); Edgar Edwards (*First Reporter*); John Harron (*Second Reporter*); Robert Homans (*Jailer*); John Ridgely (*Radio Announcer*)

Production began December 27, 1938

[Smoking inventory = one cigarette]

[Original theatrical trailer available to download from Turner Classic Movies]

12. ***Sons of Liberty***
(Warner Bros., First National)

Credits: Director: Michael Curtiz; Producer: Gordon Hollingshead, Original Screen Play: Crane Wilbur; Photography: Sol Polito and Ray Rennahan (Technicolor); Dialogue Director: Ted Thomas; Film Editor: Thomas Pratt; Sound: E.A. Brown; Art Director: Hugh Reticker; Makeup Artist: Perc Westmore; Musical Director: Leo F. Forbstein; Costumes: Milo Anderson; Released May 20, 1939; Historical; 2 reel short; Production #48

Synopsis: Set during the American Revolution the story tells of Haym Salomon American patriot and financier of the revolution that founded the United States.

Cast: Claude Rains (*Haym Salomon*); Gale Sondergaard (*Rachel Salomon*); Donald Crisp (*Alexander McDougall*); Montagu Love (*George Washington*); Henry O'Neil (*Member of Continental Congress*); **James Stephenson** (***Colonel Tillman***); [*Uncredited Cast List*] Sidney Bracey (*Bookeeper in Montage*); Egon Brecher (*Rabbi*); Al Bridge (*Prisoner*); Harry Cording (*Arresting British Trooper*); Alec Craig (*Angus*); Henry Hall (*Congressman*); Boyd Irwin (*British Inquiry Board Officer*); Wilfrid Lucas (*Physician*); Jack Mower (*Messenger*); Leonard Mudie (*Accusing British Officer*); Moroni Olsen (*Robert Morris, Superintendent of Finance*); Sarah Padden (*Widow in Temple*); Frank Reicher (*Lyons, the Storekeeper*); Vladimir Sokoloff (*Jacob*); John Sutton (*Hessian Courier*); Larry Williams (*Natan Hale*)

Won 1940 Oscar for Best Short Subject

Production Began January 24, 1939 [Released as a supplementary extra on *Dodge City* Warner DVD]

"A Picture the Whole World Will Talk About and Remember"
13. ***The Old Maid***
(Warner Bros., First National)

Credits: Director: Edmund Goulding; Executive Producer: Hal B. Wallis; Associate Producer: Henry Blanke; Screen Play: Casey Robinson, Based on the Pulitzer Prize Play by Zoe Atkins from the novel by Edith Wharton; Music: Max Steiner; Photography: Tony Gaudio; Film Editor: George Amy; Art director: Robert Haas; Sound: C.A. Riggs; Costumes: Orry-Kelly; Makeup: Perc Westmore; Orchestral Arrangements: Hugo Friedhofer; Musical director: Leo F. Forbstein; Released August 11, 1939; Drama; 95m; b/w; Production #262

Synopsis: Just prior to the outbreak of the American Civil War in the 1860s, Delia Lovell ends her engagement to the impetuous Clem Spender, in favour of the reliable and wealthy James Ralston. On the eve of Delia's wedding Clem reappears and Delia's cousin Charlotte, offers him her affections. Clem offers to marry Charlotte on his return from fighting in the Civil War. Clem is killed in battle and Charlotte later bears his child. With the help of Dr. Lanskell, she hides the stigma of unmarried motherhood, withdraws from society during the birth of her baby and later establishes a foundling home for war orphans. Though Charlotte plans to marry James Ralston's brother, Joe, Delia learns of Charlotte's motherhood and maliciously informs Joe Charlotte is in fragile health and cannot marry. This causes a rift between the two women which is only resolved when Delia's husband dies in a riding accident. Charlotte and her daughter, Tina, come to live with Delia and her young family. As the years pass, and Tina grows to be a young adult she addresses Delia as mother, and Charlotte as her old maid aunt. Tina's aspirations to marry the prosperous and eligible Lanning Halsey appear hopeless as she is legally an orphan. Tina resents bitterly her aunt's attempts to interfere with her life. Delia, prevails upon Charlotte to let her legally adopt Tina and so bring about the marriage. This Charlotte eventually agrees to, but on the eve of Tina's wedding Charlotte is poised to tell Tina all about her background. However, when the moment arrives she is unable to go through with her revelation. Delia asks Tina to perform an act of reconciliation and love for Charlotte. On the day of her wedding after Tina says goodbye to friends and relatives she follows Delia's instruction, and saves her last farewell kiss for Aunt Charlotte.

Cast: Bette Davis (*Charlotte Lovell*); Miriam Hopkins (*Delia Lovell*); George Brent (*Clem Spender*); Jane Bryan (*Tina*); Donald Crisp (*Dr. Lanskell*); Louise Fazenda (*Dora*); **James Stephenson (*Jim Ralston*)**; Jerome Cowan (*Joe Ralston*); William Lundigan (*Lanning Halsey*); Cecilia Loftus (*Grandmother Lovell*); Rand Brooks (*Jim*); Janet Shaw (*Dee*); DeWolf Hopper [William Hopper] (*John*); [*Uncredited Cast List*] Marlene Burnett (*Tina as a Child*); Sidney Bracey (*Charles, the Butler*); Doris Lloyd (*Miss Ford*); Jack George (*Orchestra Leader/Violinist*); Winifred Harris (*Mrs Halsey*); Frederick Burton (*Mr Halsey*)

Film began production on March 15, 1939 and finished on May 9, 1939

[Original trailer available to download from Turner Classic Movies, feature available on Bette Davis Box Set Vol. II Warner DVD]

"The Stirring Story of the Love of Brother for Brother!"

14. *Beau Geste*
(Paramount)

Credits: Director and Producer: William A[ugustus] Wellman; Screen Play: Robert Carson, from the novel by Percival Christopher Wren; Photography: Theodor Sparkuhl and Archie Stout; Art direction: Hans Dreier and Robert Odell; Film Editor: Thomas Scott; Sound Recording: Hugo Grenzbach and Walter Oberst; Music: Alfred Newman; Orchestral Arrangements: Edward Powell; Second Unit Director: Richard Talmadge; Costumes: Edith Head; Interior Decorations: A.E. Freudeman Released September 15, 1939; Adventure; 120m; b/w; Production #1214

Synopsis: A relief column of French legionnaires headed by Major Henri de Beaujolais arrives at the desert fort at Zinderneuf. Though sentries are on the fort battlements there is an eerie silence, and when Beaujolais fires pistol shots in the air to signal entry, two hostile rifle shots ricochet in the sand. Beaujolais approaches the perimeter of the fort and sees only dead legionaires. He then decides to scale the fort wall and open the gate, instead the company bugler volunteers, but he fails to return. After scaling the wall himself, Beaujolais finds the place deserted. Before he can investigate such strange circumstances an Arab attack from the desert occurs, and the whole relief column retreat to desert dunes nearby. There follows a flashback some fifteen years before to an English country estate owned by Lady Patricia Brandon. In a pond in the grounds a group of young boys are burning a toy boat, in the fashion of a Viking funeral. These are the Geste brothers: Beau, John and Digby. As the years pass by Lady Brandon is forced to sell a valuable family jewel "The Blue Water" which is replaced by an imitation. The lord of the manor wishes to inspect the diamond and rather than Lady Brandon having to admit its provenance Beau Geste decides to take the fake diamond leaving a note admitting the theft, and to fulfil a boyhood dream has gone to join the foreign legion. The two remaining brothers soon join Beau in the legion. During their period of rigorous training the brothers encounter the sadistic sergeant Markoff. Another raw recruit, the sly Rasinoff, hears about the Blue Water jewel and passes the information on to Markoff who is determined to acquire the jewel for himself. Two of the Geste Brothers Beau and John are packed off with Markoff to Fort Zinderneuf. When the commanding officer dies of fever Markoff takes command and his brutality leads to a planned mutiny. Markoff is warned about the coming insurrection and the mutineers are sentenced to execution by firing squad. However, before the executions can take place the fort comes under heavy bombardment by desert tribes. Markoff responds by ensuring every

a coffee house, and overhear the verdict of ordinary citizens as they read about the outcome of the spy trials.

Cast: Edward G. Robinson (*Edward Renard*); Francis Lederer (*Schneider*); George Sanders (*Schlager*); Paul Lukas (*Dr. Kassell*); Henry O'Neill (*Attorney Kellogg*); Dorothy Tree (*Hilda Keinhauer*); Lya Lys (*Erika Wolf*); Grace Stafford (*Mrs. Schneider*); **James Stephenson (*British Military Intelligence Agent*)**; Celia Sibelius (*Mrs. Kassell*); Joe Sawyer (*Werner Renz*); Sig Ruman (*Krogman*); Lionel Royce (*Hintze*); Henry Victor (*Wildebrandt*); Hans Heinrich von Twardowsky (*Helldorf*); John Voigt (*Westphal*); Frederick Vogeding (*Captain Richter*); Willy Kaufman (*Greutzwald*); Robert Davis (*Captain Straubel*); William Vaughn (*Captain von Eichen*); George Rosener (*Klauber*); Frederick Burton (*U.S. District Court Judge*); Ely (sic) [Eily] Malyon (*Mrs. McLaughlin*); Bodil Rosing (*Passenger on Boat*); John Deering (*Narrator*); [*Uncredited Cast List*] Lotte Palfi Andor (*Kassel's Nurse*); Sherwood Bailey (*Newsboy in Diner*); Ward Bond (*American Legionnaire*); Walter Bonn (*Naval Officer Seeing Renard at Seaplane*); Egon Brecher (*Fritz Muller, German Agent*); Tommy Bupp (*Shoeshine Boy*); Glen Cavender (*Man in Montage Filing Mailboxes*); John Conte (*Radio Announcer*); Alec Craig (*McGregor, Scottish Postman*); Lisa Golm (*Mrs Anna Westphal*); William Gould (*FBI Agent*); Fred Graham (*American Legionnaire at American Bund Meeting*); Creighton Hale (*Draftsman*); John Hamilton (*FBI Chief*); John Harron (*Man in Montage with Propaganda*); Max Hoffman Jr (*Soldier at Renz's Arrest*); Stuart Holmes (*Draftsman*); Selmer Jackson (*Customs Official*); Edward Keane (*FBI Agent*); Robert Emmett Keane (*Harrison Passport Official*); Milton Kibbee (*Man Greeting Waiter Bill*); Martin Kosleck (*Dr Paul Goebbels*); Frank Mayo (*FBI Agent Phillips*); Walter Miller (*Bill Waiter with Coffee*); Jack Mower (*FBI Agent 'Mac' MacDonald*); George Offerman (*Western Union Messenger*); Lucien Prival (*Kranz*); Otto Reichow (*Driver of Crashed Nazi Car*); John Ridgely (*Army Hospital Clerk*); Hans Schumm (*Bismarck Officer with Crew List*); Charles Sherlock (*FBI Agent Fred Young*); Edwin Stanley (*US Official*); Frederic Tozere (*FBI Agent Staunton*); Charles Trowbridge (*Major Williams, Intelligence Officer*); Sol Gorss (*Nazi Goon at Bund Meeting*); Emmett Vogan, (*Hotel Desk Clerk*)

Working Title: *Storm over Germany*

Film began production February 1, 1939 and finished March 18, 1939

[Original theatrical trailer and film clips are available to download from Turner Classic Movies and the feature film is available on DVD from the Warner Archive Collection]

"Crossing Forbidden Frontiers into the Danger-Zones!"
"Reporting for Action and Adventure"

16. *Espionage Agent*
(Warner Bros., First National)

Credits: Director: Lloyd Bacon; Executive Producer: Hal B. Wallis; Associate Producer: Louis F. Edelman; Screenplay: Frank Donaghue, Warren Duff, Michael Fessier; Based on the Story "Career Man" by Robert Henry Buckner; Director of Photography: Charles Rosher; Art direction; Carl Jules Weyl; Film Editor: Ralph Dawson; Wardrobe: Milo Anderson; Music: Adolph Deutsch; Musical Director: Leo F. Forbstein; Release date September 22, 1939; Spy Drama; 83m; b/w; Production # 272

Synopsis: The United States consulate in Tangier is overwhelmed by American citizens as they frantically try to return home following the outbreak of war in North Africa. Beautiful Brenda Ballard, who has agreed to spy for Germany in exchange for an American passport, meets Barry Corvall who works at the consulate. They both set sail for the United States on the same ship, and although Barry is captivated by Brenda and he proposes marriage she spurns his advances, knowing her past would damage his career in the diplomatic service. Back in Washington he successfully completes his diplomatic studies and upon graduation is transferred to the consulate in Paris. Against parental opposition, Barry ultimately persuades Brenda to marry. But before they can do so, German spy, Karl Muller appears and reminds Brenda of the debt of service she owes his organisation. Rather than go through with stealing military plans, she confronts Barry and confesses everything to him. Forced to resign from the diplomatic service and realising that as a foreign citizen the United States government has little defense against spies such as Muller, Barry and Brenda decide to go to Geneva to attempt to infiltrate an international spy ring. They manage to locate the command centre of a spy ring headed by Dr. Rader, and learn there are major plans afoot to spread disinformation across the United States. Dr. Rader suspects the couple are bent on destroying his organisation, and he kidnaps Brenda holding her hostage on a train destined for Germany. Before they cross the German border Barry successfully rescues Brenda, and they are able to make good their escape by air. In Washington Barry contacts his old boss and presents evidence of the seditious nature of foreign powers, and the need for America to be vigilant in the fight against espionage agents.

Cast: Joel McCrea (*Barry Corvall*); Brenda Marshall (*Brenda Ballard*); Jeffrey Lynn (*Lowell Warrington*); George Bancroft (*Dudley Garrett*); Stanley Ridges (*Hamilton Peyton*); **James Stephenson** (*Dr Rader*);

Howard Hickman (*Walter Forbes*); Martin Kosleck (*Karl Mullen*); Nana Bryant (*Mrs. Corvall*); Robert O. Davis (*Paul Strawn*); Hans Von Twardowsky (*Dr. Heim*); Addison Richards (*Bruce Corvall*); Edwin Stanley (*Secretary of State*); Granville Bates (*Phineas T. O'Grady*); Grace Hayle (*Mrs. O'Grady*); Egon Brecher (*Larsch*); Emmett Vogan (*Instructor*); [*Uncredited Cast List*] William Hopper (*Student*); Glenn Langan (*Student*); Lionel Royce (*Hoffmeyer*); Henry Victor (*Foreign Official*); Lucien Prival (*Decker*); George Reeves (*Warrington's Secretary*); Chris-Pin Martin (*Tunisian Guard*); Stuart Holmes (*American Tourist*); John Harron (*American Tourist*); Fern Barry (*American Tourist*); Al Lloyd (*American Tourist*); Eddie Graham (*Extra Dancing at Ball*); Sally Sage (*American Tourist*); Alice Connors (*American Tourist*); Frederick Vogeding (*Friend of Muller*); Arno Frey (*Foreign Officer*); Sarah Edwards (*Militant American Tourist*); Jack Mower (*Man Opening Door*); Lottie Williams (*American Tourist Wanting Boat Out*); Louis Adlon (*Youth*); Vera Lewis (*American Tourist Going to Desert*); Dorothy Vaughan (*Stout Woman Bumped by Garrett*); Sidney Bracy (*Ship Steward*); Don Turner (*Pilot with Map*); George Irving (*State Department Official*); William Worthington (*Instructor in Montage*); Selmer Jackson (*Instructor*); John Hamilton (*Code Room Instructor*); Rolf Lindau (*Foreign Agent*); Nella Walker (*Mrs. Peyton*); Jean De Briac (*Waiter*); Henry Von Zynda (*Guard*); Billy McCain (*Manservant at Ball*); Winifred Harris (*Lady Ashford*); Frederick Lindsley (*Announcer*); Wolfgang Zilzer (*Heinrich*)

Working Title: *Career Man*

Production began May 17, 1939

[Smoking inventory = one cigarette]

[Original theatrical trailer available to download from Turner Classic Movies]

17. *The Monroe Doctrine*
(Warner Bros., First National)

Credits: Director: Crane Wilbur; Producer: [*uncredited*]; Original Screen Play: Charles L. Tedford; Director of Photography: Wilfrid M. Cline; Technicolor Color Director: Natalie Kalmus; Art Director: Hugh Reticker; Film Editor: Everett Dodd; Sound: Dolph Thomas; Costumes: Leah Rhodes; Makeup Artist: Perc Westmore; Music: Howard Jackson [*uncredited*]; Released October 14, 1939; Historical; 16m; 2 reel short; Production #53

Synopsis: The story of how President Monroe responded to Spanish attempts to interfere in the affairs of South America.

Cast: Grant Mitchell (*James Quincy Adams*); **James Stephenson** (***Signor De La Torre***), Sidney Blackmer (*President Theodore Roosevelt*); Charles Waldron (*President James Monroe*); Nanette Fabares (*Rosita De La Torre*); George Reeves (*John Sturgis*); Frank Wilcox (*Henry Clay*); Ted Osborne (*John C. Calhoun*); [*Uncredited Cast List*] Erville Alderson (*William Seward*); Mary Currier (*Mrs Henry Clay*); Frederick Giermann (*Austrian Envoy*); Frank Puglia (*King Ferdinand II*); Edwin Stanley (*President James K. Polk*); Emmett Vogan (*Daniel Webster*); Frederick Vogeding (*German Envoy*)

Production began July 19, 1939

[Available as a supplementary extra on *Invisible Stripes* in *Warner Bros. Gangsters Collection Vol. 4* DVD Box Set]

"The Most Feared Ruler in All Europe"
"One Word from Her Can Mean War or Peace Life or Death!"

18. ***The Private Lives of Elizabeth and Essex* also known as *Elizabeth the Queen* and *The Lady and the Knight***
(Warner Bros., First National)

Credits: Director: Michael Curtiz; Executive Producer: Hal B. Wallis; Associate Producer: Robert Lord; Screen Play: Norman Reilly Raine and Aeneas MacKenzie, based on the Theatre Guild Stage Play "Elizabeth the Queen" by Maxwell Anderson; Dialogue Director: Stanley Logan; Director of Photography: Sol Polito; Associate W. Howard Greene (Technicolor); Art Director: Anton Grot; Film Editor: Owen Marks; Sound: C.A. Riggs; Costumes: Orry-Kelly; Special Effects: Byron Haskin and H.F. Koenekamp; Technical Adviser: Ali Hubert; Makeup Artist: Perc Westmore; Orchestrations: Hugo Friedhofer and Milan Roder; Musical Director: Leo F. Forbstein; Music: Erich Wolfgang Korngold; Released November 11, 1939; Romance/Historical Epic; 106m; Production #267

Synopsis: In 1596, all of London turns out to greet Robert Deveraux, the Earl of Essex on his return from his victory over the Spanish fleet at Cadiz. In his audience with sovereign Queen Elizabeth she chides Essex for his hollow victory, and failing to stop Spain from sinking its treasure fleet while he stormed Cadiz revelling in personal triumph. The Queen makes her displeasure official by promoting Essex's old enemy Sir Walter Raleigh. Insulted, Essex retreats to his estate. Essex's friend at court, Francis Bacon, tries to persuade him to return to London where courtiers are plotting against Essex. Only when the Queen herself summons him to court and offers an apology does he return. At the suggestion of Bacon

Elizabeth appoints Essex as Master of the Ordinance to keep him from suppressing rebellion in Ireland under the leadership of the Earl of Tyrone. Unfortunately, Essex is manoeuvred by the intrigues of the royal court into leading an army into Ireland against the wishes of Elizabeth who, though she realises Essex's thirst for political power, holds him high in her private affection. Though he returns from Ireland defeated, his requests for arms and men to the Queen are met with silence, the people cheer him on. Believing he has been betrayed and abandoned he and his men force their way into the sovereign's palace. Elizabeth puts up little resistance and appears amicable with her lover Essex. However, when Essex dismisses his men she has him arrested for treason. In a final meeting Elizabeth offers to spare his life if he should agree to forfeit the throne, but he steadfastly refuses. Having no choice Elizabeth orders his execution, and sobs alone on her throne when the sentence has been carried out.

Cast: Bette Davis (*Queen Elizabeth*); Errol Flynn (*Earl of Essex*); Olivia de Havilland (*Lady Penelope Gray*); Donald Crisp (*Francis Bacon*); Alan Hale (*Earl of Tyrone*); Vincent Price (*Sir Walter Raleigh*); Henry Stephenson (*Lord Burghley*); Henry Daniell (*Sir Robert Cecil*); **James Stephenson (*Sir Thomas Egerton*)**; Nanette Fabares [Nanette Fabray] (*Mistress Margaret Radcliffe*); Ralph Forbes (*Lord Knollys*); Robert Warwick (*Lord Mountjoy*); Leo G. Carroll (*Sir Edward Coke*); [*Uncredited Cast List*] Guy Bellis (*Lord Charles Howard*); Doris Lloyd (*Handmaiden*); Maris Wrixon (*Lady of the Court*); Rosella Towne (*Lady of the Court*); John Sutton (*Captain Armand of the Queen's Guard*); I. Stanford Jolley (*Spectator Outside Whitehall Palace*)

Academy Award Nominations: best photography: Sol Polito & William Howard Greene; music: Erich Wolfgang Korngold; art direction: Anton Grot

Film began May 11, 1939

[Original theatrical trailer and film clips available to download from Turner Classic Movies, the feature film is available on DVD in *Errol Flynn Signature Collection Volume One* Warner DVD Box Set]

"The Genius of Paul Muni The Greatness of James Hilton"
"Brilliantly Moulded into an Unforgettable Screen Experience"

19. *We Are Not Alone*
(Warner Bros., First National)

Credits: Director: Edmund Goulding; Executive Producer: Hal B. Wallis; Producer: Henry Blanke; Screen Play: James Hilton, Milton Krims; Novel by James Hilton; Director of Photography: Tony Gaudio A.S.C.; Technical

Adviser: Dr. Leo Schulman; Editor: Warren Low; Sound: C.A. Riggs; Art Direction: Carl Jules Weyl; Gowns: Milo Anderson; Makeup Artist: Perc Westmore; Special Effects: Byron Haskin A.S.C. H.F. Koenekamp A.S.C.; Orchestral Arrangements: Hugo Friedhofer; Musical Direction: Leo F. Forbstein; Music: Max Steiner; Released November 25, 1939; Drama; 112m; b/w; Production #280

Synopsis: On the eve of the outbreak of war in 1914, Dr. David Newcome, his wife Jessica and son Gerald live in the English town of Calderbury. Jessica, a conventional and harsh woman, is unable to understand her sensitive little son, and her unsympathetic disciplinarian attitude aggravates the child's nervousness. A solution appears when the doctor meets Leni, a young Austrian dancer, stranded in England after an injury while dancing. Later after she attempts suicide, and with Jessica's consent the doctor engages Leni's services as a governess for the boy. The doctor and Leni are oddly drawn towards each other, but their friendship remains platonic. When Jessica learns the truth about Leni's background she insists on her dismissal. Unable to dissuade his wife, the doctor arranges a position for Leni at a local music school. Meanwhile Gerald who has been sent away to his uncle, slips back home to the surgery to retrieve a toy his mother has confiscated. In reaching for the toy he accidentally knocks and breaks a bottle of pills. He puts the spilled contents into another bottle to cover up his misdemeanour. Jessica returns home shortly after and goes to the surgery for tablets to cure a headache. Shortly after, Jessica is found dead by the housemaid. Unaware of inpending tragedy awaiting them, Leni and the doctor are saying farewell when they receive news of the outbreak of the World War. Realising that Leni's nationality will place her in imminent danger should she remain in England, the doctor offers to take her to a nearby town where she can catch a train to begin the journey back to her homeland. Before they reach their destination they are arrested and tried for Jessica's murder. The appearance of flight tells against them, and Gerald, the only person who could have proved their innocence, has been told nothing of what has happened, at the doctor's request. After the couple have been sentenced to death by hanging they are granted a final meeting. The doctor kisses Leni for the first and last time and tells her they are not alone in injustice.

Cast: Paul Muni (*Dr David Newcome*); Jane Bryan (*Leni*); Flora Robson (*Jessica*); Raymond Severn (*Gerald*); Una O'Connor (*Susan*); Henry Daniell ([*Sir Ronald*] *Dawson*); Montagu Love (*Major Millman*); **James Stephenson** (***Sir William Clintock***); Stanley Logan (*Sir Guy Lockhead*); Cecil Kellaway (*Judge*); Alan Napier (*Archdeacon*); Eily Malyon (*Archdeacon's Wife*); Douglas Scott (*Tommy Baker*); Crauford Kent (*Dr.*

Stacey); May Beatty (*Mrs. Patterson*); Billy Bevan (*Mr Jones*); Holmes Herbert (*Police Inspector*); John Powers (*Charley*); Colin Kenny (*George*); Ethel Griffies (*Mrs. Raymond*); [*Uncredited Cast List*] Doris Lloyd (*Mrs. Jaeggers*); Clarence Derwent (*Stage Manager*); Charles Irwin (*Working Man with Apron*); Joseph Crehan (*American at Train Station*); David Clyde (*Ticket Collector*); Sidney Bracey (*Ben, the Lamplighter*); Viola Moore (*Second Chorus Girl*); Phyllis Barry (*First Chorus Girl*); Lowden Adams (*Detective*); Leyland Hodgson (*Detective*); Harry Cording (*Man Carrying Leni*); Cyril Thornton (*Man*); Douglas Gordon (*Mr Selby*); Olaf Hytten (*Mr Clark*); Rita Carlyle (*Mrs. Deane*); Barlowe Borland (*Tom Briggs*); Egon Brecher (*Mr Adolf Schiller*); Lillian Kemble-Cooper (*Mrs. Stacey*); Boyd Irwin (*Police Officer*); Keith Hitchcock (*Policeman*); Thomas R. Mills (*Judge's Chaplain*)

Production began July 14, 1939

[Smoking inventory = one cigar]

[Original theatrical trailer available to download from Turner Classic Movies]

"The powerful drama of a lawyer
who helped thieves and murderers cheat justice"

20. ***Wolf of New York***
(Republic)

Credits: Director: William McGann; Producer: Robert North; Screenplay: Gordon Kahn, Lionel Houser; Original Story: Leslie T. White, Arnold Belgard; Photography: Reggie T. Lanning; Musical Direction: Cy Feur; Film Editor: Ernest J. Nims; Art Director: John Victor Mackay; Wardrobe: Adele Palmer; Released January 25, 1940; Crime Drama; 69m; b/w; Production # 955

Synopsis: Hiram Rogers, a smooth, urbane racketeer, instructs members of his organisation to rob an insurance company. Unfortunately, the police catch one of the gang, but Rogers merely calls on the services of a crooked lawyer Christopher Faulkner. In court he is able to employ dubious legal means to win his client's case. After the case Peggy Nolan, secretary to the District Attorney and Chris's ex-girl friend, asks him to consider giving up his underhanded practice and go straight. Chris declines, but he is soon embroiled even more in Roger's criminal organisation when Peggy's father, a police inspector, is murdered during a police investigation of Roger's dishonest business affairs. Suspect Frankie Mason is indicted for the murder and, although he is completely innocent, is found guilty and executed. Several months later the real killer confesses and the District

Attorney is obliged to resign. This miscarriage of justice hits Chris hard, and he severs all past relations with Rogers and his rotten organisation. Peggy is able to persuade the state governor that Chris is the best person to take over as District Attorney. She then persuades Chris he should accept the position as this would enable him to track down her father's murderer. Accepting the appointment, Chris takes on gambling and vice rackets in the town. A key suspect emerges that may shed light on the killing of Peggy's father, but before the suspect can be arrested and questioned he is murdered. However, when the body is examined Chris finds a piece of paper with the name "Hugo Stout" written on it. Checking the name with criminal authorities in Washington and abroad, Bill Ennis, an assistant at the DA's office, confirms that Hugo Stout is an infamous criminal wanted in England. At this point both Bill and Peggy are kidnapped by Rogers and taken to his house. There he reveals that he is Hugo Stout and his plans to kill Bill and Peggy are disturbed by the arrival of the police. Though he attempts to make a getaway he is eventually apprehended after a car chase, and he is later convicted of ordering the murder of Peggy's father. Now justice has been seen to be done, Chris and Peggy are free to marry.

Cast: Edmund Lowe (*Chris Faulkner*); Rose Hobart (*Peggy Nolan*); **James Stephenson** (***Hiram Rogers***); Jerome Cowan (*Cosgrave*); William Demarest (*Bill Ennis*); Maurice Murphy (*Frank Mason*); Charles D. Brown (*Constable Nolan*); Edward Gargan (*W. Thornton Upshaw*); Andrew Tombes (*Sylvester Duncan*); Ben Welden (*Owney McGill*); Ann Baldwin (*Gladys*); [*Uncredited Cast List*] Roy Gordon (*Governor*); Hooper Atchley (*Detective*) Clyde Cook (*Jenkins*); Ray Cooke (*Messenger*); Edward Hearn (*Cop*); Milton Kibbee (*Reporter*); Forbes Murray (*Judge*); Archie Twitchell (*Cop*)

Working Title: *The Wolf of Wall Street*

Produced November 1939

"There's Only One Man Who Can Solve This Murder!"
"The Most Famous Detective in the World Returns to "Break"
the Most Baffling Crime of His Career!"

21. *Calling Philo Vance*

(Warner Bros., First National)

Credits: Director: William Clemens; Producer: Bryan Foy [uncredited]; Screen Play: Tom Reed, from the novel "The Kennel Murder Case" by S.S. Van Dine; Dialogue Director: Jo Graham; Director of Photography: L. William O'Connell; Film Editors: Benjamin Liss, Louis Lindsay; Art director: Ted Smith; Sound: Charles Lang; Gowns: Howard Shoup; Music:

Heinz Roemheld [*uncredited*]; Released January 27, 1940; Mystery; 62m; b/w; Production # 283

Synopsis: In Vienna the United States government unofficially approaches detective Philo Vance about investigating aircraft manufacturer Archer Coe, alleged to be involved in espionage. In disguise, Vance steals plans of Coe's latest bomber plane and manages to escape from Austria to the United States, but the plans are misplaced en route. Though Vance has no real proof of Coe's treachery, he decides to take up the case. With his business associate, Ryan, and faithful canine McTavish, Vance pays a visit to Archer Coe's home only to find a crime scene with Coe dead by gunshot. The room of the homicide is locked from the inside, indicating suicide, but Vance believes Coe was murdered. Coe's niece thinks there was sufficient motive to warrant his murder. When the coroner examines the body he finds the cause of death was not a gunshot wound, but a knife wound. Later Vance finds the body of Brisbane Coe the victim's brother in a closet and suggests it was he who killed Coe. From hereon various suspects are paraded and discounted until Vance is able to relate the unique circumstances of the murder and reveal the identity of the killer who was trying to steal blueprints of a prototype aircraft to sell to a foreign government.

Cast: **James Stephenson** (*Philo Vance*); Margot Stevenson (*Hilda Lane*); Henry O'Neill (*Markham*); Edward Brophy (*Ryan*); Sheila Bromley (*Doris*); Ralph Forbes (*Tom MacDonald*); Donald Douglas (*Philip Wrede*); Martin Kosleck (*Gamble*); Jimmy Conlin (*Doctor*); Edward Raquello (*Grassi*); Creighton Hale (*Du Bois*); Harry Strang (*Hennessey*); Richard Kipling (*Archer Coe*); Wedgwood Nowell (*Brisbane Coe*); Bo Ling (*Ling Toy*); [*Uncredited Cast List*] Herbert Anderson (*First Reporter*); Henry Blair (*Hans Snauble*); Egon Brecher (*Austrian Judge*); Harry Burns (*Captain Lugo of the Sorrento*); Yakima Canutt (*Sailor on the Sorrento*); Nat Carr (*Second Photographer*); Loia Cheaney (*Markham's Secretary*); Frederick Giermann (*Austrian Sergeant*); Eddie Graham (*Coroner's Assistant*); John Harron (*Third Reporter*); Stuart Holmes (*Hertz, the Train Conductor*); William Hopper (*Hotel Clerk*); Olaf Hytten (*Charles*); George Irving (*Avery*); Marion Lessing (*Mrs Fritz Snauble*); Rolph Lindau (*Aeronautics Sentry*); Frank Mayo (*Doorman*); George Reeves (*Steamship Clerk*); Jack Richardson (*Fourth Reporter*); Cliff Saum (*Investigator Snitken*); Hans Schumm (*Nazi Officer at Dock*); Frank Wilcox (*Second Reporter*); Jack Wise (*First Photographer*); Maris Wrixon (*Long Distance Operator*); Henry Zynda (*Austrian Lieutenant*); Terry the Cairn Terrier (*McTavish*)

Remake of *The Kennel Murder Case* (Warner, Michael Curtiz, 1933)

Working title: *Philo Vance Comes Back*

Produced July 27, 1939

[Smoking inventory = three cigarettes]

[Original theatrical trailer available to download from Turner Classic Movies and the feature film is available on DVD in *The Philo Vance Murder Case Collection* released by the Warner Archive Collection]

"This is the Most Terrifying Weapon Ever Invented! The Death Ray Projector"
"Join Ronald Reagan (Operative 207)"
"Battling 20,000 Unseen Enemies to Protect Its Amazing Secret!"

22. *Murder in the Air*
(Warner Bros., First National)

Credits: Director: Lewis Seiler; Producer: Bryan Foy; Screenplay: Raymond L. Schrock; Dialogue Director: Harry Seymour; Director of Photography: Ted D. McCord; Music: William Lava; Art Director: Stanley Fleischer; Film Editor: Frank Magee; Gowns: Howard Shoup; Released June 1, 1940; Crime; 55m; b/w; Production #289

Synopsis: Waves of sabotage across the United States lead security chief, Saxby, to assign agent Brass Bancroft to uncover a spy ring. Brass impersonates deceased spy Steve Swenko and a message found in the dead spy's shoe leads Brass and his assistant Gabby Watters, to Joe Garvey, the leader of a nationalistic society that is a front for Unamerican Activities. Before he can contact Garvey he comes into contact with Hilda Riker, the late Swenko's wife. When told by Brass Svenko is dead and he is carrying out his assignment, she recognises him as a federal operative. She immediately warns a Garvey operative, Otto Brennerman. Before the pair can set a trap for Brass they are arrested. Unsuspecting, Garvey orders Brass to board a dirigible which has on board a powerful new defense weapon, the inertia projector. He makes contact with an agent who is posing as a secretary to a League of Nations official. Brass is ordered to destroy the dirigible while the agent steals plans for the inertia projector. However, before he can act Otto Brennerman escapes FBI custody and informs Garvey and his associates of Brass's true identity. There is a violent storm and the dirigible crashes, leaving Brass unconscious and the agent free to steal the secret plans of the inertia projector. Brass is rescued and taken to hospital and the agent tells Garvey he is in imminent danger. Garvey then attempts to make good his escape by flying the plans and himself across the border. The authorites are alerted to Garvey's attempted breakout and following an aerial dogfight, Garvey's plane is fatally shot down using the inertia projector.

Cast: Ronald Reagan (*Brass Bancroft*); John Litel (*Saxby*); Lya Lys (*Hilda Riker*); **James Stephenson** (*Joe Garvey – Agent 321*); Eddie Foy Jr (*Gabby Watters*); Robert Warwick (*Doctor Finchley*); Victor Zimmerman (*Rumford*); William Gould (*Admiral Winfield*); Kenneth Harlan (*Commander Wayne*); Frank Wilcox (*Hotel Clerk*); Owen King (*George Hayden*); Dick Rich (*John Kramer*); Charles Brokaw (*Otto*); Helen Lynd (*Dolly*); [*Uncredited Cast List*] Lane Chandler (*Flagship Radio Operator*); Cliff Clark (*Police Chief at Morgue*); Richard Clayton (*Sailor Bringing Radiogram*); Alan Davis (*Dirigible Lieutenant C.O. Bell*); John Deering (*Radio Announcer*); John Hamilton (*Agent Hargrave*); Selmer Jackson (*Captain Riddell, Naval Hospital Doctor*); Reid Kilpatrick (*Continental Airport Radio Operator*); Mike Lally (*Hargrave's Radio Operator*); Alexander Lockwood (*Dirigible Officer*); Frank Mayo (*Dr. Delby Prison Hospital Doctor*); John 'Skins' Miller (*Taxi Driver*); Clayton Moore Jr. (*Sunnyvale Radio Operator*); Jack Mower (*Collins, Police Chemist*); Charles Marsh (*Sunnyvale Radio Officer*); Wedgewood Nowell (*Flagship Admiral*); Paul Panzer (*Hans, a Henchman*); Paul Phillips (*Sailor*); Jeffrey Sayre (*Prescott Dirigible Radio Officer*); Charles Sherlock (*Zepplin Navigator*); Garland Smith (*Dirigible Officer*); Edwin Stanley (*Congressman Courtney Rice*); Julie Stevens (*Naval Hospital Nurse*); Claude Wisberg (*Hotel Bellhop*)

Working titles: *Uncle Sam's Awakens; Enemy Within*

[Smoking inventory = one cigarette]

Production began September 18, 1939 and finished October 9, 1939

[Original theatrical trailer available to download from Turner Classic Movies and the feature film is available in *Brass Bancroft of the Secret Service Mysteries Collection* DVD Box set available from the Warner Archive Collection]

"Never Before So Many Giant Thrills in One Picture!"
23. *The Sea Hawk*
(Warner Bros., First National)

Credits: Director: Michael Curtiz; Executive Producer: Hal B. Wallis; Associate Producer: Henry Blanke; Screen Play: Howard Koch and Seton I. Miller, based on the novel by Rafael Sabatini; Director of Photography: Sol Polito; Dialogue Director: Jo Graham; Film Editor: George Amy; Sound: Francis J. Scheid; Art director: Anton Grot;

Technical Advisers: Ali Hubert, Thomas Manners and William Kiel; Costumes. Orry-Kelly; Makeup Artist: Perc Westmore: Special Effects: Byron Haskin and H.F. Koenekamp; Orchestrations: Hugo Friedhofer, Milan Roder and Ray Heindorf; Musical Director: Leo F. Forbstein; Music: Erich Wolfgang Korngold; Released July 1, 1940; Swashbuckler; 123m; b/w; Production # 296

Synopsis: In 1585 King Philip II of Spain, who has designs on world conquest, sends ambassador, Don José Alvarez de Cordoba, to England, the one kingdom that threatens his grand ambitions. The ambassador and his beautiful niece, Doña Maria, set sail for England, but as their Spanish Galleon approaches the English coast, it is attacked and plundered by The Albatross, a British ship. The ship's captain, Geoffrey Thorpe, despite his well-mannered civility and offer of safe escort to England for the ambassador and his niece is the leader of the "Sea Hawks," a band of fearless British buccaneers who plunder Spanish treasures in order to finance the building of a British naval fleet to protect their islands against the threat of invasion from the Spanish Armada. Though Queen Elizabeth tacitly supports the intentions behind the Sea Hawks their actions cause her political embarrassment. Though Thorpe is rebuked in public by the Queen, in private she admires his lighthearted and zestful approach to life.Thorpe conceives a daring plan to plunder Spanish gold held in Panama to help build up the royal coffers. Though the sovereign witholds royal approval, she does express her private regard for the venture and wishes him every success. Unfortunately there are enemies in the royal court who soon discover Thorpe's Panama escapade. A trap is waiting for Thorpe and his crew when they reach Panama. Captured, Thorpe and his men are taken away, manacled and forced to toil as Spanish galley slaves. Despite atrocious treatment Thorpe manages to make a daring escape and returns to his old ship and bears written plans for the Spanish sea invasion of England. Returning to England Thorpe manages with the help of Doña Maria who has fallen in love with England and Thorpe, to slip into the palace. He confronts turncoat Lord Wolfingham and a duel to the death ensues. Trying to fight his way to gain an audience with the Queen Thorpe is hopeless outnumbered by her guards. When she appears the Queen is presented with the evidence of Wolfingham's treachery. Thorpe is exonerated and with gratitude Queen Elizabeth orders a new British fleet to be commanded by The Sea Hawks. She concludes with a rousing speech of defiance against the personal ambition of dictatorship.

Cast: Errol Flynn (*Geoffrey Thorpe*); Brenda Marshall (*Dona Maria*); Claude Rains (*Don Jose Alvarez de Cordoba*); Donald Crisp (*Sir John*

Burleson); Flora Robson (*Queen Elizabeth*); Alan Hale (*Carl Pitt*); Henry Daniell (*Lord Wolfingham*); Una O'Connor (*Miss Latham*); **James Stephenson (*Abbott*)**; Gilbert Roland (*Captain Lopez*); William Lundigan (*Danny Logan*); Julien Mitchell (*Oliver Scott*); Montagu Love (*King Phillip II*); J.M. Kerrigan (*Ell Matson*); David Bruce (*Martin Burke*); Clifford Brooke (*William Tuttle*); Clyde Cook (*Walter Boggs*); Fritz Leiber (*Inquisitor*); Ellis Irving (*Monty Preston*); Francis McDonald (*Kroner*); Pedro de Cordoba (*Captain Mendoza*); Ian Keith (*Peraita*); Jack La Rue (*Lieutenant Ortega*); Halliwell Hobbes (*Astronomer*); Alec Craig (*Chartmaker*); Victor Varconi (*General Aguirre*); Robert Warwick (*Frobisher*); Harry Cording (*Slavemaster*); [*Uncredited Cast List*] Herbert Anderson (*Eph Winters*); Edgar Buchanan (*Ben Rollins*); Charles Irwin (*Arnold Cross*); Frank Lackteen (*Captain Ortiz*); Guy Bellis (*John Hawkins*); Lester Matthews (*Lieutenant*); Art Miles (*Drum Beater*); Nestor Paiva (*Slave Master*); Michael Harvey (*Sea Hawk*); Harry Silversmith (*Native*); Elizabeth Sifton and Mary Anderson (*Maids of Honour*); Gerald Mohr (*Spanish Officer*); Dave Kashner, J.W. Cody and Anthony Warde (*Whippers*); Whit Bissell (*Gate Guard at Palace Entrance*)

Academy Award Nominations: Best Art Direction (Anton Grot); Best Special Effects (Byron Haskin); Best Music Score (Erich Wolfgang Korngold)

Production began January 31, 1940 and finished April 19, 1940

[Re-issue theatrical trailer and film clips available to download from Turner Classic Movies and the feature is available in *Errol Flynn Signature Collection Volume One* DVD Box Set from Warner DVD]

"It Took Half a Century Before It Could Be Told!"
"See the Whole Uncensored Story of this Fugitive from Devil's Island!"
"Now Revealed for the First Time!"
"Put It on Your <u>Must See</u> List"

24. *Devil's Island*
(Warner Bros., First National)

Credits: Director: William Clemens; Producer: Bryan Foy; Screen Play: Kenneth Gamet and Don Ryan; Based on "The Return of Dr. X" by Anthony Coldeway and Raymond L. Schrock; Dialogue Director: John Langan; Photography: George Barnes; Art Director: Max Parker; Film Editor: Frank Magee; Sound: Robert B. Lee; Technical Adviser: Louis Van Der Ecker; Music: Howard Jackson; Preview: January 7, 1939 but not released until July 1940; Drama; 63m; b/w; Production #224

Synopsis: Dr. Charles Gaudet, a respected brain physician, treats a wounded escaped convict, and is tried and sentenced to the notorious penal colony Devil's Island. There he encounters the displeasure of Colonel Armand Lucien the sadistic commandant of the prison. Angered by the injustice around him Gaudet with other prisoners lead an unsuccessful revolt, and in retribution the commandant condemns them to death. Lucien's little daughter Collette suffers a head injury, and only Gaudet has the skill to save her life. Desperate, Lucien offers Gaudet his life for that of Collette. Gaudet agrees to Lucien's terms, but after saving the little girl's life, Lucien reneges on his agreement and orders Gaudet confined to a fetid pit. Madame Lucien, angered by her husband's callous actions and in gratitude for her little girl's life, helps plot the doctor's escape. Gaudet and other prisoners are able to escape the island using a small boat. Unfortunately, the craft soon runs out of fuel, and the fugitives are recaptured and returned to the island. Eager to exact his own punitive justice and restore order Lucien sentences Gaudet to death. As soon as she learns of the fate awaiting Gaudet, Madame Lucien makes contact with the newly appointed governor of the penal colonies. Swift to act, the governor returns to the island with Madame Gaudet. He successfully intervenes in stopping Gaudet's execution and arrests Lucien for gross misconduct in office. Offering a full pardon for Dr. Gaudet, the governor promises future institutional reforms to the penal system, replacing corruption with humanity.

Cast: Boris Karloff (*Dr. Charles Gaudet*); Nedda Harrigan (*Madame Lucien*); **James Stephenson** (*Colonel Armand Lucien*); Adia Kuznetzoff (*Pierre*); Rolla Courvitch (*Collette*); Will Stanton (*Bobo*); Edward Keane (*Dr. Duval*); Robert Warwick (*Demonpre*); Pedro de Cordoba (*Marcal*); Tom Wilson (*Emil*); John Harmon (*Andre*); Richard Bond (*Georges*); Earl Gunn (*Leon*); Sidney Bracey (*Soupy*); George Lloyd (*Dogface*); Charles Richman (*Governor Beaufort*); Stuart Holmes (*Gustave Le Brun*); Leonard Mudie (*Advocate General*); Egon Brecher (*Debriac*); Frank Reicher (*President of Assize Court*); [*Uncredited Cast List*] James Blaine (*Guard*); Dick Botiller (*Pilot of Escape Boat*); Al Bridge (*Captain of the Guards*); Nat Carr (*Court Clerk*); Glen Cavender (*Gendarme on Train*); Davison Clark (*Captain of Gendarmes*); Neal Clisby (*Jules*); Harry Cording (*Guard Accepting Bribe*); Earl Dwire (*Priest*); Eddie Foster (*Supply Clerk*); Galan Galt (*Guard*); Sol Gorss (*Guard Escorting Gaudet After Operation*); Frank Hagney (*Guard*); John Hamilton (*Captain of Second Convict Ship*); Ben Hendricks Jr (*Francois, Sergeant of the Guards*); Stanley King (*Guard*); Vera Lewis (*Gaudet's Housekeeper*);

Billy McClain (*Governor's Servant*); Henry Otho (*Guard Handcuffing Pierre*); Paul Panzer (*Jury Foreman*); Alonzo Price (*Captain Edvard Fearreau of the First Convict Ship*); Dick Rich (*Guard Drugged by Gaudet*); Cliff Saum (*Uniformed Gendarme*); Francis Sayles (*Boatman Taking Madame Lucien to Mainland*); Earl Smith (*Daniel, Madame Lucien's Servant*); Walter Soderling (*Wagon Driver*); Don Turner (*Guard Escorting Gaudet After Operation*); Douglas Williams (*Guard*)

Production began June 22, 1938

[Smoking inventory = two cigarettes + two cigars]

[Original theatrical trailer available to download from Turner Classic Movies and the feature film is available in *The Boris Karloff Triple Feature* DVD box set released by the Warner Archive Collection]

"It's the Most Fascinating Story Ever Told!"
"The Strangest Adventure that Ever Swept Across the Screen!!"
25. *A Dispatch from Reuter's* **also known as** *This Man From Reuter*
(Warner Bros., First National)

Credits: Director: William Dieterle; Executive Producer: Hal B. Wallis; Associate Producer: Henry Blanke; Screen Play: Milton Krims, From a Story by Valentine Williams and Wolfgang Wilhelm; Director of Photography: James Wong Howe; Dialogue Director: Jo Graham; Art direction: Anton Grot; Sound: C.A. Riggs; Film Editor: Warren Low; Gowns: Orry-Kelly. Makeup Artist: Perc Westmore; Orchestral Arrangements: Hugo Friedhofer; Special Effects: Byron Haskin and Robert Burks; Musical Director: Leo F. Forbstein; Music: Max Steiner; Released October 19, 1940; Historical; 89m; b/w; Production No: #312

Synopsis: In 1833 in the small German village of Gottingen, thirteen year old Julius Reuter and friend Max Wagner watch the Hanover express coach bringing a special courier for the overland service of the London *Times*. Julius is immediately impressed with the importance of the rapid transmission of news. Sixteen years Julius and Max start a business in Brussels to deliver messages by carrier pigeon between towns without the new electric telegraph. The pigeon business saves many children's lives at an Aachen hospital when news breaks that poison rather than medicine has been accidentally sent. Reuter learns publicity has been surpressed by Ida Magnus, the daughter of a prominent physician who is worried the repercussions this news will have on the medical profession. Despite their initial differences Julius and Ida are soon reconciled and they marry. With the expansion of telegraph wires Julius goes with Max to

Paris to search for new business opportunities. Learning Louis Napoleon is due to make an important speech gives him an important idea. He is able to bring the news of the speech to all newspapers across the wire as it is delivered. This scoop establishes the Reuter's news agency for fast, efficient, truthful and accurate news information. Despite stiff competition and accusations of fraud from other news agencies, Reuter is able to fend off challenges by bringing the astonishing news of the assassination of President Abraham Lincoln even before the American ambassador learns of it. The future of the Reuter's News Agency, based on the solid foundation of truth is assured.

Cast: Edward G. Robinson (*Julius Reuter*); Edna Best (*Ida Magnus*); Eddie Albert (*Max Wagner*); Albert Basserman (*Franz Geller*); Gene Lockhart (*Bauer*); Otto Kruger (*Dr. Magnus*); Nigel Bruce (*Sir Randolph Persham*); Montagu Love (*Delane*); **James Stephenson** (**Carew**); Walter Kingsford (*Napoleon III*); David Bruce (*Bruce*); Dickie Moore (*Reuter, as a Boy*); Billy Dawson (*Max Wagner, as a Boy*); Richard Nichols (*Herbert Reuter, aged 5*); Lumsden Hare (*Chairman*); [*Uncredited Cast List*] Norman Ainsley (*Cockney Newspaper Vendor*); Mary Anderson (*Girl with Max*); Hazel Boyne (*Companion*); Egon Brecher (*Von Konstat*); Alec Craig (*Editor Grant of the Morning Advertiser*); Cyril Delevanti (*Newspaper Vendor*); Gilbert Emery (*Lord Palmerston in Parliament*); Lawrence Grant (*Member of Parliament*); Bobby Hale, Ernst Hausman (*Heinrich*); Holmes Herbert (*Member of Parliament*); Stuart Holmes (*Coach Attendant*); Kenneth Hunter (*Member of Parliament*); Ellis Irving (*Parliamentary Speaker*); Paul Irving (*J. Bender*); Frank Jacquet (*Mr Stein*); Edward McWade (*Chemist who Poisoned Medicine*); Frederic Mellinger (*Man*); Leonard Mudie (*Member of Parliament*); Pat O'Malley (*Labourer*); Henry Roquemore (*Otto, Directing Carew to Bank*); Frank Shannon (*Mr O'Malley, Captain of the Nova Scotian*); Grace Stafford (*Woman Dancing with Geller*); Robert Warwick (*Opposition Parliamentary Speaker*); Paul Weigel (*Professor Gauss*); Wolfgang Zilzer (*Clerk at Post Office*); Theodore von Eltz (*Actor in "Our American Cousin"*); Georgia Caine (*Mother in "Our American Cousin"*); Mildred Coles (*Augusta in "Our American Cousin"*)

Produced early May 1940

Working titles: *The Man from Fleet Street*; *Man from Fleet Street*; *A Man from Fleet Street*

[Original theatical trailer and film clips available to download from Turner Classic Movies]

"This is Your Guide to Glorious Adventure!!"
"Filmed Against the Mighty Panorama of North America's Last Frontier!"
26. *River's End* also known as *Double Identity*
    (Warner Bros., First National)

Credits: Director: Ray Enright; Producer: Bryan Foy; Associate Producer: William Jacobs; Screen Play: Barry Trivers and Bertram Millhauser; Based on the novel by James Oliver Curwood; Dialogue Director: Robert Foulk; Director of Photography: Arthur L. Todd; Music: Howard Jackson; Clifford Vaughan; Art director: Esdras Hartley; Film Editor: Clarence Kolster; Sound: Robert B. Lee; Special Effects: Edwin A. DuPar; Special Advisor: Robert Watson; Costumes: Milo Anderson; Makeup Artist: Perc Westmore; Released August 10, 1940; Drama; 69m; b/w; Production #317

Synopsis: A convicted murderer, John Keith, escapes from River's End in Alberta, Canada and heads to the frozen north of Canada. He is pursued by Sergeant Derry Conniston an inexperienced Royal Canadian Mountie, who after several months he apprehends Keith, but not before the hostile environment takes it toil on Conniston's health. As he lies dying he is convinced of Keith's innocence and he also notes their striking resemblance when Keith shaves his beard. He urges Keith to swap places and put on his Mountie uniform. This will permit him to seek out the real murderer. Two Mounties arrive and Keith impersonating Conniston tells them he is to investigate Keith's case. On his return to River's End Keith searches out his friend Andy Dijon to assist him in proving his innocence. When Keith goes to Conniston's cabin he is astonished to find Conniston's sister, Linda, waiting for him. As luck would have it she has not seen her brother for many years and does not realise any deception. Despite Keith's warning Linda falls in love with Norman Talbot the man responsible for the crime he had been convicted of. When Linda announces she is to marry Talbot, Keith confronts her with the truth regarding Talbot and his true identity. Linda distraught at the news and thinking Keith had murdered her brother informs the Mounties who arrest Keith. Linda then decides to flee with Talbot in order to elope. Meanwhile Keith's friend, Andy, obtains a confession from Talbot's associate which identifies his guilt and this gains Keith freedom to pursue the runaway couple. Keith is able to find the couple before the Mounties, and after a spectacular chase and struggle aboard a speeding wagon Talbot is caught so he can face a jury. He is convicted and sentenced to be hanged, and Linda is presented with a posthumous award for her brother by Mountie Inspector McDowell. Linda and Keith then bid farewell to Andy, who in a moment of weakness has decided to marry his fiery girlfriend, Cheeta.

Cast: Dennis Morgan (*John Keith / Sergeant Derry Conniston*); Elizabeth Earl (*Linda Conniston*); George Tobias (*Andy Dijon*); Victor Jory (*Norman Talbot*); **James Stephenson (*Inspector McDowell*)**; Steffi Duna (*Cheeta*); Edward Pawley (*Frank Crandall*); John Ridgely (*Constable Jeffers*); Frank Wilcox (*Constable Kentish*); David Bruce (*Balt*); Gilbert Emery (*Justice*); Stuart Robinson (*Sergeant Cruze*); [*Uncredited Cast List*] Glen Cavender (*Bartender in Saloon*); Stuart Holmes (*Jury Foreman*); Milton Kibbee (*Man in Saloon*); Jim Mason (*Man at Dance*); Frank Mayo (*Barn Dance Bartender*); Jack Mower (*Courtroom Spectator/Saloon Fighter*); Pat O'Malley (*The Turnkey*); Paul Panzer (*Man Attending to Horse*); Cliff Saum (*Bathing Miner*); Sailor Vincent (*Man in Saloon*); Jack Wise (*Attorney*); Tom Wilson (*Square Dance Caller*)

Remake of earlier 1930 version directed by Michael Curtiz

Production began May 13, 1940

[Original theatrical trailer available to download from Turner Classic Movies]

> "What are the Forbidden Secrets in the Letter?"
> "What is the Strange Spell that Made this Woman
> Defy the Unwritten Law of the Orient?"
> "A Lady One Minute A Tigress the Next!"

27. *The Letter*

(Warner Bros., First National)

Credits: Director: William Wyler; Executive Producer: Hal B. Wallis; Associate Producer: Robert Lord; Screen Play: Howard Koch from the novel by W. Somerset Maugham; Director of Photography: Tony Gaudio; Film Editors: George Amy and Warren Low; Art director: Carl Jules Weyl; Sound: Dolph Thomas; Gowns: Orry-Kelly; Makeup Artist: Perc Westmore; Technical Advisers: Louis Vincenot and John Villasin; Orchestral Arrangements: Hugo Friedhofer; Musical Director: Leo F. Forbstein; Music: Max Steiner; Released November 22, 1940; 95m; b/w; Production #315

Synopsis: In the middle of a still tropical night Leslie Crosbie, the wife of a British rubber planter in Malaya, shoots and kills Geoff Hammond, an intimate family acquaintance. Leslie insists she killed Hammond in self-defence to defend her honour. Her husband, Robert, does not question the veracity of her story, but family friend and attorney Howard Joyce appears to cast doubt on Leslie's story. His suspicions appear justified when Ong Chi Seng, his confidential clerk, informs him of the existence of a letter written by Leslie to Hammond on the day of his death, in which she requests him to visit her urgently. In the jail awaiting trial for murder, Howard confronts Leslie with the damning evidence. Though she confesses to Hammond's cold-blooded killing, Leslie deviously schemes against her attorney and manages to get him to consent into buying back the letter, despite the fact he may be disbarred from his profession for this action. The incriminating document is in the possession of Hammond's widow, who demands a ransom of $10,000 handed to her in person by Leslie. Once the exchange has taken place, the resulting trial is straightforward and Leslie is acquitted of all charges. After the trial Robert learns his life savings of $10,000 which he had hoped to start a fresh life by buying a rubber plantation in Sumatra has been taken to pay for the incriminating letter. Leslie agrees Robert should see the letter and he is then confronted with his wife's complicity in murder and the true duplicity of her character. Though broken in spirit Robert is willing to forgive her, but waiting to take her revenge is Hammond's widow. Mrs. Hammond and an accomplice stab Leslie to death just beyond the garden of the Crosbie bungalow. Moments later the assailants are apprehended by two passing policemen.

Cast: Bette Davis (*Leslie Crosbie*); Herbert Marshall (*Robert Crosbie*); **James Stephenson (*Howard Joyce*)**; Frieda Inescort (*Dorothy Joyce*); Gale Sondergaard (*Mrs. Hammond*); Bruce Lester (*John Withers*); Elizabeth Earl (*Adele Ainsworth*); Cecil Kellaway (*Prescott*); Sen Yung (*Ong Chi Seng*); Doris Lloyd (*Mrs. Cooper*); Willie Fung (*Chung Hi*); Tetsu Komai (*Head Boy*); [*Uncredited Cast List*] Roland Got (*Second Boy*); Otto Hahn (*Fourth Boy*); Holmes Herbert (*Bob's Friend*); Charles Irwin (*Bob's Friend*); Pete G. Katchenaro (*Third Boy*); Leonard Mudie (*Fred*); David Newell (*Geoffrey Hammond*); John Ridgely (*Driver*); Douglas Walton (*Well Wisher*); Ray Flynn; Thomas Pogue; Zita Baca; David Bruce; Lillian Kemble-Cooper; Ottola Nesmith.

Academy Award Nominations: best picture; William Wyler; Tony Gaudio; Max Steiner; Bette Davis; **James Stephenson (*best supporting actor*)**; Warren Low

Production began May 27, 1940 and finished July 19, 1940

Remake of earlier version starring Jeanne Eagels (Paramount, Jean de Limur, 1929)

[Smoking inventory = six cigarettes]

[Original theatrical trailer and film extracts available to download from Turner Classic Movies and the feature film is released on Warner DVD]

"Where He Finds Adventure You'll find Thrills!"

28. *South of Suez*

(Warner Bros., First National)

Credits: Director: Lewis Seiler; Associate Producer: William Jacobs; Screen Play: Barry Trivers, story by Sheridan Gibney; Director of Photography: Arthur Todd; Dialogue Director: Robert Foulk; Film Editor: Clarence Kolster; Art Director: Esdras Hartley; Sound: Francis J. Scheid; Gowns: Howard Shoup; Technical Adviser: Clifford Severn; Makeup Artist: Perc Westmore; Special Effects: Byron Haskin and Edwin A DuPar; Music: Frederick Hollander; Musical Director: Leo F. Forbstein; Released December 19, 1940; Drama; 85m; b/w; Production #327

Synopsis: Persuaded by his wife, Delia, Eli Snedeker, a diamond mine owner in East Africa, hires John Gamble, as mine foreman. Delia, who is infatuated with John regrets marrying Snedeker. Infuriatied when John ignores her, she throws herself at him in the presence of her husband. Snedeker reacts by angrily discharging John. The following day John intefers in Snedeker's purchase of a valuable mine owned by Roger Smythe for a derisory sum. He tears up the bill of sale and accuses his ex-employer of robbing Smythe through his native workers. John becomes Smythe's partner, and watches the natives so intently that the thefts cease. In confidence Smythe tells John that his real name is Sheffield, and that he left England under a cloud, having taken the blame for a fault committed by his younger brother.When John sees a native secreting a stone, he takes it away. It is a large, star-shaped diamond worth a fortune. The native escapes and tells Snedeker of his find. Snedeker pays a call on Smythe in John's absence and persuades him to show him the stone, which he claims is really his. Smythe and John decide to sell their diamonds and retire. Smythe plans to join his daughter, Katherine, in Alexandria. After John has taken the stones to show to a dealer in order to get an offer for the claim, Snedeker arrives to steal the big diamond. Furiously angry at not finding the diamonds he kills Smythe, and then reports finding the body and puts the blame on John. John returns to find his partner dead. Delia still seething from her rejection tells John she will swear he did commit the murder. John goes on the run and he escapes from pursuing miners by setting the veldt alight. He manages to swim out to a river steamer where he befriends a Cockney sailor. In trying to search for Katherine to give her half of the diamonds he adopts the name of Bradley and Limey the Cockney sailor. Though John Bradley succeeds in business as a famous financier he does not succeed in tracing Katherine. However, while in London he discovers Katherine is living with some distant relatives. He is able to gain access to the house and falls in love with Katherine. Though he wishes to disclose his identity he refrains from doing so when he learns Katherine wishes to bring John Gamble, the murderer of her father, to justice. Sadly he returns to London and while out walking on the embankment sees a man pushed into the water by another. John dives in and brings the man ashore. Finding the man dead he puts John Gamble's old wallet on the body and the unknown man is buried as John Gamble. John returns to Katherine and wins her love. He decides to have the star diamond cut for her wedding present. The jeweller calls in Snedeker, who is in London to supervise the cutting of the stone. He instantly recognises John and denounces him, who is arrested and sent for trial for murder. However, at the height of the trial when Snedeker's evidence seems to condemn John outright, Delia insists on taking the stand and admitting it was her husband rather than John who murdered Smythe. Mad with rage, Snedeker shoots Delia and thereby condemns himself. John and Katherine are now free to live united in happiness.

Cast: George Brent (*John Gamble*); Brenda Marshall (*Katherine Sheffield*); George Tobias (*Eli Snedeker*); **James Stephenson (*Inspector Thornton*)**; Lee Patrick (*Delia Snedeker*); Eric Blore (*Limey*); Miles Mander (*Roger Smythe*); Cecil Kellaway (*Henry Putnam*); Mary Forbes (*Mrs. Putnam*); Gilbert Emery (*Manders*); Stanley Logan (*Prosecutor*); Frederick Worlock (*Defense Counsel*); Edward Fielding (*Judge*); Leonard Mudie (*Registrar*); Crauford Kent (*Sedley*); Holmes Herbert (*Simpson*); Prince Modupe (*Lano*); [*Uncredited Cast List*] Frank Baker (*Guard*); Sidney Bracey (*Putnam's Butler*); Nathan Curry (*First Guard*); Fern Emmett (*Mrs Wemsley*); David Clyde (*Detective Sergeant in Thornton's Office*); Alec Harford (*Pidgeon*); Leyland Hodgson (*Simpson's Assistant*); Charles Irwin (*Constable at Bridge*); James Davis (*Miner*); James 'Hambone' Robinson (*Spying Native Boy*); Hassan Said (*Mechanic who is Beaten*); Ernie Stanton (*Private Detective*)

Production began September 4, 1940 and finished October 10, 1940

[Original theatrical trailer available to download from Turner Classic Movies]

"A Picture as Great as It's Title!"
29. *Flight from Destiny*
(Warner Bros., First National)

Credits: Director: Vincent Sherman; Screen Play: Barry Trivers, from the story "Trial and Error" by Anthony Berkeley; Associate Producer: Edmund Grainger; Director of Photography: James Van Trees; Art Director: Esdras Hartley; Film Editor: Thomas Richards; Sound: Charles

Lang; Gowns: Damon Giffard; Makeup Artist: Perc Westmore; Music: H[einz] Roemheld; Orchestral Arrangements: Ray Heindorf; Musical Director: Leo F. Forbstein; Released February 8, 1941; Drama; 75m; b/w; Production #331

Synopsis: Professor Henry Todhunter learns from his friend and physician, Dr. Lawrence Stevens, he has incurable heart disease and has only six months to live. Returning to the university where he lectures at the faculty of philosophy, the dean informs him that he must leave as it would be a misfortune if he should die in the classroom. At the University Club, the professor asks former students what they would do if they had only six months to live. One answer given strikes his immediate interest. It is suggested a murder should be committed according to its social usefulness, by killing a person whose crimes have evaded the law. Todhunter considers the intriguing idea with Dr. Stevens. Though the doctor disagrees stating no one should be entitled to act as judge and jury, the professor thinks that a person facing the prospect of death is able through immortality to act without self interest for the benefit of society as a whole. The professor is visited by Betty, wife of Michael Farroway, an artist who had been the professor's prize student. Anxiously, she explains that Michael is worried, but refuses to tell her why. While agreeing to talk to Michael he accompanies Betty home by taxi. Whilst in stationary traffic they see Michael being affectionately greeted by a glamorous woman outside an exclusive art gallery. Later the professor visits the art gallery, and confronts the glamorous woman who is Ketti Moret, the gallery owner. The professor goes on to meet Michael at the University club and tries to reason with him, but resenting his interference Michael rushes out and is hit and injured by a passing car. Investigating the professor finds Michael has been inveigled by Ketti Moret into forging paintings by renowned master painters. The professor investigates Ketti's life and finds she is disliked by her family and friends. She appears the perfect victim for the professor's homicide. The professor begs Michael to ask Ketti to release him from his contract and he himself asks Ketti to restore Michael's self-respect. Both requests are ignored and when Michael leaves, the professor returns and gives Ketti a last chance to perform a generous action. Refusing he shoots her dead. When he hears Michael has been arrested on suspicion of her murder, he confesses all to the district attorney. He is disbelieved, but when he induces Dr. Stevens to testify he had discussed the possibility of a "socially useful" murder, he is charged and convicted of her murder. Following Todhunter's execution, Dr. Stevens reads to Michael and Betty, now reunited, the professor's valedictory letter.

Cast: Geraldine Fitzgerald (*Betty Farroway*); Thomas Mitchell (*Professor Todhunter*); Jeffrey Lynn (*Michael Farroway*); **James Stephenson (*Dr Lawrence 'Larry' Stevens*)**; Mona Maris (*Ketti Moret*); Jonathan Hale (*District Attorney*); David Bruce (*Saunders*); Thurston Hall (*Dean Somers*); Mary Gordon (*Martha*); John Eldredge (*Peterson*); Hardie Albright (*Ferrers*); William Forrest (*Prentiss*); Weldon Heyburn (*Brooks*); DeWolf Hopper [William Hopper] (*Travin*); Alexander Lockwood (*Conway*); Frank Reicher (*Edward Kreindling*); Willie Best (*George*); Libby Taylor (*Maid*); [*Uncredited Cast List*] Sam Ash (*Desk Clerk at Club*); Peter Ashley (*Young Man*); Romaine Callender (*Psychiatrist*); Eddy Chandler (*Eddy Head Keeper*); Alden 'Stephen' Chase (*Walter Sender, Keti's Husband*); Ann Edmonds (*Nurse*); Edward Gargan (*Hotel Doorman*); Sol Gorss (*First Cab Driver*); John Hamilton (*Judge*); Robert Homans (*Jailer*); Richard Kipling (*Elderly Man*); Manart Kippen (*Detective Fereti*); Al Lloyd (*Extra Walking Out of Hotel*); Inez Palange (*Mrs Moraciagos, Keti's Mother*); Paul Panzer (*Jim's Café Waiter*); Alexis Smith (*Young Woman*); Edwin Stanley (*Doctor*); Rolla Stewart (*Ketti's Daughter*); Rafael Storm (*Monsieur Lascaut, Art Gallery Clerk*); Elliott Sullivan (*Second Cab Driver in Accident*)

Production began September 30, 1940 and finished early November 1940

[Original theatrical trailer available to download from Turner Classic Movies]

"A Citadel of Mystery Hiding its Dark Secrets from the World!"
30. *Shining Victory*
(Warner Bros., First National)

Credits: Director: Irving Rapper; Executive Producer: Hal B. Wallis; Associate Producer: Robert Lord; Screen Play: Howard Koch and Anne Froelick; Based on the play "Jupiter Laughs" by A.J. Cronin; Director of Photography: James Wong Howe; Film Editor: Warren Low; Art Director: Carl Jules Weyl: Sound: Dolph Thomas: Gowns: Howard Shoup: Makeup Artist: Perc Westmore; Technical Adviser: Dr. George C. McDaniel; Orchestral Arrangements: Hugo Friedhofer; Musical Director: Leo F. Forbstein; Music: Max Steiner; Released June 7, 1941; Drama; 80m; b/w; Production #345

Synopsis: In 1935 Dr. Paul Venner, a medical scientist in Budapest, is embittered when Professor Hermann von Reiter, head of an important hospital in the Hungarian capital, claims his pioneering discoveries in the field of psycho-biology as his own. Furthermore, Venner is forced from the country and all his research materials are confiscated. Later, in London,

Venner finds his personal funds have been blocked and he is unable to draw money out of his account in Hungary. Down on his luck Venner encounters his old teacher, Dr. Drewett, who is a psychiatrist at a private sanitarium, Hopewell Towers, in Scotland. At Drewett's suggestion he accepts a modest paid position at the sanitarium. Though he dislikes the head of the institute, Dr. Blake, he is pleased when told his time will be spent between clinical care of patients and research work. When Venner requests an assistant he is annoyed that a young inexperienced woman, Dr. Mary Murray, is assigned the position. Though aware of his hostility she works hard to turn Venner's opinion around to her favour. Dr. Murray arouses feelings of jealousy in Miss Leeming, Dr. Blake's secretary, who harbours repressed emotions for Dr. Venner. Venner works Mary very hard and her positive attitude and quiet efficiency wins over his respect for her. When she informs him she is to leave for China to become a medical missionary he realises he has fallen in love with her. She reciprocates his feelings of love and by way of celebration they pick an engagement ring and then go on a picnic. When they return they learn a patient has died. Venner is determined to arrange a hasty post-morten in order to prove his new method of neurological treatment. Though the results validate his research theories, Venner's autopsy has broken the coroner's laws of Scotland, and places him in a precarious position something Dr. Blake, aware of the reputational damage to the sanatorium, is at pains to point out. Miss Leeming hoping to take advantage of his predicament tells Venner to give up Mary, but Venner shuns her remarks and declares she is mentally unstable. When Venner later leaves his laboratory Miss Leeming starts a fire in the room, and then tries to prevent Mary from entering. Suspicious Mary enters the room now engulfed in flames and manages to retrieve the invaluable research notes in a drawer which she then throws out of the window onto the ground safely below. Unfortunately she is unable to save herself, and she perishes in the fire. Some time later Venner's experiments are publicised in medical journals and are acclaimed, but while Dr. Blake and other doctors at Hopewell Towers bask in the glory of publicity, Dr. Venner rejects the numerous offers of prestigious positons. Instead he decides to pack for China and take up the work Dr. Mary Murray had originally intended.

Cast: **James Stephenson** (*Dr Paul Venner*); Geraldine Fitzgerald (*Dr Mary Murray*); Donald Crisp (*Dr Drewett*); Barbara O'Neil (*Miss Leeming*); Montagu Love (*Dr Blake*); Sig Ruman (*Professor Hermann von Reiter*); George P. Huntley Jr. (*Dr Thornton*); Richard Ainley (*Dr Hale*); Bruce Lester (*Dr Bentley*); Leonard Mudie (*Foster*), Doris Lloyd (*Mrs Foster*), Frank Reicher (*Dr Esterhazy*); Hermine Sterler (*Miss*

Hoffman); Billy Bevan (*Chivers*); Clara Verdera (*Miss Dennis*); Crauford Kent (*Dr Corliss*); [*Uncredited Cast List*] Alec Craig (*Shopkeeper*); Rudolf Anders (*First Police Officer*); Bette Davis (*Nurse, Allegedly*); Paul Panzer (*Mailman*); Mary Taylor (*Mrs Kent, a Patient*); Hans Von Morhart (*Second Police Officer*); Ian Wolfe (*Mr Carew, a Banker*); Wolfgang Zilzer (*Subordinate*); Tempe Piggott (*Miss Weatherby, a Patient*); Hilda Plowright (*Nurse*); Ottola Nesmith (*Nurse*); Dickie Leon (*Boy at Jewellers*); Carlotta Jelm (*Girl at Jewelers*); Helena Grant (*Jenny, a Patient*); Barlowe Borland (*Old Patient Drawing*); Louise Brien (*Nurse*); Bunny Beatty (*Nancy Hormiston*)

Working title: *Winged Victory*

[Smoking inventory = five cigarettes]

Production began late December 1940 and finished late January 1941

[Original theatrical trailer available to download from Turner Classic Movies]

"First Big Story of the RAF's "Foreign Legion"!"
31. *International Squadron*
(Warner Bros., First National)

Credits: Director: Lewis Seiler (and Lothar Mendes) [*Uncredited*]; Associate Producer: Edmund Grainger; Screen Play: Barry Trivers and Kenneth Gamet; Based on a Play "Ceiling Zero" by Frank Wead; Dialogue Director: Harold Winston: Directors of Photography: Ted McCord and James Van Trees; Music: William Lava; Film Editor: Frank Magee; Art Director: Esdras Hartley; Sound: Robert B. Lee; Special Effects: Robert Burks; Gowns: Howard Shoup; Makeup Artist: Perc Westmore; Technical Adviser: Byron F. Kennerly; Released October 11, 1941; War/Aviation; Drama; 85m; b/w; Production #360

Synopsis: Jimmy Grant a reckless aviation test pilot makes a perfect landing with a new prototype plane following gruelling testing. His employer, Saunders, requests he fly the first Saunders bomber to England. Initially he refuses, but when he is threatened with breach of contract he changes his mind. Jimmy takes off with his mechanic, Omaha. As he nears the airport near London Wing Commander Severn radios him to bale out, as thick fog surrounds the landing field. Jimmy orders Omaha to jump, but decides to take his chances and makes a successful landing. He is greeted by two old friends Charles Wyatt and Rog Wilkins. Wyatt is squadron leader of the flight in which Wilkins is a lieutenant. After meeting the other members of the squadron, Jimmy spots a pretty girl, and bets Wyatt he'll take her to dinner. This is Jeanette Benoit, a W.A.A.F. and sweetheart of

Michele Edme. He soon wins his bet and as Jeanette and Jimmy leave the restaurant an air raid begins and a little girl is injured. Jeanette and Jimmy rush her to hospital, but she dies on the way. Jimmy is deeply touched and decides to enlist in the International Squadron. Despite all his vast experience Jimmy has first to go back to flying school. When he officially graduates Wyatt and Wilkins give him a party. Wyatt's wife, Mary, and Wilkins's wife, Connie, attend the celebration. Jimmy once jilted Mary and though she has forgiven him, she keeps their old friendship secret from Wyatt. On his first mission with the squadron Jimmy breaks formation and attacks a German bomber which he successfully brings down. Expecting nothing but praise, he is told that as a result of his actions Lt. Torrence was shot down. Wyatt pleads to senior commanders that Jimmy be given another chance and assumes responsibility for him. Out on the spree one night, Jimmy phones Wilkins, who has just come off duty in sore need for sleep to take his early morning patrol. Wilkins makes a crash landing and later dies in hospital. Connie bitterly reproaches Jimmy for his death and he requests a transfer. Unable to bear meeting Connie, Jimmy realises Jeanette is in love with him. Wyatt manages to persuade Jimmy not to quit. Jimmy avoids Jeanette and when they finally meet, tells her that Michele is the man for her. Wyatt, now promoted to Flight Commander, calls the Squadron to his office. A munitions dump on the French coast must be destroyed, and it's a one man job. All identification tags are put in a bag and it is Michele's name which is drawn. Jimmy wishes him luck and shakes his hand, but as he does so knocks Michele unconscious and takes his place. Jimmy successfully completes his bombing mission, but as he returns home he is caught by an enemy patrol. Back at base Wyatt leads the tribute to Jimmy by honouring him with a toast in the bar of the officer's mess.

Cast: Ronald Reagan (*Jimmy Grant*); Olympe Bradna (*Jeanette*); **James Stephenson (*Squadron Leader Charles Wyatt*)**; William Lundigan (*Lt. Rog Wilkins*); Joan Perry (*Connie*); Reginald Denny (*Wing Commander Severn*); Cliff Edwards ("*Omaha*" *McGrath*); Julie Bishop (*Mary*); Michael Ames [Tod Andrews] (*Michele Edme*); John Ridgely (*Lt. Bill Torrence*); Charles Irwin (*Biddle*); Addison Richards (*Chief Engineer*); Selmer Jackson (*Saunders*); Holmes Herbert (*Sir Basil Wryxton*); Crauford Kent (*Major Fresney*); [*Uncredited Cast List*] Lowden Adams (*Doctor*); Jean Ames (*Blonde*); Frank Baker (*Warden*); Sonny Bupp (*Boy*); Shirley Coates (*Girl*); Eddie Conrad (*Greek Waiter*); Helmut Dantine (*Flyer*); Leslie Denison (*Ground Chief*); Ann Edmonds (*French Girl*); Frank Faylen (*Process Server*); Gerald Gavin (*Officer*); Frederick Giermann (*German*); Brenda Henderson (*Child*); Leyland Hodgson (*Warden*);

William Hopper (*Radio Operator*); Hugh Huntley (*Instructor*); Knud Kreuger (*Flyer*); Martin Lamont (*Officer*); Ernest Lennart (*Flyer*); Harry Lewis (*Pilot*); Doris Lloyd (*Mother*); John Meredith (*Flyer*); Ivan Molnar (*Flyer*); Ottola Nesmith (*Mrs Harris*); Pat O'Hara (*Instructor*); Henry Rowland (*German*); Tom Skinner (*Officer*); Tom Stevenson (*Officer*); Cyril Thornton (*Instructor*); David Thursby (*Instructor*); Richard Travis (*Radio Operator*); Marjorie Whatley (*Girl*)

Remake of *Ceiling Zero* (Warner Bros., Howard Hawks, 1935)

Working Title: *Flight Patrol*

[Smoking inventory = five cigarettes]

Production began late March 1941 and finished June 5, 194

MISCELLANEOUS FILMS

1. *Breakdowns of 1940*

Credits: Miscellaneous comedy short; 1 Reel; b/w

Cast: **James Stephenson**, Ronald Reagan

Synopsis: Annual studio bloopers reel compilation. Stephenson is shown in a brief scene taken from *Murder in the Air*. Ronald Reagan delivers his lines to camera and fluffs his delivery. Stephenson sits in armchair back to the camera. His reaction shot is not shown as we move along to another out-take.

[Available as supplementary extra on *City for Conquest* in the Tough Guys Box Set Warner DVD]

2. *Breakdowns of 1941*

Credits: Miscellaneous comedy short; 1 Reel b/w

Cast: **James Stephenson**, Barbara O'Neil

Synopsis: Among this annual compilation of studio bloopers is a studio tribute to the late star. A short extract shows a scene from *Shining Victory*. After feeding his lines to Barbara O'Neil she doesn't respond whereupon Stephenson, back to camera, reacts in a brief fit of laughter.

[Available as supplementary extra on disc two of *The Maltese Falcon* (1941) on Warner DVD]

APPENDIX V

LIST OF PERFORMERS APPEARING IN PRODUCTIONS FEATURING JAMES STEPHENSON

The following is an alphabetical record of principal performers who appeared in amateur and professional stage productions, radio and films in Britain and Hollywood featuring James Stephenson. Where known, details of dates of birth and death, and full or alternate names are given.

1. Richard Ainley (1910-1967) [Warners Burbank] x 1 *Shining Victory* (1941)

2. Norman Ainsley (1881-1948) [Warners Burbank] x 1 *A Dispatch from Reuter's* (1940)

3. Muriel Aked (1887-1955) [Liverpool Playhouse] x 1 *Fun While It Lasts* (1933)

4. Eddie Albert (1906-2005) [Edward Albert Heimberger] [Warners Burbank] x 1 *A Dispatch from Reuter's* (1940)

5. Hardie Albright (1903-1975) [Warners Burbank] x 1 *Flight from Destiny* (1941)

6. Erville Alderson (1882-1957) [Warners Burbank] x 1 *The Monroe Doctrine* (1939)

7. Jack Allen (1907-1995) [Liverpool Playhouse and BBC Radio] x 15 *Hollywood Holiday* (1932); *Lean Harvest* (1932); *The Long Christmas*

Dinner (1932); *Lady in Waiting* (1932); *The Roundabout* (1932); *What Happened to George* (1932); *Inquest* (1933); *Don't Tell England* (1933); *Mourning Becomes Electra* [Overseas League, Liverpool] (1933); *The Crime at Blossoms* (1933); *The Kingdom of God* (1933); *Laying the Devil* (1933); *The Queen's Husband* (1933); *Never Come Back* (1933); *Death of a First Mate* (1937) [BBC Radio]

8. Miss Lily Allen [Mrs Lily Phillips] [Burnley Amateur Soprano Singer and Pianist] x 8 *Operatic Evening* [Burnley Clef Club, Mechanics Institute] (1920); *Savitri* [Burnley Clef Club, Mechanics Institute] (1924); *Madam Butterfly* [Burnley Clef Club, Mechanics Institute] (1925); *Song Recital* [Tudor Gardens, Deansgate, Manchester] (1926); *A Persian Garden* [Burnley Clef Club, Mechanics Institute] (1927); *Don Giovanni* [Burnley Clef Club, Mechanics Institute] (1928); *Don Giovanni* [Burnley Clef Club, Mechanics Institute] (1929); *Grand Concert* [St Catherine's Church, Burnley] (1929)

9. Murray Alper (1904-1984) [Warners Burbank] x 1 *King of the Underworld* (1939)

10. Glen Alyn (1913-?) [Glenora Pointing] [Warners Teddington] x 4 *Perfect Crime* (1937); *You Live and Learn* (1938); *The Dark Stairway* (1938); *It's in the Blood* (1938)

11. Rudolf Anders (1895-1987) [also known as Robert O. Davis / Rudolph F. Amendt] [Warners Burbank] x 3 *Confessions of a Nazi Spy* (1939); *Espionage Agent* (1939); *Shining Victory* (1941)

12. Herbert Anderson (1917-1994) [Warners Burbank] x 2 *Calling Philo Vance* (1940); *The Sea Hawk* (1940)

13. Mary Anderson (1920-) [Bebe Anderson] [Warners Burbank] x 2 *The Sea Hawk* (1940); *A Dispatch from Reuter's* (1940)

14. Harry [Fleetwood] Andrews (1911-1989) [Liverpool Playhouse and Winter Gardens, New Brighton] x 25 *The Long Christmas Dinner* (1932); *Lady In Waiting* (1932); *What Happened to George* (1932) *Inquest* (1933); *The Crime at Blossoms* (1933); *Another Language* (1933); *The Kingdom of God* (1933); *The Queen's Husband* (1933); *Never Come Back* (1933); *Inquest* [Winter Gardens, New Brighton] (1933); *The Queen's Husband* [Winter Gardens, New Brighton] (1933); *Winsome Winnie* (1933); *The*

Road to Rome (1933); *The Lake* (1933); *The Cathedral* (1933); *Shall We Join the Ladies?* (1933); *Is Life Worth Living?* (1933); *Fun While It Lasts* (1933); *The Rose Without a Thorn* (1934); *Smoke Screen* (1934); *Cabbages and Kings* (1934); *Gallows Glorious* (1934); *Macbeth* (1934); *Lover's Leap* (1934); *The Cathedral* [Winter Gardens, New Brighton] (1934)

15. Tod Andrews (1914-1972) [also known as Michael Ames] [Warners Burbank] x 1 *International Squadron* (1941)

16. William Armstrong (1887-1952) [BBC Radio] x 1 *Round the Northern Repertories: The Liverpool Playhouse* (1935)

17. Hooper Atchley (1887-1943) [Republic Studios] x 1 *Wolf of New York* (1940)

18. Marion Atkinson [Burnley Amateur] x 1 *The School for Scandal* [Clef Club, Mechanics Institute] (1930)

19. Marie Ault (1870-1951) [Mary Cragg] [Liverpool Playhouse] x 2 *Cabbages and Kings* (1934); *Gallows Glorious* (1934)

20. Anthony Averill (1911-1982) [Alexander Averill] [Warners Burbank] x 3 *When Were You Born* (1938); *Heart of the North* (1938); *Secret Service of the Air* (1939)

21. Arthur Aylesworth (1883-1946) [Warners Burbank and Paramount Studios] x 2 *King of the Underworld* (1939); *Beau Geste* (1939)

22. Buddy Baer (1915-1986) [Jacob Henry Baer] [Warners Teddington] x 1 *Take It From Me* (1938)

23. Raymond Bailey (1904-1980) [Warners Burbank] x 2 *Secret Service of the Air* (1939); *The Adventures of Jane Arden* (1939)

24. Sherwood Bailey (1923-1987) [Warners Burbank] x 2 *King of the Underworld* (1939); *Confessions of a Nazi Spy* (1939)

25. Fay [Okell] Bainter (1893-1968) [Fay Venable] [Warners Burbank] x 1 *White Banners* (1938)

26. Frank Baker (1892-1980) [Warners Burbank] x 2 *South of Suez* (1940); *International Squadron* (1941)

27. George Bancroft (1882-1956) [Warners Burbank] x 1 *Espionage Agent* (1939)

28. Harry Barris (1905-1962) [Warners Burbank] x 1 *Cowboy from Brooklyn* (1938)

29. Fern Barry (1909-1981) [Warners Burbank] x 1 *Espionage Agent* (1939)

30. Charles Barton (1902-1981) [Paramount Studios] x 1 *Beau Geste* (1939)

31. Dora Barton (1884-1966) [The Queens, London and BBC Radio] x 2 *Post Road* (1937); *The Children's Hour: Jack and the Beanstalk* (1937)

32. Albert Bassermann (1867-1952) [Warners Burbank] x 1 *A Dispatch from Reuter's* (1940)

33. Granville Bates (1882-1940) [Warners Burbank] x 2 *Cowboy from Brooklyn* (1938); *Espionage Agent* (1939)

34. Jane Baxter (1909-1996) [Feodora Forde] [Liverpool Playhouse and BBC Radio] x 4 *Youth at the Helm* (1935); *Barnet's Folly* (1935); *Round the Northern Repertories: The Liverpool Playhouse* (1935) [BBC Radio]; *Cornelius* (1935)

35. Stewart Baxter [Liverpool Playhouse and Winter Gardens, New Brighton] x 9 *Sheppey* (1934); *Libel* (1935); *Hamlet* (1935); *Libel* [Winter Gardens, New Brighton] (1935); *Cornelius* (1935); *Circus Boy* (1935); *Richard of Bordeaux* (1936); *Storm in a Teacup* (1936); *Twelfth Night* (1936)

36. Sam Beazley (1916-) [Liverpool Playhouse and Winter Gardens, New Brighton] x 4 *Gallows Glorious* (1934); *Macbeth* (1934); *The Cathedral* [Winter Gardens, New Brighton] (1934); *The Lake* [Winter Gardens, New Brighton] (1934)

37. Ralph [Rexford] Bellamy (1904-1991) [Warners Burbank] x 1 *Boy Meets Girl* (1938)

38. Guy Bellis (1886-1980) [Warners Burbank] x 1 *The Private Lives of Elizabeth and Essex* (1939)

39. Brooks Benedict (1896-1968) [Warners Burbank] x 3 *Cowboy from Brooklyn* (1938); *The Letter* (1940); *South of Suez* (1940)

40. Edna Best (1900-1974) [Warners Burbank] x 1 *A Dispatch from Reuter's* (1940)

41. Willie Best (1916-1962) [also known as "Sleep 'n' Eat"] [Warners Burbank] x 1 *Flight from Destiny* (1941)

42. Billy Bevan (1887-1957) [William Bevan Harris] [Warners Burbank] x 1 *Shining Victory* (1941)

43. Clem Bevans (1879-1963) [Warners Burbank] x 1 *King of the Underworld* (1939)

44. Julie Bishop (1914-2001) [Jacqueline Brown also known as Diane Duval and Jacqueline Wells] [Warners Burbank] x 1 *International Squadron* (1941)

45. Whit Bissell (1909-1996) [Whitner Nutting Bissell] [Warners Burbank] x 1 *The Sea Hawk* (1940)

46. Sidney Blackmer (1895-1973) [Warners Burbank] x 1 *The Monroe Doctrine* (1939)

47. Brian Blades (1919-2003) [Liverpool Playhouse] x 5 *Lean Harvest* (1932); *The Kingdom of God* (1933); *Ferry Inn* (1935); *Hamlet* (1935); *Circus Boy* (1935)

48. Eric Blore (1887-1959) [Warners Burbank] x 1 *South of Suez* (1940)

49. Bob the Wonder Dog [Warners Teddington] x 1 *Mr. Satan* (1938)

50. Humphrey [DeForest] Bogart (1899-1957) [Warners Burbank] x 1 *King of the Underworld* (1939)

51. Curt [Boas] Bois [1901-1991] [Warners Burbank] x 1 *Boy Meets Girl* (1938)

52. May Boley (1881-1963) [Warners Burbank] x 1 *Cowboy from Brooklyn* (1938)

53. Richard Bond [Warners Burbank] x 4 *Devil's Island* (1938); *King of the Underworld* (1939); *Torchy Blane in Chinatown* (1939); *Secret Service of the Air* (1939)

54. Ward Bond (1903-1960) [Wardell E. Bond] [Warners Burbank] x 1 *Confessions of a Nazi Spy* (1939)

55. Barlowe Borland (1877-1948) [Warners Burbank] x 2 *We Are Not Alone* (1939); *Shining Victory* (1941)

56. Wade Boteler (1888-1943) [Warners Burbank] x 1 *The Adventures of Jane Arden* (1939)

57. Chili Bouchier (1909-1999) [Dorothy Irene Boucher] [Warners Teddington] x 2 *Mr. Satan* (1938); *The Dark Stairway* (1938)

58. Walter Guy [Robert] Boys OBE (1890-1961) [Burnley Amateur, Building Society Financier] x 6 *Merchant of Venice Readings* [1] [Burnley Drama Guild, Burnley Central Library] (1931); *Merchant of Venice Readings* [2] [Burnley Drama Guild, Burnley Central Library] (1931); *Annajanska* [Free Trade Hall, Manchester] (1931); *"Pompey" the Great* [Burnley Drama Guild, Burnley Central Library] (1931); *The Plays of George Bernard Shaw* [Burnley Rotary Club, Café Royal] (1931); *Scenes from A Midsummer Night's Dream* [English Folk Festival, Quernmore Park, Lancaster] (1932)

59. Sidney Bracey (1887-1942) [Warners Burbank] x 8 *When Were You Born* (1938); *Devil's Island* (1938); *King of the Underworld* (1939); *Secret Service of the Air* (1939); *On Trial* (1939); *The Old Maid* (1939); *Espionage Agent* (1939); *South of Suez* (1940)

60. Leslie Bradley (1907-1974) [The Queens, London] x 1 *Post Road* (1937)

61. Olympe Bradna (1920-2012) [Antoinette Olympe Bradna Wilhoit] [Warners Burbank] x 1 *International Squadron* (1941)

62. Henry Brandon (1912-1990) [Heinrich von Kleinbach] [Paramount Studios] x 1 *Beau Geste* (1939)

63. Egon Brecher (1880-1946) [Warners Burbank] x 7 *Devil's Island* (1938); *Confessions of a Nazi Spy* (1939); *Sons of Liberty* (1939); *Espionage Agent* (1939); *We Are Not Alone* (1939); *Calling Philo Vance* (1940); *A Dispatch from Reuter's* (1940)

64. George Brent (1899-1979) [George Brendan Nolan] [Warners Burbank] x

2 *The Old Maid* (1939); *South of Suez* (1940)

65. Al Bridge (1891-1957) [Warners Burbank] x 2 *Devil's Island* (1938); *Sons of Liberty* (1939)

66. Harry Bristow [Liverpool Playhouse] x 6 *Hollywood Holiday* (1932); *The Road to Rome* (1933); *Gallows Glorious* (1934); *Macbeth* (1934); *The Lake* (1934); *Counsellor-at-Law* (1934)

67. Sheila Bromley (1911-2003) [Warners Burbank] x 1 *Calling Philo Vance* (1940)

68. Lesley Brook (1917-2009) [Lesley Learoyd / Lesley Spencer] [Warners Teddington] x 3 *The Man Who Made Diamonds* (1937); *The Dark Stairway* (1938); *It's in the Blood* (1938)

69. Rand Brooks (1918-2003) [Warners Burbank] x 1 *The Old Maid* (1939)

70. A[rthur] Rought Brooks (1879-1947) [Burnley Amateur, Journalist / Editor of the *Burnley News*] x 1 *Merchant of Venice Readings* [2] [Burnley Drama Guild, Burnley Central Library] (1931)

71. Edward [S.] Brophy (1895-1960) [Warners Burbank] x 1 *Calling Philo Vance* (1940)

72. Miss Florence Broughton [Burnley Amateur] x 7 *The School for Scandal* [Clef Club, Mechanics Institute] (1930); *The Beaux' Stratagem* [Burnley Drama Guild, Victoria Theatre] (1930); *Merchant of Venice Readings* [1] [Burnley Drama Guild, Burnley Central Library] (1931); *Merchant of Venice Readings* [2] [Burnley Drama Guild, Burnley Central Library] (1931); *Oedipus the King* [Burnley Drama Guild, Burnley Central Library] (1931); *Pompey the Great* [Burnley Drama Guild, Burnley Central Library] (1931); *Scenes from a Midsummer Night's Dream* [English Folk Festival, "Four Oaks," Higher Reedley] (1931)

73. Charles D. Brown (1887-1948) [Republic Studios] x 1 *Wolf of New York* (1940)

74. David Bruce (1914-1976) [Marden McBroom] [Warners Burbank] x 5 *The Sea Hawk* (1940); *River's End* (1940); *A Dispatch from Reuter's* (1940); *The Letter* (1940); *Flight from Destiny* (1941)

75. Edgar K. Bruce (1893-1971) [The Garrick, London] x 1 *Storm in a Teacup* (1936)

76. [William] Nigel [Ernle] Bruce (1895-1953) [Warners Burbank] x 1 *A Dispatch from Reuter's* (1940)

77. Jane Bryan (1918-2009) [Jane O'Brien / Jane Dart] [Warners Burbank] x 2 *The Old Maid* (1939); *We Are Not Alone* (1939)

78. [William] Edgar Buchanan (1903-1979) [Warners Burbank] x 1 *The Sea Hawk* (1940)

79. Tommy Bupp (1924-1983) [Warners Burbank] x 3 *Nancy Drew, Detective* (1938); *Confessions of a Nazi Spy* (1939); *International Squadron* (1941)

80. James Burke (1886-1968) [Paramount Studios] x 1 *Beau Geste* (1939)

81. Harry Burns (1885-1948) [Warners Burbank] x 1 *Calling Philo Vance* (1940)

82. Ena Burrill (c.1908-1999) [Ena Childs] [Liverpool Playhouse and Winter Gardens, New Brighton] x 34 *Hollywood Holiday* (1932); *Lean Harvest* (1932); *The Long Christmas Dinner* (1932); *The Roundabout* (1933); *Mourning Becomes Electra* [Overseas League, Liverpool] (1933); *The Crime at Blossoms* (1933); *Another Language* (1933); *The Kingdom of God* (1933); *Laying the Devil* (1933); *Never Come Back* (1933); *Inquest* [Winter Gardens, New Brighton] (1933); *The Queen's Husband* [Winter Gardens, New Brighton] (1933); *Art and Mrs. Bottle* [Winter Gardens, New Brighton] (1933); *Anthony and Anna* [Winter Gardens, New Brighton] (1933); *The Road to Rome* (1933); *Britannia of Billingsgate* (1933); *The Lake* (1933); *Shall We Join the Ladies?* (1933); *Fun While It Lasts* (1933); *Dangerous Corner* (1934); *The Rose Without a Thorn* (1934); *Smoke Screen* (1934); *Gallows Glorious* (1934); *Macbeth* (1934); *Lovers' Leap* (1934); *The Cathedral* [Winter Gardens, New Brighton] (1934); *The Lake* [Winter Gardens, New Brighton] (1934); *Smoke Screen* [Winter Gardens, New Brighton] (1934); *Britannia of Billingsgate* [Winter Gardens, New Brighton] (1934); *The Distaff Side* (1934); *A Sleeping Clergyman* (1934); *Something In the City* (1934); *Sheppey* (1934); *Biography* (1935)

83. Benny Burt (1900-1980) [Benny Sachs] [Warners Burbank] x 1 *The Adventures of Jane Arden* (1939)

84. Frederick Burton (1871-1957) [Warners Burbank] x 2 *Confessions of a Nazi Spy* (1939); *The Old Maid* (1939)

85. [Annie] Mae Busch (1891-1946) [Warners Burbank] x 1 *Nancy Drew Detective* (1938)

86. Jessie Busley (1869-1950) [Warners Burbank] x 1 *King of the Underworld* (1939)

87. James Cagney (1899-1986) [James Francis Cagney Jr] [Warners Burbank] x 1 *Boy Meets Girl* (1938)

88. Wilfrid Caithness (1890-1954) [Warners Teddington] x 1 *Perfect Crime* (1937)

89. Alfredo Campoli (1906-1991) [Welwyn Studios] x 1 *Dangerous Fingers* (1938)

90. Candy Candido (1913-1999) [Jonathan Joseph Candido] [Warners Burbank] x 1 *Cowboy from Brooklyn* (1938)

91. Yakima Canutt (1895-1986) [Enos Edward Canutt] [Warners Burbank] x 1 *Calling Philo Vance* (1940)

92. Richard Carey [Liverpool Playhouse] x 4 *Hollywood Holiday* (1932); *Lean Harvest* (1932); *The Long Christmas Dinner* (1932); *Lady in Waiting* (1932)

93. John Carol (1910-1968) [Warners Teddington] x 3 *Perfect Crime* (1937); *You Live and Learn* (1938); *The Dark Stairway* (1938)

94. Nat Carr (1886-1944) [Warners Burbank] x 5 *King of the Underworld* (1939); *Secret Service of the Air* (1939); *The Adventures of Jane Arden* (1939); *On Trial* (1939); *Calling Philo Vance* (1940)

95. Leo G[ratten]. Carroll (1886-1972) [Warners Burbank] x 1 *The Private Lives of Elizabeth and Essex* (1939)

96. Bruce Carruthers (1901-1953) [Harold Bruce Callbeck Carruthers] [Warners Burbank] x 1 *Heart of the North* (1938)

97. Maurice Cass (1884-1954) [Warners Burbank] x 1 *When Were You Born* (1938)

98. Christopher Casson (1912-1996) [Liverpool Playhouse] x 10 *After the Event* (1933); *The Cathedral* (1933); *Is Life Worth Living?* (1933); *Fun While It Lasts* (1933); *Winsome Winnie* (1933); *The Road to Rome* (1933); *The Rose Without a Thorn* (1934); *Smoke Screen* (1934); *Cabbages and Kings* (1934); *Gallows Glorious* (1934)

99. Hobart Cavanaugh (1886-1950) [Warners Burbank] x 2 *Cowboy from Brooklyn* (1938); *The Adventures of Jane Arden* (1939)

100. Glen Cavender (1883-1962) [Warners Burbank] x 9 *Heart of the North* (1938); *Devil's Island* (1938); *King of the Underworld* (1939); *Secret Service of the Air* (1939); *The Adventures of Jane Arden* (1939); *Confessions of a Nazi Spy* (1939); *Espionage Agent* (1939); *The Monroe Doctrine* (1939); *River's End* (1940)

101. Dr. Hitchon Chadwick (1892-1958) [Burnley Amateur, General Medical Practitioner] x 4 *The Best People* [The Burnley Players, Victoria Theatre] (1930); *It Pays to Advertise* [The Burnley Players, Victoria Theatre] (1930); *Plunder* [The Burnley Players, Victoria Theatre] (1931); *Thark* [The Burnley Players, Victoria Theatre] (1932)

102. Eddy Chandler (1894-1948) [Warners Burbank] x 4 *Cowboy from Brooklyn* (1938); *Torchy Blane in Chinatown* (1939); *Secret Service of the Air* (1939); *Flight from Destiny* (1941)

103. George Chandler (1898-1985) [Paramount Studios] x 1 *Beau Geste* (1939)

104. Lane Chandler (1899-1972) [Warners Burbank] x 3 *Heart of the North* (1938); *Secret Service of the Air* (1939); *Murder in the Air* (1940)

105. Janet Chapman (1932-) [Warners Burbank] x 2 *Heart of the North* (1938); *On Trial* (1939)

106. Lola Cheaney [Warners Burbank] x 4 *Boy Meets Girl* (1938); *Espionage Agent* (1939); *On Trial* (1939); *Calling Philo Vance* (1940)

107. Cliff Clark (1889-1953) [Warners Burbank] x 2 *Murder in the Air* (1940); *A Dispatch from Reuter's* (1940)

108. Davison Clark (1881-1972) [Warners Burbank] x 4 *Devil's Island* (1938*); King of the Underworld* (1939); *Secret Service of the Air* (1939); *The Adventures of Jane Arden* (1939)

109. D[ouglas].A. Clarke-Smith (1888-1959) [BBC Radio and Welwyn Studios] x 2 *Money with Menaces* (1937); *Dangerous Fingers* (1938)

110. Peter Claughton [Liverpool Playhouse] x 10 *The Rose Without a Thorn* (1934); *Cabbages and Kings* (1934); *Gallows Glorious* (1934); *Fun While It Lasts* (1934); *Macbeth* (1934); *Sheppey* (1934); *Counsellor-at-Law* (1934); *Ferry Inn* (1934); *Hamlet* (1935); *The Matriarch* (1935)

111. Eric Clavering (1901-1989) [Warners Teddington] x 1 *Mr. Satan* (1937)

112. Julian Clay [Liverpool Playhouse] x 10 *Hollywood Holiday* (1932); *Lean Harvest* (1932); *Lady in Waiting* (1932); *What Happened to George* (1932); *Don't Tell England* (1933); *The Crime at Blossoms* (1933); *The Kingdom of God* (1933); *Laying the Devil* (1933); *The Queen's Husband* (1933); *Never Come Back* (1933)

113. Richard Clayton [Warners Burbank] x 2 *Murder in the Air* (1940); *South of Suez* (1940)

114. Joseph William Cody [Paramount Studios] x 1 *Beau Geste* (1939)

115. Mary Cole (1913-1975) [Warners Teddington] x 1 *Mr. Satan* (1937)

116. James Collinge (1888-1965) [Burnley Amateur] [Wholesale Purveyor of Cooked Meats] x 1 *The School for Scandal* [Clef Club, Mechanics Institute] (1930)

117. Jimmy Conlin (1884-1962) [Warners Burbank] x 1 *Calling Philo Vance* (1940)

118. Eddie Conrad (1891-1941) [Warmers Burbank] x 3 *Boy Meets Girl* (1938); *The Adventures of Jane Arden* (1939); *International Squadron* (1941)

119. John Conte (1915-2006) [Warners Burbank] x 1 *Confessions of a Nazi Spy* (1939)

120. Morgan Conway (1903-1981) [Warners Burbank] x 1 *Secret Service of the Air* (1939)

121. Tom Conway (1904-1967) [Thomas Charles Sanders] [BBC Radio] x 1
     The Blue Danube (1937)

122. Clyde [Wilford] Cook (1891-1984) [Republic Studios and Warners
     Burbank] x 2 *Wolf of New York* (1940); *The Sea Hawk* (1940)

123. Joan Cooke [Liverpool Playhouse] x 3 *The Lake* (1933); *The Rose Without
     a Thorn* (1934); *Cabbages and Kings* (1934)

124. Gary Cooper (1901-1961) [Frank James Cooper] [Paramount Studios] x
     1 *Beau Geste* (1939)

125. Jackie Cooper (1922-2011) [John Cooper Jnr.] [Warners Burbank] x 1
     White Banners (1938)

126. Lillian Kemble Cooper (1892-1977) [Warners Burbank] x 2 *We Are Not
     Alone* (1939); *The Letter* (1940)

127. Miss Florence Copeland [Burnley Amateur] x 6 *The Beaux' Stratagem*
     [Burnley Drama Guild, Victoria Theatre] (December 1930); *Man and
     Superman* [Burnley Drama Guild, Victoria Theatre] (1930); *Oedipus, the
     King* [Burnley Drama Guild, Burnley Central Library] (1931); *Scenes
     from A Midsummer Night's Dream* [English Folk Festival, "Four Oaks"
     Higher Reedley] (1931); *Man and Superman* [Burnley Drama Guild,
     Victoria Theatre] (1931); *Scenes from A Midsummer Night's Dream*
     [English Folk Festival, Quernmore Park, Lancaster] (1932)

128. Alan Coppock (1898-1983) [Burnley Amateur, Businessman] x 6
     Plunder [The Burnley Players, Victoria Theatre] (1931); *Pompey the
     Great* [Burnley Drama Guild, Burnley Central Library] (1931); *Electra*
     [Burnley Drama Guild, Burnley Central Library] (1931); *The Devil's
     Disciple* [Burnley Drama Guild, Victoria Theatre] (1931); *A Cup of
     Kindness* [The Burnley Players, Victoria Theatre] (1932); *Plunder* [The
     Burnley Players, Victoria Theatre] (1932)

129. Harry Cording (1891-1954) [Warners Burbank] x 6 *Heart of the North*
     (1938); *Devil's Island* (1938); *Sons of Liberty* (1939); *We Are Not Alone*
     (1939); *The Sea Hawk* (1940); *A Dispatch from Reuter's* (1940)

130. Peggy Corkish [Liverpool Playhouse] x 4 *The Lake* (1933); *Fun While It
     Lasts* (1933); *The Rose Without a Thorn* (1934); *Cabbages and Kings* (1934)

131. Gino Corrado (1893-1982) [Gino Corrado Liserani] [Warners Burbank and Paramount Studios] x 2 *Devil's Island* (1938); *Beau Geste* (1939)

132. Jerome [Palmer] Cowan (1897-1972) [Warners Burbank and Republic Studios] x 2 *The Old Maid* (1939); *Wolf of New York* (1940)

133. Alec Craig (1884-1945) [Warners Burbank] x 5 *Confessions of a Nazi Spy* (1939); *Sons of Liberty* (1939); *The Sea Hawk* (1940); *A Dispatch from Reuter's* (1940); *Shining Victory* (1941)

134. Hal Craig (1894-1964) [Warners Burbank] x 2 *Secret Service of the Air* (1939); *The Adventures of Jane Arden* (1939)

135. [William] Broderick Crawford (1911-1986) [Paramount Studios] x 1 *Beau Geste* (1939)

136. John Cresswell [Liverpool Playhouse] x 4 *Counsellor-At-Law* (1934); *Hamlet* (1935); *Boyd's Shop* (1936); *Storm in a Teacup* (1936)

137. Edgar Criddle [Liverpool Playhouse and Winter Gardens, New Brighton] x 11 *The Lake* (1933); *Fun While It Lasts* (1933); *The Rose Without A Thorn* (1934); *Cabbages and Kings* (1934); *Gallows Glorious* (1934); *Macbeth* (1934); *Counsellor-at-Law* (1934); *The Cathedral* [Winter Gardens, New Brighton] (1934); *A Sleeping Clergyman* (1934); *Laburnum Grove* (1934); *Hamlet* (1935)

138. Donald [William] Crisp (1884-1974) [Warners Burbank] x 4 *The Private Lives of Elizabeth and Essex* (1939); *The Old Maid* (1939); *The Sea Hawk* (1940); *Shining Victory* (1941)

139. Mrs [Marjorie] Croasdale [Burnley Players, Amateur Producer and Retired Professional Actress] x 6 *The Best People* [The Burnley Players, Victoria Theatre] (1930); *It Pays to Advertise* [The Burnley Players, Victoria Theatre] (1930); *Plunder* [The Burnley Players, Victoria Theatre] (1931); *A Cup of Kindness* [The Burnley Players, Victoria Theatre] (1932); *Thark* [The Burnley Players, Victoria Theatre] [as actor] (1932); *Plunder* [The Burnley Players, Victoria Theatre] (1932)

140. Kate Cutler (1870-1955) [Warners Teddington] x 1 *Perfect Crime* (1937)

141. Mary Daniel [Liverpool Playhouse and Winter Gardens, New Brighton] x

12 *The Rose Without a Thorn* (1934); *Cabbages and Kings* (1934); *Smoke Screen* (1934); *A Sleeping Clergyman* (1934); *Hamlet* (1935); *Counsellor-at-Law* [Winter Gardens, New Brighton] (1935); *The Matriarch* (1935); *Cornelius* (1935); *Miss Linley of Bath* (1935); *Circus Boy* (1935); *Death Takes a Holiday* (1936); *Richard of Bordeaux* (1936)

142. Henry [Charles] Daniell (1894-1963) [Warners Burbank] x 3 *The Private Lives of Elizabeth and Essex* (1939); *We Are Not Alone* (1939); *The Sea Hawk* (1940)

143. Helmut Dantine (1917-1982) [Helmut Guttman] [Warners Burbank] x 1 *International Squadron* (1941)

144. William B. Davidson (1888-1947) [Warners Burbank] x 2 *Cowboy from Brooklyn* (1938); *On Trial* (1939)

145. [Byron] Alan Davis (1913-1943) [Warners Burbank] x 2 *King of the Underworld* (1939); *Murder in the Air* (1940)

146. Bette Davis (1908-1989) [Ruth Elizabeth Davis] [Warners Burbank and CBS Radio] x 4½ *The Private Lives of Elizabeth and Essex* (1939); *The Old Maid* (1939); *The Letter* (1940); *Lux Radio Theatre: The Letter* (1941); *Shining Victory* (1941) [Appearance unverifiable]

147. Johnnie Davis (1910-1983) [John Gustave Davis] [Warners Burbank] x 1 *Cowboy from Brooklyn* (1938)

148. Richard Davis [CBS Radio] x 1 *Lux Radio Theatre: The Letter* (1941)

149. Billy Dawson (1927-1996) [Warners Burbank] x 1 *A Dispatch from Reuter's* (1940)

150. Pedro de Cordoba (1881-1950) [Warners Burbank] x 2 *Heart of the North* (1938); *The Sea Hawk* (1940)

151. Terence de Marney (1908-1971) [BBC Radio] x 1 *Twenty Years After* (1937)

152. Cecil B[lount]. DeMille (1881-1959) [CBS Radio] x 1 *Lux Radio Theatre: The Letter* (1941)

153. Edgar Dearing (1893-1974) [Warners Burbank] x 1 *King of the*

Underworld (1939)

154. John Deering (1904-1959) [Warners Burbank] x 2 *Confessions of a Nazi Spy* (1939); *Murder in the Air* (1940)

155. Albert [Van] Dekker (1905-1968) [Paramount Studios] x 1 *Beau Geste* (1939)

156. Cyril Delevanti (1887-1975) [Warners Burbank] x 1 *A Dispatch from Reuter's* (1940)

157. [Carl] William Demarest (1892-1983) [Republic Studios] x 1 *Wolf of New York* (1940)

158. Hugh Dempster (1900-1987) [BBC Radio] x 1 *For the Children: The King's Chair* (1937)

159. Reginald Denny (1891-1967) [Reginald Leigh Dugmore] [Warners Burbank] x 1 *International Squadron* (1941)

160. Ivy Des Voeux [The Garrick, London] x 1 *Storm in a Teacup* (1936)

161. Joe Devlin (1894-1973) [Warners Burbank] x 2 *King of the Underworld* (1939); *The Adventures of Jane Arden* (1939)

162. Gloria Dickson (1916-1945) [Thais Dickerson] [Warners Burbank] x 1 *Heart of the North* (1938)

163. Don Douglas (1905-1945) [Warners Burbank] x 1 *Calling Philo Vance* (1940)

164. Eileen Douglas [Liverpool Playhouse, Winter Gardens, New Brighton] x 8 *The Distaff Side* (1934); *Hamlet* (1935); *Counsellor-at-Law* [Winter Gardens, New Brighton] (1935); *Barnet's Folly* (1935); *Cornelius* (1935); *Miss Linley of Bath* (1935); *Boyd's Shop* (1936); *Richard of Bordeaux* (1936)

165. Mrs Nellie Down (1870-1954) [Burnley Amateur] x 5 *The Best People* [The Burnley Players, Victoria Theatre] (1930); *Man and Superman* [Burnley Drama Guild, Victoria Theatre] (1930); *Man and Superman* [Burnley Co-operative Players, Co-op Hall, Todmorden] (1931); *Plunder* [The Burnley Players, Victoria Theatre] (1931); *Plunder* [The Burnley Players, Victoria Theatre] (1932)

166. Deidre Doyle [Liverpool Playhouse, Winter Gardens, New Brighton and BBC Radio] x 17 *Counsellor-at-Law* (1934); *The Distaff Side* (1934); *Sheppey* (1934); *Laburnum Grove* (1934); *Ferry Inn* (1934); *Flowers of the Forest* (1935); *Too Young to Marry* (1935); *The Matriarch* (1935); *Barnet's Folly* (1935); *Round the Northern Repertories: The Liverpool Playhouse* [BBC Radio] (1935); *Too Young to Marry* [Winter Gardens, New Brighton] (1935); *Counsellor-at-Law* [Winter Gardens, New Brighton] (1935); *Miss Linley of Bath* (1935); *Circus Boy* (1935); *Death Takes a Holiday* (1936); *Boyd's Shop* (1936); *Storm in a Teacup* (1936)

167. Edgar Driver (1887-1964) [The Queens, London] x 1 *Post Road* (1937)

168. Edward [Ted] Dudgeon [Liverpool Playhouse] x 8 *Hollywood Holiday* (1932); *Lean Harvest* (1932); *Lady In Waiting* (1932); *What Happened to George* (1932); *Inquest* (1933); *The Crime at Blossoms* (1933); *The Queen's Husband* (1933); *Never Come Back* (1933)

169. Penelope Dudley-Ward (1914-1982) [Liverpool Playhouse] x 1 *Death Takes a Holiday* (1936)

170. Steffi Duna (1910-1992) [Stephanie Berindey] [Warners Burbank] x 1 *River's End* (1940)

171. Kenneth Duncan (1903-1972) [The Queens, London] x 1 *Post Road* (1937)

172. Emma Dunn (1875-1966) [Emma Ruth Wilcox] [Warners Burbank] x 1 *Cowboy from Brooklyn* (1938)

173. Earl Dwire (1883-1940) [Warners Burbank] x 2 *Devil's Island* (1938); *On Trial* (1939)

174. Franklin Dyall (1874-1950) [Warners Teddington] x 1 *Mr. Satan* (1938)

175. Ann Edmonds [Warners Burbank] x 2 *Flight from Destiny* (1941); *International Squadron* (1941)

176. Cliff Edwards (1895-1971) [Warners Burbank] x 1 *International Squadron* (1941)

177. Edgar Edwards [Warners Burbank] x 3 *Secret Service of the Air* (1939);

The Adventures of Jane Arden (1939); *On Trial* (1939)

178. Geoffrey Edwards [Liverpool Playhouse and Winter Gardens, New Brighton] x 43 *Hollywood Holiday* (1932); *Twelfth Night* (1932); *Lady in Waiting* (1932); *The Roundabout* (1932); *What Happened to George* (1932); *Inquest* (1933); *Don't Tell England* (1933); *Mourning Becomes Electra* [Overseas League, Liverpool] (1933); *The Crime at Blossoms* (1933); *Another Language* (1933); *The Kingdom of God* (1933); *The Queen's Husband* (1933); *Never Come Back* (1933); *Inquest* [Winter Gardens, New Brighton] (1933); *The Queen's Husband* [Winter Gardens, New Brighton] (1933); *Art and Mrs. Bottle* [Winter Gardens, New Brighton] (1933); *Anthony and Anna* [Winter Gardens, New Brighton] (1933); *The Road to Rome* (1933); *Britannia of Billingsgate* (1933); *The Lake* (1933); *The Cathedral* (1933); *Shall We Join the Ladies?* (1933); *Is Life Worth Living?* (1933); *Fun While It Lasts* (1933); *Dangerous Corner* (1934); *The Rose Without a Thorn* (1934); *Smoke Screen* (1934); *Cabbages and Kings* (1934); *Gallows Glorious* (1934); *Macbeth* (1934); *The Cathedral* [Winter Gardens, New Brighton] (1934); *The Lake* [Winter Gardens, New Brighton] (1934); *Smoke Screen* [Winter Gardens, New Brighton] (1934); *Britannia of Billingsgate* [Winter Gardens, New Brighton] (1934); *Counsellor-at-Law* (1934); *The Distaff Side* (1934); *A Sleeping Clergyman* (1934); *Something in the City* (1934); *Sheppey* (1934); *Biography* (1935); *Libel* (1935); *Flowers of the Forest* (1935); *Hamlet* (1935)

179. John Eldredge (1904-1961) [Warners Burbank] x 2 *King of the Underworld* (1939); *Flight from Destiny* (1941)

180. Miss Grace Elford [Burnley Amateur] x 5 *The Beaux' Stratagem* [Burnley Drama Guild, Victoria Theatre] (1930); *Merchant of Venice* [1] [Burnley Drama Guild, Burnley Central Library] (1931); *Merchant of Venice* [2] [Burnley Drama Guild, Burnley Central Library] (1931); *The Devil's Disciple* [Burnley Drama Guild, Victoria Theatre] (1931); *The Devil's Disciple* [Burnley Drama Guild, Co-op Hall, Todmorden] (1932)

181. Derek Elphinstone (1913-1999) [Liverpool Playhouse and BBC Radio] x 7 *Macbeth* (1934); *Sheppey* (1934); *Libel* (1935); *Youth at the Helm* (1935); *Round the Northern Repertories: Liverpool Playhouse* [BBC Radio] (1935); *Cornelius* (1935); *Circus Boy* (1935)

182. Gilbert Emery (1875-1945) [Gilbert Emery Bensley Pottle] [Warners

Burbank] x 3 *River's End* (1940); *A Dispatch from Reuter's* (1940); *South of Suez* (1940)

183. Joy Erskine Young [Liverpool Playhouse and Winter Gardens, New Brighton] x 25 *Hollywood Holiday* (1932); *Lean Harvest* (1932); *The Long Christmas Dinner* (1932); *The Lake* (1933); *Shall We Join the Ladies?* (1933); *The Crime at Blossoms* (1933); *The Rose Without a Thorn* (1934); *Smoke Screen* (1934); *Cabbages and Kings* (1934); *Macbeth* (1934); *The Cathedral* [Winter Gardens, New Brighton] (1934); *Smoke Screen* [Winter Gardens, New Brighton] (1934); *Counsellor-at-Law* (1934); *The Distaff Side* (1935); *A Sleeping Clergyman* (1934); *Libel* (1935); *Hamlet* (1935); *Too Young to Marry* (1935); *Libel* [Winter Gardens, New Brighton] (1935); *Counsellor-at-Law* [Winter Gardens, New Brighton] (1935); *Barnet's Folly* (1935); *Circus Boy* (1935); *Boyd's Shop* (1936); *Storm in a Teacup* (1936); *Twelfth Night* (1936)

184. Helena Phillips Evans (1875-1955) [Warners Burbank] x 1 *Nancy Drew Detective* (1938)

185. Wallace Evenett (1887-1973) [BBC Radio and Warners Teddington] x 2 *Scotland Yard: Life in the Metropolitan Police* (1936); *You Live and Learn* (1938)

186. Nanette Fabray (1920-) [also known as Nanette Fabares / Ruby Bernadette Nanette Teresa Fabares MacDougall] [Warners Burbank] x 2 *The Private Lives of Elizabeth and Essex* (1939); *The Monroe Doctrine* (1939)

187. Glenda Farrell (1903-1971) [Glenda Farrell Richards] [Warners Teddington and Warners Burbank] x 2 *You Live and Learn* (1938); *Torchy Blane in Chinatown* (1939)

188. W[illiam]G.[eorge] Fay (1872-1947) [The Garrick, London] x 1 *Storm in a Teacup* (1936)

189. Frank Faylen (1905-1985) [Warners Burbank] x 1 *International Squadron* (1941)

190. Louise Fazenda (1895-1962) [Warners Burbank] x 1 *The Old Maid* (1939)

191. Mary Field (1909-1996) [Warners Burbank] x 2 *Cowboy from Brooklyn* (1938); *White Banners* (1938)

192. Marjorie Fielding (1892-1956) [Liverpool Playhouse and Winter Gardens, New Brighton] x 25 *Hollywood Holiday* (1932); *Twelfth Night* (1932); *The Long Christmas Dinner* (1932); *The Roundabout* (1932); *What Happened to George* (1932); *Inquest* (1933); *Don't Tell England* (1932); *A Bite of the Apple* (1933); *Mourning Becomes Electra* [Overseas League, Liverpool] (1933); *Crime at Blossoms* (1933); *Another Language* (1933); *The Kingdom of God* (1933); *Laying the Devil* (1933); *The Queen's Husband* (1933); *Never Come Back* (1933); *Inquest* [Winter Gardens, New Brighton] (1933); *The Queen's Husband* [Winter Gardens, New Brighton] (1933); *Art and Mrs. Bottle* [Winter Gardens, New Brighton] (1933); *The Road to Rome* (1933); *Britannia of Billingsgate* (1933); *The Lake* (1933); *The Cathedral* (1933); *Shall We Join the Ladies?* (1933); *Is Life Worth Living?* (1933); *Britannia of Billingsgate* [Winter Gardens, New Brighton] (1934)

193. Geraldine Fitzgerald (1913-2005) [Warners Burbank] x 2 *Flight from Destiny* (1941); *Shining Victory* (1941)

194. Betty Fleetwood [Liverpool Playhouse] x 3 *Ferry Inn* (1934); *Miss Linley of Bath* (1935); *Circus Boy* (1935)

195. Robert Flemyng (1912-1995) [Liverpool Playhouse and Winter Gardens, New Brighton] x 36 *Hollywood Holiday* (1932); *Lean Harvest* (1932); *Lady in Waiting* (1932); *The Roundabout* (1932); *What Happened to George* (1932); *Inquest* (1933); *Mourning Becomes Electra* [Overseas League, Liverpool] (1933); *The Crime at Blossoms* (1933); *The Kingdom of God* (1933); *Never Come Back* (1933); *Anthony and Anna* [Winter Gardens, New Brighton] (1933); *The Queen's Husband* [Winter Gardens, New Brighton] (1933); *Art and Mrs. Bottle* [Winter Gardens, New Brighton] (1933); *The Road to Rome* (1933); *Britannia of Billingsgate* (1933); *The Cathedral* (1933); *Shall We Join the Ladies?* (1933); *Is Life Worth Living?* (1933); *Fun While It Lasts* (1933); *The Rose Without a Thorn* (1934); *Smoke Screen* (1934); *Cabbages and Kings* (1934); *Gallows Glorious* (1934); *Macbeth* (1934); *Counsellor-at-Law* (1934); *The Cathedral* (1934) [Winter Gardens, New Brighton]; *The Lake* [Winter Gardens, New Brighton] (1934); *Smoke Screen* [Winter Gardens, New Brighton] (1934); *Britannia of Billingsgate* [Winter Gardens, New Brighton] (1934); *The Distaff Side* (1934); *A Sleeping Clergyman* (1934); *Something in the City* (1934); *Sheppey* (1934); *Laburnum Grove* (1934); *Ferry Inn* (1934); *Biography* (1935)

196. Errol Flynn (1909-1959) [Warners Burbank] x 2 *The Private Lives of Elizabeth and Essex* (1939); *The Sea Hawk* (1940)

197. Reginald Foort (1893-1980) [BBC Radio] x 1 *Palace of Varieties* (1937)

198. Dick Foran (1910-1979) [John Nicholas Foran] [Warners Burbank] x 3 *Cowboy from Brooklyn* (1938); *Heart of the North* (1938); *Boy Meets Girl* (1938)

199. Mary Forbes (1879-1974) [Warners Burbank] x 1 *South of Suez* (1940)

200. Ralph Forbes (1896-1951) [Warners Burbank] x 2 *The Private Lives of Elizabeth and Essex* (1939); *Calling Philo Vance* (1940)

201. Miss Doris Foulds [Burnley Amateur] x 8 *The Beaux' Stratagem* [Burnley Drama Guild, Victoria Theatre] (1930); *Man and Superman* [Burnley Co-operative Players, Co-op Hall, Todmorden] (1931); *Merchant of Venice Readings* [1] [Burnley Drama Guild, Burnley Central Library] (1931); *Merchant of Venice Readings* [2] [Burnley Drama Guild, Burnley Central Library] (1931); *The Devil's Disciple* [Burnley Drama Guild, Victoria Theatre] (1931); *Scenes from A Midsummer Night's Dream* [English Folk Festival, "Four Oaks," Higher Reedley] (1931); *The Devil's Disciple* [Burnley Drama Guild, Co-op Hall, Todmorden] (1932); *Scenes from A Midsummer Night's Dream* [Quernmore Park, Lancaster] (1932)

202. Jimmie Fox (1891-1974) [Warners Burbank] x 1 *Cowboy from Brooklyn* (1938)

203. Bryan Foy (1896-1977) [KFWB Radio] x 1 *I Found Stella Parish* (1938)

204. Charles Foy (1898-1984) [Warners Burbank] x 1 *King of the Underworld* (1939)

205. Eddie Foy Jr (1905-1983) [Warners Burbank] x 2 *Secret Service of the Air* (1939); *Murder in the Air* (1940)

206. Kay Francis (1899-1968) [Katherine Gibbs] [Warners Burbank] x 1 *King of the Underworld* (1939)

207. Mrs Jane Freeman-Smith (188?-1938) [Burnley Amateur] x 3 *Oedipus the King* [Burnley Drama Guild, Burnley Central Library] (1931); *The*

Devil's Disciple [Burnley Drama Guild, Victoria Theatre] (1931); *The Devil's Disciple* [Burnley Drama Guild, Co-op Hall, Todmorden] (1932)

208. Louise Frodsham [Liverpool Playhouse] x 30 *Hollywood Holiday* (1932); *Lady in Waiting* (1932); *What Happened to George* (1932); *Inquest* (1933); *The Crime at Blossoms* (1933); *The Kingdom of God* (1933); *The Lake* (1933); *Shall We Join the Ladies?* (1933); *Is Life Worth Living?* (1933); *Smoke Screen* (1934); *Cabbages and Kings* (1934); *Counsellor-at-Law* (1934); *The Distaff Side* (1934); *A Sleeping Clergyman* (1934); *Laburnum Grove* (1934); *Ferry Inn* (1934); *Biography* (1935); *Libel* (1935); *Flowers of the Forest* (1935); *Too Young to Marry* (1935); *Counsellor-at-Law* [Winter Gardens, New Brighton] (1935); *The Matriarch* (1935); *Barnet's Folly* (1935); *Cornelius* (1935); *Miss Linley of Bath* (1935); *Compromise* (1935); *Circus Boy* (1935); *Boyd's Shop* (1936); *And So To War* (1936); *Twelfth Night* (1936)

209. Willie Fung (1896-1945) [Warners Burbank] x 1 *The Letter* (1940)

210. Renee Gadd (1906-2003) x 1 *The Man Who Made Diamonds* (1937)

211. [Richard] "Skeets" Gallagher (1891-1955) [Warners Teddington] x 1 *Mr. Satan* (1938)

212. George Galleon [Warners Teddington] x 3 *The Man Who Made Diamonds* (1937); *You Live and Learn* (1938); *It's in the Blood* (1938)

213. Dino Galvani (1890-1960) [Dino Galvanoni] [Warners Teddington] x 2 *The Man Who Made Diamonds* (1937); *Mr. Satan* (1938)

214. Edward Gargan (1902-1964) [Republic Studios] x 1 *Wolf of New York* (1940)

215. Phyllis Garge [Liverpool Playhouse] x 2 *The Crime at Blossoms* (1933); *The Kingdom of God* (1933)

216. Sonia Garmian [Liverpool Playhouse] x 5 *Barnet's Folly* (1935); *Circus Boy* (1935); *Death Takes a Holiday* (1936); *Richard of Bordeaux* (1936); *Twelfth Night* (1936)

217. Alexander Gauge (1914-1960) [Winter Gardens, New Brighton] x 1 *Too Young to Marry* (1935)

218. Bud Geary (1898-1946) [S. Maine Geary] [Warners Burbank] x 1 *Torchy Blane in Chinatown* (1939)

219. Amabel Gibson [Liverpool Playhouse] x 10 *Hollywood Holiday* (1932); *Lean Harvest* (1932); *Twelfth Night* (1932); *The Long Christmas Dinner* (1932); *Lady In Waiting* (1932); *The Roundabout* (1932); *The Crime at Blossoms* (1933); *Another Language* (1932); *The Kingdom of God* (1933); *Never Come Back* (1933)

220. Frederick Giermann (1902-1985) [Warners Burbank] x 5 *Espionage Agent* (1939); *Confessions of a Nazi Spy* (1939); *The Monroe Doctrine* (1939); *Calling Philo Vance* (1940); *International Squadron* (1941)

221. Ann Gillis (1927-) [Alma Mabel Conner] [Paramount Studios] x 1 *Beau Geste* (1939)

222. Ethel Glendinning (1910-1986) [The Garrick, London] x 1 *Storm in a Teacup* (1936)

223. [Frank] Wyndham Goldie (1897-1957) [Liverpool Playhouse] x 21 *Hollywood Holiday* (1932); *Lean Harvest* (1932); *The Roundabout* (1932); *What Happened to George* (1932); *Inquest* (1933); *Don't Tell England* (1933); *The Crime at Blossoms* (1933); *Another Language* (1933); *Laying the Devil* (1933); *The Queen's Husband* (1933); *Never Come Back* (1933); *The Road to Rome* (1933); *The Lake* (1933); *The Cathedral* (1933); *Shall We Join the Ladies?* (1933); *Fun While It Lasts* (1933); *Dangerous Corner* (1934); *The Rose Without a Thorn* (1934); *Cabbages and Kings* (1934); *Gallows Glorious* (1934); *Macbeth* (1934); *Lover's Leap* (1934)

224. Douglas Gordon [Warners Burbank] x 1 *We Are Not Alone* (1939); *A Dispatch from Reuter's* (1940)

225. Mary Gordon (1882-1963) [Mary Gilmour] [Warners Burbank] x 2 *Cowboy from Brooklyn* (1938); *Flight from Destiny* (1941)

226. Sol Gorss (1908-1966) [Warners Burbank] x 7 *When Were You Born* (1938); *Heart of the North* (1938); *Torchy Blane in Chinatown* (1939); *Secret Service of the Air* (1939); *The Adventures of Jane Arden* (1939); *Confessions of a Nazi Spy* (1939); *Flight from Destiny* (1941)

227. William Gould [Warners Burbank] x 4 *King of the Underworld* (1939); *The Adventures of Jane Arden* (1939); *Confessions of a Nazi Spy* (1939); *Murder in the Air* (1940)

228. Eddie Graham [Warners Burbank] x 4 *Cowboy from Brooklyn* (1938*); The Adventures of Jane Arden* (1939); *Espionage Agent* (1939); *Calling Philo Vance* (1940)

229. Lawrence Grant (1870-1952) [Percy Reginald Lawrence-Grant] [Warners Burbank] x 2 *Devil's Island* (1938); *A Dispatch from Reuter's* (1940)

230. Bonita Granville (1923-1988) [Warners Burbank] x 2 *White Banners* (1938); *Nancy Drew Detective* (1938)

231. Duke Green (1900-1984) [Warners Burbank and Paramount Studios] x 2 *Secret Service of the Air* (1939); *Beau Geste* (1939)

232. Paul [Sylvester] Greenwood (1900-?) [Burnley Amateur, Clerk] x 15 *The School for Scandal* [Clef Club, Mechanics Institute] (1930); *The Beaux' Stratagem* [Burnley Drama Guild, Victoria Theatre] (1930); *Man and Superman* [Burnley Drama Guild, Victoria Theatre] (1930); *Man and Superman* [Burnley Co-operative Players, Co-op Hall, Todmorden] (1931); *Merchant of Venice Readings* [Burnley Drama Guild, Burnley Central Library] (1931); *Act I of Man and Superman* [Burnley Drama Guild, Burnley Central Library] (1931): *"Pompey" the Great* [Burnley Drama Guild, Burnley Central Library] (1931); *Scenes from a Midsummer Night's Dream* [English Folk Festival, "Four Oaks" Higher Reedley] (1931); *Electra* [Burnley Drama Guild, Burnley Central Library] (1931); *Man and Superman* [Burnley Drama Guild, Victoria Theatre] (1931); *The Devil's Disciple* [Burnley Drama Guild, Victoria Theatre] (1931); *Plunder* [The Burnley Players, Victoria Theatre] (1932); *Man and Superman* [Burnley Drama Guild, Central Library] (1932); *The Devil's Disciple* [Burnley Drama Guild, Co-op Hall, Todmorden] (1932); *Scenes from A Midsummer Night's Dream* [Quernmore Park, Lancaster] (1932)

233. Hubert [Robert] Gregg (1914-2004) [BBC Radio] x 1 *The Blue Danube* (1937)

234. Dorothy Grey (1903-1993) [Dorothy Eleanor Eadie] [Burnley Amateur, Professional Pianist] x 1 *Rigoletto* [The Burnley Operatic Society, Victoria Theatre] (1932)

235. John Grey A[ssociate] C[hartered] I[nsurance] B[rokers] (1904-
     1993) [Burnley Amateur, Insurance Broker] x 19 *The Magic Flute*
     [Burnley Operatic Society, Victoria Theatre] (1929); *Aida* [Burnley
     Operatic Society, Palace Theatre] (1930); *The Beaux' Stratagem*
     [Burnley Drama Guild, Victoria Theatre] (1930); *Man and Superman*
     [Burnley Drama Guild, Victoria Theatre] (1930); *Man and Superman*
     [Burnley Co-operative Players, Co-op Hall, Todmorden] (1931);
     Merchant of Venice Readings [1] [Burnley Drama Guild, Burnley
     Central Library] (1931); *Merchant of Venice Readings* [2] [Burnley
     Drama Guild, Burnley Central Library] (1931); *The Father* [Burnley
     Drama Guild, Victoria Theatre] (1931); *Oedipus the King* [Burnley
     Drama Guild, Burnley Central Library] (1931); *"Pompey" The Great*
     [Burnley Drama Guild, Burnley Central Library] (1931); *Scenes from
     A Midsummer Night's Dream* [English Folk Festival, "Four Oaks,"
     Higher Reedley] (1931); *Electra* [Burnley Drama Guild, Burnley
     Central Library] (1931); *Man and Superman* [Burnley Drama
     Guild, Victoria Theatre] (1931); *The Plays of George Bernard Shaw*
     [Burnley Rotary Club, Café Royal] (1931); *The Devil's Disciple*
     [Burnley Drama Guild, Victoria Theatre] (1931); *Rigoletto* [Burnley
     Operatic Soceity, Victoria Theatre] (1932); *The Devil's Disciple*
     [Co-op Hall, Todmorden] (1932); *Scenes from A Midsummer Night's
     Dream* [Quernmore Park, Lancaster] (1932); *Plunder* [The Burnley
     Players, Victoria Theatre] (1932)

236. Ethel Griffies (1878-1975) [Ethel Woods] [Warners Burbank] x 1 *We Are
     Not Alone* (1939)

237. Deryck Guyler (1914-1999) [Liverpool Playhouse] x 2 *Richard of
     Bordeaux* (1936); *Twelfth Night* (1936)

238. Alan Hale (1892-1950) [Rufus Alan MacKahan] [Warners Burbank] x 2
     The Private Lives of Elizabeth and Essex (1939); *The Sea Hawk* (1940)

239. Bobby Hale (1886-1977) [Warners Burbank] x 1 *A Dispatch from
     Reuter's* (1940)

240. Creighton Hale (1882-1965) [Patrick Fitzgerald] [Warners Burbank] x 2
     Confessions of a Nazi Spy (1939); *Calling Philo Vance* (1940)

241. Jonathan Hale (1891-1966) [Jonathan Hatley] [Warners Burbank] x 1
     Flight from Destiny (1941)

242. Thurston Hall (1882-1958) [Warners Burbank] x 1 *Flight from Destiny* (1941)

243. C.[harles]M.[aitland] Hallard (1865-1942) [The Garrick, London] x 1 *Storm in a Teacup* (1936)

244. Henry Hallett (1888-1952) [BBC Radio] x 1 *The Blue Danube* (1937)

245. Margaret Halstan (1879-1967) [Winter Gardens, New Brighton] x 1 *The Lake* (1934)

246. John Hamilton (1887-1958) [Warners Burbank] x 5 *Devil's Island* (1938); *Secret Service of the Air* (1939); *Confessions of a Nazi Spy* (1939); *Espionage Agent* (1939); *Flight from Destiny* (1941)

247. Lindisfarne [Christodora] Hamilton [Liverpool Playhouse] x 13 *Laying the Devil* (1933); *The Queen's Husband* (1933); *Never Come Back* (1933); *Macbeth* (1934); *Dangerous Corner* (1934); *The Rose Without a Thorn* (1934); *Smoke Screen* (1934); *Counsellor-at-Law* (1934); *The Distaff Side* (1934); *A Sleeping Clergyman* (1934); *Something in the City* (1934); *Biography* (1935); *Libel* (1935)

248. Louise Hampton (1881-1954) [The Queens, London] x 1 *Post Road* (1937)

249. James Harcourt (1873-1951) [Winter Gardens, New Brighton] x 1 *Anthony and Anna* (1933)

250. [Francis] Lumsden Hare (1875-1964) [Warners Burbank] x 1 *A Dispatch from Reuter's* (1940)

251. Alec Harford (1888-1955) [Warners Burbank] x 4 *Heart of the North* (1938); *We Are Not Alone* (1939); *A Dispatch from Reuter's* (1940); *South of Suez* (1940)

252. Kenneth Harlan (1895-1967) [Warners Burbank] x 2 *On Trial* (1939); *Murder in the Air* (1940)

253. Nedda Harrigan (1899-1989) [Grace Harrigan] [Warners Burbank] x 2 *Devil's Island* (1938); *On Trial* (1939)

254. John Harron (1903-1939) [Warners Burbank] x 13 *Cowboy from Brooklyn* (1938); *Heart of the North* (1938); *Boy Meets Girl* (1938); *White Banners* (1938); *When Were You Born* (1938); *King of the Underworld* (1939);

Torchy Blane in Chinatown (1939); *Secret Service of the Air* (1939); *The Adventures of Jane Arden* (1939); *On Trial* (1939); *Confessions of a Nazi Spy* (1939); *Espionage Agent* (1939); *Calling Philo Vance* (1940)

255. Gordon Hart (1884-1973) [Warners Burbank] x 4 *When Were You Born* (1938); *Torchy Blane in Chinatown* (1939); *On Trial* (1939); *A Dispatch from Reuter's* (1940)

256. Forrester Harvey (1884-1945) [Warners Burbank] x 1 *The Private Lives of Elizabeth and Essex* (1939)

257. Stanley Haworth [Burnley Amateur] x 5 *The Best People* [The Burnley Players, Victoria Theatre] (1930); *It Pays to Advertise* [The Burnley Players, Victoria Theatre] (1930); *Plunder* [The Burnley Players, Victoria Theatre] (1931); *Thark* [The Burnley Players, Victoria Theatre] (1932) *Plunder* [The Burnley Players, Victoria Theatre] (1932)

258. Anthony Hawtrey (1909-1954) [Liverpool Playhouse] x 11 *The Road to Rome* (1933); *Britannia of Billingsgate* (1933); *Shall We Join the Ladies?* (1933); *Is Life Worth Living?* (1933); *Macbeth* (1934); *Cabbages and Kings* (1934); *Gallows Glorious* (1934); *The Cathedral* (1934); *The Lake* (1934); *Fun While It Lasts* (1934); *The Rose Without a Thorn* (1934)

259. Patricia Hayes (1909-1998) [Liverpool Playhouse and BBC Radio] x 2 *Circus Boy* (1935); *The Children's Hour: Jack and the Beanstalk* (1937)

260. Susan Hayward (1917-1975) [Edythe Marrenner] [Paramount Studios] x 1 *Beau Geste* (1939)

261. Miss Eva Heap [Burnley Amateur] x 1 *Aida* [Burnley Operatic Society, Victoria Theatre] (1930)

262. Bryan Herbert [Denis Herbert Doyle] [Welwyn Studios] x 1 *Dangerous Fingers* (1938)

263. Holmes Herbert (1882-1956) [Edward Jenner] [Warners Burbank] x 6 *The Private Lives of Elizabeth and Essex* (1939); *We Are Not Alone* (1939); *A Dispatch from Reuter's* (1940); *The Letter* (1940); *South of Suez* (1940); *International Squadron* (1941)

264. Herbert Heywood (1881-1964) [Warners Burbank] x 2 *King of the Underworld* (1939); *A Dispatch from Reuter's* (1940)

265. George Hickman (1906-1984) [Warners Burbank] x 2 *Cowboy from Brooklyn* (1938); *Boy Meets Girl* (1938)

266. Howard Hickman (1880-1949) [Warners Burbank] x 1 *Espionage Agent* (1939)

267. Wilfred Hindle [Burnley Amateur Singer] x 3 *A Persian Garden* [Burnley Clef Club, Mechanics Institute] (1927); *Don Giovanni* [Burnley Clef Club, Mechanics Institute] (1928); *Don Giovanni* [Burnley Clef Club, Mechanics Institute] (1929)

268. Keith Hitchcock (1887-1966) [Warners Burbank] x 2 *We Are Not Alone* (1939); *South of Suez* (1940)

269. Rose Hobart (1906-2000) [Republic Studios] x 1 *Wolf of New York* (1940)

270. Carleton Hobbs (1898-1978) [BBC Radio] x 5 *Scotland Yard: Life in the Metropolitan Police* (1936); *Twenty Years After* (1937); *Money with Menaces* (1937); *News, History of the Fourth Estate* (1937); *Death of a First Mate* (1937)

271. [Herbert] Halliwell Hobbes (1877-1962) [Warners Burbank] x 1 *The Sea Hawk* (1940)

272. Leyland Hodgson (1892-1949) [Warners Burbank] x 6 *Cowboy from Brooklyn* (1938); *The Adventures of Jane Arden* (1939); *We Are Not Alone* (1939); *The Sea Hawk* (1940); *South of Suez* (1940); *International Squadron* (1941)

273. Iris Hoey (1885-1979) [Warners Teddington] x 1 *Perfect Crime* (1937)

274. Max Hoffman Jr (1902-1945) [Warners Burbank] x 2 *King of the Underworld* (1939); *Confessions of a Nazi Spy* (1939)

275. Gloria Holden (1908-1991) [CBS Radio] x 1 *Lux Radio Theatre: The Letter* (1941)

276. Miss Dorothy Holgate [Burnley Amateur] x 6 *The Beaux' Stratagem* [The

Drama Guild, Victoria Theatre] (1930); *Merchant of Venice Readings* [1] [Burnley Drama Guild, Burnley Central Library] (1931); *Merchant of Venice Readings* [2] [Burnley Drama Guild, Burnley Central Library] (1931); *Oedipus the King* [The Drama Guild, Burnley Central Library] (1931); *Scenes from A Midsummer Night's Dream* [English Folk Festival, "Four Oaks," Higher Reedley] (1931); *Scenes from A Midsummer Night's Dream* [English Folk Festival, Quernmore Park, Lancaster] (1932)

277. Stuart Holmes (1884-1971) [Warners Burbank] x 17 *Cowboy from Brooklyn* (1938); *Heart of the North* (1938); *Nancy Drew, Detective* (1938); *Devil's Island* (1938); *King of the Underworld* (1939); *Torchy Blane in Chinatown* (1939); *Secret Service of the Air* (1939); *The Adventures of Jane Arden* (1939); *On Trial* (1939); *Confessions of a Nazi Spy* (1939); *Espionage Agent* (1939); *We Are Not Alone* (1939); *The Monroe Doctrine* (1939); *Calling Philo Vance* (1940); *River's End* (1940); *A Dispatch from Reuter's* (1940); *South of Suez* (1940)

278. Robert Homans (1877-1947) [Warners Burbank] x 5 *Heart of the North* (1938); *The Adventures of Jane Arden* (1939); *On Trial* (1939); *A Dispatch from Reuter's* (1940); *Flight from Destiny* (1941)

279. [Ellen] Miriam Hopkins (1902-1972) [Warners Burbank] x 1 *The Old Maid* (1939)

280. William [DeWolf] Hopper [Jr] (1915-1970) [Warners Burbank] x 5 *The Old Maid* (1939); *Espionage Agent* (1939); *Calling Philo Vance* (1940); *Flight from Destiny* (1940); *International Squadron* (1941)

281. Evelyn Howarth [Burnley Amateur turned Professional Singer] x 1 *The Magic Flute* (1929)

282. Harold Huber (1904-1959) [Paramount Studios] x 1 *Beau Geste* (1939)

283. Claude Hulbert (1900-1964) [Warners Teddington] x 2 *You Live and Learn* (1938); *It's in the Blood* (1938)

284. George P. Huntley Jr (1904-1971) [Paramount Studios and Warners Burbank] x 2 *Beau Geste* (1939); *Shining Victory* (1941)

285. Leila Hyams [McIntyre] (1905-1977) [CBS Radio] x 1 *Lux Radio Theatre: The Letter* (1941)

286. Olaf Hytten (1888-1955) [Warners Burbank] x 2 *We Are Not Alone* (1939); *Calling Philo Vance* (1940)

287. Ralph [Waldo] Ince (1887-1937) [Warners Teddington] x 1 *Perfect Crime* (1937)

288. Frieda Inescort (1901-1976) [Frieda Wrightman] [Warners Burbank] x 1 *The Letter* (1940)

289. Elizabeth Inglis (1913-2007) [also known as Elizabeth Earl / Desiree Mary Lucy Hawkins] [Warners Burbank] x 2 *River's End* (1940); *The Letter* (1940)

290. Ellis Irving (1902-1983) [Warners Burbank] x 2 *The Sea Hawk* (1940); *A Dispatch from Reuter's* (1940)

291. Boyd Irwin (1880-1957) [Warners Burbank] x 5 *Sons of Liberty* (1939); *We Are Not Alone* (1939); *The Letter* (1940); *A Dispatch from Reuter's* (1940); *South of Suez* (1940)

292. Charles Irwin (1887-1969) [Warners Burbank] x 6 *We Are Not Alone* (1939); *The Sea Hawk* (1940); *A Dispatch from Reuter's* (1940); *South of Suez* (1940); *The Letter* (1940); *International Squadron* (1941)

293. Stephen Jack (1902-1987) [Liverpool Playhouse and BBC Radio] x 49 *Hollywood Holiday* (1932); *Lean Harvest* (1932); *Twelfth Night* (1932); *The Long Christmas Dinner* (1932); *Lady In Waiting* (1932); *What Happened to George* (1932); *Inquest* (1933); *Don't Tell England* (1933); *The Crime at Blossoms* (1933); *Another Language* (1933); *The Kingdom of God* (1933); *Laying the Devil* (1933); *The Queen's Husband* (1933); *Never Come Back* (1933); *The Queen's Husband* [Winter Gardens, New Brighton] (1933); *Winsome Winnie* (1933); *The Road to Rome* (1933); *Britannia of Billingsgate* (1933); *The Cathedral* (1933); *Is Life Worth Living?* (1933); *Fun While It Lasts* (1933); *The Rose Without a Thorn* (1934); *Cabbages and Kings* (1934); *Gallows Glorious* (1934); *Macbeth* (1934); *The Distaff Side* (1934); *A Sleeping Clergyman* (1934); *Somewhere in the City* (1934); *Sheppey* (1934); *Laburnum Grove* (1934); *Ferry Inn* (1934); *Biography* (1935); *Libel* (1935); *The Seventh Man* (1935); *Too Young to Marry* (1935); *The Matriarch* (1935); *Youth at the Helm* (1935); *Barnet's Folly* (1935); *Cornelius* (1935); *Round the Northern Repertories: The Liverpool Playhouse* [BBC Radio] (1935); *Miss Linley*

of Bath (1935); *Compromise* (1935); *Circus Boy* (1935); *Death Takes a Holiday* (1936)*; And So To War* (1936); *Boyd's Shop* (1936); *Richard of Bordeaux* (1936); *Storm in a Teacup* (1936); *Twelfth Night* (1936)

294. Selmer Jackson (1888-1971) [Warners Burbank] x 4 *Espionage Agent* (1939); *Confessions of a Nazi Spy* (1939); *Murder in the Air* (1940); *International Squadron* (1941)

295. Thomas E[dward]. Jackson (1886-1967) [Paramount Studios] x 1 *Beau Geste* (1939)

296. Frank Jaquet (1885-1958) [Warners Burbank] x 2 *When Were You Born* (1938); *A Dispatch from Reuter's* (1940)

297. Allen Jenkins (1900-1974) [Alfred McGonegal] [Warners Burbank] x 1 *Heart of the North* (1938)

298. Megs Jenkins (1917-1998) [Muguette Mary Jenkins] [Liverpool Playhouse and Winter Gardens, New Brighton] x 11 *The Lake* (1933); *After the Event* (1933); *Fun While It Lasts* (1933); *The Rose Without a Thorn* (1934); *Cabbages and Kings* (1934); *Smoke Screen* [Winter Gardens, New Brighton] (1934); *Barnet's Folly* (1935); *Circus Boy* (1935); *Hamlet* (1935); *The Matriarch* (1935); *Richard of Bordeaux* (1936)

299. Kay Johnson (1904-1975) [Warners Burbank] x 1 *White Banners* (1938)

300. I[saac]. Stanford Jolley (1900-1978) [Warners Burbank] x 1 *The Private Lives of Elizabeth and Essex* (1939)

301. Victor Jory (1902-1982) [Warners Burbank] x 1 *River's End* (1940)

302. John Justin (1917-2002) [John Justinian de Ledesma] [Liverpool Playhouse and Winter Gardens, New Brighton] x 7 *Cabbages and Kings* (1934); *Gallows Glorious* (1934); *Macbeth* (1934); *Counsellor-at-Law* (1935); *Libel* (1935); *Hamlet* (1935); *Libel* [Winter Gardens, New Brighton] (1935)

303. Suzanne Kaaren (1912-2004) [CBS Radio] x 1 *Lux Radio Theatre: The Letter* (1941)

304. Boris Karloff (1887-1969) [William Henry Pratt] [Warners Burbank] x 1

Devil's Island (1938)

305. Willy Kaufman (1891-1966) [Warners Burbank] x 2 *Confessions of a Nazi Spy* (1939); *Espionage Agent* (1939)

306. Edward Keane (1884-1959) [Edward Kelley] [Warners Burbank] x 4 *Nancy Drew Detective* (1938); *Devil's Island* (1938); *Confessions of a Nazi Spy* (1939); *A Dispatch from Reuter's* (1940)

307. Cecil Kellaway (1893-1973) [Warners Burbank] x 3 *We Are Not Alone* (1939); *South of Suez* (1940); *The Letter* (1940) [Scenes Deleted]

308. Miss Dorothy Kellett (1903-?) [Burnley Amateur] x 14 *The Best People* [The Burnley Players, Victoria Theatre] (1930); *It Pays to Advertise* [The Burnley Players, Victoria Theatre] (1930); *Aida* [The Burnley Operatic Society, Palace Theatre] (1930); *Man and Superman* [The Burnley Drama Guild, Victoria Theatre] (1930); *Man and Superman* [Burnley Co-operative Players, Co-op Hall, Todmorden] (1931); *The Father* [The Burnley Drama Guild, Victoria Theatre] (1931); *Oedipus the King* [The Burnley Drama Guild, Burnley Central Library] (1931); *Plunder* [The Burnley Players, Victoria Theatre] (1931); *The Devil's Disciple* [The Burnley Drama Guild, Victoria Theatre] (1931); *Rigoletto* [The Burnley Operatic Society, Victoria Theatre] (1932); *The Devil's Disciple* [The Burnley Drama Guild, Co-op Hall, Todmorden] (1932); *A Cup of Kindness* [The Burnley Players, Victoria Theatre] (1932); *Thark* [The Burnley Players, Victoria Theatre] (1932); *Plunder* [The Burnley Players, Victoria Theatre] (1932)

309. Rachel Kempson (1910-2003) [Liverpool Playhouse] x 10 *Flowers of the Forest* (1935); *Youth At The Helm* (1935); *Barnet's Folly* (1935); *Miss Linley of Bath* (1935); *Circus Boy* (1935); *Death Takes a Holiday* (1936); *Boyd's Shop* (1936) *Richard of Bordeaux* (1936); *Storm in a Teacup* (1936); *Twelfth Night* (1936)

310. Colin Kenny (1888-1968) [Oswald Joseph Collins] [Warners Burbank] x 3 *We Are Not Alone* (1939); *The Sea Hawk* (1940); *South of Suez* (1940)

311. Crauford Kent (1881-1953) [Warners Burbank] x 7 *We Are Not Alone* (1939); *The Sea Hawk* (1940); *A Dispatch from Reuter's* (1940); *South of Suez* (1940); *The Letter* (1940); *Shining Victory* (1941); *International Squadron* (1941)

312. Milton Kibbee (1896-1970) [Warners Burbank and Republic Studios] x 3
Confessions of a Nazi Spy (1939); *Wolf of New York* (1940); *River's End* (1940)

313. John Kidd [Liverpool Playhouse and BBC Radio] x 12 *Hollywood Holiday* (1932); *The Road to Rome* (1933); *Counsellor-at-Law* (1935); *Round the Northern Repertories: The Liverpool Playhouse* [BBC Radio] (1935); *Miss Linley of Bath* (1935); *Circus Boy* (1935); *Youth at the Helm* (1935); *Barnet's Folly* (1935); *Cornelius* (1935); *Richard of Bordeaux* (1936); *Storm in a Teacup* (1936); *Twelfth Night* (1936)

314. Percy Kilbride (1888-1964) [The Queens, London] x 1 *Post Road* (1937)

315. D.W. King [BBC Radio] x 5 *Boss* (1932); *The Children's Hour: The Shield of Malchus, The Magician* (1932); *The Children's Hour: The Theft of the Crown Jewels* (1932); *The Children's Hour: Timkins Minor and the Vikings* (1932); *Robinson Crusoe: His Life and Adventures Reviewed in Eight Scenes* (1932)

316. Walter Kingsford (1881-1958) [Warners Burbank] x 1 *A Dispatch from Reuter's* (1940)

317. Douglas Kirk (1895-?) [James Kirkbright] [Burnley Amateur Singer] x 2 *Don Giovanni* [Burnley Clef Club, Mechanics Institute] (1928); *Don Giovanni* [Burnley Clef Club, Mechanics Institute] (1929)

318. Miss Elsie Kirk [Burnley Amateur Singer] x 3 *The Magic Flute* [The Burnley Operatic Society, Victoria Theatre] (1929); *Aida* [The Burnley Operatic Society, Palace Theatre] (1930); *Rigoletto* [The Burnley Operatic Society, Victoria Theatre] (1932)

319. Patric Knowles (1911-1995) [Reginald Lawrence Knowles] [Warners Burbank] x 2 *Heart of the North* (1938); *Torchy Blane in Chinatown* (1939)

320. Tetsu Komai (1894-1970) [Warners Burbank] x 2 *Torchy Blane in Chinatown* (1939); *The Letter* (1940)

321. Martin Kosleck (1904-1994) [Nicolaie Yoshkin] [Warners Burbank] x 3 *Confessions of a Nazi Spy* (1939); *Espionage Agent* (1939); *Calling Philo Vance* (1940)

322. Kurt Kreuger (1916-2006) [Warners Burbank] x 1 *International*

Squadron (1941)

323. Otto Kruger (1885-1974) [Warners Burbank] x 1 *A Dispatch from Reuter's* (1940)

324. Nanette Lafayette [Warners Burbank x 1 *Boy Meets Girl* (1938)

325. Mike Lally (1900-1985) [Warners Burbank] x 2 *Heart of the North* (1938); *Murder in the Air* (1940)

326. [Edward Harrison MacGregor] "Jimmie" Landless (1900-1978) [Burnley Amateur, Bank Hall Pit Transport Manager / Tivoli Cinema Manager] x 5 *The Best People* (1930); *It Pays to Advertise* [Victoria Theatre] (1930); *Plunder* [Victoria Theatre] (1931); *Thark* [Victoria Theatre] (1932); *A Cup of Kindness* [Victoria Theatre] (1932)

327. Lola Lane [Dorothy Mullican] (1906-1981) [Warners Burbank] x 1 *When Were You Born* (1938)

328. Priscilla Lane (1915-1995) [Priscilla Mullican] [Warners Burbank] x 1 *Cowboy from Brooklyn* (1938)

329. Betty Langley [Liverpool Playhouse and Winter Gardens, New Brighton] x 14 *Hollywood Holiday* (1932); *Lean Harvest* (1932); *Lady in Waiting* (1932); *The Roundabout* (1932); *What Happened to George* (1932) *The Crime at Blossoms* (1933); *The Kingdom of God* (1933); *The Road to Rome* (1933); *Shall We Join the Ladies?* (1933); *The Rose Without a Thorn* (1934); *Smoke Screen* (1934); *Macbeth* (1934); *Smoke Screen* (1934) [Winter Gardens, New Brighton]; *Hamlet* (1935)

330. Anderson Lawler (1902-1959) [Warners Burbank] x 2 *Heart of the North* (1938); *Torchy Blane in Chinatown* (1939)

331. Arthur Lawrence [Liverpool Playhouse] x 9 *Inquest* (1933); *The Kingdom of God* (1933); *The Road to Rome* (1933); *Cabbages and Kings* (1934); *Gallows Glorious* (1934); *Macbeth* (1934); *Hamlet* (1935); *Circus Boy* (1935); *Twelfth Night* (1936)

332. Joan Lawson [Liverpool Playhouse] x 11 *Hollywood Holiday* (1932); *The Long Christmas Dinner* (1932); *What Happened to George* (1932); *The Crime at Blossoms* (1933); *The Kingdom of God* (1933); *The Lake* (1933);

Is Life Worth Living? (1933); *Smoke Screen* (1934); *Gallows Glorious* (1934); *Macbeth* (1934); *Sheppey* (1934)

333. Wilfrid Lawson (1900-1966) [Wilfrid Worsnop] [Warners Teddington] x 1 *The Man Who Made Diamonds* (1937)

334. Victor Ledder [Liverpool Playhouse] x 5 *Cornelius* (1935); *Circus Boy* (1935); *And So To War* (1936); *Richard of Bordeaux* (1936); *Twelfth Night* (1936)

335. Francis Lederer (1899-2000) [Warners Burbank] x 1 *Confessions of a Nazi Spy* (1939)

336. Eddie Lee [Warners Burbank] x 1 *Torchy Blane in Chinatown* (1939)

337. Max Leeds [Mashiter Leeds] [Warners Teddington] x 1 *It's in the Blood* (1938)

338. Fritz Leiber (1882-1949) [Warners Burbank] x 1 *The Sea Hawk* (1940)

339. Ernest Lennart [Warners Burbank] x 1 *International Squadron* (1941)

340. Miss Shannon Leslie L.R. A.M. (Hons) A.T.C.L. (1900-1979) [Dieudonnee Glebe] [Burnley Amateur, Professor of Elocution and Voice Production] x 10 *The School for Scandal* [Clef Club, Mechanics Institute] (1930); *The Beaux' Stratagem* [Burnley Drama Guild, Victoria Theatre] (1930); *Man and Superman* [Burnley Drama Guild, Victoria Theatre] (1930); *Man and Superman* [Burnley Co-operative Players, Co-op Hall, Todmorden] (1931); *The Merchant of Venice* [Burnley Drama Guild, Burnley Central Library] (1931); *The Father* [Burnley Drama Guild, Victoria Theatre] (1931); *Annajanska* [Free Trade Hall, Manchester] (1931); *Scenes from A Midsummer Night's Dream* [English Folk Festival, "Four Oaks," Higher Reedley] (1931); *Electra* [Burnley Drama Guild, Burnley Central Library] (1931); *Scenes from A Midsummer Night's Dream* [Quernmore Park, Lancaster] (1932)

341. Marion Lessing (1901-1988) [Warners Burbank] x 1 *Calling Philo Vance* (1940)

342. Bruce Lester (1912-2008) [also known as Bruce Lister / Rowland Bruce Somerset Lister] [Warners Teddington and Warners Burbank] x 4 *Mr. Satan* (1938); *Boy Meets Girl* (1938); *The Letter* (1940); *Shining Victory* (1941)

343. Harry Lewis (1920-) [Warners Burbank] x 1 *International Squadron* (1941)

344. Vera Lewis (1873-1956) [Warners Burbank] x 7 *Boy Meets Girl* (1938); *Nancy Drew, Detective* (1938); *Devil's Island* (1938); *King of the Underworld* (1939); *Torchy Blane in Chinatown* (1939); *On Trial* (1939); *Espionage Agent* (1939)

345. Margaret Lindsay [Margaret Kies] (1910-1981) [Warners Burbank] x 2 *When Were You Born* (1938); *On Trial* (1939)

346. Bo Ling [Warners Burbank] x 1 *Calling Philo Vance* (1940)

347. Cyril Lister [Liverpool Playhouse, Winter Gardens, New Brighton and BBC Radio] x 19 *Macbeth* (1934); *Something in the City* (1934); *Laburnum Grove* (1934); *Counsellor-at-Law* (1934); *Sheppey* (1934); *Flowers of the Forest* (1935); *Hamlet* (1935); *Too Young to Marry* (1935); *The Matriarch* (1935); *Libel* (1935) [Winter Gardens, New Brighton]; *Youth at the Helm* (1935); *Barnet's Folly* (1935); *Cornelius* (1935); *Round the Northern Repertories: The Liverpool Playhouse* [BBC Radio] (1935); *Miss Linley of Bath* (1935); *Circus Boy* (1935); *And So To War* (1936); *Richard of Bordeaux* (1936); *Storm in a Teacup* (1936); *Twelfth Night* (1936)

348. Moira Lister (1923-2007) [The Queens, London] x 1 *Post Road* (1937)

349. John [Beach] Litel (1892-1972) [Warners Burbank] x 4 *Nancy Drew Detective* (1938); *Secret Service of the Air* (1939); *On Trial* (1939); *Murder in the Air* (1940)

350. Roger Livesey (1906-1976) [The Garrick, London] x 1 *Storm in a Teacup* (1936)

351. Hessy] Doris Lloyd (1896-1968) [Warners Burbank] x 4 *The Old Maid* (1939); *The Letter* (1940); *Shining Victory* (1941); *International Squadron* (1941)

352. Gene Lockhart (1891-1957) [Eugene Lockhart] [Warners Burbank] x 1 *A Dispatch from Reuter's* (1940)

353. Alexander Lockwood (1902-1990) [Warners Burbank] x 2 *Murder in the Air* (1940); *Flight from Destiny* (1941)

354. Frank Lofthouse [Burnley Amateur] x 5 *The School for Scandal* [Clef

Club, Mechanics Institute] (1930); *Man and Superman* [The Drama Guild, Victoria Theatre] (1931); *The Devil's Disciple* [The Drama Guild, Victoria Theatre] (1931); *The Devil's Disciple* [The Drama Guild, Co-op Hall, Todmorden] (1932); *Scenes from A Midsummer Night's Dream* [Quernmore Park, Lancaster] (1932)

355. Cecilia Loftus (1876-1943) [Warners Burbank] x 1 *The Old Maid* (1939)

356. Stanley Logan (1885-1953) [Warners Burbank] x 2 *We Are Not Alone* (1939); *South of Suez* (1940)

357. Montagu Love (1877-1943) [Warners Burbank] x 3 *Sons of Liberty* (1939); *The Sea Hawk* (1940); *Shining Victory* (1941)

358. Edmund Lowe (1890-1971) [Edmund Dantes Lowe] [Republic Studios] x 1 *Wolf of New York* (1940)

359. Wilfred Lucas (1871-1940) [Warners Burbank] x 2 *Sons of Liberty* (1939); *A Dispatch from Reuter's* (1940)

360. Paul Lukas (1891-1971) [Pal Lukacs] [Warners Burbank] x 1 *Confessions of a Nazi Spy* (1939)

361. William Lundigan (1914-1975) [Warners Burbank] x 3 *The Old Maid* (1939); *The Sea Hawk* (1940); *International Squadron* (1941)

362. Charlie Lung (1897-1974) [Bernard Clerc Davey] [CBS Radio] x 1 *Lux Radio Theatre: The Letter* (1941)

363. Helen Lynd (1902-1992) [Warners Burbank] x 1 *Murder in the Air* (1940)

364. Jeffrey Lynn (1909-1995) [Ragnar Lind] [Warners Burbank] x 4 *Cowboy from Brooklyn* (1938); *When Were You Born* (1938); *Espionage Agent* (1939); *Flight from Destiny* (1941)

365. Betty Lynne (1911-2011) [Margaret Helen Betty Kracklinnis / Betty Suter] [Warners Teddington and Welwyn Studios] x 3 *Take It From Me* (1938); *Mr. Satan* (1938); *Dangerous Fingers* (1938)

366. Lya Lys (1908-1986) [Natalia Lyecht] [Warners Burbank] x 2 *Confessions of a Nazi Spy* (1939); *Murder in the Air* (1940)

367. Lon McCallister (1923-2005) [Herbert Alonzo McCallister Jr] [Warners Burbank] x 1 *Confessions of a Nazi Spy* (1939)

368. Francis McDonald (1891-1968) [Paramount Studios and Warners Burbank] x 2 *Beau Geste* (1939); *The Sea Hawk* (1940)

369. J.[oseph] Farrell McDonald (1875-1952) [Warners Burbank] x 1 *White Banners* (1938)

370. Gibb McLaughlin (1884-1960) [Warner Teddington] x 1 *You Live and Learn* (1938)

371. Edward McWade (1865-1943) [Warners Burbank] x 2 *White Banners* (1938); *A Dispatch from Reuter's* (1940)

372. Noel Madison (1897-1975) [Warners Teddington] x 1 *The Man Who Made Diamonds* (1937)

373. [Joan] Prudence Magor (1911-2007) [Prudence Wallace] [Liverpool Playhouse] x 2 *Hollywood Holiday* (1932); *Lean Harvest* (1932)

374. Wally Maher (1908-1951) [CBS Radio] x 1 *Lux Radio Theatre: The Letter* (1941)

375. Eily Malyon (1879-1961) [Eily Sophie Lees-Craston] [Warners Burbank] x 2 *Confessions of a Nazi Spy* (1939); *We Are Not Alone* (1939)

376. Miles Mander (1888-1946) [Lionel Mander] [Warners Burbank] x 1 *South of Suez* (1940)

377. Nadine March (1898-1944) [Welwyn Studios] x 1 *Dangerous Fingers* (1938)

378. Howard Marion-Crawford (1914-1969) [Liverpool Playhouse and BBC Radio] x 2 *Hamlet* (1935); *Death of a First Mate* (1937)

379. Brenda Marshall (1915-1992) [Ardis Ankerson Gaines] [Warners Burbank] x 3 *Espionage Agent* (1939); *The Sea Hawk* (1940); *South of Suez* (1940)

380. Herbert [Brough Falcon] Marshall (1890-1966) [Warners Burbank and CBS Radio] x 2 *The Letter* (1940); *Lux Radio Theatre: The Letter* (1941)

381. Chris-Pin Martin (1893-1953) [Ysabel Ponciana Chris-Pin Martin Piaz] [Warners Burbank] x 1 *Espionage Agent* (1939)

382. Edie Martin (1880-1964) [Liverpool Playhouse] x 1 *Counsellor-at-Law* (1934)

383. Lester Matthews (1900-1975) [Warners Burbank] x 1 *The Sea Hawk* (1940)

384. Frank Mayo (1886-1963) [Warners Burbank] x 9 *Cowboy from Brooklyn* (1938); *Heart of the North* (1938); *Torchy Blane in Chinatown* (1939); *Secret Service of the Air* (1939); *Confessions of a Nazi Spy* (1939); *The Monroe Doctrine* (1939); *Calling Philo Vance* (1940); *Murder in the Air* (1940); *River's End* (1940)

385. Mary Merrall (1890-1973) [Mary Lloyd] [The Queens, London] x 1 *Post Road* (1937)

386. George Merritt (1890-1977) [Welwyn Studios] x 1 *Dangerous Fingers* (1938)

387. Marcus Merwin [The Queens, London] x 1 *Post Road* (1937)

388. Ray Milland (1905-1986) [Reginald Alfred Truscott-Jones] [Paramount Studios] x 1 *Beau Geste* (1939)

389. Max Miller (1894-1963) [Thomas Henry Sargent] [Warners Teddington] x 1 *Take It From Me* (1938)

390. Donald Mills [Liverpool Playhouse] x 6 *Youth at the Helm* (1935); *Cornelius* (1935); *Circus Boy* (1935); *And So To War* (1936); *Richard of Bordeaux* (1936); *Twelfth Night* (1936)

391. Grant Mitchell (1874-1957) [Warners Burbank] x 1 *The Monroe Doctrine* (1939)

392. Julien Mitchell (1888-1954) [Warners Burbank] x 1 *The Sea Hawk* (1940)

393. Thomas Mitchell (1892-1962) [Warners Burbank] x 1 *Flight from Destiny* (1941)

394. Prince Modupe [Warners Burbank] x 1 *South of Suez* (1940)

395. Gerald Mohr (1914-1968) [Warners Burbank] x 1 *The Sea Hawk* (1940)

396. Miss Florence Moon [Burnley Amateur] x 17 *The Best People* [The Burnley Players, Victoria Theatre] (1930); *It Pays to Advertise* [The Burnley Players, Victoria Theatre] (1930); *Aida* [The Burnley Operatic Society, Palace Theatre] (1930); *Man and Superman* [The Drama Guild, Victoria Theatre] (1930); *Act I of Man and Superman* [Burnley Drama Guild, Burnley Central Library] (1931) *Man and Superman* [Burnley Co-operative Players, Co-op Hall, Todmorden] (1931*); The Father* [Burnley Drama Guild, Victoria Theatre] (1931); *Merchant of Venice Readings* [1] [Burnley Drama Guild, Burnley Central Library] (1931); *Merchant of Venice Readings* [2] [Burnley Drama Guild, Burnley Central Library] (1931); *Oedipus the King* [Burnley Drama Guild, Burnley Central Library] (1931); *Plunder* [The Burnley Players, Victoria Theatre] (1931); *Pompey the Great* [Burnley Drama Guild, Burnley Central Library] (1931) *Man and Superman* [Burnley Drama Guild, Burnley Central Library] (1932); *Rigoletto* [The Burnley Operatic Society, Victoria Theatre] (1932); *A Cup of Kindness* [The Burnley Players, Victoria Theatre] (1932); *Thark* [The Burnley Players, Victoria Theatre] (1932); *Plunder* [The Burnley Players, Victoria Theatre] (1932)

397. Clayton Moore (1914-1999) [Warners Burbank] x 2 *Cowboy from Brooklyn* (1938); *When Were You Born* (1938)

398. Dennie Moore (1907-1978) [Warners Burbank] x 3 *Cowboy from Brooklyn* (1938); *Boy Meets Girl* (1938); *The Adventures of Jane Arden* (1939)

399. Dickie Moore (1925-) [John Richard Moore Jr] [Warners Burbank] x 1 *A Dispatch from Reuter's* (1940)

400. Peggy Moran (1918-2002) [Warners Burbank] x 2 *Boy Meets Girl* (1938); *King of the Underworld* (1939)

401. Dennis Morgan (1908-1994) [Earl Stanley Morner] [Warners Burbank] x 1 *River's End* (1940)

402. Edmund Mortimer (1874-1944) [Warners Burbank] x 1 *Torchy Blane in Chinatown* (1939)

403. Eve Mortimer [Liverpool Playhouse] x 17 *What Happened to George* (1932); *Shall We Join the Ladies?* (1933); *Is Life Worth Living?* (1933); *Crime at Blossoms* (1933); *The Kingdom of God* (1933); *What Happened to George* (1933); *The Rose Without a Thorn* (1934); *Cabbages and Kings*

(1934); *Macbeth* (1934); *Sheppey* (1934); *The Matriarch* (1935); *Hamlet* (1935); *Barnet's Folly* (1935); *Cornelius* (1935); *Circus Boy* (1935); *Death Takes a Holiday* (1936); *Twelfth Night* (1936)

404. Jack Mower (1890-1965) [Warners Burbank] x 13 *Cowboy from Brooklyn* (1938); *Heart of the North* (1938); *Nancy Drew Detective* (1938); *King of the Underworld* (1939); *Torchy Blane in Chinatown* (1939); *Secret Service of the Air* (1939); *On Trial* (1939); *Confessions of a Nazi Spy* (1939); *Sons of Liberty* (1939); *Espionage Agent* (1939); *The Monroe Doctrine* (1939); *Murder in the Air* (1940); *River's End* (1940)

405. Leonard Mudie (1883-1965) [Leonard Mudie Cheetham] [Warners Burbank] x 7 *When Were You Born* (1938); *Sons of Liberty* (1939); *The Sea Hawk* (1940); *A Dispatch from Reuter's* (1940); *South of Suez* (1940); *The Letter* (1940); *Shining Victory* (1941)

406. Paul Muni (1895-1967) [Meshilem Meier Weisenfreund) [Warners Burbank] x 1 *We Are Not Alone* (1939)

407. Maurice Murphy (1913-1978) [Republic Studios] x 1 *Wolf of New York* (1940)

408. Forbes Murray (1884-1982) [Republic Studios] x 1 *Wolf of New York* (1940)

409. J[oseph Patrick] Carroll Naish (1896-1973) [Paramount Studios] x 1 *Beau Geste* (1939)

410. Alan Napier (1903-1988) [Alan Napier-Clavering] [Warners Burbank] x 1 *We Are Not Alone* (1939)

411. [George] Eric [Grinham] Nayler (1908-?) [Burnley Amateur, Printing Firm Manager] x 6 *It Pays to Advertise* [The Burnley Players, Victoria Theatre] (1930); *The Father* [Burnley Drama Guild, Victoria Theatre] (1931); *Plunder* [The Burnley Players, Victoria Theatre] (1931); *A Cup of Kindness* [The Burnley Players, Victoria Theatre] (1932); *Thark* [The Burnley Players, Victoria Theatre] (1932); *Plunder* [The Burnley Players, Victoria Theatre] (1932)

412. Ottola Nesmith (1889-1972) [Warners Burbank] x 3 *The Letter* (1940); *Shining Victory* (1941); *International Squadron* (1941)

413. David Newell (1905-1980) [Warners Burbank] x 3 *Heart of the North*

(1938); *We Are Not Alone* (1939); *The Letter* (1940)

414. Frank A. Nichols (1884-?) [BBC Radio] x 4 *The Spectral Dog* (1932); *The Children's Hour: The Shield of Malchus, The Magician* (1932); *The Children's Hour: The Theft of the Crown Jewels* (1932); *The Pigeon* (1932)

415. Arthur Nightingale (1900-?) [Burnley Amateur, Cashier] x 11 *The Magic Flute* [The Burnley Operatic Society, Victoria Theatre] (1929); *The School for Scandal* [Clef Club, Mechanics Institute] (1930); *The Beaux' Stratagem* [Burnley Drama Guild, Victoria Theatre] (1930); *Merchant of Venice Readings* [1] [Burnley Drama Guild, Burnley Central Library] (1931); *Merchant of Venice Readings* [2] [Burnley Drama Guild, Burnley Central Library] (1931); *Annajanska* [Burnley Drama Guild, Free Trade Hall, Manchester] (1931); *Scenes from A Midsummer Night's Dream* [English Folk Festival, "Four Oaks," Higher Reedley] (1931); *Electra* [Burnley Drama Guild, Burnley Central Library] (1931); *The Devil's Disciple* [Burnley Drama Guild, Victoria Theatre] (1931); *Rigoletto* [The Burnley Operatic Society, Victoria Theatre] (1932) *The Devil's Disciple* [Burnley Drama Guild, Co-op Hall, Todmorden] (1932)

416. Eric Noels [Liverpool Playhouse] x 10 *Hollywood Holiday* (1932); *Lean Harvest* (1932); *Lady in Waiting* (1932); *What Happened to George* (1932); *Inquest* (1933); *Don't Tell England* (1933); *The Crime at Blossoms* (1933); *Another Language* (1933); *The Kingdom of God* (1933); *The Queen's Husband* (1933)

417. Wedgewood Nowell (1878-1957) [Warners Burbank] x 3 *Calling Philo Vance* (1940); *Murder in the Air* (1940); *Flight from Destiny* (1941)

418. Miss Carrie Nutter-Smith [Burnley Amateur, Soprano Singer] x 6 *Operatic Evening* [Burnley Clef Club, Mechanics Institute] (1920); *Don Giovanni* [Burnley Clef Club, Mechanics Institute] (1928); *Don Giovanni* [Burnley Clef Club, Mechanics Institute] (1929); *The Magic Flute* [The Burnley Operatic Society, Victoria Theatre] (1929); *Aida* [The Burnley Operatic Society, Palace Theatre] (1930); *Municipal Concert* [Palace Theatre] (1932)

419. Pat O'Brien (1899-1983) [William Joseph Patrick O'Brien] [Warners Burbank] x 2 *Cowboy from Brooklyn* (1938); *Boy Meets Girl* (1938)

420. Donald O'Connor (1925-2003) [Paramount Studios] x 1 *Beau Geste* (1939)

421. Una O'Connor (1880-1959) [Agnes Teresa McGlade] [Warners Burbank] x 2 *We Are Not Alone* (1939); *The Sea Hawk* (1940)

422. George O'Hanlon (1912-1989) [Warners Burbank] x 1 *The Adventures of Jane Arden* (1939)

423. Pat O'Hara (1910-1979) [Warners Burbank] x 2 *A Dispatch from Reuter's* (1940); *International Squadron* (1941)

424. Eileen Oldham [Liverpool Playhouse] x 9 *Hollywood Holiday* (1932); *Lean Harvest* (1932); *The Long Christmas Dinner* (1932); *Lady in Waiting* (1932); *What Happened to George* (1932); *Mourning Becomes Electra* [Overseas League, Liverpool] (1933); *The Crime at Blossoms* (1933); *The Kingdom of God* (1933); *The Queen's Husband* (1933)

425. Moroni Olsen (1889-1954) [Warners Burbank] x 1 *Sons of Liberty* (1939)

426. Pat O'Malley (1890-1966) [Patrick H. O'Malley Jr] [Warners Burbank] x 3 *Secret Service of the Air* (1939); *River's End* (1940); *A Dispatch from Reuter's* (1940)

427. Barbara O'Neil (1910-1980) [Warners Burbank] x 1 *Shining Victory* (1941)

428. Henry O'Neill (1891-1961) [Warners Burbank] x 5 *White Banners* (1938); *Torchy Blane in Chinatown* (1939); *Sons of Liberty* (1939); *Confessions of a Nazi Spy* (1939); *Calling Philo Vance* (1940)

429. Frank Orth (1880-1962) [Warners Burbank] x 2 *Nancy Drew, Detective* (1938); *King of the Underworld* (1939)

430. Ted Osborne (1905-1987) [Warners Burbank] x 1 *The Monroe Doctrine* (1939)

431. Henry Otho [Wright] (1888-1940) [Warners Burbank] x 2 *Devil's Island* (1938); *Secret Service of the Air* (1939)

432. Garry Owen (1902-1951) [Warners Burbank] x 1 *Heart of the North* (1938)

433. Mardale Owen [Liverpool Playhouse] x 7 *The Road to Rome* (1933); *The Lake* (1933); *After the Event* (1933); *Fun While It Lasts* (1933); *Cabbages*

and Kings (1934); *Gallows Glorious* (1934); *Macbeth* (1934)

434. Sarah Padden (1881-1967) [Warners Burbank] x 1 *Sons of Liberty* (1939)

435. Gale Page (1911-1983) [Sally Perkins Rutter] [Warners Burbank and KFW Radio] x 2 *Heart of the North* (1938); *I Found Stella Parish* (1938)

436. Nestor Paiva (1905-1966) [Paramount Studios and Warners Burbank] x 2 *Beau Geste* (1939); *The Sea Hawk* (1940)

437. Inez Palange (1889-1962) [Warners Burbank] x 1 *Flight from Destiny* (1941)

438. Paul Panzer [Paul Wolfgang Panzerbeiter] (1872-1958) x 10 *When Were You Born* (1938); *Heart of the North* (1938); *Devil's Island* (1938); *King of the Underworld* (1939); *Torchy Blane in Chinatown* (1939); *Secret Service of the Air* (1939); *Murder in the Air* (1940); *River's End* (1940); *Flight from Destiny* (1941); *Shining Victory* (1941)

439. Miss Laura Parker (1891-?) [Burnley Amateur Singer] x 3 *The Magic Flute* [The Burnley Operatic Society, Victoria Theatre] (1929); *Aida* [The Burnley Operatic Society, Palace Theatre] (1930); *Rigoletto* [The Burnley Operatic Society, Victoria Theatre] (1932)

440. Clifford [Alwyn] Parkinson (1897-1957) [Burnley Amateur, Manchester Corn Exchange Clerk / Parish Priest / RAF Padre] x 8 *The School for Scandal* [Clef Club, Mechanics Institute] (1930); *It Pays to Advertise* [The Burnley Players, Victoria Theatre] (1930); *Man and Superman* [Burnley Drama Guild, Victoria Theatre] (1930); *Man and Superman* [Burnley Co-operative Players, Co-op Hall, Todmorden] (1931); *Merchant of Venice Readings* [1] [Burnley Drama Guild, Burnley Central Library] (1931); *Annajanska* [Burnley Drama Guild, Free Trade Hall, Manchester] (1931); *Oedipus the King* [Burnley Drama Guild, Burnley Central Library] (1931); *"Pompey" the Great* [Burnley Drama Guild, Burnley Central Library] (1931)

441. Lee Patrick (1901-1982) [Warners Burbank] x 1 *South of Suez* (1940)

442. Edward Pawley (1901-1988) [Warners Burbank] x 1 *River's End* (1940)

443. William Pawley (1905-1952) [Warners Burbank] x 1 *White Banners* (1938)

444. Lloyd Pearson (1897-1966) [Liverpool Playhouse and Winter Gardens,

New Brighton] x 59 *Hollywood Holiday* (1932); *Lean Harvest* (1932); *Twelfth Night* (1932); *The Long Christmas Dinner* (1932); *Lady In Waiting* (1932); *The Roundabout* (1932); *What Happened to George* (1932); *Inquest* (1933); *Don't Tell England* (1933); *A Bite of the Apple* (1933); *Mourning Becomes Electra* [Overseas League, Liverpool] (1933); *The Crime at Blossoms* (1933); *The Kingdom of God* (1933); *Laying the Devil* (1933); *The Queen's Husband* (1933); *Never Come Back* (1933); *Inquest* [Winter Gardens, New Brighton] (1933); *The Queen's Husband* [Winter Gardens, New Brighton] (1933); *Art and Mrs. Bottle* [Winter Gardens, New Brighton] (1933); *Anthony & Anna* [Winter Gardens, New Brighton] (1933); *The Road to Rome* (1933); *Britannia of Billingsgate* (1933); *The Cathedral* (1933); *Shall We Join the Ladies?* (1933); *Is Life Worth Living?* (1933); *Fun While It Lasts* (1933); *The Rose Without a Thorn* (1934); *Cabbages and Kings* (1934); *Gallows Glorious* (1934); *Macbeth* (1934); *The Cathedral* [Winter Gardens, New Brighton] (1934); *The Lake* [Winter Gardens, New Brighton] (1934); *Britannia of Billingsgate* [Winter Gardens, New Brighton]; *Counsellor-at-Law* (1934); *A Sleeping Clergyman* (1934); *Something in the City* (1934); *Sheppey* (1934); *Laburnum Grove* (1934); *Ferry Inn* (1934); *Libel* (1935); *Hamlet* (1935); *Too Young to Marry* (1935); *The Matriarch* (1935); *Libel* [Winter Gardens, New Brighton] (1935); *Counsellor-at-Law* [Winter Gardens, New Brighton] (1935); *Too Young to Marry* [Winter Gardens, New Brighton] (1935); *The Distaff Side* [Winter Gardens, new Brighton] (1935); *Sheppey* [Winter Gardens, New Brighton] (1935); *Youth at the Helm* (1935); *Barnet's Folly* (1935); *Miss Linley of Bath* (1935); *Compromise* (1935); *Circus Boy* (1935); *Death Takes a Holiday* (1936); *And So To War* (1936); *Boyd's Shop* (1936); *Richard of Bordeaux* (1936); *Storm in a Teacup* (1936); *Twelfth Night* (1936)

445. Leslie Perrins (1902-1962) [BBC Radio and Welwyn Studios] x 2 *News, The History of the Fourth Estate* (1937); *Dangerous Fingers* (1938)

446. Joan Perry (1911-1996) [Elizabeth Rosiland Miller] [Warners Burbank] x 1 *International Squadron* (1941)

447. James Pick [Burnley Amateur, Accountant] x 4 *The Best People* [The Burnley Players, Victoria Theatre] (1930); *It Pays to Advertise* [The Burnley Players, Victoria Theatre] (1930); *Plunder* [The Burnley Players, Victoria Theatre] (1931); *A Cup of Kindness* [The Burnley Players, Victoria Theatre] (1932).

448. Tempe Pigott (1884-1962) [Warners Burbank] x 2 *Confessions of a Nazi Spy* (1939); *Shining Victory* (1941)

449. Audrey Pimblett [Liverpool Playhouse] x 9 *Hollywood Holiday* (1932); *Lean Harvest* (1932); *What Happened to George* (1932); *The Crime at Blossoms* (1933); *The Kingdom of God* (1933); *Fun While It Lasts* (1933); *The Rose Without a Thorn* (1934); *Cabbages and Kings* (1934); *Gallows Glorious* (1934)

450. Harold Pollard [Burnley Amateur] x 6 *The Beaux' Stratagem* [The Drama Guild, Victoria Theatre] (1930); *Man and Superman* [The Drama Guild, Victoria Theatre] (1930); *Man and Superman* [Burnley Co-operative Players, Co-op Hall, Todmorden] (1931); *Merchant of Venice Readings* [1] [Burnley Drama Guild, Burnley Central Library] (1931); *Merchant of Venice Readings* [2] [Burnley Drama Guild, Burnley Central Library] (1931); *Scenes from a Midsummer Night's Dream* [English Folk Festival, "Four Oaks," Higher Reedley] (1931)

451. Dick Powell (1904-1963) [Richard Ewing Powell] [Warners Burbank] x 1 *Cowboy from Brooklyn* (1938)

452. Bryan Powley (1871-1962) [Warners Teddington] x 1 *Mr. Satan* (1938)

453. Robert Preston (1918-1987) [Robert Preston Meservey] [Paramount Studios] x 1 *Beau Geste* (1939)

454. Vincent Price (1911-1993) [Warners Burbank] x 1 *The Private Lives of Elizabeth and Essex* (1939)

455. Lucien Prival (1900-1994) [Warners Burbank] x 2 *Espionage Agent* (1939); *Confessions of a Nazi Spy* (1939)

456. Frank Puglia (1892-1975) [Warners Burbank] x 1 *The Monroe Doctrine* (1939)

457. Dick Purcell. (1908-1944) [Warners Burbank] x 1 *Nancy Drew Detective* (1938)

458. Reginald Purdell (1895-1953) [Reginald W.H. Grasdorff] [Warners Teddington] x 2 *Perfect Crime* (1937); *The Dark Stairway* (1938)

459. Richard Quine (1920-1989) [Warners Burbank] x 1 *King of the*

Underworld (1939)

460. Margaret Radcliffe [Liverpool Playhouse] x 8 *Fun While It Lasts* (1933); *Winsome Winnie* (1933); *Britannia of Billingsgate* (1933); *The Lake* (1933); *The Cathedral* (1933); *Shall we Join the Ladies?* (1933); *The Rose Without a Thorn* (1934); *Smoke Screen* (1934)

461. [William] Claude Rains (1889-1967) [Warners Burbank] x 3 *White Banners* (1938); *Sons of Liberty* (1939); *The Sea Hawk* (1940)

462. Edward Raquello (1900-1976) [Warners Burbank] x 1 *Calling Philo Vance* (1940)

463. Herbert Rawlinson (1885-1953) [Warners Burbank] x 1 *Secret Service of the Air* (1939)

464. Philip Ray (1898-1976) [Warners Teddington and Welwyn Studios] x 3 *Perfect Crime* (1937); *The Man Who Made Diamonds* (1937); *Dangerous Fingers* (1938)

465. Ronald [Wilson] Reagan (1911-2004) [Warners Burbank] x 5 *Cowboy from Brooklyn* (1938); *Boy Meets Girl* (1938); *Secret Service of the Air* (1939); *Murder in the Air* (1940); *International Squadron* (1941)

466. Michael Redgrave (1908-1985) [Liverpool Playhouse, Winter Gardens, New Brighton and BBC Radio] x 24 *Counsellor-at-Law* (1934); *The Distaff Side* (1934); *A Sleeping Clergyman* (1934); *Sheppey* (1934); *Biography* (1935); *Libel* (1935); *Flowers of the Forest* (1935); *Hamlet* (1935); *Too Young to Marry* (1935); *The Matriarch* (1935); *Counsellor-at-Law* [Winter Gardens, New Brighton] (1935); *Libel* [Winter Gardens, New Brighton] (1935); *Too Young to Marry* [Winter Gardens, New Brighton] (1935); *Youth at the Helm* (1935); *Barnet's Folly* (1935); *Cornelius* (1935); *Round the Northern Repertories: The Liverpool Playhouse* [BBC Radio] (1935); *Miss Linley of Bath* (1935); *Circus Boy* (1935); *And So To War* (1936); *Boyd's Shop* (1936); *Richard of Bordeaux* (1936); *Storm in a Teacup* (1936); *Twelfth Night* (1936)

467. George Reeves (1914-1959) [George Keefer Brewer] [Warners Burbank] x 3 *Espionage Agent* (1939); *The Monroe Doctrine* (1939); *Calling Philo Vance* (1940)

468. George Regas (1890-1940) [Paramount Studios] x 1 *Beau Geste* (1939)

469. Frank Reicher (1875-1965) [Franz Reichert] [Warners Burbank] x 2 *Flight from Destiny* (1941); *Shining Victory* (1941)

470. Hedwiga Reicher (1884-1971) [Warners Burbank] x 1 *Confessions of a Nazi Spy* (1939)

471. George Renavent (1894-1969) [Georges de Cheux] [Warners Burbank] x 2 *The Adventures of Jane Arden* (1939); *A Dispatch from Reuter's* (1940)

472. Robert Rendel (1890-1973) [BBC Radio and Warners Teddington] x 3 *The Blue Danube* (1937); *Mr. Satan* (1938); *The Dark Stairway* (1938)

473. Ernest Retlaw [BBC Radio] x 7 *The Spectral Dog* (1932); *The Children's Hour: The Siege of Malchus The Magician* (1932); *Hunt the Tiger* (1932); *The Children's Hour: The Theft of the Crown Jewels* (1932); *Robinson Crusoe: His Life and Adventures in Eight Scenes* (1932); *The Pigeon* (1932); *The Ship* (1932)

474. Dick Rich (1909-1967) [Warners Burbank] x 2 *Devil's Island* (1938); *Murder in the Air* (1940)

475. Addison Richards (1887-1964) [Warner Burbank] x 2 *Espionage Agent* (1939); *International Squadron* (1941)

476. Jack Richardson (1883-1957) [Warners Burbank] x 8 *Heart of the North* (1938); *King of the Underworld* (1939); *Torchy Blane in Chinatown* (1939); *Secret Service of the Air* (1939); *The Adventures of Jane Arden* (1939); *Espionage Agent* (1939); *Calling Philo Vance* (1940); *South of Suez* (1940)

477. John Ridgely (1909-1968) [John Huntington Rea] [Warners Burbank] x 8 *When Were You Born?* (1938); *White Banners* (1938); *Torchy Blane in Chinatown* (1939); *Secret Service of the Air* (1939); *Confessions of a Nazi Spy* (1939); *River's End* (1940); *The Letter* (1940); *International Squadron* (1941)

478. Stanley Ridges (1890-1951) [Warners Burbank] x 1 *Espionage Agent* (1939)

479. Elizabeth Risdon [Elisabeth Evans] (1887-1958) [Warners Burbank] x 1

Cowboy from Brooklyn (1938)

480. J. Edward Roberts [BBC Radio] x 3 *The Spectral Dog* (1932); *The Children's Hour: The Theft of the Crown Jewels* (1932); *Robinson Crusoe: His Life and Adventures in Eight Scenes* (1932)

481. Stuart Robertson (1901-1958) [Warners Burbank] x 1 *River's End* (1940)

482. Bernard Robinson [Liverpool Playhouse and Winter Gardens, New Brighton] x 10 *Macbeth* (1934); *Counsellor-at-Law* (1934); *A Sleeping Clergyman* (1934); *Libel* (1935); *Hamlet* (1935); *Libel* [Winter Gardens, New Brighton] (1935); *Cornelius* (1935); *Circus Boy* (1935); *Richard of Bordeaux* (1936); *Storm in a Teacup* (1936)

483. Edward G. Robinson (1893-1973) [Emmanuel Goldenberg] [Warners Burbank] x 2 *Confessions of a Nazi Spy* (1939); *A Dispatch from Reuter's* (1940)

484. Flora Robson (1902-1984) [Warners Burbank] x 2 *We Are Not Alone* (1939); *The Sea Hawk* (1940)

485. Gilbert Roland (1905-1994) [Luis Antonio Dámaso de Alonso] [Warners Burbank] x 1 *The Sea Hawk* (1940)

486. Bodil Rosing (1878-1942) [Warners Burbank] x 1 *Confessions of a Nazi Spy* (1939)

487. Lionel Royce (1891-1946) [Warners Burbank] x 2 *Espionage Agent* (1939); *Confessions of a Nazi Spy* (1939)

488. Sig Ruman (1884-1967) [Siegfrid Albon Rumann] [Warners Burbank] x 2 *Confessions of a Nazi Spy* (1939); *Shining Victory* (1941)

489. Miss Teresa Russell [Burnley Professional Soprano Singer] x 2 *Don Giovanni* [Burnley Clef Club, Mechanics Institute] (1928); *The Magic Flute* [The Burnley Operatic Society, Victoria Theatre] (1929)

490. Edmond Ryan (1905-1984) [Edmon Ryan Mossbarger] [The Queens, London] x 1 *Post Road* (1937)

491. Sally Sage (1914-2000) [Warners Burbank] x 1 *Espionage Agent* (1939)

492. George Sanders (1906-1972) [Warners Burbank] x 1 *Confessions of a Nazi Spy* (1939)

493. Alfred Sangster (1880-1972) [Liverpool Playhouse and Winter Gardens, New Brighton] x 14 *Libel* (1935); *Hamlet* (1935); *Too Young to Marry* (1935); *Libel* [Winter Gardens, New Brighton] (1935); *Too Young to Marry* [Winter Gardens, New Brighton] (1935); *Cornelius* (1935); *Miss Linley of Bath* (1935); *Compromise* (1935); *Circus Boy* (1935); *Death Takes a Holiday* (1936); *Boyd's Shop* (1936); *And So To War* (1936); *Richard of Bordeaux* (1936); *Storm in a Teacup* (1936)

494. Cliff Saum (1882-1943) [Warners Burbank] x 14 *Cowboy from Brooklyn* (1938); *White Banners* (1938); *When Were You Born* (1938); *Heart of the North* (1938); *Boy Meets Girl* (1938); *Nancy Drew Detective* (1938); *Devil's Island* (1938); *King of the Underworld* (1939); *Torchy Blane in Chinatown* (1939); *Secret Service of the Air* (1939); *The Adventures of Jane Arden* (1939); *On Trial* (1939); *Calling Philo Vance* (1940); *River's End* (1940)

495. Joe Sawyer (1906-1982) [Joseph Sauers] [Warners Burbank] x 2 *Heart of the North* (1938); *Confessions of a Nazi Spy* (1939)

496. Francis Sayles (1891-1944) [Warners Burbank] x 1 *Devil's Island* (1938); *King of the Underworld* (1939)

497. Ferdinand Schumann-Heink (1893-1958) [Warners Burbank] x 2 *Confessions of a Nazi Spy* (1939); *Espionage Agent* (1939)

498. Hans Schumm (1896-1990) [Warners Burbank] x 3 *Espionage Agent* (1939); *Confessions of a Nazi Spy* (1939); *Calling Philo Vance* (1940)

499. Sara Seegar (1914-1990) [The Queens, London] x 1 *Post Road* (1937)

500. Frank [Connolly] Shannon (1874-1959) [Warners Burbank] x 2 *Torchy Blane in Chinatown* (1939); *A Dispatch from Reuter's* (1940)

501. Peggy Shannon (1910-1941) [Warners Burbank] x 1 *The Adventures of Jane Arden* (1939)

502. Lester Sharpe (1894-1962) [Warners Burbank] x 1 *Confessions of a Nazi Spy* (1939)

503. [Thomas] Alan Shaw [Burnley Amateur, Bank Cashier] (1904-?) x 15 *The Best People* [The Burnley Players, Victoria Theatre] (1930), *It Pays to Advertise* [The Burnley Players, Victoria Theatre] (1930); *The Beaux' Stratagem* [Burnley Drama Guild, Victoria Theatre] (1930); *Man and Superman* [Burnley Drama Guild, Victoria Theatre] (1930); *Man and Superman* [Burnley Co-operative Players, Co-op Hall, Todmorden] (1931); *Merchant of Venice* [1] [Burnley Drama Guild, Burnley Central Library] (1931); *Merchant of Venice* [2] [Burnley Drama Guild, Burnley Central Library] (1931); *Oedipus, The King* [Burnley Drama Guild, Burnley Central Library] (1931); *The Father* [Burnley Drama Guild, Victoria Theatre] (1931); *"Pompey" The Great* [Burnley Drama Guild, Burnley Central Library] (1931); *Electra* [Burnley Drama Guild, Burnley Central Library] (1931); *Man and Superman* [Burnley Drama Guild, Victoria Theatre] (1931); *The Devil's Disciple* [Burnley Drama Guild, Victoria Theatre] (1931); *A Cup of Kindness* [The Burnley Players, Victoria Theatre] (1932); *The Devil's Disciple* [Burnley Drama Guild, Co-op Hall, Todmorden] (1932)

504. Janet Shaw (1919-2001) [Ellen Martha Clancy Stuart] [Warners Burbank] x 3 *King of the Underworld* (1939); *Torchy Blane in Chinatown* (1939); *The Old Maid* (1939)

505. Sebastian Shaw (1905-1994) [BBC Radio] x 1 *Twenty Years After* (1937)

506. Norman Shelley (1903-1980) [BBC Radio] x 4 *Scotland Yard: Life in the Metropolitan Police* (1936); *Twenty Years After* (1937); *News, The History of the Fourth Estate* (1937); *For the Children: The King's Chair* (1937)

507. Ann Sheridan (1915-1967) [Clara Lou Sheridan] [Warners Burbank] x 1 *Cowboy from Brooklyn* (1938)

508. Charles Sherlock (1900-1983) [Warners Burbank] x 2 *Confessions of a Nazi Spy* (1939); *Murder in the Air* (1940)

509. Larry Silverstone [Liverpool Playhouse, Winter Gardens, New Brighton and BBC Radio] x 22 *The Lake* (1933); *Fun While It Lasts* (1933); *The Road to Rome* (1933); *The Lake* [Winter Gardens, New Brighton] (1934); *Cabbages and Kings* (1934); *Gallows Glorious* (1934); *Macbeth* (1934); *A Sleeping Clergyman* (1934); *Counsellor-at-Law* (1934); *Hamlet* (1935); *The Seventh Man* (1935); *The Matriarch* (1935); *Counsellor-at-Law* [Winter Gardens, New Brighton] (1935); *Too Young to Marry*

[Winter Gardens, New Brighton] (1935); *Sheppey* [Winter Gardens, New Brighton] (1935); *Cornelius* (1935); *Round the Northern Repertories: The Liverpool Playhouse* [BBC Radio] (1935); *Circus Boy* (1935); *And So To War* (1936); *Death Takes a Holiday* (1936); *Storm in a Teacup* (1936); *Twelfth Night* (1936)

510. Russell [McCaskill] Simpson (1880-1959) [Warners Burbank] x 1 *Heart of the North* (1938)

511. Penny Singleton (1908-2003) [Mariana Dorothy Agnes McNulty] [Warners Burbank] x 1 *Boy Meets Girl* (1938)

512. Albert Smith [Burnley Amateur] x 6 *The Beaux' Stratagem* [Burnley Drama Guild, Victoria Theatre] (1930); *Merchant of Venice Readings* [1] [Burnley Drama Guild, Burnley Central Library] (1931); *Merchant of Venice Readings* [2] [Burnley Drama Guild, Burnley Central Library] (1931); *Annajanska* [Burnley Drama Guild, Free Trade Hall, Manchester] (1931); *Scenes from A Midsummer Night's Dream* [English Folk Festival, "Four Oaks," Higher Reedley] (1931); *Scenes from A Midsummer Night's Dream* [Quernmore Park, Lancaster] (1932)

513. Alexis Smith (1921-1993) [Gladys Smith] [Warners Burbank] x 1 *Flight From Destiny* (1941)

514. Eric Snowden (1888-1979) [CBS Radio] x 1 *Lux Radio Theatre: The Letter* (1941)

515. Walter Soderling (1872-1948) [Warners Burbank] x 1 *Devil's Island* (1938)

516. Vladimir Sokoloff (1889-1962) [Warners Burbank] x 1 *Sons of Liberty* (1939)

517. Gale Sondergaard (1899-1985) [Edith Holm Sondergaard] [Warners Burbank] x 2 *Sons of Liberty* (1939); *The Letter* (1940)

518. George Sorel (1901-1948) [Warners Burbank] x 2 *Secret Service of the Air* (1939); *A Dispatch from Reuter's* (1940)

519. Grace Stafford (1903-1992) [Grace Boyle] [Warners Burbank] x 2 *Confessions of a Nazi Spy* (1939); *A Dispatch from Reuter's* (1940)

520. Edwin Stanley (1880-1944) [Warners Burbank] x 5 *King of the Underworld*

(1939); *Confessions of a Nazi Spy* (1939); *The Monroe Doctrine* (1939); *Murder in the Air* (1940); *Flight from Destiny* (1941)

521. Eric Stanley [Warners Burbank] x 1 *When Were You Born* (1938)

522. Ernie Stanton (1890-1944) [Warners Burbank] x 2 *A Dispatch from Reuter's* (1940); *South of Suez* (1940)

523. Graham Stark (1922-) [Liverpool Playhouse] x 1 *Macbeth* (1934)

524. Rudolf Steinboeck (1908-1996) [Warners Burbank] x 1 *Confessions of a Nazi Spy* (1939)

525. Harvey Stephens (1901-1986) [Paramount Studios] x 1 *Beau Geste* (1939)

526. Henry Stephenson (1871-1956) [Harry Stephenson Garraway] [Warners Burbank] x 1 *The Private Lives of Elizabeth and Essex* (1939)

527. Hermine Sterler (1894-1982) [Warners Burbank] x 1 *Shining Victory* (1941)

528. Julie Stevens (1916-1984) [Harriet Foote] [Warners Burbank] x 1 *Murder in the Air* (1940)

529. Margot Stevenson (1912-2011) [Margaret Helen Stevenson] [Warners Burbank] x 1 *Calling Philo Vance* (1940)

530. Eleanor Stewart (1913-2007) [CBS Radio] x 1 *Lux Radio Theatre: The Letter* (1941)

531. Sally Stewart [Welwyn Studios] x 1 *Dangerous Fingers* (1938)

532. Carl Stockdale (1874-1953) [Warners Burbank] x 1 *King of the Underworld* (1939)

533. Harry Strang (1892-1972) [Warners Burbank] x 1 *Calling Philo Vance* (1940)

534. John [Hind] Stuttard [Burnley Amateur, Cotton Manufacturer] (1908-1971) x 2 *The Best People* [The Burnley Players, Victoria Theatre] (1930); *Plunder* [The Burnley Players, Victoria Theatre] (1931)

535. Carmen Sugars [Liverpool Playhouse] x 10 *Hollywood Holiday* (1932); *The Long Christmas Dinner* (1932); *Lady in Waiting* (1932); *What Happened to George* (1932); *A Bite of the Apple* (1933); *Mourning Becomes Electra* [Overseas League, Liverpool] (1933); *The Crime at Blossoms* (1933); *Another Language* (1933); *The Kingdom of God* (1933); *Gallows Glorious* (1934)

536. Elliott Sullivan (1907-1974) [Warners Burbank] x 3 *Devil's Island* (1938); *King of the Underworld* (1939); *Flight from Destiny* (1941)

537. John Sutton (1908-1963) [Warners Burbank] x 2 *Sons of Liberty* (1939); *The Private Lives of Elizabeth and Essex* (1939)

538. Donald Taylor [Burnley Amateur] x 6 *The School for Scandal* [Clef Club, Mechanics Institute] (1930); *Merchant of Venice Readings* [2] [Burnley Drama Guild, Burnley Central Library] (1931); *Oedipus the King* [Burnley Drama Guild, Burnley Central Library] (1931); *"Pompey" the Great* [Burnley Drama Guild, Burnley Central Library] (1931); *The Devil's Disciple* [Burnley Drama Guild, Victoria Theatre] (1931); *The Devil's Disciple* [Burnley Drama Guild, Co-op Hall, Todmorden] (1932)

539. Terry the Cairn Terrier (1933-c.1944) [Warners Burbank] x 1 *Calling Philo Vance* (1940)

540. Heather [Mary] Thatcher (1896-1987) [Paramount Studios] x 1 *Beau Geste* (1939)

541. Lee Thistlethwaite (1885-1973) [Burnley Amateur, Semi-professional Baritone Singer and Musician / Cotton Merchant] x 4 *Operatic Evening* [The Burnley Clef Club, Mechanics Institute] (1920); *The Magic Flute* [The Burnley Operatic Society, Victoria Theatre] (1929); *Aida* [The Burnley Operatic Society, Palace Theatre] (1930); *Rigoletto* [The Burnley Operatic Society, Victoria Theatre] (1932)

542. Frankie Thomas (1921-2006) [Warners Burbank] x 1 *Nancy Drew Detective* (1938)

543. David Thursby (1889-1977) [Warners Burbank] x 5 *We Are Not Alone* (1939); *The Sea Hawk* (1940); *A Dispatch from Reuter's* (1940); *South of Suez* (1940); *International Squadron* (1941)

544. George Tobias (1901-1980) [Warners Burbank] x 1 *River's End* (1940)

545. Andrew Tombes (1885-1976) [Republic Studios] x 1 *Wolf of New York* (1940)

546. Rosella Towne (1918-) [Rosella Townsend / Rosella Kronman] [Warners Burbank] x 5 *Cowboy from Brooklyn* (1938); *Boy Meets Girl* (1938); *Secret Service of the Air* (1939); *The Adventures of Jane Arden* (1939); *The Private Lives of Elizabeth and Essex* (1939)

547. Richard Travis (1913-1989) [William Justice] [Warners Burbank] x 1 *International Squadron* (1941)

548. Peter Trent (1917-?) [Liverpool Playhouse] x 7 *Youth at the Helm* (1935); *Cornelius* (1935); *Barnet's Folly* (1935); *Circus Boy* (1935); *Death Takes a Holiday* (1936); *Richard of Bordeaux* (1936); *Twelfth Night* (1936)

549. Charles Trowbridge (1882-1967) [Warners Burbank] x 4 *Nancy Drew Detective* (1938); *King of the Underworld* (1939); *On Trial* (1939); *Confessions of a Nazi Spy* (1939)

550. Valerie Tudor (1910-1997) [Enid Valerie Samuel] [Liverpool Playhouse and Winter Gardens, New Brighton] x 27 *The Road to Rome* (1933); *Britannia of Billingsgate* (1933); *The Lake* (1933); *After the Event* (1933); *The Cathedral* (1933); *Shall We Join the Ladies?* (1933); *Is Life Worth Living* (1933); *Dangerous Corner* (1934); *The Rose Without a Thorn* (1934); *Cabbages and Kings* (1934); *Macbeth* (1934); *The Cathedral* [Winter Gardens, New Brighton] (1934); *Smoke Screen* [Winter Gardens, New Brighton] (1934); *Britannia of Billingsgate* [Winter Gardens, New Brighton] (1934); *Counsellor-at-Law* (1934); *The Distaff Side* (1934); *A Sleeping Clergyman* (1934); *Sheppey* (1934); *Laburnum Grove* (1934); *Flowers of the Forest* (1935); *Hamlet* (1935); *Too Young to Marry* (1935); *The Matriarch* (1935); *Libel* [Winter Gardens, New Brighton] (1935); *Counsellor-at-Law* [Winter Gardens, New Brighton] (1935); *Too Young to Marry* [Winter Gardens, New Brighton] (1935); *Sheppey* [Winter Gardens, New Brighton] (1935);

551. Norah Turley [Burnley Amateur] x 5 *Merchant of Venice Readings* [1] [Burnley Drama Guild, Burnley Central Library] (1931); *Merchant of Venice Readings* [2] [Burnley Drama Guild, Burnley Central Library] (1931); *Oedipus, the King* [Burnley Drama Guild, Burnley Central

Library] (1931); *"Pompey" the Great* [Burnley Drama Guild, Burnley Central Library] (1931); *Scenes from A Midsummer Night's Dream* [English Folk Festival, "Four Oaks," Higher Reedley] (1931)

552. Don Turner (1910-1982) [Warners Burbank] x 5 *Heart of the North* (1938); *Devil's Island* (1938); *Secret Service of the Air* (1939); *The Adventures of Jane Arden* (1939); *Espionage Agent* (1939)

553. Neil Tuson [Liverpool Playhouse and Winter Gardens, New Brighton] x 24 *Hollywood Holiday* (1932); *Lean Harvest* (1932); *What Happened to George* (1932); *Inquest* (1933); *The Kingdom of God* (1933); *The Queen's Husband* (1933); *Anthony and Anna* [Winter Gardens, New Brighton] (1933); *The Road to Rome* (1933); *The Lake* (1933); *Fun While It Lasts* (1933); *The Rose Without a Thorn* (1934); *Smoke Screen;* (1934); *Cabbages and Kings* (1934); *Macbeth* (1934); *Counsellor-at-Law* (1934); *The Cathedral* [Winter Gardens, New Brighton] (1934); *Smoke Screen* [Winter Gardens, New Brighton] (1934); *Britannia of Billingsgate* [Winter Gardens, New Brighton] (1934); *A Sleeping Clergyman* (1934); *Sheppey* (1934); *Libel* (1935); *Hamlet* (1935); *Libel* [Winter Gardens, New Brighton] (1935); *Counsellor at Law* [Winter Gardens, New Brighton] (1935)

554. Jane Vaughan [Liverpool Playhouse and Winter Gardens, New Brighton] x 9 *Hollywood Holiday* (1932); *Lean Harvest* (1932); *Lady in Waiting* (1932); *The Roundabout* (1932); *Don't Tell England* (1933); *The Crime at Blossoms* (1933); *The Kingdom of God* (1933); *Never Come Back* (1933); *Art and Mrs. Bottle* [Winter Gardens, New Brighton] (1933)

555. Henry Victor (1892-1945) [Warners Burbank] x 2 *Espionage Agent* (1939); *Confessions of a Nazi Spy* (1939)

556. [Charles] Emmett Vogan (1893-1969) [Warners Burbank] x 5 *Cowboy from Brooklyn* (1938); *Heart of the North* (1938); *Confessions of a Nazi Spy* (1939); *Espionage Agent* (1939); *The Monroe Doctrine* (1939)

557. Frederick Vogeding (1887-1942) [Warners Burbank] x 3 *Confessions of a Nazi Spy* (1939); *Espionage Agent* (1939); *The Monroe Doctrine* (1939)

558. Theodore Von Eltz (1893-1964) [Warners Burbank] x 2 *Devil's Island* (1938); *A Dispatch from Reuter's* (1940)

559. Hans Von Twardowsky (1898-1958) [Warners Burbank] x 2 *Espionage*

Agent (1939); *Confessions of a Nazi Spy* (1939)

560. Philip Wade (1896-1950) [BBC Radio] x 3 *Scotland Yard: Life in the Metropolitan Police* (1936); *Money with Menaces* (1937); *Death of a First Mate* (1937)

561. Charles Waldron (1874-1946) [Warners Burbank] x 1 *The Monroe Doctrine* (1939)

562. Nella Walker (1886-1971) [Warners Burbank] x 1 *Espionage Agent* (1939)

563. Percy Walsh (1888-1952) [Warners Teddington] x 1 *It's In the Blood* (1938)

564. Douglas Walton (1910-1961) [J. Douglas Dunder] [Warners Burbank] x 1 *The Letter* (1940)

565. Robert Warwick (1878-1964) [Robert Taylor Bien] [Warners Burbank] x 5 *Devil's Island* (1938); *The Private Lives of Elizabeth and Essex* (1939); *Murder in the Air* (1940); *The Sea Hawk* (1940); *A Dispatch from Reuter's* (1940)

566. Pierre Watkin (1889-1960) [Warners Burbank] x 3 *King of the Underworld* (1939); *The Adventures of Jane Arden* (1939); *Secret Service of the Air* (1939)

567. Denis Webb [Liverpool Playhouse, Winter Gardens, New Brighton and BBC Radio] x 16 *Hamlet* (1935); *The Seventh Man* (1935); *The Matriarch* (1935); *Libel* [Winter Gardens, New Brighton] (1935); *Counsellor-at-Law* [Winter Gardens, New Brighton] (1935); *The Distaff Side* [Winter Gardens, New Brighton] 1935; *Sheppey* [Winter Gardens, New Brighton] (1935); *Youth at the Helm* (1935); *Barnet's Folly* (1935); *Cornelius* (1935); *Round the Northern Repertories: The Liverpool Playhouse* [BBC Radio] (1935); *Miss Linley of Bath* (1935); *Circus Boy* (1935); *Death Takes a Holiday* (1936); *Richard of Bordeaux* (1936); *Twelfth Night* (1936)

568. Ben Welden (1901-1997) [Benjamin Weinblatt] [Republic Studios] x 1 *Wolf of New York* (1940)

569. Leo White (1882-1948) [Warners Burbank] x 3 *Torchy Blane in Chinatown* (1939); *On Trial* (1939); *River's End* (1940) [Scenes Deleted]

570. Miss Edith [Jane] Whittaker [Burnley Amateur, Infant School Teacher] x 5 *The Magic Flute* [The Burnley Operatic Society, Victoria Theatre]

(1929); *Aida* [The Burnley Operatic Society, Palace Theatre] (1930);
Scenes from A Midsummer Night's Dream [English Folk Festival, "Four
Oaks," Higher Reedley] (1931); *Rigoletto* [The Burnley Operatic Society,
Victoria Theatre] (1932); *Scenes from A Midsummer Night's Dream*
[Quernmore Park, Lancaster] (1932)

571. Frank Wilcox (1907-1974) [Warners Burbank] x 5 *The Monroe Doctrine*
(1939); *Calling Philo Vance* (1940); *Murder in the Air* (1940); *The Sea
Hawk* (1940); *River's End* (1940)

572. Hugh [Anthony Glanmor] Williams (1904-1969) [Warners Teddington] x
2 *Perfect Crime* (1937); *The Dark Stairway* (1938)

573. Larry Williams (1913-1956) [Warners Burbank] x 3 *Secret Service of the
Air* (1939); *On Trial* (1939); *Sons of Liberty* (1939)

574. Lottie Williams (1874-1962) [Warners Burbank] x 5 *When Were You Born*
(1938); *Nancy Drew, Detective* (1938); *King of the Underworld* (1939);
Espionage Agent (1939); *A Dispatch from Reuter's* (1940)

575. Stanley Williams (1920-2000) [Liverpool Playhouse] x 2 *And So To War*
(1936); *Richard of Bordeaux* (1936)

576. Marie Wilson (1916-1972) [Katherine Elizabeth Wilson] [Warners
Burbank and KWF Radio] x 2 *Boy Meets Girl* (1938); *I Found Stella
Parish* (1938)

577. Tom Wilson (1880-1965) [Warners Burbank] x 7 *Heart of the North*
(1938); *Nancy Drew, Detective* (1938); *Devil's Island* (1938); *King of the
Underworld* (1939); *We Are Not Alone* (1939); *River's End* (1940); *South
of Suez* (1940)

578. Jack Wise (1888-1954) [Warners Burbank] x 7 *Cowboy from Brooklyn*
(1938); *Devil's Island* (1938); *Torchy Blane in Chinatown* (1939); *Secret
Service of the Air* (1939); *The Adventures of Jane Arden* (1939); *Calling
Philo Vance* (1940); *River's End* (1940)

579. Anna May Wong (1905-1961) [Wong Liu Tsong] [Warners Burbank] x 1
When Were You Born (1938)

580. Frederick Worlock (1886-1973) [Warners Burbank] x 2 *The Sea Hawk*

(1940); *South of Suez* (1940)

581. Harry J. Worth (1903-1975) [Paramount Studios] x 1 *Beau Geste* (1939)

582. William Worthington (1872-1941) [Warners Burbank] x 1 *Espionage Agent* (1939)

583. Maris Wrixon (1916-1999) [Warners Burbank] x 3 *The Adventures of Jane Arden* (1939); *The Private Lives of Elizabeth and Essex* (1939); *Calling Philo Vance* (1940)

584. [Victor] Sen Yung (1915-1980) [Sen Yew Cheung] [Warners Burbank] x 2 *Torchy Blane in Chinatown* (1939); *The Letter* (1940)

585. Wolfgang Zilzer (1901-1991) [Warners Burbank] x 4 *Confessions of a Nazi Spy* (1939); *Espionage Agent* (1939); *A Dispatch from Reuter's* (1940); *Shining Victory* (1941)

586. Henry [Von] Zynda (1904-1961) [Warners Burbank] x 2 *Espionage Agent* (1939); *Calling Philo Vance* (1940)

BIBLIOGRAPHY

PRIMARY SOURCES
ARCHIVAL AND UNPUBLISHED DOCUMENTS

Burnley Local History Library

ERB 20 / R.P.E. 11 p.85: County Borough of Burnley: Register of Parochial Electors 1912-1913; Burnley Wood Polling District K South Ward (Parochial)

ERB 22 / K1757 p.65: County Borough of Burnley Register of Voters 1914; Burnley Wood Polling District South Ward (Parochial)

ERB 32: Parliamentary Borough of Burnley Register of Electors 1928-1929; Burnley Wood Ward Polling District No. 1

REF 54: Burnley Grammar School Booklet, George Anderson, Burnley, 1906

Coventry Archives

CCA/CD/1/112/6,7: Bomb Damage Schedules 1940

CCA/CD/1/113/6,7: Bomb Damage Schedules 1941

Lancashire Record Office

DDX 2523/2: The Papers of Rev. Harry Battye, Scrapbook 1928-1936

DDX 2523/6: The Papers of Rev. Harry Battye, St Catherine's Burnley Monthly Magazine 1929-1941

DDX 2523/9: The Papers of Rev. Harry Battye, Scrapbook 1936-1941

UDPA 32/3: Padiham Urban District Council General Rate Book April 16 1930

UDPA 32/4: Padiham Urban District Council General Rate Book April 16 1931

UDPA 32/5: Padiham Urban District Council General Rate Book April 18 1932

VLBU 2/3: County Borough of Burnley Register of Motor Cars and Motor Cycles

VLBU 2/6: County Borough of Burnley Register of Motor Cycles

VLBU 2/12: Register of Burnley Motor Car Numbers 1925-1935

VLBU/4/1: CW7918: Burnley Vehicle License Registration Documents 1927-1936

Manchester City Council Archives and Local Studies

M9/40/2/10563 Manchester Business Rates Books - Great Ancoats Street 1921-1922 (District 9)

M9/40/2/10563 Manchester Business Rates Books - Princess Street1921-1922 (District 9)

M9/40/2/10595 Manchester Business Rates Books - Princess Street 1926-1927 (District 2)

M9/40/2/10636 Manchester Business Rates Books - Sackville Street 1928-1929 (District 9)

M9/40/2/10671 Manchester Business Rates Books - Sackville Street 1931-1932 (District 9)

Margaret Herrick Library Academy of Motion Picture Arts and Sciences

Beau Geste (1939) Production File

The Letter (1940) Production File

FC 25-111: *Wanted by Scotland Yard* Motion Picture Association of America, Production Code Administration Records

Michael Redgrave Archive

THM/31/4/1/3: 1935 Diary

THM/31/4/1/4: 1936 Diary

National Archives of the UK (Public Record Office)

BT26/818/154: Board of Trade, Inward Passenger Lists 1925

BT26 /849/79: Board of Trade, Inward Passenger Lists 1927

BT26/879: Board of Trade, Inwards Passenger Lists 1928

BT26/925/13: Board of Trade, Inwards Passenger Lists 1930

BT26/944: Board of Trade, Inwards Passenger Lists 1930

BT26/965: Board of Trade, Inwards Passenger Lists 1931

BT26/1210: Board of Trade, Inward Passenger Lists 1945

BT27/1084: Board of Trade, Outwards Passenger Lists 1925

BT27/1081: Board of Trade, Outwards Passenger Lists 1928

BT27/1403: Board of Trade, Outwards Passenger Lists 1934

BT27/1489: Board of Trade, Outwards Passenger Lists 1937

WO9 /1270: War Office: First World War and Army of Occupation War Diaries:
2 Infantry Brigade: 1 Battalion Loyal North Lancashire Regiment 1914-1918

WO374/14779: War Office: Officer's Services, First World War, Personal Files: Lieutenant S. Collier

WO374/65170: War Office: Officer's Services, First World War, Personal Files: Lieutenant A. Stephenson

WO329/65205: War Office: Officer's Services, First World War, Personal Files: Lieutenant J.A. Stephenson

In the Possession of Mrs. Jane Blain

Diary of Adela R. Wilkinson: January 1923 - December 1927

Diary of Adela R. Stephenson: January 1928 - December 1932

Diary of Adela R. Stephenson: January 1933 - December 1937

Diary of Adela R. Stephenson: January 1938 - December 1942

In the Possession of Dr. Peter Stephenson

Letters from James Stephenson to Lorna Hewitt Kilby Dinn: August1935 to July 1936

Letters from James Stephenson to Lorna Stephenson: August 1936 to September 1939

University of Southern California, Los Angeles (USC) Warner Bros. Archives

Box 1985: *The Adventures of Jane Arden*: Daily Production and Progress Reports

Box 1495: *Boy Meets Girl*: Daily Production and Progress Reports

Box 1745: *Boy Meets Girl*: Story; Memos and Correspondence

Box 2743: *Bruce Lister*: Legal File

Box 2019B: *Calling Philo Vance*: Story; Memos and Correspondence

Box 1485: *Confessions of a Nazi Spy*: Daily Production and Progress Reports

Box 1495: *Cowboy from Brooklyn*: Daily Production and Progress Reports

Box 1891: *The Dark Stairway*: Story Final Script

Box 1785B: *A Dispatch from Reuter's*: Daily Production and Progress Reports

Box 1485: *Espionage Agent*: Daily Production and Progress Reports

Box 2302B: *Flight from Destiny*: Story; Memos and Correspondence

Box 1485: *Flight from Destiny*: Daily Production and Progress Reports

Box 1790: *International Squadron*: Story; Memos and Correspondence

Box 1487: *International Squadron*: Daily Production and Progress Reports

Box 2817: *Irving Asher*: Legal File

Box 1746: *It's in the Blood*: Final Script

Box 2746B: *James Stephenson*: Legal File: May 8 1937 to June 22 1938

Box 2746B: *James Stephenson*: Legal File: June 27 1938 to July 15 1940

Box 2746B: *James Stephenson*: Legal File: July 26 1940 to November 13 1952

Box 1485: *The Letter*: Daily Production and Progress Reports

Box 12734: *The Letter*: Legal Files

Box 1014: *The Letter*: Research File

Box 2042: *The Letter*: Story; Memos and Correspondence

Box 2078: *The Man Who Made Diamonds*: Final Script

Box 1455A: *The Monroe Doctrine*: Daily Production and Progress Reports

Box 2399A: *The Monroe Doctrine*: Story; Memos and Correspondence

Box 2337: *Murder in the Air*: Story; Memos and Correspondence

Box 2170: *Nancy Drew Detective*: Story; Memos and Correspondence

Box 1495A: *Nancy Drew Detective*: Daily Production and Progress Reports

Box 2142: *The Old Maid*: Story Memos and Correspondence

Box 1711B: *On Trial*: Story Memos and Correspondence

Box 1485: *The Private Lives of Elizabeth and Essex*: Daily Production and Progress Reports

Box 1880: *The Private Lives of Elizabeth and Essex*: Story; Memos and Correspondence

Box 2187: *River's End*: Story; Memos and Correspondence

Box 1485: *Secret Service of the Air*: Daily Production and Progress Reports

Box 2015: *Shining Victory*: Story Memos and Correspondence

Box 2403B: *Sons of Liberty*: Story Memos and Correspondence

Box 1485: *South of Suez*: Daily Production and Progress Reports

Box 2161: *Torchy Blane in Chinatown*: Story Memos and Correspondence

Box 2360: *We Are Not Alone*: Story Memos and Correspondence

Box 1495A: *When Were You Born*: Daily Production and Progress Reports

Box 2358A: *When Were You Born*: Story; Memos and Correspondence

ARTICLES

Balcon, Michael. "Interview - Call up the Hollywood Britons," *Picturegoer*, May 11, 1940, p. 11

Bazin, André. "William Wyler, or the Jansenist of Directing," *Bazin at Work: Major Essays and Reviews from the Forties and Fifties*, (ed.) Bert Cardullo, London, Routledge, 1997, pp.1-22

Jenkinson, Philip. "The Letter," *Radio Times*, May 18, 1975, p.15

Karr, Jeanne. "He Earned His Letter," *Modern Screen*, March 1941, Vol. 22, No. 4 pp. 36-37, 73-75

McFee, Frederick. "Man of the Hour," *Hollywood*, March 1941, pp37-39

Mulvey, Laura. "Visual Pleasure and Narrative Cinema," *Contemporary Film Theory,* (ed.) Anthony Easthope, London, Longman, 1993

Orwell, George. "The Lion and the Unicorn: Socialism and the English Genius: Part I: England Your England," *Collected Essays and Journalism: 1940-1943*, London, Octopus, 1981

Proctor, Kay. "Newest Star," *Screen Life*, March 1941

Schrott, Eugene. "The Remarkable Mr. Stephenson," *Screenland*, May 1941, p.96

Shaw, George Bernard. "Whither Britain? – V," *The Listener*, February 7, 1934, p.216

Smith, Frederick James. "Opportunity Finally Knocked," *Silver Screen*, March 1941, Vol. 11, No. 5 pp. 24-25, 70

Surmelian, Leon. "Keep Your Eyes on Stephenson!," *Motion Picture*, April 1941, Vol. 61, No. 3, pp. 33, 91, 92, 96

Usai, Paolo Cherchi. "The Shakedown," *1998 Pordenone Silent Film Festival Programme*, p.38

Wallace, Inez. "Inez Predicts Stardom for James Stephenson, Found in "Letter," Within Six Months," March 30 1941, Stephenson Archive

Zeitlin, Ida. "The Last Hours of James Stephenson," *Photoplay*, October 1941, Vol. 19, No. 5, pp. 65, 109

BOOKS
GENERAL

Aaker, Everett. *Encyclopaedia of Early Television Crime Fighters*, Jefferson, McFarland, 2006

Affron, Charles. *Star Acting: Gish, Garbo, Davis*, New York, Dutton, 1977

Agate, James. *Around Cinemas*, London, Home & Van Thal, 1946

Arnold, Matthew. *Culture and Anarchy*, Cambridge, Cambridge University Press, 1981

Balio, Tino. *History of the American Cinema Volume 5 - Grand Design: Hollywood as a Modern Business Enterprise, 1930-1939*, New York, Scribner, 1995

Behlmer, Rudy (ed.) *Inside Warner Bros. (1935-1951)*, New York, Simon and Schuster, 1987

Behlmer, Rudy (ed.) *Wisconsin/Warner Bros. Screenplay Series: The Sea Hawk*, Wisconsin, University of Wisconsin Press, 1982

Benjamin, Walter. *The Work of Art in the Age of Mechanical Reproduction*, Hammondsworth, Penguin, 2008

Bennett, Walter. *A History of the Grammar School Burnley*, Burnley, Burnley Press, 1940

Bouchier, Chili. *Shooting Stars: The Last of the Silent Film Stars*, Leicester, Ulverscroft, 1996

Cagney, James. *Cagney by Cagney*, London, New English Library, 1976

Carey, John. *The Intellectuals and the Masses: Pride and Prejudice among the Literary Intellegentsia (1880-1939)*, London, Faber and Faber, 1992

Castle, Roy. *Roy Castle: Now and Then*, London, Robson, 1994

Chaplin, Charles. *My Autobiography*, Hammondsworth, Penguin, 1966

Chibnall, Steve. *Quota Quickies: The Birth of the British B Film*, London, British Film Institute, 2007

Coué, Émil. *Self Mastery through Conscious Autosuggestion*, New York, Cosimo, 2007

Cunliffe, James W. *Wheel of Friendship: The History of the Burnley Rotary Club (1920-1945)*, Manchester, 1945

Davis, Ronald L. *The Glamour Factory: Inside Hollywood's Big Studio System*, Dallas, Southern Methodist University Press, 1993

Dimbleby, David and Reynolds, David. *An Ocean Apart: The Relationship Between Britain and America in the Twentieth Century*, London, Hodder and Stoughton / BBC Books, 1988

Dunning, John. *Tune in Yesterday: The Ultimate Encyclopaedia of Old-Time Radio 1925-1926*, New Jersey, Prentice-Hall, 1976

Everson, William K. *The Detective in Film*, New Jersey, Citadel, 1972

Eyles, Allen and Meeker, David. *Missing Believed Lost: The Great British Film Search*, London, British Film Institute, 1992

Gifford, Denis. *The British Film Catalogue 1895-1970*, Newton Abbot, David & Charles, 1973

Glancy, H. Mark. *When Hollywood Loved Britain: The Hollywood 'British' Film 1939-45*, Manchester, Manchester University Press, 1999

Goldie, Grace Wyndham. *The Liverpool Repertory Theatre*, London, Hodder and Stoughton, 1935

Graves, Robert and Hodge, Alan. *The Long Weekend: A Social History of Great Britain 1918-1939*, London, Cardinal, 1991

Halliwell, Leslie. *Halliwell's Hundred: A Nostalgic Choice of Films from the Golden Age*, London, Granada, 1982

Higham, Charles and Greenberg, Joel. *Hollywood in the Forties*, London, Tantivy Press, 1968

Hirschhorn, Clive. *The Warner Bros. Story*, London, Octopus, 1979

Hunnings, Neville March. *Film Censors and the Law*, London, Allen and Unwin, 1967

Jackson, George. *Collier of Manchester: A Friend's Tribute*, London, Hodder and Stoughton, 1923

Jones, Thomas. *A Diary with Letters, 1931-50*, London, Oxford University Press, 1954

Kael, Pauline. *5001 Nights at the Movies*, London, Zenith, 1984

Kennedy Matthew. *Edmund Goulding's Dark Victory: Hollywood's Genius Bad Boy*, Wisconsin, University of Wisconsin Press, 2004

Kirkpatrick, Ivone. *The Inner Circle*, London, Macmillan, 1959

Koszarski, Richard. *Hollywood on the Hudson: Film and Television in New York from Griffith to Sarnoff*, New Brunswick, Rutgers University Press, 2008

Liddell Hart, Basil Henry. *Through the Fog of War*, London, Faber and Faber, 1938

Lloyd George, David. *War Memoirs*, London, Ivor Nicholson & Watson, 1934

Low, Rachael. *Film Making in 1930s Britain*, London, Allen and Unwin, 1985

McClelland, Doug. *Forties Film Talk: Oral Histories of Hollywood, with 120 Lobby Posters*, Jefferson, McFarland, 1992

McFarlane, Brian (ed.) *The Encyclopaedia of British Film* (2nd ed.), London, British Film Institute, 2006

MacMahon, Pelham and Brooks, Pam. *An Actor's Place: The Liverpool Repertory Company at Liverpool Playhouse, 1911-1998*, Liverpool, Bluecoat Press, 2000

Maltin, Leonard. *Leonard Maltin's Classic Movie Guide* (2nd ed.), New York, Plume, 2010

Maugham, W. Somerset. *The Casuarina Tree*, Singapore, Oxford University Press, 1985

Melly, George. *Scouse Mouse, Or I Never Got Over It*, London, Weidenfeld and Nicholson, 1984

Morley, Sheridan. *Gladys Cooper: A Biography*, London, Book Club Associates, 1979

Nietzsche, Friedrich. *Beyond Good and Evil: Prelude to a Philosophy of the Future*, ed. Marion Faber, Oxford, Oxford University Press, 1998

Niven, David. *Bring on the Empty Horses*, London, Hamish Hamilton, 1975

Niven, David. *The Moon's a Balloon*, London, Penguin, 1994

Nuttall, George. *A Seventy Years' Review 1849-1919 "Musical Worthies" of Burnley and District Vol II*, Burnley, Nuttall, 1919

Overy, Richard. *The Morbid Age: Britain Between the Wars*, London, Penguin, 2009

Palmer, Scott. *A Who's Who of British Film Actors*, New Jersey, Scarecrow Press, 1981

Phillips, Alastair and Vincendeau (eds.) *Journeys of Desire: European Actors in Hollywood a Critical Companion*, London, British Film Institute, 2006

Powdermaker, Hortense. *Hollywood The Dream Factory: An Anthropologist Looks at the Movie-Makers*, London, Secker and Warburg, 1951

Powell, Michael. *A Life in the Movies*, London, Methuen, 1987

Priestley, John Boynton. *The Good Companions*, London, Arrow, 2000

Pugh, Martin. *We Danced All Night: A Social History of Britain Between the Wars*, London, Bodley Head, 2008

Quinlan, David. *Quinlan's Film Stars* (5th ed.), London, B.T. Batsford, 2000

Quirk, Lawrence. *The Passionate Life of Bette Davis*, London, Robson, 1990

Reagan, Ronald. *An American Life: The Autobiography*, London, Hutchinson, 1990

Redgrave, Michael. *In My Mind's Eye: An Autobiography*, London, Weidenfeld & Nicholson, 1984

Richards, Jeffrey. *Cinema and Radio in Britain and America, 1920-60*, Manchester, Manchester University Press, 2010

Richards, Jeffrey. *Swordsman of the Silver Screen*, London, Routledge and Kegan Paul, 1977

Richards, Jeffrey. *Visions of Yesterday*, London, Routledge and Kegan Paul, 1973

Riese, Randall. *All About Bette: Her Life from A to Z*, Chicago, Contemporary, 1993

Roberts, Anthony. *'The Holy Fox': A Biography of Lord Halifax*, London, Weidenfeld and Nicolson, 1991

Robertson, James C. *The Hidden Cinema: British Film Censorship in Action 1913-1972*, London, Routledge, 1989

Robinson, David. *Chaplin*, Harmondsworth, Penguin, 2000

Roddick, Nick. *A New Deal in Entertainment: Warner Brothers in the 1930s*, London, British Film Institute, 1983

Sarris, Andrew. *The American Cinema: Directors and Direction 1929-1968*, New York, E.P. Dutton, 1968

Schatz, Thomas. *Boom and Bust: American Cinema in the 1940s*, California, University of California, 1999

Schmidt, Paul. *Hitler's Interpreter*, London, William Heinemann, 1951

Sherman, Vincent. *Studio Affairs: My Life as a Film Director*, Kentucky, University Press of Kentucky, 1996

Shindler, Colin. *Hollywood Goes to War: Films and American Society 1939-1952*, London, Routledge and Kegan Paul, 1979

Shipman, David. *The Great Movie Stars: The Golden Years*, London, Argus & Robertson, 1979

Shirer, William L. *The Nightmare Years: 1930-1940*, Edinburgh, Birlinn, 1984

Speer, Albert. *Inside the Third Reich*, London, Phoenix, 1995

Spencer, Lesley and Terence. *Living Dangerously*, Odiham, Percival, 2002

Stalin, J.V. *Problems of Leninism*, Peking, Foreign Language Press, 1976

Stine, Whitney and Davis Bette. *Bette Davis: Mother Goddam*, London, Star, 1982

Strachan, Alan. *Secret Dreams: The Biography of Michael Redgrave*, London,

Weidenfeld & Nicolson, 2004

Swanson, Gloria. *Swanson on Swanson*, London, Michael Joseph, 1981

Thistlethwaite, Frank. *A Lancashire Family Inheritance*, Cambridge, Ipswich, 1996

Thomson, David. *The New Biographical Dictionary of Film* (5th ed.), London, Little Brown, 2010

Vasey, Ruth. *The World According to Hollywood 1918-1939*, Exeter, University of Exeter, 1997

Walker, John (ed.) *Halliwell's Film Video & DVD Guide* (19th ed.), London, Harper Collins, 2004

BOOKS
STEPHENSON ARCHIVE
PLAYS

Ervine, St. John. *Boyd's Shop*, London, Allen & Unwin, 1936

Gilbert, W.S. and Sullivan, Arthur. *The Plays of Gilbert and Sullivan*, New York, Book League of America, 1941

Gow, Ronald. *Gallows Glorious*, London, Gollancz, 1933

Ibsen, Henrik. *The Best Known Works of Ibsen: Including Ghosts, Hedda Gabler, Peer Gynt, A Doll's House*, New York, Book League of America, 1941

Maugham, Somerset. *The Plays of W. Somerset Maugham: Collected Edition*, London, Heinemann, 1934. – A set of six volumes

Volume I *Lady Frederick; Mrs. Dot; Jack Straw*

Volume II *Penelope, Smith; The Land of Promise*

Volume III *Our Betters; The Unattainable; Home and Beauty*

Volume IV *The Circle; The Constant Wife; The Breadwinner*

Volume V *Caesar's Wife; East of Suez; The Sacred Flame*

Volume VI *The Unknown; For Services Rendered; Sheppey*

Redgrave, Michael. *The Seventh Man*, London, Samuel French, 1936

Sangster, Alfred. *By the Order of the King*, London, Thomas Nelson, 1937

Sangster, Alfred. *Massacre!*, London, Constable, 1935

Shaw. Bernard. *Androcles & The Lion, Overruled, Pygmalion*, London, Constable, 1931

Shaw, Bernard. *Back to Methuselah A metabiological Pentateuch*, London, Constable, 1931

Shaw, Bernard. *The Complete Plays of Bernard Shaw*, London, Odhams, 1934

Shaw, Bernard. *The Doctor's Dilemma, Getting Married, The Shewing-Up of Blanco Posnet*, London, Constable, 1932

Shaw, Bernard. *Heartbreak House, Great Catherine, Playlets of the War*, London, Constable, 1933

Shaw, Bernard. *Man and Superman: A Comedy and a Philosophy*, London, Constable, 1931

Shaw, Bernard. *Misalliance, The Dark Lady of the Sonnets and Fanny's First Play*, London, Constable, 1932

Shaw, Bernard. *St Joan: A Chronicle The Apple Cart a Political Extravaganza*, London, Constable, 1932

Shaw, Bernard. *The Simpleton, The Six & The Millionairess, Three Plays*, London, Constable, 1936

Shaw, Bernard. *Too True To Be Good, Village Wooing & On the Rocks: Three Plays*, London, Constable, 1934

Steele, Wilbur Daniel and Mitchell, Norma. *Post Road*, New York, Samuel French, 1936

Synge, John M. *Plays of John M. Synge*, Woking, Unwin, 1932

Wilder, Thornton. *The Long Christmas Dinner*, London, Samuel French, 1933

Wooll, Edward. *Libel! A Play in Three Acts*, London, Heinemann, 1934

BOOKS
STEPHENSON ARCHIVE
POETRY

Kipling, Rudyard. *Rudyard Kipling's Verse*, London, Hodder and Stoughton, 1919

Miller, Alan. *Mixed Grill*, Birkenhead, Willmer, 1932

Miller, Alice Duer. *The White Cliffs*, London, Methuen, 1941

Ward, Thomas Humphrey (ed.) *The English Poets*, London, Macmillian, 1920. A set of five volumes:

> Volume One   *Chaucer to Donne*
>
> Volume Two   *Ben Jonson to Dryden*
>
> Volume Three   *Addison to Blake*
>
> Volume Four   *Wordsworth to Rossetti*
>
> Volume Five   *Browning to Rupert Brooke*

BOOKS
STEPHENSON ARCHIVE
PROSE

Austen, Jane. *Pride and Prejudice*, New York, Book League of America, 1940

Beaumont, Major W.S. *66th East Lancashire Division Dinner Club*, Manchester, George Falkner, 1924

Cerf, Bennett C and Moriarty, Henry C. *The Bedside Book of Famous British Stories*, New York, Literary Guild of America, 1940

Coyle, David Cushman. *America*, Washington, National Home Library Foundation, 1941

De Maupassant, Guy. *Short Stories of De Maupassant*, New York, Book League of America, 1941

Emerson, Ralph Waldo. *Essays of Ralph Waldo Emerson*, New York, Book League of America, 1941

Fielding, Henry. *The Adventures of Joseph Andrews Parts I and II*, New York, Doubleday, [no date given]

Fielding, Henry. *Amelia Part I II and III*, New York, Doubleday, [no date given]

Fielding, Henry. *The History of the Life Of The Late Mr. Jonathan Wild The Great*, New York, Doubleday, [no date given]

Fielding, Henry. *Miscellaneous Writings Part I and Part II*, New York, Doubleday, [no date given]

Fielding, Henry. *Tom Jones A Foundling Part I-Part IV*, New York, Doubleday, [no date given]

Fowler, H.W. *The Concise Oxford Dictionary of Current English* (5th Ed.), Oxford, 1917

Frankau, Gilbert. *Tip'apa" (What Does It Matter?)*, London, Chatto & Windus, 1924

Gibbon, Frederick P. *The 42nd East Lancashire Division 1914-1918*, London, Country Life Library, 1920

Henderson, Archibald. *Bernard Shaw: Playboy and Prophet (Authorised)*, New York, Appleton, 1932

Kipling, Rudyard. *Many Inventions*, New York, Doubleday Page, 1916

Krause, René. *Winston Churchill*, New York, Literary Guild of America, 1941

Lothian, Nicholson. *History of the East Lancashire Regiment, 1914-1918*, Liverpool, Littlebury Bros, 1936

Marden, Orison Swett. *The Secret of Achievement: A Book Designed to Teach*, Thomas Nelson & Sons, 1899

Marriott, J.W. *The Theatre*, London, Harrap, 1931

Sassoon, Siegfried. *The Memoirs of George Sherston*, New York, Literary Guild of America, 1937

Shaw, Bernard. *Our Theatres in the Nineties Vol I*, London, Constable, 1932

Shaw, Bernard. *Prefaces*, London, Constable, 1934

Shaw, Bernard. *What I Really Wrote About the War*, London, Constable, 1931.

Sniff, Fannie (ed.) *Famous Stars: Favourite Foods*, Los Angeles, 1938

Stansfield, John. *History of the Family of Stansfeld of Stansfield in the Parish of Halifax and Its Numerous Branches*, Leeds, 1885

Stevenson, Robert, Louis. *The Best Known Works of R.L. Stevenson Including: Treasure Island; Kidnapped; Dr Jekyll and Mr. Hyde and New Arabian Nights*, New York, Book League of America, 1941

Strachey, Lytton. *Eminent Victorians: Cardinal Newman, Florence Nightingale, Dr Arnold, General Gordon*, London, Chatto & Windus, 1922

Treynor, Blair. *She Ate Her Cake*, New York, William Morrow, 1946

Voltaire *The Best Known Works of Voltaire*, New York, Book League of America, 1941

Weeks, Edward. *Great Short Novels: An Anthology*, New York, The Literary Guild of America, 1941

Wyld, Henry Cecil (ed.) *The Universal Dictionary of the English Language*, London, Amalgamated Press, 1932

Zola, Emil. *The Best Known Works of Emil Zola Including: Nana; The Miller's Daughter and Nantas*, New York, 1941

NEWSPAPERS

Birkenhead Advertiser (1937)

Birkenhead News (1932-1933)

Birmingham Gazette (1937)

Birmingham Post (1937)

Bolton Journal and Guardian (1937)

Brighton and Hove Herald (1937)

Burnley Express (1899-1983)

Burnley News (1900-1933)

Bury Times (1931)

Chiswick Times (1937)

Daily Express (1937)

Daily Film Renter (1937)

Daily Sketch (1931-1936)

Daily Telegraph (1933-1937)

Daily Worker (1937)

Eastbourne Chronicle (1937)

Evening Express (1932-1936)

Evening Standard (1937)

Finchley Press (1937)

Golders Green Gazette (1937)

Hoylake and West Kirby Advertiser (1936)

Lancaster Guardian (1932)

Leeds Mercury (1937)

Liverpool Echo (1932-1941)

Liverpool Evening Post and Mercury (1932-1941)

Los Angeles Times (1939-1941)

Manchester Daily Dispatch (1932-1941)

Manchester Evening Chronicle (1929-1941)

Manchester Evening News (1932-1941)

Manchester Guardian (1923-1941)

Morecambe and Heysham Visitor and Lancashire Advertiser (1941-1950)

New York Times (1937-1941)

Morning Post (1933)

Northern Daily Telegraph (1929-1932)

Observer (1937)

Singapore Free Press and Mercantile Advertiser (1911)

Southport Guardian (1932-1937)

Streatham News (1937)

Thames Valley Times (1937)

Sunderland Echo (1937)

The Times (1911-1941)

Todmorden Advertiser (1931-1932)

Todmorden and District News (1931-1932)

Wallasey Chronicle (1933-1935)

Wallasey News (1933-1935)

Yorkshire Post (1937)

DIRECTORIES, JOURNALS, PERIODICALS AND TRADE PAPERS

Barrett's General and Commercial Directory of Burnley, Nelson, Colne, Padiham, Barrowfield, Cliviger, Trawden, Barnoldswick and other Adjacent Districts issues of 1896-1941

Cinema issues of 1937-1941

Film Pictorial issue of 1937

Film Weekly issues of 1937-1939

Flight issue of 1937

Kinematograph Weekly issues of 1937-1941

Kinematograph Year Books issues of 1938-1942

The Listener issue of 1934

Liverpolitan issues of 1932-1936

Monthly Film Bulletin issues of 1937-1942

Motion Picture Almanac issues of 1936-37 and 1944-45

Picturegoer issues of 1937-1940

Picture Show issue of 1937

Radio Times issues of 1929-1975

Sight and Sound issues of 1937-1941

Skinners' Cotton Trade Directory of the World issues of 1924-1929

Slater's Commercial Directory of Manchester issues of 1921-1929

Spotlight Casting Directory issues of 1930, 1932 and 1937

Stage issues of 1932-1937

Today's Cinema issue of 1937

Variety issue of 1937

World Film News issue of 1937

WEBSITES

www.afi.com
American Film Institute

www.ancestry.com
Ancestry Genealogy

www.bfi.org.uk
British Film Institute

http://www.cwgc.org/
Commonwealth War Graves Commission

www.imdb.com
Internet Movie Database

INDEX

Numbers in bold indicate photographs